"The Stile of
This Confederacy ...

ISBN 978-0-9839189-0-5

Library of Congress Control Number: 2013907139

Printed in the United States of America

Published by:

Hailstonesouth
Louisville, Kentucky

www.hailstonesouth.com

"The Stile of This Confederacy …

Carl B. Nett

⚜ HAILSTONESOUTH

… shall be
'The United States of America.'"

—Article I: *Articles of Confederation*

"A nation must believe in three things. It must believe in the past. It must believe in the future. It must, above all, believe in the capacity of its own people so to learn from the past that they can gain in judgment in creating their own future."

—FRANKLIN D. ROOSEVELT

Preface

We live in the present. We focus most of our time and energy on planning for and worrying about the future. Why should we care about the past? Specifically, why should we, as Americans, care about our nation's past? Given all the demands of daily life and the often stressful anticipation over what is yet to come, why bother with what has been?

History is too often reduced to an exercise in remembering names and dates. History is about so much more. Among the great lessons and wisdom to be discovered from history are ideas, a philosophy of how one should live life, and about what works and what doesn't work in creating a society where each individual is free to achieve his or her own highest potential. Understanding our history allows us to recognize and value those defining factors that fostered the most free, most prosperous, and most creative people to walk the earth. The people who displayed this uniquely "American" character came from different races, different continents, different cultural backgrounds, and different historical experiences. Lacking the ethnic homogeneity that defines most nations, our forebearers had a sameness of spirit that made a difference in the fate of their nation and, as a result, the fate of mankind itself. Knowledge of our past validates the just pride we have in our country. National pride not rooted in knowledge of national identity is nothing more than blind nationalism.

The Stile of This Confederacy seeks to foster an informed patriotism through historical literacy. Gathered within are the documents, speeches, declarations, poems, arguments, and songs that have shaped centuries of American life. Here, readers are introduced to the very people who influenced and guided our country's formation—in their own words, rather than an interpretation of their words.

In compiling this anthology, I was mindful of President Reagan's 1989 farewell address, the first political speech I remember paying attention to and really taking note of.

"We've got to teach history based not on what's in fashion, but what's important: Why the Pilgrims came here, who Jimmy Doolittle was, and what those thirty seconds over Tokyo meant." The president went on to warn of "an eradication of the American memory that could result, ultimately, in an erosion of the American spirit."

With this in mind, my goal was to do more than simply throw together a collection of disparate works. Given our history, I could have undoubtedly produced several volumes of material. Reagan's farewell address is one of the many works that, while obviously memorable, did not make its way into the finished version. Combing through a wealth of information and considering a multitude of speakers who deserve to be heard, I made my final selections based largely on eloquence and literary quality. In some cases, I chose selections for the opportunity they present to expound on a particular theme or be used to teach a particular point. I looked for words that have been instrumental in weaving the great American fabric and therefore have, either demonstrably or with great anticipation, a timeless quality for the listener and reader. I included some selections simply because I liked them and found them to be worthy of introduction to later generations. Not every selection fits an exact criterion.

It is important to note that this collection does not represent every significant event in American history—some did not inspire either great oratory or artistic expression. Nor does it seek to represent every point of view relative to every issue addressed. Nor does it represent every major voice—not every notable figure produced noteworthy oratory. Many of the longer pieces had to be condensed, but the words belong to the original speaker. They have not been sanitized for contemporary consumption.

This work began as a purely intellectual pursuit on my part many years ago, and developed into a commercial ambition when I realized just how little a great many people—often brilliant, successful people—know about our country. Ignorance in such trivial pursuits as sports is one thing. We hear all the time that so-and-so is the best basketball player, the greatest baseball player, the most skilled boxer "of all time"—yet such pronouncements are often made by casual sports fans whose historical knowledge is limited to their own lifetimes and the athletic contests they have personally witnessed. Ignorance in such matters as the development of our nation—where we've been—can adversely affect where we're going. The importance of knowing the past can't be overstated, for, as George Santayana warned, "Those who cannot remember the past are condemned to repeat it."

This book was written for the general reader. It is not necessarily meant to be read from cover to cover, though doing so may provide valuable insight into the individual author's perspective relative to the times. Suitable for parents, children (save perhaps Patton's "Speech to the Third Army") and students alike, this work may be used for reference, for marking favorite passages, or for using as a guide to call upon other sources for a more thorough exploration of our past. It may even inspire others to create similar collections of their own favorite works. Such an undertaking, I can readily attest, provides an education unto itself.

The biggest challenge encountered was in choosing contemporary selections—say, those originating since 1990. The inclusion or omission of recent partisan ideas and personalities, or the manner in which such partisans are presented, will meet with favor or disfavor by their critics and supporters alike. It has, of course, always been this way. Revolution was once a partisan idea. Abolition was once a partisan idea. Suffrage was a partisan idea. The issues surrounding war and peace often center around partisan ideas—and there have been many wars in our history. The contemporary issues and contests must be viewed in a broad historical context and, above all, appreciated as one of the great benefits of living in a free and open society where the exchange of ideas can be made without fear or violence. Whether these modern selections stand the test of time and are remembered beyond their speakers' lifetimes is a question for future anthologists.

In a larger sense, the amount of noteworthy—and quote worthy—material seems to have narrowed in recent years. This is probably because we now live in the hustle and bustle of the information age where people are disinterested in anything but the present moment, growing quickly bored and ever in search of new distractions. Twenty-four-hour news channels now fill a role once accomplished by thirty-minute newscasts, yet never seem to have time for their invited guests to finish a thought. We live increasingly in a visual age, where people learn from televisions, laptops, and a variety of hand-held devices, not from books or academic journals. Political oratory also seems to be losing its prominence in American life. Politicians rarely craft a stump speech, instead trying to conjure a thirty-second sound bite. Congressmen and senators campaign for C-Span cameras in an empty chamber, rather than engage in the back and forth with a live audience.

Some argue that reading, too, is going out of style. There is no doubt that the manner in which people consume information is changing. Nationwide, newspapers are going out of business or significantly shrinking their publications. There is an increasing use of interactive technology in schools and the workplace. Video games and movies on demand further compete with books for individuals' attention, particularly the young. With the growing popularity of e-readers, it may be that books themselves will become obsolete.

Whatever the benefits or distractions posed by the electronic media, and whatever the future of the printed word, the written word will continue to be indispensable to the continued progress of civilization. Those who cannot effectively speak and write will find themselves at the mercy of those who can—by calculating politicians, by unscrupulous lenders, by predators of every ilk.

The inability to clearly express ideas excludes individuals not only from job opportunities, but from virtually every other avenue of advancement and life fulfillment. Words matter.

The words here collected represent a mostly chronological, though not all-inclusive narrative of American life. The words of our most articulate men and women—in some cases a reflection of popular sentiment and, in others, a significant influence in shaping popular sentiment—have been instrumental in the continued evolution of our society. Understanding where we've been and listening to the voices of those who created and developed our country will enable us to better understand ourselves and the age in which we live.

"This is not [just] history," said former House Speaker Newt Gingrich. "This is *identity*. It's who we are."

Providing more than a history of our republic, this book also serves as the ultimate self-help guide. This nation was founded, developed, and sustained by great people, many of whom dealt with far more substantive challenges than those we now confront. All of these people faced personal problems and setbacks that are universal to the human condition. This book does more than tell a nation's story. This book reinforces those old-fashioned, indeed timeless, lessons—that nothing worthwhile comes without struggle; that difficulties and injustices, however daunting, must be overcome by patience and perseverance; that worldly success is meaningless without a moral foundation. As beneficiaries of those who have gone before us, we are duty-bound to confront the challenges of our time and "secure the blessings of liberty to ourselves and our posterity."

Addressing the Young Men's Lyceum of Springfield, Illinois, on January 27, 1838, Abraham Lincoln spoke of the importance of doing exactly that—perpetuating our values and political institutions:

We, the American people...find ourselves in the peaceful possession of the fairest portion of the earth as regards extent of territory, fertility of soil, and salubrity of climate. We find ourselves under the government of a system of political institutions conducing more essentially to the ends of civil and religious liberty than any of which the history of former times tells us. We, when mounting the stage of existence, found ourselves the legal inheritors of these fundamental blessings. We toiled not in the acquirement or establishment of them; they are a legacy bequeathed us by a once hardy, brave, and patriotic, but now lamented and departed, race of ancestors. Theirs was the task (and nobly they performed it) to possess themselves, and through themselves, us, of this goodly land, and to uprear upon its hills and its valleys a political edifice of liberty and equal rights; 'tis ours only to transmit these—the former unprofaned by the foot of an invader, the latter undecayed by the lapse of time and untorn by usurpation—to the latest generation that fate shall permit the world to know. This task of gratitude to our fathers, justice to ourselves, duty to posterity, and love for our species in general, all imperatively require us faithfully to perform.

How then shall we perform it? At what point shall we expect the approach of danger? By what means shall we fortify against it? Shall we expect some transatlantic military giant to step the ocean and crush us at a blow? Never! All the armies of Europe, Asia, and Africa combined, with all the treasure of the earth (our own excepted) in their military chest, with a Bonaparte for a commander, could not by force take a drink from the Ohio or make a track on the Blue Ridge in a trial of a thousand years.

At what point, then, is the approach of danger to be expected? I answer, if it ever reach us, it must spring up amongst us. It cannot come from abroad. If destruction be our lot, we must ourselves be its author and finisher. As a nation of freemen, we must live through all time, or die by suicide.

As Lincoln's words are timeless, it is hoped—for the newly arrived and the native alike—that this book will spark a deeper exploration of the men and women who have shaped our common country, most especially the Founding Fathers.

In writing this book, as in all of life's other pursuits, I am indebted to many people. Most of all, my parents, Carl Anthony and Barbara Wimsatt Nett, whose love and support made me the upstanding citizen that I am. My brothers, Joe and Tim, and my sister, Jenny—adversaries in a competitive youth and my closest friends in adulthood. My wife, Kate, whose patience and moral support saw me through the rigors of recent life challenges. I also extend a heartfelt thanks to Butler Books for affording non-celebrity types like me the opportunity to contribute to the national dialogue. Without Carol Butler's generous counsel and unwavering support, this book would not be possible. Thanks, as well, to all those at HAILSTONESOUTH Publishing. Finally, I am indebted to those who have borne the burdens and made the sacrifices that enable me to live in peace and freedom—none more so than those who have made the ultimate sacrifice, from Concord Bridge to my fallen brethren in Iraq and Afghanistan.

—CARL NETT

At the close of the Constitutional Convention, Benjamin Franklin rose and made an observation about the chair from which General Washington had been presiding. On the chair was the design of a sun low on the horizon, and many of the delegates had wondered whether it was a rising or a setting sun. "We know now," Franklin said. "It is a rising sun and the beginning of a great new day!"

Contents

Preface   *ix*

Foreword   *xxv*

Colonial Life and the War Inevitable

The Mayflower Compact 2

BENJAMIN FRANKLIN: *Poor Richard's Almanack* 3

ANDREW HAMILTON: Freedom of the Press 7

JONATHAN EDWARDS: Sinners in the Hands of an Angry God 9

JAMES OTIS: Against Writs of Assistance 14

JOHN DICKINSON: The Liberty Song 16

GEORGE R. T. HEWES: Recollections of the Boston Tea Party 17

Slaves' Appeal to the Royal Governor of Massachusetts 20

PATRICK HENRY: An Appeal to Arms 21

George Washington: Answer to Congress on His Appointment as Commander-in-Chief 23

THOMAS PAINE: *Common Sense* 23

THOMAS PAINE: Liberty Tree 27

THOMAS JEFFERSON: The Declaration of Independence 28

JOHN ADAMS: Letter to Abigail 31

THOMAS PAINE: *The American Crisis* 32

Yankee Doodle 34

FRANCIS MILES FINCH: Nathan Hale 35

Valley Forge 37

Articles of Confederation 38

THOMAS JEFFERSON: A Bill for Establishing Religious Freedom in Virginia 43

MICHEL-GUILLAUME JEAN DE CRÈVECOEUR: *Letters from an American Farmer* 45

The Emerging Republic

GEORGE WASHINGTON: Rejecting a Crown 50

The Constitution of the United States 51

ALEXANDER HAMILTON, JAMES MADISON, AND JOHN JAY: The Federalist Papers 58

PATRICK HENRY: Against Ratification 64

Amendments to the Constitution 67

GEORGE WASHINGTON: First Inaugural Address 72

ARTHUR GUITERMAN: Daniel Boone 74

GEORGE WASHINGTON: Second Inaugural Address 76

GEORGE WASHINGTON: Farewell Address 77

JOSEPH HOPKINSON: Hail, Columbia 80

THOMAS JEFFERSON: First Inaugural Address 82

JOHN MARSHALL: *Marbury v. Madison* 85

JIMMY DRIFTWOOD: Battle of New Orleans 89

FRANCIS SCOTT KEY: The Star-Spangled Banner 90

SAMUEL WOODWORTH: The Old Oaken Bucket 91

JOSEPH RODMAN DRAKE: The American Flag 92

JAMES MONROE: The Monroe Doctrine 93

JOHN HOWARD PAYNE: Home, Sweet Home 95

DANIEL WEBSTER: Bunker Hill Oration 96

Reform and Expansion

OLIVER WENDELL HOLMES: The Flower of Liberty 100

OLIVER WENDELL HOLMES: Old Ironsides 100

GEORGE POPE MORRIS: Woodman, Spare That Tree 101

SAMUEL F. SMITH: America 102

BLACK HAWK: Speeches of Surrender and Reconciliation 103

WILLIAM BARRET TRAVIS: Dispatch from the Alamo 105

THEODORE O'HARA: The Bivouac of the Dead 106

RALPH WALDO EMERSON: Self-Reliance 107

RALPH WALDO EMERSON: Concord Hymn 110

HENRY WADSWORTH LONGFELLOW: Paul Revere's Ride 112

HENRY WADSWORTH LONGFELLOW: A Psalm of Life 112

HENRY WADSWORTH LONGFELLOW: The Village Blacksmith 112

HENRY WADSWORTH LONGFELLOW: The Ship of State 112

On Top of Old Smoky 116

Columbia, the Gem of the Ocean 116

HORACE MANN: The Case for Public Schools 118

Seneca Falls Declaration of Sentiments and Resolutions 120

SOJOURNER TRUTH: Address to the Ohio Women's Rights Convention 122

FREDERICK DOUGLASS: Fourth of July Address 123

FREDERICK DOUGLASS: Letter to His Former Master 126

HENRY DAVID THOREAU: Civil Disobedience 130

HENRY DAVID THOREAU: *Walden* 134

CHIEF SEE-YAHTLH: Address to the White Man 139

STEPHEN FOSTER: Oh! Susanna 141

STEPHEN FOSTER: Old Folks at Home 141

STEPHEN FOSTER: Camptown Races 141

STEPHEN FOSTER: My Old Kentucky Home, Good Night 141

A House Divided

DAVID WALKER: Walker's Appeal 146

ROBERT HAYNE: States' Rights 149

DANIEL WEBSTER: Against Nullification 152

JOHN C. CALHOUN: Fort Hill Address 154

WILLIAM LLOYD GARRISON: Prospectus for *The Liberator* 160

JAMES RUSSELL LOWELL: The Present Crisis 161

HENRY HIGHLAND GARNET: An Address to the Slaves of the United States of America 165

ABRAHAM LINCOLN: The House Divided Speech 169

JOSIAH GILBERT HOLLAND: God, Give Us Men! 172

JOHN BROWN: Last Statement to the Court 173

ABRAHAM LINCOLN: The Cooper Union Speech 174

Go Down Moses 180

Swing Low, Sweet Chariot 180

The Irrepressible Conflict

JEFFERSON DAVIS: Farewell to the U.S. Senate 184

ABRAHAM LINCOLN: First Inaugural Address 187

FRANCIS DE HAES JANVIER: God Save Our President 191

WILLIAM CULLEN BRYANT: Oh Mother of a Mighty Race 192

WILLIAM CULLEN BRYANT: Our Country's Call 192

SULLIVAN BALLOU: Letter to His Wife 194

THOMAS BUCHANAN READ: The Flag of the Constellation 196

DANIEL DECATUR EMMETT: Dixie 197

HARRY MCCARTHY: The Bonnie Blue Flag 198

GEORGE F. ROOT: Battle Cry of Freedom 199

JAMES RYDER RANDALL: Maryland, My Maryland 201

John Brown's Body 202

JULIA WARD HOWE: Battle Hymn of the Republic 203

WALTER KITTREDGE: Tenting on the Old Camp Ground 204

PATRICK S. GILMORE: When Johnny Comes Marching Home 205

ABRAHAM LINCOLN: Emancipation Proclamation 206

JOHN GREENLEAF WHITTIER: Stanzas for the Times 207

JOHN GREENLEAF WHITTIER: Maud Muller 207

JOHN GREENLEAF WHITTIER: Barbara Frietchie 207

ABRAHAM LINCOLN: The Gettysburg Address 212

NATHANIEL GRAHAM SHEPHERD: Roll-Call 213

ABRAHAM LINCOLN: Second Inaugural Address 214

FREDERICK DOUGLASS: Speech to the American Anti-Slavery Society 215

ULYSSES S. GRANT: Appomattox 217

ROBERT E. LEE: Farewell to His Army 218

FREDERICK DOUGLASS: In Memory of Abraham Lincoln 219

WALT WHITMAN: I Hear America Singing 221

WALT WHITMAN: O Captain! My Captain! 221

FRANCIS MILES FINCH: The Blue and the Gray 223

Postwar Society: The Progressive Age

The Ballad of John Henry 226

HIRAM R. REVELS: On Readmission of Georgia to the Union 228

CARTER GLASS: The Court-Packing Plan 338

ROBERT A. TAFT: Against the New Deal 342

IRVING BERLIN: Oh, How I Hate to Get Up in the Morning 345

IRVING BERLIN: God Bless America 345

LOU GEHRIG: Farewell 346

Flag Day 347

WOODY GUTHRIE: This Land Is Your Land 348

FRANKLIN D. ROOSEVELT: The Four Freedoms 350

FRANKLIN D. ROOSEVELT: War Message to Congress 353

ROBERT CRAWFORD: The U.S. Air Force 356

CHARLES A. ZIMMERMAN AND ALFRED H. MILES: Anchors Aweigh 357

LEARNED HAND: The Spirit of Liberty 359

Letter from a Navy Pilot 360

GEORGE S. PATTON, JR.: Speech to the Third Army 361

GEORGE S. PATTON, JR.: Through a Glass, Darkly 364

FRANK LOESSER: Praise the Lord and Pass the Ammunition 366

KARL SHAPIRO: Elegy for a Dead Soldier 367

ROSEMARY AND STEPHEN VINCENT BENÉT: U.S.A 370

Cold War Conflict

BERNARD BARUCH: The Baruch Plan for Control of Atomic Energy 374

GEORGE C. MARSHALL: The Marshall Plan Speech 375

HARRY S. TRUMAN: Inaugural Address 378

MARGARET CHASE SMITH: Declaration of Conscience 381

LANGSTON HUGHES: Dark Youth of the U.S.A. 384

LANGSTON HUGHES: Let America Be America Again 384

LANGSTON HUGHES: Refugee in America 384

GWENDOLYN BROOKS: The Mother 387

STAN JONES: Riders in the Sky 388

ROY ROGERS AND DALE EVANS: Happy Trails 389

ADLAI E. STEVENSON: The Nature of Patriotism 390

DOUGLAS MACARTHUR: Farewell Address at West Point 393

DWIGHT D. EISENHOWER: Farewell Address 396

Troubled Times

JOHN F. KENNEDY: Speech to the Greater Houston Ministerial Association 402

JOHN F. KENNEDY: Inaugural Address 405

PETE SEEGER: Where Have All the Flowers Gone? 407

MARTIN LUTHER KING, JR.: Letter from Birmingham City Jail 408

JOHN F. KENNEDY: Speech at the Berlin Wall 412

MARTIN LUTHER KING, JR.: March on Washington Address 414

We Shall Overcome 416

DUDLEY RANDALL: Ballad of Birmingham 417

BOB DYLAN: Blowin' in the Wind 418

LYNDON B. JOHNSON: The American Promise 419

ROBERT F. KENNEDY: Ending the War in Vietnam 422

EUGENE MCCARTHY: Kilroy 426

ROBERT F. KENNEDY: On the Death of Martin Luther King, Jr. 429

BARRY SADLER AND ROBERT L. MOORE: Ballad of the Green Berets 430

THOMAS B. ALLEN: A Place for Memories 431

RICHARD NIXON: Final Remarks at the White House 436

JOHNNY CASH: Ragged Old Flag 438

The Shining City

RONALD REAGAN: First Inaugural Address 442

MILTON AND ROSE FRIEDMAN: Free to Choose 445

A Nation at Risk 448

RONALD REAGAN: Speech on the *Challenger* Disaster 450

RONALD REAGAN: Brandenburg Gate Speech 452

GEORGE J. MITCHELL: The Iran-Contra Hearings 455

JESSE JACKSON: Speech to the Democratic National Convention 457

RONALD REAGAN: Speech at Moscow State University 460

Rendezvous with Destiny

NEWTON MINOW: Address to the Broadcasting Industry 466

HILLARY CLINTON: Women's Rights Are Human Rights 468

CLARENCE THOMAS: Remarks to the National Bar Association 471

HENRY HYDE: The Rule of Law 476

AL GORE: Concession Speech 479

BRUCE SPRINGSTEEN: My City of Ruins 482

GEORGE W. BUSH: War Message to Congress 483

BARACK OBAMA: A More Perfect Union 488

DAVID MCCULLOUGH: The Course of Human Events 493

Author Index   *501*

Premissions and Credits   *505*

Illustrations   *509*

Foreword

"These are the times that try men's souls," said Thomas Paine at the time of the American Revolutionary War. At once both topical and timeless, Paine's words were influential in the eighteenth century, and eloquently connect with the modern crises facing America. We, the American people, once again face threats to our freedom and liberty—a war to defeat a tyrannical and medieval ideology, and political and economic events that threaten the very existence of the United States.

September 11, 2001—9/11. What a tragic moment in time; perhaps the defining moment for a generation. Islamic terrorists from al Qaeda hijacked commercial jets and used them to destroy the World Trade Center and hit the Pentagon. A third jet, destined for either the White House or the U.S. Capitol, crashed in Shanksville, Pennsylvania, after passengers courageously attempted to foil the hijacking and retake the aircraft. All told, more than 3,000 innocent lives were extinguished—Americans and foreigners of all sizes, colors, languages, and religions. Americans were shocked, mortified, and caught completely off guard. Around the world, some mourned, but others cheered our fate.

Those of us of age remember what happened, and we vowed to never forget. But the true meaning of "never forget" is to not forget what 9/11 means to our nation and to free people around the world, and to never forget our historic and unending mission.

I had never really tried to put together what 9/11 meant to me, despite the far-reaching impact it had on my life and where I was in my life at that time. It's like being asked, "What was the BUD/S (Basic Underwater Demolition/SEAL) training course like?" or "What's it like to be a Navy SEAL?" The questions are just unanswerable in one sitting. My quick and ready answer is the first line of a Dickens novel—"It was the best of times, it was the worst of times." Then I just walk away.

The truth is, the catastrophe ripped me to the core because I grew up only forty miles away from the World Trade Center, in upstate New Jersey, and I knew people in the area—as most did from that part of the country. I could see New York City on the horizon from the top of a mountain behind my house. I used to visit my grandparents and cousins, who lived out on Remsen Avenue in the

Canarsie neighborhood of Brooklyn, and we would see the towers as we went past Yankee Stadium. Occasionally, we'd go into the city to ride in the elevators in the towers and jump when we got to the top. We felt like we were going to slam into the ceiling; we could feel the weightlessness as we moved so quickly. The buildings were huge; but for those who had never seen them or been in them, it's impossible to get the full scope of what happened there.

About four days before 9/11, I was a young Navy SEAL and had just graduated from SEAL Qualification Training (SQT), the last hurdle to jump before reporting to my assigned team. I was happy and excited to be a "Frogman" and didn't have a care in the world. Like firemen, you don't wish for people to get into accidents or for their houses to burn down, but you want to get out there and do something because you just made it to the big leagues. I wanted to test my skills somewhere in the world, and there really wasn't much going on anywhere. I wanted something to happen so the SEALs could save someone from the bad guys. I remember thinking that my generation had nothing to show for itself other than the advent of computers and video games. Little did I know of the horror that awaited a nation—my nation, that I signed on to protect.

In more recent years, with my SEAL career behind me, I've come to realize that there is another battle waging. It's a battle for the heart and soul of our nation and, largely, it's a battle between those who have learned the lessons of history and those who haven't.

There was a study done not too long ago that surveyed students from fifty of the elite colleges and universities. The students were asked questions taken from a high school curriculum, and the lack of historical knowledge was truly appalling. Sixty-six percent of the students tested could not place the Civil War in the proper half-century; close to 40 percent thought the Missouri Compromise settled a border dispute; only 45 percent could identify Samuel Gompers; only 23 percent of college seniors correctly identified James Madison as the "Father of the Constitution." According to the survey, the results demonstrate that "little more than half of college seniors know general information about American democracy and the Constitution," and most "do not know specifics about major wars the United States participated in." Two-thirds of the students failed to pass the multiple choice test and only one of 500 answered all thirty-four questions correctly.

This strikes me as something that the tragedy of 9/11 brings home. That is, our country has been attacked. Not only the Twin Towers and the Pentagon, but really the idea of our country; the ideas generated by the Founding Fathers. How are we going to defend this if we really don't know much about it? Students in our institutions of higher learning have less grasp, less understanding, less knowledge of American history than ever before. (What of all those who don't go to our "elite" colleges and universities, or pursue higher education at all?) We are raising a generation of young Americans who are, to a very large degree, historically illiterate. Handicapped by their ignorance, they lack the perspective to separate what is important from what is trivial, what is durable from what is ephemeral.

This isn't just something that we should be sad about, or worried about, that these young people don't know any history. We should be angry. They are being cheated, and our way of life could very well be in jeopardy because of this.

It's ironic, really. We face an enemy who believes in enforced ignorance; an enemy opposed to all that we stand for—the exercise of a free mind, the spirit of generosity, the ideas of tolerance, freedom, education, and opportunity. Yet, the traditional understanding of citizenship is being challenged here, on the home front, by contemporary forces and ideas that regard individuals more as helpless victims than as personally responsible, self-governing citizens. Consequently, authority and accountability tend to flow away from citizens, toward centralized "service-providing" bureaucracies that treat individuals as clients. This systematic disenfranchisement of the citizen, aided and abetted by a lack of historical literacy and the overall erosion of the education system, poses a grave threat to the hard-won freedoms of centuries past.

No less than Thomas Jefferson recognized the importance of education. He wrote, "If a nation expects to be ignorant and free in a state of civilization, it expects what never was and never will be." Interestingly, Jefferson proposed that education be "chiefly historical":

History, by apprising them [citizens] of the past, will enable them to judge of the future; it will avail them of the experience of other times, and other nations; it will qualify them as judges of the actions and designs of men; it will enable them to know

ambition under every disguise it may assume: and knowing it, to defeat its views. In every Government on earth is some trace of human weakness, some germ of corruption and degeneracy, which cunning will discover, and wickedness insensibly open, cultivate, and improve. Every Government degenerates when trusted to the rulers of the people alone. The people themselves, therefore, are its only safe depositories. And to render even them safe, their minds must be improved to a certain degree. This, indeed, is not all that is necessary, though it be essentially necessary…. The influence over Government must be shared among all the people. If every individual which composes their mass participates of the ultimate authority, the Government will be safe; because the corrupting the whole mass will exceed any private resources of wealth, and public ones cannot be provided but by levies on the people.

Jefferson and all of the Founding Fathers were, themselves, students of history. These men who declared our independence from England, who invented a new nation, who shaped and formed its constitution, were the heirs of the Age of Reason. They turned to Thomas Hobbes who, in his *Leviathan*, put forth his idea of the structure of society and legitimate government. They considered John Locke's view of man as a creature possessed of certain natural and inherent rights which it is the duty of government to ensure. They benefited from Francis Bacon's contribution to the scientific method and advances in the study and understanding of the human mind and behavior. They were influenced by the writings of Adam Smith, who believed that there was an invisible hand guiding the economic development of society, which was best left to function independently. At the core of his belief was the view of man as an essentially rational creature who was able to identify and pursue his needs. They likewise studied the writings of Montesquieu and his theory of separation of powers; Voltaire and his advocacy of civil liberties, including freedom of religion, freedom of expression, free trade, and religious pluralism; Rousseau and *The Social Contract*—"Man is born free, and everywhere he is in chains."

The statement, "We hold these truths to be self-evident…" implies that man is able to grasp truths, and beyond this, that all men are capable of living their own lives, pursuing happiness as they define it, and living freely. Reason is the beating heart of a constitutional republic, for only beings who are inherently free and rational are able to live under such a system of government, one which complements human nature. Freedom without reason gives us terror, anarchy, and fear. Reason without freedom leads, as our Founding Fathers demonstrated, to rebellion and revolution.

This fundamental understanding of our civilization is under attack today as never before. The forces that run contrary to our history know that the battle of ideas cannot be won head to head, so clandestine warfare—something I know a great deal about—is their logical choice. They are careful to subvert rather than overthrow institutions, leaving ordinary Americans "fat and happy" while the termites nibble the floor out from under them. Schools are the key to the future of their ideology, and the education strategy of those who seek to "fundamentally transform" America is in high gear. It begins slowly by omitting the history that makes our country great. Take WWII, for instance. A very important time in our history when the very *world* that we live in was almost taken over by evil and resulted in a Cold War that lasted for many years. Quiz a youth. You'll find them as lacking in history and civics as the participants in that collegiate study.

Now, since September 11, 2001, it seems to me that never in our lifetime, except possibly in the early stages of World War II, has it been clearer that we have as a source of strength, a source of direction, a source of inspiration— our story. It's a story worth reminding ourselves of and, in the case of others, worth *informing* them of. Yes, this is a dangerous time. Yes, this is a time full of shadows and fear. But we have been through worse before, and we have faced more difficult days. We have shown courage and determination, and demonstrated skillful and inventive responses to crisis. We should draw on our story; we should draw on our history as we've never drawn before. If we don't know who we are; if we don't know how we became what we are, we're going to start suffering from all the obvious detrimental effects of historical amnesia.

The Stile of This Confederacy is aimed at getting people in all walks of life thinking about what it means to be an American—our liberties, all those things we were attacked for. After 9/11, it seems to me that this is something essential.

Carl Nett, uniquely qualified to write this book, has lived his adult life on the frontlines of history. He grew up in Louisville, Kentucky, and, like me, he was profoundly affected by the events of 9/11. Just one day before the attack on our country, his application with the U.S. Secret Service arrived in the mail. Motivated as never before, he completed and submitted that application on 9/11 itself. Exactly one year later, just before entering the first of two training academies (the Federal Law Enforcement Training Center in Artesia, New Mexico, and, later, the U.S. Secret Service Academy in Beltsville, Maryland), he found himself working at the Pentagon alongside his Secret Service colleagues for the rededication ceremony after completion of the Phoenix Project—the name given to the project to repair the damage to the Pentagon, caused when American Airlines Flight 77 was deliberately crashed into the building on September 11, 2001. Carl spent the next five years traversing our country, and the world, protecting a war-time president. His Secret Service tenure only scratches the surface of his service to our nation since that fateful day. From Afghanistan to Guantanamo Bay to the corridors of power inside the Capital Beltway, Carl Nett has served in the most sensitive areas of our government and has been directly involved in the most important issues of our time.

But what both Carl and I realize is that you don't have to live our lifestyle to make a contribution. Nor do you *have* to read Hobbes, Locke, Smith, Montesquieu, Voltaire, Rousseau, et al. You don't have to enlist in the military or serve in law enforcement or obtain a top-secret security clearance. You don't have to carry a gun, travel to distant lands, or place yourself in harm's way to do your duty as an American. You are no less important than our troops fighting overseas, or our intelligence officers collecting and mining data, or our first responders keeping us safe on the home front.

Carl and I took an oath to "support and defend the Constitution of the United States against all enemies, foreign and domestic." This oath has been required of soldiers, representatives, senators, judges, and countless other government officials since it was expanded during the time of the Civil War to include "domestic" enemies. Historically, those who falsely swore this oath were prosecuted for perjury and forever denied federal employment. Surveying the landscape today, one may rightly question if that oath means something else in political-speak. As for Carl and I, we meant every word of that oath; it's an oath with no expiration date.

You pledge that same oath, less formally, when you recognize the dignity and worth of each human being, and when you commit yourself to preserving and defending the institutions of free, representative government and private enterprise that have enabled America and the entire Western world to realize that dignity. You fulfill that oath when you strengthen the institutions, principles, and values that nurture and sustain the American Experiment.

Our republic is fragile. Benjamin Franklin knew this all too well. At the close of the Constitutional Convention in Philadelphia in 1787, anxious citizens gathered outside Independence Hall when the proceedings ended in order to learn what had been produced behind closed doors. A Mrs. Powell of Philadelphia reportedly approached Franklin and asked, "Well, Doctor, what have we got, a republic or a monarchy?" Franklin responded, "A republic, if you can keep it."

"If you can keep it." Those five words by Franklin suggest that a republic is not something that can be expected to survive without nurturing and constant attention. What Franklin's admonition to Mrs. Powell means to today's Americans is that a freedom-affirming republic not only costs a great deal to obtain, it also requires continuing investment if the republic is to long endure. Maintaining a free republic requires an informed and engaged citizenry to actively pursue righteousness in our elected officials, and to remain alert to the goings on at every level of government.

"Freedom is never more than one generation away from extinction," said Ronald Reagan. "We didn't pass it to our children in the bloodstream. It must be fought for, protected, and handed on for them to do the same."

In short, *you* have a duty. *You* have an obligation as an American to serve your country and to do what is best for it. The United States of America is the greatest nation in the history of mankind, and it is our duty as Americans, guided by a knowledge of our history—the "informed patriotism" Carl speaks of, and which *The Stile of This Confederacy* cultivates—to live lives worthy of our inheritance and to transmit to our posterity, that liberty, which we received from our ancestors.

Of you, fellow citizen, much is required. "The summer soldier and the sunshine patriot will, in this crisis, shrink from the service of his country," concluded Paine, "but he that stands it now, deserves the love and thanks of man and woman. Tyranny, like hell, is not easily conquered; yet we have this consolation with us, that the harder the conflict, the more glorious the triumph. What we obtain too cheap, we esteem too lightly; 'tis dearness only that gives everything its value. Heaven knows how to put a proper price upon its goods; and it would be strange indeed, if so celestial an article as FREEDOM should not be highly rated."

—BENJAMIN SMITH

Columbus Before the Queen *(Isabella)*, as imagined by Emanuel Leutze. *The Norse explorer Leif Ericson is regarded as the first European to land in mainland North America, nearly five hundred years before Columbus. Giovanni Caboto, known in English as John Cabot, was a Genoese navigator and explorer whose 1497 discovery of North America is commonly held to be the first European voyage to the continent since that Norse exploration. Spanish explorer and conquistador Hernando De Soto led the first European expedition deep into the territory of the modern-day United States and became the first European to discover the Mississippi River. Columbus, who made the first of four voyages to the New World in 1492, is regarded more accurately as the person who brought the Americas into the forefront of Western attention and paved the way for these and later explorers like Ferdinand Magellan, Vasco de Gama, Sir Francis Drake, Sir Walter Raleigh, Hernando Cortes, Samuel de Champlain, Louis Joliet, Vasco Núñez de Balboa, Francisco Pizarro, Juan Ponce de León, Bartolomeu Dias, and many others. Veneration of Columbus in America dates back to the colonial era. Following the American Revolution, the name "Columbia" was given to the federal capital District of Columbia, South Carolina's new capital city Columbia, the Columbia River, and numerous other places. In 1812, the name "Columbus" was given to the newly founded capital of Ohio. The moniker "America," however, derives from explorer Amerigo Vespucci, who correctly believed that the place he discovered was not India, as Columbus believed, but a new continent entirely. German cartographer Martin Waldseemüller (who read Vespucci's travel journals, but had not then heard of Christopher Columbus's earlier travels) published a world map in 1507 calling the new continent America for Vespucci's Latinized name "Americus."*

Colonial Life
and the
War Inevitable

The Mayflower Compact

We whose names are underwriten ... doe by these presents solemnly & mutualy in ye presence of God, and one of another, covenant & combine our selves togeather into a civill body politick ...

"Americans are a nation born of an idea," wrote historian Theodore H. White. "Not the place, but the idea, created the United States Government." The idea was that citizens could join freely and govern themselves according to a set of laws designed to protect the common good.

On November 21, 1620, after sixty-six days at sea, the *Mayflower* anchored in what is now Provincetown Harbor just inside Cape Cod Bay. Aboard ship were 102 passengers, about a third of whom were Separatists—puritans who had separated from the Church of England. Before going ashore, the forty-one male passengers joined together and signed a covenant known as the Mayflower Compact—what John Adams would one day refer to, figuratively, as the foundation of the Constitution. It served as an early basis for self-government in America, whereby a body politic was created that was based on the consent of the governed and the rule of law.

On December 21, after nearly a month of exploring, the passengers—now collectively referred to as the Pilgrims—landed at what is now Plymouth, Massachusetts. They sailed the *Mayflower* across Cape Cod Bay, anchored in Plymouth Harbor, and established the second permanent English settlement in America. (Jamestown, settled in 1607, was the first.) Those who had signed the compact became the governing body of Plymouth Colony with the power to elect officers, make laws, levy taxes, admit new voting members, and call town meetings. The seeds of democracy had been sown in the new world.

In ye name of God Amen. We whose names are underwriten, the loyall subjects of our dread soveraigne Lord King James by ye grace of God, of great Britaine, Franc, & Ireland king, defender of ye faith, &c.

Haveing undertaken, for ye glorie of God, and advancements of ye Christian faith and honour of our king & countrie, a voyage to plant ye first colonie in ye Northerne parts of Virginia, doe by these presents solemnly & mutualy in ye presence of God, and one of another, covenant & combine our selves togeather into a civill body politick; for our better ordering, & preservation & furtherance of ye ends aforesaid; and by vertue hearof, to enacte, constitute, and frame shuch just & equall lawes, ordinances, Acts, constitutions, & offices, from time to time, as shall be thought most meete & convenient for ye generall good of ye Colonie: unto which we promise all due submission and obedience.

In witnes wherof we have hereunder subscribed our names at Cap-Codd ye ·11· of November, in ye year of ye raigne of our soveraigne Lord King James of England, France, & Ireland ye eighteenth and of Scotland ye fiftie fourth. An°: Dom. 1620.

John Carver, William Bradford, Edward Winslow, William Brewster, Isaac Allerton, Myles Standish, John Alden, Samuel Fuller, Christopher Martin, William Mullins, William White, Richard Warren, John Howland, Stephen Hopkins, Edward Tilley, John Tilley, Francis Cooke, Thomas Rogers, John Turner, Francis Eaton, James Chilton, John Crakston, John Billington, Moses Fletcher, John Goodman, Degory Priest, Thomas Tinker, John Rigdale, Edward Fuller, Thomas Williams, Gilbert Winslow, Edmund Margeson, Peter Brown, Richard Britterige, George Soule, Richard Clarke, Richard Gardiner, John Allerton, Thomas English, Edward Doty, Edward Leister.

Here comes the Orator! with his Flood of Words, and his Drop of Reason.

If what most men admire, they would despise,
'Twould look as if mankind were growing wise.

Are you angry that others disappoint you? remember you cannot depend upon yourself.

Fish & Visitors stink in 3 days.

Never praise your Cyder, Horse, or Bedfellow.

God helps them that help themselves.

Why does the blind man's wife paint herself?

Don't throw stones at your neighbours, if your own windows are glass.

Three things are men most liable to be cheated in, a Horse, a Wig, and a Wife.

God heals, and the Doctor takes the Fees.

The greatest monarch on the proudest throne, is oblig'd to sit upon his own arse.

The nearest way to come at glory, is to do that for conscience which we do for glory.

After crosses and losses men grow humbler & wiser.

Well done is better than well said.

At the working man's house hunger looks in but dares not enter.

The worst wheel of the cart makes the most noise.

To whom thy secret thou dost tell,
To him thy freedom thou dost sell.

Don't go to the doctor with every distemper, nor to the lawyer with every quarrel, nor to the pot with every thirst.

The noblest question in the world is *What good may I do in it?*

There are three faithful friends, an old wife, an old dog, and ready money.

He that would have a short Lent, let him borrow Money to be repaid at Easter.

If you wou'd not be forgotten
As soon as you are dead and rotten,
Either write things worth reading,
or do things worth the writing.

If you do what you should not, you must hear what you would not.

There is much difference between imitating a good man, and counterfeiting him.

Each year one vicious habit rooted out,
In time might make the worst Man good throughout.

When Death puts out our Flame, the Snuff will tell,
If we were Wax, or Tallow by the Smell.

Let thy Child's first Lesson be Obedience, and the second may be what thou wilt.

A Man of Knowledge like a rich Soil, feeds
If not a world of Corn, a world of Weeds.

Thirst after Desert, not Reward.

Proclaim not all thou knowest, all that owest, all thou hast, nor all thou canst.

Fear not Death; for the sooner we die, the longer we shall be immortal.

Those who in quarrels interpose,
Must often wipe a bloody nose.

Marry above thy match, and thou'lt get a Master.

A Flatterer never seems absurd:
The Flatter'd always take his word.

He that teaches himself, hath a fool for his master.

Well done, is twice done.

Quarrels never could last long,
If on one side only lay the wrong.

He that hath a Trade, hath an Estate.

The painful Preacher, like a candle bright,
Consumes himself in giving others Light.

Against Diseases here, the strongest Fence,
Is the defensive Virtue, Abstinence.

Write with the learned, pronounce with the vulgar.

In prosperous fortunes be modest and wise,
The greatest may fall, and the lowest may rise:
But insolent People that fall in disgrace,
Are wretched and no-body pities their Case.

'Tis easy to frame a good bold resolution;
but hard is the Task that concerns execution.

What you would seem to be, be really.

Tart Words make no Friends: a spoonful of honey will catch
more flies than a Gallon of Vinegar.

Fear God, and your Enemies will fear you.

A light purse is a heavy curse.

When the Well's dry, we know the Worth of Water.

Dost though love Life? then do not squander Time; for
that's the Stuff Life is made of.

Write Injuries in Dust, Benefits in Marble.

A Mob's a Monster; Heads enough, but no Brains.

Nature and nature's laws lay hid in night;
God said, Let NEWTON be, and all was light.

Having been poor is no shame, but being ashamed of it, is.

The Art of getting Riches consists very much in THRIFT.
All men are not equally qualified for getting Money, but it
is in the Power of every one alike to practice this Virtue.

Pay what you owe, and what you're worth you'll know.

Genius without Education is like Silver in the Mine.

Tim was so learned, that he could name a Horse in nine
Languages; So ignorant, that he bought a Cow to ride on.

The Golden Age never was the present age.

If worldly Goods cannot save me from Death, they ought
not to hinder me of eternal life.

'Tis against some Mens Principle to pay Interest, and
seems against others Interest to pay the Principal.

Haste makes Waste.

He that is of Opinion Money will do every Thing, may
well be suspected of doing every Thing for Money.

A Pair of good Ears will drain dry a hundred Tongues.

Gifts much expected, are paid, not given.

The Horse thinks one thing, and he that saddles him another.

Some make Conscience of wearing a Hat in the Church,
who make none of robbing the Altar.

Learning to the Studious; Riches to the Careful; Power to
the Bold; Heaven to the Virtuous.

When the Wine enters, out goes the Truth.

The hasty Bitch brings forth blind Puppies.

The Wolf sheds his Coat once a Year, his Disposition never.

A long Life may not be good enough, but a good Life is long enough.

Love your Enemies, for they tell you your Faults.

He that sows Thorns, should never go barefoot.

... to be proud of Virtue, is to poison yourself with the Antidote.

Nothing dries sooner than a Tear.

It is Ill-Manners to silence a Fool, and Cruelty to let him go on.

One To-day is worth two To-morrows.

Little Strokes,
Fell great Oaks.

Retirement does not always secure Virtue; Lot was upright in the City, wicked in the Mountain.

The royal Crown cures not the Head-ach.

Great Estates may venture more,
But little Boats should keep near Shore.

Fools need Advice most, but wise Men only are the better for it.

The Honey is sweet, but the Bee has a Sting.

Reader, farewel, all Happiness attend thee:
May each New-Year better and richer find thee.

ANDREW HAMILTON

Freedom of the Press

I differ very widely from him when he would insinuate that the just complaints of a number of men, who suffer under a bad administration, is libeling that administration.

Andrew Hamilton (1676-1741) was born in Scotland and migrated to Virginia as an indentured servant. He taught school while studying for admission to the bar, served in the Maryland Assembly, and then briefly studied law in London before settling in Philadelphia.

One of the most prominent lawyers in colonial America, Hamilton argued his most significant case in 1735 when he defended John Peter Zenger, who routinely criticized the policies of the colonial governor in the *New York Weekly Journal*. Upset with the criticism, the governor had Zenger arrested on the charge of seditious libel. Hamilton successfully argued that Zenger's comments could not be libelous because they were true, and he further challenged the established precedent of judges, not juries, deciding the truthfulness of written materials. This case signaled an early victory for freedom of the press and served as a building block for the First Amendment.

May it please your honors, I agree with Mr. Attorney [Richard Bradley] that government is a sacred thing, but I differ very widely from him when he would insinuate that the just complaints of a number of men, who suffer under a bad administration, is libeling that administration. Had I believed that to be law, I should not have given the court the trouble of hearing anything that I could say in this cause. ...

There is heresy in law as well as in religion, and both have changed very much; and we well know that it is not two centuries ago that a man would have burned as a heretic for owning such opinions in matters of religion as are publicly written and printed at this day. They were fallible men, it seems, and we take the liberty, not only to differ from them in religious opinion, but to condemn them and their opinions too; and I must presume that in taking these freedoms in thinking and speaking about matters of faith or religion, we are in the right; for, though it is said there are very great liberties of this kind taken in New York, yet I have heard of no information preferred by Mr. Attorney for an offense of this sort. From which I think it is pretty clear that in New York a man may make very free with his God, but he must take special care what he says of his Governor. It is agreed upon by all men that this is a reign of liberty, and while men keep within the bounds of truth, I hope they may with safety both speak and write their sentiments of the conduct of men of power; I mean of that part of their conduct only which affects the liberty or property of the people under their administration; were this to be denied, then the next step may make them slaves. For what notions can be entertained of slavery beyond that of suffering the greatest injuries and oppressions without the liberty of complaining; or if they do, to be destroyed, body and estate, for so doing?

It is said, and insisted upon by Mr. Attorney, that government is a sacred thing; that it is to be supported and reverenced; it is government that protects our persons and estates; that prevents treasons, murders, robberies, riots, and all the train of evils that overturn kingdoms and states and ruin particular persons; and if those in the administration, especially the supreme magistrates, must have all their conduct censured by private men, government cannot subsist. This is called a licentiousness not to be tolerated. It is said that it brings the rulers of the people into contempt so that their authority is not regarded, and so that in the end the laws cannot be put in execution. These, I say, and such as these, are the general topics insisted upon by men in power and their advocates. But I wish it might be considered at the same time how often it has happened that the abuse of power has been the primary cause of these evils, and that it was the injustice and oppression of these great men which has commonly brought them into contempt with the people. The craft and art of such men are great, and who that is the least acquainted with history or with law can be ignorant of the specious pretenses which have often been made use of by men in power to introduce arbitrary rule and destroy the liberties of a free people. …

The loss of liberty to a generous mind is worse than death; and yet we know there have been those in all ages who, for the sakes of preferment or some imaginary honor, have freely lent a helping hand to oppress, nay, to destroy, their country.

This brings to my mind that saying of the immortal Brutus, when he looked upon the creatures of Caesar, who were very great men, but by no means good men: "You Romans," said Brutus, "if yet I may call you so, consider what you are doing; remember that you are assisting Caesar to forge those very chains which one day he will make yourselves wear." This is what every man that values freedom ought to consider; he should act by judgment and not by affection or self-interest; for where those prevail, no ties of either country or kindred are regarded; as, upon the other hand, the man who loves his country prefers its liberty to all other considerations, well knowing that without liberty life is misery. …

Power may justly be compared to a great river; while kept within its bounds, it is both beautiful and useful, but when it overflows its banks, it is then too impetuous to be stemmed; it bears down all before it, and brings destruction and desolation wherever it comes. If, then, this be the nature of power, let us at least do our duty, and, like wise men who value freedom, use our utmost care to support liberty, the only bulwark against lawless power, which, in all ages, has sacrificed to its wild lust and boundless ambition the blood of the best men that ever lived.

I hope to be pardoned, sir, for my zeal upon this occasion. It is an old and wise caution that "when our neighbor's house is on fire, we ought to take care of our own." For though, blessed be God, I live in a government where liberty is well understood and freely enjoyed, yet experience has shown us all (I am sure it has to me) that a bad precedent in one government is soon set up for an authority in another; and therefore I cannot but think it mine and every honest man's duty that, while we pay all due obedience to men in authority, we ought, at the same time, to be upon our guard against power wherever we apprehend that it may affect ourselves or our fellow subjects.

I am truly very unequal to such an undertaking, on many accounts. And you see I labor under the weight of many years and am borne down with great infirmities of body; yet old and weak as I am, I should think it my duty, if required, to go to the utmost part of the land, where my service could be of any use in assisting to quench the flame of prosecutions upon informations, set on foot by the government to deprive a people of the right of remonstrating, and complaining too, of the arbitrary attempts of men in power. Men who injure and oppress the people under their administration provoke them to cry out and complain, and then make that very complaint the foundation for new oppressions and prosecutions. I wish I could say there were no instances of this kind. But, to conclude, the question before the court, and you, gentlemen of the jury, is not of small nor private concern; it is not the cause of a poor printer, nor of New York alone, which you are now trying. No! It may, in its consequence, affect every free man that lives under a British government on the main continent of America. It is the best cause; it is the cause of liberty; and I make no doubt but your upright conduct, this day, will not only entitle you to the love and esteem of your fellow citizen, but every man who prefers freedom to a life of slavery will bless and honor you as men who have baffled the attempt of tyranny, and, by an impartial and uncorrupt verdict, have laid a noble foundation for securing to ourselves, our posterity, and our neighbors that to which nature and the laws of our country have given us a right—the liberty of both exposing and opposing arbitrary power (in these parts of the world at least) by speaking and writing truth. ...

JONATHAN EDWARDS

Sinners in the Hands of an Angry God

If sin was not restrained, it would immediately turn the soul into a fiery oven, or a furnace of fire and brimstone.

The religious persecution that drove settlers from Europe to the British North American colonies sprang from the conviction, held by numerous denominations, that uniformity of religion was a necessary component of civilized society. This conviction rested on the belief that there was "one true religion" and that it was the duty of the civil authorities to impose that religion, by force if necessary, in the interest of saving the souls of all citizens.

In seventeenth and eighteenth century America, as in Europe, religious life and political life were intimately linked. As many of the persecuted became persecutors, debates over religious toleration generally concerned whether people holding minority beliefs should be allowed to practice their religion without criminal sanction—or worse. The Salem Witch Trials of the 1690s serve as perhaps the most widely known cautionary tale of religious extremism, lack of due process, and government intrusion on individual liberties.

As more and more people seeking religious freedom came to America, bringing with them a variety of beliefs, the colonies became a patchwork of religiously diverse communities. As a result, this religious persecution diminished and religious freedom became more widely accepted. A significant influence on American religion during this time was the Great Awakening, a religious revitalization movement that swept through the English-speaking world in the 1730s and 1740s. It resulted from powerful preaching that gave listeners a sense of personal guilt for their sins and stressed the need for individual salvation through Jesus Christ. The Great Awakening brought Christianity to African slaves, challenged established authority, and served as an affront to traditionalists by supplanting rituals and ceremony with a more personalized call for introspection and a commitment to personal morality. The revival also stimulated a concern for higher education and a desire on the part of more young men to enter the ministry.

A leading organizer of the Great Awakening was Jonathan Edwards (1703–1758), a Congregationalist minister in Northampton, Massachusetts, and the leading theologian of the colonial era. "Sinners in the Hands of an Angry God," Edwards's most famous sermon, emphasized the widely held belief that hell is a real and functional place. His vivid imagery combined with an emotional, highly engaged preaching style served to "awaken" his audience to the horrific reality that, in his view, awaited the sinful and unrepentant.

The effect of Great Awakening unity was a rejection of the deferential thinking that characterized English politics and religion. No longer accepting the long-held belief that God's will was necessarily interpreted by the monarch or his bishops, the colonists viewed themselves as more capable of performing the task. Thus, it was a religious and self-assured people who rose in rebellion during the American Revolution. The signers of the Declaration of Independence made their appeal, not to any church or potentate, but directly to the "Supreme Judge of the World."

Deuteronomy 32:35
Their foot shall slide in due time.

In this verse is threatened the vengeance of God on the wicked unbelieving Israelites. …

The expression that I have chosen for my text, "Their foot shall slide in due time," seems to imply the following things, relating to the punishment and destruction that these wicked Israelites were exposed to.

1. That they were *always* exposed to destruction; as one that stands or walks in slippery places is always exposed to fall. …

2. It implies that they were always exposed to *sudden* unexpected destruction. As he that walks in slippery places is every moment liable to fall; he can't foresee one moment whether he shall stand or fall the next; and when he does fall, he falls at once, without warning. …

3. Another thing implied is that they are liable to fall *of themselves*, without being thrown down by the hand of another. As he that stands or walks on slippery ground, needs nothing but his own weight to throw him down.

4. That the reason why they are not fallen already, and don't fall now, is only that God's appointed time is not come…. Then they shall be left to fall as they are inclined by their own weight. God won't hold them up in these slippery places any longer, but will let them go …

[DOCTRINE.]
There is nothing that keeps wicked men, at any one moment, out of hell, but the mere pleasure of God.

By "the mere pleasure of God," I mean his sovereign pleasure, his arbitrary will, restrained by no obligation, hindered by no manner of difficulty, any more than if nothing else but God's mere will had in the least degree, or in any respect whatsoever, any hand in the preservation of wicked men one moment.

The truth of this observation may appear by the following considerations.

I. There is no want of *power* in God to cast wicked men into hell at any moment. …

He is not only able to cast wicked men into hell, but he can most *easily* do it. …

There is no fortress that is any defense from the power of God. Though hand join in hand, and vast multitudes of God's enemies combine and associate themselves, they are easily broken in pieces. …

II. They *deserve* to be cast into hell; so that divine justice never stands in the way, it makes no objection against God's using his power at any moment to destroy them. Yea, on the contrary, justice calls aloud for an infinite punishment of their sins … The sword of divine justice is every moment brandished over their heads, and 'tis nothing but the hand of arbitrary mercy, and God's mere will, that holds it back.

III. They are *already* under a sentence of condemnation to hell … So that every unconverted man properly belongs to hell; that is his place; from thence he is. …

IV. They are now the objects of that very *same* anger and wrath of God that is expressed in the torments of hell: and the reason why they don't go down to hell at each moment, is not because God, in whose power they are, is not then very angry with them … The wrath of God burns against them, their damnation don't slumber, the pit is prepared, the fire is made ready, the furnace is now hot, ready to receive them, the flames do now rage and glow. The glittering sword is whet, and held over them, and the pit hath opened her mouth under them.

V. The *devil* stands ready to fall upon them, and seize them as his own, at what moment God shall permit him. They belong to him; he has their souls in his possession, and under his dominion … if God should withdraw his hand, by which they are restrained, they would in one moment fly upon their poor souls. …

VI. There are in the souls of wicked men those hellish *principles* reigning, that would presently kindle and flame out into hell fire, if it were not for God's restraints … Sin is the ruin and misery of the soul; it is destructive in its nature; and if God should leave it without restraint, there would need nothing else to make the soul perfectly miserable. The corruption of the heart of man is a thing that is immoderate and boundless in its fury; and while wicked men live here, it is like fire pent up by God's restraints, whenas if it were let loose it would set on fire the course of nature; and as the heart is now a sink of sin, so, if sin was not restrained, it would immediately turn the soul into a fiery oven, or a furnace of fire and brimstone.

VII. It is no security to wicked men for one moment, that there are no *visible means of death* at hand … The manifold and continual experience of the world in all ages, shows that this is no evidence that a man is not on the very brink of eternity, and that the next step won't be into another world … Unconverted men walk over the pit of hell on a rotten covering, and there are innumerable places in this covering so weak that they won't bear their weight, and these places are not seen. The arrows of death fly unseen at noonday; the sharpest sight can't discern them. God has so many different unsearchable ways of taking wicked men out of the world and sending 'em to hell, that there is nothing to make it appear that God had need to be at the expense of a miracle, or go out of the ordinary course of his providence, to destroy any wicked man, at any moment. …

VIII. Natural men's prudence and care to preserve their own lives, or the care of others to preserve them, don't secure 'em a moment … There is this clear evidence that men's own wisdom is no security to them from death. …

IX. All wicked men's pains and contrivance they use to escape hell, while they continue to reject Christ, and so remain wicked men, don't secure 'em from hell one moment. Almost every natural man that hears of hell, flatters himself that he shall escape it; he depends upon himself for his own security; he flatters himself in what he has done, in what he is now doing, or what he intends to do; everyone lays out matters in his own mind how he shall avoid damnation, and flatters himself that he contrives well for himself, and that his schemes won't fail. …

But the foolish children of men miserably delude themselves in their own schemes, and in their confidence in their own strength and wisdom; they trust to nothing but a shadow … If it were so, that we could come to speak with them, and could inquire of them, one by one, whether they expected when alive, and when they used to hear about hell, ever to be the subjects of that misery, we doubtless, should hear one and another reply, "No, I never intended to come here: I had laid out matters otherwise in my mind; I thought I should contrive well for myself; I thought my scheme good; I intended to take effectual care; but it came upon me unexpected; I did not look for it at that time, and in that manner; it came as a thief; death outwitted me; God's wrath was too quick for me; O my cursed foolishness! I was flattering myself, and pleasing myself with vain dreams of what I would do hereafter, and when I was saying, 'Peace and safety,' then suddenly destruction came upon me."

X. God has laid himself under *no obligation* by any promise to keep any natural man out of hell one moment. God certainly has made no promises either of eternal life, or of any deliverance or preservation from eternal death, but what are contained in the covenant of grace, the promises that are given in Christ, in whom all the promises are yea and amen. But surely they have no interest in the promises of the covenant of grace that are not the children of the covenant, and that don't believe in any of the promises of the covenant, and have no interest in the *Mediator* of the covenant. …

Whatever pains a natural man takes in religion, whatever prayers he makes, till he believes in Christ, God is under no manner of obligation to keep him a *moment* from eternal destruction.

So that thus it is, that natural men are held in the hand of God over the pit of hell; they have deserved the fiery pit, and are already sentenced to it; and God is dreadfully provoked, his anger is as great towards them as to those that are actually suffering the executions of the fierceness of his wrath in hell, and they have done nothing in the least to appease or abate that anger, neither is God in the least bound by any promise to hold 'em up one moment; the devil is waiting for them, hell is gaping for them, the flames gather and flash about them, and would fain lay hold on them, and swallow them up; the fire pent up in their own hearts is struggling to break out; and they have no interest in any mediator, there are no means within reach that can be any security to them. In short, they have no refuge, nothing to take hold of, all that preserves them every moment is the mere arbitrary will, and uncovenanted unobliged forbearance of an incensed God.

APPLICATION

The *Use* may be of *Awakening* to unconverted persons in this congregation. This that you have heard is the case of everyone of you that are out of Christ. That world of misery, that lake of burning brimstone is extended abroad under you. *There* is the dreadful pit of the glowing flames of the wrath of God; there is hell's wide gaping mouth open; and you have nothing to stand upon, nor any thing to take hold of: there is nothing between you and hell but the air; 'tis only the power and mere pleasure of God that holds you up.

You probably are not sensible of this; you find you are kept out of hell, but don't see the hand of God in it, but look at other things, as the good state of your bodily constitution, your care of your own life, and the means you use for your own preservation. But indeed these things are nothing; if God should withdraw his hand, they would avail no more to keep you from falling, than the thin air to hold up a person that is suspended in it. …

If God should let you go, you would immediately sink and swiftly descend and plunge into the bottomless gulf, and your healthy constitution, and your own care and prudence, and best contrivance, and all your righteousness, would have no more influence to uphold you and keep you out of hell, than a spider's web would have to stop a falling rock. …

The bow of God's wrath is bent, and the arrow made ready on the string, and Justice bends the arrow at your heart, and strains the bow, and it is nothing but the mere pleasure of God, and that of an angry God, without any promise or obligation at all, that keeps the arrow one moment from being made drunk with your blood.

Thus all you that never passed under a great change of heart, by the mighty power of the Spirit of God upon your souls; all that were never born again, and made new creatures, and raised from being dead in sin, to a state of new, and before altogether unexperienced light and life (however you may have reformed your life in many things, and may have had religious affections, and may keep up a form of religion in your families and closets, and in the house of God, and may be strict in it), you are thus in the hands of an angry God; 'tis nothing but his mere pleasure that keeps you from being this moment swallowed up in everlasting destruction.

However unconvinced you may now be of the truth of what you hear, by and by you will be fully convinced of it. …

The God that holds you over the pit of hell, much as one holds a spider, or some loathsome insect, over the fire, abhors you, and is dreadfully provoked; his wrath towards you burns like fire; he looks upon you as worthy of nothing else, but to be cast into the fire; he is of purer eyes than to bear to have you in his sight; you are ten thousand times so abominable in his eyes as the most hateful venomous serpent is in ours. You have offended him infinitely more than ever a stubborn rebel did his prince; and yet 'tis nothing but his hand that holds you from falling into the fire every moment. …

O sinner! Consider the fearful danger you are in … You hang by a slender thread, with the flames of divine wrath flashing about it, and ready every moment to singe it, and burn it asunder; and you have no interest in any mediator, and nothing to lay hold of to save yourself, nothing to keep off the flames of wrath, nothing of your own, nothing that you ever have done, nothing that you can do, to induce God to spare you one moment.

And consider here more particularly several things concerning that wrath you are in such danger of.

First. *Whose* wrath it is: it is the wrath of the infinite God … The greatest earthly potentates, in their greatest majesty and strength, and when clothed in their greatest terrors, are but feeble despicable worms of the dust, in comparison of the great and almighty Creator and King of heaven and earth. …

Second. 'Tis the *fierceness* of his wrath that you are exposed to … The fury of God! the fierceness of Jehovah! Oh how dreadful must that be! Who can utter or conceive what such expressions carry in them! But it is not only said so, but "the fierceness and wrath of *almighty God.*" …

Consider this, you that are here present, that yet remain in an unregenerate state. That God will execute the fierceness of his anger, implies that he will inflict wrath without any pity … he will have no regard to your welfare, nor be at all careful lest you should suffer too much, in any other sense than only that you shall not suffer beyond what strict justice requires: nothing shall be withheld, because it's so hard for you to bear … Now God stands ready to pity you; this is a day of mercy; you may cry now with some encouragement of obtaining mercy: but when once the day of mercy is past, your most lamentable and dolorous cries and shrieks will be in vain; you will be wholly lost and thrown away of God as to any regard to your welfare; God will have no other use to put you to but only to suffer misery; you shall be continued in being to no other end; for you will be a vessel of wrath fitted to destruction; and there will be no other use of this vessel but only to be filled full of wrath. …

Third. The misery you are exposed to is that which God will inflict to that end, that he might show what the wrath of Jehovah is. God hath had it on his heart to show to angels and men, both how excellent his love is, and also how terrible his wrath is …When the great and angry God hath risen up and executed his awful vengeance on the poor sinner; and the wretch is actually suffering the infinite weight and power of his indignation, then will God call upon the whole universe to behold that awful majesty, and mighty power that is to be seen in it. …

Thus it will be with you that are in an unconverted state, if you continue in it; the infinite might, and majesty and terribleness of the omnipotent God shall be magnified upon you, in the ineffable strength of your torments: you shall be tormented in the presence of the holy angels, and in the presence of the Lamb; and when you shall be in this state of suffering, the glorious inhabitants of heaven shall go forth and look on the awful spectacle, that they may see what the wrath and fierceness of the Almighty is, and when they have seen it, they will fall down and adore that great power and majesty. …

Fourth. 'Tis *everlasting* wrath. It would be dreadful to suffer this fierceness and wrath of almighty God one moment; but you must suffer it to all eternity: there will be no end to this exquisite horrible misery. When you look forward, you shall see a long forever, a boundless duration before you, which will swallow up your thoughts, and amaze your soul; and you will absolutely despair of ever having any deliverance, any end, any mitigation, any rest at all; you will know certainly that you must wear out long ages, millions of millions of ages, in wrestling and conflicting with this almighty merciless vengeance; and then when you have so done, when so many ages have actually been spent by you in this manner, you will know that all is but a point to what remains. …

How dreadful is the state of those that are daily and hourly in danger of this great wrath, and infinite misery! But this is the dismal case of every soul in this congregation, that has not been born again, however moral and strict, sober and religious they may otherwise be. Oh that you would consider it, whether you be young or old. There is reason to think, that there are many in this congregation now hearing this discourse, that will actually be the subjects of this very misery to all eternity … If we knew that there was one person, and but one, in the whole congregation that was to be the subject of this misery, what an awful thing would it be to think of! … And it would be a wonder if some that are now present, should not be in hell in a very short time, before this year is out … Those of you that finally continue in a natural condition, that shall keep out of hell longest, will be there in a little time! your damnation don't slumber; it will come swiftly, and in all probability very suddenly upon many of you … But here you are in the land of the living, and in the house of God, and have an opportunity to obtain salvation. What would not those poor damned, hopeless souls give for one day's opportunity such as you now enjoy!

And now you have an extraordinary opportunity, a day wherein Christ has flung the door of mercy wide open, and stands in the door calling and crying with a loud voice to poor sinners; a day wherein many are flocking to him, and pressing into the kingdom of God; many are daily coming from the east, west, north and south; many that were very lately in the same miserable condition that you are in, are now in a happy state, with their hearts filled with love to him that has loved them and washed them from their sins in his own blood, and rejoicing in hope of the glory of God. How awful is it to be left behind at such a day! To see so many others feasting, while you are pining and perishing! … Are there not many here that have lived *long* in the world, that are not to this day born again, and so are aliens from the commonwealth of Israel, and have done nothing ever since they have lived, but treasure up wrath against the day of wrath? …

And let everyone that is yet out of Christ, and hanging over the pit of hell, whether they be old men and women, or middle aged, or young people, or little children, now hearken to the loud calls of God's Word and providence … God seems now to be hastily gathering in his elect in all parts of the land; and probably the bigger part of adult persons that ever shall be saved, will be brought in now in a little time, and that it will be as it was on that great outpouring of the Spirit upon the Jews in the apostles' days, the election will obtain, and the rest will be blinded. …

Therefore let everyone that is out of Christ, now awake and fly from the wrath to come. The wrath of almighty God is now undoubtedly hanging over great part of this congregation: let everyone fly out of Sodom. "Haste and escape for your lives, look not behind you, escape to the mountain, lest you be consumed" [Gen. 19:17].

"Join, or Die," created by Benjamin Franklin, was first published in his Pennsylvania Gazette *in 1754 and accompanied his editorial about the "disunited state" of the colonies. Showing a snake severed into eighths, with each segment labeled with the initials of a British American colony or region, the cartoon helped make his point about the importance of colonial unity. At that time, the colonists were divided on whether to fight the French and their Indian allies for control of the land west of the Appalachian Mountains, in what came to be known as the French and Indian War. Franklin had proposed his Albany Plan of Union, an early attempt to form a union of the colonies that would remain under the authority of the British crown, and his cartoon suggested that such a union was necessary to avoid destruction. A popular superstition of the era was that a snake that had been cut into pieces would come back to life if the pieces were put together before sunset.*

JAMES OTIS

Against Writs of Assistance

A man's house is his castle; and whilst he is quiet, he is as well guarded as a prince in his castle.

James Otis (1725-1783) served as the king's advocate general of the vice admiralty from 1756 until 1761, when he resigned his position rather than supervise orders empowering British customs officials to search any house at will for smuggled goods. Arguing eloquently before the court, Otis claimed that these "writs of assistance" violated the rights of colonials as Englishmen and that any act of Parliament violating those rights was void. Although not successful, the British government eventually withdrew the orders.

Otis went on to become one of the leading agitators against Great Britain. He organized colonial meetings and relentlessly criticized British revenue officers, declaring, "Taxation without representation is tyranny." Frequently denounced in the British Parliament, Otis's career ended abruptly in 1769 when a savage beating by British officers left him insane. He was later killed by lightning, an ironic death for a man whom John Adams described as a rhetorical "flame of fire." Commenting on Otis's eloquent demand to limit search and seizure, Adams stated: "American independence was there and then born; the seeds of patriots and heroes were then and there sown. Then and there was the first scene of the first act of opposition to the arbitrary claims of Great Britain."

May it please your honors, I was desired by one of the court to look into the books, and consider the question now before them concerning writs of assistance. I have, accordingly, considered it, and now appear not only in obedience to your order, but likewise in behalf of the inhabitants of this town, who have presented another petition, and out of regard to the liberties of the subject. And I take this opportunity to declare that, whether under a fee or not (for in such a case as this I despise a fee), I will to my dying day oppose with all the powers and faculties God has given me all such instruments of slavery, on the one hand, and villainy, on the other, as this writ of assistance is.

It appears to me the worst instrument of arbitrary power, the most destructive of English liberty and the fundamental principles of law that ever was found in an English lawbook. I must, therefore, beg your honors' patience and attention to the whole range of an argument, that may, perhaps, appear uncommon in many things, as well as to points of learning that are more remote and unusual: that the whole tendency of my design may the more easily be perceived, the conclusions better descend, and the force of them be better felt. I shall not think much of my pains in this cause, as I engaged in it from principle. I was solicited to argue this case as Advocate General; and because I would not, I have been charged with desertion from my office. To this charge I can give a very sufficient answer. I renounced that office, and I argue this cause from the same principle; and I argue it with the greater pleasure, as it is in favor of British liberty, at a time when we hear the greatest monarch upon earth declaring from his throne that he glories in the name of Briton, and that the privileges of his people are dearer to him than the most valuable prerogatives of his crown; and as it is in opposition to a kind of power the exercise of which, in former periods of history, cost one king of England his head and another his throne. I have taken more pains in this cause than I ever will take again, although my engaging in this and another popular cause has raised much resentment. But I think I can sincerely declare that I cheerfully submit myself to every odious name for conscience's sake; and from my soul I despise all those whose guilt, malice, or folly has made them my foes. Let the consequences be what they will, I am determined to proceed. The only principles of public conduct that are worthy of a gentlemen or a man are to sacrifice estate, ease, health, and applause, and even life, to the sacred calls of his country.

These manly sentiments, in private life, make the good citizen; in public life, the patriot and the hero. I do not say

that when brought to the test I shall be invincible. I pray God I may never be brought to the melancholy trial; but if ever I should, it will be then known how far I can reduce to practice principles which I know to be founded in truth. In the meantime I will proceed to the subject of this writ.

Your honors will find in the old books concerning the office of a justice of the peace precedents of general warrants to search suspected houses. But in more modern books you will find only special warrants to search such and such houses, specially named, in which the complainant has before sworn that he suspects his goods are concealed; and will find it adjudged that special warrants only are legal. In the same manner I rely on it that the writ prayed for in this petition, being general, is illegal. It is a power that places the liberty of every man in the hands of every petty officer. I say I admit that special writs of assistance, to search special places, may be granted to certain persons on oath; but I deny that the writ now prayed for can be granted, for I beg leave to make some observations on the writ itself, before I proceed to other acts of Parliament. In the first place, the writ is universal, being directed "to all and singular justices, sheriffs, constables, and all other officers and subjects;" so that, in short, it is directed to every subject in the king's dominions. Everyone with this writ may be a tyrant; if this commission be legal, a tyrant in a legal manner, also, may control, imprison, or murder anyone within the realm. In the next place, it is perpetual; there is no return. A man is accountable to no person for his doings. Every man may reign secure in his petty tyranny, and spread terror and desolation around him, until the trump of the archangel shall excite different emotions in his soul. In the third place, a person with this writ, in the daytime, may enter all houses, shops, etc., at will, and command all to assist him. Fourthly, by this writ, not only deputies, etc., but even their menial servants, are allowed to Lord it over us. What is this but to have the curse of Canaan with a witness on us; to be the servant of servants, the most despicable of God's creation? Now, one of the most essential branches of English liberty is the freedom of one's house. A man's house is his castle; and whilst he is quiet, he is as well guarded as a prince in his castle. This writ, if it should be declared legal, would totally annihilate this privilege. Customhouse officers may enter our houses when they please; we are commanded to permit their entry. Their menial servants may enter, may break locks, bars, and everything in their way; and whether they break through malice or revenge, no man, no court, can inquire. Bare suspicion without oath is sufficient. This wanton exercise of this power is not a chimerical suggestion of a heated brain. I will mention some facts. Mr. Pew had one of these writs, and when Mr. Ware succeeded him, he indorsed this writ over to Mr. Ware; so that these writs are negotiable from one officer to another; and so your honors have no opportunity of judging the persons to whom this vast power is delegated. Another instance is this: Mr. Justice Walley had called this same Mr. Ware before him, by a constable, to answer for a breach of the Sabbath Day Acts, or that of profane swearing. As soon as he had finished, Mr. Ware asked him if he had done. He replied: "Yes." "Well, then," said Mr. Ware, "I will show you a little of my power. I command you to permit me to search your house for uncustomed goods;" and went on to search the house from the garret to the cellar, and then served the constable in the same manner! But to show another absurdity in this writ, if it should be established, I insist upon it that every person, by the 14th of Charles II, has this power as well as the customhouse officers. The words are: "It shall be lawful for any person or persons authorized," etc. What a scene does this open! Every man prompted by revenge, ill-humor, or wantonness to inspect the inside of his neighbor's house may get a writ of assistance. Others will ask it from self-defense; one arbitrary exertion will provoke another, until society be involved in tumult and in blood. …

JOHN DICKINSON

The Liberty Song

John Dickinson (1732-1808), among the most knowledgeable and influential of American statesmen, served as a Pennsylvania delegate to the Continental Congress. A proponent of conciliation with Great Britain, Dickinson had expressed his moderate political views in his *Letters from a Farmer in Pennsylvania to the Inhabitants of the British Colonies*. He opposed the Declaration of Independence, drafted by the Second Continental Congress, but nonetheless served in the militia and went on to serve his fledgling country as chief author of the Articles of Confederation. As a delegate from Delaware, Dickinson also attended the Constitutional Convention, which drafted the Constitution, and he worked tirelessly for its ratification.

"The Liberty Song," written by Dickinson in 1768, was the first patriotic American ballad and was sung on nearly all public occasions to the annoyance of British soldiers and loyalists.

Come join hand in hand brave Americans all,
And rouse your bold hearts at fair Liberty's call;
No tyrannous acts shall suppress your just claim,
Or stain with dishonour America's name.

Chorus:
    In Freedom we're born and in Freedom we'll live,
    Our purses are ready,
    Steady, Friends, Steady.
    Not as slaves, but as Freemen our money we'll give.

Our worthy Forefathers—Let's give them a cheer
To Climates unknown did courageously steer;
Thro' Oceans, to deserts, for freedom they came,
And dying bequeath'd us their freedom and Fame.

Their generous bosoms all dangers despis'd,
So highly, so wisely, their *Birthrights* they priz'd;
We'll keep what they gave, we will piously keep,
Nor frustrate their toils on the land and the deep.

The Tree their own hands had to Liberty rear'd;
They liv'd to behold growing strong and rever'd;
With transport they cry'd, "Now our wishes we gain
For our children shall gather the fruits of our pain."

Swarms of placemen and pensioners soon will appear
Like locusts deforming the charms of the year;
Suns vainly will rise, Showers vainly descend,
If we are to drudge for what others shall spend.

Then join hand in hand brave Americans all,
By uniting we stand, by dividing we fall;
In so Righteous a cause let us hope to succeed,
For Heaven approves of each generous deed.

All ages shall speak with amaze and applause,
Of the courage we'll show in support of our laws;
To die we can bear—but to serve we disdain,
For shame is to freedom more dreadful than pain.

This bumper I crown for our Sovereign's health,
And this for Britannia's glory and wealth;
That wealth and that glory immortal may be,
If she is but just—and we are but Free.

GEORGE R. T. HEWES

Recollections of the Boston Tea Party

There appeared to be an understanding that each individual should volunteer his services, keep his own secret, and risk the consequence for himself.

George Robert Twelves Hewes (1742-1840) was initially quite passive about the independence movement. The occupation of Boston by British soldiers in 1768, however, transformed the twenty-six-year-old shoemaker into a zealous revolutionary. He was angered by the refusal of several soldiers to pay for shoes and grew angrier still when others moonlighted, taking jobs away from colonists. On March 5, 1770, when the British attempted to clear the streets of rowdy civilians, Hewes joined his fellow townspeople. In what came to be known as "The Boston Massacre," the soldiers fired into the crowd, wounding six and killing five others—including Crispus Attucks, a runaway slave who historians believe was a leader of the patriot mob. Personally acquainted with four of the men shot down that night, Hewes armed himself with a cane, but was quickly subdued by club-wielding soldiers. In a legal deposition, Hewes stated: "I told [the soldiers] I had as good a right to carry a cane as they had to carry clubs." The British commanding officer, Captain Preston, was brought to trial but acquitted due to the efforts of his defense counsel, John Adams, who believed the soldiers were acting in self-defense. "Facts are stubborn things," said Adams. "Whatever may be our wishes, our inclinations, or the dictates of our passions, they cannot alter the state of facts and evidence."

On the night of December 16, 1773, Hewes turned up as a participant in another famous protest. He was one of approximately fifty patriots who raided British ships anchored in Boston Harbor and destroyed 340 chests of tea as a means of protesting taxes imposed by the British government. "There is a dignity, a majesty, a sublimity, in this last effort of the patriots that I greatly admire," wrote Adams. "The people should never rise without doing something to be remembered—something notable and striking. This destruction of the tea is so bold, so daring, so firm, intrepid and inflexible, and it must have so important consequences, and so lasting, that I can't but consider it as an epoch in history!"

Hewes played as active a role in the war effort as he had played in the agitation for war. He enlisted in the militia four different times and also served as a sailor, shipping out twice—about two years of military service in all. Hewes did not win fame or fortune or even adequate pay for his contributions to the independence movement. What's more, his shop in Boston was burned to the ground by British troops. He did, however, win the affection of posterity. In 1835, as one of the last surviving participants in the Tea Party, Hewes was brought back to Boston as the guest of honor on Independence Day.

The tea destroyed was contained in three ships, lying near each other, at what was called at that time Griffin's wharf, and were surrounded by armed ships of war; the commanders of which had publicly declared, that if the rebels, as they were pleased to style the Bostonians, should not withdraw their opposition to the landing of the tea before a certain day, the 17th day of December, 1773, they should on that day force it on shore, under the cover of their cannon's mouth.

On the day preceding the seventeenth, there was a meeting of the citizens of the county of Suffolk, convened at one of the churches in Boston, for the purpose of consulting on what measures might be considered expedient to prevent the landing of the tea, or secure the people from the collection of the duty. At that meeting a committee was appointed to wait on Governor Hutchinson, and request him to inform them whether he would take any measures to satisfy the people on the object of the meeting. To the first application of this committee, the Governor told them he would give them a definite answer by five o'clock in the afternoon. At the hour appointed, the committee again repaired to the Governor's house, and on inquiry found he had gone to his country seat at Milton, a distance of about six miles. When the committee returned and informed the meeting of the absence of the Governor, there was a confused murmur among the members, and the meeting was immediately dissolved, many of them crying out, "Let every man do his duty, and be true to his country"; and there was a general huzza for Griffin's wharf. It was now evening, and I immediately dressed myself in the costume of an Indian, equipped with a small hatchet, which I and my associates denominated the tomahawk, with which, and a club, after having painted my face and hands with coal dust in the shop of a blacksmith, I repaired to Griffin's wharf, where the ships lay that contained the tea. When I first appeared in the street after being thus disguised, I fell in with many who were dressed, equipped and painted as I was, and who fell in with me and marched in order to the place of our destination.

When we arrived at the wharf, there were three of our number who assumed an authority to direct our operations, to which we readily submitted. They divided us into three parties, for the purpose of boarding the three ships which contained the tea at the same time. The name of him who commanded the division to which I was assigned was Leonard Pitt. The names of the other commanders I never knew. We were immediately ordered by the respective commanders to board all the ships at the same time, which we promptly obeyed. The commander of the division to which I belonged, as soon as we were on board the ship, appointed me boatswain, and ordered me to go to the captain and demand of him the keys to the hatches and a dozen candles. I made the demand accordingly, and the captain promptly replied, and delivered the articles; but requested me at the same time to do no damage to the ship or rigging. We then were ordered by our commander to open the hatches and take out all the chests of tea and throw them overboard, and we immediately proceeded to execute his orders, first cutting and splitting the chests with our tomahawks, so as thoroughly to expose them to the effects of the water.

In about three hours from the time we went on board, we had thus broken and thrown overboard every tea chest to be found in the ship, while those in the other ships were disposing of the tea in the same way, at the same time. We were surrounded by British armed ships, but no attempt was made to resist us.

We then quietly retired to our several places of residence, without having any conversation with each other, or taking any measures to discover who were our associates; nor do I recollect of our having had the knowledge of the name of a single individual concerned in that affair, except that of Leonard Pitt, the commander of my division, whom I have mentioned. There appeared to be an understanding that each individual should volunteer his services, keep his own secret, and risk the consequence for himself. No disorder took place during that transaction, and it was observed at that time that the stillest night ensued that Boston had enjoyed for many months.

During the time we were throwing the tea overboard, there were several attempts made by some of the citizens of Boston and its vicinity to carry off small quantities of it for their family use. To effect that object, they would watch their opportunity to snatch up a handful from the deck, where it became plentifully scattered, and put it into their pockets. One Captain O'Connor, whom I well knew, came on board for that purpose, and when he supposed he was not noticed, filled his pockets, and also the lining of his coat. But I had detected him, and gave information to the captain of what he was doing. We were ordered to take him into custody, and just as he was stepping from the vessel, I seized him by the skirt of his coat, and in attempting to pull him back, I tore it off; but springing forward, by a rapid effort, he made his escape. He had, however, to run a gauntlet through the crowd upon the wharf; each one, as he passed, giving him a kick or a stroke.

Another attempt was made to save a little tea from the ruins of the cargo by a tall, aged man who wore a large cocked hat and white wig, which was fashionable at that time. He had slightly slipped a little into his pocket, but being detected, they seized him, and taking his hat and wig from his head, threw them, together with the tea, of which they had emptied his pockets, into the water. In

Declaration of Independence *by John Trumbull, an artist of the Revolutionary War era noted for his historical paintings. This scene depicts the five-man drafting committee presenting their finished work. This is one of four Trumbull paintings displayed in the United States Capitol and is the source of the picture on the reverse of the U.S. two-dollar bill.*

JOHN ADAMS

Letter to Abigail

Posterity will tryumph in that Days Transaction …

Called the "Atlas of American independence" by New Jersey delegate Richard Stockton, John Adams (1735-1826) played a leading role in the adoption of the Declaration of Independence. In a July 3, 1776, letter to his wife, Abigail, he excitedly shared news of the adopted Resolution of Independence, proposed by Richard Henry Lee of Virginia. Although Adams incorrectly envisioned the second of July as Independence Day, he accurately predicted the manner in which the event would be celebrated by posterity.

… Yesterday, the greatest Question was decided which ever was debated in America, and a greater, perhaps, never was nor will be decided among Men. … The Second Day of July 1776 will be the most memorable Epocha, in the history of America. I am apt to believe that it will be celebrated, by succeeding Generations, as the great anniversary Festival. It ought to be commemorated, as the Day of Deliverance by solemn Acts of Devotion to God Almighty. It ought to be solemnized with Pomp and Parade, with Shews, Games, Sports, Guns, Bells, Bonfires and Illuminations, from one End of this Continent to the other from this Time forward forevermore.

You will think me transported with Enthusiasm, but I am not. I am well aware of the Toil and Blood and Treasure that it will cost us to maintain this Declaration and support and defend these States. Yet, through all the Gloom, I can see the Rays of ravishing Light and Glory. I can see that the End is more than worth all the Means. And that Posterity will tryumph in that Days Transaction, even altho We should rue it, which I trust in God We shall not.

spirit up her countrymen, and save her fair fellow sufferers from ravage and ravishment! …

I call not upon a few, but upon all: not on THIS state or THAT state, but on EVERY state; up and help us; lay your shoulders to the wheel; better have too much force than too little, when so great an object is at stake. Let it be told to the future world, that in the depth of winter, when nothing but hope and virtue could survive, that the city and the country, alarmed at one common danger, came forth to meet and to repulse it. Say not that thousands are gone, turn out your tens of thousands; throw not the burden of the day upon Providence, but *"shew your faith by your works,"* that God may bless you. It matters not where you live, or what rank of life you hold, the evil or the blessing will reach you all. The far and the near, the home counties and the back, the rich and the poor, will suffer or rejoice alike. The heart that feels not now, is dead: the blood of his children will curse his cowardice, who shrinks back at a time when a little might have saved the whole, and made *them* happy. I love the man that can smile in trouble, that can gather strength from distress, and grow brave by reflection. 'Tis the business of little minds to shrink; but he whose heart is firm, and whose conscience approves his conduct, will pursue his principles unto death. My own line of reasoning is to myself as straight and clear as a ray of light. Not all the treasures of the world, so far as I believe, could have induced me to support an offensive war, for I think it murder; but if a thief breaks into my house, burns and destroys my property, and kills or threatens to kill me, or those that are in it, and to *"bind me in all cases whatsoever,"* to his absolute will, am I to suffer it? What signifies it to me, whether he who does it is a king or a common man; my countryman or not my countryman: whether it be done by an individual villain, or any army of them? If we reason to the root of things we shall find no difference; neither can any just cause be assigned why we should punish in the one case and pardon in the other. Let them call me rebel, and welcome, I feel no concern from it; but I should suffer the misery of devils, were I to make a whore of my soul by swearing allegiance to one whose character is that of a sottish, stupid, stubborn, worthless, brutish man. I conceive likewise a horrid idea in receiving mercy from a being, who at the last day shall be shrieking to the rocks and mountains to cover him, and fleeing with terror from the orphan, the widow, and the slain of America.

There are cases which cannot be overdone by language, and this is one. There are persons, too, who see not the full extent of the evil which threatens them; they solace themselves with hopes that the enemy, if he succeed, will be merciful. It is the madness of folly, to expect mercy from those who have refused to do justice; and even mercy, where conquest is the object, is only a trick of war; the cunning of the fox is as murderous as the violence of the wolf; and we ought to guard equally against both. …

I thank GOD that I fear not. I see no real cause for fear. I know our situation well, and can see the way out of it … By perseverance and fortitude we have the prospect of a glorious issue; by cowardice and submission, the sad choice of a variety of evils—a ravaged country—a depopulated city—habitations without safety, and slavery without hope—our homes turned into barracks and bawdy-houses for Hessians, and a future race to provide for, whose fathers we shall doubt of. Look on this picture and weep over it! and if there yet remains one thoughtless wretch who believes it not, let him suffer it unlamented. …

Yankee Doodle

The tune "Yankee Doodle," believed to have originated in Holland in the sixteenth century, was popular with Englishmen who wrote several different stanzas, often with the intent of poking fun at colonial Americans. The word "Yankee," for example, was a derogatory term for a New Englander, and a "doodle" was an individual of limited intelligence. Nevertheless, Americans adopted the song as their own (with further changes) and made it one of the most popular patriotic songs of the Revolutionary War. Many American soldiers, in fact, whistled "Yankee Doodle" in battle, prompting General Gage to declare upon his retreat from Concord: "I hope [we] shall never hear that tune again!" The British did hear it again, however—at the surrender of General Cornwallis at Yorktown.

Yankee Doodle went to town,
A-ridin' on a pony,
Stuck a feather in his cap
And called it Macaroni.

Chorus:
 Yankee Doodle, keep it up,
 Yankee Doodle Dandy,
 Mind the music and the step
 And with the girls be handy.

Father and I went down to camp,
Along with Captain Gooding,
And there we saw the men and boys
As thick as hasty pudding.

And there we saw a thousand men,
As rich as Squire David;
And what they wasted every day,
I wish it could be saved.

And there was Captain Washington
Upon a slapping stallion,
A-giving orders to his men;
I guess there was a million.

And there I saw a little keg,
Its head was made of leather;
They knocked upon it with two sticks
To call the men together.

And there I saw a swamping gun,
As big as a log of maple,
Upon a mighty little cart,
A load for father's cattle.

And every time they fired it off,
It took a horn of powder,
And made a noise like father's gun,
Only a nation louder.

I can't tell you half I saw,
They kept up such a smother,
So I took my hat off, made a bow
And scampered home to mother.

Yankee Doodle is the tune
Americans delight in,
'Twill do to whistle, sing or play
And just the thing for fightin'.

Spirit of '76 *by Archibald M. Willard, an Ohio-born painter who fought in the American Civil War. This 1875 painting, also known as* Yankee Doodle, *was a patriotic tribute to the heroes of the Revolutionary War.*

FRANCIS MILES FINCH

Nathan Hale

Nathan Hale (1755-1776), one of twelve children, was born in Coventry, Connecticut, graduated from Yale, and earned a living as a schoolteacher. When the Revolutionary War began, he immediately joined the conflict, receiving a lieutenant's commission in the Connecticut militia. Hale then became a captain in an elite fighting group called the Rangers. In September 1776, General Washington asked for a member of the Rangers to cross enemy lines and obtain information. Hale volunteered and was successful in his mission, but was captured before he could return. Many historians believe that he was betrayed by a cousin with British sympathies.

Hale, without a trial, was sentenced to be hanged. Captain Montresor, an English officer, recorded the events that followed: "On the morning of the execution, my station being near the fatal spot, I requested the Provost-Marshal to permit the prisoner to sit in my marquee while he was making the necessary preparations. Captain Hale entered. He asked for writing materials, which I furnished him. He wrote two letters; one to his mother and one to a brother officer. The Provost-Marshal destroyed the letters, and assigned as reason that the rebels should not know that they had a man in their army who could die with so much firmness."

Hale asked for a Bible, but his request was refused. He was marched out by a guard and hanged. Asked to make his dying "speech and confession," Hale responded, saying, "I only regret that I have but one life to lose for my country."

The following tribute to the revolutionary hero was written by Francis Miles Finch (1827-1907), a New York judge and law professor at Cornell University.

To drumbeat, and heartbeat,
A soldier marches by;
There is color in his cheek,
There is courage in his eye,
Yet to drumbeat and heartbeat
In a moment he must die.

By the starlight and moonlight,
He seeks the Briton's camp;
He hears the rustling flag,
And the armed sentry's tramp;
And the starlight and moonlight
His silent wanderings lamp.

With slow tread and still tread,
He scans the tented line;
And he counts the battery guns,
By the gaunt and shadowy pine;
And his slow tread and still tread
Gives no warning sign.

The dark wave, the plumed wave,
It meets his eager glance;
And it sparkles 'neath the stars,
Like the glimmer of a lance
A dark wave, a plumed wave,
On an emerald expanse.

A sharp clang, a steel clang,
And terror in the sound!
For the sentry, falcon-eyed,
In the camp a spy hath found;
With a sharp clang, a steel clang,
The patriot is bound.

With calm brow, and steady brow,
He listens to his doom;
In his look there is no fear,
Nor a shadow-trace of gloom;
But with calm brow and steady brow,
He robes him for the tomb.

In the long night, the still night,
He kneels upon the sod;
And the brutal guards withhold
E'en the solemn Word of God!
In the long night, the still night,
He walks where Christ hath trod.

'Neath the blue morn, the sunny morn,
He dies upon the tree;
And he mourns that he can lose
But one life for Liberty;
And in the blue morn, the sunny morn,
His spirit wings are free.

But his last words, his message-words,
They burn, lest friendly eye
Should read how proud and calm
A patriot could die,
With his last words, his dying words,
A soldier's battle cry.

From the Fame-leaf and Angel-leaf,
From the monument and urn,
The sad of earth, the glad of heaven,
His tragic fate shall learn;
But on Fame-leaf and Angel-leaf
The name of HALE shall burn!

ANONYMOUS

Valley Forge

In the winter of 1777, Washington and 11,000 soldiers in the Continental Army set up winter camp at Valley Forge, Pennsylvania. Coming on the heels of defeats at Brandywine and Germantown, Washington's soldiers suffered from shortages of food and clothing and bitter cold. To make matters worse, a smallpox epidemic broke out in the camp and, by winter's end, more than 3,000 men had died.

Valley Forge tested both the loyalty of American soldiers and the leadership of General Washington, who suffered harsh criticism. By early spring of 1778, however, Washington's troops were better disciplined thanks to months of instruction from Baron von Steuben, a former Prussian soldier, and morale was boosted in May 1778 by news of an American alliance with France.

The following tribute to the winter encampment was a popular inclusion in early American anthologies.

Our path is traced by a crimson stain,
We leave our mark on the snow-clad plain,
As onward to Valley Forge we press,
Where all will be bleak and verdureless.

Our wives are sighing by hearthstones drear,
Our babes are sobbing and we not near,
The tempest rages through the rifted wood,
But grief keeps time in her wildest mood.

We go with the ax our huts to raise,
And then to creep to the camp-fire's blaze,
And talk, as our heart-strings closer twine,
Of comrades we lost at Brandywine.

We will know what famine means, and wish
For the nook of home and the smoking dish;
And our aching limbs, as they shrink with cold,
Will feel how scant is the garment's fold.

Our path is traced by a ruddy dye,
But we turn our thoughts to the distant sky
And the snow-clad plain seems a vernal sod,
When we feel our cause is the cause of God.

The foe will lodge in the city gay,
And Howe and his troops keep cares away,
And the feast and the dance will loudly tell
How St. George's sons hold carnival.

But we in the rude-built huts will wait
For a brighter day and a nobler fate;
And, as clings to the sire the trusting son,
We will nestle close to our Washington.

Our path is traced by a crimson stain,
Our blood pours out like the April rain,
But a Spartan heart and an iron will
Shall be the portion of freemen still.

Then, brothers, on to the forest wild,
Let the axes ring,—be the timber piled,—
The cheek of the Briton will burn with shame
When Valley Forge has a deathless name

Washington and Lafayette at Valley Forge during the winter of 1777-78, as depicted by Alonzo Chappel. The Marquis de Lafayette was a French aristocrat and military officer who became a confidant of General Washington due to his heroism and fierce loyalty to the Commander-in-Chief. The youngest general to fight on either side in the War of Independence, Lafayette was just nineteen when commissioned by Congress.

Articles of Confederation

The Stile of this confederacy shall be "The United States of America."

While still engaged in a life-or-death struggle with Great Britain, the newly independent united states decided to formalize their relationship with one another via a written constitution. *The Articles of Confederation and Perpetual Union*, as it was formally known, established a confederacy—a coalition of sovereign states, which would act on behalf of those states only in certain limited areas and only when the states were in unanimous agreement.

The final draft of the Articles was approved on November 15, 1777, by the Second Continental Congress and submitted to the states for ratification. The final copy was signed by the delegates on July 9, 1778. The ratification process dragged on for over three years, however, as several states refused to rescind their claims to lands in the West. The final draft of the Articles therefore served as the de facto system of government used by the Congress, which exercised an unprecedented level of political, diplomatic, military, and economic authority over the states. The Congress oversaw the conduct of the war, issued money, created a military code of law, adopted commercial codes, defined crimes, and conducted diplomatic relations. Article XIII of the new government stipulated that its provisions "shall be inviolably observed by every State" and that "the Union shall be perpetual."

To all to whom these Presents shall come, we the undersigned Delegates of the States affixed to our Names send greeting. Whereas the Delegates of the United States of America in Congress assembled did on the fifteenth day of November in the Year of our Lord One Thousand Seven Hundred and Seventy seven, and in the Second Year of the Independence of America agree to certain articles of Confederation and perpetual Union between the States of New Hampshire, Massachusetts-bay, Rhode Island and Providence Plantations, Connecticut, New York, New Jersey, Pennsylvania, Delaware, Maryland, Virginia, North Carolina, South Carolina, and Georgia in the Words following, viz. Articles of Confederation and perpetual Union between the States of New Hampshire, Massachusetts-bay, Rhode Island and Providence Plantations, Connecticut, New York, New Jersey, Pennsylvania, Delaware, Maryland, Virginia, North Carolina, South Carolina and Georgia.

Article I. The Stile of this confederacy shall be "The United States of America."

Article II. Each state retains its sovereignty, freedom and independence, and every Power, Jurisdiction and right, which is not by this confederation expressly delegated to the United States, in Congress assembled.

Article III. The said States hereby severally enter into a firm league of friendship with each other, for their common defence, the security of their Liberties, and their mutual and general welfare, binding themselves to assist each other, against all force offered to, or attacks made upon them, or any of them, on account of religion, sovereignty, trade, or any other pretence whatever.

Article IV. The better to secure and perpetuate mutual friendship and intercourse among the people of the different States in this Union, the free inhabitants of each of these States, paupers, vagabonds and fugitives from Justice excepted, shall be entitled to all privileges and immunities of free citizens in the several States; and the people of each State shall have free ingress and regress to and from any other State, and shall enjoy therein all the privileges of trade and commerce, subject to the same duties, impositions and restrictions as the inhabitants thereof respectively, provided that such restriction shall not extend so far as to prevent the removal of property imported into any State, to any other State of which the owner is an inhabitant; provided also that no imposition, duties or restriction shall be laid by any State, on the property of the United States, or either of them.

If any Person guilty of, or charged with treason, felony, or other high misdemeanor in any State, shall flee from Justice, and be found in any of the United States, he shall upon demand of the Governor or executive power, of the State from which he fled, be delivered up and removed to the State having jurisdiction of his offence.

Full faith and credit shall be given in each of these States to the records, acts and judicial proceedings of the courts and magistrates to every other State.

Article V. For the more convenient management of the general interests of the United States, delegates shall be annually appointed in such manner as the legislature of each State shall direct, to meet in Congress on the first Monday in November, in every year, with a power reserved to each State, to recall its delegates, or any of them, at any time within the year, and to send others in their stead, for the remainder of the Year.

No State shall be represented in Congress by less than two, nor by more than seven Members; and no person shall be capable of being a delegate for more than three years in any term of six years; nor shall any person, being a delegate, be capable of holding any office under the United States, for which he, or another for his benefit receives any salary, fees or emolument of any kind.

Each State shall maintain its own delegates in a meeting of the States, and while they act as members of the committee of the States.

In determining questions in the United States, in Congress assembled, each State shall have one vote.

Freedom of speech and debate in Congress shall not be impeached or questioned in any Court, or place out of Congress, and the members of Congress shall be protected in their persons from arrests and imprisonments, during the time of their going to and from, and attendance on Congress, except for treason, felony, or breach of the peace.

Article VI. No State, without the consent of the United States in Congress assembled, shall send any embassy to, or receive any embassy from, or enter into any conference, agreement, or alliance or treaty with any King, Prince or State; nor shall any person holding any office of profit or trust under the United States, or any of them, accept of any present, emolument, office or title of any kind whatever from any King, Prince or foreign State; nor shall the United States in Congress assembled, or any of them, grant any title of nobility.

No two or more States shall enter into any treaty, confederation or alliance whatever between them, without the consent of the United States in Congress assembled, specifying accurately the purposes for which the same is to be entered into, and how long it shall continue.

No State shall lay any imposts or duties, which may interfere with any stipulations in treaties, entered into by the United States in Congress assembled, with any King, Prince or State, in pursuance of any treaties already proposed by Congress, to the courts of France and Spain.

No vessels of war shall be kept up in time of peace by any State, except such number only, as shall be deemed necessary by the United States in Congress assembled, for the defence of such State, or its trade; nor shall any body of forces be kept up by any State in time of peace, except such number only, as in the judgment of the United States, in Congress assembled, shall be deemed requisite to garrison the forts necessary for the defence of such State; but every State shall always keep up a well regulated and disciplined militia, sufficiently armed and accoutered, and shall provide and constantly have ready for use, in public stores, a due number of field pieces and tents, and a proper quantity of arms, ammunition and camp equipage.

No State shall engage in any war without the consent of the United States in Congress assembled, unless such State be actually invaded by enemies, or shall have received certain advice of a resolution being formed by some nation of Indians to invade such State, and the danger is so imminent as not to admit of a delay, till the United States in Congress assembled can be consulted: nor shall any State grant commissions to any ships or vessels of war, nor letters of marque or reprisal, except it be after a declaration of war by the United States in Congress assembled, and then only against the kingdom or State and the subjects thereof, against which war has been so declared, and under such regulations as shall be established by the United States in Congress assembled, unless such State be infested by pirates, in which case vessels of war may be fitted out for that occasion, and kept so long as the danger shall continue, or until the United States in Congress assembled shall determine otherwise.

Article VII. When land-forces are raised by any State for the common defence, all officers of or under the rank of colonel, shall be appointed by the legislature of each State respectively by whom such forces shall be raised, or in such manner as such State shall direct, and all vacancies shall be filled up by the State which first made the appointment.

Article VIII. All charges of war, and all other expenses that shall be incurred for the common defence or general welfare, and allowed by the United States in Congress assembled, shall be defrayed out of a common treasury, which shall be supplied by the several States, in proportion to the value of all land within each State, granted to or surveyed for any person, as such land and the buildings and improvements thereon shall be estimated according to such mode as the United States in Congress assembled, shall from time to time direct and appoint. The taxes for paying that proportion shall be laid and levied by the authority and direction of the legislatures of the several States within the time agreed upon by the United States in Congress assembled.

Article IX. The United States in Congress assembled shall have the sole and exclusive right and power of determining on peace and war, except in the cases mentioned in the sixth article—of sending and receiving ambassadors—entering into treaties and alliances, provided that no treaty of commerce shall be made whereby the legislative power of the respective States shall be restrained from imposing such imposts and duties on foreigners, as their own people are subjected to, or from prohibiting the exportation or importation of any species of goods or commodities whatsoever—of establishing rules for deciding in all cases, what captures on land or water shall be legal, and in what manner prizes taken by land or naval forces in the service of the United States shall be divided or appropriated—of granting letters of marque and reprisal in times of peace—appointing courts for the trial of piracies and felonies committed on the high seas and establishing courts for receiving and determining finally appeals in all cases of captures, provided that no member of Congress shall be appointed a judge of any of the said courts.

The United States in congress assembled shall also be the last resort on appeal in all disputes and differences now subsisting or that hereafter may arise between two or more States concerning boundary, jurisdiction or any other cause whatever; which authority shall always be exercised in the manner following: Whenever the legislative or executive authority or lawful agent of any State in controversy with another shall present a petition to Congress, stating the matter in question and praying for a hearing, notice thereof shall be given by order of Congress to the legislative or executive authority of the other State in controversy, and a day assigned for the appearance of the parties by their lawful agents, who shall then be directed to appoint, by joint consent, commissioners or judges to constitute a court for hearing and determining the matter in question; but if they cannot agree, Congress shall name three persons out of each of the United States, and from the list of such persons each party shall alternately strike out one, the petitioners beginning, until the number shall be reduced to thirteen; and from that number not less than seven, nor more than nine names as Congress shall direct, shall in the presence of Congress be drawn out by lot, and the persons whose names shall be so drawn or any five of them, shall be commissioners or judges, to hear and finally determine the controversy, so always as a major part of the judges who shall hear the cause shall agree in the determination; and if either party shall neglect to attend at the day appointed, without showing reasons which Congress shall judge sufficient, or being present shall refuse to strike, the Congress shall proceed to nominate three persons out of each State, and the secretary of Congress shall strike in behalf of such party absent or refusing; and the judgment and sentence of the court to be appointed, in the manner before prescribed, shall be final and conclusive; and if any of the parties shall refuse to submit to the authority of such court, or to appear to defend their claim or cause, the court shall nevertheless proceed to pronounce sentence, or judgment, which shall in like manner be final and decisive, the judgment or sentence and other proceedings being in either case transmitted to Congress, and lodged among the Acts of Congress for the security of the parties concerned: provided that every commissioner, before he sits in judgment, shall take an oath to be administered by one of the judges of the supreme or superior court of the State, where the cause shall be tried, "well and truly to hear and determine the matter in question, according to the best of his judgment, without favor, affection or hope of reward": provided also that no State shall be deprived of territory for the benefit of the United States.

All controversies concerning the private right of soil claimed under different grants of two or more States, whose jurisdictions as they may respect such lands, and the States which passed such grants are adjusted, the said grants or either of them being at the same time claimed to have originated antecedent to such settlement of jurisdiction, shall on the petition of either party to the Congress of the United States, be finally determined as near as may be in the same manner as is before prescribed for deciding disputes respecting territorial jurisdiction between different States.

The United States in Congress assembled shall also have the sole and exclusive right and power of regulating the alloy and value of coin struck by their own authority, or by that of the respective States—fixing the standard of weights and measures throughout the United States—regulating the trade and managing all affairs with the Indians, not members of any of the States, provided that the legislative right of any State within its own limits be not infringed or violated—establishing and regulating post-offices from one State to another, throughout all the United States, and exacting such postage on the papers passing thro' the same as may be requisite to defray the expenses of the said office—appointing all officers of the land forces, in the service of the United States, excepting regimental officers—appointing all the officers of the naval forces, and commissioning all officers whatever in the service of the United States—making rules for the government and regulation of the said land and naval forces, and directing their operations.

The United States in Congress assembled shall have authority to appoint a committee, to sit in the recess of Congress, to be denominated "A Committee of the States," and to consist of one delegate from each State; and to appoint such other committees and civil officers as may be necessary for managing the general affairs of the United States under their direction—to appoint one of their number to preside, provided that no person be allowed to serve in the office of president more than one year in any term of three years; to ascertain the necessary sums of money to be raised for the service of the United States, and to appropriate and apply the same for defraying the public expenses—to borrow money, or emit bills on the credit of the United States, transmitting every half year to the respective States an account of the sums of money so borrowed or emitted—to build and equip a navy—to agree upon the number of land forces, and to make requisitions from each State for its quota, in proportion to the number of white inhabitants in such State; which requisition shall be binding, and thereupon the legislature of each State shall appoint the regimental officers, raise the men and cloath, arm and equip them in a soldier like manner, at the expense of the United States, and the officers and men so cloathed, armed and equipped shall march to the place appointed, and within the time agreed on by the United States in Congress assembled. But if the United States in Congress assembled shall, on consideration of circumstances, judge proper that any State should not raise men, or should raise a smaller number than its quota, and that any other State should raise a greater number of men than the quota thereof, such extra number shall be raised, officered, cloathed, armed and equipped in the same manner as the quota of such State, unless the legislature of such State shall judge that such extra number cannot be safely spared out of the same, in which case they shall raise officers, cloath, arm and equip as many of such extra number as they judge can be safely spared. And the officers and men so cloathed, armed and equipped, shall march to the place appointed, and within the time agreed on by the United States in Congress assembled.

The United States in Congress assembled shall never engage in a war, nor grant letters of marque and reprisal in time of peace, nor enter into any treaties or alliances, nor coin money, nor regulate the value thereof, nor ascertain the sums and expenses necessary for the defence and welfare of the United States, or any of them, nor emit bills, nor borrow money on the credit of the United States, nor appropriate money, nor agree upon the number of vessels of war, to be built or purchased, or the number of land or sea forces to be raised, nor appoint a commander in chief of the army or navy, unless nine States assent to the same; nor shall a question on any other point, except for adjourning from day to day be determined, unless by the votes of a majority of the United States in Congress assembled.

The Congress of the United States shall have power to adjourn to any time within the year, and to any place within the United States, so that no period of adjournment be for a longer duration than the space of six months, and shall publish the Journal of their proceedings monthly, except such parts thereof relating to treaties, alliances or military operations as in their judgment require secrecy; and the yeas and nays of the delegates of each State on any question shall be entered on the Journal, when it is desired by any delegate; and the delegates of a State, or any of them, at his or their request shall be furnished with a transcript of the said Journal, except such parts as are above excepted, to lay before the legislatures of the several States.

Article X. The Committee of the States, or any nine of them, shall be authorized to execute, in the recess of Congress, such of the powers of Congress as the United States in Congress assembled, by the consent of nine States, shall from time to time think expedient to vest them with; provided that no power be delegated to the said committee, for the exercises of which, by the articles of confederation,

the voice of nine States in the Congress of the United States assembled is requisite.

Article XI. Canada acceding to this confederation, and joining in the measures of the United States, shall be admitted into, and entitled to all the advantages of this Union; but no other colony shall be admitted into the same, unless such admission be agreed to by nine States.

Article XII. All bills of credit emitted, monies borrowed and debts contracted by, or under the authority of Congress, before the assembling of the United States, in pursuance of the present confederation, shall be deemed and considered as a charge against the United States, for payment and satisfaction whereof the said United States, and the public faith are hereby solemnly pledged.

Article XIII. Every State shall abide by the determinations of the United States in Congress assembled, on all questions which by this confederation are submitted to them. And the Articles of this Confederation shall be inviolably observed by every State, and the Union shall be perpetual; nor shall any alteration at any time hereafter be made in any of them; unless such alteration be agreed to in a Congress of the United States, and be afterwards confirmed by the legislatures of every State.

And whereas it hath pleased the Great Governor of the World to incline the hearts of the legislatures we respectively represent in Congress, to approve of, and to authorize us to ratify the said Articles of Confederation and perpetual Union. Know Ye that we the undersigned delegates, by virtue of the power and authority to us given for that purpose, do by these presents, in the name and in behalf of our respective constituents, fully and entirely ratify and confirm each and every of the said Articles of Confederation and perpetual Union, and all and singular the matters and things therein contained. And we do further solemnly plight and engage the faith of our respective constituents, that they shall abide by the determinations of the United States in Congress assembled, on all questions, which by the said confederation are submitted to them. And that the articles thereof shall be inviolably observed by the States we respectively represent, and that the union shall be perpetual. In Witness whereof we have hereunto set our hands in Congress. Done at Philadelphia in the State of Pennsylvania the ninth Day of July in the Year of our Lord One Thousand Seven Hundred and Seventy-eight, and in the third year of the independence of America.

THOMAS JEFFERSON

A Bill for Establishing Religious Freedom in Virginia

To compel a man to furnish contributions of money for the propagation of opinions which he disbelieves and abhors is sinful and tyrannical.

Thomas Jefferson resigned from Congress in September 1776. He chose not to fight in the Revolutionary War, believing that his talents could best be utilized in the Virginia House of Delegates. Passionately committed to the exercise of a free mind, Jefferson worked for land reform, the expansion of voting privileges and educational opportunities, freedom of speech, freedom of the press, and religious toleration. In 1779, he offered the following bill, which became a precursor to the First Amendment's establishment clause and free exercise clause. Jefferson was able to disestablish the Anglican Church, take clergymen off the public payroll, and exempt Virginians from paying taxes to support the church.

The epitaph on Jefferson's grave, which he himself wrote, reads: "Here was buried Thomas Jefferson, author of the Declaration of American Independence, of the statute of Virginia for religious freedom, and father of the University of Virginia."

Well aware that the opinions and belief of men depend not on their own will, but follow involuntarily the evidence proposed to their minds; that Almighty God hath created the mind free, and manifested his supreme will that free it shall remain by making it altogether insusceptible of restraint; that all attempts to influence it by temporal punishments, or burthens, or by civil incapacitations, tend only to beget habits of hypocrisy and meanness, and are a departure from the plan of the holy author of our religion, who being lord both of body and mind, yet chose not to propagate it by coercions on either, as was in his almighty power to do, but to exalt it by its influence on reason alone; that the impious presumption of legislature and ruler, civil as well as ecclesiastical, who, being themselves but fallible and uninspired men, have assumed dominion over the faith of others, setting up their own opinions and modes of thinking as the only true and infallible, and as such endeavoring to impose them on others, hath established and maintained false religions over the greatest part of the world and through all time: that to compel a man to furnish contributions of money for the propagation of opinions which he disbelieves and abhors is sinful and tyrannical; that even the forcing him to support this or that teacher of his own religious persuasion is depriving him of the comfortable liberty of giving his contributions to the particular pastor whose morals he would make his pattern and whose powers he feels most persuasive to righteousness, and is withdrawing from the ministry those temporary rewards which, proceeding from an approbation of their personal conduct, are an additional incitement to earnest and unremitting labors for the instruction of mankind; that our civil rights have no dependence on our religious opinions, any more than our opinions in physics or geometry; and therefore the proscribing any citizen as unworthy the public confidence by laying upon him an incapacity of being called to offices of trust or emolument, unless he profess or renounce this or that religious opinion, is depriving him injudiciously of those privileges and advantages to which, in common with his fellow citizens, he has a natural right; that it tends also to corrupt the principles of that very religion it is meant to encourage, by bribing with a monopoly of worldly honors and emoluments those who will externally profess and conform to it; that though indeed these are criminals who do not withstand such temptation, yet neither are those innocent who lay the bait in their way; that the opinions of men are not the object of civil government, nor under its jurisdiction; that to suffer the civil magistrate to intrude his powers into the field of opinion and to restrain the profession or propagation of principles on supposition of their ill tendency is a dangerous fallacy, which at once destroys all religious liberty, because he being of course judge of that tendency will make his opinions the rule of judgment and approve or condemn the sentiments of others only as they shall square with or suffer from his own; that is time enough for the rightful purposes of civil government for its officers to interfere when principles break out into overt acts against peace and good order; and finally, that the truth is great and will prevail if left to herself; that she is the proper and sufficient antagonist to error, and has nothing to fear from the conflict unless by human interposition disarmed of her natural weapons, free argument and debate; errors ceasing to be dangerous when it is permitted freely to contradict them.

We the General Assembly of Virginia do enact that no man shall be compelled to frequent or support any religious worship, place, or ministry whatsoever, nor shall be enforced, restrained, molested, or burthened in his body or goods, or shall otherwise suffer, on account of his religious opinions or beliefs; but that all men shall be free to profess, and by argument to maintain, their opinions in matters of religion, and that the same shall in no wise diminish, enlarge, or affect their civil capacities.

And though we well know that this Assembly, elected by the people for their ordinary purposes of legislation only, have no power to restrain the acts of succeeding Assemblies, constituted with powers equal to our own, and that therefore to declare this act to be irrevocable would be of no effect in law; yet we are free to declare, and do declare, that the rights hereby asserted are of the natural rights of mankind, and that if any act shall be hereafter passed to repeal the present or to narrow its operations, such act will be an infringement of natural right.

Washington Crossing the Delaware, *by Emanuel Leutze. This 1851 painting commemorates General Washington's crossing of the Delaware River on December 25, 1776. That action was the first move in a surprise attack against the Hessian forces at Trenton, New Jersey, in the Battle of Trenton. The painting contains many historical inaccuracies to include the depiction of the original flag of the United States (the "Stars and Stripes"), the design of which did not exist at the time of Washington's crossing.*

MICHEL-GUILLAUME JEAN DE CRÈVECOEUR

Letters from an American Farmer

Here individuals of all nations are melted into a new race of men, whose labours and posterity will one day cause great changes in the world.

Michel-Guillaume Jean de Crèvecoeur (1735-1813), also known as J. Hector St. Jean de Crèvecoeur, emigrated to the United States from France prior to the Revolutionary War. He earned his living as a farmer in Orange County, New York, but gained international fame as a writer. Always modest about his literary success, Crèvecoeur said, "There is something truly ridiculous in a farmer quitting his plow and his axe, and then flying to his pen." Nonetheless, Crèvecoeur preceded Alexis de Tocqueville as one of the great commentators on early America, publishing twelve essays known as *Letters from an American Farmer*. The following excerpt, which helped advance the popular image of America as a melting pot for the people of many nations, is taken from Letter III—*What is an American?*

I wish I could be acquainted with the feelings and thoughts which must agitate the heart and present themselves to the mind of an enlightened Englishman, when he first lands on this continent. He must greatly rejoice that he lived at a time to see this fair country discovered and settled; he must necessarily feel a share of national pride, when he views the chain of settlements which embellishes these extended shores. When he says to himself, this is the work of my countrymen, who, when convulsed by factions, afflicted by a variety of miseries and wants, restless and impatient, took refuge here. They brought along with them their national genius, to which they principally owe what liberty they enjoy, and what substance they possess. Here he sees the industry of his native country displayed in a new manner, and traces in their works the embryos of all the arts, sciences, and ingenuity which flourish in Europe. Here he beholds fair cities, substantial villages, extensive fields, an immense country filled with decent houses, good roads, orchards, meadows, and bridges, where an hundred years ago all was wild, woody and uncultivated! What a train of pleasing ideas this fair spectacle must suggest; it is a prospect which must inspire a good citizen with the most heartfelt pleasure. The difficulty consists in the manner of viewing so extensive a scene. He is arrived on a new continent; a modern society offers itself to his contemplation, different from what he had hitherto seen. It is not composed, as in Europe, of great lords who possess every thing and of a herd of people who have nothing. Here are no aristocratical families, no courts, no kings, no bishops, no ecclesiastical dominion, no invisible power giving to a few a very visible one; no great manufacturers employing thousands, no great refinements of luxury. The rich and the poor are not so far removed from each other as they are in Europe. Some few towns excepted, we are all tillers of the earth, from Nova Scotia to West Florida. We are a people of cultivators, scattered over an immense territory communicating with each other by means of good roads and navigable rivers, united by the silken bands of mild government, all respecting the laws, without dreading their power, because they are equitable. We are all animated with the spirit of an industry which is unfettered and unrestrained, because each person works for himself. If he travels through our rural districts he views not the hostile castle, and the haughty mansion, contrasted with the clay-built hut and miserable cabin, where cattle and men help to keep each other warm, and dwell in meanness, smoke, and indigence. A pleasing uniformity of decent competence appears throughout our habitations. The meanest of our log-houses is a dry and comfortable habitation. Lawyer or merchant are the fairest titles our towns afford; that of a farmer is the only appellation of the rural inhabitants of our country. It must take some time ere he can reconcile himself to our dictionary, which is but short in words of dignity, and names of honour. There, on a Sunday, he sees a congregation of respectable farmers and their wives, all clad in neat homespun, well mounted, or riding in their own humble waggons. There is not among them an esquire, saving the unlettered magistrate. There he sees a parson as simple as his flock, a farmer who does not riot on the labour of others. We have no princes, for whom we toil, starve, and bleed: we are the most perfect society now existing in the world. Here man is free; as he ought to be;

nor is this pleasing equality so transitory as many others are. Many ages will not see the shores of our great lakes replenished with inland nations, nor the unknown bounds of North America entirely peopled. Who can tell how far it extends? Who can tell the millions of men whom it will feed and contain? for no European foot has as yet travelled half the extent of this mighty continent!

The next wish of this traveller will be to know whence came all these people? they are a mixture of English, Scotch, Irish, French, Dutch, Germans, and Swedes. From this promiscuous breed, that race now called Americans have arisen. The eastern provinces must indeed be excepted, as being the unmixed descendants of Englishmen. I have heard many wish that they had been more intermixed also: for my part, I am no wisher, and think it much better as it has happened. They exhibit a most conspicuous figure in this great and variegated picture; they too enter for a great share in the pleasing perspective displayed in these thirteen provinces. I know it is fashionable to reflect on them, but I respect them for what they have done; for the accuracy and wisdom with which they have settled their territory; for the decency of their manners; for their early love of letters; their ancient college, the first in this hemisphere; for their industry; which to me who am but a farmer, is the criterion of everything. There never was a people, situated as they are, who with so ungrateful a soil have done more in so short a time. Do you think that the monarchical ingredients which are more prevalent in other governments, have purged them from all foul stains? Their histories assert the contrary.

In this great American asylum, the poor of Europe have by some means met together, and in consequence of various causes; to what purpose should they ask one another what countrymen they are? Alas, two thirds of them had no country. Can a wretch who wanders about, who works and starves, whose life is a continual scene of sore affliction or pinching penury; can that man call England or any other kingdom his country? A country that had no bread for him, whose fields procured him no harvest, who met with nothing but the frowns of the rich, the severity of the laws, with jails and punishments; who owned not a single foot of the extensive surface of this planet? No! urged by a variety of motives, here they came. Every thing has tended to regenerate them; new laws, a new mode of living, a new social system; here they are become men: in Europe they were as so many useless plants, wanting vegetative mould,

and refreshing showers; they withered, and were mowed down by want, hunger, and war; but now by the power of transplantation, like all other plants they have taken root and flourished! Formerly they were not numbered in any civil lists of their country, except in those of the poor; here they rank as citizens. By what invisible power has this surprising metamorphosis been performed? By that of the laws and that of their industry. The laws, the indulgent laws, protect them as they arrive, stamping on them the symbol of adoption; they receive ample rewards for their labours; these accumulated rewards procure them lands; those lands confer on them the title of freemen, and to that title every benefit is affixed which men can possibly require. This is the great operation daily performed by our laws. ...

What attachment can a poor European emigrant have for a country where he had nothing? The knowledge of the language, the love of a few kindred as poor as himself, were the only cords that tied him: his country is now that which gives him land, bread, protection, and consequence: Ubi panis ibi patria, is the motto of all emigrants. What then is the American, this new man? He is either an European, or the descendant of an European, hence that strange mixture of blood, which you will find in no other country. I could point out to you a family whose grandfather was an Englishman, whose wife was Dutch, whose son married a French woman, and whose present four sons have now four wives of different nations. He is an American, who leaving behind him all his ancient prejudices and manners, receives new ones from the new mode of life he has embraced, the new government he obeys, and the new rank he holds.

He becomes an American by being received in the broad lap of our great Alma Mater. Here individuals of all nations are melted into a new race of men, whose labours and posterity will one day cause great changes in the world. Americans are the western pilgrims, who are carrying along with them that great mass of arts, sciences, vigour, and industry which began long since in the east; they will finish the great circle. The Americans were once scattered all over Europe; here they are incorporated into one of the finest systems of population which has ever appeared, and which will hereafter become distinct by the power of the different climates they inhabit. The American ought therefore to love this country much better than that wherein either he or his forefathers were born. Here the rewards of his industry follow with equal steps the progress of his labour; his labour is founded on the basis of nature, self-interest;

can it want a stronger allurement? Wives and children, who before in vain demanded of him a morsel of bread, now, fat and frolicsome, gladly help their father to clear those fields whence exuberant crops are to arise to feed and to clothe them all; without any part being claimed, either by a despotic prince, a rich abbot, or a mighty lord. Here religion demands but little of him; a small voluntary salary to the minister, and gratitude to God; can he refuse these? The American is a new man, who acts upon new principles; he must therefore entertain new ideas, and form new opinions. From involuntary idleness, servile dependence, penury, and useless labour, he has passed to toils of a very different nature, rewarded by ample subsistence.—This is an American. …

* * *

Surrender of Lord Cornwallis, *by John Trumbull, depicting the British surrendering to French and American forces at Yorktown, Virginia, on October 19, 1781, in what would be the last military engagement of the American Revolution. Feigning illness, Cornwallis refused to meet formally with General Washington and also refused to come to the ceremony of surrender. British General Charles O'Hara offered the sword of surrender to French General Comte de Rochambeau, who shook his head and pointed to Washington. Because Cornwallis was not present, Washington ordered the British to present the sword to his second in command, General Benjamin Lincoln. In November of 1782, the British Parliament recognized U.S. independence and agreed to a preliminary peace treaty later formalized as the Treaty of Paris.*

The Emerging Republic

Rejecting a Crown

If I am not deceived in the knowledge of myself, you could not have found a person to whom your schemes are more disagreeable.

In May 1782, Washington received a letter from Colonel Lewis Nichola written on behalf of his officers. The men complained of injustices suffered from Congress—most notably, a shortage of pay. The solution, the officers argued, was to use the army to establish a monarchy with Washington as king. Printed here is Washington's stern rebuke of such a notion.

The following year, 1783, discontent in the army again threatened the young nation. With most of the Continental Army camped near Newburgh, New York, a group of officers began lobbying for a coup d'état against Congress. The so-called Newburgh Conspirators were frustrated that Congress was not paying them what had been promised. On March 15—the Ides of March, a date rich in irony for its association with the tyranny and assassination of Julius Caesar—Washington called his men together and sternly reprimanded them for losing faith. The new nation had a chance to succeed, he argued, only through adherence to the rule of law. Washington then took a letter from his pocket, one drafted by a member of Congress to be read to the officers. With a great sense of drama, Washington fumbled with the letter before taking a pair of reading glasses from his pocket. He then said: "Gentlemen, you will permit me to put on my spectacles, for I have not only grown gray but almost blind in the service of my country." The meaning was clear. Washington had sacrificed as much for the revolution as any of them. His fellow officers, most of them having served with him for years, were reportedly moved to tears. The conspiracy collapsed as he read the letter. On December 23, 1783, Washington returned his commission to Congress and pledged loyalty to the civilian government he had served. He thereby established the principle that our nation's military would always be under civilian rule.

Sir,

With a mixture of great surprise and astonishment I have read with attention the sentiments you have submitted to my perusal. Be assured sir, no occurrence in the course of the war has given me more painful sensations than your information of there being such ideas existing in the army as you have expressed, and I must view with abhorrence, and reprehend with severity—for the present, the communication of them will rest in my own bosom, unless some further agitation of the matter shall make a disclosure necessary.

I am much at a loss to conceive what part of my conduct could have given encouragement to an address which to me seems big with the greatest mischiefs that can befall my country. If I am not deceived in the knowledge of myself, you could not have found a person to whom your schemes are more disagreeable—at the same time in justice to my own feelings I must add, that no man possesses a more sincere wish to see ample justice done to the army than I do, and as far as my powers and influence, in a constitution, may extend, they shall be employed to the utmost of my abilities to effect it, should there be any occasion—Let me conjure you then, if you have any regard for your country—concern for yourself or posterity—or respect for me, to banish these thoughts from your mind, and never communicate, as from yourself, or anyone else, a sentiment of the like nature.

With esteem I am, Sir,
Your Most Obedient Servant
G. Washington

The Constitution of the United States

We the People …

Not long after securing victory in the Revolutionary War, it became obvious that the Second Continental Congress, in attempting to limit the power of the central government, created one without sufficient power to govern effectively. The greatest weakness of the federal government under the Articles of Confederation was its inability to regulate trade and levy taxes. The government could not pay off the debts it had incurred during the revolution, to include paying soldiers who had fought in the war and citizens who had provided supplies. States often refused to give the government the money it needed, leading to an inability to defend against foreign encroachments, and they nearly paralyzed commerce by engaging in tariff wars with one another. Additionally, there was no national court system and no executive branch. Frustration further arose over the depreciation of the federal currency ("not worth a continental"), and amendments were difficult to pass because they required approval of all thirteen states.

On February 21, 1787, Congress adopted a resolution calling for a convention "for the sole and express purpose of revising the Articles of Confederation, and reporting to Congress, and the several Legislatures, such alterations and provisions therein as shall, when agreed to in Congress, and confirmed by the states, render the Federal Constitution adequate to the exigencies of government and the preservation of the Union."

Convening in Philadelphia in May of that year, the Constitutional Convention quickly discarded its stated goal of revising the Articles and focused on more sweeping changes. Discussion turned to two competing concepts of how a new government should be formed —the Virginia Plan, setting forth the idea of population-weighted representation in the proposed national legislature, and the New Jersey Plan, calling for equal representation among the states. The final draft of the Constitution, the product of numerous compromises, retained some of the features of the Articles of Confederation, but gave considerably more power to the federal government, thus setting the stage for a prolonged national debate on the meaning of federalism.

We the People of the United States, in Order to form a more perfect Union, establish Justice, insure domestic Tranquility, provide for the common defence, promote the general Welfare, and secure the Blessings of Liberty to ourselves and our Posterity, do ordain and establish this Constitution for the United States of America.

ARTICLE I

Section 1. All legislative Powers herein granted shall be vested in a Congress of the United States, which shall consist of a Senate and House of Representatives.

Section 2. The House of Representatives shall be composed of Members chosen every second Year by the People of the several States, and the Electors in each State shall have the Qualifications requisite for Electors of the most numerous Branch of the State Legislature.

No Person shall be a Representative who shall not have attained to the Age of twenty five Years, and been seven Years a Citizen of the United States, and who shall not, when elected, be an inhabitant of that State in which he shall be chosen.

Representatives and direct Taxes shall be apportioned among the several States which may be included within this Union, according to their respective Numbers, which shall be determined by adding to the whole Number of free Persons, including those bound to Service for a Term of Years, and excluding Indians not taxed, three fifths of all other Persons. The actual Enumeration shall be made within three Years after the first Meeting of the Congress of the United States, and within every subsequent Term of ten Years, in such Manner as they shall by Law direct. The Number of Representatives shall not exceed one for every thirty Thousand, but each State shall have at least one Representative; and until such enumerations shall be made, the State of New Hampshire shall be entitled to chuse three, Massachusetts eight, Rhode Island and Providence Plantations one, Connecticut five, New York six, New Jersey four, Pennsylvania eight, Delaware one, Maryland six, Virginia ten, North Carolina five, South Carolina five, and Georgia three.

When vacancies happen in the Representation from any State, the Executive Authority thereof shall issue Writs of Election to fill such Vacancies.

The House of Representatives shall chuse their speaker and other Officers; and shall have the sole Power of Impeachment.

Section 3. The Senate of the United States shall be composed of two Senators from each State, chosen by the Legislature thereof, for six Years; and each Senator shall have one Vote.

Immediately after they shall be assembled in Consequence of the first Election, they shall be divided as equally as may be into three Classes. The Seats of the Senators of the first Class shall be vacated at the Expiration of the second Year, of the second Class at the Expiration of the fourth Year, and of the third Class at the Expiration of the sixth Year, so that one third may be chosen every second Year; and if Vacancies happen by Resignation, or otherwise, during the Recess of the Legislature of any State, the Executive thereof may make temporary Appointments until the next Meeting of the Legislature, which shall then fill such Vacancies.

No Person shall be a Senator who shall not have attained to the Age of thirty Years, and been nine Years a Citizen of the United States, and who shall not, when elected, be an Inhabitant of that State for which he shall be chosen.

The Vice President of the United States shall be President of the Senate, but shall have no Vote, unless they be equally divided.

The Senate shall chuse their other Officers, and also a President pro tempore, in the Absence of the Vice President, or when he shall exercise the Office of President of the United States.

The Senate shall have the sole Power to try all Impeachments. When sitting for that Purpose, they shall be on Oath or Affirmation. When the President of the United States is tried, the Chief Justice shall Preside: And no Person shall be convicted without the concurrence of two thirds of the Members present.

Judgment in Cases of Impeachment shall not extend further than to removal from Office, and disqualification to hold and enjoy any Office of honor, Trust or Profit under the United States: but the Party convicted shall nevertheless be liable and subject to Indictment, Trial, Judgment and Punishment, according to Law.

Section 4. The Times, Places and Manner of holding Elections for Senators and Representatives, shall be prescribed in each State by the Legislature thereof; but the Congress may at any time by law make or alter such Regulations, except as to the Places of chusing Senators.

The Congress shall assemble at least once every Year, and such Meeting shall be on the first Monday in December, unless they shall by Law appoint a different Day.

Section 5. Each House shall be the Judge of the Elections, Returns and Qualifications of its own Members, and a Majority of each shall constitute a Quorum to do Business; but a smaller Number may adjourn from day to day, and may be authorized to compel the Attendance of absent Members, in such Manner, and under such Penalties as each House may provide.

Each House may determine the Rules of its Proceedings, punish its Members for disorderly Behavior, and, with the Concurrence of two thirds, expel a Member.

Each House shall keep a Journal of its Proceedings, and from time to time publish the same, excepting such Parts as may in their Judgment require Secrecy; and the Yeas and Nays of the Members of either House on any question shall, at the Desire of one fifth of those Present, be entered on the Journal.

Neither House, during the Session of Congress, shall, without the Consent of the other, adjourn for more than three days, nor to any other place than that in which the two Houses shall be sitting.

Section 6. The Senators and Representatives shall receive a Compensation for their Services, to be ascertained by Law, and paid out of the Treasury of the United States. They shall in all Cases, except Treason, Felony and Breach of the Peace, be privileged from Arrest during their Attendance at the Session of their respective Houses, and in going to and returning from the same; and for any Speech or Debate in either House, they shall not be questioned in any other Place.

No Senator or Representative shall, during the Time for which he was elected, be appointed to any civil Office under the Authority of the United States, which shall have been created, or the Emoluments whereof shall have been increased during such time; and no Person holding any Office under the United States, shall be a Member of either House during his Continuance in Office.

for the Case of Removal, Death, Resignation or Inability, both of the President and Vice President, declaring what Officer shall then act as President, and such Officer shall act accordingly, until the Disability be removed, or a President shall be elected.

The President shall, at stated Times, receive for his Services, a Compensation, which shall neither be increased nor diminished during the Period for which he shall have been elected, and he shall not receive within that Period any other Emolument from the United States, or any of them.

Before he enter on the Execution of his Office, he shall take the following Oath or Affirmation:—"I do solemnly swear (or affirm) that I will faithfully execute the Office of President of the United States, and will to the best of my Ability, preserve, protect and defend the Constitution of the United States."

Section 2. The President shall be Commander in Chief of the Army and Navy of the United States, and of the Militia of the several States, when called into the actual Service of the United States; he may require the Opinion, in writing, of the principal Officer in each of the executive Departments, upon any Subject relating to the Duties of their respective Offices, and he shall have Power to grant Reprieves and Pardons for Offences against the United States, except in Cases of Impeachment.

He shall have Power, by and with the Advice and Consent of the Senate, to make Treaties, provided two thirds of the Senators present concur; and he shall nominate, and by and with the Advice and Consent of the Senate, shall appoint Ambassadors, other public Ministers and Consuls, Judges of the supreme Court, and all other Officers of the United States, whose Appointments are not herein otherwise provided for, and which shall be established by Law: but the Congress may by Law vest the Appointment of such inferior Officers, as they think proper, in the President alone, in the Courts of Law, or in the Heads of Departments.

The President shall have Power to fill up all Vacancies that may happen during the Recess of the Senate, by granting Commissions which shall expire at the End of their next Session.

Section 3. He shall from time to time give to the Congress Information of the State of the Union, and recommend to their Consideration such Measures as he shall judge necessary and expedient; he may, on extraordinary Occasions, convene both Houses, or either of them, and in Case of Disagreement between them, with Respect to the Time of Adjournment, he may adjourn them to such Time as he shall think proper; he shall receive Ambassadors and other public Ministers; he shall take Care that the Laws be faithfully executed, and shall Commission all the Officers of the United States.

Section 4. The President, Vice President and all civil Officers of the United States, shall be removed from Office on Impeachment for, and Conviction of, Treason, Bribery, or other high Crimes and Misdemeanors.

ARTICLE III

Section 1. The judicial Power of the United States, shall be vested in one supreme Court, and in such inferior Courts as the Congress may from time to time ordain and establish. The Judges, both of the supreme and inferior Courts, shall hold their Offices during good Behaviour, and shall, at stated Times, receive for their Services a Compensation, which shall not be diminished during their Continuance in Office.

Section 2. The judicial Power shall extend to all Cases, in Law and Equity, arising under this Constitution, the Laws of the United States, and Treaties made, or which shall be made, under their Authority;—to all Cases affecting Ambassadors, other public Ministers and Consuls;—to all Cases of admiralty and maritime Jurisdiction;—to Controversies to which the United States shall be a Party;—to Controversies between two or more States;—between a State and Citizens of another State,—between Citizens of different States,—between Citizens of the same State claiming Lands under Grants of different States, and between a State, or the Citizens thereof, and foreign States, Citizens or Subjects.

In all Cases affecting Ambassadors, other public Ministers and Consuls, and those in which a State shall be Party, the supreme Court shall have original Jurisdiction. In all the other Cases before mentioned, the supreme Court shall have appellate Jurisdiction, both as to Law and Fact, with such Exceptions, and under such Regulations as the Congress shall make.

The Trial of all Crimes, except in Cases of Impeachment, shall be by Jury; and such Trial shall be held in the State where the said Crimes shall have been committed; but when not committed within any State, the Trial shall be at such Place or Places as the Congress may by Law have directed.

Section 3. Treason against the United States, shall consist only in levying War against them, or in adhering to their Enemies, giving them Aid and Comfort. No Person shall be convicted of Treason unless on the Testimony of two Witnesses to the same overt Act, or on Confession in open Court.

The Congress shall have Power to declare the Punishment of Treason, but no Attainder of Treason shall work Corruption of Blood, or Forfeiture except during the Life of the Person attainted.

ARTICLE IV

Section 1. Full Faith and Credit shall be given in each State to the public Acts, Records, and judicial Proceedings of every other State. And the Congress may by general Laws prescribe the Manner in which such Acts, Records and Proceedings shall be proved, and the Effect thereof.

Section 2. The Citizens of each State shall be entitled to all Privileges and Immunities of Citizens in the several States.

A Person charged in any State with Treason, Felony, or other Crime, who shall flee from Justice, and be found in another State, shall on Demand of the executive Authority of the State from which he fled, be delivered up, to be removed to the State having Jurisdiction of the Crime.

No person held to Service or Labour in one State, under the Laws thereof, escaping into another, shall, in Consequence of any Law or Regulation therein, be discharged from such Service or Labour, but shall be delivered up on Claim of the Party to whom Service or Labour may be due.

Section 3. New States may be admitted by the Congress into this Union; but no new State shall be formed or erected within the Jurisdiction of any other State; nor any State be formed by the Junction of two or more States, or Parts of States, without the Consent of the Legislatures of the States concerned as well as of the Congress.

The Congress shall have Power to dispose of and make all needful Rules and Regulations respecting the Territory or other Property belonging to the United States; and nothing in this Constitution shall be so construed as to Prejudice any Claims of the United States, or of any particular State.

Section 4. The United States shall guarantee to every State in this Union a Republican Form of Government, and shall protect each of them against Invasion; and on Application of the Legislature, or of the Executive (when the Legislature cannot be convened), against domestic Violence.

ARTICLE V

The Congress, whenever two thirds of both Houses shall deem it necessary, shall propose Amendments to this Constitution, or, on the Application of the Legislatures of two thirds of the several States, shall call a Convention for proposing Amendments, which, in either Case, shall be valid to all Intents and Purposes, as Part of this Constitution, when ratified by the Legislatures of three fourths of the several States, or by Conventions in three fourths thereof, as the one or the other Mode of Ratification may be proposed by the Congress; Provided that no Amendment which may be made prior to the Year One thousand eight hundred and eight shall in any Manner affect the first and fourth Clauses in the Ninth Section of the first Article; and that no State, without its Consent, shall be deprived of its equal Suffrage in the Senate.

ARTICLE VI

All Debts contracted and Engagements entered into, before the Adoption of this Constitution, shall be as valid against the United States under this Constitution, as under the Confederation.

This Constitution, and the Laws of the United States which shall be made in Pursuance thereof; and all Treaties made, or which shall be made, under the Authority of the United States, shall be the supreme Law of the Land; and the Judges in every State shall be bound thereby, any Thing in the Constitution or Laws of any State to the Contrary notwithstanding.

The Senators and Representatives before mentioned, and the Members of the several State Legislatures, and all executive and judicial Officers, both of the United States and of the several States, shall be bound by Oath or Affirmation, to support this Constitution; but no religious Test shall ever be required as a Qualification to any Office or public Trust under the United States.

ARTICLE VII

The Ratification of the Conventions of nine States, shall be sufficient for the Establishment of this Constitution between the States so ratifying the Same.

Done in Convention by the Unanimous Consent of the States present the Seventeenth Day of September in the Year of our Lord one thousand seven hundred and Eighty seven and of the Independence of the United States of America the Twelfth. In witness whereof We have hereunto subscribed our Names.

George Washington—President and deputy from Virginia
William Jackson—Secretary

Delaware: *George Read, Gunning Bedford Jr., John Dickinson, Richard Bassett, Jacob Broom*

Maryland: *James McHenry, Daniel of St. Thomas Jenifer, Daniel Carroll*

Virginia: *John Blair, James Madison Jr.*

North Carolina: *William Blount, Richard Dobbs Spaight, Hugh Williamson*

South Carolina: *J. Rutledge, Charles Cotesworth Pinckney, Charles Pinckney, Pierce Butler*

Georgia: *William Few, Abraham Baldwin*

New Hampshire: *John Langdon, Nicholas Gilman*

Massachusetts: *Nathaniel Gorham, Rufus King*

Connecticut: *William Samuel Johnson, Roger Sherman*

New York: *Alexander Hamilton*

New Jersey: *William Livingston, David Brearley, William Paterson, Jonathan Dayton*

Pennsylvania: *Benjamin Franklin, Thomas Mifflin, Robert Morris, George Clymer, Thomas FitzSimons, Jared Ingersoll, James Wilson, Gouverneur Morris*

Scene at the Signing of the Constitution of the United States, *by Howard Chandler Christy, depicting the Constitutional Convention at Independence Hall in Philadelphia.*

ALEXANDER HAMILTON, JAMES MADISON, AND JOHN JAY

The Federalist Papers

Justice is the end of government. It is the end of civil society. It ever has been and ever will be pursued until it be obtained, or until liberty be lost in the pursuit.

The argument over Constitutional ratification resulted in the creation of the first political parties in America. The supporters of the Constitution, known as *Federalists*, were opposed by the *Anti-Federalists*. The two factions presented their arguments to the American people in pamphlets and newspapers, on the floor of representative assemblies, and in public meeting houses.

Some Anti-Federalists were altogether opposed to adopting the Constitution, while others demanded amendments or pressed for a second convention to correct what they regarded as the errors of the first. They were not, as their name suggests, opposed to a federal system of government. They simply believed that the proposed Constitution granted too much authority to the central government, usurped state sovereignty, and failed to guarantee individual liberties. These concerns were voiced by numerous writers, none more passionately than in New York where the Constitution was under siege from multiple Anti-Federalist writings. From October of 1787 through April of 1788, for example, a series of sixteen essays were published in the *New York Journal* under the pseudonym "Brutus." Named in honor of the Roman senator who conspired to assassinate Julius Caesar in order to prevent him from overthrowing the Roman Republic, these essays were widely reprinted and commented on throughout the American states. The author is thought by most scholars to have been Robert Yates, a delegate to the Constitutional Convention and a political ally of New York Governor George Clinton (himself believed to be "Cato," the pseudonymous author of another series of Anti-Federalist essays that appeared in New York newspapers).

The most famous of the counterarguments in support of the Constitution are *The Federalist Papers*, a series of eighty-five letters written in 1787 and 1788 under the pseudonym "Publius" and later published collectively as *The Federalist*. The principle author was Alexander Hamilton, who penned fifty-one of the letters, with James Madison writing twenty-nine and John Jay contributing five. *The Federalist Papers*, which did not seek to defend every point in the Constitution but rather make the argument that it was the best plan upon which a general agreement could be reached, played a prominent role in gaining acceptance of the Constitution and remain an important tool in interpreting it. The following excerpts provide important statements of the principles of the Constitution and of republican government in general.

Federalist No. 1—Alexander Hamilton
General Introduction

After an unequivocal experience of the inefficiency of the subsisting federal government, you are called upon to deliberate on a new Constitution for the United States of America. The subject speaks its own importance; comprehending in its consequences nothing less than the existence of the UNION, the safety and welfare of the parts of which it is composed, the fate of an empire in many respects the most interesting in the world. It has been frequently remarked that it seems to have been reserved to the people of this country, by their conduct and example, to decide the important question, whether societies of men are really capable or not of establishing good government from reflection and choice, or whether they are forever destined to depend for their political constitutions on accident and force. If there be any truth in the remark, the crisis at which we are arrived may with propriety be regarded as the era in which that decision is to be made; and a wrong election of the part we shall act may, in this view, deserve to be considered as the general misfortune of mankind.

This idea will add the inducements of philanthropy to those of patriotism, to heighten the solicitude which all considerate and good men must feel for the event. Happy will it be if our choice should be directed by a judicious estimate of our true interests, unperplexed and unbiased by considerations not connected with the public good. …

Federalist No. 10—James Madison

The Same Subject Continued: The Union as a Safeguard Against Domestic Faction and Insurrection

Among the numerous advantages promised by a well-constructed Union, none deserves to be more accurately developed than its tendency to break and control the violence of faction. The friend of popular governments never finds himself so much alarmed for their character and fate, as when he contemplates their propensity to this dangerous vice. He will not fail, therefore, to set a due value on any plan which, without violating the principles to which he is attached, provides a proper cure for it. The instability, injustice, and confusion introduced into the public councils, have, in truth, been the mortal diseases under which popular governments have everywhere perished. …

By a faction, I understand a number of citizens, whether amounting to a majority or a minority of the whole, who are united and actuated by some common impulse of passion, or of interest, adversed to the rights of other citizens, or to the permanent and aggregate interests of the community.

There are two methods of curing the mischiefs of faction: the one, by removing its causes; the other, by controlling its effects.

There are again two methods of removing the causes of faction: the one, by destroying the liberty which is essential to its existence; the other, by giving to every citizen the same opinions, the same passions, and the same interests.

It could never be more truly said than of the first remedy, that it was worse than the disease. Liberty is to faction what air is to fire, an aliment without which it instantly expires. But it could not be less folly to abolish liberty, which is essential to political life, because it nourishes faction, than it would be to wish the annihilation of air, which is essential to animal life, because it imparts to fire its destructive agency.

The second expedient is as impracticable as the first would be unwise. As long as the reason of man continues fallible, and he is at liberty to exercise it, different opinions will be formed. As long as the connection subsists between his reason and his self-love, his opinions and his passions will have a reciprocal influence on each other; and the former will be objects to which the latter will attach themselves. The diversity in the faculties of men, from which the rights of property originate, is not less an insuperable obstacle to a uniformity of interests. The protection of these faculties is the first object of government. From the protection of different and unequal faculties of acquiring property, the possession of different degrees and kinds of property immediately results; and from the influence of these on the sentiments and views of the respective proprietors, ensues a division of the society into different interests and parties …

When a majority is included in a faction, the form of popular government, on the other hand, enables it to sacrifice to its ruling passion or interest both the public good and the rights of other citizens. To secure the public good and private rights against the danger of such a faction, and at the same time to preserve the spirit and the form of popular government, is then the great object to which our inquiries are directed. Let me add that it is the great desideratum by which this form of government can be rescued from the opprobrium under which it has so long labored, and be recommended to the esteem and adoption of mankind. …

A republic, by which I mean a government in which the scheme of representation takes place, opens a different prospect, and promises the cure for which we are seeking. Let us examine the points in which it varies from pure democracy, and we shall comprehend both the nature of the cure and the efficacy which it must derive from the Union. …

The … point of difference is, the greater number of citizens and extent of territory which may be brought within the compass of republican than of democratic government; and it is this circumstance principally which renders factious combinations less to be dreaded in the former than in the latter. The smaller the society, the fewer probably will be the distinct parties and interests composing it; the fewer the distinct parties and interests, the more frequently will a majority be found of the same party; and the smaller the number of individuals composing a majority, and the smaller the compass within which they are placed, the more easily will they concert and execute their plans of oppression. Extend the sphere, and you take in a greater variety of parties and interests; you make it less probable that a majority of the whole will have a common motive to invade the rights of other citizens; or if such a common motive exists, it will be more difficult for all who feel it to discover their own strength, and to act in unison with each other. Besides other impediments, it may be remarked that, where there is a consciousness of unjust or dishonorable purposes, communication is always checked by distrust in proportion to the number whose concurrence is necessary. …

In the extent and proper structure of the Union, therefore, we behold a republican remedy for the diseases most incident to republican government. And according to the degree of pleasure and pride we feel in being republicans, ought to be our zeal in cherishing the spirit and supporting the character of Federalists.

Federalist No. 11—Alexander Hamilton
The Utility of the Union in Respect to Commercial Relations and a Navy

The importance of the Union, in a commercial light, is one of those points about which there is least room to entertain a difference of opinion, and which has, in fact, commanded the most general assent of men who have any acquaintance with the subject. This applies as well to our intercourse with foreign countries as with each other. ...

I shall briefly observe, that our situation invites and our interests prompt us to aim at an ascendant in the system of American affairs. The world may politically, as well as geographically, be divided into four parts, each having a distinct set of interests. Unhappily for the other three, Europe, by her arms and by her negotiations, by force and by fraud, has, in different degrees, extended her dominion over them all. Africa, Asia, and America, have successively felt her domination. The superiority she has long maintained has tempted her to plume herself as the Mistress of the World, and to consider the rest of mankind as created for her benefit. Men admired as profound philosophers have, in direct terms, attributed to her inhabitants a physical superiority, and have gravely asserted that all animals, and with them the human species, degenerate in America—that even dogs cease to bark after having breathed awhile in our atmosphere. Facts have too long supported these arrogant pretensions of the Europeans. It belongs to us to vindicate the honor of the human race, and to teach that assuming brother, moderation. Union will enable us to do it. Disunion will add another victim to his triumphs. Let Americans disdain to be the instruments of European greatness! Let the thirteen States, bound together in a strict and indissoluble Union, concur in erecting one great American system, superior to the control of all transatlantic force or influence, and able to dictate the terms of the connection between the old and the new world!

Federalist No. 14—James Madison
Objections to the Proposed Constitution From Extent of Territory Answered

... Hearken not to the unnatural voice which tells you that the people of America, knit together as they are by so many cords of affection, can no longer live together as members of the same family; can no longer continue the mutual guardians of their mutual happiness; can no longer be fellow citizens of one great, respectable, and flourishing empire. Hearken not to the voice which petulantly tells you that the form of government recommended for your adoption is a novelty in the political world; that it has never yet had a place in the theories of the wildest projectors; that it rashly attempts what it is impossible to accomplish. No, my countrymen, shut your ears against this unhallowed language. Shut your hearts against the poison which it conveys; the kindred blood which flows in the veins of American citizens, the mingled blood which they have shed in defense of their sacred rights, consecrate their Union, and excite horror at the idea of their becoming aliens, rivals, enemies. And if novelties are to be shunned, believe me, the most alarming of all novelties, the most wild of all projects, the most rash of all attempts, is that of rendering us in pieces, in order to preserve our liberties and promote our happiness. But why is the experiment of an extended republic to be rejected, merely because it may comprise what is new? Is it not the glory of the people of America, that, whilst they have paid a decent regard to the opinions of former times and other nations, they have not suffered a blind veneration for antiquity, for custom, or for names, to overrule the suggestions of their own good sense, the knowledge of their own situation, and the lessons of their own experience? To this manly spirit, posterity will be indebted for the possession, and the world for the example, of the numerous innovations displayed on the American theatre, in favor of private rights and public happiness. Had no important step been taken by the leaders of the Revolution for which a precedent could not be discovered, no government established of which an exact model did not present itself, the people of the United States might, at this moment have been numbered among the melancholy victims of misguided councils, must at best have been laboring under the weight of some of those forms which have crushed the liberties of the rest of mankind. Happily for America, happily, we trust, for the whole human race, they pursued a new and more noble course. They accomplished a revolution which has no parallel in the annals of human society. They reared the fabrics of governments which have no model on the face of the globe. They formed the design of a great Confederacy, which it is incumbent on their successors to improve and perpetuate. If their works betray imperfections, we wonder at the fewness of them. If they erred most in the structure of the Union, this was the work most difficult to be executed; this is the work which has been new modelled by the act of your convention, and it is that act on which you are now to deliberate and to decide.

Federalist No. 30—Alexander Hamilton
Concerning the General Power of Taxation

It has been already observed that the federal government ought to possess the power of providing for the support of the national forces; in which proposition was intended to be included the expense of raising troops, of building and equipping fleets, and all other expenses in any wise connected with military arrangements and operations. But these are not the only objects to which the jurisdiction of the Union, in respect to revenue, must necessarily be empowered to extend. It must embrace a provision for the support of the national civil list; for the payment of the national debts contracted, or that may be contracted; and, in general, for all those matters which will call for disbursements out of the national treasury. The conclusion is, that there must be interwoven, in the frame of the government, a general power of taxation, in one shape or another.

Money is, with propriety, considered as the vital principle of the body politic; as that which sustains its life and motion, and enables it to perform its most essential functions. A complete power, therefore, to procure a regular and adequate supply of it, as far as the resources of the community will permit, may be regarded as an indispensable ingredient in every constitution. From a deficiency in this particular, one of two evils must ensue; either the people must be subjected to continual plunder, as a substitute for a more eligible mode of supplying the public wants, or the government must sink into a fatal atrophy, and, in a short course of time, perish. …

Federalist No. 42—James Madison
The Powers Conferred by the Constitution Further Considered

… It were doubtless to be wished, that the power of prohibiting the importation of slaves had not been postponed until the year 1808, or rather that it had been suffered to have immediate operation. But it is not difficult to account, either for this restriction on the general government, or for the manner in which the whole clause is expressed. It ought to be considered as a great point gained in favor of humanity, that a period of twenty years may terminate forever, within these States, a traffic which has so long and so loudly upbraided the barbarism of modern policy; that within that period, it will receive a considerable discouragement from the federal government, and may be totally abolished, by a concurrence of the few States which continue the unnatural traffic, in the prohibitory example which has been given by so great a majority of the Union. Happy would it be for the unfortunate Africans, if an equal prospect lay before them of being redeemed from the oppressions of their European brethren!

Attempts have been made to pervert this clause into an objection against the Constitution, by representing it on one side as a criminal toleration of an illicit practice, and on another as calculated to prevent voluntary and beneficial emigrations from Europe to America. I mention these misconstructions, not with a view to give them an answer, for they deserve none, but as specimens of the manner and spirit in which some have thought fit to conduct their opposition to the proposed government …

Federalist No. 51—James Madison
The Structure of the Government Must Furnish the Proper Checks and Balances Between the Different Departments

… If men were angels, no government would be necessary. If angels were to govern men, neither external nor internal controls on government would be necessary. In framing a government which is to be administered by men over men, the great difficulty lies in this: you must first enable the government to control the governed; and in the next place oblige it to control itself …

Justice is the end of government. It is the end of civil society. It ever has been and ever will be pursued until it be obtained, or until liberty be lost in the pursuit. In a society under the forms of which the stronger faction can readily unite and oppress the weaker, anarchy may as truly be said to reign as in a state of nature, where the weaker individual is not secured against the violence of the stronger; and as, in the latter state, even the stronger individuals are prompted, by the uncertainty of their condition, to submit to a government which may protect the weak as well as themselves; so, in the former state, will the more powerful factions or parties be gradually induced, by a like motive, to wish for a government which will protect all parties, the weaker as well as the more powerful. ...

Federalist No. 55—James Madison
The Total Number of the House of Representatives

The number of which the House of Representatives is to consist, forms another and a very interesting point of view, under which this branch of the federal legislature may be contemplated. ...

The truth is, that in all cases a certain number at least seems to be necessary to secure the benefits of free consultation and discussion, and to guard against too easy a combination for improper purposes; as, on the other hand, the number ought at most to be kept within a certain limit, in order to avoid the confusion and intemperance of a multitude. In all very numerous assemblies, of whatever character composed, passion never fails to wrest the sceptre from reason. Had every Athenian citizen been a Socrates, every Athenian assembly would still have been a mob. ...

As there is a degree of depravity in mankind which requires a certain degree of circumspection and distrust, so there are other qualities in human nature which justify a certain portion of esteem and confidence. Republican government presupposes the existence of these qualities in a higher degree than any other form. Were the pictures which have been drawn by the political jealousy of some among us faithful likenesses of the human character, the inference would be, that there is not sufficient virtue among men for self-government; and that nothing less than the chains of despotism can restrain them from destroying and devouring one another.

Federalist No. 57—James Madison
The Alleged Tendency of the New Plan to Elevate the Few at the Expense of the Many Considered in Connection with Representation

The third charge against the House of Representatives is, that it will be taken from that class of citizens which will have least sympathy with the mass of the people, and be most likely to aim at an ambitious sacrifice of the many to the aggrandizement of the few. Of all the objections which have been framed against the federal Constitution, this is perhaps the most extraordinary.

Whilst the objection itself is levelled against a pretended oligarchy, the principle of it strikes at the very root of republican government. The aim of every political constitution is, or ought to be, first to obtain for rulers men who possess most wisdom to discern, and most virtue to pursue, the common good of the society; and in the next place, to take the most effectual precautions for keeping them virtuous whilst they continue to hold their public trust. The elective mode of obtaining rulers is the characteristic policy of republican government. The means relied on in this form of government for preventing their degeneracy are numerous and various. The most effectual one, is such a limitation of the term of appointments as will maintain a proper responsibility to the people. Let me now ask what circumstance there is in the constitution of the House of Representatives that violates the principles of republican government, or favors the elevation of the few on the ruins of the many? Let me ask whether every circumstance is not, on the contrary, strictly conformable to these principles, and scrupulously impartial to the rights and pretensions of every class and description of citizens? Who are to be the electors of the federal representatives? Not the rich, more than the poor; not the learned, more than the ignorant; not the haughty heirs of distinguished names, more than the humble sons of obscurity and unpropitious fortune. The electors are to be the great body of the people of the United States. They are to be the same who exercise the right in every State of electing the corresponding branch of the legislature of the State. Who are to be the objects of popular choice? Every citizen whose merit may recommend him to the esteem and confidence of his country. No qualification of wealth, of birth, of religious faith, or of civil profession is permitted to fetter the judgement or disappoint the inclination of the people. ...

Federalist No. 64—John Jay
The Powers of the Senate

... They who make laws may, without doubt, amend or repeal them; and it will not be disputed that they who make treaties may alter or cancel them; but still let us not forget that treaties are made, not by only one of the contracting parties, but by both; and consequently, that as the consent of both was essential to their formation at first, so must it ever afterwards be to alter or cancel them. The proposed Constitution, therefore, has not in the least extended the obligation of treaties. They are just as binding, and just as far beyond the lawful reach of legislative acts now, as they will be at any future period, or under any form of government.

However useful jealousy may be in republics, yet when like bile in the natural, it abounds too much in the body politic, the eyes of both become very liable to be deceived by the delusive appearances which that malady casts on surrounding objects. From this cause, probably, proceed the fears and apprehensions of some, that the President and Senate may make treaties without an equal eye to the interests of all the States. Others suspect that two thirds will oppress the remaining third, and ask whether those gentlemen are made sufficiently responsible for their conduct; whether, if they act corruptly, they can be punished; and if they make disadvantageous treaties, how are we to get rid of those treaties?

As all the States are equally represented in the Senate, and by men the most able and the most willing to promote the interests of their constituents, they will all have an equal degree of influence in that body, especially while they continue to be careful in appointing proper persons, and to insist on their punctual attendance. In proportion as the United States assume a national form and a national character, so will the good of the whole be more and more an object of attention, and the government must be a weak one indeed, if it should forget that the good of the whole can only be promoted by advancing the good of each of the parts or members which compose the whole. It will not be in the power of the President and Senate to make any treaties by which they and their families and estates will not be equally bound and affected with the rest of the community; and, having no private interests distinct from that of the nation, they will be under no temptations to neglect the latter.

As to corruption, the case is not supposable. He must either have been very unfortunate in his intercourse with the world, or possess a heart very susceptible of such impressions, who can think it probable that the President and two thirds of the Senate will ever be capable of such unworthy conduct. The idea is too gross and too invidious to be entertained. But in such a case, if it should ever happen, the treaty so obtained from us would, like all other fraudulent contracts, be null and void by the law of nations.

With respect to their responsibility, it is difficult to conceive how it could be increased. Every consideration that can influence the human mind, such as honor, oaths, reputations, conscience, the love of country, and family affections and attachments, afford security for their fidelity. In short, as the Constitution has taken the utmost care that they shall be men of talents and integrity, we have reason to be persuaded that the treaties they make will be as advantageous as, all circumstances considered, could be made; and so far as the fear of punishment and disgrace can operate, that motive to good behavior is amply afforded by the article on the subject of impeachments.

Federalist No. 78—Alexander Hamilton
The Judiciary Department

… The complete independence of the courts of justice is peculiarly essential in a limited Constitution. By a limited Constitution, I understand one which contains certain specified exceptions to the legislative authority; such, for instance, as that it shall pass no bills of attainder, no ex-post-facto laws, and the like. Limitations of this kind can be preserved in practice no other way than through the medium of courts of justice, whose duty it must be to declare all acts contrary to the manifest tenor of the Constitution void. Without this, all the reservations of particular rights or privileges would amount to nothing.

Some perplexity respecting the rights of the courts to pronounce legislative acts void, because contrary to the Constitution, has arisen from an imagination that the doctrine would imply a superiority of the judiciary to the legislative power. It is urged that the authority which can declare the acts of another void, must necessarily be superior to the one whose acts may be declared void. As this doctrine is of great importance in all the American constitutions, a brief discussion of the ground on which it rests cannot be unacceptable.

There is no position which depends on clearer principles, than that every act of a delegated authority, contrary to the tenor of the commission under which it is exercised, is void. No legislative act, therefore, contrary to the Constitution, can be valid. To deny this, would be to affirm, that the deputy is greater than his principal; that the servant is above his master; that the representatives of the people are superior to the people themselves; that men acting by virtue of powers, may do not only what their powers do not authorize, but what they forbid.

If it be said that the legislative body are themselves the constitutional judges of their own powers, and that the construction they put upon them is conclusive upon the other departments, it may be answered, that this cannot be the natural presumption, where it is not to be collected from any particular provisions in the Constitution. It is not otherwise to be supposed, that the Constitution could intend to enable the representatives of the people to substitute their WILL to that of their constituents. It is far more rational to suppose, that the courts were designed to be an intermediate body between the people and the legislature, in order, among other things, to keep the latter within the limits assigned to their authority. The interpretation of the laws is the proper and peculiar province of the courts. A constitution is, in fact, and must be regarded by the judges, as a fundamental law. It therefore belongs to them to ascertain its meaning, as well as the meaning of any particular act proceeding from the legislative body. If there should happen to be an irreconcilable variance between the two, that which has the superior obligation and validity ought, of course, to be preferred; or, in other words, the Constitution ought to be preferred to the statute, the intention of the people to the intention of their agents.

Nor does this conclusion by any means suppose a superiority of the judicial to the legislative power. It only supposes that the power of the people is superior to both; and that where the will of the legislature, declared in its statutes, stands in opposition to that of the people, declared in the Constitution, the judges ought to be governed by the latter rather than the former. They ought to regulate their decisions by the fundamental laws, rather than by those which are not fundamental. ...

PATRICK HENRY

Against Ratification

The first thing I have at heart is American liberty; the second thing is American union.

In order to be ratified, the Constitution needed the approval of nine states. Delaware became the first state to ratify on December 7, 1787, and, on June 21, 1788, New Hampshire became the ninth. Despite the legality of the Constitution, the Founding Fathers worried about popular acceptance of the new government because the heavy populated states of Virginia and New York had not ratified. The State of Rhode Island had even refused to send representatives to the Constitutional Convention because it did not want the federal government to infringe on Rhode Island sovereignty.

Support for the final draft of the Constitution at the Federal Convention had been far from unanimous, with sixteen of the fifty-five delegates refusing to sign the document. Among the detractors were Elbridge Gerry, George Mason, and Edmund Randolph, all of whom objected to the powers delegated to the proposed national government. Luther Martin, delegate from Maryland, outlined his objections in his nearly 30,000-word "Genuine Information," an address to the Maryland legislature in which he lamented the ascension of the national government over the states and condemned what he saw as unequal representation in Congress. Revolutionary hero Richard Henry Lee actively campaigned against ratification, despaired by the lack of provisions to protect "those essential rights of mankind without which liberty cannot exist." Thomas Jefferson, who was serving as minister to France during the Convention, characterized the delegates as an assembly of "demi-gods" and likewise opposed ratification.

Patrick Henry, who had again served as governor of Virginia after the revolution, declined to attend the Constitutional Convention of 1787 saying that he "smelt a rat in Philadelphia, tending toward the monarchy." An ardent supporter of states' rights, Henry led the opposition at the Virginia Ratifying Convention of 1788, expressing concern that the untested office of the presidency could devolve into a monarchy, and he protested with vehemence against the proposed new Constitution's lack of sufficient safeguards against governmental abuses due to human weakness among its officials.

Henry's passionate demands for a constitutional bill of rights led to assurances that the Constitution would be amended after ratification, which secured the necessary support among the states and greatly pacified his opposition to the new government.

... I rose yesterday to ask a question which arose in my own mind. When I asked that question, I thought the meaning of my interrogation was obvious. The fate of this question and of America may depend on this. Have they said, We, the states? Have they made a proposal of a compact between states? If they had, this would be a confederation. It is otherwise most clearly a consolidated government. The question turns, sir, on that poor little thing—the expression, We, the *people*, instead of the *states*, of America. I need not take much pains to show that the principles of this system are extremely pernicious, impolitic, and dangerous. Is this a monarchy, like England—a compact between prince and people, with checks on the former to secure the liberty of the latter? Is this a confederacy, like Holland—an association of a number of independent states, each of which retains its individual sovereignty? It is not a democracy, wherein the people retain all their rights securely. Had these principles been adhered to, we should not have been brought to this alarming transition, from a confederacy to a consolidated government. We have no detail of these great considerations, which, in my opinion, ought to have abounded before we should recur to a government of this kind. Here is a resolution as radical as that which separated us from Great Britain. It is radical in this transition; our rights and privileges are endangered, and the sovereignty of the states will be relinquished: and cannot we plainly see that this is actually the case? The rights of conscience, trial by jury, liberty of the press, all your immunities and franchises, all pretensions to human rights and privileges, are rendered insecure, if not lost, by this change, so loudly talked of by some, and inconsiderately by others. Is this tame relinquishment of rights worthy of freemen? Is it worthy of that manly fortitude that ought to characterize republicans? It is said eight states have adopted this plan. I declare that if twelve states and a half had adopted it, I would, with manly firmness, and in spite of an erring world, reject it. You are not to inquire how your trade may be increased, nor how you are to become a great and powerful people, but how your liberties can be secured; for liberty ought to be the direct end of your government.

Having premised these things, I shall, with the aid of my judgment and information, which, I confess, are not extensive, go into the discussion of this system more minutely. Is it necessary for your liberty that you should abandon those great rights by the adoption of this system?

Is the relinquishment of the trial by jury and the liberty of the press necessary for your liberty? Will the abandonment of your most sacred rights tend to the security of your liberty? Liberty, the greatest of all earthly blessing—give us that precious jewel, and you may take every thing else! But I am fearful I have lived long enough to become an old-fashioned fellow. Perhaps an invincible attachment to the dearest rights of man may, in these refined, enlightened days, be deemed old-fashioned; if so, I am contented to be so. I say, the time has been when every pulse of my heart beat for American liberty, and which, I believe, had a counterpart in the breast of every true American ... There are many on the other side, who possibly may have been persuaded to the necessity of these measures, which I conceive to be dangerous to your liberty. Guard with jealous attention the public liberty. Suspect every one who approaches that jewel. Unfortunately, nothing will preserve it but downright force. Whenever you give up that force, you are inevitably ruined. I am answered by gentlemen, that, though I might speak of terrors, yet the fact was, that we were surrounded by none of the dangers I apprehended. I conceive this new government to be one of those dangers: it has produced those horrors which distress many of our best citizens. We are come hither to preserve the poor commonwealth of Virginia, if it can be possibly done: something must be done to preserve your liberty and mine. The Confederation, this same despised government, merits, in my opinion, the highest encomium: it carried us through a long and dangerous war; it rendered us victorious in that bloody conflict with a powerful nation; it has secured us a territory greater than any European monarch possesses: and shall a government which has been thus strong and vigorous, be accused of imbecility, and abandoned for want of energy? Consider what you are about to do before you part with the government. Take longer time in reckoning things; revolutions like this have happened in almost every country in Europe; similar examples are to be found in ancient Greece and ancient Rome—instances of the people losing their liberty by their own carelessness and the ambition of a few. ...

In some parts of the plan before you, the great rights of freemen are endangered; in other parts, absolutely taken away. How does your trial by jury stand? In civil cases gone—not sufficiently secured in criminal—this best privilege is gone. But we are told that we need not fear; because those in power, being our representatives, will not abuse the powers we put in their hands. I am not well versed in history, but I will submit to your recollection, whether liberty has been destroyed most often by the licentiousness of the people, or by the tyranny of rulers. I imagine, sir, you will find the balance on the side of tyranny. Happy will you be if you miss the fate of those nations, who, omitting to resist their oppressors, or negligently suffering their liberty to be wrested from them, have groaned under intolerable despotism! Most of the human race are now in this deplorable condition; and those nations who have gone in search of grandeur, power, and splendor, have also fallen a sacrifice, and been the victims of their own folly. While they acquired those visionary blessings, they lost their freedom. …

What, sir, is the genius of democracy? Let me read that clause of the bill of rights of Virginia which relates to this: 3d clause:—"That government is, or ought to be, instituted for the common benefit, protection, and security of the people, nation, or community. Of all the various modes and forms of government, that is best, which is capable of producing the greatest degree of happiness and safety, and is most effectually secured against the danger of maladministration; and that whenever any government shall be found inadequate, or contrary to those purposes, a majority of the community hath an indubitable, unalienable, and indefeasible right to reform, alter, or abolish it, in such manner as shall be judged most conducive to the public weal."

This, sir, is the language of democracy—that a majority of the community have a right to alter government when found to be oppressive. But how different is the genius of your new Constitution from this! How different from the sentiments of freemen, that a contemptible minority can prevent the good of the majority! If, then, gentlemen, standing on this ground, are come to that point, that they are willing to bind themselves and their posterity to be oppressed, I am amazed and inexpressibly astonished. If this be the opinion of the majority, I must submit; but to me, sir, it appears perilous and destructive. … The honorable gentleman who presides told us that, to prevent abuses in our government, we will assemble in Convention, recall our delegated powers, and punish our servants for abusing the trust reposed in them. O sir, we should have fine times, indeed, if, to punish tyrants, it were only sufficient to assemble the people! Your arms, wherewith you could defend yourselves, are gone; and you have no longer an aristocratical, no longer a democratical spirit. Did you ever read of any revolution in a nation, brought about by the punishment of those in power, inflicted by those who had

no power at all? You read of a riot act in a country which is called one of the freest in the world, where a few neighbors cannot assemble without the risk of being shot by a hired soldiery, the engines of despotism. We may see such an act in America. …

Will the oppressor let go the oppressed? Was there ever an instance? Can the annals of mankind exhibit one single example where rulers overcharged with power willingly let go the oppressed, though solicited and requested most earnestly? The application for amendments will therefore be fruitless. Sometimes, the oppressed have got loose by one of those bloody struggles that desolate a country; but a willing relinquishment of power is one of those things which human nature never was, nor ever will be, capable of. …

When the American spirit was in its youth, the language of America was different: liberty, sir, was then the primary object. We are descended from a people whose government was founded on liberty: our glorious forefathers of Great Britain made liberty the foundation of every thing. That country is become a great, mighty, and splendid nation; not because their government is strong and energetic, but, sir, because liberty is its direct end and foundation. We drew the spirit of liberty from our British ancestors: by that spirit we have triumphed over every difficulty. But now, sir, the American spirit, assisted by the ropes and chains of consolidation, is about to convert this country into a powerful and mighty empire. If you make the citizens of this country agree to become the subjects of one great consolidated empire of America, your government will not have sufficient energy to keep them together. …

The voice of tradition, I trust, will inform posterity of our struggles for freedom. If our descendants be worthy the name of Americans, they will preserve, and hand down to their latest posterity, the transactions of the present times; and, though I confess my exclamations are not worthy the hearing, they will see that I have done my utmost to preserve their liberty; for I never will give up the power of direct taxation but for a scourge. I am willing to give it conditionally; that is, after non-compliance with requisitions. I will do more, sir, and what I hope will convince the most skeptical man that I am a lover of the American Union—that, in case Virginia shall not make punctual payment, the control of our custom-houses, and the whole regulation of trade, shall be given to Congress, and that Virginia shall depend on Congress even for passports, till Virginia shall have paid the last

State, Territory, or possession of the United States for delivery or use therein of intoxicating liquors, in violation of the laws thereof, is hereby prohibited.

Section 3. This article shall be inoperative unless it shall have been ratified as an amendment to the Constitution by conventions in the several States, as provided in the Constitution, within seven years from the date of the submission hereof to the States by the Congress.

Amendment XXII (Ratified February 27, 1951)

Section 1. No person shall be elected to the office of the President more than twice, and no person who has held the office of President, or acted as President, for more than two years of a term to which some other person was elected President shall be elected to the office of the President more than once. But this Article shall not apply to any person holding the office of President, or acting as President, during the term within which this Article becomes operative from holding the office of President or acting as President during the remainder of such term.

Section 2. This article shall be inoperative unless it shall have been ratified as an amendment to the Constitution by the legislatures of three-fourths of the several States within seven years from the date of its submission to the States by the Congress.

Amendment XXIII (Ratified March 29, 1961)

Section 1. The District constituting the seat of Government of the United States shall appoint in such manner as the Congress may direct:

A number of electors of President and Vice President equal to the whole number of Senators and Representatives in Congress to which the District would be entitled if it were a State, but in no event more than the least populous State; they shall be in addition to those appointed by the States, but they shall be considered, for the purposes of the election of President and Vice President, to be electors appointed by a State; and they shall meet in the District and perform such duties as provided by the twelfth article of amendment.

Section 2. The Congress shall have power to enforce this article by appropriate legislation.

Amendment XXIV (Ratified January 23, 1964)

Section 1. The right of citizens of the United States to vote in any primary or other election for President or Vice President, for electors for President or Vice President, or for Senator or Representative in Congress, shall not be denied or abridged by the United States or any State by reason of failure to pay any poll tax or other tax.

Section 2. The Congress shall have power to enforce this article by appropriate legislation.

Amendment XXV (Ratified February 10, 1967)

Section 1. In case of the removal of the President from office or of his death or resignation, the Vice President shall become President.

Section 2. Whenever there is a vacancy in the office of the Vice President, the President shall nominate a Vice President who shall take office upon confirmation by a majority vote of both Houses of Congress.

Section 3. Whenever the President transmits to the President protempore of the Senate and the Speaker of the House of Representatives his written declaration that he is unable to discharge the powers and duties of his office, and until he transmits to them a written declaration to the contrary, such powers and duties shall be discharged by the Vice President as Acting President.

Section 4. Whenever the Vice President and a majority of either the principal officers of the executive departments or of such other body as Congress may by law provide, transmit to the President pro tempore of the Senate and the Speaker of the House of Representatives their written declaration that the President is unable to discharge the powers and duties of his office, the Vice President shall immediately assume the powers and duties of the office as Acting President.

Thereafter, when the President transmits to the President pro tempore of the Senate and the Speaker of the House of Representatives his written declaration that no inability exists, he shall resume the powers and duties of his office unless the Vice President and a majority of either the principal officers of the executive department or of such other body as Congress may by law provide, transmit within four days to the President pro tempore of the Senate and the Speaker of the House of Representatives their written declaration that the President is unable to discharge the powers and duties of his office. Thereupon Congress shall decide the issue, assembling within forty-eight hours for that purpose if not in session. If the Congress, within twenty-one days after receipt of the latter written declaration, or, if Congress is not in session, within twenty-one days after Congress is required to assemble, determines by two-thirds vote of both Houses that the President is unable to discharge the powers and duties of his office, the Vice President shall continue to discharge the same as Acting President; otherwise, the President shall resume the powers and duties of his office.

Amendment XXVI (Ratified July 1, 1971)

Section 1. The right of citizens of the United States, who are eighteen years of age or older, to vote shall not be denied or abridged by the United States or by any State on account of age.

Section 2. The Congress shall have the power to enforce this article by appropriate legislation.

Amendment XXVII (Ratified May 7, 1992)

No law, varying the compensation for the services of the Senators and Representatives, shall take effect, until an election of Representatives shall have intervened.

GEORGE WASHINGTON

First Inaugural Address

No people can be bound to acknowledge and adore the Invisible Hand which conducts the affairs of men more than those of the United States.

On April 30, 1789, the fifty-seven-year-old George Washington stood on the balcony at Federal Hall in New York City and was sworn in as the first president of the United States. He placed his hand on an open Bible and repeated the oath of office administered by Robert R. Livingston. Washington then added the words, "So help me God!" and kissed the Bible before walking into the Senate chamber where he delivered his inaugural address.

Fellow-Citizens of the Senate and of the House of Representatives:

Among the vicissitudes incident to life no event could have filled me with greater anxieties than that of which the notification was transmitted by your order, and received on the 14th day of the present month. On the one hand, I was summoned by my country, whose voice I can never hear but with veneration and love, from a retreat which I had chosen with the fondest predilection, and, in my flattering hopes, with an immutable decision, as the asylum of my declining years—a retreat which was rendered every day more necessary as well as more dear to me by the addition of habit to inclination, and of frequent interruptions in my health to the gradual waste committed on it by time. On the other hand, the magnitude and difficulty of the trust to which the voice of my country called me, being sufficient to awaken in the wisest and most experienced of her citizens a distrustful scrutiny into his qualifications, could not but overwhelm with despondence one who (inheriting inferior endowments from nature and unpracticed in the duties of civil administration) ought to be peculiarly conscious of his own deficiencies. In this conflict of emotions all I dare aver is that it has been my faithful study to collect my duty from a just appreciation of every circumstance by which it might be affected. All I dare hope is that if, in executing this task, I have been too much swayed by a grateful remembrance of former instances, or by an affectionate sensibility to this transcendent proof of the confidence of my fellow-citizens, and have thence too little consulted my incapacity as well as disinclination for the weighty and untried cares before me, my error will be palliated by the motives which mislead me, and its consequences be judged by my country with some share of the partiality in which they originated.

Such being the impressions under which I have, in obedience to the public summons, repaired to the present station, it would be peculiarly improper to omit in this first official act my fervent supplications to that Almighty Being who rules over the universe, who presides in the councils of nations, and whose providential aids can supply every human defect, that His benediction may consecrate to the liberties and happiness of the people of the United States a Government instituted by themselves for these essential purposes, and may enable every instrument employed in its administration to execute with success the functions allotted to his charge. In tendering this homage to the Great Author of every public and private good, I assure myself that it expresses your sentiments not less than my own, nor those of my fellow-citizens at large less than either. No people can be bound to acknowledge and adore the Invisible Hand which conducts the affairs of men more than those of the United States. Every step by which they have advanced to the character of an independent nation seems to have been distinguished by some token of providential agency; and in the important revolution just accomplished in the system of their united government the tranquil deliberations and voluntary consent of so many distinct communities from which the event has resulted can not be compared with the means by which most governments have been established without some return of pious gratitude, along with an humble anticipation of the future blessings which the past seem to presage. These reflections, arising out of the present crisis, have forced themselves too strongly on my mind to be suppressed. You will join with me, I trust, in thinking that there are none under the influence of which the proceedings of a new and free government can more auspiciously commence.

By the article establishing the executive department it is made the duty of the President "to recommend to your consideration such measures as he shall judge necessary and expedient." The circumstances under which I now meet you will acquit me from entering into that subject further than to refer to the great constitutional charter under which you are assembled, and which, in defining your powers, designates the objects to which your attention is to be given. It will be more consistent with those circumstances, and far more congenial with the feelings which actuate me, to substitute, in place of a recommendation of particular measures, the tribute that is due to the talents, the rectitude, and the patriotism which adorn the characters selected to devise and adopt them. In these honorable qualifications I behold the surest pledges that as on one side no local prejudices or attachments, no separate views nor party animosities, will misdirect the comprehensive and equal eye which ought to watch over this great assemblage of communities and interests, so, on another, that the foundation of our national policy will be laid in the pure and immutable principles of private morality, and the preeminence of free government be exemplified by all the attributes which can win the affections of its citizens and command the respect of the world. I dwell on this prospect with every satisfaction which an ardent love for my country can inspire, since there is no truth more thoroughly established than that there exists in the economy and course of nature an indissoluble union between virtue and happiness; between duty and advantage; between the genuine maxims of an honest and magnanimous policy and the solid rewards of public prosperity and felicity; since we ought to be no less persuaded that the propitious smiles of Heaven can never be expected on a nation that disregards the eternal rules of order and right which Heaven itself has ordained; and since the preservation of the sacred fire of liberty and the destiny of the republican model of government are justly considered, perhaps, as deeply, as finally, staked on the experiment entrusted to the hands of the American people.

Besides the ordinary objects submitted to your care, it will remain with your judgment to decide how far an exercise of the occasional power delegated by the fifth article of the Constitution is rendered expedient at the present juncture by the nature of objections which have been urged against the system, or by the degree of inquietude which has given birth to them. Instead of undertaking particular recommendations on this subject, in which I could be guided by no lights derived from official opportunities, I shall again give way to my entire confidence in your discernment and pursuit of the public good; for I assure myself that whilst you carefully avoid every alteration which might endanger the benefits of an united and effective government, or which ought to await the future lessons of experience, a reverence for the characteristic rights of freemen and a regard for the public harmony will sufficiently influence your deliberations on the question how far the former can be impregnably fortified or the latter be safely and advantageously promoted.

To the foregoing observations I have one to add, which will be most properly addressed to the House of Representatives. It concerns myself, and will therefore be as brief as possible. When I was first honored with a call into the service of my country, then on the eve of an arduous struggle for its liberties, the light in which I contemplated my duty required that I should renounce every pecuniary compensation. From this resolution I have in no instance departed; and being still under the impressions which produced it, I must decline as inapplicable to myself any share in the personal emoluments which may be indispensably included in a permanent provision for the executive department, and must accordingly pray that the pecuniary estimates for the station in which I am placed may during my continuance in it be limited to such actual expenditures as the public good may be thought to require.

Having thus imparted to you my sentiments as they have been awakened by the occasion which brings us together, I shall take my present leave; but not without resorting once more to the benign Parent of the Human Race in humble supplication that, since He has been pleased to favor the American people with opportunities for deliberating in perfect tranquillity, and dispositions for deciding with unparalleled unanimity on a form of government for the security of their union and the advancement of their happiness, so His divine blessing may be equally conspicuous in the enlarged views, the temperate consultations, and the wise measures on which the success of this Government must depend.

ARTHUR GUITERMAN

Daniel Boone

Daniel Boone (1734-1820), the subject of Austrian-born American Arthur Guiterman's (1871-1943) celebrated poem, was born in a log cabin near Reading, Pennsylvania, and, with the help of friendly Indians, grew into a skilled hunter and woodsman. He later moved with his family to North Carolina along the Yadkin River and, at the age of twenty, fought in the French and Indian War. Boone married, had children and lived the pioneer life, hunting game and fighting Indians with his Kentucky rifle, *Tick-Licker*. Whenever more and more people would settle near his North Carolina cabin, Daniel pushed deeper into the woods where the hunting was better.

In 1768, Boone became reacquainted with John Finley, an old friend and former supply wagon driver who had learned of an Indian trail, the Warrior's Path, that led into Kentucky. Intrigued, Boone soon followed the Warrior's Path through the Cumberland Mountains and explored the region for two years before returning home. He then gathered his family and persuaded his neighbors to settle the area. The group began their journey in 1773, but turned back when Daniel's eldest son, James, was captured and killed by Indians. In 1775, under the employ of the Transylvania Company, Boone once more set out to settle the region; he successfully connected Indian trails to form a route that became known as the Wilderness Road.

After the Revolutionary War ended, Boone worked as a surveyor along the Ohio River and eventually settled in present-day Missouri. Despite an abundance of courage and resourcefulness, Boone did not prosper. He established extensive land claims, but lost them because of invalid titles. The U.S. Congress did, however, return a portion of Boone's land as a reward for his lifetime contribution to westward expansion. He spent the rest of his life in Missouri and, when the opportunity presented itself, ventured further west to hunt and explore new territory.

Daniel Boone, who had faced death many times in an adventurous life, died at the age of eighty-six. His remains were removed to Frankfort, Kentucky, where a monument stands in memory of the greatest frontiersman in history. A legendary figure even at the time of his death, Boone's fame spread worldwide when Lord Byron devoted seven stanzas to him in "Don Juan."

Daniel Boone at twenty-one
Came with his tomahawk, knife and gun
Home from the French and Indian War
To North Carolina and the Yadkin shore.
He married his maid with a golden band,
Builded his house and cleared his land;
But the deep woods claimed their son again
And he turned his face from the homes of men.
Over the Blue Ridge, dark and lone,
The Mountains of Iron, the Hills of Stone,
Braving the Shawnee's jealous wrath,
He made his way on the Warrior's Path.
Alone he trod the shadowed trails;
But he was the lord of a thousand vales
As he roved Kentucky, far and near,
Hunting the buffalo, elk and deer.
What joy to see, what joy to win
So fair a land for his kith and kin,
Of streams unstained and woods unhewn!
"Elbowroom!" laughed Daniel Boone.

On the Wilderness Road that his axmen made
The settlers flocked to the first stockade;
The deerskin shirts and the coonskin caps
Filed through the glens and the mountain gaps;
And hearts were high in the fateful spring
When the land said "Nay!" to the stubborn king.
While the men of the East of farm and town
Strove with the troops of the British Crown,
Daniel Boone from a surge of hate
Guarded a nation's westward gate.
Down on the fort in a wave of flame
The Shawnee horde and the Mingo came,
And the stout logs shook in a storm of lead;
But Boone stood firm and the savage fled.
Peace! And the settlers flocked anew,
The farm lands spread, the town lands grew;
But Daniel Boone was ill at ease
When he saw the smoke in his forest trees.
"There'll be no game in the country soon.
Elbowroom!" cried Daniel Boone.

Straight as a pine at sixty-five—
Time enough for a man to thrive—
He launched his bateau on Ohio's breast
And his heart was glad as he oared it west;
There were kindly folk and his own true blood
Where great Missouri rolls his flood;
New woods, new streams and room to spare,
And Daniel Boone found comfort there.
Yet far he ranged toward the sunset still,
Where the Kansas runs and the Smoky Hill,
And the prairies toss, by the south wind blown;
And he killed his bear on the Yellowstone.
But ever he dreamed of new domains
With vaster woods and wider plains;
Ever he dreamed of a world-to-be
Where there are no bounds and the soul is free.
At four-score-five, still stout and hale,
He heard a call to a farther trail;
So he turned his face where the stars are strewn;
"Elbowroom!" sighed Daniel Boone.

Down the Milky Way in its banks of blue
Far he has paddled his white canoe
To the splendid quest of the tameless soul—
He has reached the goal where there is no goal.
Now he rides and rides an endless trail
On the Hippogriff of the flaming tail
Or the Horse of the Stars with the golden mane,
As he rode the first of the blue-grass strain.
The joy that lies in the Search he seeks
On breathless hills with crystal peaks;
He makes his camp on heights untrod,
The steps of the Shrine, alone with God.
Through the woods of the vast, on the plains of Space
He hunts the pride of the Mammoth race
And the Dinosaur of the triple horn,
The manticore and the Unicorn,
As once by the broad Missouri's flow
He followed the elk and the buffalo.
East of the Sun and west of the Moon,
"Elbowroom!" laughs Daniel Boone.

Second Inaugural Address

I am again called upon by the voice of my country …

Washington's second inauguration took place in Philadelphia on March 4, 1793, making him the only president to be inaugurated in two cities. His inaugural address was a short, but heartfelt acceptance of "this distinguished honor." Later in the year, he traveled to Washington, D.C., then known as Federal City, to lay the cornerstone of the U.S. Capitol.

Fellow citizens: I am again called upon by the voice of my country to execute the functions of its Chief Magistrate. When the occasion proper for it shall arrive, I shall endeavor to express the high sense I entertain of this distinguished honor, and of the confidence which has been reposed in me by the people of united America.

Previous to the execution of any official act of the President the Constitution requires an oath of office. This oath I am now about to take, and in your presence: That if it shall be found during my administration of the Government I have in any instance violated willingly or knowingly the injunctions thereof, I may (besides incurring constitutional punishment) be subject to the upbraidings of all who are now witnesses of the present solemn ceremony.

George Washington reviews the troops near Fort Cumberland, Maryland, before their march to suppress the Whiskey Rebellion, as depicted by Frederick Kemmelmeyer. Having succeeded in gaining independence from Great Britain, many citizens of the new republic assumed they would never again pay direct taxes to support a distant government. The first secretary of the Treasury, Alexander Hamilton, successfully prevailed on Congress his plan to finance the national debt by creating an excise tax on spirits distilled in the United States. Opposition to the act was widespread, but most violent in western Pennsylvania where opponents tarred and feathered tax collectors and attacked the home of General John Neville, local inspector of the excise. President George Washington, refusing to tolerate the escalating defiance of federal authority, called out the militia to restore order. This act demonstrated the ability of the national government to enforce national law. On the other hand, the rebellion showed the depth of American citizens' hostility to a central government intent upon taxing them and regulating their lives. This hostility was demonstrated more peacefully in the 1800 election of Thomas Jefferson, under whose administration Congress repealed the Whiskey Tax.

GEORGE WASHINGTON

Farewell Address

*Citizens, by birth or choice, of a common country, that country has a right to concentrate your affections. The name of
AMERICAN, which belongs to you, in your national capacity, must always exalt the just pride of Patriotism.*

The following is an excerpt from Washington's 6,000-word farewell address, published on September 17, 1796. Offering
the "counsels of an old and affectionate friend," Washington spoke of political parties, religion, education, international
relations, taxes, and morality. Realizing that the transfer of power was the true test of democracy, Washington's refusal
to accept a third term ensured that the young republic was off to a good start. Washington spoke not only to the
Americans of the day, but to posterity—setting the precedent of using farewell addresses as an occasion to offer warnings.

Today, not only is the capital city of the United States named for Washington, but also an entire state and a
towering obelisk built in his honor. In addition, thousands of counties, parks, bridges, streets, and schools across the
country bear his name. Washington's image can be found on the quarter, the one-dollar bill, and numerous postage
stamps. His was the first birthday to be celebrated as a federal holiday (now observed on Presidents' Day), and due to
an act of Congress in 1976, the bicentennial year, George Washington holds in perpetuity the nation's highest military
title—"General of the Armies of the United States."

George Washington is, as Henry Lee stated, "first in war, first in peace, first in the hearts of his countrymen." He is
the indispensable American.

Friends and Fellow-Citizens: The period for a new election of a citizen, to administer the executive government of the United States, being not far distant, and the time actually arrived, when your thoughts must be employed designating the person, who is to be clothed with that important trust, it appears to me proper, especially as it may conduce to a more distinct expression of the public voice, that I should now apprise you of the resolution I have formed, to decline being considered among the number of those out of whom a choice is to be made …

The unity of Government, which constitutes you one people, is also now dear to you. It is justly so; for it is a main pillar in the edifice of your real independence, the support of your tranquillity at home, your peace abroad; of your safety; of your prosperity; of that very Liberty, which you so highly prize. But as it is easy to foresee, that, from different causes and from different quarters, much pains will be taken, many artifices employed, to weaken in your minds the conviction of this truth; as this is the point in your political fortress against which the batteries of internal and external enemies will be most constantly and actively (though often covertly and insidiously) directed, it is of infinite moment, that you should properly estimate the immense value of your national Union to your collective and individual happiness; that you should cherish a cordial, habitual, and immovable attachment to it; accustoming yourselves to think and speak of it as of the Palladium of your political safety and prosperity; watching for its preservation with jealous anxiety; discountenancing whatever may suggest even a suspicion, that it can in any event be abandoned; and indignantly frowning upon the first dawning of every attempt to alienate any portion of our country from the rest, or to enfeeble the sacred ties which now link together the various parts.

For this you have every inducement of sympathy and interest. Citizens, by birth or choice, of a common country, that country has a right to concentrate your affections. The name of AMERICAN, which belongs to you, in your national capacity, must always exalt the just pride of Patriotism, more than any appellation derived from local discriminations. With slight shades of difference, you have the same religion, manners, habits, and political principles. You have in a common cause fought and triumphed together; the Independence and Liberty you possess are the work of joint counsels, and joint efforts, of common dangers, sufferings, and successes …

In contemplating the causes which may disturb our Union, it occurs as matter of serious concern that any ground should have been furnished for characterizing parties by geographical discriminations, Northern and Southern, Atlantic and Western; whence designing men may endeavor to excite a belief that there is a real difference of local interests and views. One of the expedients of party to acquire influence within particular districts is to misrepresent the opinions and aims of other districts. You cannot shield yourselves too much against the jealousies and heartburnings which spring from these misrepresentations; they tend to render alien to each other those who ought to be bound together by fraternal affection …

To the efficacy and permanency of your Union, a government for the whole is indispensable. No alliance, however strict, between the parts can be an adequate substitute; they must inevitably experience the infractions and interruptions which all alliances in all times have experienced. Sensible of this momentous truth, you have improved upon your first essay, by the adoption of a constitution of government better calculated than your former for an intimate union, and for the efficacious management of your common concerns. This government, the offspring of our own choice, uninfluenced and unawed, adopted upon full investigation and mature deliberation, completely free in its principles, in the distribution of its powers, uniting security with energy, and containing within itself a provision for its own amendment, has a just claim to your confidence and your support. Respect for its authority, compliance with its laws, acquiescence in its measures, are duties enjoined by the fundamental maxims of true liberty. The basis of our political systems is the right of the people to make and to alter their constitutions of government. But the Constitution which at any time exists, till changed by an explicit and authentic act of the whole people, is sacredly obligatory upon all. The very idea of the power and the right of the people to establish government presupposes the duty of every individual to obey the established government. …

Toward the preservation of your government, and the permanency of your present happy state, it is requisite, not only that you steadily discountenance irregular oppositions to its acknowledged authority, but also that you resist with care the spirit of innovation upon its principles, however specious the pretexts. One method of assault may be to effect, in the forms of the Constitution, alterations which will impair the energy of the system, and thus to undermine what cannot be directly overthrown. In all the changes to which you may be invited, remember that time and habit are at least as necessary to fix the true character of governments as of other human institutions; that experience is the surest standard by which to test the real tendency of the existing constitution of a country; that facility in changes, upon the credit of mere hypothesis and opinion, exposes to perpetual change, from the endless variety of hypothesis and opinion; and remember, especially, that for the efficient management of your common interests, in a country so extensive as ours, a government of as much vigor as is consistent with the perfect security of liberty is indispensable. Liberty itself will find in such a government, with powers properly distributed and adjusted, its surest guardian. It is, indeed, little else than a name, where the government is too feeble to withstand the enterprises of faction, to confine each member of the society within the limits prescribed by the laws, and to maintain all in the secure and tranquil enjoyment of the rights of person and property.

I have already intimated to you the danger of parties in the State, with particular reference to the founding of them on geographical discriminations. Let me now take a more comprehensive view, and warn you in the most solemn manner against the baneful effects of the spirit of party generally.

This spirit, unfortunately, is inseparable from our nature, having its root in the strongest passions of the human mind. It exists under different shapes in all governments, more or less stifled, controlled, or repressed; but, in those of the popular form, it is seen in its greatest rankness, and is truly their worst enemy.

The alternate domination of one faction over another, sharpened by the spirit of revenge, natural to party dissension, which in different ages and countries has perpetrated the most horrid enormities, is itself a frightful despotism. But this leads at length to a more formal and permanent despotism. The disorders and miseries, which result, gradually incline the minds of men to seek security and repose in the absolute power of an individual; and sooner or later the chief of some prevailing faction, more able or more fortunate than his competitors, turns this disposition to the purposes of his own elevation, on the ruins of Public Liberty. …

There is an opinion, that parties in free countries are useful checks upon the administration of the Government, and serve to keep alive the spirit of Liberty. This within certain limits is probably true; and in Governments of a Monarchical cast, Patriotism may look with indulgence, if not with favor, upon the spirit of party. But in those of the popular character, in Governments purely elective, it is a spirit not to be encouraged. …

Of all the dispositions and habits which lead to political prosperity, Religion and Morality are indispensable supports. In vain would that man claim the tribute of Patriotism, who should labor to subvert these great pillars of human happiness, these firmest props of the duties of Men and Citizens. The mere Politician, equally with the pious man, ought to respect and to cherish them. A volume could not trace all their connections with private and public felicity. Let it simply be asked, Where is the security for property, for reputation, for life, if the sense of religious obligation desert the oaths, which are the instruments of investigation in Courts of Justice? And let us with caution indulge the supposition, that morality can be maintained without religion. Whatever may be conceded to the influence of refined education on minds of peculiar structure, reason and experience both forbid us to expect, that national morality can prevail in exclusion of religious principles.

It is substantially true, that virtue or morality is a necessary spring of popular government. The rule, indeed, extends with more or less force to every species of free government. Who, that is a sincere friend to it, can look with indifference upon attempts to shake the foundation of the fabric?

Promote, then, as an object of primary importance, institutions for the general diffusion of knowledge. In proportion as the structure of a government gives force to public opinion, it is essential that public opinion should be enlightened.

As a very important source of strength and security, cherish public credit. One method of preserving it is, to use it as sparingly as possible; avoiding occasions of expense by cultivating peace, but remembering also that timely disbursements to prepare for danger frequently prevent much greater disbursements to repel it; avoiding likewise the accumulation of debt, not only by shunning occasions of expense, but by vigorous exertions in time of peace to discharge the debts, which unavoidable wars may have occasioned, not ungenerously throwing upon posterity the burthen, which we ourselves ought to bear ...

Against the insidious wiles of foreign influence (I conjure you to believe me, fellow-citizens,) the jealousy of a free people ought to be constantly awake; since history and experience prove, that foreign influence is one of the most baneful foes of Republican Government. But that jealousy, to be useful, must be impartial; else it becomes the instrument of the very influence to be avoided, instead of a defense against it. Excessive partiality for one foreign nation, and excessive dislike of another, cause those whom they actuate to see danger only on one side, and serve to veil and even second the arts of influence on the other. Real patriots, who may resist the intrigues of the favorite, are liable to become suspected

and odious; while its tools and dupes usurp the applause and confidence of the people, to surrender their interests.

The great rule of conduct for us, in regard to foreign nations, is, in extending our commercial relations, to have with them as little political connection as possible. So far as we have already formed engagements, let them be fulfilled with perfect good faith. Here let us stop ...

'Tis our true policy to steer clear of permanent alliances with any portion of the foreign world; so far, I mean, as we are now at liberty to do it; for let me not be understood as capable of patronizing infidelity to existing engagements. I hold the maxim no less applicable to public than to private affairs, that honesty is always the best policy. I repeat it, therefore, let those engagements be observed in their genuine sense. But, in my opinion, it is unnecessary and would be unwise to extend them.

Taking care always to keep ourselves, by suitable establishments, on a respectable defensive posture, we may safely trust to temporary alliances for extraordinary emergencies.

Harmony, liberal intercourse with all nations, are recommended by policy, humanity, and interest. But even our commercial policy should hold an equal and impartial hand; neither seeking nor granting exclusive favors or preferences; consulting the natural course of things; diffusing and diversifying by gentle means the streams of commerce, but forcing nothing; establishing, with powers so disposed, in order to give trade a stable course, to define the rights of our merchants, and to enable the government to support them, conventional rules of intercourse, the best that present circumstances and mutual opinion will permit, but temporary, and liable to be from time to time abandoned or varied, as experience and circumstances shall dictate; constantly keeping in view, that it is folly in one nation to look for disinterested favors from another; that it must pay with a portion of its independence for whatever it may accept under that character; that, by such acceptance, it may place itself in the condition of having given equivalents for nominal favors, and yet of being reproached with ingratitude for not giving more. There can be no greater error than to expect or calculate upon real favors from nation to nation. It is an illusion, which experience must cure, which a just pride ought to discard.

In offering to you, my countrymen, these counsels of an old and affectionate friend, I dare not hope they will make the strong and lasting impression I could wish; that they will control the usual current of the passions, or prevent our nation from running the course, which has hitherto marked the destiny of nations. But, if I may even flatter myself, that they may be productive of some partial benefit, some occasional good; that they may now and then recur to moderate the fury of party spirit, to warn against the mischiefs of foreign intrigue, to guard against the impostures of pretended patriotism; this hope will be a full recompense for the solicitude for your welfare, by which they have been dictated. …

Though, in reviewing the incidents of my administration, I am unconscious of intentional error, I am nevertheless too sensible of my defects not to think it probable that I may have committed many errors. Whatever they may be, I fervently beseech the Almighty to avert or mitigate the evils to which they may tend. I shall also carry with me the hope, that my Country will never cease to view them with indulgence; and that, after forty-five years of my life dedicated to its service with an upright zeal, the faults of incompetent abilities will be consigned to oblivion, as myself must soon be to the mansions of rest.

Relying on its kindness in this as in other things, and actuated by that fervent love towards it, which is so natural to a man, who views it in the native soil of himself and his progenitors for several generations; I anticipate with pleasing expectation that retreat, in which I promise myself to realize, without alloy, the sweet enjoyment of partaking, in the midst of my fellow-citizens, the benign influence of good laws under a free government—the ever-favorite object of my heart, and the happy reward, as I trust, of our mutual cares, labors, and dangers.

JOSEPH HOPKINSON

Hail, Columbia

"Hail, Columbia" was written in 1798 by Joseph Hopkinson (1770-1842), the son of Francis Hopkinson, a signer of the Declaration of Independence. Originally titled "The Favorite New Federal Song," the lyrics were set to the tune of "The President's March," which had been composed for Washington's first inaugural. The last stanza paid homage to newly elected President John Adams, who had defeated Thomas Jefferson in a hard-fought and often bitter election. Those with strong anti-Federalist sentiments derided the song as a pompous tribute to a party with "monarchical pretensions." Hopkinson, however, had intended "Hail, Columbia" to heal the party divide by appealing to the shared heritage of all Americans, regardless of political opinion. Much to his delight, the song was embraced by the public with patriotic fervor. "Hail, Columbia" now serves as the official song of the vice president of the United States and is played whenever he enters a ceremonial occasion unaccompanied by the president.

Hail! Columbia, happy land!
Hail! ye heroes, heaven-born band,
Who fought and bled in freedom's cause,
And when the storm of war was gone,
Enjoyed the peace your valor won;
Let Independence be our boast,
Ever mindful what it cost,
Ever grateful for the prize,
Let its Altar reach the Skies.

Chorus:
Firm, united let us be,
Rallying round our Liberty,
As a band of Brothers joined,
Peace and safety we shall find.

Immortal Patriots, rise once more!
Defend your rights, defend your shore;
Let no rude foe with impious hand,
Invade the shrine where sacred lies
Of toil and blood the well-earned prize;
While offering peace, sincere and just,
In heaven we place a manly trust,
That truth and justice may prevail,
And every scheme of bondage fail.

Sound, sound the trump of fame!
Let Washington's great name
Ring through the world with loud applause!
Let every clime to freedom dear
Listen with a joyful ear;
With equal skill, with steady power,
He governs in the fearful hour
Of horrid war, or guides with ease
The happier times of honest peace.

Behold the Chief, who now commands,
Once more to serve his country stands,
The rock on which the storms will beat!
But armed in virtue, firm and true,
His hopes are fixed on Heaven and you.
When hope was sinking in dismay,
When glooms obscured Columbia's day,
His steady mind, from changes free,
Resolved on death or liberty.

This engraving by Alonzo Chappel depicts American heroes Stephen Decatur, Jr. and Reuben James during the First Barbary War. Also known as the Tripolitan Wars, the United States fought two wars against the Barbary States of North Africa in the early nineteenth century. At issue was the Barbary pirates' demand of tribute from American merchant vessels in the Mediterranean Sea. During the first war (1801-1805), the American frigate Philadelphia *was captured by the Barbary pirates when it ran aground in the city of Tripoli. Lieutenant Stephen Decatur, along with a group of volunteers that included Reuben James, entered the harbor of Tripoli under the cover of darkness in an attempt to burn the* Philadelphia *so that the pirates could not use her. In the ensuing hand-to-hand combat, Reuben James, with both of his hands already wounded, positioned himself between Lieutenant Decatur and a sword-wielding pirate. Willing to give his life for his captain, James took a blow from the sword and survived.*

THOMAS JEFFERSON

First Inaugural Address

If there be any among us who would wish to dissolve this Union or to change its republican form, let them stand undisturbed as monuments of the safety with which error of opinion may be tolerated where reason is left free to combat it.

The election of 1800—a rematch of the 1796 election in which the Federalist nominee John Adams had defeated the Republican (or Democratic-Republican) nominee Thomas Jefferson—was the most confusing and hotly contested presidential election in American history. By 1800, the Federalist Party was divided by a rift between Adams and Alexander Hamilton. The party divide, coupled with the unpopularity of the Federalist-supported Alien and Sedition Acts, which Jefferson and James Madison had severely criticized in the Kentucky and Virginia Resolutions, led to a narrow victory for Jefferson. Republican electors, however, had each cast one vote for Jefferson and one vote for Aaron Burr, intending to make Burr vice president. Technically a candidate for the presidency, however, Burr refused to remove his name from contention, meaning that the election was a tie and would have to be decided by the House of Representatives. Alexander Hamilton, who distrusted Burr, threw his considerable influence in support of Jefferson, who was finally elected president by the Federalist controlled House on February 17, 1801, on the thirty-sixth ballot. The election of 1800 led to the Twelfth Amendment whereby each elector would cast one vote for president and one vote for vice president. (Burr would later kill Hamilton in a duel when Hamilton successfully opposed his bid for the governorship of New York and exposed a covert plot of Burr's to break up the Union. Burr would be arrested by Jefferson and tried for treason, but acquitted.)

Jefferson's election represented the first transfer of political power from one party to another. His inaugural address, the first to be delivered in Washington, D.C., was a conciliatory speech in which he tried to unify the country, stating: "Every difference of opinion is not a difference of principle. We have called by different names brethren of the same principle. We are all republicans, we are all federalists." Under Jefferson's administration, the United States greatly increased in size due to the Louisiana Purchase and the exploration of western lands by Meriwether Lewis and William Clark. The U.S. also fought a successful naval war against marauding Barbary pirates in the Mediterranean.

In time, Jefferson and Adams reconciled their differences and renewed their friendship through a stream of steady correspondence. By a remarkable coincidence, both men died on July 4, 1826—fifty years after the adoption of the Declaration of Independence.

Friends and Fellow Citizens: Called upon to undertake the duties of the first executive office of our country, I avail myself to the presence of that portion of my fellow citizens which is here assembled, to express my grateful thanks for the favor with which they have been pleased to look toward me, to declare a sincere consciousness that the task is above my talents, and that I approach it with those anxious and awful presentiments which the greatness of the charge and the weakness of my powers so justly inspire. A rising nation, spread over a wide and fruitful land, traversing all the seas with the rich productions of their industry, engaged in commerce with nations who feel power and forget right, advancing rapidly to destinies beyond the reach of mortal eye—when I contemplate these transcendent objects, and see the honor, the happiness and the hopes of this beloved country committed to the issue and the auspices of this day, I shrink from the contemplation, and humble myself before the magnitude of the undertaking. Utterly indeed, should I despair, did not the presence of many whom I here see remind me, that in the other high authorities provided by our constitution, I shall find resources of wisdom, of virtue, and of zeal on which to rely under all difficulties. To you, then, gentlemen, who are charged with the sovereign functions of legislation, and to those associated with you, I look with encouragement for that guidance and support which may enable us to steer with safety the vessel in which we are all embarked amid the conflicting elements of a troubled world.

During the contest of opinion through which we have passed, the animation of discussion and of exertions

JOHN MARSHALL

Marbury v. Madison

The constitution of the United States confirms and strengthens the principle, supposed to be essential to all written constitutions, that a law repugnant to the constitution is void; and that courts, as well as other departments, are bound by that instrument.

Though defeated in the election of 1800, losing control of both the executive and legislative branches, the Federalists had no intention of going quietly. In the interim between the election and the expiration of their terms in office, President John Adams and the lame-duck Congress passed the Judiciary Act of 1801. Modifying the Judiciary Act of 1789, this new act was an attempt to extend the Federalist Party influence and hamper the incoming Democratic-Republicans through a number of last-minute federal appointments.

Among the judicial appointments Adams made during the closing weeks of his administration was that of John Marshall (1755-1835) to be chief justice of the United States, replacing the ailing Chief Justice Oliver Ellsworth. One of those whom Adams had appointed to the office of justice of the peace was William Marbury, but time ran out before his commission could be delivered. The individual responsible for delivering Marbury's commission was John Marshall, who, despite his judicial appointment, was still serving as secretary of state.

Upon taking office, President Jefferson promptly took steps to gain the repeal of the Judiciary Act of 1801, which he accomplished the following year. As for Marbury, Jefferson simply instructed his new secretary of state, James Madison, to withhold Marbury's commission. Predictably, Marbury then filed suit asking the Supreme Court, under its original jurisdiction, to issue a writ of mandamus to compel Madison to give him his commission.

In deciding *Marbury*, Marshall and his fellow justices faced a dilemma. The Jefferson administration would likely ignore any writ of mandamus, thereby hurting the standing of the Supreme Court. On the other hand, refusing to hear Marbury's petition would be seen as weakness in the face of presidential power and likewise damage the court. Marshall followed neither course. Instead, he ruled that while Madison should have delivered the commission and Marbury was therefore entitled to seek legal remedy, the Supreme Court had no right to issue writs of mandamus. He reasoned that the section of the Judiciary Act of 1789 granting the court such powers violated the Constitution and was therefore null and void.

Marbury v. Madison was the first time the Supreme Court declared something "unconstitutional" and established the concept of judicial review—the idea that courts may oversee and nullify the actions of another branch of government. Thomas Jefferson argued that if this ruling became accepted, it would be "placing us under the despotism of an oligarchy." Nonetheless, the principle of judicial review has been accepted in the American legal community.

… The very essence of civil liberty certainly consists in the right of every individual to claim the protection of the laws, whenever he receives an injury. One of the first duties of government is to afford that protection. The government of the United States has been emphatically termed a government of laws, and not of men. It will certainly cease to deserve this high appellation, if the laws furnish no remedy for the violation of a vested legal right.

By the constitution of the United States, the President is invested with certain important political powers, in the exercise of which he is to use his own discretion, and is accountable only to his country in his political character, and to his own conscience. To aid him in the performance of these duties, he is authorized to appoint certain officers, who act by his authority and in conformity with his orders.

In such cases, their acts are his acts; and whatever opinion may be entertained of the manner in which executive discretion may be used, still there exists, and can exist, no power to control that discretion. The subjects are political. They respect the nation, not individual rights, and being entrusted to the executive, the decision of the executive is conclusive. The application of this remark will be perceived by adverting to the act of congress for establishing the department of foreign affairs. This office, as his duties were prescribed by that act, is to conform precisely to the will of the President. He is the mere organ by whom that will is communicated. The acts of such an officer, as an officer, can never be examinable by the courts.

But when the legislature proceeds to impose on that officer other duties; when he is directed peremptorily to perform certain acts; when the rights of individuals are dependent on the performance of those acts; he is so far the officer of the law; is amenable to the laws for his conduct; and cannot at his discretion sport away the vested rights of others.

The conclusion from this reasoning is, that where the heads of departments are the political or confidential agents of the executive, merely to execute the will of the President, or rather to act in cases in which the executive possesses a constitutional or legal discretion, nothing can be more perfectly clear than that their acts are only politically examinable. But where a specific duty is assigned by law, and individual rights depend upon the performance of that duty, it seems equally clear that the individual who considers himself injured, has a right to resort to the laws of his country for a remedy. …

The constitution vests the whole judicial power of the United States in one supreme court, and such inferior courts as congress shall, from time to time, ordain and establish. This power is expressly extended to all cases arising under the laws of the United States; and consequently, in some form, may be exercised over the present case; because the right claimed is given by a law of the United States.

In the distribution of this power it is declared that "the supreme court shall have original jurisdiction in all cases affecting ambassadors, other public ministers and consuls, and those in which a state shall be a party. In all other cases, the supreme court shall have appellate jurisdiction."

It has been insisted, at the bar, that as the original grant of jurisdiction, to the supreme and inferior courts, is general, and the clause, assigning original jurisdiction to the supreme court, contains no negative or restrictive words; the power remains to the legislature, to assign original jurisdiction to that court in other cases than those specified in the article which has been recited; provided those cases belong to the judicial power of the United States.

If it had been intended to leave it to the discretion of the legislature to apportion the judicial power between the supreme and inferior courts according to the will of that body, it would certainly have been useless to have proceeded further than to have defined the judicial powers, and the tribunals in which it should be vested. The subsequent part of the section is mere surplusage, is entirely without meaning, if such is to be the construction. If congress remains at liberty to give this court appellate jurisdiction, where the constitution has declared their jurisdiction shall be original; and original jurisdiction where the constitution has declared it shall be appellate; the distribution of jurisdiction, made in the constitution, is form without substance. Affirmative words are often, in their operation, negative of other objects than those affirmed; and in this case, a negative or exclusive sense must be given to them or they have no operation at all. It cannot be presumed that any clause in the constitution is intended to be without effect; and therefore such a construction is inadmissible, unless the words require it.

When an instrument organizing fundamentally a judicial system, divides it into one supreme, and so many inferior courts as the legislature may ordain and establish; then enumerates its powers, and proceeds so far to distribute them, as to define the jurisdiction of the supreme court by declaring the cases in which it shall take original jurisdiction, and that in others it shall take appellate jurisdiction; the plain import of the words seems to be, that in one class of cases its jurisdiction is original, and not appellate; in the other it is appellate, and not original. If any other construction would render the clause inoperative, that is an additional reason for rejecting such other construction, and for adhering to their obvious meaning. …

The question, whether an act, repugnant to the constitution, can become the law of the land, is a question deeply interesting to the United States; but, happily, not of an intricacy proportioned to its interest. It seems only necessary to recognize certain principles, supposed to have been long and well established, to decide it.

That the people have an original right to establish, for their future government, such principles as, in their opinion, shall most conduce to their own happiness, is the basis, on which the whole American fabric has been erected. The exercise of this original right is a very great exertion; nor can it, nor ought it to be frequently repeated. The principles, therefore, so established, are deemed fundamental. And as the authority, from which they proceed, is supreme, and can seldom act, they are designed to be permanent.

This original and supreme will organizes the government, and assigns, to different departments, their respective powers. It may either stop here; or establish certain limits not to be transcended by those departments.

The government of the United States is of the latter description. The powers of the legislature are defined, and limited; and that those limits may not be mistaken, or forgotten, the constitution is written. To what purpose are powers limited, and to what purpose is that limitation committed to writing, if these limits may, at any time, be passed by those intended to be restrained? The distinction, between a government with limited and unlimited powers, is abolished, if those limits do not confine the persons on whom they are imposed, and if acts prohibited and acts allowed, are of equal obligation. It is a proposition too plain to be contested, that the constitution controls any legislative act repugnant to it; or, that the legislature may alter the constitution by an ordinary act.

Between these alternatives there is no middle ground. The constitution is either a superior, paramount law, unchangeable by ordinary means, or it is on a level with ordinary legislative acts, and like other acts, is alterable when the legislature shall please to alter it.

If the former part of the alternative be true, then a legislative act contrary to the constitution is not law: if the latter part be true, then written constitutions are absurd attempts, on the part of the people, to limit a power, in its own nature illimitable.

Certainly all those who have framed written constitutions contemplate them as forming the fundamental and paramount law of the nation, and consequently the theory of every such government must be, that an act of the legislature, repugnant to the constitution, is void.

If an act of the legislature, repugnant to the constitution, is void, does it, notwithstanding its invalidity, bind the courts, and oblige them to give it effect? Or, in other words, though it be not law, does it constitute a rule as operative as if it was a law? This would be to overthrow in fact what was established in theory; and would seem, at first view, an absurdity too gross to be insisted on. It shall, however, receive a more attentive consideration.

It is emphatically the province and duty of the judicial department to say what the law is. Those who apply the rule to particular cases, must of necessity expound and interpret that rule. If two laws conflict with each other, the courts must decide on the operation of each.

So if a law be in opposition to the constitution; if both the law and the constitution apply to a particular case, so that the court must either decide that case conformably to the law, disregarding the constitution; or conformably to the constitution, disregarding the law; the court must determine which of these conflicting rules governs the case. This is of the very essence of judicial duty.

If then the courts are to regard the constitution; and

the constitution is superior to any ordinary act of the legislature; the constitution, and not such ordinary act, must govern the case to which they both apply.

Those then who controvert the principle that the constitution is to be considered, in court, as a paramount law, are reduced to the necessity of maintaining that courts must close their eyes on the constitution, and see only the law.

This doctrine would subvert the very foundation of all written constitutions. It would declare that an act, which, according to the principles and theory of our government, is entirely void; is yet, in practice, completely obligatory. It would declare, that if the legislature shall do what is expressly forbidden, such act, notwithstanding the express prohibition, is in reality effectual. It would be giving to the legislature a practical and real omnipotence, with the same breath which professes to restrict their powers within narrow limits. It is prescribing limits, and declaring that those limits may be passed at pleasure.

That it thus reduces to nothing what we have deemed the greatest improvement on political institutions—a written constitution—would of itself be sufficient, in America, where written constitutions have been viewed with so much reverence, for rejecting the construction. But the peculiar expressions of the constitution of the United States furnish additional arguments in favor of its rejection.

The judicial power of the United States is extended to all cases arising under the constitution. Could it be the intention of those who gave this power, to say that, in using it, the constitution should not be looked into? That a case arising under the constitution should be decided without examining the instrument under which it arises? This is too extravagant to be maintained.

In some cases then, the constitution must be looked into by the judges. And if they can open it at all, what part of it are they forbidden to read, or to obey? …

The oath of office, too, imposed by the legislature, is completely demonstrative of the legislative opinion on the subject. It is in these words, "I do solemnly swear that I will administer justice without respect to persons, and do equal right to the poor and to the rich; and that I will faithfully and impartially discharge all the duties incumbent on me as according to the best of my abilities and understanding, agreeably to the constitution, and laws of the United States."

Why does a judge swear to discharge his duties agreeably to the constitution of the United States, if that constitution forms no rule for his government? if it is closed upon him, and cannot be inspected by him?

If such be the real state of things, this is worse than solemn mockery. To prescribe, or to take this oath, becomes equally a crime.

Thus, the particular phraseology of the constitution of the United States confirms and strengthens the principle, supposed to be essential to all written constitutions, that a law repugnant to the constitution is void; and that courts, as well as other departments, are bound by that instrument.

"April 27, 1805. After a bombardment of Derne, Tripoli, by the Hornet, Nautilus *and* Argus, *a landing party with Lieutenant O'Bannon of the Marines in command hauled down the Tripolitan flag and hoisted Old Glory for the first time over a fort in the old world." After achieving victory in the First Barbary War, the attention of the United States was diverted to its worsening relationship with Great Britain over trade with France, which culminated in the War of 1812. The Barbary pirate states took this opportunity to return to their practice of attacking American and European merchant vessels in the Mediterranean Sea and holding their crews and officers for ransom. Unable to devote military resources and political will to the situation, the United States quietly recommenced paying ransom for return of the prisoners. At the conclusion of the War of 1812, however, America could once again turn its sights on North Africa. On March 3, 1815, the U.S. Congress authorized deployment of naval power against Algiers, and a force of ten ships was dispatched under the command of Commodores Stephen Decatur, Jr. and William Bainbridge, both veterans of the First Barbary War.*

JIMMY DRIFTWOOD

Battle of New Orleans

On June 1, 1812, President James Madison asked Congress for a formal declaration of war against Great Britain. He cited as reasons the impressment of United States seamen and interference with U.S. trade. At the time, Great Britain and France were involved in a bitter struggle in Europe and were both guilty of interrupting American shipping in an attempt to enforce embargoes against one another. Napoleon Bonaparte eased the pressure on American vessels, however, hoping to draw the United States into the war. On June 18, in response to continuing British offenses, the United States declared war on Great Britain. Unbeknownst to Americans, the British had repealed the very laws that caused the conflict just two days prior.

The War of 1812 featured such notable engagements as the Battle of Lake Erie, won by American forces under the leadership of Oliver Hazard Perry. The most memorable battle of the war, however, was the last. In 1814, the British made plans to capture New Orleans and recruited the services of Jean Lafitte, a New Orleans pirate. Lafitte refused a British offer of $30,000 and informed the U.S. government of the plans. On January 8, 1815, more than 8,000 British soldiers arrived in New Orleans. The Americans, led by General Andrew Jackson who had begun fortifications in December of 1814, won a decisive victory—killing, wounding, and capturing nearly 2,000 British, including the commanding officer, Sir Edward Packenham, who was fatally shot.

The Battle of New Orleans, like the entire war itself, was the result of poor communication. Although a peace treaty was not formally ratified until February 1815, the Treaty of Ghent, which ended the war, had been signed by British and American representatives in Belgium fifteen days before "the needless battle."

"The Battle of New Orleans" was written by an Arkansas teacher named Jimmy Driftwood (born James Morris, 1907-1998) who, as a teaching tool, wrote poems about historical events and set them to music. The song became the number one hit of 1959 when it appeared on an album of songs by country music singer Johnny Horton.

Well, in 18 and 14, we took a little trip
Along with Colonel Jackson down the mighty Missisip.
We took a little bacon and we took a little beans
And we met the bloody British in the town of New Orleans.

We fired our guns and the British kept a comin'
There wasn't nigh as many as there was a while ago.
We fired once more and they began a running
Down the Mississippi to the Gulf of Mexico.

Well, I seed Marse Jackson come a-walkin' down the street
And a-talkin' to a pirate by the name of Jean Lafitte;
He gave Jean a drink that he brung from Tennessee,
And the pirate said he'd help us drive the British to the sea.

Well the French told Andrew, "You had better run
For Packenham's a'comin' with a bullet in his gun."
Old Hickory said he didn't give a damn
He's a-gonna whup the britches off of Colonel Packenham.

Well, we looked down the river and we seed the British come
And there must have been a hundred of them beating on the drum.
They stepped so high and they made their bugles ring
While we stood behind our cotton bales and didn't say a thing

Old Hickory said we could take 'em by surprise
If we didn't fire a musket till we looked 'em in the eyes.
We held our fire till we seed their faces well
Then we opened up our squirrel guns and really gave 'em well …

Well they ran through the briars and they ran through the brambles
And they ran through the bushes where a rabbit couldn't go.
They ran so fast the hounds couldn't catch 'em
Down the Mississippi to the Gulf of Mexico

Well we fired our cannons till the barrels melted down
So we grabbed an alligator and we fought another round.
We filled his head with minie balls and powdered his behind
And when we touched the powder off, the 'gator lost his mind.

They lost their pants and their pretty shiny coats
And their tails was all a-showin' like a bunch of billy goats.
They ran down the river with their tongues a-hanging out
And they said they got a lickin', which there wasn't any doubt.

Well we marched back to town in our dirty ragged pants
And we danced all night with the pretty girls from France;
We couldn't understand 'em, but they had the sweetest charms
And we understood 'em better when we got 'em in our arms.

Well, the guide who brung the British from the sea
Come a-limping into camp just as sick as he could be,
He said the dying words of Colonel Packenham
Was, "You better quit your foolin' with your cousin Uncle Sam."

Well, we'll march back home, but we'll never be content
Till we make Old Hick'ry the people's president.
And every time we think about the bacon and the beans
We'll think about the fun we had way down in New Orleans.

FRANCIS SCOTT KEY

The Star-Spangled Banner

In September 1814, British troops captured Washington, D.C., and set fire to the Capitol, the White House, and several other government buildings. During the British withdrawal from Washington, an elderly physician named William Beanes was taken prisoner. Dr. Beanes was a personal friend of Francis Scott Key (1779-1843), a respected Maryland attorney who would later become district attorney of the District of Columbia.

After receiving permission from President Madison to intercede on his friend's behalf, Key boarded the British prison exchange boat under a flag of truce and made a plea for Beanes's release. The British granted the request, but refused to allow the Americans to leave right away, as they were planning a naval bombardment of Fort McHenry in Baltimore Harbor that very night—September 13, 1814. Through the haze of cannon fire, Key noticed a huge American flag flying over the fort's ramparts. As dawn arrived, and the bombardment ended, Key observed that "our flag was still there." The event inspired him to write a poem—"The Star-Spangled Banner"—which he later set to the tune "To Anacreon in Heaven," a popular English song.

One of America's best-loved patriotic songs for decades, "The Star-Spangled Banner" was especially popular in the military during morning and evening colors and, in 1931, was adopted by Congress as the official national anthem.

Oh, say, can you see, by the dawn's early light,
What so proudly we hailed at the twilight's last gleaming,
Whose broad stripes and bright stars through the perilous fight,
O'er the ramparts we watched were so gallantly streaming?
And the rockets' red glare, the bombs bursting in air,
Gave proof thro' the night that our flag was still there.
Oh, say, does that star-spangled banner yet wave
O'er the land of the free, and the home of the brave?

On the shore, dimly seen thro' the mists of the deep,
Where the foe's haughty host in dread silence reposes,
What is that which the breeze o'er the towering steep,
As it fitfully blows, half conceals, half discloses?
Now it catches the gleam of the morning's first beam,
In full glory reflected, now shines on the stream.
'Tis the star-spangled banner; oh, long may it wave
O'er the land of the free, and the home of the brave!

And where is that band who so vauntingly swore
That the havoc of war and the battle's confusion
A home and a country should leave us no more?
Their blood has washed out their foul footsteps' pollution.
No refuge could save the hireling and slave
From the terror of flight, or the gloom of the grave:
And the star-spangled banner in triumph doth wave
O'er the land of the free, and the home of the brave!

Oh, thus be it ever when freemen shall stand
Between their loved homes and the war's desolation;
Blest with victory and peace, may the heaven-rescued land
Praise the power that hath made and preserved us a nation!
Then conquer we must, when our cause it is just,
And this be our motto: "In God is our trust!"
And the star-spangled banner in triumph doth wave,
O'er the land of the free, and the home of the brave!

Battle of Lake Erie, *by William Henry Powell, depicts Oliver Hazard Perry transferring command from the disabled* Lawrence *to the* Niagara *during this famous battle of the War of 1812. From his flagship, Perry flew a large blue battle ensign stitched with the phrase "DONT GIVE UP THE SHIP" [sic] in bold white letters. This was the dying command of Captain James Lawrence, the American naval officer mortally wounded just months earlier. Perry's battle report to General William Henry Harrison proved equally memorable: "We have met the enemy and they are ours …" One of the great American naval heroes, Perry had previously commanded the* Nautilus *in the capture of Derne during the First Barbary War. His younger brother, Matthew Calbraith Perry, was the commodore of the U.S. Navy who compelled the opening of Japan to the West with the Convention of Kanagawa in 1854.*

SAMUEL WOODWORTH

The Old Oaken Bucket

Samuel Woodworth (1785-1842), a Massachusetts playwright, is remembered for one work—"The Old Oaken Bucket." First published in 1818, the poem expresses sadness over the disappearance of simple country life due to industrialization. The poem was found in most schoolbooks through the nineteenth century and, when set to music, gained increased popularity as a hit song.

How dear to my heart are the scenes of my childhood,
When fond recollection presents them to view!
The orchard, the meadow, the deep tangled wildwood,
And every loved spot which my fancy knew,
The wide-spreading pond and the mill that stood by it,
The bridge and the rock where the cataract fell;
The cot of my father, the dairy house nigh it,
And e'en the rude bucket that hung in the well.

That moss-covered bucket I hailed as a treasure,
For often at noon, when returned from the field,
I found it the source of an exquisite pleasure,
The purest and sweetest that nature can yield.
How ardent I seized it, with hands that were glowing,
And quick to the white-pebbled bottom it fell.
Then soon, with the emblem of truth overflowing,
And dripping with coolness, it rose from the well.

How sweet from the green, mossy brim to receive it,
As, poised on the curb, it inclined to my lips!
Not a full, blushing goblet could tempt me to leave it,
Tho' filled with the nectar that Jupiter sips,
And now, far removed from the loved habitation,
The tear of regret will intrusively swell,
As fancy reverts to my father's plantation,
And sighs for the bucket that hung in the well.

JOSEPH RODMAN DRAKE

The American Flag

Joseph Rodman Drake (1795-1820), an amateur poet, earned his medical degree in 1816, but died just four years later of tuberculosis. On his deathbed, he ordered his unpublished verses destroyed. His wife, Sarah, saved those works, however, and later published them. "The American Flag" is not only one of Drake's best poems, but one of the best ever written about "Old Glory."

When Freedom, from her mountain height,
Unfurled her standard to the air,
She tore the azure robe of night,
And set the stars of glory there!
She mingled with its gorgeous dyes
The milky baldric of the skies,
And striped its pure, celestial white
With streakings of the morning light;
Then, from his mansion in the sun,
She called her eagle-bearer down,
And gave into his mighty hand
The symbol of her chosen land!

Majestic monarch of the cloud!
Who rear'st aloft thy regal form,
To hear the tempest trumping loud,
And see the lightning lances driven,
When strive the warriors of the storm,
And rolls the thunder-drum of heaven,—
Child of the sun! to thee 'tis given
To guard the banner of the free,
To hover in the sulphur smoke,
To ward away the battle-stroke,
And bid its blendings shine afar,
Like rainbows on the cloud of war,
The harbingers of victory!

Flag of the brave! thy folds shall fly,
The sign of hope and triumph high!
When speaks the signal-trumpet tone,
And the long line comes gleaming on,
Ere yet the life-blood, warm and wet,
Has dimmed the glistening bayonet,
Each soldier's eye shall brightly turn
To where thy sky-born glories burn,
And, as his springing steps advance,
Catch war and vengeance from the glance.
And when the cannon-mouthings loud
Heave in wild wreaths the battle shroud,
And gory sabers rise and fall
Like shoots of flame on midnight's pall,
Then shall thy meteor-glances glow,
And cowering foes shall shrink beneath
Each gallant arm that strikes below
That lovely messenger of death.

Flag of the seas! on ocean wave
Thy stars shall glitter o'er the brave;
When death, careering on the gale,
Sweeps darkly round the bellied sail,
And frighted waves rush wildly back
Before the broadside's reeling rack,
Each dying wanderer of the sea
Shall look at once to heaven and thee,
And smile to see thy splendors fly
In triumph o'er his closing eye.

Flag of the free heart's hope and home,
By angel hands to valor given!
Thy stars have lit the welkin dome,
And all thy hues were born in heaven.
Forever float that standard sheet!
Where breathes the foe but falls before us,
With Freedom's soil beneath our feet,
And Freedom's banner streaming o'er us!

JAMES MONROE

The Monroe Doctrine

We ... declare that we should consider any attempt on their part to extend their system to any portion of this hemisphere as dangerous to our peace and safety.

James Monroe (1758-1831) served in the Revolutionary War as a lieutenant at the age of eighteen and, in 1782, began his political career by winning a seat in the Virginia Assembly. He was elected to the U.S. Senate in 1790, governor of Virginia in 1799 and, during the War of 1812, served as both secretary of state and secretary of war. In 1816, Monroe was elected fifth president of the United States, ushering in "the era of good feeling"—a period of relative peace, industrial growth, and westward settlement. In 1820, due in large part to the disappearance of the Federalist Party, Monroe ran for re-election unopposed, receiving every vote cast in the electoral college but one.

On December 2, 1823, as part of his annual message to Congress, Monroe put forth what proved to be his most lasting legacy—the Monroe Doctrine—in which he proclaimed before Congress the independence of the Americas against European interference. The doctrine came about after Russia abandoned its claims in the Pacific Northwest, Spain ceded Florida, and Great Britain abandoned fortifications on the Great Lakes—and at a time when many South American colonies had taken advantage of the Napoleonic Wars by declaring their independence from colonial overlords. Monroe stated that the Americas were "henceforth not to be considered as subjects for future colonization by any European powers." The doctrine had the support of Great Britain (upon whose power the doctrine was actually dependent) because of widespread rumors that France, aided by "The Holy Alliance" of Russia, Austria, and Prussia, intended to reestablish control of revolting Spanish colonies in South America, thereby reducing trade with Great Britain.

While Monroe continued to abide by "The Great Rule" of Washington—that of the United States staying out of world affairs—the doctrine itself was not an instrument of isolation. It was simply an argument that while America was content to stay out of European affairs, Europe should likewise stay out of American affairs. The Monroe Doctrine has remained a standard of American foreign policy ever since.

Fellow-citizens of the Senate and House of Representatives … At the proposal of the Russian Imperial Government, made through the minister of the Emperor residing here, a full power and instructions have been transmitted to the minister of the United States at St. Petersburg to arrange by amicable negotiation the respective rights and interests of the two nations on the northwest coast of this continent. A similar proposal has been made by His Imperial Majesty to the Government of Great Britain, which has likewise been acceded to. The Government of the United States has been desirous, by this friendly proceeding, of manifesting the great value which they have invariably attached to the friendship of the Emperor and their solicitude to cultivate the best understanding with his Government. In the discussion to which this interest has given rise and in the arrangements by which they may terminate, the occasion has been judged proper for asserting, as a principle in which the rights and interests of the United States are involved, that the American continents, by the free and independent condition which they have assumed and maintain, are henceforth not to be considered as subjects for future colonization by any European powers. …

It was stated at the commencement of the last session that a great effort was then making in Spain and Portugal to improve the condition of the people of those countries, and that it appeared to be conducted with extraordinary moderation. It need scarcely be remarked that the result has been so far very different from what was then anticipated.

Of events in that quarter of the globe, with which we have so much intercourse and from which we derive our origin, we have always been anxious and interested spectators. The citizens of the United States cherish sentiments the most friendly in favor of the liberty and happiness of their fellow-men on that side of the Atlantic. In the wars of the European powers in matters relating to themselves we have never taken any part, nor does it comport with our policy so to do. It is only when our rights are invaded or seriously menaced that we resent injuries or make preparations for our defense.

With the movements in this hemisphere we are of necessity more immediately connected, and by causes which must be obvious to all enlightened and impartial observers. The political system of the allied powers is essentially different in this respect from that of America. This difference proceeds from that which exists in their respective Governments; and to the defense of our own, which has been achieved by the loss of so much blood and treasure, and matured by the wisdom of their most enlightened citizens, and under which we have enjoyed unexampled felicity, this whole nation is devoted.

We owe it, therefore, to candor and to the amicable relations existing between the United States and those powers to declare that we should consider any attempt on their part to extend their system to any portion of this hemisphere as dangerous to our peace and safety. With the existing colonies or dependencies of any European power we have not interfered and shall not interfere. But with the Governments who have declared their independence and maintained it, and whose independence we have, on great consideration and on just principles, acknowledged, we could not view any interposition for the purpose of oppressing them, or controlling in any other manner their destiny, by any European power in any other light than as the manifestation of an unfriendly disposition toward the United States. In the war between those new Governments and Spain, we declared our neutrality at the time of their recognition, and to this we have adhered, and shall continue to adhere, provided no change shall occur which, in the judgment of the competent authorities of this Government, shall make a corresponding change on the part of the United States indispensable to their security.

The late events in Spain and Portugal show that Europe is still unsettled. Of this important fact no stronger proof can be adduced than that the allied powers should have thought it proper, on any principle satisfactory to themselves, to have interposed by force in the internal concerns of Spain. To what extent such interposition may be carried, on the same principle, is a question in which all independent powers whose governments differ from theirs are interested, even those most remote, and surely none more so than the United States. Our policy in regard to Europe, which was adopted at an early stage of the wars which have so long agitated that quarter of the globe, nevertheless remains the same, which is, not to interfere in the internal concerns of any of its powers; to consider the government *de facto* as the legitimate government for us; to cultivate friendly relations with it, and to preserve those relations by a frank, firm, and manly policy, meeting in all instances the just claims of every power, submitting to injuries from none. But, in regard to these continents, circumstances are eminently and conspicuously different. It is impossible that the allied powers should extend their political system to any portion of either continent without endangering our peace and happiness; nor can anyone believe that our southern brethren, if left to themselves, would adopt it of their own accord. It is equally impossible, therefore, that we should behold such interpositions in any form with indifference. If we look to the comparative strength and resources of Spain and those new Governments, and their distance from each other, it must be obvious that she can never subdue them. It is still the true policy of the United States to leave the parties to themselves, in the hope that other powers will pursue the same course. …

JOHN HOWARD PAYNE

Home, Sweet Home

John Howard Payne (1791-1852) was a popular actor and playwright who had his first play performed when he was only fourteen years old. He went on to write more than sixty plays and had the opportunity to work with Washington Irving on several productions. His play *Brutus*, perhaps his greatest achievement, was popular in both America and Great Britain and was performed long after his death. Despite the popularity of his works, however, Payne received few royalties and frequently landed in debtors' prison. His name long forgotten to the public, Payne's song "Home, Sweet Home," included in his play *Clari: or the Maid of Milan* (1823), survives courtesy of its sentimental phrase, "There's no place like home."

'Mid pleasures and palaces though we may roam,
Be it ever so humble, there's no place like home;
A charm from the sky seems to hallow us there,
Which, seek through the world, is ne'er met with elsewhere.
Home, home, sweet, sweet home!
There's no place like home, oh, there's no place like home!

An exile from home, splendor dazzles in vain;
Oh, give me my lowly thatched cottage again!
The birds singing gayly, that came at my call—
Give me them—and the peace of mind, dearer than all!
Home, home, sweet, sweet home!
There's no place like home, oh, there's no place like home!

I gaze on the moon as I tread the drear wild,
And I feel that my mother now thinks of her child,
As she looks on that moon from our own cottage door
Thro' the woodbine, whose fragrance shall cheer me no more.
Home, home, sweet, sweet home!
There's no place like home, oh, there's no place like home!

How sweet 'tis to sit 'neath a fond father's smile,
And the caress of a mother to soothe and beguile!
Let others delight 'mid new pleasure to roam,
But give me, oh, give me, the pleasures of home!
Home, home, sweet, sweet home!
There's no place like home, oh, there's no place like home!

To thee I'll return, overburdened with care;
The heart's dearest solace will smile on me there;
No more from that cottage again will I roam;
Be it ever so humble, there's no place like home.
Home, home, sweet, sweet home!
There's no place like home, oh, there's no place like home!

DANIEL WEBSTER

Bunker Hill Oration

We are not propagandists … Our history hitherto proves, however, that the popular form is practicable and that, with wisdom and knowledge, men may govern themselves.

On June 17, 1825, a monument to the heroes of Bunker Hill was dedicated in Charlestown, Massachusetts. The first major engagement of the Revolutionary War, the Battle of Bunker Hill was actually fought on nearby Breed's Hill. From this vantage point, New England militia bombarded the British, who had occupied Boston. British Major General William Howe led three charges against the American fortifications before finally breaking through. The American commanding officer, Colonel William Prescott, conscious of the fact that his men were low on gun powder, reportedly ordered: "Don't fire until you see the whites of their eyes." Although the British drove the Americans away, theirs was a Pyrrhic victory, as they suffered more than 1,000 causalities compared to 400 American losses.

Representative Daniel Webster (1782-1852), the featured speaker at the dedication ceremony, reminded his fellow citizens of the cost of freedom and expounded on the international significance of the American Revolution.

… We are among the sepulchers of our fathers. We are on ground distinguished by their valor, their constancy, and the shedding of their blood. We are here, not to fix an uncertain date in our annals, nor to draw into notice an obscure and unknown spot. If our humble purpose had never been conceived, if we ourselves had never been born, the seventeenth of June, 1775, would have been a day on which all subsequent history would have poured its light, and the eminence where we stand, a point of attraction to the eyes of successive generations. But we are Americans. We live in what may be called the early age of this great continent; and we know that our posterity, through all time, are here to suffer and enjoy the allotments of humanity. We see before us a probable train of great events; we know that our own fortunes have been happily cast; and it is natural, therefore, that we should be moved by the contemplation of occurrences which have guided our destiny before many of us were born, and settled the condition in which we should pass that portion of our existence which God allows to men on earth. …

The great event, in the history of the continent, which we are now met here to commemorate—that prodigy of modern times, at once the wonder and the blessing of the world—is the American Revolution. In a day of extraordinary prosperity and happiness, of high national honor, distinction, and power, we are brought together, in this place, by our love of country, by our admiration of exalted character, by our gratitude for signal services and patriotic devotion. …

The great wheel of political revolution began to move in America. Here its rotation was guarded, regular, and safe. Transferred to the other continent, from unfortunate but natural causes, it received an irregular and violent impulse; it whirled along with a fearful celerity, till at length, like the chariot wheels in the races of antiquity, it took fire from the rapidity of its own motion and blazed onward, spreading conflagration and terror around. …

When Louis XIV said, "I am the state," he expressed the essence of the doctrine of unlimited power. By the rules of that system, the people are disconnected from the state; they are its subjects; it is their lord. These ideas, founded in the love of power, and long supported by the excess and the abuse of it, are yielding in our age to other opinions; and the civilized world seems at last to be proceeding to the conviction of that fundamental and manifest truth, that the powers of government are but a trust, and that they cannot be lawfully exercised but for the good of the community.…

We may hope that the growing influence of enlightened sentiments will promote the permanent peace of the world. Wars, to maintain family alliances, to uphold or to cast down dynasties, to regulate successions to thrones, which have occupied so much room in the history of modern times, if not less likely to happen at all, will be less likely to become general and involve many nations, as the great principle shall be more and more established, that the interest of the world is peace, and its first great statute, that every nation possesses the power of establishing a government for itself. But public opinion has attained also an influence over governments which do not admit the popular principle into their organization. A necessary respect for the judgment of the world operates, in some measure, as a control over the most unlimited forms of authority. ... Let us thank God that we live in an age when something has influence besides the bayonet, and when the sternest authority does not venture to encounter the scorching power of public reproach. ...

When the Battle of Bunker Hill was fought, the existence of South America was scarcely felt in the civilized world. The thirteen little colonies of North America habitually called themselves the "continent." Borne down by colonial subjugation, monopoly, and bigotry, these vast regions of the South were hardly visible above the horizon. But in our day there hath been, as it were, a new creation. The Southern Hemisphere emerges from the sea. Its lofty mountains begin to lift themselves into the light of heaven; its broad and fertile plains stretch out in beauty to the eye of civilized man, and at the mighty being of the voice of political liberty the waters of darkness retire.

And now let us indulge an honest exultation in the conviction of the benefit which the example of our country has produced and is likely to produce on human freedom and human happiness. And let us endeavor to comprehend in all its magnitude and to feel in all its importance the part assigned to us in the great drama of human affairs. We are placed at the head of the system of representative and popular governments. Thus far our example shows that such governments are compatible, not only with respectability and power, but with repose, with peace, with security of personal rights, with good laws and a just administration.

We are not propagandists. Wherever other systems are preferred, either as being thought better in themselves or as better suited to existing conditions, we leave the preference to be enjoyed. Our history hitherto proves, however, that the popular form is practicable and that, with wisdom and knowledge, men may govern themselves; and the duty incumbent on us is to preserve the consistency of this cheering example and take care that nothing may weaken its authority with the world. If in our case the representative system ultimately fail, popular governments must be pronounced impossible. No combination of circumstances more favorable to the experiment can ever be expected to occur. The last hopes of mankind, therefore, rest with us;

and if it should be proclaimed that our example had become an argument against the experiment, the knell of popular liberty would be sounded throughout the earth.

These are incitements to duty; but they are not suggestions of doubt. Our history and our condition, all that is gone before us and all that surrounds us, authorize the belief that popular governments, though subject to occasional variations, perhaps not always for the better in form, may yet in their general character be as durable and permanent as other systems. We know, indeed, that in our country any other is impossible. The principle of free governments adheres to the American soil. It is bedded in it—immovable as its mountains.

And let the sacred obligations which have devolved on this generation and on us sink deep into our hearts. Those are daily dropping from among us who established our liberty and our government. The great trust now descends to new hands. Let us apply ourselves to that which is presented to us as our appropriate object. We can win no laurels in a war for independence. Earlier and worthier hands have gathered them all. Nor are there places for us by the side of Solon, and Alfred, and other founders of states. Our fathers have filled them. But there remains to us a great duty of defense and preservation; and there is opened to us also a noble pursuit to which the spirit of the times strongly invites us.

Our proper business is improvement. Let our age be the age of improvement. In a day of peace let us advance the arts of peace and the works of peace. Let us develop the resources of our land, call forth its powers, build up its institutions, promote all its great interests, and see whether we also, in our day and generation, may not perform something worthy to be remembered. Let us cultivate a true spirit of union and harmony. In pursuing the great objects which our condition points out to us, let us act under a settled conviction, and a habitual feeling that these twenty-four states are one country. Let our conceptions be enlarged to the circle of our duties. Let us extend our ideas over the whole of the vast field in which we are called to act. Let our object be our country, our whole country, and nothing but our country. And by the blessing of God may that country itself become a vast and splendid monument, not of oppression and terror, but of wisdom, of peace, and of liberty, upon which th e world may gaze with admiration, forever.

* * *

Mirage on the Prairie, *by Alfred Jacob Miller. Traveling with the American Fur company expedition to the annual fur trappers' and traders' rendezvous of 1837, Miller produced a notable series of works that provided a visual record of the soon-to-be heavily traveled Oregon Trail and the American West.*

Reform and Expansion

OLIVER WENDELL HOLMES

The Flower of Liberty and Old Ironsides

Oliver Wendell Holmes (1809-1894) was a physician and medical researcher who served as dean of the Harvard Medical School. One of his sons, Oliver Wendell Holmes, Jr., became one of the most famous jurists in American history, serving as an associate justice of the United States Supreme Court for nearly thirty years.

The elder Holmes's fame, however, came from his writing—specifically, from such patriotic poems as "The Flower of Liberty." His most famous work, and the one that made him a national figure at the age of twenty-one when published in a Boston paper, was "Old Ironsides." The poem was written as an appeal to the Department of the Navy to abandon plans to scrap the USS *Constitution*, a frigate that had been launched in 1797 and seen action in the Tripolitan War and the War of 1812. The ship earned her nickname when British cannonballs bounced off her hull, causing the Americans to shout, "Her sides are made of iron!" (They were actually made of wood from part of the more than 1,500 trees used in its construction.) The poem set off such a national fervor that money was appropriated to restore the ship, which has been a part of the U.S. Navy ever since. It is now the oldest commissioned warship afloat in the world. On July 21, 1997, the USS *Constitution* sailed under her own power for the first time in 116 years.

The Flower of Liberty

What flower is this that greets the morn,
Its hues from Heaven so freshly born?
With burning star and flaming band
It kindles all the sunset land:
Oh, tell us what its name may be—
Is this the Flower of Liberty?
It is the banner of the free,
The starry Flower of Liberty!

In savage Nature's far abode
Its tender seed our fathers sowed;
The storm-winds rocked its swelling bud,
Its opening leaves were streaked with blood,
Till lo! earth's tyrants shook to see
The full-blown Flower of Liberty!
Then hail the banner of the free,
The starry Flower of Liberty!

Behold its streaming rays unite,
One mingling flood of braided light—
The red that fires the Southern rose
With spotless white from Northern snows,
And, spangled o'er its azure, see
The sister Stars of Liberty!
Then hail the banner of the free,
The starry Flower of Liberty!

The blades of heroes fence it round,
Where'er it springs is holy ground;
From tower and dome its glories spread;
It waves where lonely sentries tread;
It makes the land as ocean free,
And plants an empire on the sea!
Then hail the banner of the free,
The starry Flower of Liberty!

Thy sacred leaves, fair Freedom's flower,
Shall ever float on dome and tower,
To all their heavenly colors true,
In blackening frost or crimson dew—
And God love us as we love thee,
Thrice holy Flower of Liberty!
Then hail the banner of the free,
The starry Flower of Liberty!

Old Ironsides

Ay, tear her tattered ensign down!
Long has it waved on high,
And many an eye has danced to see
That banner in the sky;
Beneath it rung the battle-shout,
And burst the cannon's roar;—
The meteor of the ocean air
Shall sweep the clouds no more!

Her deck, once red with heroes' blood,
Where knelt the vanquished foe,
When winds were hurrying o'er the flood
And waves were white below,
No more shall feel the victor's tread,
Or know the conquered knee;—
The harpies of the shore shall pluck
The eagle of the sea!

Oh, better that her shattered hulk
Should sink beneath the wave!
Her thunders shook the mighty deep,
And there should be her grave;
Nail to the mast her holy flag,
Set every threadbare sail,
And give her to the god of storms,
The lightning and the gale!

GEORGE POPE MORRIS

Woodman, Spare That Tree

George Pope Morris (1802-1864), a journalist and poet, served as editor of the *New York Mirror*, a newspaper he co-founded with Samuel Woodworth. His best-known work, "Woodman, Spare That Tree," was published in 1830 and became the hit song of 1837 when Henry Russell, an English-born songwriter, set the lyrics to music. The poem, like other works of the day, was an expression of sadness over the "progress" of industrialization and a sentimental yearning for the days of yore.

Woodman, spare that tree!
Touch not a single bough!
In youth it sheltered me,
And I'll protect it now.
'Twas my forefather's hand
That placed it near his cot;
There, woodman, let it stand,
Thy axe shall harm it not!

That old familiar tree,
Whose glory and renown
Are spread o'er land and sea,
And wouldst thou hew it down?
Woodman, forbear thy stroke!
Cut not its earth-bound ties;
O, spare that aged oak,
Now towering to the skies!

When but an idle boy
I sought its grateful shade;
In all their gushing joy
Here too my sisters played
My mother kissed me here;
My father pressed my hand—
Forgive this foolish tear,
But let that old oak stand!

My heart-strings round thee cling.
Close as thy bark, old friend!
Here shall the wild-bird sing,
And still thy branches bend.
Old Tree! the storm still brave!
And, woodman, leave the spot,
While I've a hand to save,
Thy axe shall hurt it not.

The Trail of Tears, *a painting by Robert Lindneux, commemorates the suffering of American Indians on their reluctant march West. On May 26, 1830, President Andrew Jackson signed into law the Indian Removal Act calling for the relocation and movement of American Indians from their homelands to Indian Territory in the unsettled western United States. Prior to the Removal Act, the "Five Civilized Tribes" of the Cherokee, Chickasaw, Choctaw, Muscogee-Creek, and Seminole were living as autonomous nations in what would be called the American Deep South. The Removal Act received strong public support, with states eager to gain access to additional lands for white settlement. Thousands died from exposure, disease, and starvation while en route to their destinations.*

SAMUEL F. SMITH

America

Reverend Samuel Francis Smith (1808-1895) wrote the lyrics to "America" (also known as "My Country 'Tis of Thee") and set them to the music of the English national anthem, "God Save the King," which was well known to Americans who had already adopted the tune for such patriotic airs as "God Save America" and "God Save the Thirteen States." Smith's song debuted in 1832 at a Fourth of July celebration in Boston and was quickly embraced throughout the country. Its continued popularity, accompanied by frequent requests for personally autographed copies, prompted an ever-modest Smith to write: "I did not design it for a national hymn, nor did I think it would gain such notoriety." Oliver Wendell Holmes, a Harvard classmate of Smith's, offered this tribute at a reunion for the class of 1829:

> *There's a nice youngster of excellent pith,*
> *Fate tried to conceal him by naming him Smith;*
> *But he shouted a song for the brave and the free,*
> *Just read on his medal, "My country," "of thee."*

My country, 'tis of thee,
Sweet land of liberty,
Of thee I sing;
Land where my fathers died,
Land of the pilgrims' pride,
From every mountain-side
Let freedom ring.

My native country, thee,
Land of the noble free,
Thy name I love;
I love thy rocks and rills,
Thy woods and templed hills;
My heart with rapture thrills
Like that above.

Let music swell the breeze,
And ring from all the trees
Sweet Freedom's song;
Let mortal tongues awake,
Let all that breathe partake,
Let rocks their silence break,
The sound prolong.

Our fathers' God, to Thee,
Author of liberty,
To Thee we sing;
Long may our land be bright
With Freedom's holy light;
Protect us by Thy might,
Great God, our King.

BLACK HAWK

Speeches of Surrender and Reconciliation

Black Hawk is an Indian. He has done nothing for which an Indian ought to be ashamed.

The quarter century following the War of 1812 was a major period of warfare between whites and American Indians. One of the principal opponents of the westward movement of white settlers was Black Hawk (1767-1838), chief of the Sauk Indians. Black Hawk had allied himself with the British during the War of 1812 and, in 1832, battled settlers in what was known as the Black Hawk War, claiming that Indian lands had been signed away by chiefs who had been given intoxicating liquors as a prelude to negotiations. The brief conflict resulted in Black Hawk's capture and confinement to Fortress Monroe, Virginia; he later joined his tribe on a reservation near Fort Des Moines, Iowa. In his speech of surrender, delivered to General J. M. Street at Prairie du Chien, Wisconsin, Black Hawk was proud and defiant, and later greeted President Jackson in a similar tone, saying, "I am a man and you are another! I took up the hatchet to revenge injuries which my people could no longer endure."

Shortly before his death, Black Hawk accepted the inevitable defeat of his people and agreed to make a speech at a Fourth of July celebration near Fort Madison. Upon his death, Black Hawk was decorated with medals from President Jackson and former President John Quincy Adams—symbols of reconciliation between one-time enemies. A fifty-foot statue of the Indian chief now stands on the Rock River near Oregon, Illinois.

You have taken me prisoner with my warriors. I am much grieved; for I expected, if I did not defeat you, to hold out much longer and give you more trouble before I surrendered. ...

Black Hawk is now a prisoner of the white men; they will do with him as they wish. But he can stand torture, and is not afraid of death. He is no coward.

Black Hawk is an Indian. He has done nothing for which an Indian ought to be ashamed. He has fought for his countrymen against white men who came, year after year, to cheat them and take away their lands.

You know the cause of our making war. It is known to all white men. The white men despise the Indians, and drive them from their homes. They smile in the face of the poor Indian, to cheat him; they shake him by the hand, to gain his confidence; they make him drunk, to deceive him.

We told them to let us alone, and keep away from us; but

they followed on and beset our paths, and coiled themselves among us like the snake. They poisoned us by their touch. We were not safe. We lived in danger. We looked up to the Great Spirit. We went to our Father (in Washington). We were encouraged. His council gave us fair words and big promises, but we got no satisfaction; things were growing worse. There were no deer in the forest. The opossum and beaver fled. The springs were drying up, and our squaws and papooses were without food to keep them from starving. …

We set up the war whoop, and dug up the tomahawk; our knives were ready, and the heart of Black Hawk swelled high in his bosom when he led his warriors to battle. He is satisfied. He will go to the world of spirits contented. He has done his duty. His father will meet him there and command him. …

Farewell, my nation! … He can do no more. He is near his end. His sun is setting, and will rise no more.

Farewell to Black Hawk!

Brothers! It has pleased the Great Spirit that I am here today. I have eaten with my white friends. The earth is our mother; we are on it, with the Great Spirit above us. It is good. I hope we are all friends here.

A few winters ago I was fighting against you. I did wrong perhaps; but that is past; it is buried; let it be forgotten.

Rock River was a beautiful country. I liked my towns, my cornfields, and the home of my people. I fought for it. It is now yours; keep it as we did; it will produce you good crops.

I thank the Great Spirit that I am now friendly with my white brothers. We are here together; we have eaten together; we are friends. It is His wish and mine.

I was once a great warrior. I am now poor. …

I have looked upon the Mississippi since I have been a child. I love the Great River. I have dwelt upon its banks from the time I was an infant. I look upon it now. I shake hands with you, and as it is my wish, I hope you are my friends.

The first presidential assassination attempt took place on January 30, 1835. As depicted in this etching by an unknown artist, President Andrew Jackson departed the U.S. Capitol and was confronted by a deranged man bearing two derringer pistols. Both guns misfired, and the man ended up being beaten down by a cane-wielding Jackson. The assailant, an unemployed house painter who believed himself to be a former king of England, told investigators that he only felt genuine fear when he saw the sixty-seven-year-old president turn to attack. Indeed, no president lived through more violence than Andrew Jackson. As a thirteen-year-old courier in the Revolutionary War, Jackson received his first wound. Taken prisoner by the British, he was scarred on his head and hands by a saber blow from an irate British officer whose boots he refused to shine. Orphaned at age fourteen and schooled on the Appalachian frontier, his life was one of perpetual conflict defending his nation and his honor. As a duelist, Jackson fought at least thirteen battles and once killed a man from eight paces. As a general, he defeated British, Spanish, and American Indian armies.

WILLIAM BARRET TRAVIS

Dispatch from the Alamo

I shall never surrender nor retreat ... Victory or Death.

In 1835, American settlers in Texas engaged in armed rebellion against Mexican authorities and, soon thereafter, proclaimed an independent republic. Mexico's dictator, General Antonio López de Santa Anna, assembled a large army and marched into Texas to suppress the independence movement. Santa Anna's forces entered San Antonio in early 1836, and the city force of 150 Texans under the command of William Barret Travis (1809-1836) held up in a Spanish mission called *San Antonio de Valero*, which would later be known as the *Alamo*. Travis sent a dispatch for help which was responded to by a small contingency of less than forty men who crossed through Mexican lines and joined the Texas defenders. A force of nearly 400 men under the command of Colonel J. W. Fannin left Goliad to offer relief, but had equipment trouble and never made it.

On February 23, 1836, Santa Anna laid siege to the Alamo and, by March 5, ammunition was so low the Texans could not return fire. The Mexicans then scaled the walls, forcing the Texans to defend themselves using their muskets as clubs. By the following day, all of the defenders, including border heroes James Bowie and Davy Crockett, were dead.

"Remember the Alamo!" became the battle cry of General Sam Houston and his men, who would eventually defeat the Mexican Army and capture Santa Anna, forcing him to sign a treaty granting independence to Texas. The inscription on the Alamo in San Antonio reads: "In memory of the heroes who sacrificed their lives at the Alamo, March 6, 1836, in the defense of Texas. They chose never to surrender nor retreat. These brave hearts, with flag still proudly waving, perished in the flames of immortality that their high sacrifice might lead to the founding of this Texas. From the fire that burned their bodies rose the eternal spirit of the sublime, heroic sacrifice which gave birth to an empire state."

To the people of Texas and all Americans in the world. Fellow citizens and compatriots: I am besieged by a thousand or more of the Mexicans under Santa Anna. I have sustained a continual bombardment and cannonade for twenty-four hours and have not lost a man. The enemy has demanded a surrender at discretion; otherwise the garrison are to be put to the sword if the fort is taken. I have answered the demand with a cannon shot, and our flag still waves proudly from the walls. *I shall never surrender nor retreat.* Then, I call on you in the name of liberty, of patriotism, and everything dear to the American character, to come to our aid with all dispatch. The enemy is receiving reinforcements daily and will no doubt increase to three or four thousand in four or five days. If this call is neglected, I am determined to sustain myself as long as possible and die like a soldier who never forgets what is due to his own honor and that of his country. Victory or Death.

William Barret Travis
Lieutenant Colonel Commandant

The Bivouac of the Dead

In 1845, Texas was admitted into the Union as the twenty-eighth state. Disputes with Mexico over the Texas boundary and an increasing American belief in "manifest destiny" led to a two-year war in which American forces, under the leadership of General Winfield Scott, occupied Mexico City. The result of the war was the *Mexican Cession* in which the U.S. gained all of California, Nevada and Utah, most of Arizona, and parts of New Mexico, Colorado, and Wyoming in exchange for $15 million and a cancellation of all claims made against the Mexican government by American citizens. (The Gadsden Purchase in 1853 finalized the present-day Mexican/American border.)

One of the most memorable battles of the Mexican-American War was the Battle of Buena Vista, in which a Kentucky regiment of 5,000 men under the command of General Zachary Taylor, who would become the twelfth president of the United States, achieved a costly victory over a much larger Mexican force. The remains of those killed at Buena Vista, including Henry Clay, Jr., son of the great statesman, were removed to Frankfort. To commemorate the completion of a monument built in their honor, Theodore O'Hara (1820-1867), a Kentuckian who served in the war as a captain, wrote "The Bivouac of the Dead." Despite local references within the poem, such as "the Dark and Bloody Ground"—a reference to Kentucky, alluding to the frequent wars waged there between Indians—O'Hara's work gained nationwide acclaim. Considered "the greatest martial elegy in our language," lines from "The Bivouac of the Dead" can be found inscribed on headstones throughout Arlington National Cemetery.

The muffled drum's sad roll has beat
The soldier's last tattoo;
No more on life's parade shall meet
The brave and fallen few.
On Fame's eternal camping-ground
Their silent tents are spread,
And Glory guards, with solemn round,
The bivouac of the dead.

No rumor of the foe's advance
Now swells upon the wind;
Nor troubled thought at midnight haunts,
Of loved ones left behind;
No vision of the morrow's strife
The warrior's dreams alarms,
No braying horn nor screaming fife
At dawn to call to arms.

Their shivered swords are red with rust,
Their plumed heads are bowed;
Their haughty banner, trailed in dust,
Is now their martial shroud;
And plenteous funeral tears have washed
The red stains from each brow,
And the proud forms, by battle gashed,
Are free from anguish now.

The neighing troop, the flashing blade,
The bugle's stirring blast,
The charge, the dreadful cannonade,
The din and shout are past;
Nor war's wild note, nor glory's peal
Shall thrill with fierce delight
Those breasts that nevermore may feel
The rapture of the fight.

Like the fierce Northern hurricane
That sweeps his great plateau,
Flushed with the triumph yet to gain,
Came down the serried foe.
Who heard the thunder of the fray
Break o'er the field beneath,
Knew well the watchword of that day
Was "Victory or death."

Long did the doubtful conflict rage
O'er all that stricken plain,
For never fiercer fight did wage
The vengeful blood of Spain.
And still the storm of battle blew,
Still swelled the gory tide—
Not long our stout old chieftain knew
Such odds his strength could bide.

'Twas at that hour his stern command
Called to a martyr's grave
The flower of his own loved land,
The Nation's flag to save,
By rivers of their father's gore
His first-born laurels grew,
And well he deemed the sons would pour
Their lives for glory too.

Full many a norther's breath has swept
O'er Angostura's plain—
And long the pitying sky has wept
Above its mouldering slain.
The raven's screams, or eagle's flight,
Or shepherd's pensive lay,
Alone awakens each sullen height
That frowned o'er that dread fray.

Sons of the Dark and Bloody Ground,
Ye must not slumber there,
Where stranger steps and tongues resound
Along the heedless air.
Your own proud land's heroic soil
Shall be your fitter grave;
She claims from War its richest spoil—
The ashes of her brave.

Thus 'neath their parent turf they rest,
Far from the gory field,
Borne to a Spartan mother's breast
On many a bloody shield;
The sunshine of their native sky
Smiles sadly on them here,
And kindred eyes and hearts watch by
The heroes' sepulcher.

Rest on, embalmed and sainted dead,
Dear as the blood ye gave,
No impious footstep here shall tread
The herbage of your grave;
Nor shall your glory be forgot
While Fame her record keeps,
Or Honor points the hallowed spot
Where Valor proudly sleeps.

Yon Marble Minstrel's voiceful stone
In deathless song shall tell,
When many a vanquished age hath flown,
The story how ye fell;
Nor wreck, nor change, nor winter's blight,
Nor Time's remorseless doom,
Shall dim one ray of Glory's light
That gilds your deathless tomb.

RALPH WALDO EMERSON

Self-Reliance

Nothing is at last sacred but the integrity of your own mind.

Born in Boston and educated at Harvard, Ralph Waldo Emerson (1803-1882) was an ordained Unitarian minister who left the pulpit to pursue a career as a philosopher, essayist, and lecturer. He is best known as the leading advocate of *transcendentalism*—a philosophy that appealed to reason rather than the acceptance of tradition and social codes. Transcendentalists valued individuality and viewed society as an evil, although a necessary one. "Self-Reliance," published in 1841, is the best representation of Emerson's personal philosophy.

... I read the other day some verses written by an eminent painter which were original and not conventional. The soul always hears an admonition in such lines, let the subject be what it may. The sentiment they instil is of more value than any thought they may contain. To believe your own thought, to believe that what is true for you in your private heart is true for all men,—that is genius. Speak your latent conviction, and it shall be the universal sense; for the inmost in due time becomes the outmost,—and our first thought is rendered back to us by the trumpets of the Last Judgment. Familiar as the voice of the mind is to each, the highest merit we ascribe to Moses, Plato, and Milton is, that they set at naught books and traditions, and spoke not what men but what they thought. A man should learn to detect and watch that gleam of light which flashes across his mind from within, more than the lustre of the firmament of bards and sages. Yet he dismisses without notice his thought, because it is his. In every work of genius we recognize our own rejected thoughts: they come back to us with a certain alienated majesty. Great works of art have no more affecting lesson for us than this. They teach us to abide by our spontaneous impression with good-humored inflexibility the most when the whole cry of voices is on the other side. Else, to-morrow a stranger will say with masterly good sense precisely what we have thought and felt all the time, and we shall be forced to take with shame our own opinion from another.

There is a time in every man's education when he arrives at the conviction that envy is ignorance; that imitation is suicide; that he must take himself for better, for worse, as his portion; that though the wide universe is full of good, no kernel of nourishing corn can come to him but through his toil bestowed on that plot of ground which is given to him to till. The power which resides in him is new in nature, and none but he knows what that is which he can do, nor does he know until he has tried. Not for nothing one face, one character, one fact, makes much impression on him, and another none. This sculpture in the memory is not without preestablished harmony. The eye was placed where one ray should fall, that it might testify of that particular ray. We but half express ourselves, and are ashamed of that divine idea which each of us represents. It may be safely trusted as proportionate and of good issues, so it be faithfully imparted, but God will not have his work made manifest by cowards. A man is relieved and gay when he has put his heart into his work and done his best; but what he has said or done otherwise, shall give him no peace. It is a deliverance which does not deliver. In the attempt his genius deserts him; no muse befriends; no invention, no hope.

Trust thyself: every heart vibrates to that iron string. Accept the place the divine providence has found for you, the society of your contemporaries, the connection of events. Great men have always done so, and confided themselves childlike to the genius of their age, betraying their perception that the absolutely trustworthy was seated at their heart, working through their hands, predominating in all their being. And we are now men, and must accept in the highest mind the same transcendent destiny; and not minors and invalids in a protected corner, not cowards fleeing before a revolution, but guides, redeemers, and benefactors, obeying the Almighty effort, and advancing on Chaos and the Dark. …

These are the voices which we hear in solitude, but they grow faint and inaudible as we enter into the world. Society everywhere is in conspiracy against the manhood of every one of its members. Society is a joint-stock company, in which the members agree, for the better securing of his bread to each shareholder, to surrender the liberty and culture of the eater. The virtue in most requests is conformity. Self-reliance is its aversion. It loves not realities and creators, but names and customs.

Whoso would be a man must be a nonconformist. He who would gather immortal palms must not be hindered by the name of goodness, but must explore if it be goodness. Nothing is at last sacred but the integrity of your own mind. Absolve you to yourself, and you shall have the suffrage of the world. I remember an answer which when quite young I was prompted to make to a valued adviser, who was wont to importune me with the dear old doctrines of the church. On my saying, What have I to do with the sacredness of traditions, if I live wholly from within? my friend suggested,—"But these impulses may be from below, not from above." I replied, "They do not seem to me to be such; but if I am the Devil's child, I will live then from the Devil." No law can be sacred to me but that of my nature. Good and bad are but names very readily transferable to that or this; the only right is what is after my constitution, the only wrong what is against it. A man is to carry himself in the presence of all opposition, as if every thing were titular and ephemeral but he. I am ashamed to think how easily we capitulate to badges and names, to large societies and dead institutions. Every decent and well-spoken individual affects and sways me more than is right. I ought to go upright and vital, and speak the rude truth in all ways. …

What I must do is all that concerns me, not what the people think. This rule, equally arduous in actual and in intellectual life, may serve for the whole distinction between greatness and meanness. It is the harder because you will always find those who think they know what is your duty better than you know it. It is easy in the world to live after the world's opinion; it is easy in solitude to live after our own; but the great man is he who in the midst of the crowd keeps with perfect sweetness the independence of solitude.

The objection to conforming to usages that have become dead to you is that it scatters your force. It loses your time and blurs the impression of your character. If you maintain a dead church, contribute to a dead Bible Society, vote with a great party either for the Government or against it, spread your table like base housekeepers,—under all these screens

I have difficulty to detect the precise man you are. And of course so much force is withdrawn from your proper life. But do your thing, and I shall know you. Do your work, and you shall reinforce yourself. A man must consider what a blindman's-buff is this game of conformity. If I know your sect I anticipate your argument. I hear a preacher announce for his text and topic the expediency of one of the institutions of his church. Do I not know beforehand that not possibly can he say a new and spontaneous word? Do I not know that with all this ostentation of examining the grounds of the institution he will do no such thing? Do I not know that he is pledged to himself not to look but at one side, the permitted side, not as a man, but as a parish minister? He is a retained attorney, and these airs of the bench are the emptiest affectation. Well, most men have bound their eyes with one or another handkerchief, and attached themselves to some one of these communities of opinion. This conformity makes them not false in a few particulars, authors of a few lies, but false in all particulars. Their every truth is not quite true. Their two is not the real two, their four not the real four; so that every word they say chagrins us and we know not where to begin to set them right. Meantime nature is not slow to equip us in the prison-uniform of the party to which we adhere. We come to wear one cut of face and figure, and acquire by degrees the gentlest asinine expression. There is a mortifying experience in particular, which does not fail to wreck itself also in the general history; I mean "the foolish face of praise," the forced smile which we put on in company where we do not feel at ease, in answer to conversation which does not interest us. The muscles, not spontaneously moved but moved by a low usurping wilfulness, grow tight about the outline of the face, with the most disagreeable sensation; a sensation of rebuke and warning which no brave young man will suffer twice.

For nonconformity the world whips you with its displeasure. And therefore a man must know how to estimate a sour face. The by-standers look askance on him in the public street or in the friend's parlor. If this aversation had its origin in contempt and resistance like his own he might well go home with a sad countenance; but the sour faces of the multitude, like their sweet faces, have no deep cause, but are put on and off as the wind blows and a newspaper directs. Yet is the discontent of the multitude more formidable than that of the senate and the college. It is easy enough for a firm man who knows the world to brook the rage of the cultivated classes. Their rage is decorous and prudent, for they are timid, as being very vulnerable themselves. But when to their feminine rage the indignation of the people is added, when the ignorant and the poor are aroused, when the unintelligent brute force that lies at the bottom of society is made to growl and mow, it needs the habit of magnanimity and religion to treat it godlike as a trifle of no concernment.

The other terror that scares us from self-trust is our consistency; a reverence for our past act or word because the eyes of others have no other data for computing our orbit than our past acts, and we are loath to disappoint them.

But why should you keep your head over your shoulder? Why drag about this monstrous corpse of your memory, lest you contradict somewhat you have stated in this or that public place? Suppose you should contradict yourself; what then? It seems to be a rule of wisdom never to rely on your memory alone, scarcely even in acts of pure memory, but to bring the past for judgment into the thousand-eyed present, and live ever in a new day. In your metaphysics you have denied personality to the Deity, yet when the devout motions of the soul come, yield to them heart and life, though they should clothe God with shape and color. Leave your theory, as Joseph his coat in the hand of the harlot, and flee.

A foolish consistency is the hobgoblin of little minds, adored by little statesmen and philosophers and divines. With consistency a great soul has simply nothing to do. He may as well concern himself with his shadow on the wall. Speak what you think now in hard words and to-morrow speak what to-morrow thinks in hard words again, though it contradict every thing you said to-day.—Ah, so you shall be sure to be misunderstood.—Is it so bad then to be misunderstood? Pythagoras was misunderstood, and Socrates, and Jesus, and Luther, and Copernicus, and Galileo, and Newton, and every pure and wise spirit that ever took flesh. To be great is to be misunderstood. ...

Concord Hymn

"Concord Hymn" was written by Emerson as a tribute to the heroes of the battle of Concord who, on April 19, 1775, engaged the British at the North Bridge and "fired the shot heard round the world." The hymn was sung at a ceremony in 1837 to commemorate the completion of a monument built in honor of the revolutionary heroes.

By the rude bridge that arched the flood,
Their flag to April's breeze unfurled,
Here once the embattled farmers stood
And fired the shot heard round the world.

The foe long since in silence slept;
Alike the conqueror silent sleeps;
And Time the ruined bridge has swept
Down the dark stream which seaward creeps.

On this green bank, by this soft stream,
We set to-day a votive stone;
That memory may their deed redeem,
When, like our sires, our sons are gone.

Spirit, that made those heroes dare
To die, and leave their children free,
Bid Time and Nature gently spare
The shaft we raise to them and thee.

Charles Wilkes, commander of the United States Exploring Expedition, an exploring and surveying expedition of the Pacific Ocean conducted by the United States Navy from 1838-1842. The voyage was authorized by Congress in 1836 at the behest of President John Quincy Adams for the purpose of promoting commerce, surveying newly discovered areas, and revisiting previously discovered territory about which there was insufficient knowledge. Commonly known as the Wilkes Expedition, the voyage included naturalists, botanists, mineralogists, taxidermists, and artists. The Wilkes Expedition played a major role in development of nineteenth-century science, particularly in the growth of the U.S. scientific establishment. Many of the species and other items found by the expedition helped form the basis of collections at the new Smithsonian Institution.

Paul Revere's Ride, A Psalm of Life, The Village Blacksmith, and The Ship of State

Henry Wadsworth Longfellow (1807-1882) was born in Portland, Maine, graduated from Bowdoin College, and lived most of his life in Massachusetts where he taught at Harvard and wrote prolifically. He had his first poem published at the age of thirteen and became noted for such works as "The Song of Hiawatha," "The Courtship of Miles Standish," and "Evangeline." The most accomplished and most famous poet of the nineteenth century, Longfellow became the first American honored with a memorial bust in the Poet's Corner of Westminster Abbey.

Longfellow's first volume of poetry appeared in 1839 and included two of his most often reprinted works—"A Psalm of Life" and "The Village Blacksmith." "Paul Revere's Ride," perhaps the most widely anthologized and oft-recited poem in history, first appeared in 1863 as part of *Tales of a Wayside Inn*. "The Ship of State," taken from *The Building of the Ship*, gained increased popularity years later when President Franklin Roosevelt sent the first five lines, written in his own hand, as a message of encouragement to Winston Churchill during World War II.

Paul Revere's Ride

Listen, my children, and you shall hear
Of the midnight ride of Paul Revere,
On the eighteenth of April, in Seventy-five;
Hardly a man is now alive
Who remembers that famous day and year.

He said to his friend, "If the British march
By land or sea from the town tonight,
Hang a lantern aloft in the belfry arch
Of the North Church tower as a signal light—
One, if by land, and two, if by sea;
And I on the opposite shore will be,
Ready to ride and spread the alarm
Through every Middlesex village and farm,
For the country folk to be up and to arm."

Then he said, "Good night!" and with muffled oar
Silently rowed to the Charlestown shore,
Just as the moon rose over the bay,
Where swinging wide at her moorings lay
The Somerset, British man-of-war;
A phantom ship, with each mast and spar
Across the moon like a prison bar,
And a huge black hulk, that was magnified
By its own reflection in the tide.

Meanwhile, his friend, through alley and street,
Wanders and watches with eager ears,
Till in the silence around him he hears
The muster of men at the barrack door,
The sound of arms, and the tramp of feet,
And the measured tread of the grenadiers,
Marching down to their boats on the shore.

Then he climbed the tower of the Old North Church,
By the wooden stairs, with stealthy tread,
To the belfry-chamber overhead,
And startled the pigeons from their perch
On the somber rafters, that round him made
Masses and moving shapes of shade—
By the trembling ladder, steep and tall,
To the highest window in the wall,
Where he paused to listen and look down
A moment on the roofs of the town,
And the moonlight flowing over all.

Beneath, in the churchyard, lay the dead,
In their night-encampment on the hill,
Wrapped in silence so deep and still
That he could hear, like a sentinel's tread,
The watchful night-wind, as it went
Creeping along from tent to tent,
And seeming to whisper, "All is well!"
A moment only he feels the spell
Of the place and the hour, and the secret dread
Of the lonely belfry and the dead;
For suddenly all his thoughts are bent
On a shadowy something far away,
Where the river widens to meet the bay—
A line of black that bends and floats
On the rising tide, like a bridge of boats.

Meanwhile, impatient to mount and ride,
Booted and spurred, with a heavy stride
On the opposite shore walked Paul Revere.
Now he patted his horse's side,
Now gazed at the landscape far and near,
Then, impetuous, stamped the earth,
And turned and tightened his saddle-girth;
But mostly he watched with eager search
The belfry-tower of the Old North Church,
As it rose above the graves on the hill,
Lonely and spectral and somber and still.
And lo! as he looks, on the belfry's height
A glimmer, and then a gleam of light!
He springs to the saddle, the bridle he turns,
But lingers and gazes, till full on his sight
A second lamp in the belfry burns!

A hurry of hoofs in a village street,
A shape in the moonlight, a bulk in the dark,
And beneath, from the pebbles, in passing, a spark
Struck out by a steed flying fearless and fleet;
That was all! And yet, through the gloom and the light
The fate of a nation was riding that night;
And the spark struck out by that steed in his flight,
Kindled the land into flame with its heat.

He has left the village and mounted the steep,
And beneath him, tranquil and broad and deep,
Is the Mystic, meeting the ocean tides;
And under the alders, that skirt its edge,
Now soft on the sand, now loud on the ledge,
Is heard the tramp of his steed as he rides.

It was twelve by the village clock,
When he crossed the bridge into Medford town.
He heard the crowing of the cock,
And the barking of the farmer's dog,
And felt the damp of the river fog,
That rises after the sun goes down.

It was one by the village clock,
When he galloped into Lexington.
He saw the gilded weathercock
Swim in the moonlight as he passed,
And the meeting-house windows, blank and bare,
Gaze at him with a spectral glare,
As if they already stood aghast
At the bloody work they would look upon.

It was two by the village clock,
When he came to the bridge in Concord town.
He heard the bleating of the flock,
And the twitter of birds among the trees,
And felt the breath of the morning breeze
Blowing over the meadows brown.
And one was safe and asleep in his bed
Who at the bridge would be first to fall,
Who that day would be lying dead,
Pierced by a British musket-ball.

You know the rest. In the books you have read,
How the British Regulars fired and fled—
How the farmers gave them ball for ball,
From behind each fence and farmyard wall,
Chasing the redcoats down the lane,
Then crossing the fields to emerge again
Under the trees at the turn of the road,
And only pausing to fire and load.

So through the night rode Paul Revere;
And so through the night went his cry of alarm
To every Middlesex village and farm—
A cry of defiance, and not of fear,
A voice in the darkness, a knock at the door,
And a word that shall echo forevermore!
For, borne on the night-wind of the Past,
Through all our history, to the last,
In the hour of darkness and peril and need,
The people will waken and listen to hear
The hurrying hoofbeats of that steed,
And the midnight message of Paul Revere.

A Psalm of Life

WHAT THE HEART OF THE YOUNG MAN SAID TO THE PSALMIST

Tell me not, in mournful numbers,
"Life is but an empty dream!"
For the soul is dead that slumbers,
And things are not what they seem.

Life is real! Life is earnest!
And the grave is not its goal;
"Dust thou art, to dust returnest,"
Was not spoken of the soul.

Not enjoyment, and not sorrow,
Is our destined end or way;
But to act, that each to-morrow
Finds us farther than to-day

Art is long, and Time is fleeting,
And our hearts, though stout and brave,
Still, like muffled drums, are beating
Funeral marches to the grave.

In the world's broad field of battle,
In the bivouac of Life,
Be not like dumb, driven cattle!
Be a hero in the strife!

Trust no Future, howe'er pleasant!
Let the dead Past bury its dead!
Act,—act in the living Present!
Heart within, and God o'erhead!

Lives of great men all remind us
We can make our lives sublime,
And, departing, leave behind us
Footprints on the sands of time;

Footprints, that perhaps another,
Sailing o'er life's solemn main,
A forlorn and shipwrecked brother,
Seeing, shall take heart again.

Let us, then, be up and doing,
With a heart for any fate;
Still achieving, still pursuing,
Learn to labour and to wait.

The Village Blacksmith

Under a spreading chestnut tree
The village smithy stands;
The smith, a mighty man is he,
With large and sinewy hands;
And the muscles of his brawny arms
Are strong as iron bands.

His hair is crisp, and black, and long,
His face is like the tan;
His brow is wet with honest sweat,
He earns whate'er he can,
And looks the whole world in the face,
For he owes not any man.

Week in, week out, from morn till night,
You can hear his bellows blow;
You can hear him swing his heavy sledge,
With measured beat and slow,
Like a sexton ringing the village bell,
When the evening sun is low.

And children coming home from school
Look in at the open door;
They love to see the flaming forge,
And hear the bellows roar,
And catch the burning sparks that fly
Like chaff from a threshing floor.

He goes on Sunday to the church,
And sits among his boys;
He hears the parson pray and preach,
He hears his daughter's voice,
Singing in the village choir,
And it makes his heart rejoice.

It sounds to him like her mother's voice,
Singing in Paradise!
He needs must think of her once more,
How in the grave she lies;
And with his hard, rough hands he wipes
A tear out of his eyes.

Toiling—rejoicing—sorrowing
Onward through life he goes;
Each morning sees some task begin,
Each evening sees it close;
Something attempted, something done,
Has earned a night's repose.

Thanks, thanks to thee, my worthy friend,
For the lesson thou hast taught!
Thus at the flaming forge of life
Our fortunes must be wrought;
Thus on its sounding anvil shaped
Each burning deed and thought!

The Ship of State

Thou, too, sail on, O Ship of State!
Sail on, O UNION, strong and great!
Humanity with all its fears,
With all the hopes of future years,
Is hanging breathless on thy fate!
We know what Master laid thy keel,
What Workmen wrought thy ribs of steel,
Who made each mast, and sail, and rope,
What anvils rang, what hammers beat,
In what a forge and what a heat
Were shaped the anchors of thy hope!
Fear not each sudden sound and shock,
'Tis of the wave and not the rock;
'Tis but the flapping of the sail,
And not a rent made by the gale!
In spite of rock and tempest's roar,
In spite of false lights on the shore,
Sail on, nor fear to breast the sea!
Our hearts, our hopes, are all with thee,
Our hearts, our hopes, our prayers, our tears,
Our faith triumphant o'er our fears,
Are all with thee,—are all with thee!

On Top of Old Smoky

"On Top of Old Smoky" was a popular folksong of the early settlers of the Southern Appalachians—most of whom were of English, Scottish, and Irish descent. Old Smoky is a reference to one of the peaks in the Blue Ridge Mountains near Asheville, North Carolina. This song became a favorite of the pioneers of the westward movement.

On top of Old Smoky,
All covered with snow,
I lost my true lover
For courtin' too slow.

Now courtin's a pleasure
But partin' is grief,
A false-hearted lover
is worse than a thief.

A thief will just rob you
And take what you have,
But a false-hearted lover
Will send you to the grave.

They'll hug you and kiss you
And tell you more lies
Than cross-ties on the railroad
Or stars in the skies.

On top of Old Smoky,
All covered with snow,
I lost my true lover
For courtin' too slow.

Columbia, the Gem of the Ocean

"Columbia, the Gem of the Ocean," an American patriotic song, is believed to have been written by David Shaw, an actor and singer who first performed the song in 1843. Thomas Becket, who arranged the music, also claimed authorship of the lyrics, however. It is probable that the two men, both English born, first introduced an alternate version of the song in England where it was known as "Britannia, the Pride of the Ocean."

O Columbia! the gem of the ocean,
The home of the brave and the free,
The shrine of each patriot's devotion,
A world offers homage to thee!
Thy mandates make heroes assemble,
When Liberty's form stands in view;
Thy banners make tyranny tremble,
When borne by the red, white and blue!
When borne by the red, white and blue,
When borne by the red, white and blue,
Thy banners make tyranny tremble,
When borne by the red, white and blue!

When war wing'd its wide desolation,
And threatened the land to deform,
The ark then of freedom's foundation,
Columbia, rode safe thro' the storm;
With the garlands of vict'ry around her,
When so proudly she bore her brave crew,
With her flag proudly floating before her,
The boast of the red, white and blue!
The boast of the red, white and blue,
The boast of the red, white and blue,
With her flag proudly floating before her,
The boast of the red, white, and blue!

arbitrary law, is unequally divided among men; and the problem presented for solution is, how to transfer a portion of this property from those who are supposed to have too much, to those who feel and know that they have too little. At this point, both their theory and their expectation is of reform stop. But the beneficent power of education would not be exhausted, even though it should peaceably abolish all the miseries that spring from the coexistence, side by side, of enormous wealth and squalid want. It has a higher function. Beyond the power of diffusing old wealth, it has the prerogative of creating new. It is a thousand times more lucrative than fraud; and adds a thousand fold more to a nation's resources than the most successful conquests. Knaves and robbers can obtain only what was before possessed by others. But education creates or develops new treasures,—treasures not before possessed or dreamed of by any one. …

If a savage will learn how to swim, he can fasten a dozen pounds' weight to his back, and transport it across a narrow river, or other body of water of moderate width. If he will invent an ax, or other instrument, by which to cut down a tree, he can use the tree for a float, and one of its limbs for a paddle, and can thus transport many times the former weight, many times the former distance. Hollowing out his log, he will increase, what may be called, its tonnage,—or, rather, its *poundage*,—and, by sharpening its ends, it will cleave the water both more easily and more swiftly. Fastening several trees together, he makes a raft, and thus increases the buoyant power of his embryo water-craft. Turning up the ends of small poles, or using knees of timber instead of straight pieces, and grooving them together, or filling up the interstices between them, in some way, so as to make them water-tight, he brings his rude raft literally into *ship-shape*. Improving upon hull below and rigging above, he makes a proud merchantman, to be wafted by the winds from continent to continent. But, even this does not content the adventurous naval architect. He frames iron arms for his ship; and, for oars, affixes iron wheels, capable of swift revolution, and stronger than the strong sea. Into iron-walled cavities in her bosom, he puts iron organs of massive structure and strength, and of cohesion insoluble by fire. Within these, he kindles a small volcano; and then, like a sentinent and rational existence, this wonderful creation of his hands cleaves oceans, breasts tides, defies tempests, and bears its living and jubilant freights around the globe. Now, take away intelligence from the ship-builder, and the steamship,—that miracle of human art,—falls back into a floating log; the log itself is lost; and the savage swimmer, bearing his dozen pounds on his back, alone remains.

And so it is, not in one department only, but in the whole circle of human labors. The annihilation of the sun would no more certainly be followed by darkness, than the extinction of human intelligence would plunge the race at once into the weakness and helplessness of barbarism. To have created such beings as we are, and to have placed them in this world, without the light of the sun, would be no more cruel than for a government to suffer its laboring classes to grow up without knowledge….

For the creation of wealth, then,—for the existence of a wealthy people and a wealthy nation,—intelligence is the grand condition. The number of improvers will increase, as the intellectual constituency, if I may so call it, increases. In former times, and in most parts of the world even at the present day, not one man in a million has ever had such a development of mind, as made it possible for him to become a contributor to art or science. Let this development precede, and contributions, numberless, and of inestimable value, will be sure to follow. That Political Economy, therefore, which busies itself about capital and labor, supply and demand, interest and rents, favorable and unfavorable balance of trade; but leaves out of account the element of a wide-spread mental development, is nought but stupendous folly. The greatest of all the arts in political economy is, to change a consumer into a producer; and the next greatest is to increase the producer's producing power;—an end to be directly attained, by increasing his intelligence.

Seneca Falls Declaration of Sentiments and Resolutions

The history of mankind is a history of repeated injuries and usurpations on the part of man toward woman, having in direct object the establishment of an absolute tyranny over her.

In July 1848, Elizabeth Cady Stanton and Lucretia Mott organized a convention in Seneca Falls, New York, for the purpose of discussing women's rights. The convention drafted the following Declaration of Sentiments and Resolutions, modeled after the Declaration of Independence. The goal was to acquire equal rights for women in educational opportunities, property rights and, most importantly, women's suffrage.

When the Constitution was written, the Founding Fathers left the decision of who could vote with the states. Originally, only white adult male property owners could participate in elections. The first step toward expanded suffrage came in 1830, when every state had finally eliminated the property requirement. The first state to allow women the vote was Wyoming in 1869, and Utah followed in 1870—the same year the Fifteenth Amendment was ratified granting black men the vote. Women finally gained nationwide suffrage in 1920 with ratification of the Nineteenth Amendment.

When, in the course of human events, it becomes necessary for one portion of the family of man to assume among the people of the earth a position different from that which they have hitherto occupied, but one to which the laws of nature and of nature's God entitle them, a decent respect to the opinions of mankind requires that they should declare the causes that impel them to such a course.

We hold these truths to be self-evident: that all men and women are created equal; that they are endowed by their Creator with certain inalienable rights; that among these are life, liberty, and the pursuit of happiness; that to secure these rights governments are instituted, deriving their just powers from the consent of the governed. Whenever any form of Government becomes destructive of these ends, it is the right of those who suffer from it to refuse allegiance to it, and to insist upon the institution of a new government, laying its foundation on such principles, and organizing its powers in such form as to them shall seem most likely to effect their safety and happiness. Prudence, indeed, will dictate that governments long established should not be changed for light and transient causes; and accordingly, all experience hath shown that mankind are more disposed to suffer, while evils are sufferable, than to right themselves by abolishing the forms to which they are accustomed. But when a long train of abuses and usurpations, pursuing invariably the same object, evinces a design to reduce them under absolute despotism, it is their duty to throw off such government, and to provide new guards for their future security. Such has been the patient sufferance of the women under this government, and such is now the necessity which constrains them to demand equal station to which they are entitled.

The history of mankind is a history of repeated injuries and usurpations on the part of man toward woman, having in direct object the establishment of an absolute tyranny over her. To prove this, let facts be submitted to a candid world.

He has never permitted her to exercise her inalienable right to the elective franchise.

He has compelled her to submit to laws, in the formation of which she had no voice.

He has withheld from her rights which are given to the most ignorant and degraded men—both natives and foreigners.

Having deprived her of this first right of a citizen, the elective franchise, thereby leaving her without representation in the halls of legislation, he has oppressed her on all sides.

He has made her, if married, in the eye of the law, civilly dead.

He has taken from her all right in property, even to the wages she earns.

He has made her, morally, an irresponsible being, as she can commit many crimes with impunity, provided they be done in the presence of her husband. In the covenant of marriage, she is compelled to promise obedience to her husband, he becoming, to all intents and purposes, her master—the law giving him power to deprive her of her liberty, and to administer chastisement.

He has so framed the laws of divorce, as to what shall be the proper causes of divorce; in case of separation, to whom the guardianship of the children shall be given; as to be wholly regardless of the happiness of women—the law, in all cases, going upon the false supposition of the supremacy of man, and giving all power into his hands.

After depriving her of all rights as a married woman, if single and the owner of property, he has taxed her to support a government which recognizes her only when her property can be made profitable to it.

He has monopolized nearly all the profitable employments, and from those she is permitted to follow, she receives but a scanty remuneration.

He closes against her all avenues to wealth and distinction, which he considers most honorable to himself. As a teacher of theology, medicine, or law, she is not known.

He has denied her the facilities for obtaining a thorough education—all colleges being closed against her.

He allows her in Church as well as State, but a subordinate position, claiming Apostolic authority for her exclusion from the ministry, and, with some exceptions, from any public participation in the affairs of the Church.

He has created a false public sentiment, by giving to the world a different code of morals for men and women, by which moral delinquencies which exclude women from society, are not only tolerated but deemed of little account in man.

He has usurped the prerogative of Jehovah himself, claiming it as his right to assign for her a sphere of action, when that belongs to her conscience and her God.

He has endeavored, in every way that he could to destroy her confidence in her own powers, to lessen her self-respect, and to make her willing to lead a dependent and abject life.

Now, in view of this entire disfranchisement of one-half the people of this country, their social and religious degradation,—in view of the unjust laws above mentioned, and because women do feel themselves aggrieved, oppressed, and fraudulently deprived of their most sacred rights, we insist that they have immediate admission to all the rights and privileges which belong to them as citizens of these United States.

In entering upon the great work before us, we anticipate no small amount of misconception, misrepresentation, and ridicule; but we shall use every instrumentality within our power to effect our object. We shall employ agents, circulate tracts, petition the State and national Legislatures, and endeavor to enlist the pulpit and the press in our behalf.

We hope this Convention will be followed by a series of Conventions, embracing every part of the country.

Firmly relying upon the final triumph of the Right and the True, we do this day affix our signatures to this declaration.

RESOLUTIONS

Whereas, the great precept of nature is conceded to be, "that man shall pursue his own true and substantial happiness." Blackstone, in his Commentaries, remarks, that this law of Nature being coeval with mankind, and dictated by God himself, is of course superior in obligation to any other. It is binding over all the globe, in all countries, and at all times; no human laws are of any validity if contrary to this, and such of them as are valid, derive all their force, and all their validity, and all their authority, mediately and immediately, from this origin; Therefore,

Resolved, That such laws as conflict, in any way, with the true and substantial happiness of woman, are contrary to the great precept of nature, and of no validity; for this is "superior in obligation to any other."

Resolved, That all laws which prevent women from occupying such a station in society as her conscience shall dictate, or which place her in a position inferior to that of man, are contrary to the great precept of nature, and therefore of no force or authority.

Resolved, That woman is man's equal—was intended to be so by the Creator, and the highest good of the race demands that she should be recognized as such.

Resolved, That the women of this country ought to be enlightened in regard to the laws under which they live, that they may no longer publish their degradation, by declaring themselves satisfied with their present position, nor their ignorance, by asserting that they have all the rights they want.

Resolved, That inasmuch as man, while claiming for himself intellectual superiority, does accord to woman moral superiority, it is pre-eminently his duty to encourage her to speak, and teach, as she has an opportunity, in all religious assemblies.

Resolved, That the same amount of virtue, delicacy, and refinement of behavior, that is required of woman in the social state, should also be required of man, and the same transgressions should be visited with equal severity on both man and woman.

Resolved, That the objection of indelicacy and impropriety, which is so often brought against woman when she addresses a public audience, comes with a very ill grace from those who encourage, by their attendance, her appearance on the stage, in the concert, or in the feats of the circus.

Resolved, That woman has too long rested satisfied in the circumscribed limits which corrupt customs and a perverted application of the Scriptures have marked out for her, and that it is time she should move in the enlarged sphere which her great Creator has assigned her.

Resolved, That it is the duty of the women of this country to secure to themselves their sacred right to the elective franchise.

Resolved, That the equality of human rights results necessarily from the fact of the identity of the race in capabilities and responsibilities.

Resolved, therefore, That, being invested by the Creator with the same capabilities, and the same consciousness of responsibility for their exercise, it is demonstrably the right and duty of woman, equally with man, to promote every righteous cause, by every righteous means; and especially in regard to the great subjects of morals and religion, it is self-evidently her right to participate with her brother in teaching them, both in private and in public, by writing and by speaking, by any instrumentalities proper to be used, and in any assemblies proper to be held; and this being a self-evident truth, growing out of the divinely implanted principles of human nature, any custom or authority adverse to it, whether modern or wearing the hoary sanction of antiquity, is to be regarded as self-evident falsehood, and at war with the interests of mankind.

Resolved, That the speedy success of our cause depends upon the zealous and untiring efforts of both men and women, for the overthrow of the monopoly of the pulpit, and for the securing to woman an equal participation with men in the various trades, professions and commerce.

SOJOURNER TRUTH

Address to the Ohio Women's Rights Convention

And ain't I a woman?

Born into slavery in New York, Isabella Baumfree (1797?-1883) gained her freedom when that state passed an anti-slavery law. Shortly thereafter, she changed her name to Sojourner Truth and began lecturing throughout the Northeast and Midwest. In 1864, she was received at the White House by President Lincoln and stayed on in Washington, D.C., where she worked to improve the living conditions of slaves who had escaped from the South.

In addition to being a leading abolitionist, Truth also embraced the women's rights movement. Speaking before the Ohio Women's Rights Convention in Akron in 1851, she successfully won over critics who did not wish to mix the issue of women's rights with the unpopular abolitionist cause.

Well, children, where there is so much racket there must be something out of kilter. I think that 'twixt the Negroes of the South and the women at the North, all talking about rights, the white men will be in a fix pretty soon. But what's all this here talking about?

That man over there says that women need to be helped into carriages, and lifted over ditches, and to have the best place everywhere. Nobody ever helps me into carriages, or over mud-puddles, or gives me any best place! And ain't I a woman? Look at me! Look at my arm. I have ploughed and planted, and gathered into barns, and no man could head me! And ain't I a woman? I could work as much and eat as much as a man—when I could get it—and bear the lash as well! And ain't I a woman? I have borne thirteen children, and seen them most all sold off to slavery, and when I cried out with my mother's grief, none but Jesus heard me! And ain't I a woman?

Then they talk about this thing in the head; what's this they call it? [Intellect, someone whispers.] That's it, honey. What's that got to do with women's rights or Negro's rights? If my cup won't hold but a pint, and yours holds a quart, wouldn't you be mean not to let me have my little half-measure full?

Then that little man in black there, he says women can't have as much rights as men, 'cause Christ wasn't a woman! Where did your Christ come from? Where did your Christ come from? From God and a woman! Man had nothing to do with Him.

If the first woman God ever made was strong enough to turn the world upside down all alone, these women together ought to be able to turn it back, and get it right side up again! And now they is asking to do it, the men better let them.

Obliged to you for hearing me, and now old Sojourner ain't got nothing more to say.

FREDERICK DOUGLASS

Fourth of July Address

What, to the American slave, is your Fourth of July? I answer: a day that reveals to him, more than all other days in the year, the gross injustice and cruelty to which he is the constant victim.

The child of a white father and a plantation field hand, Frederick Augustus Washington Bailey (1818-1895) was born into slavery in Maryland. At the age of eight, Frederick was sent to work as a house slave for a relative of his master. There, his mistress taught him to read, an act forbidden by law. He began to educate himself and, in 1838, escaped into Massachusetts and changed his name to Frederick Douglass. He became involved in the Massachusetts Anti-Slavery Society and gained fame as a noted lecturer and writer. In 1845, Douglass published the first version of his autobiography, but, fearing exposure of his identity as a runaway slave, fled to England where he continued to speak against slavery while raising money to purchase his freedom. Upon returning to the United States in 1847, he founded the *North Star*, an anti-slavery newspaper in Rochester, New York.

Speaking in Corinthian Hall in Rochester on July 5, 1852, Douglass praised the accomplishments of the Founding Fathers, but reminded his white audience of the nation's hypocrisy with regard to blacks who did not enjoy independence.

… Fellow citizens, pardon me, allow me to ask, why am I called upon to speak here today? What have I, or those I represent, to do with your national independence? Are the great principles of political freedom and of natural justice, embodied in that Declaration of Independence, extended to us? And am I, therefore, called upon to bring our humble offering to the national altar, and to confess the benefits and express devout gratitude for the blessings resulting from your independence to us?

Would to God, both for your sakes and ours, that an affirmative answer could be truthfully returned to these questions! Then would my task be light, and my burden easy and delightful. For *who* is there so cold that a nation's sympathy could not warm him? Who so obdurate and dead to the claims of gratitude that would not thankfully acknowledge such priceless benefits? Who so stolid and selfish that would not give his voice to swell the hallelujahs of a nation's jubilee, when the chains of servitude had been torn from his limbs? I am not that man. In a case like that the dumb might eloquently speak and the "lame man leap as an hart."

But, such is not the state of the case. I say it with a sad sense of the disparity between us. I am not included within the pale of this glorious anniversary! Your high independence only reveals the immeasurable distance between us. The blessings in which you, this day, rejoice, are not enjoyed in common. The rich inheritance of justice, liberty, prosperity and independence, bequeathed by your fathers, is shared by you, not by me. The sunlight that brought life and healing to you, has brought stripes and death to me. This Fourth of July is *yours*, not *mine. You* may rejoice, I must mourn. To drag a man in fetters into the grand illuminated temple of liberty, and call upon him to join you in joyous anthems, were inhuman mockery and sacrilegious irony. Do you mean, citizens, to mock me, by asking me to speak to-day? If so, there is a parallel to your conduct. And let me warn you that it is dangerous to copy the example of a nation whose crimes, lowering up to heaven, were thrown down by the breath of the Almighty, burying that nation in irrecoverable ruin! I can to-day take up the plaintive lament of a peeled and woe-smitten people!

"By the rivers of Babylon, there we sat down. Yea! we wept when we remembered Zion. We hanged our harps upon the willows in the midst thereof. For there, they that carried us away captive, required of us a song; and they who wasted us required of us mirth, saying, sing us one of the songs of Zion. How can we sing the Lord's song in a strange land? If I forget thee, O Jerusalem, let my right hand forget her cunning. If I do not remember thee, let my tongue cleave to the roof of my mouth."

Fellow-citizens; above your national, tumultuous joy, I hear the mournful wail of millions! whose chains, heavy and grievous yesterday, are, to-day, rendered more intolerable by the jubilee shouts that reach them. If I do forget, if I do not faithfully remember those bleeding children of sorrow this day, "may my right hand forget her cunning, and may my tongue cleave to the roof of my mouth!" To forget them, to pass lightly over their wrongs, and to chime in with the popular theme, would be treason most scandalous and shocking, and would make me a reproach before God and the world. My subject, then fellow-citizens, is AMERICAN SLAVERY. I shall see, this day, and its popular characteristics, from the slave's point of view. Standing, there, identified with the American bondman, making his wrongs mine, I do not hesitate to declare, with all my soul, that the character and conduct of this nation never looked blacker to me than on this 4th of July! Whether we turn to the declarations of the past, or to the professions of the present, the conduct of the nation seems equally hideous and revolting. America is false to the past, false to the present, and solemnly binds herself to be false to the future. Standing with God and the crushed and bleeding slave on this occasion, I will, in the name of humanity which is outraged, in the name of liberty which is fettered, in the name of the constitution and the Bible, which are disregarded and trampled upon, dare to call in question and to denounce, with all the emphasis I can command, everything that serves to perpetuate slavery—the great sin and shame of America! "I will not equivocate; I will not excuse;" I will use the severest language I can command; and yet not one word shall escape me that any man, whose judgment is not blinded by prejudice, or who is not at heart a slaveholder, shall not confess to be right and just.

But I fancy I hear someone of my audience say, "It is just in this circumstance that you and your brother abolitionists fail to make a favorable impression on the public mind. Would you argue more and denounce less, would you persuade more and rebuke less, your cause would be much more likely to succeed." But, I submit, where all is plain, there is nothing to be argued. What point in the antislavery creed would you have me argue? On what branch of the subject do the people of this country need light? Must I undertake to prove that the slave is a man? That point is conceded already. Nobody doubts it. The slaveholders themselves acknowledge it in the enactment of laws for their government. They acknowledge it when they punish disobedience on the part of the slave. There are seventy-two crimes in the state of Virginia which, if committed by a black man (no matter how ignorant he be), subject him to the punishment of death; while only two of the same crimes will subject a white man to the like punishment. What is this but the acknowledgment that the slave is a moral, intellectual, and responsible being? The manhood of the slave is conceded. It is admitted in the fact that the Southern statute books are covered with enactments forbidding, under severe fines and penalties, the teaching of the slave to read or to write. When you can point to any such laws in reference to the beasts of the field, then I may consent to argue the manhood of the slave. When the dogs in your streets, when the fowls of the air, when the cattle on your hills, when the fish of the sea and the reptiles that crawl shall be unable to distinguish the slave from a brute, then will I argue with you that the slave is a man!

For the present, it is enough to affirm the equal manhood of the Negro race. Is it not astonishing that, while we are plowing, planting, and reaping, using all kinds of mechanical tools, erecting houses, constructing bridges, building ships, working in metals of brass, iron, copper, silver, and gold; that, while we are reading, writing, and ciphering, acting as clerks, merchants, and secretaries, having among us lawyers, doctors, ministers, poets, authors, editors, orators, and teachers; that, while we are engaged in all manner of enterprises common to other men, digging gold in California, capturing the whale in the Pacific, feeding sheep and cattle on the hillside, living, moving, acting, thinking, planning, living in families as husbands, wives, and children, and, above all, confessing and worshiping the Christian's God, and looking hopefully for life and immortality beyond the grave, we are called upon to prove that we are men!

Would you have me argue that man is entitled to liberty? That he is the rightful owner of his own body? You have already declared it. Must I argue the wrongfulness of slavery? Is that a question for republicans? Is it to be settled by the rules of logic and argumentation, as a matter beset with great difficulty, involving a doubtful application of the principle of justice, hard to be understood? How should I look today, in the presence of Americans, dividing and subdividing a discourse, to show that men have a natural right to freedom? Speaking of it relatively and positively, negatively and affirmatively? To do so would be to make myself ridiculous and to offer an insult to your understanding. There is not a man beneath the canopy of heaven that does not know that slavery is wrong for *him*.

What, am I to argue that it is wrong to make men brutes, to rob them of their liberty, to work them without wages, to keep them ignorant of their relations to their fellow men, to beat them with sticks, to flay their flesh with the lash, to load their limbs with irons, to hunt them with dogs, to sell them at auction, to sunder their families, to knock out their teeth, to burn their flesh, to starve them into obedience and submission to their masters? Must I argue that a system thus marked with blood, and stained with pollution, is *wrong*? No! I will not. I have better employment for my time and strength than such arguments would imply.

What, then, remains to be argued? Is it that slavery is not divine; that God did not establish it; that our doctors of divinity are mistaken? There is blasphemy in the thought. That which is inhuman cannot be divine! *Who* can reason on such a proposition? They that can may; I cannot. The time for such argument is past.

At a time like this, scorching iron, not convincing argument, is needed. O! had I the ability, and could I reach the nation's ear, I would today pour out a fiery stream of biting ridicule, blasting reproach, withering sarcasm, and stern rebuke. For it is not light that is needed, but fire; it is not the gentle shower, but thunder. We need the storm, the whirlwind, and the earthquake. The feeling of the nation must be quickened; the conscience of the nation must be roused; the propriety of the nation must be startled; the hypocrisy of the nation must be exposed; and its crimes against God and man must be proclaimed and denounced.

What, to the American slave, is your Fourth of July? I answer: a day that reveals to him, more than all other days in the year, the gross injustice and cruelty to which he is the constant victim. To him, your celebration is a sham; your boasted liberty, an unholy license; your national greatness, swelling vanity; your sounds of rejoicing are empty and heartless; your denunciation of tyrants, brass-fronted impudence; your shouts of liberty and equality, hollow mockery; your prayers and hymns, your sermons and thanksgivings, with all your religious parade and solemnity, are, to Him, mere bombast, fraud, deception, impiety, and hypocrisy—a thin veil to cover up crimes which would disgrace a nation of savages. There is not a nation of savages. There is not a nation on the earth guilty of practices more shocking and bloody than are the people of the United States at this very hour.

Go where you may, search where you will, roam through all the monarchies and despotisms of the Old World, travel through South America, search out every abuse, and when you have found the last, lay your facts by the side of the everyday practices of this nation, and you will say with me that, for revolting barbarity and shameless hypocrisy, America reigns without a rival. ...

One of the most significant figures in American history, Frederick Douglass, shown here in 1856, devoted his life to the cause of freedom and human rights. A firm believer in the equality of all people, Douglass said, "I would unite with anybody to do right and with nobody to do wrong."

FREDERICK DOUGLASS

Letter to His Former Master

The very first mental effort that I now remember on my part, was an attempt to solve the mystery—why am I a slave?

While in England, Frederick Douglass wrote the following letter to his former master, Captain Thomas Auld, and openly published it in the *North Star* on September 8, 1848. Thirty years later, the two men, who had long since reconciled, met at Auld's deathbed in a reunion that Douglass described as "deeply emotional." He was pleased to learn that Auld had, in fact, taken his sickly grandmother into his own home to care for her.

Sir—The long and intimate, though by no means friendly, relation which unhappily subsisted between you and myself, leads me to hope that you will easily account for the great liberty which I now take in addressing you in this open and public manner. The same fact may remove any disagreeable surprise which you may experience on again finding your name coupled with mine, in any other way than in an advertisement, accurately describing my person, and offering a large sum for my arrest. In thus dragging you again before the public, I am aware that I shall subject myself to no inconsiderable amount of censure. I shall probably be charged with an unwarrantable, if not a wanton and reckless disregard of the rights and properties of private life. There are those north as well as south who entertain a much higher respect for rights which are merely conventional, than they do for rights which are personal and essential. Not a few there are in our country, who, while they have no scruples against robbing the laborer of the hard earned results of his patient industry, will be shocked by the extremely indelicate manner of bringing your name before the public. Believing this to be the case, and wishing to meet every reasonable or plausible objection to my conduct, I will frankly state the ground upon which I justify myself in this instance, as well as on former occasions when I have thought proper to mention your name in public. All will agree that a man guilty of theft, robbery, or murder, has forfeited the right to concealment and private life; that the community have a right to subject such persons to the most complete exposure. However much they may desire retirement, and aim to conceal themselves and their movements from the popular gaze, the public have a right to ferret them out, and bring their conduct before the proper tribunals of the country for investigation. Sir, you will undoubtedly make the proper application of these generally admitted principles, and will easily see the light in which you are regarded by me; I will not therefore manifest ill temper, by calling you hard names. I know you to be a man of some intelligence, and can readily determine the precise estimate which I entertain of your character. I may therefore indulge in language which may seem to others indirect and ambiguous, and yet be quite well understood by yourself.

I have selected this day on which to address you, because it is the anniversary of my emancipation; and knowing no better way, I am led to this as the best mode of celebrating that truly important event. Just ten years ago this beautiful September morning, yon bright sun beheld me a slave—a poor degraded chattel—trembling at the sound of your voice, lamenting that I was a man, and wishing myself a brute. The hopes which I had treasured up for weeks of a safe and successful escape from your grasp, were powerfully confronted at this last hour by dark clouds of doubt and fear, making my person shake and my bosom to heave with the heavy contest between hope and fear. I have no words to describe to you the deep agony of soul which I experienced on that never-to-be-forgotten morning—for I left by daylight. I was making a leap in the dark. The probabilities, so far as I could by reason determine them, were stoutly against the undertaking. The preliminaries and precautions I had adopted previously, all worked badly. I was like one going to war without weapons—ten chances of defeat to one of victory. One in whom I had confided, and one who had promised me assistance, appalled by fear at the trial hour, deserted me, thus leaving the responsibility of success or failure solely with myself. You, sir, can never know my feelings. As I look back to them, I can scarcely realize that I have passed through a scene so trying. Trying, however, as they were, and gloomy as was the prospect, thanks be to the Most High, who is ever the God of the oppressed, at the moment which was to determine my whole earthly career, His grace was sufficient; my mind was made up. I embraced the golden opportunity, took the morning tide at the flood, and a free man, young, active, and strong, is the result.

I have often thought I should like to explain to you the grounds upon which I have justified myself in running away from you. I am almost ashamed to do so now, for by this time you may have discovered them yourself. I will, however, glance at them. When yet but a child about six years old, I imbibed the determination to run away. The very first mental effort that I now remember on my part, was an attempt to solve the mystery—why am I a slave? and with this question my youthful mind was troubled for many days, pressing upon me more heavily at times than others. When I saw the slave-driver whip a slave-woman, cut the blood out of her neck, and heard her piteous cries, I went away into the corner of the fence, wept and pondered over the mystery. I had, through some medium, I know not what, got some idea of God, the Creator of all mankind, the black and the white, and that he had made the blacks to serve the whites as slaves. How he could do this and be *good*, I could not tell. I was not satisfied with this theory, which made God responsible for slavery, for it pained me greatly, and I have wept over it long and often. At one time, your first wife, Mrs. Lucretia, heard me sighing and saw me shedding tears, and asked of me the matter, but I was afraid to tell her. I was puzzled with this question, till one night while sitting in the kitchen, I heard some of the old slaves talking of their parents having been stolen from Africa by white men, and were sold here as slaves. The whole mystery was solved at once. Very soon after this, my Aunt Jinny and Uncle Noah ran away, and the great noise made about it by your father-in-law, made me for the first time acquainted with the fact, that there were free states as well as slave states. From that time, I resolved that I would some day run away. The morality of the act I dispose of as follows: I am myself; you are yourself; we are two distinct persons, equal persons. What you are, I am. You are a man, and so am I. God created both, and made us separate beings. I am not by nature bond to you, or you to me. Nature does not make your existence depend upon me, or mine to depend upon yours. I cannot walk upon your legs, or you upon mine. I cannot breathe for you, or you for me; I must breathe for myself, and you for yourself. We are distinct persons, and are each equally provided with faculties necessary to our individual existence. In leaving you, I took nothing but what belonged to me, and in no way lessened your means for obtaining an honest living. Your faculties remained yours, and mine became useful to their rightful owner. I therefore see no wrong in any part of the transaction. It is true, I went off secretly; but that was more your fault than mine. Had I let you into the secret, you would have defeated the enterprise entirely; but for this, I should have been really glad to have made you acquainted with my intentions to leave.

You may perhaps want to know how I like my present condition. I am free to say, I greatly prefer it to that which I occupied in Maryland. I am, however, by no means prejudiced against the state as such. Its geography, climate, fertility, and products, are such as to make it a very desirable abode for any man; and but for the existence of slavery there, it is not impossible that I might again take up my abode in that state. It is not that I love Maryland less, but freedom more. You will be surprised to learn that people at the north labor under the strange delusion that if the slaves were emancipated at the south, they would flock to the north. So far from this being the case, in that event, you would see many old and familiar faces back again to the south. The fact is, there are few here who would not return to the south in the event of emancipation. We want to live in the land of our birth, and to lay our bones by the side of our fathers; and nothing short of an intense love of personal freedom keeps us from the south. For the sake of this, most of us would live on a crust of bread and a cup of cold water.

Since I left you, I have had a rich experience. I have occupied stations which I never dreamed of when a slave. Three out of the ten years since I left you, I spent as a common laborer on the wharves of New Bedford, Massachusetts. It was there I earned my first free dollar. It was mine. I could spend it as I pleased. I could buy hams or herring with it, without asking any odds of anybody. That was a precious dollar to me. You remember when I used to make seven, or eight, or even nine dollars a week in Baltimore, you would take every cent of it from me every Saturday night, saying that I belonged to you, and my earnings also. I never liked this conduct on your part—to say the best, I thought it a little mean. I would not have served you so. But let that pass. I was a little awkward about counting money in New England fashion when I first landed in New Bedford. I came near betraying myself several times. I caught myself saying phip, for fourpence; and at one time a man actually charged me with being a runaway, whereupon I was silly enough to become one by running away from him, for I was greatly afraid he might adopt measures to get me again into slavery, a condition I then dreaded more than death.

I soon learned, however, to count money, as well as to make it, and got on swimmingly. I married soon after leaving you; in fact, I was engaged to be married before I left you; and instead of finding my companion a burden, she was truly a helpmate. She went to live at service, and I to work on the wharf, and though we toiled hard the first winter, we never lived more happily. After remaining in New Bedford for three years, I met with William Lloyd Garrison, a person of whom you have possibly heard, as he is pretty generally known among slaveholders. He put it into my head that I might make myself serviceable to the cause of the slave, by devoting a portion of my time to telling my own sorrows, and those of other slaves, which had come under my observation. This was the commencement of a higher state of existence than any to which I had ever aspired. I was thrown into society the most pure, enlightened, and benevolent, that the country affords. Among these I have never forgotten you, but have invariably made you the topic of conversation—thus giving you all the notoriety I could do. I need not tell you that the opinion formed of you in these circles is far from being favorable. They have little respect for your honesty, and less for your religion.

But I was going on to relate to you something of my interesting experience. I had not long enjoyed the excellent society to which I have referred, before the light of its excellence exerted a beneficial influence on my mind and heart. Much of my early dislike of white persons was removed, and their manners, habits, and customs, so entirely unlike what I had been used to in the kitchen-quarters on the plantations of the south, fairly charmed me, and gave me a strong disrelish for the coarse and degrading customs of my former condition. I therefore made an effort so to improve my mind and deportment, as to be somewhat fitted to the station to which I seemed almost providentially called. The transition from degradation to respectability was indeed great, and to get from one to the other without carrying some marks of one's former condition, is truly a difficult matter. I would not have you think that I am now entirely clear of all plantation peculiarities, but my friends here, while they entertain the strongest dislike to them, regard me with that charity to which my past life somewhat entitles me, so that my condition in this respect is exceedingly pleasant. So far as my domestic affairs are concerned, I can boast of as comfortable a dwelling as your own. I have an industrious and neat companion, and four dear children—the oldest a girl of nine years, and three fine boys, the oldest eight, the next six, and the youngest four years old. The three oldest are now going regularly to school—two can read and write, and the other can spell, with tolerable correctness, words of two syllables. Dear fellows! they are all in comfortable beds, and are sound asleep, perfectly secure under my own roof. There are no slaveholders here to rend my heart by snatching them from my arms, or blast a mother's dearest hopes by tearing them from her bosom. These dear children are ours—not to work up into rice, sugar, and tobacco, but to watch over, regard, and protect, and to rear them up in the nurture and admonition of the gospel—to train them up in the paths of wisdom and virtue, and, as far as we can, to make them useful to the world and to themselves. Oh! sir, a slaveholder never appears to me so completely an agent of hell, as when I think of and look upon my dear children. It is then that my feelings rise above my control. I meant to have said more with respect to my own prosperity and happiness, but thoughts and feelings which this recital has quickened, unfit me to proceed further in that direction. The grim horrors of slavery rise in all their ghastly terror before me; the wails of millions pierce my heart and chill my blood. I remember the chain, the gag, the bloody whip;

the death-like gloom overshadowing the broken spirit of the fettered bondman; the appalling liability of his being torn away from wife and children, and sold like a beast in the market. Say not that this is a picture of fancy. You well know that I wear stripes on my back, inflicted by your direction; and that you, while we were brothers in the same church, caused this right hand, with which I am now penning this letter, to be closely tied to my left, and my person dragged, at the pistol's mouth, fifteen miles, from the Bay Side to Easton, to be sold like a beast in the market, for the alleged crime of intending to escape from your possession. All this, and more, you remember, and know to be perfectly true, not only of yourself, but of nearly all of the slaveholders around you.

At this moment, you are probably the guilty holder of at least three of my own dear sisters, and my only brother, in bondage. These you regard as your property. They are recorded on your ledger, or perhaps have been sold to human flesh-mongers, with a view to filling your own ever-hungry purse. Sir, I desire to know how and where these dear sisters are. Have you sold them? or are they still in your possession? What has become of them? are they living or dead? And my dear old grandmother, whom you turned out like an old horse to die in the woods—is she still alive? Write and let me know all about them. If my grandmother be still alive, she is of no service to you, for by this time she must be nearly eighty years old—too old to be cared for by one to whom she has ceased to be of service; send her to me at Rochester, or bring her to Philadelphia, and it shall be the crowning happiness of my life to take care of her in her old age. Oh! she was to me a mother and a father, so far as hard toil for my comfort could make her such. Send me my grandmother! that I may watch over and take care of her in her old age. And my sisters—let me know all about them. I would write to them, and learn all I want to know of them, without disturbing you in any way, but that, through your unrighteous conduct, they have been entirely deprived of the power to read and write. You have kept them in utter ignorance, and have therefore robbed them of the sweet enjoyments of writing or receiving letters from absent friends and relatives. Your wickedness and cruelty, committed in this respect on your fellow-creatures, are greater than all the stripes you have laid upon my back or theirs. It is an outrage upon the soul, a war upon the immortal spirit, and one for which you must give account at the bar of our common Father and Creator.

The responsibility which you have assumed in this regard is truly awful, and how you could stagger under it these many years is marvelous. Your mind must have become darkened, your heart hardened, your conscience seared and petrified, or you would have long since thrown off the accursed load, and sought relief at the hands of a sin-forgiving God. How, let me ask, would you look upon me, were I, some dark night, in company with a band of hardened villains, to enter the precincts of your elegant dwelling, and seize the person of your own lovely daughter, Amanda, and carry her off from your family, friends, and all the loved ones of her youth—make her my slave—compel her to work, and I take her wages—place her name on my ledger as property—disregard her personal rights—fetter the powers of her immortal soul by denying her the right and privilege of learning to read and write—feed her coarsely—clothe her scantily, and whip her on the naked back occasionally; more, and still more horrible, leave her unprotected—a degraded victim to the brutal lust of fiendish overseers, who would pollute, blight, and blast her fair soul—rob her of all dignity—destroy her virtue, and annihilate in her person all the graces that adorn the character of virtuous womanhood? I ask, how would you regard me, if such were

my conduct? Oh! the vocabulary of the damned would not afford a word sufficiently infernal to express your idea of my God-provoking wickedness. Yet, sir, your treatment of my beloved sisters is in all essential points precisely like the case I have now supposed. Damning as would be such a deed on my part, it would be no more so than that which you have committed against me and my sisters.

I will now bring this letter to a close; you shall hear from me again unless you let me hear from you. I intend to make use of you as a weapon with which to assail the system of slavery—as a means of concentrating public attention on the system, and deepening the horror of trafficking in the souls and bodies of men. I shall make use of you as a means of exposing the character of the American church and clergy—and as a means of bringing this guilty nation, with yourself, to repentance. In doing this, I entertain no malice toward you personally. There is no roof under which you would be more safe than mine, and there is nothing in my house which you might need for your comfort, which I would not readily grant. Indeed, I should esteem it a privilege to set you an example as to how mankind ought to treat each other.

I am your fellow-man, but not your slave.

HENRY DAVID THOREAU
Civil Disobedience

There will never be a really free and enlightened State until the State comes to recognize the individual as a higher and independent power, from which all its own power and authority are derived, and treats him accordingly.

Henry David Thoreau (1817-1862) was born in Concord, Massachusetts, and graduated from Harvard College. He soon met and gained employment with Ralph Waldo Emerson, who introduced Thoreau to transcendentalism and encouraged him to pursue his writing interests. "Civil Disobedience," the most famous social protest ever written, is an account of Thoreau's refusal to pay poll taxes as a means of protesting the U.S. government's acceptance of slavery and involvement in a war against Mexico which Thoreau considered to be imperialistic. His nonconformity earned him a night in jail, and he was released when a relative paid the tax for him. Thoreau's doctrine of passive resistance became the model for such reformers as Leo Tolstoy of Russia, Mahatma Gandhi of India, and Martin Luther King, Jr. during the civil rights movement.

I heartily accept the motto, "That government is best which governs least;" and I should like to see it acted up to more rapidly and systematically. Carried out, it finally amounts to this, which also I believe—"That government is best which governs not at all;" and when men are prepared for it, that will be the kind of government which they will have. Government is at best but an expedient; but most governments are usually, and all governments are sometimes, inexpedient. The objections which have been brought against a standing army, and they are many and weighty, and deserve to prevail, may also at last be brought against a standing government. The standing army is only an arm of the standing government. The government itself, which is only the mode which the people have chosen to execute their will, is equally liable to be abused and perverted before the people can act through it. Witness the present Mexican war, the work of comparatively a few individuals using the standing government as their tool; for in the outset, the people would not have consented to this measure.

This American government—what is it but a tradition, though a recent one, endeavoring to transmit itself unimpaired to posterity, but each instant losing some of its integrity? It has not the vitality and force of a single living man; for a single man can bend it to his will. It is a sort of wooden gun to the people themselves. But it is not the less necessary for this; for the people must have some complicated machinery or other, and hear its din, to satisfy that idea of government which they have. Governments show thus how successfully men can be imposed upon, even impose on themselves, for their own advantage. It is excellent, we must all allow; yet this government never of itself furthered any enterprise, but by the alacrity with which it got out of its way. *It* does not keep the country free. *It* does not settle the West. *It* does not educate. The character inherent in the American people has done all that has been accomplished; and it would have done somewhat more, if the government had not sometimes got in its way. For government is an expedient, by which men would fain succeed in letting one another alone; and, as has been said, when it is most expedient, the governed are most let alone by it. Trade and commerce, if they were not made of India rubber, would never manage to bounce over obstacles which legislators are continually putting in their way; and if one were to judge these men wholly by the effects of their actions and not partly by their intentions, they would deserve to be classed and punished with those mischievous persons who put obstructions on the railroads.

But, to speak practically and as a citizen, unlike those who call themselves no-government men, I ask for, not at once no government, but *at once* a better government. Let every man make known what kind of government would command his respect, and that will be one step toward obtaining it.

After all, the practical reason why, when the power is once in the hands of the people, a majority are permitted, and for a long period continue, to rule is not because they are most likely to be in the right, nor because this seems fairest to the minority, but because they are physically the strongest. But a government in which the majority rule in all cases can not be based on justice, even as far as men understand it. Can there not be a government in which the majorities do not virtually decide right and wrong, but conscience?—in which majorities decide only those questions to which the rule of expediency is applicable? Must the citizen ever for a moment, or in the least degree, resign his conscience to the legislator? Why has every man a conscience then? I think that we should be men first, and subjects afterward. It is not desirable to cultivate a respect for the law, so much as for the right. ...

How does it become a man to behave toward the American government today? I answer, that he cannot without disgrace be associated with it. I cannot for an instant recognize that political organization as *my* government which is the *slave's* government also.

All men recognize the right of revolution; that is, the right to refuse allegiance to, and to resist, the government, when its tyranny or its inefficiency are great and unendurable. But almost all say that such is not the case now. But such was the case, they think, in the Revolution of '75. If one were to tell me that this was a bad government because it taxed certain foreign commodities brought to its ports, it is most probable that I should not make an ado about it, for I can do without them. All machines have their friction; and possibly this does enough good to counter-balance the evil. At any rate, it is a great evil to make a stir about it. But when the friction comes to have its machine, and oppression and robbery are organized, I say, let us not have such a machine any longer. In other words, when a sixth of the population of a nation which has undertaken to be the refuge of liberty are slaves, and a whole country is unjustly overrun and conquered by a foreign army, and subjected to military law, I think that it is not too soon for honest men to rebel and revolutionize. What makes this duty the more urgent is that fact that the country so overrun is not our own, but ours is the invading army. ...

Practically speaking, the opponents to a reform in Massachusetts are not a hundred thousand politicians at the South, but a hundred thousand merchants and farmers here, who are more interested in commerce and agriculture than they are in humanity, and are not prepared to do justice to the slave and to Mexico, *cost what it may*. I quarrel not with far-off foes, but with those who, neat at home, co-operate with, and do the bidding of, those far away, and without whom the latter would be harmless. We are accustomed to say, that the mass of men are unprepared; but improvement is slow, because the few are not as materially wiser or better than the many. It is not so important that many should be good as you, as that there be some absolute goodness somewhere; for that will leaven the whole lump. There are thousands who are *in opinion* opposed to slavery and to the war, who yet in effect do nothing to put an end to them; who, esteeming themselves children of Washington and Franklin, sit down with their hands in their pockets, and say that they know not what to do, and do nothing; who even postpone the question of freedom to the question of free trade, and quietly read the prices-current along with the latest advices from Mexico, after dinner, and, it may be, fall asleep over them both. …

The American has dwindled into an Odd Fellow—one who may be known by the development of his organ of gregariousness, and a manifest lack of intellect and cheerful self-cilliancy; whose first and chief concern, on coming into the world, is to see that the almshouses are in good repair; and, before yet he has lawfully donned the virile garb, to collect a fund to the support of the widows and orphans that may be; who, in short, ventures to live only by the aid of the Mutual Insurance company, which has promised to bury him decently. …

Unjust laws exist: shall we be content to obey them, or shall we endeavor to amend them, and obey them until we have succeeded, or shall we transgress them at once? Men, generally, under such a government as this, think that they ought to wait until they have persuaded the majority to alter them. They think that, if they should resist, the remedy would be worse than the evil. But it is the fault of the government itself that the remedy *is* worse than the evil. *It* makes it worse. Why is it not more apt to anticipate and provide for reform? Why does it not cherish its wise minority? Why does it cry and resist before it is hurt? Why does it not encourage its citizens to put out its faults, and *do* better than it would have them? Why does it always crucify Christ and excommunicate Copernicus and Luther, and pronounce Washington and Franklin rebels? …

If the injustice is part of the necessary friction of the machine of government, let it go, let it go: perchance it will wear smooth—certainly the machine will wear out. If the injustice has a spring, or a pulley, or a rope, or a crank, exclusively for itself, then perhaps you may consider whether the remedy will not be worse than the evil; but if it is of such a nature that it requires you to be the agent of injustice to another, then I say, break the law. Let your life be a counter-friction to stop the machine. What I have to do is to see, at any rate, that I do not lend myself to the wrong which I condemn.

As for adopting the ways which the State has provided for remedying the evil, I know not of such ways. They take too much time, and a man's life will be gone. I have other affairs to attend to. I came into this world, not chiefly to make this a good place to live in, but to live in it, be it good or bad. A man has not everything to do, but something; and because he cannot do *every thing*, it is not necessary that he should do *something* wrong. It is not my business to be petitioning the Governor or the Legislature any more than it is theirs to petition me; and if they should not hear my petition, what should I do then? But in this case the State has provided no way: its very Constitution is the evil. This may seem to be harsh and stubborn and unconcilliatory; but it is to treat with the utmost kindness and consideration the only spirit that can appreciate or deserves it. So is all change for the better, like birth and death which convulse the body.

I do not hesitate to say, that those who call themselves Abolitionists should at once effectually withdraw their support, both in person and property, from the government of Massachusetts, and not wait till they constitute a majority of one, before they suffer the right to prevail through them. I think that it is enough if they have God on their side, without waiting for that other one. Moreover, any man more right than his neighbors constitutes a majority of one already. …

Under a government which imprisons unjustly, the true place for a just man is also a prison. The proper place today, the only place which Massachusetts has provided for her freer and less despondent spirits, is in her prisons, to be put out and locked out of the State by her own act, as they have already put themselves out by their principles. It is there that the fugitive slave, and the Mexican prisoner on parole, and the Indian come to plead the wrongs of his race should find them; on that separate but more free and honorable ground, where the State places those who are not *with* her, but *against* her—the only house in a slave State in which a free man can abide with honor. If any think that their influence would be lost there, and their voices no longer afflict the ear of the State, that they would not be as an enemy within its walls, they do not know by how much truth is stronger than error, nor how much more eloquently and effectively he can combat injustice who has experienced a little in his own person. Cast your whole vote, not a strip of paper merely, but your whole influence. A minority is powerless while it conforms to the majority; it is not even a minority then; but it is irresistible when it clogs by its whole weight. If the alternative is to keep all just men in prison, or give up war and slavery, the State will not hesitate which to choose. If a thousand men were not to pay their tax bills this year, that would not be a violent and bloody measure, as it would be to pay them, and enable the State to commit violence and shed innocent blood. This is, in fact, the definition of a peaceable revolution, if any such is possible. If the tax-gatherer, or any other public officer, asks me, as one has done, "But what shall I do?" my answer is, "If you really wish to do anything, resign your office." When the subject has refused allegiance, and the officer has resigned from office, then the revolution is accomplished. But even suppose blood shed when the conscience is wounded? Through this wound a man's real manhood and immortality flow out, and he bleeds to an everlasting death. I see this blood flowing now. …

I have paid no poll tax for six years. I was put into a jail once on this account, for one night; and, as I stood considering the walls of solid stone, two or three feet thick, the door of wood and iron, a foot thick, and the iron grating which strained the light, I could not help being struck with the foolishness of that institution which treated me as if I were mere flesh and blood and bones, to be locked up. I wondered that it should have concluded at length that this was the best use it could put me to, and had never thought to avail itself of my services in some way. I saw that, if there was a wall of stone between me and my townsmen, there was a still more difficult one to climb or break through before they could get to be as free as I was. I did not for a moment feel confined, and the walls seemed a great waste of stone and mortar. I felt as if I alone of all my townsmen had paid my tax. They plainly did not know how to treat me, but behaved like persons who are underbred. In every threat and in every compliment there was a blunder; for they thought that my chief desire was to stand the other side of that stone wall. I could not but smile to see how

industriously they locked the door on my meditations, which followed them out again without let or hindrance, and *they* were really all that was dangerous. As they could not reach me, they had resolved to punish my body; just as boys, if they cannot come at some person against whom they have a spite, will abuse his dog. I saw that the State was half-witted, that it was timid as a lone woman with her silver spoons, and that it did not know its friends from its foes, and I lost all my remaining respect for it, and pitied it.

Thus the state never intentionally confronts a man's sense, intellectual or moral, but only his body, his senses. It is not armed with superior wit or honesty, but with superior physical strength. I was not born to be forced. I will breathe after my own fashion. Let us see who is the strongest. What force has a multitude? They only can force me who obey a higher law than I. They force me to become like themselves. I do not hear of *men* being *forced* to live this way or that by masses of men. What sort of life were that to live? When I meet a government which says to me, "Your money or your life," why should I be in haste to give it my money? It may be in a great strait, and not know what to do: I cannot help that. It must help itself; do as I do. It is not worth the while to snivel about it. I am not responsible for the successful working of the machinery of society. I am not the son of the engineer. I perceive that, when an acorn and a chestnut fall side by side, the one does not remain inert to make way for the other, but both obey their own laws, and spring and grow and flourish as best they can, till one, perchance, overshadows and destroys the other. If a plant cannot live according to nature, it dies; and so a man. …

I do not wish to quarrel with any man or nation. I do not wish to split hairs, to make fine distinctions, or set myself up as better than my neighbors. I seek rather, I may say, even an excuse for conforming to the laws of the land. I am but too ready to conform to them. Indeed, I have reason to suspect myself on this head; and each year, as the tax-gatherer comes round, I find myself disposed to review the acts and position of the general and State governments, and the spirit of the people to discover a pretext for conformity. …

I believe that the State will soon be able to take all my work of this sort out of my hands, and then I shall be no better a patriot than my fellow-countrymen. Seen from a lower point of view, the Constitution, with all its faults, is very good; the law and the courts are very respectable; even this State and this American government are, in many respects, very admirable, and rare things, to be thankful for, such as a great many have described them; but seen from a point of view a little higher, they are what I have described them; seen from a higher still, and the highest, who shall say what they are, or that they are worth looking at or thinking of at all?

However, the government does not concern me much, and I shall bestow the fewest possible thoughts on it. It is not many moments that I live under a government, even in this world. If a man is thought-free, fancy-free, imagination-free, that which *is not* never for a long time appearing *to be* to him, unwise rulers or reformers cannot fatally interrupt him. ...

The authority of government, even such as I am willing to submit to—for I will cheerfully obey those who know and can do better than I, and in many things even those who neither know nor can do so well—is still an impure one: to be strictly just, it must have the sanction and consent of the governed. It can have no pure right over my person and property but what I concede to it. The progress from an absolute to a limited monarchy, from a limited monarchy to a democracy, is a progress toward a true respect for the individual. Even the Chinese philosopher was wise enough to regard the individual as the basis of the empire. Is a democracy, such as we know it, the last improvement possible in government? Is it not possible to take a step further towards recognizing and organizing the rights of man? There will never be a really free and enlightened State until the State comes to recognize the individual as a higher and independent power, from which all its own power and authority are derived, and treats him accordingly. I please myself with imagining a State at last which can afford to be just to all men, and to treat the individual with respect as a neighbor; which even would not think it inconsistent with its own repose if a few were to live aloof from it, not meddling with it, nor embraced by it, who fulfilled all the duties of neighbors and fellow men. A State which bore this kind of fruit, and suffered it to drop off as fast as it ripened, would prepare the way for a still more perfect and glorious State, which I have also imagined, but not yet anywhere seen.

HENRY DAVID THOREAU

Walden

I went to the woods because I wished to live deliberately, to front only the essential facts of life, and see if I could not learn what it had to teach, and not, when I came to die, discover that I had not lived.

In 1845, Thoreau built a cabin on Emerson's land on Walden Pond near Concord. He lived there for two years—not withdrawn from society, but on the outskirts of society—where he wrote *Walden* (1854), an account of a man who, surrounded by nature, had stripped life down to its essentials. *Walden* was one of only two books Thoreau published in his lifetime and, like most of his works, was not a financial success. It has since come to be recognized as one of the classics in American literature and the work most responsible for Thoreau's literary reputation.

... Some of you, we all know, are poor, find it hard to live, are sometimes, as it were, gasping for breath. I have no doubt that some of you who read this book are unable to pay for all the dinners which you have actually eaten, or for the coats and shoes which are fast wearing or are already worn out, and have come to this page to spend borrowed or stolen time, robbing your creditors of an hour. It is very evident what mean and sneaking lives many of you live, for my sight has been whetted by experience; always on the limits, trying to get into business and trying to get out of debt, a very ancient slough, called by the Latins *aes alienum*, another's brass, for some of their coins were made of brass; still living, and dying, and buried by this other's brass; always promising to pay, promising to pay, tomorrow, and dying today, insolvent; seeking to curry favor, to get custom, by how many modes, only not state-prison offenses; lying, flattering, voting, contracting yourselves into a nutshell of civility or dilating into an atmosphere of thin and vaporous generosity, that you may persuade your neighbor to let you make his shoes, or his hat, or his coat, or his carriage, or import his groceries for him; making yourselves sick, that you may lay up something against a sick day, something to be tucked away in an old chest, or in a stocking behind the plastering, or, more safely, in the brick bank; no matter where, no matter how much or how little. ...

The mass of men lead lives of quiet desperation. What is called resignation is confirmed desperation. From the desperate city you go into the desperate country, and have to console yourself with the bravery of minks and muskrats. A stereotyped but unconscious despair is concealed even under what are called the games and amusements of mankind. There is no play in them, for this comes after work. But it is a characteristic of wisdom not to do desperate things.

When we consider what, to use the words of the catechism, is the chief end of man, and what are the true necessaries and means of life, it appears as if men had deliberately chosen the common mode of living because they preferred it to any other. Yet they honestly think there is no choice left. But alert and healthy natures remember that the sun rose clear. It is never too late to give up our prejudices. No way of thinking or doing, however ancient, can be trusted without proof. What everybody echoes or in silence passes by as true today may turn out to be falsehood tomorrow, mere smoke of opinion, which some had trusted for a cloud that would sprinkle fertilizing rain on their fields. What old people say you cannot do, you try and find that you can. Old deeds for old people, and new deeds for new. Old people did not know enough once, perchance, to fetch fresh fuel to keep the fire a-going; new people put a little dry wood under a pot, and are whirled round the globe with the speed of birds, in a way to kill old people, as the phrase is. Age is no better, hardly so well, qualified for an instructor as youth, for it has not profited so much as it has lost. One may almost doubt if the wisest man has learned anything of absolute value by living. Practically, the old have no very important advice to give the young, their own experience has been so partial, and their lives have been such miserable failures, for private reasons, as they must believe; and it may be that they have some faith left which belies that experience, and they are only less young than they were. I have lived some thirty years on this planet, and I have yet to hear the first syllable of valuable or even earnest advice from my seniors. They have told me nothing, and probably cannot tell me anything to the purpose. Here is life, an experiment to a great extent untried by me; but it does not avail me that they have tried it. If I have any

experience which I think valuable, I am sure to reflect that this my Mentors said nothing about. ...

When first I took up my abode in the woods, that is, began to spend my nights as well as days there, which, by accident, was on Independence Day, or the Fourth of July, 1845, my house was not finished for winter, but was merely a defence against the rain, without plastering or chimney, the walls being of rough, weather-stained boards, with wide chinks, which made it cool at night. The upright white hewn studs and freshly planed door and window casings gave it a clean and airy look, especially in the morning, when its timbers were saturated with dew, so that I fancied that by noon some sweet gum would exude from them. To my imagination it retained throughout the day more or less of this auroral character, reminding me of a certain house on a mountain which I had visited a year before. This was an airy and unplastered cabin, fit to entertain a traveling god, and where a goddess might trail her garments. The winds which passed over my dwelling were such as sweep over the ridges of mountains, bearing the broken strains, or celestial parts only, of terrestrial music. The morning wind forever blows, the poem of creation is uninterrupted; but few are the ears that hear it. Olympus is but the outside of the earth everywhere. ...

I went to the woods because I wished to live deliberately, to front only the essential facts of life, and see if I could not learn what it had to teach, and not, when I came to die, discover that I had not lived. I did not wish to live what was not life, living is so dear; nor did I wish to practise resignation, unless it was quite necessary. I wanted to live deep and suck out all the marrow of life, to live so sturdily and Spartan-like as to put to rout all that was not life, to cut a broad swath and shave close, to drive life into a corner, and reduce it to its lowest terms, and, if it proved to be mean, why then to get the whole and genuine meanness of it, and publish its meanness to the world; or if it were sublime, to know it by experience, and be able to give a true account of it in my next excursion. For most men, it appears to me, are in a strange uncertainty about it, whether it is of the devil or of God, and have *somewhat hastily* concluded that it is the chief end of man here to "glorify God and enjoy him forever."

Still we live meanly, like ants; though the fable tells us that we were long ago changed into men; like pygmies we fight with cranes; it is error upon error, and clout upon clout, and our best virtue has for its occasion a superfluous and evitable wretchedness. Our life is frittered away by detail. An honest man has hardly need to count more than his ten fingers, or in extreme cases he may add his ten toes, and lump the rest. Simplicity, simplicity, simplicity! I say, let your affairs be as two or three, and not a hundred or a thousand; instead of a million count half a dozen, and keep your accounts on your thumb-nail. In the midst of this chopping sea of civilized life, such are the clouds and storms and quicksands and thousand-and-one items to be allowed for, that a man has to live, if he would not founder and go to the bottom and not make his port at all, by dead reckoning, and he must be a great calculator indeed who succeeds. Simplify, simplify. Instead of three meals a day, if it be necessary eat but one; instead of a hundred dishes, five; and reduce other things in proportion. Our life is like a German Confederacy, made up of petty states, with its boundary forever fluctuating, so that even a German cannot tell you how it is bounded at any moment. The nation itself, with all its so-called internal improvements, which, by the way are all external and superficial, is just such an unwieldy and overgrown establishment, cluttered with furniture and tripped up by its own traps, ruined by luxury and heedless expense, by want of calculation and a worthy aim, as the million households in the land; and the only cure for it, as for them, is in a rigid economy, a stern and more than Spartan simplicity of life and elevation of purpose. It lives too fast. Men think that it is essential that the *Nation* have commerce, and export ice, and talk through a telegraph, and ride thirty miles an hour, without a doubt, whether *they* do or not; but whether we should live like baboons or like men, is a little uncertain. If we do not get out sleepers, and forge rails, and devote days and nights to the work, but go to tinkering upon our lives to improve them, who will build railroads? And if railroads are not built, how shall we get to heaven in season? But if we stay at home and mind our business, who will want railroads? We do not ride on the railroad; it rides upon us. Did you ever think what those sleepers are that underlie the railroad? Each one is a man, an Irishman, or a Yankee man. The rails are laid on them, and they are covered with sand, and the cars run smoothly over them. They are sound sleepers, I assure you. And every few years a new lot is laid down and run over; so that, if some have the pleasure of riding on a rail, others have the misfortune to be ridden upon. And when they run over a man that is walking in his sleep, a supernumerary sleeper in the wrong position, and wake him up, they suddenly stop the cars, and make a hue and cry about it, as if this were an exception. I am glad to know that it takes a gang of men for every five miles to keep the sleepers down and level in their beds as it is, for this is a sign that they may sometime get up again.

Why should we live with such hurry and waste of life? We are determined to be starved before we are hungry. Men say that a stitch in time saves nine, and so they take a thousand stitches today to save nine tomorrow. As for *work*, we haven't any of any consequence. We have the Saint Vitus' dance, and cannot possibly keep our heads still. If I should only give a few pulls at the parish bell-rope, as for a fire, that is, without setting the bell, there is hardly a man on his farm in the outskirts of Concord, notwithstanding that press of engagements which was his excuse so many times this morning, nor a boy, nor a woman, I might almost say, but would forsake all and follow that sound, not mainly to save property from the flames, but, if we will confess the truth, much more to see it burn, since burn it must, and we, be it known, did not set it on fire—or to see it put out, and have a hand in it, if that is done as handsomely; yes, even if it were the parish church itself. Hardly a man takes a half-hour's nap after dinner, but when he wakes he holds up his head and asks, "What's the news?" as if the rest of mankind had stood his sentinels. Some give directions to be waked every half-hour, doubtless for no other purpose; and then, to pay for it, they tell what they have dreamed. After a night's sleep the news is as indispensable as the breakfast. "Pray tell me anything new that has happened to a man anywhere on this globe"—and he reads it over his coffee and rolls, that a man has had his eyes gouged out this morning on the Wachito River; never dreaming the while that he lives in the dark unfathomed mammoth cave of this world, and has but the rudiment of an eye himself.

For my part, I could easily do without the post-office. I think that there are very few important communications made through it. To speak critically, I never received more than one or two letters in my life—I wrote this some years ago—that were worth the postage. The penny-post is, commonly, an institution through which you seriously offer a man that penny for his thoughts which is so often safely offered in jest. And I am sure that I never read any memorable news in a newspaper. If we read of one man robbed, or murdered, or killed by accident, or one house burned, or one vessel wrecked, or one steamboat blown up, or one cow run over on the Western Railroad, or one mad dog killed, or one lot of grasshoppers in the winter—we never need read of another. One is enough. If you are acquainted with the principle, what do you care for a myriad instances and applications? To a philosopher all *news*, as it is called, is gossip, and they who edit and read it are old women over their tea. …

Let us spend one day as deliberately as Nature, and not be thrown off the track by every nutshell and mosquito's wing that falls on the rails. Let us rise early and fast, or break fast, gently and without perturbation; let company come and let company go, let the bells ring and the children cry—determined to make a day of it. Why should we knock under and go with the stream? Let us not be upset and overwhelmed in that terrible rapid and whirlpool called a dinner, situated in the meridian shallows. Weather this danger and you are safe, for the rest of the way is down hill. With unrelaxed nerves, with morning vigor, sail by it, looking another way, tied to the mast like Ulysses. If the engine whistles, let it whistle till it is hoarse for its pains. If the bell rings, why should we run? We will consider what kind of music they are like. Let us settle ourselves, and work and wedge our feet downward through the mud and slush of opinion, and prejudice, and tradition, and delusion, and appearance, that alluvion which covers the globe, through Paris and London, through New York and Boston and Concord, through Church and State, through poetry and philosophy and religion, till we come to a hard bottom and rocks in place, which we can call *reality*, and say, This is, and no mistake. … Be it life or death, we crave only reality. If we are really dying, let us hear the rattle in our throats and feel cold in the extremities; if we are alive, let us go about our business.

Time is but the stream I go a-fishing in. I drink at it; but while I drink I see the sandy bottom and detect how shallow it is. Its thin current slides away, but eternity remains. I would drink deeper; fish in the sky, whose bottom is pebbly with stars. I cannot count one. I know not the first letter of the alphabet. I have always been regretting that I was not as wise as the day I was born. The intellect is a cleaver; it discerns and rifts its way into the secret of things. I do not wish to be any more busy with my hands than is necessary. My head is hands and feet. I feel all my best faculties concentrated in it. My instinct tells me that my head is an organ for burrowing, as some creatures use their snout and fore paws, and with it I would mine and burrow my way through these hills. I think that the richest vein is somewhere hereabouts; so by the divining-rod and thin rising vapors I judge; and here I will begin to mine. …

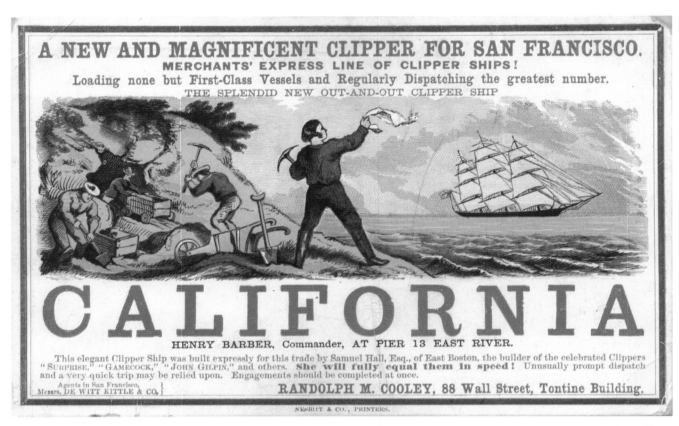

The above advertisement for sailing to California appeared at the onset of the California Gold Rush, which began on January 24, 1848, when gold was discovered at John Sutter's mill in Coloma. News of the discovery quickly spread and was confirmed by President James K. Polk in a December 5 address to Congress. By spring 1849, the stampede was well underway. An estimated 300,000 people came rushing to California from the rest of the United States and abroad. Approximately half this number arrived by sea while the others traveled overland by covered wagon. After a period of rule by the U.S. Army, the burgeoning population wrote a constitution and California was granted statehood in 1850.

CHIEF SEE-YAHTLH

Address to the White Man

The white man will never be alone. Let him be just and deal kindly with my people, for the dead are not altogether powerless.

Chief See-Yahtlh (1780?-1866) was leader of the Duwamish and Suquamish Indian tribes in the Pacific Northwest. On January 12, 1854, he addressed an assemblage of Indians and white settlers at the site of what would become the city of Seattle. The chief directed his speech to Isaac Ingalls Stevens, governor of the Washington Territory, who had been directed by the federal government to buy Indian land and establish reservations. Chief See-Yahtlh signaled acceptance of the governor's offer and expressed a desire for peace, realizing that resistance to the overwhelming strength of the government would be futile. He maintained that the red man and white man "are two distinct races and must ever remain so," but recognized their common destiny, saying, "We *may* be brothers after all." Although armed conflicts still occurred between Indians and white settlers—the battles of Little Bighorn and Wounded Knee among the bloodiest encounters—the American Indian, at this point in history, was no longer vilified as a cruel savage. Instead, American Indians were increasingly looked upon as sympathetic figures relegated to a more domesticated life, inevitable victims of an expanding nation.

The following account of Chief See-Yahtlh's speech was provided by Dr. Henry A. Smith, an early settler of Seattle who served as the chief's translator on that historic occasion. The speech was first printed in the *Seattle Sunday Star* newspaper in 1887 and endures as a moving statement from an Indian leader about the relationship between his people and the land.

Yonder sky, which has wept tears of compassion on our fathers for centuries untold, and which to us looks eternal, may change. Today it is fair; tomorrow it may be overcast with clouds. My words are like stars that never set. What Seattle says, the great chief Washington can rely upon, with as much certainty as our paleface brothers can rely upon the return of the seasons. The son of the white chief says his father sends us greetings of friendship and good will. This is kind, for we know he has little need of our friendship in return, because his people are many. They are like the grass that covers the vast prairies, while my people are few, and resemble the scattering trees of a windswept plain.

The great, and I presume also good, white chief sends us word that he wants to buy our lands but is willing to allow us to reserve enough to live on comfortably. This indeed appears generous, for the red man no longer has rights that he need respect, and the offer may be wise, also, for we are no longer in need of a great country. There was a time when our people covered the whole land, as the waves of a wind-ruffled sea cover its shell floor. But that time has long since passed away with the greatness of tribes now almost forgotten. I will not mourn over our untimely decay, nor reproach my paleface brothers for hastening it, for we, too, may have been somewhat to blame.

When our young men grow angry at some real or imaginary wrong and disfigure their faces with black paint, their hearts also are disfigured and turn black, and then their cruelty is relentless and knows no bounds, and our old men are not able to restrain them.

But let us hope that hostilities between the red man and his paleface brothers may never return. We would have everything to lose and nothing to gain.

True it is that revenge, with our young braves, is considered gain, even at the cost of their own lives, but old men who stay at home in times of war, and old women who have sons to lose, know better.

Our great father in Washington, for I presume he is now our father as well as yours, since George has moved his boundaries to the north; our great and good father, I say, sends us word by his son, who, no doubt, is a great chief among his people, that if we do as he desires, he will protect us. His brave armies will be to us a bristling wall of strength, and his great ships of war will fill our harbors so that our ancient enemies far to the northward, the Simsians and Hydas, will no longer frighten our women and old men. Then he will be our father and we will be his children.

But can this ever be? Your God loves your people and hates mine; he folds his strong arms lovingly around the white man and leads him as a father leads his infant son, but he has forsaken his red children; he makes your people wax strong every day, and soon they will fill the land; while my people are ebbing away like a fast receding tide that will never flow again. The white man's God cannot love his red children, or he would protect them. They seem to be orphans and can look nowhere for help. How, then, can we become brothers? How can your father become our father and bring us prosperity and awaken in us dreams of returning greatness?

Your God seems to be partial. He came to the white man. We never saw him; never even heard his voice; he gave the white man laws, but he had no word for his red children, whose teeming millions filled this vast continent as the stars fill the firmament. No, we are two distinct races and must ever remain so. There is little in common between us. The ashes of our ancestors are sacred, and their final resting place is hallowed ground, while you wander away from the tombs of your fathers seemingly without regret.

Your religion was written on tables of stone by the iron finger of an angry God, lest you might forget it. The red man could never remember nor comprehend it.

Our religion is the traditions of our ancestors, the dreams of our old men, given them by the great Spirit, and the visions of our sachems, and is written in the hearts of our people.

Your dead cease to love you and the homes of their nativity as soon as they pass the portals of the tomb. They wander far off beyond the stars, are soon forgotten, and never return. Our dead never forget the beautiful world that gave them being. They still love its winding rivers, its great mountains and its sequestered vales, and they ever yearn in tenderest affection over the lonely-hearted living and often return to visit and comfort them.

Day and night cannot dwell together. The red man has ever fled the approach of the white man, as the changing mists on the mountainside flee before the blazing morning sun.

However, your proposition seems a just one, and I think my folks will accept it and will retire to the reservation you offer them, and we will dwell apart and in peace, for the words of the great white chief seem to be the voice of nature speaking to my people out of the thick darkness that is fast gathering around them like a dense fog floating inward from a midnight sea.

It matters but little where we pass the remainder of our days. They are not many. The Indian's night promises to be dark. No bright star hovers about the horizon. Sad-voiced winds moan in the distance. Some grim Nemesis of our race is on the red man's trail, and wherever he goes he will still hear the sure approaching footsteps of the fell destroyer and prepare to meet his doom, as does the wounded doe that hears the approaching footsteps of the hunter. A few more moons, a few

more winters, and not one of all the mighty hosts that once filled this broad land or that now roam in fragmentary bands through these vast solitudes will remain to weep over the tombs of a people once as powerful and as hopeful as your own.

But why should we repine? Why should I murmur at the fate of my people? Tribes are made up of individuals and are no better than they. Men come and go like the waves of the sea. A tear, a tamanawus, a dirge, and they are gone from our longing eyes forever. Even the white man, whose God walked and talked with him, as friend to friend, is not exempt from the common destiny. We *may* be brothers after all. We shall see.

We will ponder your proposition, and when we have decided we will tell you. But should we accept it, I here and now make this the first condition: That we will not be denied the privilege, without molestation, of visiting at will the graves of our ancestors and friends. Every part of this country is sacred to my people. Every hillside, every valley, ever plain and grove has been hallowed by some fond memory or some sad experience of my tribe. Even the rocks that seem to lie dumb as they swelter in the sun along the silent seashore in solemn grandeur thrill with memories of past events connected with the fate of my people, and the very dust under your feet responds more lovingly to our footsteps than to yours, because it is the ashes of our ancestors, and our bare feet are conscious of the sympathetic touch, for the soil is rich with the life of our kindred.

The sable braves, and fond mothers, and glad-hearted maidens, and the little children who lived and rejoiced here, and whose very names are now forgotten, still love these solitudes, and their deep fastnesses at eventide grow shadowy with the presence of dusky spirits. And when the last red man shall have perished from the earth and his memory among white men shall have become a myth, these shores shall swarm with the invisible dead of my tribe, and when your children's children shall think themselves alone in the field, the store, the shop, upon the highway or in the silence of the woods, they will not be alone.

In all the earth there is no place dedicated to solitude. At night, when the streets of your cities and villages shall be silent, and you think them deserted, they will throng with the returning hosts that once filled and still love this beautiful land. The white man will never be alone. Let him be just and deal kindly with my people, for the dead are not altogether powerless. Dead, did I say? There is no death, only a change of worlds.

STEPHEN FOSTER

Oh! Susanna, Old Folks at Home, Camptown Races, and My Old Kentucky Home, Good Night

Stephen Collins Foster (1826-1864), one of America's greatest songwriters, was born on July 4, 1826, in what is now Pittsburgh, Pennsylvania. Yielding to family pressure, he worked briefly as a bookkeeper in his brother's Cincinnati business. His interest in music, however, could not be repressed. In a life cut short by poverty and alcoholism, Foster wrote the words and music for nearly 200 songs, including "Jeannie with the Light Brown Hair," "Old Black Joe," and "Beautiful Dreamer." "Oh! Susanna," written in 1846, was a favorite of the forty-niners during the California gold rush. "Camptown Races" and "Old Folks at Home," also known as "Swanee River," served as popular features in minstrel shows throughout the country. Foster's most recognized song, and one of the surprising few that was a financial success, was "My Old Kentucky Home, Good Night." The official song of the Bluegrass State was written by Foster while visiting the mansion of his uncle, Senator Rowan, in Bardstown, Kentucky. Each year, thousands of tourists visit the mansion (My Old Kentucky Home) on Federal Hill and attend a performance of *The Stephen Foster Story*, a musical which has been performed in such far away venues as Japan.

Oh! Susanna

I come from Alabama with a banjo on my knee,
I'm gone to Lou'siana,
My true love for to see,
It rained all night the day I left,
The weather it was dry,
The sun so hot I froze to death;
Susanna, don't you cry.

Chorus:

Oh! Susanna, don't you cry for me,
I come from Alabama with a banjo on my knee.

I had a dream the other night,
When everything was still,
I thought I saw Susanna dear,
a'coming down the hill.
The buckwheat cake was in her mouth,
The tear was in her eye.
Says I, I'm coming from the South,
Susanna, don't you cry.

I soon will be in New Orleans,
And then I'll look all 'round,
And when I find Susanna,
I'll fall upon the ground.
But if I do not find her,
This darkey'll surely die,
And when I'm dead and buried,
Susanna, don't you cry.

Old Folks at Home

'Way down upon the Swanee River,
Far far away,
There's where my heart is turning ever,
There's where the old folks stay.
All up and down the whole creation,
Sadly I roam,
Still longing for the old plantation,
And for the old folks at home.

Chorus:

All the world is sad and dreary
Everywhere I roam,
Oh, darkies, how my heart grows weary,
Far from the old folks at home.

All 'round the little farm I wandered
When I was young,
Then many happy days I squandered,
Many the songs I sung.
When I was playing with my brother
Happy was I.
Oh! take me to my kind old mother,
There let me live and die.

One little hut among the bushes,
One that I love,
Still sadly to my mem'ry rushes,
No matter where I rove.
Where will I see the bees a-humming
All 'round the comb?
When will I hear the banjo strumming
Down in my good old home?

Camptown Races

De Camptown ladies sing this song,
Doo-da, Doo-da
De Camptown racetrack's two miles long
Oh, de doo-da day

Chorus:
 Gwine to run all night
 Gwine to run all day
 I bet my money on a bob-tailed nag
 Somebody bet on the gray

Oh, de long tailed filly and de big black horse,
Doo-da, doo-da
Come to a mud hole and dey all cut across,
Oh, de doo-da day

I went down South with my hat caved in,
Doo-da, doo-da
I came back North with a pocket full of tin
Oh, de doo-da day

My Old Kentucky Home, Good Night

The sun shines bright in the old Kentucky home
'Tis summer, the darkies are gay,
The corn top's ripe and the meadow's in the bloom
While the birds make music all the day.
The young folks roll on the little cabin floor
All merry, all happy, and bright.
By'n by hard times comes a-knocking at the door,
Then my old Kentucky home, good night.

Chorus:
 Weep no more, my lady,
 Oh weep no more today.
 We will sing one song for the old Kentucky home,
 For the old Kentucky home far away.

They hunt no more for the 'possum and the coon
On meadow, the hill and the shore.
They sing no more by the glimmer of the moon
On the bench by that old cabin door.
The day goes by like a shadow o'er the heart
With sorrow where all was delight.
The time has come when the darkies have to part
Then my old Kentucky home, good night.

The head must bow and the back will have to bend
Wherever the darky may go.
A few more days and the trouble all will end
In the field where sugar-canes may grow.
A few more days for to tote the weary load.
No matter, 'twill never be light.
A few more days till we totter on the road,
Then my old Kentucky home, good night.

* * *

Peter F. Rothermel's painting, The United States Senate, A.D. 1850, *shows Senator Henry Clay of Kentucky addressing the U.S. Senate. Arguing for what came to be known as the Compromise of 1850, Clay proposed a series of resolutions that he saw as amenable to both Northern and Southern viewpoints. As with the Missouri Compromise of 1820, he successfully quieted the controversy between Northerners and Southerners over the expansion of slavery and delayed secession and civil war for another decade. Upon his death in 1852, Clay became the first person to lie in state in the United States Capitol. "I know no South, no North, no East, no West, to which I owe any allegiance," said Clay. "The Union, sir, is my country."*

A House Divided

DAVID WALKER

Walker's Appeal

They are so happy to keep in ignorance and degradation, and to receive the homage and the labor of the slaves, they forget that God rules in the armies of heaven and among the inhabitants of the earth, having his ears continually open to the cries, tears, and groans of his oppressed people.

David Walker (1785-1830), the son of a slave father and free mother, was born in Wilmington, North Carolina. As a young man, Walker went north and settled in Boston, where he found employment as a clothier and set about writing abolitionist papers and aiding fugitive slaves. In 1829, he published *Walker's Appeal in Four Articles, Together with a Preamble to the Coloured Citizens of the World, but in Particular and very Expressly to Those of the United States of America*. The work was banned in the Southern states and slaves caught possessing his essay were subject to death. Several bounties were placed on Walker's head and, in 1830, he was found dead near his shop, the apparent victim of poisoning.

Walker's appeal was unique from early abolitionist writings in that his argument against slavery was not a political judgment against the institution, but a prediction of its ultimate destruction by the hand of God. Walker expresses hope that slaves and white Americans can one day become a united people, but states that violence is inevitable if slavery is continued.

Having travelled over a considerable portion of these United States, and having, in the course of my travels taken the most accurate observations of things as they exist—the result of my observations has warranted the full and unshakened conviction, that we, (colored people of these United States) are the most degraded, wretched, and abject set of beings that ever lived since the world began, and I pray God, that none like us ever may live again until time shall be no more. They tell us of the Israelites in Egypt, the Helots in Sparta, and of the Roman Slaves, which last, were made up from almost every nation under heaven, whose sufferings under those ancient and heathen nations were, in comparison with ours, under this enlightened and Christian nation, no more than a cypher—or in other words, those heathen nations of antiquity, had but little more among them than the name and form of slavery, while wretchedness and endless miseries were reserved, apparently in a phial, to be poured out upon our fathers, ourselves and our children by *Christian* Americans!

These positions, I shall endeavour, by the help of the Lord, to demonstrate in the course of this *appeal*, to the satisfaction of the most incredulous mind—and may God Almighty who is the father of our Lord Jesus Christ, open your hearts to understand and believe the truth.

The *causes*, my brethren, which produce our wretchedness and miseries, are so very numerous and aggravating, that I believe the pen only of a Josephus or a Plutarch, can well enumerate and explain them. Upon subjects then, of such incomprehensible magnitude, so impenetrable, and so notorious, I shall be obliged to omit a large class of, and content myself with giving you an exposition of a few of those, which do indeed rage to such an alarming pitch, that they cannot but be a perpetual source of terror and dismay to every reflecting mind.

I am fully aware, in making this appeal to my much afflicted and suffering brethren, that I shall not only be assailed by those whose greatest earthly desires are, to keep us in abject ignorance and wretchedness, and who are of the firm conviction that heaven has designed us and our children to be slaves and *beasts of burden* to them and their children. I say, I do not only expect to be held up to the public as an ignorant, impudent and restless disturber of the public peace, by such avaricious creatures, as well as a mover of insubordination—and perhaps put in prison or to death, for giving a superficial exposition of our miseries, and exposing tyrants. But I am persuaded, that many of my brethren, particularly those who are ignorantly in league with slave-holders or tyrants, who acquire their daily bread by the blood and sweat of their more ignorant brethren—and not a few of those too, who are too ignorant to see an inch beyond their noses, will rise up and call me cursed—Yea, the jealous ones among us will perhaps use more abject subtlety by affirming that this work is not worth perusing; that we are well situated and there is no use in trying to better our condition, for we cannot. I will ask one question here.—Can our condition be any worse?—Can it be more mean and abject? If there are any changes, will they not be for the better though they may appear for the worst at first? Can they get us any lower? Where can they get us? They are afraid to treat us worse, for they know well, the day they do it they are gone. But against all accusations which may or can be preferred against me, I appeal to heaven for my motive in writing—who knows that my object is, if possible, to awaken in the breasts of my afflicted, degraded and slumbering brethren, a spirit of inquiry and investigation respecting our miseries and wretchedness in this *Republican Land of Liberty!!!!!*

The sources from which our miseries are derived and on which I shall comment, I shall not combine in one, but shall put them under distinct heads and expose them in their turn; in doing which, keeping truth on my side, and not departing from the strictest rules of morality, I shall endeavor to penetrate, search out, and lay them open for your inspection. If you cannot or will not profit by them, I shall have done *my* duty to you, my country and my God.

And as the inhuman system of *slavery*, is the *source* from which most of our miseries proceed, I shall begin with that *curse to nations;* which has spread terror and devastation through so many nations of antiquity, and which is raging to such a pitch at the present day in Spain and in Portugal. It had one tug in England, in France, and in the United States of America; yet the inhabitants thereof, do not learn wisdom, and erase it entirely from their dwellings and from all with whom they have to do. The fact is, the labor of slaves comes so cheap to the avaricious usurpers, and is (as they think) of such great utility to the country where it exists, that those who are actuated by sordid avarice only, overlook the evils, which will as sure as the Lord lives, follow after their good. In fact, they are so happy to keep in ignorance and degradation, and to receive the homage and the labor of the slaves, they forget that God rules in the armies of heaven and among the inhabitants of the earth, having his ears continually open to the cries, tears, and groans of his oppressed people; and being a just and holy Being will at one day appear fully in behalf of the oppressed, and arrest the progress of the avaricious oppressors; for although the destruction of the oppressors God may not effect by the oppressed, yet the Lord our God will bring other destructions upon them—for not unfrequently will he cause them to rise up one against another, to be split

and divided, and to oppress each other, and sometimes to open hostilities with sword in hand. Some may ask, what is the matter with this enlightened and happy people?—Some say it is the cause of political usurpers, tyrants, oppressors, etc. But has not the Lord an oppressed and suffering people among them? Does the Lord condescend to hear their cries and see their tears in consequence of oppression? Will he let the oppressors rest comfortably and happy always? Will he not cause the very children of the oppressors to rise up against them, and oftimes put them to death? "God works in many ways his wonders to perform. …"

All persons who are acquainted with history, and particularly the Bible, who are not blinded by the God of this world, and are not actuated solely by avarice—who are able to lay aside prejudice long enough to view candidly and impartially, things as they were, are, and probably will be, who are willing to admit that God made man to serve him *alone*, and that man should have no other Lord or Lords but himself—that God Almighty is the *sole proprietor* or *master* of the WHOLE human family, and will not on any consideration admit of a colleague, being unwilling to divide his glory with another.—And who can dispense with prejudice long enough to admit that we are men, notwithstanding our *improminent noses* and *woolly heads*, and believe that we feel for our fathers, mothers, wives and children as well as they do for theirs. …I saw a paragraph, a few years since, in a South Carolina paper, which, speaking of the barbarity of the Turks, said: "The Turks are the most barbarous people in the world—they treat the Greeks more like *brutes* than human beings." And in the same paper was an advertisement, which said: "Eight well built Virginia and Maryland *Negro fellows* and four *wenches* will positively be *sold* this day, to the highest bidder!" And what astonished me still more was, to see in this same *humane* paper!! the cuts of three men, with clubs and budgets on their backs, and an advertisement offering a considerable sum of money for their apprehension and delivery. I declare, it is really amusing to hear the Southerners and Westerners of this country talk about *barbarity*, that it is positively enough to make a man *smile*. …

Men of colour, who are also of sense, for you particularly is my *Appeal* designed. Our more ignorant brethren are not able to penetrate its value. I call upon you therefore to cast your eyes upon the wretchedness of your brethren, and to do your utmost to enlighten them—*go to work and enlighten your brethren!*—Let the Lord see you doing what you can to rescue them and yourselves from degradation. There is a great work for you to do, as trifling as some of you may think of it. You have to prove to the Americans and the world, that we are *Men*, and not *brutes*, as we have been represented, and by millions treated. Remember, to let the aim of your labours among your brethren, and particularly the youths, be the dissemination of education and religion. …

What the American preachers can think of us, I aver this day before my God, I have never been able to define. They have newspapers and monthly periodicals, which they receive in continual succession, but on the pages of which, you will scarcely ever find a paragraph respecting slavery, which is ten thousand times more injurious to this country than all the other evils put together; and which will be the final overthrow of its government, unless something is very speedily done; for their cup is nearly full.—Perhaps they will laugh at or make light of this; but I tell you Americans! that unless you speedily alter your course, *you* and your Country are gone!!!!! For God Almighty will tear up the very face of the earth!!! Will not that very remarkable passage of Scripture be fulfilled on Christian Americans? Hear it Americans!! "He that is unjust, let him be unjust still:—and he which is filthy, let him be filthy still: and he that is righteous, let him be righteous still: and he that is holy, let him be holy still." I hope that the Americans may hear, but I am afraid that they have done us so much injury, and are so firm in the belief that our Creator made us to be an inheritance to them forever, that their hearts will be hardened, so that their destruction may be sure. This language, perhaps, is too harsh for the American's delicate ears. But O Americans! Americans!! I warn you in the name of the Lord (whether you will hear, or forbear,) to repent and reform, or you are ruined!!! Do you think that our blood is hiding from the Lord, because you can hide it from the rest of the world, by sending out missionaries, and by your charitable deeds to the Greeks, Irish, etc.? Will he not publish your secret crimes on the house top? Even here in Boston, pride and prejudice have got to such a pitch, that in the very houses erected to the Lord, they have built little places for the reception of coloured people, where they must sit during meeting, or keep away from the house of God, and the preachers say nothing about it—much less go into the hedges and highways seeking the lost sheep of the house of Israel, and try to bring them in to their Lord and Master. There are not a more wretched, ignorant, miserable and abject set of beings in all the world than the blacks in the southern and western sections of this country, under tyrants and devils. The preachers of America can not see them, but they can send out missionaries to convert the heathens, notwithstanding.... O Americans! Americans!! I call God—I call angels—I call men, to witness, that your *destruction* is at hand, and will be speedily consummated unless you *repent*.

States' Rights

The object of the framers of the Constitution, as disclosed in that address, was not the consolidation of the government, but "the consolidation of the Union." It was not to draw power from the states, in order to transfer it to a great national government, but, in the language of the Constitution itself, "to form a more perfect Union."

In January of 1830, Senators Robert Young Hayne (1791-1839) of South Carolina and Daniel Webster of Massachusetts engaged in "the greatest debate in the history of the Senate." The exchange was sparked by Connecticut Senator Samuel Foot's proposal to limit western land sales. This prompted an angry response from Senator Thomas Hart Benton of Missouri, a staunch defender of Western interests, who accused Foot of being part of a sinister plot to safeguard cheap labor in the Northeast by limiting opportunities in the developing West. Hayne joined the argument on January 19, expressing his view that the national tariff was yet another means by which Northeastern manufacturing interests were using the power of the federal government to serve their own interests at the expense of other sections of the country. Hayne supported Western interests by calling for an end to land sales by the federal government, arguing that states should be able to control their own lands and set aside federal laws they believed to be detrimental to their own well-being. He sought to defend Southern interests by supporting policies that favored agriculture and states' rights.

Daniel Webster's reply to Hayne was a spirited defense of Northeastern interests through the "American System"—a plan to strengthen and unify the nation through high tariffs designed to protect American industries, preservation of the Bank of the United States to stabilize currency, and land sales by the federal government to further generate revenue for infrastructure improvements.

The speech excerpted here is Hayne's reply to Webster, initiated on January 21 and, after a long weekend, concluded on January 25. Encouraged by Vice President John C. Calhoun, who was presiding over the Senate, Hayne charged that the North was seeking to destroy the South through its recent conversion to high protective tariffs and its increasingly vocal opposition to slavery. Hayne stressed the sovereignty of the individual states, which had voluntarily ceded limited power to the central government. When the government unconstitutionally encroached on a state's sovereignty, Hayne believed that state could legitimately oppose the encroachment until three-quarters of the states ratified a clarifying amendment to the Constitution. The states' rights doctrine of Hayne and Calhoun assumed great significance in the decades leading up to the Civil War and many of their arguments remain relevant in the ever-present debate over the proper relationship between state and federal sovereignty and authority.

... Sir, I questioned no man's opinions; I impeached no man's motives; I charged no party, or state, or section of country with hostility to any other, but ventured, as I thought, in a becoming spirit, to put forth my own sentiments in relation to a great national question of public policy. Such was my course. The gentleman from Missouri, [Mr. Benton] it is true, had charged upon the eastern States an early and continued hostility towards the West, and referred to a number of historical facts and documents in support of that charge. Now, Sir, how have these different arguments been met? The honorable gentleman from Massachusetts, after deliberating a whole night upon his course, comes into this chamber to vindicate New England, and, instead of making up his issue with the gentleman from Missouri, on the charges which *he*

had preferred, chooses to consider me as the author of those charges, and, losing sight entirely of that gentleman, selects me as his adversary, and pours out all the vials of his mighty wrath upon my devoted head. Nor is he willing to stop there. He goes on to assail the institutions and policy of the South, and calls in question the principles and conduct of the State which I have the honor to represent. When I find a gentleman of mature age and experience, of acknowledged talents and profound sagacity, pursuing a course like this, declining the contest offered from the West, and making war upon the unoffending South, I must believe, I am bound to believe, he has some object in view that he has not ventured to disclose. Why is this? Has the gentleman discovered in former controversies with the gentleman from

Missouri, that he is overmatched by that Senator? And does he hope for an easy victory over a more feeble adversary? …

The gentleman from Massachusetts, in reply to my remarks on the injurious operations of our land system on the prosperity of the West, pronounced an extravagant eulogium on the paternal care which the government had extended towards the West, to which he attributed all that was great and excellent in the present condition of the new States. The language of the gentleman on this topic fell upon my ears like the almost forgotten tones of the Tory leaders of the British Parliament, at the commencement of the American Revolution. They, too, discovered that the colonies had grown great under the fostering care of the mother country; and, I must confess, while listening to the gentleman, I thought the appropriate reply to his argument was to be found in the remark of a celebrated orator, made on that occasion: "They have grown great in spite of your protection." …

In 1825, the gentleman told the world that the public lands "ought not to be treated as a treasure." He now tells us that "they must be treated as so much treasure." What the deliberate opinion of the gentleman on this subject may be, belongs not to me to determine; but I do not think he can, with the shadow of justice or propriety, impugn my sentiments, while his own recorded opinions are identical with my own. When the gentleman refers to the conditions of the grants under which the United States have acquired these lands, and insists that, as they are declared to be "for the common benefit of all the States," they can only be treated as so much treasure, I think he has applied a rule of construction too narrow for the case. If, in the deeds of cession, it has been declared that the grants were intended for "the common benefit of all the States," it is clear, from other provisions, that they were not intended merely as *so much property*: for, it is expressly declared that the object of the grants is the erection of new States; and the United States, in accepting this trust, bind themselves to facilitate the foundation of these States, to be admitted into the Union with all the rights and privileges of the original States. This, Sir, was the great end to which all parties looked, and it is by the fulfillment of this high trust, that "the common benefit of all the States" is to be best promoted. Sir, let me tell the gentleman, that, in the part of the country in which I live, we do not measure political benefits by the *money standard*. We consider as more valuable than gold—liberty, principle, and justice. …

The gentleman from Massachusetts, in alluding to a remark of mine, that, before any disposition could be made of the public lands, the national *debt* (for which they stand pledged) must be first paid, took occasion to intimate "that the *extraordinary fervor* which seems to exist in a *certain* quarter, (meaning the South, sir,) for the payment of the debt, arises from a disposition *to weaken the ties which bind the people to the Union.*" While the gentleman deals us this blow, he professes an ardent desire to see the debt speedily extinguished. He must excuse me, however, for feeling some distrust on that subject until I find this disposition manifested by something stronger than professions. I shall look for acts, decided and unequivocal acts: for the performance of which an opportunity will very soon (if I am not greatly mistaken) be afforded. Sir, if were at liberty to judge of the course which that gentleman would pursue, from the principles which he has laid down in relation to this matter, I should be bound to conclude that he will be found acting with those with whom it is a darling object to prevent the payment of the public debt. He tells us he is desirous of paying the debt, "because we are under *an obligation* to discharge it." Now, Sir, suppose it should happen that the public creditors, with whom we have contracted the obligation, should release us from it, so far as to declare their willingness to wait for payment for fifty years to come, provided only the interest shall be punctually discharged. The gentleman from Massachusetts will then be released from the obligation which now makes him desirous of paying the debt; and, let me tell the gentleman, the holders of the stock will not only release us from this obligation, but they will implore, nay, they will even *pay us* not to pay them. But, adds the gentleman, "so far as the debt may have an effect in binding the debtors to the country, and thereby serving as a link to hold the States together, he would be glad that it should exist forever." Surely then, sir, on the gentleman's own principles, he must be opposed to the payment of the debt.

Sir, let me tell that gentleman, that the South repudiates the idea that *pecuniary dependence* on the federal government is one of the legitimate means of holding the States together. A moneyed interest in the government is essentially a base interest; and just so far as it operates to bind the feelings of those who are subjected to it to the government; just so far as it operates in creating sympathies and interests that would not otherwise exist; is it opposed to all the principles of free government, and at war with

undermined, NULLIFIED, it will not be, if we and those who shall succeed us here, as agents and representatives of the people, shall conscientiously and vigilantly discharge the two great branches of our public trust, faithfully to preserve, and wisely to administer it.

Mr. President, I have thus stated the reasons of my dissent to the doctrines which have been advanced and maintained. I am conscious of having detained you and the Senate much too long. I was drawn into the debate with no previous deliberation, such as is suited to the discussion of so grave and important a subject. But it is a subject of which my heart is full, and I have not been willing to suppress the utterance of its spontaneous sentiments. I cannot, even now, persuade myself to relinquish it, without expressing once more my deep conviction, that, since it respects nothing less than the Union of the States, it is of most vital and essential importance to the public happiness. I profess, Sir, in my career hitherto, to have kept steadily in view the prosperity and honor of the whole country, and the preservation of our Federal Union. It is to that Union we owe our safety at home, and our consideration and dignity abroad. It is to that Union that we are chiefly indebted for whatever makes us most proud of our country. That Union we reached only by the discipline of our virtues in the severe school of adversity. It had its origin in the necessities of disordered finance, prostrate commerce, and ruined credit. Under its benign influences, these great interests immediately awoke, as from the dead, and sprang forth with newness of life. Every year of its duration has teemed with fresh proofs of its utility and its blessings; and although our territory has stretched out wider and wider, and our population spread farther and farther, they have not outrun its protection or its benefits. It has been to us all a copious fountain of national, social, and personal happiness.

I have not allowed myself, Sir, to look beyond the Union, to see what might lie hidden in the dark recess behind. I have not coolly weighed the chances of preserving liberty when the bonds that unite us together shall be broken asunder. I have not accustomed myself to hang over the precipice of disunion, to see whether, with my short sight, I can fathom the depth of the abyss below; nor could I regard him as a safe counsellor in the affairs of this government, whose thoughts should be mainly bent on considering, not how the Union may be best preserved, but how tolerable might be the condition of the people when it should be broken up and destroyed. While the Union lasts, we have high, exciting, gratifying prospects spread out before us, for us and our children. Beyond that I seek not to penetrate the veil. God grant that, in my day, at least, that curtain may not rise! God grant that on my vision never may be opened what lies behind! When my eyes shall be turned to behold for the last time the sun in heaven, may I not see him shining on the broken and dishonored fragments of a once glorious Union; on States dissevered, discordant, belligerent; on a land rent with civil feuds, or drenched, it may be, in fraternal blood! Let their last feeble and lingering glance rather behold the gorgeous ensign of the republic, now known and honored throughout the earth, still full high advanced, its arms and trophies streaming in their original lustre, not a stripe erased or polluted, nor a single star obscured, bearing for its motto, no such miserable interrogatory as "What is all this worth?" nor those other words of delusion and folly, "Liberty first and Union afterwards"; but everywhere, spread all over in characters of living light, blazing on all its ample folds, as they float over the sea and over the land, and in every wind under the whole heavens, that other sentiment, dear to every true American heart,—Liberty *and* Union, now and forever, one and inseparable!

JOHN C. CALHOUN

Fort Hill Address

Stripped of all its covering, the naked question is, whether ours is a federal or a consolidated government; a constitutional or absolute one; a government resting ultimately on the solid basis of the sovereignty of the States or on the unrestrained will of a majority; a form of government, as in all other unlimited ones, in which injustice, and violence, and force must finally prevail.

John C. Calhoun (1782-1850) served as a congressman and senator from South Carolina, secretary of war, secretary of state, and vice president under Presidents John Quincy Adams and Andrew Jackson. Along with Henry Clay and Daniel Webster, he was part of "The Great Triumvirate"—a reference to the three statesmen who dominated the Senate in the 1830s and 1840s, with each representing one of the three major sections of the United States at that time and their respective interests.

Calhoun's interest lay in defending the South and its institutions. After the War of 1812, as manufacturing interests in the Northeast increased pressure on Congress to enact tariff legislation that would protect their products against foreign competition, the South was beginning to perceive that its economic future lay in supplying raw materials— particularly slave-cultivated cotton. Thus, as the northern states moved toward embracing protective tariffs, the South was moving away from them. This shift guaranteed sectional confrontation in the legislative arena, as demonstrated by the aforementioned Webster-Hayne debate.

An early supporter of a strong national government, Calhoun supported the War of 1812 and, in the beginning, the American System of tariffs and internal improvements. His position in regard to federal authority changed over time, however. In 1828, he anonymously authored the "South Carolina Exposition and Protest," a protest against the Tariff of 1828. Designed to protect industry in the North, it was labeled the "Tariff of Abominations" by its southern detractors because of the effects it had on the antebellum Southern economy. Calhoun's document stated that if the tariff was not repealed, South Carolina would secede. It also stated Calhoun's doctrine of nullification—the idea that a state has the right to reject federal law, first introduced by Thomas Jefferson and James Madison in their Kentucky and Virginia Resolutions.

Calhoun further elaborated on the subject in his July 26, 1831, "Fort Hill Address," written at his plantation known as Fort Hill. Here, Calhoun explains the principles that underlie South Carolina's Ordinance of Nullification and offers what has since come to be recognized as one of the strongest arguments for preserving the legitimate rights of the states.

On July 14, 1832, after Calhoun had resigned the vice presidency in order to run for the Senate, where he could more effectively defend nullification, President Jackson signed into law the Tariff of 1832. This attempt to remedy the conflict with lower tariffs was also deemed unacceptable by many in the South, however, and led to military preparations by South Carolina to resist anticipated federal enforcement. In early 1833, Congress passed a "Force Bill" authorizing the president to use military force to enforce Federal tariffs. Also passed was a new negotiated tariff satisfactory to South Carolina, which then repealed its Ordinance of Nullification. Thus ended the Nullification Crisis, allowing both sides to claim victory and maintain the Union.

The question of the relation which the States and General Government bear to each other is not of recent origin. From the commencement of our system, it had divided public sentiment. Even in the convention, while the Constitution was struggling into existence, there were two parties as to what this relation should be, whose different sentiments constituted no small impediment in forming that instrument. After the General Government went into operation, experience soon proved that the question had not terminated with the labors of the Convention. The great struggle that preceded the political revolution of 1801, which brought Mr. Jefferson into power, turned essentially on it, and the doctrines and arguments on both sides were embodied and ably sustained;—on the one, in the Virginia and Kentucky Resolutions, and the Report to the Virginia Legislature;—and on the other, in the replies of the

Legislature of Massachusetts and some of the other States....

The great and leading principle is, that the General Government emanated from the people of the several States, forming distinct political communities, and acting in their separate and sovereign capacity, and not from all of the people forming one aggregate political community; that the Constitution of the United States is, in fact, a compact, to which each State is a party, in the character already described; and that the several States, or parties, have a right to judge of its infractions; and in case of a deliberate, palpable, and dangerous exercise of power not delegated, they have the right, in the last resort, to use the language of the Virginia Resolutions, "*to interpose for arresting the progress of the evil, and for maintaining, within their respective limits, the authorities, rights, and liberties appertaining to them.*" This right of interposition, thus solemnly asserted by the State of Virginia, be it called what it may,—State-right, veto, nullification, or by any other name,—I conceive to be the fundamental principle of our system, resting on facts historically as certain as our revolution itself, and deductions as simple and demonstrative as that of any political or moral truth whatever; and I firmly believe that on its recognition depend the stability and safety of our political institutions. ...

It has been well said by one of the most sagacious men of antiquity, that the object of a constitution is, to *restrain the government, as that of laws* is to restrain *individuals.* The remark is correct; nor is it less true where the government is vested in a majority, than where it is in a single or a few individuals—in a republic, than in a monarchy or aristocracy. No one can have a higher respect for the maxim that the majority ought to govern than I have, taken in its proper sense, subject to the restrictions imposed by the Constitution, and confined to objects in which every portion of the community have similar interests; but it is a great error to suppose, as many do, that the right of a majority to govern is a natural and not a conventional right, and therefore absolute and unlimited. By nature, every individual has the right to govern himself; and governments, whether founded on majorities or minorities, must derive their right from the assent, expressed or implied, of the governed, and be subject to such limitations as they may impose. Where the interests are the same, that is, where the laws that may benefit one will benefit all, or the reverse, it is just and proper to place them under the control of the majority; but where they are dissimilar, so that the law that may benefit one portion may be ruinous to another,

it would be, on the contrary, unjust and absurd to subject them to its will; and such I conceive to be the theory on which our Constitution rests.

That such dissimilarity of interests may exist, it is impossible to doubt. They are to be found in every community, in a greater or less degree, however small or homogeneous; and they constitute every where the great difficulty of forming and preserving free institutions. To guard against the unequal action of the laws, when applied to dissimilar and opposing interests, is, in fact, what mainly renders a constitution indispensable; to overlook which, in reasoning on our Constitution, would be to omit the principal element by which to determine its character. Were there no contrariety of interests, nothing would be more simple and easy than to form and preserve free institutions. The right of suffrage alone would be a sufficient guarantee. It is the conflict of opposing interests which renders it the most difficult work of man. ...

So numerous and diversified are the interests of our country, that they could not be fairly represented in a single government, organized so as to give to each great and leading interest a separate and distinct voice, as in governments to which I have referred. A plan was adopted better suited to our situation, but perfectly novel in its character. The powers of government were divided, not, as heretofore, in reference to classes, but geographically. One General Government was formed for the whole, to which were delegated all the powers supposed to be necessary to regulate the interests common to all the States, leaving others subject to the separate control of the States, being, from their local and peculiar character, such that they could not be subject to the will of a majority of the whole Union, without the certain hazard of injustice and oppression. It was thus that the interests of the whole were subjected, as they ought to be, to the will of the whole, while the peculiar and local interests were left under the control of the States separately, to whose custody only they could be safely confided. This distribution of power, settled solemnly by a constitutional compact, to which all the States are parties, constitutes the peculiar character and excellence of our political system. It is truly and emphatically *American, without example or parallel.*

To realize its perfection, we must view the General Government and those of the States as a whole, each in its proper sphere independent; each perfectly adapted to its respective objects; the States acting separately, representing and protecting the local and peculiar interests; and acting jointly through one General Government, with the weight respectively assigned to each by the Constitution, representing and protecting the interest of the whole; and thus perfecting, by an admirable but simple arrangement, the great principle of representation and responsibility, without which no government can be free or just. To preserve this sacred distribution as originally settled, by coercing each to move in its prescribed orbit, is the great and difficult problem, on the solution of which the duration of our Constitution, of our Union, and, in all probability, our liberty depends. How is this to be effected?

The question is new, when applied to our peculiar political organization, where the separate and conflicting interests of society are represented by distinct but connected governments; but it is, in reality, an old question under a new form, long since perfectly solved. Whenever separate and dissimilar interests have been separately represented in any government; whenever the sovereign power has been divided in its exercise, the experience and wisdom of the ages have devised but one mode by which such political organization can be preserved,—the mode adopted in England, and by all governments, ancient and modern, blessed with constitutions deserving to be called free,—to give to each co-estate the right to judge of its powers, with a negative or veto on the acts of the others, in order to protect against encroachments the interests it particularly represents; a principle which all of our constitutions recognize in the distribution of power among their respective departments, as essential to maintain the independence of each; but which, to all who will duly reflect on the subject, must appear far more essential, for the same object, in that great and fundamental distribution of powers between the General and State Governments. So essential is the principle, that, to withhold the right from either, where the sovereign power is divided, is, in fact, *to annul the division* itself, and to *consolidate,* in the one left in the exclusive possession of the right, *all* powers of government; for it is not possible to distinguish, practically, between a government having all power, and one having the right to take what powers in pleases. Nor does it in the least vary the principle, whether the distribution of power be between co-estates, as in England, or between distinctly organized but connected governments, as with us. The reason is the same in both cases, while the necessity is greater in our case, as the danger of conflict is greater where the interests of a

society are divided geographically than in any other, as has already been shown.

These truths do seem to me to be incontrovertible; and I am at a loss to understand how any one, who has maturely reflected on the nature of our institutions, or who has read history or studied the principles of free government to any purpose, can call them in question. The explanation must, it appears to me, be sought in the fact that, in every free State there are those who look more to the necessity of maintaining power than guarding against its abuses. I do not intend reproach, but simply to state a fact apparently necessary to explain the contrariety of opinions among the intelligent, where the abstract consideration of the subject would seem scarcely to admit of doubt. If such be the true cause, I must think the fear of weakening the government too much, in this case, to be in a great measure unfounded, or, at least, that the danger is much less from that than the opposite side. I do not deny that a power of so high a nature may be abused by a State; but when I reflect that the States unanimously called the General Government into existence with all its powers, which they freely delegated on their part, under the conviction that their common peace, safety and prosperity required it; that they are bound together by a common origin, and the recollection of common suffering and common triumph in the great and splendid achievement of their independence; and that the strongest feelings of our nature, and among them the love of national power and distinction, are on the side of the Union, it does seem to me that the fear which would strip the States of their sovereignty, and degrade them, in fact, to mere dependent corporations, lest they should abuse a right indispensable to the peaceable protection of those interests which they reserved under their own peculiar guardianship when they created the General Government, is unnatural and unreasonable. If those who voluntarily created the system cannot be trusted to preserve it, who can?...

I yield, I trust, to few in my attachment to the Judiciary Department. I am fully sensible of its importance, and would maintain it, to the fullest extent, in its constitutional powers and independence; but it is impossible for me to believe it was ever intended by the Constitution that it should exercise the power in question, or that it is competent to do so; and, if it were, that it would be a safe depository of the power.

Its powers are judicial, and not political; and are expressly confined by the Constitution "to all *cases* in law and equity arising under the Constitution, the laws of the United States, and the treaties made, or which shall be made, under its authority;" and which I have high authority in asserting excludes political questions, and comprehends those only where there are parties amenable to the process of the Court. Nor is its incompetency less clear than its want of constitutional authority. There may be many, and the most dangerous infractions on the part of Congress, of which, it is conceded by all, the court, as a judicial tribunal, cannot, from its nature, take cognizance. The Tariff itself is a strong case in point; and the reason applies equally *to all others where Congress perverts a power from an object intended, to one not intended, the most insidious and dangerous of all infractions; and which may be extended to all of its powers, more especially to the taxing and appropriating.* But, supposing it competent to take cognizance of all infractions of every description, the insuperable objection still remains, that it would not be a safe tribunal to exercise the power in question.

It is a universal and fundamental political principle, that the power to protect can safely be confided only to those interested in protecting, or their responsible agents,—a maxim not less true in private than in public affairs. The danger in our system is, that the General Government, which represents the interests of the whole, may encroach on the States, which represent the peculiar and local interests, or that the latter may encroach on the former. …

But it is useless to multiply arguments. Were it possible that reason could settle a question where the passions and interests of men are concerned, this point would have been long since settled for ever by the State of Virginia. The report of her Legislature, to which I have already referred, has really, in my opinion, placed it beyond controversy. Speaking in reference to this subject, it says: "It has been objected" (to the right of a State to interpose for the protection of her reserved rights) "that the judicial authority is to be regarded as the sole expositor of the Constitution. On this objection it might be observed, first, that there may be instances of usurped powers which the forms of the Constitution could never draw within the control of the Judicial Department; secondly, that, if the decision of the judiciary be raised above the sovereign parties to the Constitution, the decisions of the other departments, not carried by the forms of the Constitution before the Judiciary, must be equally authoritative and final with the decision of that department. But the proper answer to the objection is, that the resolution of the General Assembly relates to those great and extraordinary cases, in which all the forms of the Constitution may prove ineffectual against infractions dangerous to the essential rights of the parties to it. The resolution supposes that dangerous powers, not delegated, may not only be usurped and executed by the other departments, but that the Judicial Department may also exercise or sanction dangerous powers, beyond the grant of the Constitution, and, consequently, that the ultimate right of the parties to the Constitution to judge whether the compact has been dangerously violated, must extend to violations by one delegated authority, as well as by another,— by the judiciary, as well as by the executive or legislative."

Against these conclusive arguments, as they seem to me, it is objected that, if one of the parties has the right to judge of infractions of the Constitution, so has the other; and that, consequently, in cases of contested powers between a State and the General Government, each would have a right to maintain its opinion, as is the case when sovereign powers differ in the construction of treaties or compacts; and that, of course, it would come to be a mere question of force. The error is in the assumption that the General Government is a party to the constitutional compact. The States, as has been shown, formed the compact, acting as sovereign and independent communities. The General Government is but its creature; and though, in reality, a government, with all the rights and authority which belong to any other government, within the orbit of its powers, it is, nevertheless, a government emanating from a compact between sovereigns, and partaking, in its nature and object, of the character of a joint commission, appointed to superintend and administer the interests in which all are jointly concerned; but having, beyond its proper sphere, no more power than if it did not exist. To deny this would be to deny the most incontestable facts and the clearest conclusions; while to acknowledge its truth is to destroy utterly the objection that the appeal would be to force, in the case supposed. For, if each party has a right to judge, then, under our system of government, the final cognizance of a question of contested power would be in the States, and not in the General Government. It would be the duty of the latter, as in all similar cases of a contest between one or more of the principals and a joint commission or agency, to refer the contest to the principals themselves. Such are the plain dictates of both reason and analogy. On no sound principle can the agents have a right to final cognizance, as against the principals, much less to use force against them to maintain their construction of their powers. Such a right would be monstrous, and has never, heretofore, been claimed in similar cases.

That the doctrine is applicable to the case of a contested power between the States and the General Government, we have the authority, not only of reason and analogy, but of the distinguished statesman already referred to. Mr. Jefferson, at a late period of his life, after long experience and mature reflection, says, "With respect to our State and Federal Governments, I do not think their relations are correctly understood by foreigners. They suppose the former are subordinate to the latter. This is not the case. They are co-ordinate departments of one simple and integral whole. But you may ask, 'If the two departments should claim each the same subject of power, where is the umpire to decide between them?' In cases of little urgency or importance, the prudence of both parties will keep them aloof from the questionable ground; but, if it can neither be avoided nor compromised, a convention of the States must be called to ascribe the doubtful power to that department which they may think best."

It is thus that our Constitution, by authorizing amendments, and by prescribing the authority and mode of making them, has, by a simple contrivance, with its characteristic wisdom, provided a power which, in the last resort, supersedes effectually the necessity, and even the pretext for force: a power to which none can fairly object; with which the interests of all are safe; which can definitely close all controversies in the only effectual mode, by freeing the compact of every defect and uncertainty, by an amendment of the instrument itself. It is impossible for human wisdom, in a system like ours, to devise another mode which shall be safe and effectual, and, at the same time, consistent with what are the relations and acknowledged powers of the two great departments of our Government. It gives a beauty and security peculiar to our system, which, if duly appreciated, will transmit its blessings to the remotest generations; but, if not, our splendid anticipations of the future will prove but an empty dream. Stripped of all its covering, the naked question is, whether ours is a federal or a consolidated government; a constitutional or absolute one; a government resting ultimately on the solid basis of the sovereignty of the States or on the unrestrained will of a majority; a form of government, as in all other unlimited ones, in which injustice, and violence, and force must finally prevail. *Let it never be forgotten that, where the majority rules without restriction, the minority is the subject;* and that, if we should absurdly attribute to the former the exclusive right of construing the Constitution, there would be, in fact, between the sovereign and subject, under such a government, no Constitution, or, at least, nothing deserving the name, or serving the legitimate object of so sacred an instrument. ...

Discovery of Nat Turner.

Discovery of Nat Turner, *a wood engraving by William Henry Shelton illustrating the capture of Nathaniel Turner by farmer Benjamin Phipps. Nat Turner's Rebellion was a slave uprising led by Turner on August 21, 1831, in Virginia that resulted in the murder of fifty-six whites, including many children and at least one infant. This was the largest number of white fatalities to occur in a single uprising in the antebellum South. Turner and fifty-six slaves accused of being part of his rebellion were subsequently executed by the state. Hundreds more blacks were beaten and killed by white militias and mobs reacting with violence. Throughout the South, state legislatures passed new laws prohibiting education of slaves and free blacks, restricting rights of assembly and other civil rights for free blacks, and requiring white ministers to be present at black worship services. Some free blacks chose to move their families north to obtain educations for their children and some individual white people chose to violate the laws and teach slaves to read. Overall, the laws enacted in the aftermath of the Turner Rebellion ensured widespread illiteracy among blacks at the end of the Civil War.*

WILLIAM LLOYD GARRISON

Prospectus for *The Liberator*

I am in earnest—I will not equivocate—I will not excuse—I will not retreat a single inch—AND I WILL BE HEARD.

William Lloyd Garrison (1805-1879) was a journalist and famed abolitionist who sought an immediate end to slavery and denounced all who did not embrace his view with the same fervor. In 1832, he founded the New England Anti-Slavery Society and, later, the American Anti-Slavery Society. Garrison even went so far as to advocate secession, arguing that the North's union with slaveholding states was "a covenant with death and an agreement with hell." In 1831, after serving two months in jail for a libel conviction, Garrison began publishing *The Liberator*—a small but influential abolitionist newspaper that he kept in circulation until 1865.

… During my recent tour for the purpose of exciting the minds of the people by a series of discourses on the subject of slavery, every place that I visited gave fresh evidence of the fact, that a greater revolution in public sentiment was to be effected in the free states—and particularly in New-England—than at the south. I found contempt more bitter, opposition more active, detraction more relentless, prejudice more stubborn, and apathy more frozen, than among the slave owners themselves. Of course, there were individual exceptions to the contrary. This state of things afflicted, but did not dishearten me. I determined, at every hazard to lift up the standard of emancipation in the eyes of the nation, within sight of Bunker Hill and in the birth place of liberty. That standard is now unfurled; and long may it float, unhurt by the spoliations of time or the missiles of a desperate foe—yea, till every chain be broken, and every bondman be set free! Let southern oppressors tremble—let their northern apologists tremble—let all the enemies of the persecuted blacks tremble.

I deem the publication of my original Prospectus unnecessary, as it has obtained a wide circulation. The principles therein inculcated will be steadily pursued in this paper, excepting that I shall not array myself as the political partisan of any man. In defending the great cause of human rights, I wish to derive the assistance of all religions and of all parties.

Assenting to the "self-evident truth" maintained in the American Declaration of Independence, "that all men are created equal and endowed by their Creator with certain inalienable rights—among which are life, liberty and the pursuit of happiness," I shall strenuously contend for the immediate enfranchisement of our slave population. In Park-street Church, on the Fourth of July, 1829, in an address on slavery, I unreflectingly assented to the popular but pernicious doctrine of *gradual* abolition. I seize this opportunity to make a full and unequivocal recantation, and thus publicly to ask pardon of my God, of my country, and of my brethren the poor slaves, for having uttered a sentiment so full of timidity, injustice and absurdity. A similar recantation, from my pen, was published in the *Genius of Universal Emancipation* at Baltimore, in September, 1829. My conscience is now satisfied.

I am aware that many object to the severity of my language; but is there not cause for severity? I *will be* as harsh as truth, and as uncompromising as justice. On this subject, I do not wish to think, or speak, or write, with moderation. No! no! Tell a man whose house is on fire, to give a moderate alarm; tell him to moderately rescue his wife from the hands of the ravisher; tell the mother to gradually extricate her babe from the fire into which it has fallen;—but urge me not to use moderation in a cause like the present. I am in earnest—I will not equivocate—I will not excuse—I will not retreat a single inch—AND I WILL BE HEARD. The apathy of the people is enough to make every statue leap from its pedestal, and to hasten the resurrection of the dead.

It is pretended, that I am retarding the cause of emancipation, by the coarseness of my invective, and the precipitancy of my measures. *The charge is not true.* On this question my influence,—humble as it is,—is felt at this moment to a considerable extent, and shall be felt in coming years—not perniciously, but beneficially—not as a curse, but as a blessing; and posterity will bear testimony that I was right. I desire to thank God, that he enables me to disregard "the fear of man which bringeth a snare," and to speak his truth in its simplicity and power. …

The Present Crisis

James Russell Lowell (1819-1891), best known as a poet, was also a literary critic, editor, teacher, reformer, and diplomat. A graduate of Harvard, he succeeded Henry Wadsworth Longfellow as professor of modern languages at the college. He also served as the first editor of the *Atlantic Monthly*, which he founded with Oliver Wendell Holmes, and co-editor of the *North American Review*. In 1877, Lowell was appointed United States minister to Spain by President Rutherford B. Hayes, whose election Lowell had actively supported. He later served as U.S. minister to England.

An ardent abolitionist, much of Lowell's poetry reflected his anti-slavery position and firm support of the Union. "The Present Crisis" (1844), perhaps his best-known poem, was embraced by the NAACP, which said: "If we had a creed to which our members, black and white, our branches North and South and East and West, our college societies, our children's circles, should all subscribe, it should be the lines of Lowell's noble verse, lines that are as true today as when they were written."

When a deed is done for Freedom, through the broad earth's aching breast
Runs a thrill of joy prophetic, trembling on from east to west,
And the slave, where'er he cowers, feels the soul within him climb
To the awful verge of manhood, as the energy sublime
Of a century bursts full-blossomed on the thorny stem of Time.

Through the walls of hut and palace shoots the instantaneous throe,
When the travail of the Ages wrings earth's systems to and fro;
At the birth of each new Era, with a recognizing start,
Nation wildly looks at nation, standing with mute lips apart,
And glad Truth's yet mightier man-child leaps beneath the Future's heart.

So the Evil's triumph sendeth, with a terror and a chill,
Under continent to continent, the sense of coming ill,
And the slave, where'er he cowers, feels his sympathies with God
In hot tear-drops ebbing earthward, to be drunk up by the sod,
Till a corpse crawls round unburied, delving in the nobler clod.

For mankind are one in spirit, and an instinct bears along,
Round the earth's electric circle, the swift flash of right or wrong;
Whether conscious or unconscious, yet Humanity's vast frame
Through its ocean-sundered fibres feels the gush of joy or shame;—
In the gain or loss of one race all the rest have equal claim.

Once to every man and nation comes the moment to decide,
In the strife of Truth with Falsehood, for the good or evil side;
Some great cause, God's new Messiah, offering each the bloom or blight,
Parts the goats upon the left hand, and the sheep upon the right,
And the choice goes by forever 'twixt that darkness and that light.

Hast thou chosen, O my people, on whose party thou shalt stand,
Ere the Doom from its worn sandals shakes the dust against our land?
Though the cause of Evil prosper, yet 'tis Truth alone is strong,
And, albeit she wander outcast now, I see around her throng
Troops of beautiful, tall angels, to enshield her from all wrong.

Backward look across the ages and the beacon-moments see,
That, like peaks of some sunk continent, jut through Oblivion's sea;
Not an ear in court or market for the low foreboding cry
Of those Crises, God's stern winnowers, from whose feet earth's chaff must fly;
Never shows the choice momentous till the judgment hath passed by.

Careless seems the great Avenger; history's pages but record
One death-grapple in the darkness 'twixt old systems and the Word;
Truth forever on the scaffold, Wrong forever on the throne,—
Yet that scaffold sways the future, and, behind the dim unknown,
Standeth God within the shadow, keeping watch above his own.

We see dimly in the Present what is small and what is great,
Slow of faith how weak an arm may turn this iron helm of fate,
But the soul is still oracular; amid the market's din,
List the ominous stern whisper from the Delphic cave within,—
"They enslave their children's children who make compromise with sin."

Slavery, the earth-born Cyclops, fellest of the giant brood,
Sons of brutish Force and Darkness, who have drenched the earth with blood,
Famished in his self-made desert, blinded by our purer day,
Gropes in yet unblasted regions for his miserable prey;—
Shall we guide his gory fingers where our helpless children play?

Then to side with Truth is noble when we share her wretched crust,
Ere her cause bring fame and profit, and 'tis prosperous to be just;
Then it is the brave man chooses, while the coward stands aside,
Doubting in his abject spirit, till his Lord is crucified,
And the multitude make virtue of the faith they had denied.

Count me o'er the earth's chosen heroes,—they were souls that stood alone,
While the men they agonized for hurled the contumelious stone,
Stood serene, and down the future saw the golden beam incline
To the side of perfect justice, mastered by their faith divine,
By one man's plain truth to manhood and to God's supreme design.

By the light of burning heretics Christ's bleeding feet I track,
Toiling up new Calvaries ever with the cross that turns not back,
And these mounts of anguish number how each generation learned
One new word of that grand *Credo* which in prophet-hearts hath burned
Since the first man stood God-conquered with his face to heaven upturned.

For Humanity sweeps onward: where to-day the martyr stands,
On the morrow, crouches Judas with the silver in his hands;
Far in front the cross stands ready and the crackling fagots burn,
While the hooting mob of yesterday in silent awe return
To glean up the scattered ashes into History's golden urn.

'Tis as easy to be heroes as to sit the idle slaves
Of a legendary virtue carved upon our father's graves,
Worshippers of light ancestral make the present light a crime;—
Was the Mayflower launched by cowards, steered by men behind their time?
Turn those tracks toward Past or Future, that make Plymouth Rock sublime?

They were men of present valor, stalwart old iconoclasts,
Unconvinced by axe or gibbet that all virtue was the Past's;
But we make their truth our falsehood, thinking that hath made us free,
Hoarding it in mouldy parchments, while our tender spirits flee
The rude grasp of that great Impulse which drove them across the sea.

They have rights who dare maintain them; we are traitors to our sires,
Smothering in their holy ashes Freedom's new-lit altar-fires;
Shall we make their creed our jailer? Shall we, in our haste to slay,
From the tombs of the old prophets steal the funeral lamps away
To light up the martyr-fagots round the prophets of to-day?

New occasions teach new duties; Time makes ancient good uncouth;
They must upward still, and onward, who would keep abreast of Truth;
Lo, before us gleam her camp-fires! we ourselves must Pilgrims be,
Launch our Mayflower, and steer boldly through the desperate winter sea,
Nor attempt the Future's portal with the Past's blood-rusted key.

Stump Speaking, by George Caleb Bingham. *This was part of a series of canvases marking elections in newly created states along the western frontier. Note that the electorate is thoroughly male and white.*

HENRY HIGHLAND GARNET

An Address to the Slaves of the United States of America

Let your motto be RESISTANCE! RESISTANCE! RESISTANCE!

Henry Highland Garnet (1815-1882) was born into slavery in Maryland and, at the age of nine, escaped with his parents to New York. He prepared for the ministry at Oneida Theological Institute and, in 1865, became the first black clergyman to deliver a sermon to the United States House of Representatives.

In 1843, Garnet addressed the National Negro Convention in Buffalo, New York. He shocked delegates by declaring that slaves should, in essence, resolve to live free or die. To Garnet's disappointment, his position was not adopted as the official resolution of the convention. Five years later, however, the substance of Garnet's address was adopted by a similar convention assembled in Troy, New York. On that occasion, Garnet prefaced his address, saying of its earlier presentation:

"The document elicited more discussion than any other paper that was ever brought before that, or any other deliberative body of colored persons, and their friends. Gentlemen who opposed the Address, based their objections on these grounds. 1) That the document was war-like, and encouraged insurrection; and 2) That if the Convention should adopt it, that those delegates who lived near the borders of the slave states, would not dare return to their homes. The Address was rejected by a small majority; and now in compliance with the earnest request of many who heard it, and in conformity to the wishes of numerous friends who are anxious to see it, the author now gives it to the public, praying God that this little book may be borne on the four winds of heaven, until the principles it contains shall be understood and adopted by every slave in the Union."

Your brethren of the north, east, and west have been accustomed to meet together in National Conventions, to sympathize with each other, and to weep over your unhappy condition. In these meetings we have addressed all classes of the free, but we have never until this time, sent a word of consolation and advice to you. We have been contented in sitting still and mourning over your sorrows, earnestly hoping that before this day, your sacred liberties would have been restored. But, we have hoped in vain. Years have rolled on, and tens of thousands have been borne on streams of blood, and tears, to the shores of eternity. While you have been oppressed, we have also been partakers with you; nor can we be free while you are enslaved. We therefore write to you as being bound with you.

Many of you are bound to us, not only by the ties of a common humanity, but we are connected by the more tender relations of parents, wives, husbands, children, brothers, and sisters, and friends. As such we most affectionately address you.

Slavery has fixed a deep gulf between you and us, and while it shuts out from you the relief and consolation which your friends would willingly render, it afflicts and persecutes you with a fierceness which we might not expect to see in the fiends of hell. But still the Almighty Father of Mercies has left to us a glimmering ray of hope, which shines out like a lone star in a cloudy sky. Mankind are becoming wiser, and better—the oppressor's power is fading, and you, every day, are becoming better informed, and more numerous. Your grievances, brethren, are many. We shall not attempt, in this short address, to present to the world, all the dark catalogue of this nation's sins, which have been committed upon an innocent people. Nor is it indeed, necessary, for you feel them from day to day, and all the civilized world look upon them with amazement.

Two hundred and twenty-seven years ago, the first of our injured race were brought to the shores of America. They came not with glad spirits to select their homes, in the New World. They came not with their own consent, to find an unmolested enjoyment of the blessings of this fruitful soil. The first dealings which they had with men calling themselves Christians, exhibited to them the worst features of corrupt and sordid hearts; and convinced them that no cruelty is too great, no villainy, and no robbery too abhorrent for even enlightened men to perform, when influenced by avarice, and lust. Neither did they come flying upon the wings of Liberty, to a land of freedom. But, they came with broken hearts, from their beloved native land, and were doomed to unrequited toil, and deep degradation. Nor did the evil of their bondage end at their emancipation by death. Succeeding generations inherited their chains, and millions have come from eternity into time, and have returned again to the world of spirits, cursed, and ruined by American Slavery.

The propagators of the system, or their immediate ancestors very soon discovered its growing evil, and its tremendous wickedness, and secret promises were made to destroy it. The gross inconsistency of a people holding slaves, who had themselves "ferried o'er the wave," for freedom's sake, was too apparent to be entirely overlooked. The voice of Freedom cried, "emancipate your Slaves." Humanity supplicated with tears, for the deliverance of the children of Africa. Wisdom urged her solemn plea. The bleeding captive pled his innocence, and pointed to Christianity who stood weeping at the cross. Jehovah frowned upon the nefarious institution, and thunderbolts, red with vengeance, struggled to leap forth to blast the guilty wretches who maintained it. But all was vain. Slavery had stretched its dark wings of death over the land, the Church stood silently by—the priests prophesied falsely, and the people loved to have it so. Its throne is established, and now it reigns triumphant.

Nearly three millions of your fellow citizens, are prohibited by law, and public opinion, (which in this country is stronger than law), from reading the Book of Life. Your intellect has been destroyed as much as possible, and every ray of light they have attempted to shut out from your minds. The oppressors themselves have become involved in the ruin. They have become weak, sensual, and rapacious. They have cursed you—they have cursed themselves—they have cursed the earth which they have trod. In the language of a Southern statesman, we can truly say, "even the wolf, driven back long since by the approach of man, now returns after the lapse of a hundred years, and howls amid the desolations of slavery."

The colonists threw the blame upon England. They said that the mother country entailed the evil upon them, and that they would rid themselves of it if they could. The world thought they were sincere, and the philanthropic pitied them. But time soon tested their sincerity. In a few years, the colonists grew strong and severed themselves from the British Government. Their independence was declared, and they took their station among the sovereign powers of the earth. The declaration was a glorious document. Sages admired it, and the patriotic of every nation reverenced the Godlike sentiments which it contained. When the power of Government returned to their hands, did they emancipate the slaves? No; they rather added new links to our chains. Were they ignorant of the principles of Liberty? Certainly they were not. The sentiments of their revolutionary orators fell in burning eloquence upon their hearts, and with one voice they cried, LIBERTY OR DEATH. O, what a sentence was that! It ran from soul to soul like electric fire, and nerved the arm of thousands to fight in the holy cause of Freedom. Among the diversity of opinions that are entertained in regard to physical resistance, there are but a few found to gainsay that stern declaration. We are among those who do not.

SLAVERY! How much misery is comprehended in that single word. What mind is there that does not shrink from its direful effects? Unless the image of God is obliterated from the soul, all men cherish the love of Liberty. The nice discerning political economist does not regard the sacred right, more than the untutored African who roams in the wilds of Congo. Nor has the one more right to the full enjoyment of his freedom than the other. In every man's mind the good seeds of liberty are planted, and he who brings his fellow down so low, as to make him contented with a condition of slavery, commits the highest crime against God and man. Brethren, your oppressors aim to do this. They endeavor to make you as much like brutes as possible. When they have blinded the eyes of your mind—when they have embittered the sweet waters of life—when they have shut out the light which shines from the word of God—then, and not till then has American slavery done its perfect work.

To such DEGRADATION IT IS SINFUL IN THE EXTREME FOR YOU TO MAKE VOLUNTARY SUBMISSION. The divine commandments, you are in duty bound to reverence, and obey. If you do not obey them you will surely meet with the displeasure of the Almighty. He requires you to love him supremely, and your neighbor as yourself—to keep the Sabbath day holy—to search the Scriptures—and bring up your children with respect for his laws, and to worship no other God but him. But slavery sets all these at naught, and hurls defiance in the face of Jehovah. The forlorn condition in which you are placed does not destroy your moral obligation to God. You are not certain of Heaven, because you suffer yourselves to remain in a state of slavery, where you cannot obey the commandments of the Sovereign of the universe. If the ignorance of slavery is a passport to heaven, then it is a blessing, and no curse, and you should rather desire its perpetuity than its abolition. God will not receive slavery, nor ignorance, nor any other state of mind, for love, and obedience to him. Your condition does not absolve you from your moral obligation. The diabolical injustice by which your liberties are cloven down, NEITHER GOD, NOR ANGELS, NOR JUST MEN, COMMAND YOU TO SUFFER FOR A SINGLE MOMENT. THEREFORE IT IS YOUR SOLEMN AND IMPERATIVE DUTY TO USE EVERY MEANS, BOTH MORAL, INTELLECTUAL, AND PHYSICAL, THAT PROMISE SUCCESS. If a band of heathen men should attempt to enslave a race of Christians, and to place their children under the influence of some false religion, surely, heaven would frown upon the men who would not resist such aggression, even to death. If, on the other hand, a band of Christians should attempt to enslave a race of heathen men and to entail slavery upon them, and to keep them in heathenism in the midst of Christianity, the God of heaven would smile upon every effort which the injured might make to disenthral themselves.

Brethren, it is as wrong for your lordly oppressors to keep you in slavery, as it was for the man thief to steal our ancestors from the coast of Africa. You should therefore now use the same manner of resistance, as would have been just in our ancestors, when the bloody foot prints of the first remorseless soul thief was placed upon the shores of our fatherland. The humblest peasant is as free in the sight of God, as the proudest monarch that ever swayed a sceptre. Liberty is a spirit sent out from God, and like its great Author, is no respecter of persons.

Brethren, the time has come when you must act for yourselves. It is an old and true saying, that "if hereditary bondmen would be free, they must themselves strike the blow." You can plead your own cause, and do the work of emancipation better than any others. The nations of the old world are moving in the great cause of universal freedom, and some of them at least, will ere long, do you justice. The combined powers of Europe have placed their broad seal of disapprobation upon the African slave trade. But in the slave holding parts of the United States, the trade is as brisk as ever. They buy and sell you as though you were brute beasts. The North has done much—her opinion of slavery in the abstract is known. But in regard to the South, we adopt the opinion of the New York Evangelist—"We have advanced so far, that the cause apparently waits for a more

effectual door to be thrown open that has been yet." We are about to point you to that more effectual door. Look around you, and behold the bosoms of your loving wives, heaving with untold agonies! Hear the cries of your poor children! Remember the stripes your fathers bore. Think of the torture and disgrace of your noble mothers. Think of your wretched sisters, loving virtue and purity, as they are driven into concubinage, and are exposed to the unbridled lusts of incarnate devils. Think of the undying glory that hangs around the ancient name of Africa—and forget not that you are native-born American citizens, and as such, you are justly entitled to all the rights that are granted to the freest. Think how many tears you have poured out upon the soil which you have cultivated with unrequited toil, and enriched with your blood; and then go to your lordly enslavers, and tell them plainly, that YOU ARE DETERMINED TO BE FREE. Appeal to their sense of justice, and tell them that they have no more right to oppress you, then you have to enslave them. Entreat them to remove the grievous burdens which they have imposed upon you, and to remunerate you for your labor. Promise them renewed diligence in the cultivation of the soil, if they will render to you an equivalent for your services. Point them to the increase of happiness and prosperity in the British West Indies, since the act of Emancipation. Tell them in language which they cannot misunderstand, of the exceeding sinfulness of slavery, and of a future judgment, and of the righteous retributions of an indignant God. Inform them that all you desire, is FREEDOM, and that nothing else will suffice. Do this, and for ever after cease to toil for the heartless tyrants, who give you no other reward but stripes and abuse. If they then commence the work of death, they, and not you, will be responsible for the consequences. You had far better all die—*die immediately*, than live slaves, and entail your wretchedness upon your posterity. …

Fellow-men! patient sufferers! behold your dearest rights crushed to the earth! See your sons murdered, and your wives, mothers, and sisters, doomed to prostitution! In the name of the merciful God! and by all that life is worth, let it no longer be a debateable question, whether it is better to choose **LIBERTY** or **DEATH!** …

We do not advise you to attempt a revolution with the sword, because it would be INEXPEDIENT. Your numbers are too small, and moreover the rising spirit of the age, and the spirit of the gospel, are opposed to war and bloodshed. But from this moment cease to labor for tyrants who will not remunerate you. Let every slave throughout the land do this, and the days of slavery are numbered. You cannot be more oppressed than you have been—you cannot suffer greater cruelties than you have already. Rather DIE FREEMEN, THAN LIVE TO BE SLAVES. Remember that you are THREE MILLIONS.

It is in your power so to torment the God cursed slaveholders, that they will be glad to let you go free. If the scale was turned and black men were the masters, and white men the slaves, every destructive agent and element would be employed to lay the oppressor low. Danger and death would hang over their heads day and night. Yes, the tyrants would meet with plagues more terrible than those of Pharaoh. But you are a patient people. You act as though you were made for the special use of these devils. You act as though your daughters were born to pamper the lusts of your masters and overseers. And worse than all, you tamely submit, while your lords tear your wives from your embraces, and defile them before your eyes. In the name of God we ask, are you men? Where is the blood of your fathers? Has it all run out of your veins? Awake, awake; millions of voices are calling you! Your dead fathers speak to you from their graves. Heaven, as with a voice of thunder, calls on you to arise from the dust.

Let your motto be RESISTANCE! RESISTANCE! RESISTANCE!—No oppressed people have ever secured their liberty without resistance. What kind of resistance you had better make, you must decide by the circumstances that surround you, and according to the suggestion of expediency. Brethren, adieu. Trust in the living God. Labor for the peace of the human race, and remember that you are three millions.

SOUTHERN CHIVALRY — ARGUMENT VERSUS CLUB'S.

An 1856 lithograph by John L. Magee depicting the May 22, 1856, attack on Senator Charles Sumner of Massachusetts by Preston Smith Brooks, Democratic congressman from South Carolina, in the Senate Chamber. Several other senators attempted to help Sumner, but were blocked by Representative Laurence Keitt, who was holding a pistol. This attack was in retaliation for insulting language Sumner used against Brooks's relative in a speech denouncing Southerners for pro-slavery violence in Kansas. Sumner, who was beaten severely and did not return to his Senate desk for three years as a result of his injuries, was regarded as an antislavery martyr.

ABRAHAM LINCOLN

The House Divided Speech

"A house divided against itself cannot stand." I believe this Government can not endure permanently half slave and half free. I do not expect the Union to be dissolved—I do not expect the house to fall—but I do expect it will cease to be divided.

Abraham Lincoln (1809-1865) was born near Hodgenville, Kentucky. Self-educated, he worked at a variety of labor-intensive occupations before settling in Illinois and studying law. Noted for his quick wit and common sense, Lincoln became a successful lawyer and was elected to the Illinois state legislature. In 1842, he married Mary Todd, the daughter of a slaveholding Kentucky banker and, four years later, was elected to the United States House of Representatives. In 1858, Lincoln challenged Stephen A. Douglas for the Senate. Speaking in Springfield, Illinois, on June 16 of that year, he accepted the Republican Party's nomination with what came to be known as "The House Divided Speech."

Lincoln concentrated his speech on the issue of slavery, highlighting three recent events. One was the passing of the Kansas-Nebraska Bill, which allowed voters in western territories to decide whether or not to allow slavery. This bill repealed the Missouri Compromise, which had prohibited slavery in those territories. A second event was the Dred Scott decision in which the Supreme Court ruled that blacks could not be citizens of the United States and that Congress had no authority to prohibit slavery in free states and territories, as it would deprive slaveowners of their property. The third event Lincoln addressed was the controversial Lecompton Constitution in Kansas, which was written by pro-slavery settlers but overwhelmingly rejected by voters who would eventually place Free Staters firmly in control of the legislature.

In highlighting these events, Lincoln sharply criticized the Democratic Party's policy of aiding and abetting the expansion of slavery. He made mention of Stephen Douglas's "care not" policy, referring to a statement by Douglas in which he said, "I care not whether slavery be voted down or voted up," and he attacked Douglas's *popular sovereignty* defense of the Kansas-Nebraska Bill, calling it *squatter sovereignty*. Lincoln also characterized these events as a "piece of machinery" manufactured by "Stephen, Franklin, Roger, and James"—referring to Democrats Stephen Douglas, former President Franklin Pierce, Chief Justice Roger Taney, and President James Buchanan.

"The House Divided Speech" served as a precursor to seven Lincoln-Douglas debates in which the two men further argued the expansion of slavery. In the end, Lincoln lost the election but became a widely recognized national figure.

… If we could first know where we are, and whither we are tending, we could better judge what to do, and how to do it. We are now far into the fifth year since a policy was initiated with the avowed object and confident promise of putting an end to slavery agitation. Under the operation of that policy that agitation has not only not ceased, but has constantly augmented. In my opinion, it will not cease until a crisis shall have been reached and passed. "A house divided against itself cannot stand." I believe this Government can not endure permanently half slave and half free. I do not expect the Union to be dissolved—I do not expect the house to fall—but I do expect it will cease to be divided. It will become all one thing, or all the other. Either the opponents of slavery will arrest the further spread of it, and place it where the public mind shall rest in the belief that it is in course of ultimate extinction; or its advocates will push it forward till it shall become alike lawful in all the States, old as well as new, North as well as South. Have we no tendency to the latter condition? Let any one who doubts carefully contemplate that now almost complete legal combination—piece of machinery, so to speak—compounded of the Nebraska doctrine and the Dred Scott decision. Let him consider not only what work the machinery is adapted to do, and how well adapted; but also let him study the history of its construction, and trace, if he can, or rather fail, if he can, to trace the evidences of design and concert of action among its chief architects from the beginning.

The new year of 1854 found slavery excluded from more than half the States by State Constitutions, and from most of the national territory by Congressional prohibition. Four days later commenced the struggle which ended in repealing that Congressional prohibition. This opened all the national territory to slavery, and was the first point gained. But, so far, Congress only had acted; and an indorsement by the people, real or apparent, was indispensable to save the point already gained and give chance for more. This necessity had not been overlooked, but had been provided for, as well as might be, in the notable argument of "squatter sovereignty," otherwise called "sacred right of self-government," which latter phrase, though expressive of the only rightful basis of any government, was so perverted in this attempted use of it as to amount to just this: that if any one man choose to enslave another, no third man shall be allowed to object. That argument was incorporated into the Nebraska Bill itself, in the language which follows: "It being the true intent and meaning of this act not to legislate slavery into any Territory or State, nor to exclude it therefrom; but to leave the people thereof perfectly free to form and regulate their domestic institutions in their own way, subject only to the Constitution of the United States." Then opened the roar of loose declamation in favor of "squatter sovereignty" and "sacred right of self-government." "But," said opposition members, "let us amend the bill so as to expressly declare that the people of the territory may exclude slavery." "Not we," said the friends of the measure; and down they voted the amendment.

While the Nebraska Bill was passing through Congress, a law case involving the question of a Negro's freedom, by reason of his owner having voluntarily taken him first into a free State and then a territory covered by the Congressional prohibition, and held him as a slave for a long time in each, was passing through the U.S. Circuit Court for the District of Missouri and both the Nebraska Bill and law suit were brought to a decision in the same month of May, 1854. The Negro's name was "Dred Scott," which name now designates the decision finally made in the case. Before the then next Presidential election, the law case came to and was argued in the Supreme Court of the United States; but the decision of it was deferred until after the election. Still, before the election, Senator Trumbull, on the floor of the Senate, requested the leading advocate of the Nebraska Bill to state his opinion whether the people of a territory can constitutionally exclude slavery from their limits; and the latter answered, "That is a question for the Supreme Court."

The election came. Mr. Buchanan was elected, and the indorsement, such as it was, secured. That was the second point gained. The indorsement, however, fell short of a clear popular majority by nearly four hundred thousand votes, and so, perhaps, was not overwhelmingly reliable and satisfactory. The outgoing President, in his last annual message, as impressively as possible echoed back upon the people the weight and authority of the indorsement. The Supreme Court met again; did not announce their decision, but ordered a re-argument. The Presidential inauguration came, and still no decision of the court; but the incoming President in his Inaugural Address fervently exhorted the people to abide by the forthcoming decision, whatever it might be. Then, in a few days came the decision. The reputed author of the Nebraska Bill finds an early occasion to make a speech at this capitol indorsing the Dred Scott decision, and vehemently denouncing all opposition to it. The new President, too, seizes the early occasion of the Silliman letter to indorse and strongly construe that decision, and to express his astonishment that any different view had ever been entertained.

At length a squabble springs up between the President and the author of the Nebraska Bill, on the mere question of fact, whether the Lecompton Constitution was or was not, in any just sense, made by the people of Kansas; and in that quarrel the latter declares that all he wants is a fair vote for the people, and that he cares not whether slavery be voted down or voted up. I do not understand his declaration that he cares not whether slavery be voted down or voted up to be intended by him other than as an apt definition of the policy he would impress upon the public mind—the principle for which he declares he has suffered much, and is ready to suffer to the end. And well may he cling to that principle. If he has any parental feeling, well may he cling to it. That principle is the only shred left of his original Nebraska doctrine. Under the Dred Scott decision "squatter sovereignty" squatted out of existence, tumbled down like temporary scaffolding,—like the mould at the foundry, served through one blast and fell back into loose sand,—helped to carry an election, and then was kicked to the winds. His late joint struggle with the Republicans against the Lecompton Constitution involves nothing of the original Nebraska doctrine. That struggle was made on a point—the right of a people to make their own Constitution—upon which he and the Republicans have never differed.

The several points of the Dred Scott decision, in connection with Senator Douglas's "care not" policy, constitute the piece of machinery in its present state of advancement. This was the third point gained. The working points of the machinery are: (1) That no Negro slave, imported as such from Africa, and no descendant of such slave, can ever be a citizen of any State, in the sense of that term as used in the Constitution of the United States. This point is made in order to deprive the Negro in every possible event of the benefit of this provision of the United States Constitution which declares that, "The citizens of each State shall be entitled to all the privileges and immunities of citizens in the several States." (2) That, "subject to the Constitution of the United States," neither Congress nor a Territorial Legislature can exclude slavery from any United States Territory. This point is made in order that individual men may fill up the Territories with slaves, without danger of losing them as property, and thus enhance the chances of permanency to the institution through all the future. (3) That whether the holding a Negro in actual slavery in a free State makes him free as against the holder, the United States courts will not decide, but will leave it to be decided by the courts of any slave State the Negro may be forced into by the master. This point is made, not to be pressed immediately, but, if acquiesced in for a while, and apparently indorsed by the people at an election, then to sustain the logical conclusion that what Dred Scott's master might lawfully do with Dred Scott in the free State of Illinois, every other master may lawfully do with any other one or one thousand slaves in Illinois or in any other free State.

Auxiliary to all this, and working hand in hand with it, the Nebraska doctrine, or what is left of it, is to educate and mould public opinion, at least Northern public opinion, not to care whether slavery is voted down or voted up. This shows exactly where we now are, and partially, also, whither we are tending.

It will throw additional light on the latter, to go back and run the mind over the string of historical facts already stated. Several things will now appear less dark and mysterious than they did when they were transpiring. The people were to be left "perfectly free," subject only to the Constitution. What the Constitution had to do with it outsiders could not then see. Plainly enough now, it was an exactly fitted niche for the Dred Scott decision afterward to come in, and declare that perfect freedom of the people to be no just freedom at all. Why was the amendment expressly declaring the right of the people to exclude slavery voted down? Plainly enough now, the adoption of it would have spoiled the niche for the Dred Scott decision. Why was the court decision held up? Why even a Senator's individual opinion withheld till after the Presidential election? Plainly enough now, the speaking

out then would have damaged the "perfectly free" argument upon which the election was to be carried. Why the outgoing President's felicitation on the indorsement? Why the delay of a re-argument? Why the incoming President's advance exhortation in favor of the decision? These things look like the cautious patting and petting of a spirited horse preparatory to mounting him, when it is dreaded that he may give the rider a fall. And why the hasty after-indorsement of the decision by the President and others?

We cannot absolutely know that all these exact adaptations are the result of pre-concert. But when we see a lot of framed timbers, different portions of which we know have been gotten out at different times and places and by different workmen,—Stephen, Franklin, Roger, and James, for instance—and when we see these timbers joined together, and see they exactly make the frame of a house or a mill, all the tenons and mortices exactly fitting, and all the lengths and proportions of the different pieces exactly adapted to their respective places, and not a piece too many or too few, not omitting even scaffolding—or, if a single piece be lacking, we see the place in the frame exactly fitted and prepared to yet bring such piece in—in such a case we find it impossible not to believe that Stephen and Franklin and Roger and James all understood one another from the beginning, and all worked upon a common plan or draft drawn up before the first blow was struck. ...

While the opinion of the court, by Chief Justice Taney, in the Dred Scott case, and the separate opinions of all the concurring judges, expressly declare that the Constitution of the United States neither permits Congress nor a Territorial Legislature to exclude slavery from any United States Territory, they all omit to declare whether or not the same Constitution permits a State, or the people of a State, to exclude it. Possibly, this was a mere omission; but who can be quite sure. ... Put this and that together, and we have another nice little niche, which we may, ere long, see filled with another Supreme Court decision, declaring that the Constitution of the United States does not permit a State to exclude slavery from its limits. And this may especially be expected if the doctrine of "care not whether slavery be voted down or voted up" shall gain upon the public mind sufficiently to give promise that such a decision can be maintained when made.

Such a decision is all that slavery now lacks of being alike lawful in all the States. Welcome, or unwelcome, such decision is probably coming, and will soon be upon us, unless the power of the present political dynasty shall be met and overthrown. We shall lie down pleasantly dreaming that the people of Missouri are on the verge of making their State free, and we shall awake to the reality instead that the Supreme Court has made Illinois a slave State. To meet and overthrow the power of that dynasty is the work now before all those who would prevent that consummation. That is what we have to do. How can we best do it?

There are those who denounce us openly to their own friends, and yet whisper us softly that Senator Douglas is the aptest instrument there is with which to effect that object. They do not tell us, nor has he told us, that he wishes any such object to be effected. They wish us to infer all from the facts that he now has a little quarrel with the present head of the dynasty; and that he has regularly voted with us on a single point upon which he and we have never differed. They remind us that he is a very great man, and that the largest of us are very small ones. Let this be granted. But "a living dog is better than a dead lion." Judge Douglas, if not a dead lion for this work, is at least a caged and toothless one. How can he oppose the advances of slavery? He doesn't care anything about it. His avowed mission is impressing the "public heart" to care nothing about it. …

Our cause, then, must be intrusted to, and conducted by, its own undoubted friends—those whose hands are free, whose hearts are in the work, who do care for the result. Two years ago the Republicans of the nation mustered over thirteen hundred thousand strong. We did this under the single impulse of resistance to a common danger, with every external circumstance against us. Of strange, discordant, and even hostile elements, we gathered from the four winds and formed and fought the battle through, under the constant hot fire of a disciplined, proud, and pampered enemy. Did we brave all then to falter now?—now, when that same enemy is wavering, dissevered, and belligerent! The result is not doubtful. We shall not fail—if we stand firm, we shall not fail. Wise counsels may accelerate or mistakes delay it, but, sooner or later, the victory is sure to come.

JOSIAH GILBERT HOLLAND

God, Give Us Men!

Born in Belchertown, Massachusetts, Josiah Gilbert Holland (1819-1881) was among the most popular Americans of his day, but was almost completely forgotten soon after his death. Having earned his M.D. degree in 1843, Holland soon abandoned the medical profession in favor of teaching. He later became editor of several newspapers and magazines and earned nationwide fame through such noteworthy writings as "God, Give Us Men!," symbolic of the times.

God, give us men! A time like this demands
Strong minds, great hearts, true faith and ready hands;
Men whom the lust of office does not kill;
Men whom the spoils of office cannot buy;
Men who possess opinions and a will;
Men who have honor; men who will not lie;
Men who can stand before a demagogue
And damn his treacherous flatteries without winking!
Tall men, sun-crowned, who live above the fog
In public duty and in private thinking;
For while the rabble, with their thumb-worn creeds,
Their large professions and their little deeds,
Mingle in selfish strife, lo! Freedom weeps,
Wrong rules the land and waiting Justice sleeps.

JOHN BROWN

Last Statement to the Court

If it is deemed necessary that I should forfeit my life for the furtherance of the ends of justice … I say, let it be done.

Born in Torrington, Connecticut, John Brown (1800-1859) was among the most zealous of abolitionists. The father of twenty children from two marriages, Brown tried his hand at several business ventures before dedicating his life to his one true passion—the destruction of slavery. Having spent his youth helping slaves escape into Canada and organizing blacks to protect themselves from slavecatchers, Brown joined five of his sons in 1855 by staking a claim in "Bleeding Kansas." There, they supported Free Staters in armed conflict against the "border ruffians"—citizens of the neighboring slave state of Missouri. In May 1856, Brown became outraged when he learned that pro-slavery forces had raided the nearby town of Lawrence. In retaliation, he and his men dragged five pro-slavery settlers from their homes and brutally murdered them. This event, known as the "Pottawatomie massacre," led to further violence.

At some point during the bloody conflicts, Brown began planning an invasion of the South, believing that slaves would rise in rebellion. In 1859, in order to secure munitions for that purpose, he and eighteen men raided and captured the United States arsenal at Harpers Ferry, Virginia (now West Virginia). They failed to escape, however, before being surrounded by the forces of Colonel Robert E. Lee, who captured the surviving raiders and delivered them for trial. On November 2, despite abolitionists' efforts to have Brown declared insane, he was convicted of murder, insurrection, and treason and hanged one month later.

The following is John Brown's last statement to the court, delivered when his sentence was pronounced and printed the following morning in the *New York Herald*.

I have, may it please the Court, a few words to say.

In the first place, I deny everything but what I have all along admitted: of a design on my part to free slaves. I intended certainly to have made a clean thing of that matter, as I did last winter, when I went into Missouri and there took slaves without the snapping of a gun on either side, moving them through the country, and finally leaving them in Canada. I designed to have done the same thing again on a larger scale. That was all I intended. I never did intend murder, or treason, or the destruction of property, or to exercise or incite slaves to rebellion, or to make insurrection.

I have another objection, and that is that it is unjust that I should suffer such a penalty. Had I interfered in the manner which I admit, and which I admit has been fairly proved—for I admire the truthfulness and candor of the greater portion of the witnesses who have testified in this case—Had I so interfered in behalf of the rich, the powerful, the intelligent, the so-called great, or in behalf of any of their friends, either father, mother, brother, sister, wife or children, or any of that class, and suffered and sacrificed what I have in this interference, it would have been all right. Every man in this Court would have deemed it an act worthy of reward rather than punishment.

This Court acknowledges, too, as I suppose, the validity of the law of God. I see a book kissed, which I suppose to be the Bible, or at least the New Testament, which teaches me that all things whatsoever I would that men should do to me, I should do even so to them. It teaches me, further, to remember them that are in bonds as bound with them. I endeavored to act up to that instruction. I say I am yet too young to understand that God is any respecter of persons. I believe that to have interfered as I have done, as I have always freely admitted I have done, in behalf of His despised poor, I did no wrong, but right. Now, if it is deemed necessary that I should forfeit my life for the furtherance of the ends of justice, and mingle my blood further with the blood of my children and with the blood of millions in this slave country whose rights are disregarded by wicked, cruel, and unjust enactments, I say, let it be done.

Let me say one word further. I feel entirely satisfied with the treatment I have received on my trial. Considering all the circumstances, it has been more generous than I expected. But I feel no consciousness of guilt. I have stated from the first what was my intention, and what was not. I never had any design against the liberty of any person, nor any disposition to commit treason or incite slaves to rebel or make any general insurrection. I never encouraged any man to do so, but always discouraged any idea of that kind.

Let me say, also, in regard to the statements made by some of those who were connected with me, I hear it has been stated by some of them that I have induced them to join me. But the contrary is true. I do not say this to injure them, but as regretting their weakness. Not one but joined me of his own accord, and the greater part at their own expense. A number of them I never saw, and never had a word of conversation with, till the day they came to me, and that was for the purpose I have stated.

Now, I have done.

ABRAHAM LINCOLN

The Cooper Union Speech

Let us have faith that right makes might, and in that faith let us to the end dare to do our duty as we understand it.

A long-shot candidate for his party's presidential nomination, Lincoln made an important breakthrough on February 27, 1860, when he delivered the following speech at the Cooper Union in New York City. Here, Lincoln challenged the assertion of Stephen Douglas, soon to be the Democratic nominee and Lincoln's opponent in the general election, that the Founding Fathers intentionally preserved slavery. Lincoln argued that the framers of the Constitution limited slavery, intending for it to end. This speech, and others made throughout New England, helped Lincoln win the support of influential eastern Republicans and crucial delegates in the Northeast. In May 1860, Lincoln secured the nomination on the third ballot at the Republican convention in Chicago, narrowly defeating Senator William H. Seward of New York.

Though Lincoln viewed slavery as "a moral, social and political evil," he was not an abolitionist. He accepted the original Constitutional protection of slavery, believing that the national chords would be too greatly strained by a sudden break with the past. He hoped to hasten slavery's demise, however, by convincing his fellow Americans of its inherent wickedness. He believed that the existence of slavery allowed the enemies of freedom to "taunt us as hypocrites" and was angered by individuals such as Douglas who refused even to admit that slavery was wrong.

Lincoln's views on the issue were best expressed in his letters. He wrote in 1858, for example: "As I would not be a *slave*, so I would not be a *master*. This expresses my idea of democracy. Whatever differs from this, to the extent of the difference, is no democracy." On another occasion, he wrote: "I have always thought that all men should be free; but if any should be slaves, it should be first those who desire it for themselves, and secondly those who desire it for others. Whenever I hear anyone arguing for slavery, I feel a strong impulse to see it tried on him personally." And in a letter to Joshua Speed dated August 24, 1855, Lincoln stated: "As a nation, we began by declaring that 'all men are created equal.' We now practically read it, 'all men are created equal except Negroes.' Soon it will read 'all men are created equal, except Negroes and foreigners and Catholics.' When it comes to this, I shall prefer emigrating to some country where they make no pretense of loving liberty—to Russia, for instance, where despotism can be taken pure and without the base alloy of hypocrisy."

The facts with which I shall deal this evening are mainly old and familiar; nor is there anything new in the general use I shall make of them. If there shall be any novelty, it will be in the mode of presenting the facts, and the inferences and observations following that presentation.

In his speech last autumn, at Columbus, Ohio, as reported in "The New-York Times," Senator Douglas said:

"Our fathers, when they framed the Government under which we live, understood this question just as well, and even better, than we do now."

I fully indorse this, and I adopt it as a text for this discourse. I so adopt it because it furnishes a precise and an agreed starting point for a discussion between Republicans and that wing of the Democracy headed by Senator Douglas.

It simply leaves the inquiry: *"What was the understanding those fathers had of the question mentioned?"*

What is the frame of government under which we live?

The answer must be: "The Constitution of the United States." That Constitution consists of the original, framed in 1787, (and under which the present government first went into operation,) and twelve subsequently framed amendments, the first ten of which were framed in 1789.

Who were our fathers that framed the Constitution? I suppose the "thirty-nine" who signed the original instrument may be fairly called our fathers who framed that part of the present Government. It is almost exactly true to say they framed it, and it is altogether true to say they fairly represented the opinion and sentiment of the whole nation at that time. Their names, being familiar to nearly all, and accessible to quite all, need not now be repeated.

I take these "thirty-nine," for the present, as being "our fathers who framed the Government under which we live."

What is the question which, according to the text, those fathers understood "just as well, and even better than we do now?"

It is this: Does the proper division of local from federal authority, or anything in the Constitution, forbid our *Federal Government* to control as to slavery in our *Federal Territories*.

Upon this, Senator Douglas holds the affirmative, and Republicans the negative. This affirmation and denial form an issue; and this issue—this question—is precisely what the text declares our fathers understood "better than we."

Let us now inquire whether the "thirty-nine," or any of them, ever acted upon this question; and if they did, how they acted upon it—how they expressed that better understanding?

In 1784, three years before the Constitution—the United States then owning the Northwestern Territory, and no other, the Congress of the Confederation had before them the question of prohibiting slavery in that Territory; and four of the "thirty-nine" who afterward framed the Constitution, were in that Congress, and voted on that question. Of these, Roger Sherman, Thomas Mifflin, and Hugh Williamson voted for the prohibition, thus showing that, in their understanding, no line dividing local from federal authority, nor anything else, properly forbade the Federal Government to control as to slavery in federal territory. The other of the four—James McHenry—voted against the prohibition, showing that, for some cause, he thought it improper to vote for it.

In 1787, still before the Constitution, but while the Convention was in session framing it, and while the Northwestern Territory still was the only territory owned by the United States, the same question of prohibiting slavery in the territory again came before the Congress of the Confederation; and two more of the "thirty-nine" who afterward signed the Constitution, were in that Congress, and voted on the question. They were William Blount and William Few; and they both voted for the prohibition. ...

In 1789, by the first Congress which sat under the Constitution, an act was passed to enforce the Ordinance of '87, including the prohibition of slavery in the Northwestern Territory. The bill for this act was reported by one of the "thirty-nine," Thomas Fitzsimmons, then a member of the House of Representatives from Pennsylvania. It went through all its stages without a word of opposition, and finally passed both branches without yeas and nays, which is equivalent to a unanimous passage. In this Congress there were sixteen of the thirty-nine fathers who framed the original Constitution. They were John Langdon, Nicholas Gilman, Wm. S. Johnson, Roger Sherman, Robert Morris, Thos. Fitzsimmons, William Few, Abraham Baldwin, Rufus King, William Paterson, George Clymer, Richard Bassett, George Read, Pierce Butler, Daniel Carroll, James Madison. ...

Again, George Washington, another of the "thirty-nine," was then President of the United States, and, as such approved and signed the bill; thus completing its validity as a law, and thus showing that, in his understanding, no line dividing local from federal authority, nor anything in the Constitution, forbade the Federal Government, to control as to slavery in federal territory.

No great while after the adoption of the original Constitution, North Carolina ceded to the Federal Government the country now constituting the State of Tennessee; and a few years later Georgia ceded that which now constitutes the States of Mississippi and Alabama. In both deeds of cession it was made a condition by the ceding States that the Federal Government should not prohibit slavery in the ceded territory. Besides this, slavery was then actually in the ceded country. Under these circumstances, Congress, on taking charge of these countries, did not absolutely prohibit slavery within them. But they did interfere with it—take control of it—even there, to a certain extent. In 1798, Congress organized the Territory of Mississippi. In the act of organization, they prohibited the bringing of slaves into the Territory, from any place without the United States, by fine, and giving freedom to slaves so bought. This act passed both branches of Congress without yeas and nays. In that Congress were three of the "thirty-nine" who framed the original Constitution. They were John Langdon, George Read and Abraham Baldwin. ...

In 1803, the Federal Government purchased the Louisiana country. Our former territorial acquisitions came from certain of our own States; but this Louisiana country was acquired from a foreign nation. In 1804, Congress gave a territorial organization to that part of it which now constitutes the State of Louisiana. New Orleans, lying within that part, was an old and comparatively large city. There were other considerable towns and settlements, and slavery was extensively and thoroughly intermingled with the people. Congress did not, in the Territorial Act, prohibit slavery; but they did interfere with it—take control of it—in a more marked and extensive way than they did in the case of Mississippi. The substance of the provision therein made, in relation to slaves, was:

First. That no slave should be imported into the territory from foreign parts.

Second. That no slave should be carried into it who had been imported into the United States since the first day of May, 1798.

Third. That no slave should be carried into it, except by the owner, and for his own use as a settler; the penalty in all the cases being a fine upon the violator of the law, and freedom to the slave.

This act also was passed without yeas and nays. In the Congress which passed it, there were two of the "thirty-nine." They were Abraham Baldwin and Jonathan Dayton. ...

In 1819-20 came and passed the Missouri question. Many votes were taken, by yeas and nays, in both branches of Congress, upon the various phases of the general question. Two of the "thirty-nine"—Rufus King and Charles Pinckney—were members of that Congress. Mr. King steadily voted for slavery prohibition and against all compromises, while Mr. Pinckney as steadily voted against slavery prohibition and against all compromises. ...

The cases I have mentioned are the only acts of the "thirty-nine," or of any of them, upon the direct issue, which I have been able to discover. ...

Here, then, we have twenty-three out of our thirty-nine fathers "who framed the government under which we live," who have, upon their official responsibility and their corporal oaths, acted upon the very question which the text affirms they "understood just as well, and even better than we do now;" and twenty-one of them—a clear majority of the whole "thirty-nine"—so acting upon it as to make them guilty of gross political impropriety and willful perjury, if, in their understanding, any proper division between local and federal authority, or anything in the Constitution they had made themselves, and sworn to support, forbade the Federal Government to control as to slavery in the federal territories. Thus the twenty-one acted; and, as actions speak louder than words, so actions, under such responsibility, speak still louder. ...

The remaining sixteen of the "thirty-nine," so far as I have discovered, have left no record of their understanding upon the direct question of federal control of slavery in the federal territories. But there is much reason to believe that their understanding upon that question would not have appeared different from that of their twenty-three compeers, had it been manifested at all.

For the purpose of adhering rigidly to the text, I have purposely omitted whatever understanding may have been manifested by any person, however distinguished, other than the thirty-nine fathers who framed the original Constitution; and, for the same reason, I have also omitted whatever understanding may have been manifested by any of the "thirty-nine" even, on any other phase of the general question of slavery. If we should look into their acts and declarations on those other phases, as the foreign slave trade, and the morality and policy of slavery generally, it would appear to us that on the direct question of federal control of slavery in federal territories, the sixteen, if they had acted at all, would probably have acted just as the twenty-three did. Among that sixteen were several of the most noted anti-slavery men of those times—as Dr. Franklin, Alexander Hamilton and Gouverneur Morris—while there was not one now known to have been otherwise, unless it may be John Rutledge of South Carolina.

The sum of the whole is, that of our thirty-nine fathers who framed the original Constitution, twenty-one—a clear majority of the whole—certainly understood that no proper division of local from federal authority, nor any part of the Constitution, forbade the Federal Government to control slavery in the federal territories; while all the rest probably had the same understanding. Such, unquestionably, was the understanding of our fathers who framed the original Constitution; and the text affirms that they understood the question "better than we." ...

It is surely safe to assume that the thirty-nine framers of the original Constitution, and the seventy-six members of the Congress which framed the amendments thereto, taken together, do certainly include those who may be fairly called "our fathers who framed the Government under which we live." And so assuming, I defy any man to show that any one of them ever, in his whole life, declared that, in his understanding, any proper division of local from federal authority, or any part of the Constitution, forbade the Federal Government to control as to slavery in the federal territories. I go a step further. I defy any one to show that any living man in the whole world ever did, prior to the beginning of the present century, (and I might almost say prior to the beginning of the last half of the present century,) declare that, in his understanding, any proper division of local from federal authority, or any part of the Constitution, forbade the Federal Government to control as to slavery in the federal territories. To those who now so declare, I give, not only "our fathers who framed the Government under which we live," but with them all other living men within the century in which it was framed, among whom to search, and they shall not be able to find the evidence of a single man agreeing with them.

Now, and here, let me guard a little against being misunderstood. I do not mean to say we are bound to follow implicitly in whatever our fathers did. To do so, would be to discard all the lights of current experience—to reject all progress—all improvement. What I do say is, that if we would supplant the opinions and policy of our fathers in any case, we should do so upon evidence so conclusive, and argument so clear, that even their great authority, fairly considered and weighed, cannot stand; and most surely not in a case whereof we ourselves declare they understood the question better than we. ...

And now, if they would listen—as I suppose they will not—I would address a few words to the Southern people.

I would say to them: You consider yourselves a reasonable and a just people; and I consider that in the general qualities of reason and justice you are not inferior to any other people. Still, when you speak of us Republicans, you do so only to denounce us a reptiles, or, at the best, as no better than outlaws. ...

You say we are sectional. We deny it. That makes an issue; and the burden of proof is upon you. You produce your proof; and what is it? Why, that our party has no existence in your section—gets no votes in your section. The fact is

substantially true; but does it prove the issue? If it does, then in case we should, without change of principle, begin to get votes in your section, we should thereby cease to be sectional. You cannot escape this conclusion; and yet, are you willing to abide by it? If you are, you will probably soon find that we have ceased to be sectional, for we shall get votes in your section this very year. You will then begin to discover, as the truth plainly is, that your proof does not touch the issue. ...

Some of you delight to flaunt in our faces the warning against sectional parties given by Washington in his Farewell Address. Less than eight years before Washington gave that warning, he had, as President of the United States, approved and signed an act of Congress, enforcing the prohibition of slavery in the Northwestern Territory, which act embodied the policy of the Government upon that subject up to and at the very moment he penned that warning; and about one year after he penned it, he wrote LaFayette that he considered that prohibition a wise measure, expressing in the same connection his hope that we should at some time have a confederacy of free States.

Bearing this in mind, and seeing that sectionalism has since arisen upon this same subject, is that warning a weapon in your hands against us, or in our hands against you? Could Washington himself speak, would he cast the blame of that sectionalism upon us, who sustain his policy, or upon you who repudiate it? ...

And how much would it avail you, if you could ... break up the Republican organization? Human action can be modified to some extent, but human nature cannot be changed. There is a judgment and a feeling against slavery in this nation, which cast at least a million and a half of votes. You cannot destroy that judgment and feeling—that sentiment—by breaking up the political organization which rallies around it. You can scarcely scatter and disperse an army which has been formed into order in the face of your heaviest fire; but if you could, how much would you gain by forcing the sentiment which created it out of the peaceful channel of the ballot-box, into some other channel? What would that other channel probably be? Would the number of John Browns be lessened or enlarged by the operation?

But you will break up the Union rather than submit to a denial of your Constitutional rights.

That has a somewhat reckless sound; but it would be palliated, if not fully justified, were we proposing, by the mere force of numbers, to deprive you of some right, plainly written down in the Constitution. But we are proposing no such thing.

When you make these declarations, you have a specific and well-understood allusion to an assumed Constitutional right of yours, to take slaves into the federal territories, and to hold them there as property. But no such right is specifically written in the Constitution. That instrument is literally silent about any such right. We, on the contrary, deny that such a right has any existence in the Constitution, even by implication.

Your purpose, then, plainly stated, is that you will destroy the Government, unless you be allowed to construe and enforce the Constitution as you please, on all points in dispute between you and us. You will rule or ruin in all events.

This, plainly stated, is your language. Perhaps you will say the Supreme Court has decided the disputed Constitutional question in your favor. Not quite so. But waiving the lawyer's distinction between dictum and decision, the Court have decided the question for you in a sort of way. The Court have substantially said, it is your Constitutional right to take slaves into the federal territories, and to hold them there as property.

When I say the decision was made in a sort of way, I mean it was made in a divided Court, by a bare majority of the Judges, and they not quite agreeing with one another in the reasons for making it; that it is so made as that its avowed supporters disagree with one another about its meaning, and that it was mainly based upon a mistaken statement of fact—the statement in the opinion that "the right of property in a slave is distinctly and expressly affirmed in the Constitution."

An inspection of the Constitution will show that the right of property in a slave is not "*distinctly* and *expressly* affirmed" in it. …

If they had only pledged their judicial opinion that such right is affirmed in the instrument by implication, it would be open to others to show that neither the word "slave" nor "slavery" is to be found in the Constitution, nor the word "property" even, in any connection with language alluding to the things slave, or slavery; and that wherever in that instrument the slave is alluded to, he is called a "person;"— and wherever his master's legal right in relation to him is alluded to, it is spoken of as "service or labor which may be due,"—as a debt payable in service or labor. Also, it would be open to show, by contemporaneous history, that this mode of alluding to slaves and slavery, instead of speaking of them, was employed on purpose to exclude from the Constitution the idea that there could be property in man....

Under all these circumstances, do you really feel yourselves justified to break up this Government unless such a court decision as yours is, shall be at once submitted to as a conclusive and final rule of political action? But you will not abide the election of a Republican president! In that supposed event, you say, you will destroy the Union; and then, you say, the great crime of having destroyed it will be upon us! That is cool. A highwayman holds a pistol to my ear, and mutters through his teeth, "Stand and deliver, or I shall kill you, and then you will be a murderer!"…

A few words now to Republicans. *It is exceedingly desirable that all parts of this great Confederacy shall be at peace, and in harmony, one with another. Let us Republicans do our part to have it so. Even though much provoked, let us do nothing through passion and ill temper. Even though the southern people will not so much as listen to us, let us calmly consider their demands, and yield to them if, in our deliberate view of our duty, we possibly can.* Judging by all they say and do, and by the subject and nature of their controversy with us, let us determine, if we can, what will satisfy them.

Will they be satisfied if the Territories be unconditionally surrendered to them? We know they will not. In all their present complaints against us, the Territories are scarcely mentioned. Invasions and insurrections are the rage now. Will it satisfy them, if, in the future, we have nothing to do with invasions and insurrections? We know it will not. We so know, because we know we never had anything to do with invasions and insurrections; and yet this total abstaining does not exempt us from the charge and the denunciation.

The question recurs, what will satisfy them?... This, and this only: cease to call slavery *wrong*, and join them in calling it *right*. And this must be done thoroughly—done in *acts* as well as in *words*. Silence will not be tolerated— we must place ourselves avowedly with them. Senator Douglas' new sedition law must be enacted and enforced, suppressing all declarations that slavery is wrong, whether made in politics, in presses, in pulpits, or in private. We must arrest and return their fugitive slaves with greedy pleasure. We must pull down our Free State constitutions. The whole atmosphere must be disinfected from all taint of opposition to slavery, before they will cease to believe that all their troubles proceed from us. …

Holding, as they do, that slavery is morally right, and socially elevating, they cannot cease to demand a full national recognition of it, as a legal right, and a social blessing.

Nor can we justifiably withhold this, on any ground save our conviction that slavery is wrong. If slavery is right, all words, acts, laws, and constitutions against it, are themselves wrong, and should be silenced, and swept away. If it is right, we cannot justly object to its nationality—its universality; if it is wrong, they cannot justly insist upon its extension—its enlargement. All they ask, we could readily grant, if we thought slavery right; all we ask, they could as readily grant, if they thought it wrong. Their thinking it right, and our thinking it wrong, is the precise fact upon which depends the whole controversy. Thinking it right, as they do, they are not to blame for desiring its full recognition, as being right; but, thinking it wrong, as we do, can we yield to them? Can we cast our votes with their view, and against our own? In view of our moral, social, and political responsibilities, can we do this?

Wrong as we think slavery is, we can yet afford to let it alone where it is, because that much is due to the necessity arising from its actual presence in the nation; but can we, while our votes will prevent it, allow it to spread into the National Territories, and to overrun us here in these Free States?

If our sense of duty forbids this, then let us stand by our duty, fearlessly and effectively. Let us be diverted by none of those sophistical contrivances wherewith we are so industriously plied and belabored—contrivances such as groping for some middle ground between the right and the wrong; vain as the search for a man who should be neither a living man nor a dead man; such as a policy of "don't care" on a question about which all true men do care; such as Union appeals beseeching true Union men to yield to Disunionists, reversing the divine rule, and calling, not the sinners, but the righteous to repentance; such as invocations to Washington, imploring men to unsay what Washington said, and undo what Washington did.

Neither let us be slandered from our duty by false accusations against us, nor frightened from it by menaces of destruction to the Government nor of dungeons to ourselves. Let us have faith that right makes might, and in that faith let us to the end dare to do our duty as we understand it.

Photograph of Abraham Lincoln taken by Mathew Brady on February 27, 1860, the day of Lincoln's Cooper Union speech. Recognized as the father of photojournalism, Brady took thousands of photographs that now serve as the primary visual history of the Civil War.

Go Down Moses and Swing Low, Sweet Chariot

The songs of the slaves are among the most enduring in the history of American folk music. These hymns were popular among Negroes working in the plantation fields and among those escaping into Canada via the Underground Railroad in the years prior to the Civil War. One of the most famous leaders of the Underground Railroad was Harriet Tubman, often referred to as the "Moses of her people." "Go Down Moses," which was widely known by the 1850s, became a tribute to her efforts. "Swing Low, Sweet Chariot"—although not nationally known until the early twentieth century—was a popular spiritual among blacks who were adjusting to American citizenship.

Go Down Moses

Go down, Moses,
Way down in Egyptland
Tell ole Pharaoh
To let my people go.

When Israel was in Egyptland
Let my people go
Oppressed so hard they could not stand
Let my people go.

Go down, Moses,
Way down in Egyptland
Tell old Pharaoh
"Let my people go."

"Thus saith the Lord," bold Moses said,
"Let my people go;
If not I'll smite your first-born dead
Let my people go."

Go down, Moses,
Way down in Egyptland,
Tell old Pharaoh,
"Let my people go!"

Swing Low, Sweet Chariot

Swing low, sweet chariot
Comin' for to carry me home;
Swing low, sweet chariot
Comin' for to carry me home

I looked over Jordan, and what did I see,
Comin' for to carry me home?
A band of angels comin' after me,
Comin' for to carry me home

Sometimes I'm up and sometimes I'd down
Comin' for to carry me home,
But still my soul feels heavenly bound
Comin' for to carry me home

The brightest day that I can say
Comin' for to carry me home,
When Jesus washed my sins away
Comin' for to carry me home

If I get there before you do
Comin' for to carry me home,
I'll cut a hole and pull you through
Comin' for to carry me home

If you get there before I do
Comin' for to carry me home,
Tell all my friends I'm comin' too
Comin' for to carry me home

* * *

The Eagle's Nest, an 1861 print by E.B. and E.C. Kellogg depicting the American flag as a nest with the various states as eggs. The eggs representing seceding states are cracked, with small creatures emerging.

The Irrepressible Conflict

JEFFERSON DAVIS

Farewell to the U.S. Senate

I hope the time may come again when a better comprehension of the theory of our Government, and the inalienable rights of the people of the States, will prevent any one from denying that each State is a sovereign, and thus may reclaim the grants which it has made to any agent whomsoever.

Jefferson Davis (1808-1889), the son of a Revolutionary War veteran, was born in that part of Christian County, Kentucky, which now forms Todd County. He attended Transylvania University and later graduated from the U.S. Military Academy. Davis's first wife, who died only months after their marriage, was the daughter of future President Zachary Taylor. He married his second wife, with whom he had six children, in 1845. A veteran of the Black Hawk War and the Mexican-American War, Davis began his political career as a U.S. Representative from Mississippi. He was later elected to the Senate and then served as secretary of war in the administration of Franklin Pierce. At the end of Pierce's administration in 1857, Davis was re-elected to the Senate where he carried on John C. Calhoun's support of states' rights.

On January 21, 1861, after Mississippi passed an Ordinance of Secession, Davis gave his resignation speech to the U.S. Senate. In this speech, he reasserted his belief in the constitutionality of secession and interpreted the Founding Fathers' view of slavery in a manner contrary to that of Abraham Lincoln. Less than one month later, Davis was sworn in as president of the Confederacy.

After Lee's surrender, Davis was imprisoned and indicted for treason, but released on bail after two years and never tried. His spent the rest of his life at his home in Biloxi, entertaining friends and defending the Confederate cause through his writings. In 1881, he published *The Rise and Fall of the Confederate Government*.

I rise, Mr. President, for the purpose of announcing to the Senate that I have satisfactory evidence that the State of Mississippi, by a solemn ordinance of her people, in convention assembled, has declared her separation from the United States. Under these circumstances, of course, my functions are terminated here. It has seemed to me proper, however, that I should appear in the Senate to announce that fact to my associates, and I will say but very little more. The occasion does not invite me to go into argument; and my physical condition would not permit me to do so, if it were otherwise; and yet it seems to become me to say something on the part of the State I here represent on an occasion as solemn as this.

It is known to Senators who have served with me here that I have for many years advocated, as an essential attribute of State sovereignty, the right of a State to secede from the Union. Therefore, if I had thought that Mississippi was acting without sufficient provocation, or without an existing necessity, I should still, under my theory of the Government, because of my allegiance to the State of which I am a citizen, have been bound by her action. I, however, may be permitted to say that I do think she has justifiable cause, and I approve of her act. I conferred with her people before that act was taken, counseled them then that, if the state of things which they apprehended should exist when their Convention met, they should take the action which they have now adopted.

I hope none who hear me will confound this expression of mine with the advocacy of the right of a State to remain in the Union, and to disregard its constitutional obligation by the nullification of the law. Such is not my theory. Nullification and secession, so often confounded, are, indeed, antagonistic principles. Nullification is a remedy which it is sought to apply within the Union, against the agent of the States. It is only to be justified when the agent has violated his constitutional obligations, and a State, assuming to judge for itself, denies the right of the agent thus to act, and appeals to the other states of the Union for a decision; but, when the States themselves and when the people of the States have so acted as to convince us that they will not regard our constitutional rights, then, and then for the first time, arises the doctrine of secession in its practical application.

A great man who now reposes with his fathers, and who has often been arraigned for want of fealty to the

Union, advocated the doctrine of nullification because it preserved the Union. It was because of his deep-seated attachment to the Union—his determination to find some remedy for existing ills short of a severance of the ties which bound South Carolina to the other States—that Mr. Calhoun advocated the doctrine of nullification, which he proclaimed to be peaceful, to be within the limits of State power, not to disturb the Union, but only to be a means of bringing the agent before the tribunal of the States for their judgement.

Secession belongs to a different class of remedies. It is to be justified upon the basis that the states are sovereign. There was a time when none denied it. I hope the time may come again when a better comprehension of the theory of our Government, and the inalienable rights of the people of the States, will prevent any one from denying that each State is a sovereign, and thus may reclaim the grants which it has made to any agent whomsoever.

I, therefore, say I concur in the action of the people of Mississippi, believing it to be necessary and proper, and should have been bound by their action if my belief had been otherwise; and this brings me to the important point which I wish, on this last occasion, to present to the Senate. It is by this confounding of nullification and secession that the name of a great man whose ashes now mingle with his mother earth has been invoked to justify coercion against a seceded State. The phrase, "to execute the laws," was an expression which General Jackson applied to the case of a State refusing to obey the laws while yet a member of the Union. That is not the case which is now presented. The laws are to be executed over the United States, and upon the people of the United States. They have no relation to any foreign country. It is a perversion of terms—at least, it is a great mis-apprehension of the case—which cites that expression for application to a State which has withdrawn from the Union. You may make war on a foreign state. If it be the purpose of gentlemen, they may make war against a State which has withdrawn from the Union; but there are no laws of the United States to be executed within the limits of a seceded State. A State, finding herself in the condition in which Mississippi has judged she is—in which her safety requires that she should provide for the maintenance of her rights out of the Union—surrenders all the benefits (and they are known to be many), deprives herself of the advantages (and they are known to be great), severs all the ties of affection (and they are close and enduring), which

have bound her to the Union; and thus divesting herself of every benefit—taking upon herself every burden—she claims to be exempt from any power to execute the laws of the United States within her limits.

I well remember an occasion when Massachusetts was arraigned before the bar of the Senate, and when the doctrine of coercion was rife, and to be applied against her, because of the rescue of a fugitive slave in Boston. My opinion then was the same that it is now. Not in a spirit of egotism, but to show that I am not influenced in my opinions because the case is my own, I refer to that time and that occasion as containing the opinion which I then entertained, and on which my present conduct is based. I then said that if Massachusetts—following her purpose through a stated line of conduct—chose to take the last step, which separates her from the Union, it is her right to go, and I will neither vote one dollar nor one man to coerce her back; but I will say to her, Godspeed, in memory of the kind associations which once existed between her and the other States.

It has been a conviction of pressing necessity—it has been a belief that we are to be deprived in the Union of the rights which our fathers bequeathed to us—which has brought Mississippi to her present decision. She has heard proclaimed the theory that all men are created free and equal, and this made the basis of an attack upon her social institutions; and the sacred Declaration of Independence has been invoked to maintain the position of the equality of the races. That Declaration is to be construed by the circumstances and purposes for which it was made. The communities were declaring their independence; the people of those communities were asserting that no man was born—to use the language of Mr. Jefferson—booted and spurred, to ride over the rest of mankind; that men were created equal—meaning the men of the political community; that there was no divine right to rule; that no man inherited the right to govern; that there were no classes by which power and place descended to families; but that all stations were equally within the grasp of each member of the body politic. These were the great principles they announced; these were the purposes for which they made their declaration; these were the ends to which their enunciation was directed. They have no reference to the slave; else, how happened it that among the items of arraignment against George III was that he endeavored to do just what the North has been endeavoring of late to do, to stir up insurrection among our slaves? Had the Declaration announced that the negroes were free and equal, how was the prince to be arraigned for raising up insurrection among them? And how was this to be enumerated among the high crimes which caused the colonies to sever their connection with the mother country? When our Constitution was formed, the same idea was rendered more palpable; for there we find provision made for that very class of persons as property; they were not put upon the equality of footing with white men—not even upon that of paupers and convicts; but, so far as representation was concerned, were discriminated against as a lower caste, only to be represented in the numerical proportion of three-fifths.

Then, Senators, we recur to the compact which binds us together; we recur to the principles upon which our Government was founded; and when you deny them, and when you deny us the right to withdraw from a Government which, thus perverted, threatens to be destructive of our rights, we but tread in the path of our fathers when we proclaim our independence and take the hazard. This is done, not in hostility to others, not to injure any section of the country, not even for our own pecuniary benefit, but from the high and solemn motive of defending and protecting the rights we inherited, and which it is our duty to transmit unshorn to our children.

I find in myself perhaps a type of the general feeling of my constituents towards yours. I am sure I feel no hostility toward you, Senators from the North. I am sure there is not one of you, whatever sharp discussion there may have been between us, to whom I cannot now say, in the presence of my God, I wish you well; and such, I feel, is the feeling of the people whom I represent toward those whom you represent. I, therefore, feel that I but express their desire when I say I hope, and they hope, for peaceable relations with you, though we must part. They may be mutually beneficial to us in the future, as they have been in the past, if you so will it. The reverse may bring disaster on every portion of the country, and, if you will have it thus, we will invoke the God of our fathers, who delivered them from the power of the lion, to protect us from the ravages of the bear; and thus, putting our trust in God and in our firm hearts and strong arms, we will vindicate the right as best we may.

In the course of my service here, associated at different times with a variety of Senators, I see now around me some with whom I have served long; there have been points of collision, but, whatever of offense there has been to me, I leave here. I carry with me no hostile remembrance. Whatever offense I have given which has not been redressed, or for which satisfaction has not been demanded, I have, Senators, in this hour of our parting, to offer you my apology for any pain which, in the heat of discussion, I have inflicted. I go hence unencumbered by the remembrance of any injury received, and having discharged the duty of making the only reparation in my power for any injury offered.

Mr. President and Senators, having made the announcement which the occasion seemed to me to require, it only remains for me to bid you a final adieu.

ABRAHAM LINCOLN

First Inaugural Address

The mystic chords of memory, stretching from every battlefield and patriot grave to every living heart and hearthstone all over this broad land, will yet swell the chorus of the Union, when again touched, as surely they will be, by the better angels of our nature.

Receiving all of his electoral votes and most of his popular votes from the North, Abraham Lincoln was elected president in 1860. Shortly thereafter, and by the time he was inaugurated, seven states—South Carolina, Mississippi, Florida, Alabama, Georgia, Louisiana, and Texas—had seceded from the Union. Representatives from these states had met in Montgomery, Alabama, where they formed the Confederate States of America.

On February 11, 1861, Lincoln left Springfield and boarded a train for Washington, D.C., saying, "I now leave, not knowing when, or whether ever, I may return, with a task before me greater than that which rested upon Washington. Without the assistance of that Divine Being who ever attended him, I cannot succeed. With that assistance I cannot fail."

On March 4, President-elect Lincoln rode with President Buchanan in an open carriage to the Capitol. There, on the East Portico, eighty-three-year-old Chief Justice Roger Taney administered the executive oath. The Capitol itself was sheathed in scaffolding because the copper and wood dome was being replaced with a cast iron dome. Lincoln's inaugural address was a final attempt at conciliation with the South, but he made it clear that secession was unlawful and that the Union would defend itself.

Lincoln's words were not heeded. On April 12, 1861, Confederate forces fired on Fort Sumter, a Union garrison in Charleston, South Carolina, and the fort was surrendered the following day. Lincoln responded by issuing a call for troops, and Virginia, Arkansas, North Carolina, and Tennessee promptly joined the Confederacy. The American Civil War had begun.

Fellow-citizens of the United States:

In compliance with a custom as old as the Government itself, I appear before you to address you briefly and to take in your presence the oath prescribed by the Constitution of the United States to be taken by the President before he enters on the execution of this office.

I do not consider it necessary at present for me to discuss those matters of administration about which there is no special anxiety or excitement.

Apprehension seems to exist among the people of the Southern States that by the accession of a Republican Administration their property and their peace and personal security are to be endangered. There has never been any reasonable cause for such apprehension. Indeed, the most ample evidence to the contrary has all the while existed and been open to their inspection. It is found in nearly all the published speeches of him who now addresses you. I do but quote from one of those speeches when I declare that I have no purpose, directly or indirectly, to interfere with the institution of slavery in the States where it exists. I believe I have no lawful right to do so, and I have no inclination to do so. ...

It is seventy-two years since the first inauguration of a President under our National Constitution. During that period fifteen different and greatly distinguished citizens have in succession administered the executive branch of the Government. They have conducted it through many perils, and generally with great success. Yet, with all this scope of precedent, I now enter upon the same task for the brief constitutional term of four years under great and peculiar difficulty. A disruption of the Federal Union, heretofore only menaced, is now formidably attempted.

I hold that in contemplation of universal law and of the Constitution, the Union of these States is perpetual. Perpetuity is implied, if not expressed, in the fundamental law of all national governments. It is safe to assert that no government proper ever had a provision in its organic law for its own termination. Continue to execute all the express provisions of our National Constitution, and the Union will endure forever, it being impossible to destroy it except by some action not provided for in the instrument itself.

Again: If the United States be not a government proper, but an association of States in the nature of contract merely, can it, as a contract, be peaceably unmade by less than all the parties who made it? One party to a contract may violate it—break it, so to speak—but does it not require all to lawfully rescind it?

Descending from these general principles, we find the proposition that in legal contemplation the Union is perpetual confirmed by the history of the Union itself. The Union is much older than the Constitution. It was formed, in fact, by the Articles of Association in 1774. It was matured and continued by the Declaration of Independence in 1776. It was further matured, and the faith of all the then thirteen States expressly plighted and engaged that it should be perpetual, by the Articles of Confederation in 1778. And finally, in 1787, one of the declared objects for ordaining and establishing the Constitution was *to form a more perfect Union.*

But if destruction of the Union by one or by a part only of the States be lawfully possible, the Union is less perfect than before the Constitution, having lost the vital element of perpetuity.

It follows from these views that no State upon its own mere motion can lawfully get out of the Union; that *resolves* and *ordinances* to that effect are legally void, and that acts of violence within any State or States against the authority of the United States are insurrectionary or revolutionary, according to circumstances.

I therefore consider that in view of the Constitution and the laws the Union is unbroken, and to the extent of my ability, I shall take care, as the Constitution itself expressly enjoins upon me, that the laws of the Union be faithfully executed in all the States. Doing this I deem to be only a simple duty on my part, and I shall perform it so far as practicable unless my rightful masters, the American people, shall withhold the requisite means or in some authoritative manner direct the contrary. I trust this will not be regarded as a menace, but only as the declared purpose of the Union that it will constitutionally defend and maintain itself.

In doing this there needs to be no bloodshed or violence, and there shall be none unless it be forced upon the national authority. The power confided to me will be used to hold, occupy, and possess the property and places belonging to the Government and to collect the duties and imposts; but beyond what may be necessary for these objects, there will be no invasion, no using of force against or among the people anywhere. Where hostility to the United States in any interior locality shall be so great and universal as to prevent competent resident citizens from holding the Federal offices, there will be no attempt to force obnoxious strangers among the people for that object. While the strict legal right may exist in the Government to enforce the exercise of these offices, the attempt to do so would be so irritating, and so nearly impracticable withal, that I deem it better to forego for the time the uses of such offices.

The mails, unless repelled, will continue to be furnished in all parts of the Union. So far as possible the people everywhere shall have that sense of perfect security which is most favorable to calm thought and reflection. The course here indicated will be followed unless current events and experience shall show a modification or change to be proper, and in every case and exigency my best discretion will be exercised, according to circumstances actually existing and with a view and a hope of a peaceful solution of the national troubles and the restoration of fraternal sympathies and affections.

That there are persons in one section or another who seek to destroy the Union at all events and are glad of any pretext to do it I will neither affirm nor deny; but if there be such, I need address no word to them. To those, however, who really love the Union may I not speak?

Before entering upon so grave a matter as the destruction of our national fabric, with all its benefits, its memories, and its hopes, would it not be wise to ascertain precisely why we do it? Will you hazard so desperate a step while there is any possibility that any portion of the ills you fly from have no real existence? Will you, while the certain ills you fly to are greater than all the real ones you fly from, will you risk the commission of so fearful a mistake?

All profess to be content in the Union if all constitutional rights can be maintained. Is it true, then, that any right plainly written in the Constitution has been denied? I think not. Happily, the human mind is so constituted that no party can reach to the audacity of doing this. Think, if you can, of a single instance in which a plainly written provision of the Constitution has ever been denied. If by the mere force of numbers a majority should deprive a minority of any clearly written constitutional right, it might in a moral point of view justify revolution; certainly would if such right were a vital one. But such is not our case. All the vital rights of minorities and of individuals are so plainly assured to them by affirmations and negations, guaranties and prohibitions, in the Constitution that controversies never arise concerning them. But no organic law can ever be framed with a provision specifically applicable to every question which may occur in practical administration. No foresight can anticipate, nor any document of reasonable length contain, express provisions for all possible questions. Shall fugitives from labor be surrendered by national or by State authority? The Constitution does not expressly say. *May* Congress prohibit slavery in the Territories? The Constitution does not expressly say. *Must* Congress protect slavery in the Territories? The Constitution does not expressly say.

From questions of this class spring all our constitutional controversies, and we divide upon them into majorities and minorities. If the minority will not acquiesce, the majority must, or the Government must cease. There is no other alternative, for continuing the Government is acquiescence on one side or the other. If a minority in such case will secede rather than acquiesce, they make a precedent which in turn will divide and ruin them, for a minority of their own will secede from them whenever a majority refuses to be controlled by such minority. For instance, why may not any portion of a new confederacy a year or two hence arbitrarily secede again, precisely as portions of the present Union now claim to secede from it? All who cherish disunion sentiments are now being educated to the exact temper of doing this.

Is there such perfect identity of interests among the States to compose a new union as to produce harmony only and prevent renewed secession?

Plainly the central idea of secession is the essence of anarchy. A majority held in restraint by constitutional checks and limitations, and always changing easily with deliberate changes of popular opinions and sentiments, is the only true sovereign of a free people. Whoever rejects it does of necessity fly to anarchy or to despotism. Unanimity is impossible. The rule of a minority, as a permanent arrangement, is wholly inadmissible; so that, rejecting the majority principle, anarchy or despotism in some form is all that is left.

I do not forget the position assumed by some that constitutional questions are to be decided by the Supreme Court, nor do I deny that such decisions must be binding in any case upon the parties to a suit as to the object of that suit, while they are also entitled to very high respect and consideration in all parallel cases by all other departments of the Government. And while it is obviously possible that such decision may be erroneous in any given case, still the evil effect following it, being limited to that particular case, with the chance that it may be overruled and never become

a precedent for other cases, can better be borne than could the evils of a different practice. At the same time, the candid citizen must confess that if the policy of the Government upon vital questions affecting the whole people is to be irrevocably fixed by decisions of the Supreme Court, the instant they are made in ordinary litigation between parties in personal actions the people will have ceased to be their own rulers, having to that extent practically resigned their Government into the hands of that eminent tribunal. Nor is there in this view any assault upon the court or the judges. It is a duty from which they may not shrink to decide cases properly brought before them, and it is no fault of theirs if others seek to turn their decisions to political purposes.

One section of our country believes slavery is *right* and ought to be extended, while the other believes it is *wrong* and ought not to be extended. This is the only substantial dispute. The fugitive-slave clause of the Constitution and the law for the suppression of the foreign slave trade are each as well enforced, perhaps, as any law can ever be in a community where the moral sense of the people imperfectly supports the law itself. The great body of the people abide by the dry legal obligation in both cases, and a few break over in each. This, I think, can not be perfectly cured; and it would be worse in both cases *after* the separation of the sections, than before. The foreign slave trade, now imperfectly suppressed, would be ultimately revived without restriction in one section, while fugitive slaves, now only partially surrendered, would not be surrendered at all by the other.

Physically speaking, we cannot separate. We cannot remove our respective sections from each other nor build an impassable wall between them. A husband and wife may be divorced and go out of the presence and beyond the reach of each other, but the different parts of our country can not do this. They can not but remain face to face, and intercourse, either amicable or hostile, must continue between them. Is it possible, then, to make that intercourse more advantageous or more satisfactory *after* separation than *before*? Can aliens make treaties easier than friends can make laws? Can treaties be more faithfully enforced between aliens than laws can among friends? Suppose you go to war, you can not fight always; and when, after much loss on both sides and no gain on either, you cease fighting, the identical old questions, as to terms of intercourse, are again upon you.

This country, with its institutions, belongs to the people who inhabit it. Whenever they shall grow weary of the existing Government, they can exercise their *constitutional* right of amending it or their *revolutionary* right to dismember or overthrow it. I can not be ignorant of the fact that many worthy and patriotic citizens are desirous of having the national Constitution amended. While I make no recommendation of amendments, I fully recognize the rightful authority of the people over the whole subject, to be exercised in either of the modes prescribed in the instrument itself; and I should, under existing circumstances, favor rather than oppose a fair opportunity being afforded the people to act upon it.

I will venture to add that to me the convention mode seems preferable, in that it allows amendments to originate with the people themselves, instead of only permitting them to take or reject propositions originated by others, not especially chosen for the purpose, and which might not be precisely such as they would wish to either accept or refuse. I understand a proposed amendment to the Constitution—which amendment, however, I have not seen—has passed Congress, to the effect that the Federal Government shall never interfere with the domestic institutions of the States, including that of persons held to service. To avoid misconstruction of what I have said, I depart from my purpose not to speak of particular amendments so far as to say that, holding such a provision to now be implied constitutional law, I have no objection to its being made express and irrevocable.

The Chief Magistrate derives all his authority from the people, and they have referred none upon him to fix terms for the separation of the States. The people themselves can do this if also they choose, but the Executive as such has nothing to do with it. His duty is to administer the present Government as it came to his hands and to transmit it unimpaired by him to his successor.

Why should there not be a patient confidence in the ultimate justice of the people? Is there any better or equal hope in the world? In our present differences, is either party without faith of being in the right? If the Almighty Ruler of Nations, with His eternal truth and justice, be on your side of the North, or on yours of the South, that truth and justice will surely prevail by the judgment of this great tribunal of the American people.

By the frame of the Government under which we live this same people have wisely given their public servants but little power for mischief, and have with equal wisdom provided for the return of that little to their own hands at very short intervals. While the people retain their virtue and vigilance no Administration by any extreme of wickedness or folly can very seriously injure the Government in the short space of four years.

My countrymen, one and all, think calmly and *well* upon this whole subject. Nothing valuable can be lost by taking time. If there be an object to *hurry* any of you in hot haste to a step which you would never take *deliberately*, that object will be frustrated by taking time; but no good object can be frustrated by it. Such of you as are now dissatisfied still have the old Constitution unimpaired, and, on the sensitive point, the laws of your own framing under it; while the new Administration will have no immediate power, if it would, to change either. If it were admitted that you who are dissatisfied hold the right side in the dispute, there still is no single good reason for precipitate action. Intelligence, patriotism, Christianity, and a firm reliance on Him who has never yet forsaken this favored land are still competent to adjust in the best way all our present difficulty.

In *your* hands, my dissatisfied fellow-countrymen, and not in *mine*, is the momentous issue of civil war. The Government will not assail *you*. You can have no conflict without being yourselves the aggressors. *You* have no oath registered in heaven to destroy the Government, while *I* shall have the most solemn one to "preserve, protect, and defend it."

I am loath to close. We are not enemies, but friends. We must not be enemies. Though passion may have strained it must not break our bonds of affection. The mystic chords of memory, stretching from every battlefield and patriot grave to every living heart and hearthstone all over this broad land, will yet swell the chorus of the Union, when again touched, as surely they will be, by the better angels of our nature.

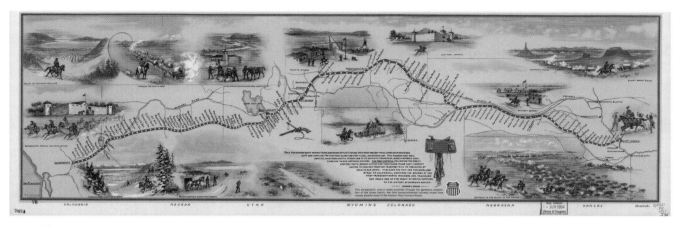

Map of the Pony Express Route in 1860, by William Henry Jackson, re-issued by the Union Pacific Railroad Company in commemoration of the Pony Express centennial. The Pony Express was a fast mail delivery service that roughly followed the Oregon Trail and the California Trail to Fort Bridger in Wyoming, the Mormon Trail to Salt Lake City, and the Central Nevada Route to Carson City before passing over the Sierras into Sacramento, California. Between April 3, 1860, and the end of 1861, when replaced by the transcontinental telegraph, riders delivered nearly 35,000 pieces of mail between Missouri and California—1,966 miles in a then lightning fast ten days while battling rough terrain, inclement weather and hostile Indians. Help wanted ads called for "expert riders willing to risk death daily. Orphans preferred." The Pony Express was vital for tying California closely with the Union just before the Civil War.

FRANCIS DE HAES JANVIER

God Save Our President

Francis de Haes Janvier (1817-1885), the descendent of a Huguenot refugee, wrote "God Save Our President" as a tribute to Abraham Lincoln. The poem gives praise to the manner in which Americans have, from the very beginning, chosen their chief executive—"Ten times ten thousand patriots greet the shrine of Liberty! … To elevate, with solemn rites, the ruler of our land!"

All hail! Unfurl the Stripes and Stars!
The banner of the free!
Ten times ten thousand patriots greet
The shrine of Liberty!
Come, with one heart, one hope, one aim,
An undivided band,
To elevate, with solemn rites,
The ruler of our land!

Not to invest a potentate
With robes of majesty,
Not to confer a kingly crown,
Nor bend a subject knee.
We bow beneath no sceptred sway,
Obey no royal nod:
Columbia's sons, erect and free,
Kneel only to their God!

Our ruler boasts no titled rank,
No ancient, princely line,
No regal right to sovereignty,
Ancestral and divine.
A patriot,—at his country's call,
Responding to her voice;
One of the people,—he becomes
A sovereign by our choice!

And now, before the mighty pile
We've reared to Liberty,
He swears to cherish and defend
The charter of the free!
God of our country! seal his oath
With Thy supreme assent.
God save the Union of the States!
God save our President!

WILLIAM CULLEN BRYANT

Oh Mother of a Mighty Race and Our Country's Call

William Cullen Bryant (1794-1878), one of the most influential and popular figures of the mid-nineteenth century, was born in Cummington, Massachusetts. Like his contemporary, Henry Wadsworth Longfellow, Bryant had his first poem published at the age of thirteen. At seventeen, he gained international acclaim for "Thanatopsis," a lengthy reflection on the meaning of death. In addition to his poetic endeavors, Bryant was also a well-known newspaper editor and civic activist in New York City. He helped establish Central Park and the Metropolitan Museum of Art and made the *Evening Post* an advocate of the Democratic Party, although he later joined the Republicans.

"Oh Mother of a Mighty Race," published in *Graham's Magazine* in 1847, was among Bryant's many great tributes to the country he loved. His fidelity to union was further evidenced by the 1861 publication of "Our Country's Call," an appeal to men of the North to take arms against secessionists.

Oh Mother of a Mighty Race

Oh mother of a mighty race,
Yet lovely in thy youthful grace!
The elder dames, thy haughty peers,
Admire and hate thy blooming years.
    With words of shame
And taunts of scorn they join thy name.

For on thy cheeks the glow is spread
That tints thy morning hills with red;
Thy step—the wild-deer's rustling feet
Within thy woods are not more fleet;
    Thy hopeful eye
Is bright as thine own sunny sky.

Ay, let them rail—those haughty ones,
While safe thou dwellest with thy sons.
They do not know how loved thou art,
How many a fond and fearless heart
    Would rise to throw
Its life between thee and the foe.

They know not, in their hate and pride,
What virtues with thy children bide;
How true, how good, thy graceful maids
Make bright, like flowers, the valley-shades;
    What generous men
Spring, like thine oaks, by hill and glen;—

What cordial welcomes greet the guest
By thy lone rivers of the West;
How faith is kept, and truth revered,
And man is loved, and God is feared,
    In woodland homes,
And where the ocean border foams.

There's freedom at thy gates and rest
For Earth's down-trodden and opprest,
A shelter for the hunted head,
For the starved laborer toil and bread.
    Power, at thy bounds,
Stops and calls back his baffled hounds.

Oh, fair young mother! on thy brow
Shall sit a nobler grace than now.
Deep in the brightness of the skies
The thronging years in glory rise,
    And, as they fleet,
Drop strength and riches at thy feet.

Thine eye, with every coming hour,
Shall brighten, and thy form shall tower;
And when thy sisters, elder born,
Would brand thy name with words of scorn,
    Before thine eye,
Upon their lips the taunt shall die.

Our Country's Call

Lay down the axe; fling by the spade;
Leave in its track the toiling plough;
The rifle and the bayonet-blade
For arms like yours were fitter now;
And let the hands that ply the pen
Quit the light task, and learn to wield
The horseman's crooked brand, and rein
The charger on the battle-field.

Our country calls; away! away!
To where the blood-stream blots the green.
Strike to defend the gentlest sway
That Time in all his course has seen.
See, from a thousand coverts—see,
Spring the armed foes that haunt her track;
They rush to smite her down, and we
Must beat the banded traitors back.

Ho! sturdy as the oaks ye cleave,
And moved as soon to fear and flight,
Men of the glade and forest! leave
Your woodcraft for the field of fight.
The arms that wield the axe must pour
An iron tempest on the foe;
His serried ranks shall reel before
The arm that lays the panther low.

And ye, who breast the mountain-storm
By grassy steep or highland lake,
Come, for the land ye love, to form
A bulwark that no foe can break.
Stand, like your own gray cliffs that mock
The whirlwind, stand in her defence;
The blast as soon shall move the rock
As rushing squadrons bear ye thence.

And ye, whose homes are by her grand
Swift rivers, rising far away,
Come from the depth of her green land,
As mighty in your march as they;
As terrible as when the rains
Have swelled them over bank and borne,
With sudden floods to drown the plains
And sweep along the woods uptorn.

And ye, who throng, beside the deep,
Her ports and hamlets of the strand,
In number like the waves that leap
On his long-murmuring marge of sand—
Come like that deep, when, o'er his brim
He rises, all his floods to pour,
And flings the proudest barks that swim,
A helpless wreck, against the shore!

Few, few were they whose swords of old
Won the fair land in which we dwell,
But we are many, we who hold
The grim resolve to guard it well.
Strike, for that broad and goodly land,
Blow after blow, till men shall see
That Might and Right move hand in hand,
And glorious must their triumph be!

Officers on deck of the USS Monitor, *on the James River. The Battle of Hampton Roads was a naval battle noted for being the first fight between two ironclad warships, the USS* Monitor *and the CSS* Virginia *(the latter rebuilt from the burned-out hull of the USS* Merrimack*). The principal confrontations took place on March 8 and March 9, 1862, off Sewell's Point, a narrow place near the mouth of Hampton Roads, Virginia. The battle, though inconclusive, received worldwide publicity. Wooden navies soon became obsolete, and new technologies were developed to improve the efficiency and the battle-power of iron-clad ships.*

SULLIVAN BALLOU

Letter to His Wife

When my last breath escapes me on the battlefield I shall whisper your name.

In 1861, comparatively few volunteers in the Northern army marched off to end slavery, but most were willing to fight and die to preserve the Union. One such individual was Sullivan Ballou, a thirty-two-year-old Providence lawyer and former speaker of the Rhode Island House of Representatives. An ardent Republican and devoted supporter of Abraham Lincoln, Ballou left a promising political career to enlist as a major in the Second Rhode Island Volunteers.

While stationed at Camp Clark, near the nation's capital, Ballou penned the following letter to his wife in Smithfield. It is at once a passionate love letter and a profound meditation on the meaning of Union in which Ballou expresses his "unbounded love" for his "darling wife and children," but confides that those feelings struggle "in fierce, though useless contest" with his love of country. Ballou's words came to prominence 129 years after he wrote them, when an abridged version of his letter was read on the widely watched public television series *The Civil War*, produced by Ken Burns. The beauty of the language and the passion of the sentiments stirred millions.

Ballou wrote the letter July 14 while awaiting orders that would take him to Manassas, where he and twenty-seven of his men would die one week later in the First Battle of Bull Run.

My Dear Sarah,

The indications are very strong that we shall move in a few days perhaps tomorrow.

Lest I shall not be able to write to you again, I feel impelled to write a few lines that may fall under your eye when I shall be no more.

Our movement may be one of a few days duration, and full of pleasure, and it may be one of severe conflict and death to me. "Not my will, but Thine Oh God, be done." If it is necessary that I should fall on the battlefield for my Country, I am ready. I have no misgivings about or lack of confidence in the cause in which I am engaged, and my courage does not halt or falter.

I know how strongly American Civilization now leans on the triumph of the Government, and how great a debt we owe to those who went before us through the blood and suffering of the Revolution, and I am willing, perfectly willing, to lay down all my joys in this life to help maintain this Government and to pay that debt, but, my dear wife, when I know that with my own joys I lay down nearly all of yours, and replace them in this life with cares and sorrows; when, after having eaten for long years the bitter fruit of orphanage myself, I must offer it as the only sustenance to my dear little children, is it weak or dishonorable, that, while the banner of my purpose floats calmly and proudly in the breeze, underneath, my unbounded love for you, my darling wife and children, I shall struggle in fierce though useless contest with my love of Country.

I cannot describe to you my feelings on this calm summer Sabbath night, when two thousand men are sleeping around me, many of them enjoying the last perhaps before that of death; and I am suspicious that death is creeping behind me with his fatal dart while I am communing with God, My Country, and Thee. I have sought most closely and diligently, and often in my breast for a wrong motive in thus hazarding the happiness of all those I loved, and I could find none. A pure love of my Country and the principles I have often advocated before the people, another name of honor that I love more than I fear death, has called upon me and I have obeyed.

Sarah, my love for you is deathless. It seems to bind me in mighty cables that nothing but Omnipotence could break, and my love of country comes over me like a strong wind, and bears me irresistibly on, with all these chains to the battlefield.

The memories of all the blissful moments I have spent with you come creeping over me, and I feel most deeply grateful to God, and you, that I have enjoyed them so long, and how hard it is for me to give them up, and burn to ashes the hopes of future years, when, God willing we might still have lived and loved together and seen our sons grow up to honorable manhood around us.

I know I have but few and small claims upon Divine Providence, but something whispers to me, perhaps it is the wafted prayer of my little Edgar, that I shall return to my loved ones unharmed. If I do not, my dear Sarah never forget how much I love you, and when my last breath escapes me on the battlefield I shall whisper your name. Forgive my many faults and the many pains I have caused you. How thoughtless, how foolish I have often times been. How gladly would I wash out with my tears every little spot upon your happiness, and struggle with all the misfortunes of this world to shield you and my children from harm, but I cannot. I must watch you from the spirit land and hover near you, while you buffet the storms with your precious little freight, and wait with sad patience till we meet to part no more. But Oh Sarah if the dead can come back to this earth, and flit unseen around those they love, I shall always be near you in the gladdest day, and in the darkest night, amidst your happiest scenes and gloomiest hours, always always; and if there be a soft breeze upon your cheek it shall be my breath, or the cool air fans your throbbing temple, it shall be my spirit passing by.

Sarah, do not mourn me dead, think I am gone and wait for me, for we shall meet again.

As for my little boys, they will grow up, as I have grown, and never know a father's love and care. Little Willie is too young to remember me long, and my blue-eyed Edgar will keep my frolics with him among the dimmest memories of his childhood.

Sarah, I have unbounded confidence in your maternal care and your development of their character, and feel that God will bless you in your holy work.

Tell my two mothers I call God's blessing upon them.

Oh Sarah I wait for you there, come to me, and lead thither my children.

The Flag of the Constellation

Thomas Buchanan Read (1822-1872), a Philadelphia poet and artist, was dedicated to the preservation of the Union and devoted much of his work to celebrating the lives and accomplishments of the Americans who fought in the war of Independence. Read was very generous with his earnings, contributing to organizations which benefited "the sick and wounded who have suffered in our country's cause."

The stars of the morn
On our banner borne,
With the Iris of Heaven are blended;
The hand of our sires,
First mingled those fires,
And by us they shall be defended.
Then hail the true
Red, White and Blue,
The flag of the Constellation;
It sails as it sailed,
By our forefathers hailed,
O'er battles that made us a nation.

What hand so bold
As Strike from its fold
One star or one stripe of its bright'ning,
For him be those stars
Each a fiery Mars,
And each stripe be a terrible lightning.
Then hail the true
Red, White and Blue,
The flag of the Constellation;
It sails as it sailed,
By our forefathers hailed,
O'er battles that made us a nation.

Its meteor form
Shall ride the storm
Till the fiercest of foes surrender;
The storm gone by,
It shall gild the sky,
A rainbow of peace and of splendor.
Then hail the true
Red, White and Blue,
The flag of the Constellation;
It sails as it sailed,
By our forefathers hailed,
O'er battles that made us a nation.

Peace, peace to the world,
Is our motto unfurled,
Though we shun not the field that is gory;
At home or abroad,
Fearing none but our God,
We will carve our own pathway to glory.
Then hail the true
Red, White and Blue,
The flag of the Constellation;
It sails as it sailed,
By our forefathers hailed,
O'er battles that made us a nation.

Dixie

Daniel Decatur Emmett (1815-1904) was an Ohio-born stage performer and songwriter who composed such memorable pieces as "Old Dan Tucker," the most popular tune of 1843. His biggest hit, "Dixie," was written in 1859 and first appeared as a music number in Bryant's Minstrel Show in New York.

When the Civil War broke out, "Dixie" became popular below the Mason-Dixon line, with the South making it the battle hymn of the Confederacy while altering the lyrics with more militaristic verses—*For faith betrayed and pledges broken. Wrongs inflicted, insults spoken. To arms! To arms! In Dixie!*

Southerners were quick to embrace Emmett's song because they had long referred to their region of the country as "Dixieland." The origin of this name is not exactly known, but popular legend refers to an exceptionally kind slaveowner named Dixie who treated his slaves with great humanity. Thus, "Dixie's Land" was known, in a propagandist way, as a genteel place.

The North, unwilling to cede one of their favorite tunes to the South, however, offered their own substitute lyrics— *Away down south in the land of traitors, Rattlesnakes and alligators. … Away down south where grows the cotton, Seventy six seems quite forgotten. …*

"Dixie" was played at Abraham Lincoln's inauguration as well as that of Jefferson Davis.

I wish I was in de land ob cotton,
Old times dar am not forgotten,
Look away! Look away! Look away, Dixie Land!
In Dixie Land where I was born in
Early on one frosty mornin'
Look away! Look away! Look away, Dixie Land!

Chorus:
>   Den I wish I was in Dixie! Hooray! Hooray!
>   In Dixie's Land I'll take my stand, to lib and die in Dixie!
>   Away! Away! Away down South in Dixie!
>   Away! Away! Away down South in Dixie!

Old Missus marry "Will-de-weaber,"
Willyum was a gay deceber,
Look away! Look away! Look away, Dixie Land!
But when he put his arm around her,
He smiled as fierce as a forty-pounder.
Look away! Look away! Look away, Dixie Land!

His face was sharp as a butcher's cleaber;
But dat did not seem to grieb 'er,
Look away! Look away! Look away, Dixie Land!
Old Missus acted de foolish part,
And died for a man dat broke her heart.
Look away! Look away! Look away, Dixie Land!

Now here's a health to de next old Missus,
An' all de gals that want to kiss us;
Look away! Look away! Look away, Dixie Land!
But if you want to drive 'way sorrow,
Come and hear dis song tomorrow.
Look away! Look away! Look away, Dixie Land!

Dar's buckwheat cakes an' Injun batter,
Makes you fat or a little fatter,
Look away! Look away! Look away, Dixie Land!
Den hoe it down and scratch your grabble,
To Dixie's Land I'm bound to trabble.
Look away! Look away! Look away, Dixie Land!

The Bonnie Blue Flag

The Bonnie Blue Flag, a solid blue field with a single white five-pointed star in its center, served unofficially as the first flag of the Confederacy. Originating in the Republic of West Florida in the early 1800s, this flag was later used by the Republic of Texas and was flown by several of the seceding states that were "taking their star out of the Union." When Mississippi's Ordinance of Secession was signed on January 9, 1861, it was marked by a ceremony in which the Bonnie Blue Flag was raised over the capitol building in Jackson.

Among those who witnessed the event was Harry McCarthy (1834-1874?), an English-born comedian and vaudevillian. Having settled in Arkansas, McCarthy performed throughout the South with a pet cockatoo that had been trained to squawk, "Three cheers for Jeff Davis!" on stage. In late 1860, he wrote "The Bonnie Blue Flag" as a tribute to South Carolina's decision to secede from the Union. Set to the tune of a well-known Irish air, "The Jaunting Car," the song became the Confederacy's national anthem as McCarthy added additional stanzas to represent the states that followed in secession. So popular was the song, the New Orleans music publishing house of A. E. Blackmar issued six editions of "The Bonnie Blue Flag" between 1861 and 1864. During the Union Army's occupation of New Orleans, General Benjamin Butler reportedly ordered Blackmar's arrest for daring to publish it and imposed fines on any civilian caught singing or whistling the tune.

We are a band of brothers, and native to the soil,
Fighting for the property we gained by honest toil;
And when our rights were threatened, the cry rose near and far:
Hurrah! for the Bonnie Blue Flag that bears a single star.

Chorus:
    Hurrah! hurrah! for Southern rights! hurrah!
    Hurrah! for the Bonnie Blue Flag that bears a single star.

As long as the Union was faithful to her trust,
Like friends and brethren, kind were we and just;
But now, when Northern treachery attempts our rights to mar,
We hoist on high, the Bonnie Blue Flag that bears a single star.

First gallant South Carolina nobly made the stand,
Then came Alabama who took her by the hand;
Next, quickly Mississippi, Georgia and Florida,
All raised on high, the Bonnie Blue Flag that bears a single star.

Ye men of valor gather 'round the banner of the right,
Texas and fair Louisiana join us in the fight;
Davis, our loved President, and Stephens, statesman rare,
Now rally 'round the Bonnie Blue Flag that bears a single star.

And here's to brave Virginia, the old Dominion State,
With the young Confederacy at length has linked her fate;
Impelled by her example now other States prepare
To hoist, on high, the Bonnie Blue Flag that bears a single star.

Then cheer, boys, cheer, raise a joyous shout,
For Arkansas and North Carolina now have both gone out;
And let another rousing cheer for Tennessee be given,
The single star of the Bonnie Blue Flag has grown to be eleven.

Then here's to our Confederacy, strong we are and brave,
Like patriots of old we'll fight, our heritage to save;
And rather than submit to shame, to die we would prefer,
So cheer for the Bonnie Blue Flag that bears a single star.

GEORGE F. ROOT

Battle Cry of Freedom

George Frederick Root (1820-1895) was born in Sheffield, Massachusetts, and, by the age of thirteen, had mastered no fewer than a dozen musical instruments. He published a music periodical, *The Song Messenger of the Northwest*, and became a partner in the Chicago-based music publishing firm of Root and Cady.

Among the most prolific of wartime songwriters, Root was responsible for the popular Union marching song "Tramp! Tramp! Tramp!" and several other period pieces, including "Just Before the Battle, Mother" and "There's Music in the Air, Boys." In 1861, he wrote two versions of what proved to be the most popular Union song of the entire war. "Battle Cry of Freedom" featured a "rallying" song for civilians and a "battle" song for soldiers. Root's autobiography, *The Story of a Musical Life*, was published in 1891.

Rallying Song

Yes, we'll rally round the flag, boys, we'll rally once again,
Shouting the battle-cry of freedom,
We will rally from the hill-side, we'll gather from the plain,
Shouting the battle-cry of freedom.

Chorus:
    The Union forever, hurrah! boys, hurrah!
    Down with the traitor, up with the star,
    While we rally round the flag, boys, rally once again,
    Shouting the battle-cry of freedom.

We are springing to the call of our Brothers gone before,
And we'll fill the vacant ranks with a million freemen more.

We will welcome to our numbers the loyal, true, and brave,
And altho' they may be poor, not a man shall be a slave.

So we're springing to the call from the East and from the West,
And we'll hurl the rebel crew from the land we love the best.

Battle Song

We are marching to the field, boys, we're going to the fight,
Shouting the battle-cry of freedom,
And we bear the glorious stars for the Union and the right,
Shouting the battle-cry of freedom.

Chorus:
    The Union forever, hurrah! boys, hurrah!
    Down with the traitor, up with the star,
    For we're marching to the field, boys, going to the fight
    Shouting the battle-cry of freedom.

We will meet the rebel host, boys, with fearless hearts and true,
And we'll show what Uncle Sam has for loyal boys to do.

If we fall amid the fray, boys, we'll face them to the last,
And our comrades brave shall hear us, as they go rushing past.

Yes, for Liberty and Union we're springing to the fight,
And the vict'ry shall be ours, for we're rising in our might!

Clara Barton, circa 1866. Known as "The Angel of the Battlefield," Barton served as a nurse on the front lines of the Civil War and worked to obtain and distribute supplies to wounded soldiers. In 1864, she was named superintendent of all Union nurses. Shortly thereafter, at the request of President Lincoln, she set up a bureau of records to aid in the search for missing men. Barton traveled to Europe after the war and became involved with the International Committee of the Red Cross. She founded the American Red Cross in 1881 and served as its president until 1904.

JAMES RYDER RANDALL

Maryland, My Maryland

On April 19, 1861, a Massachusetts regiment passing through Baltimore was attacked by pro-Confederate forces in the city. Baltimore native James Ryder Randall (1839-1908), a professor of English at Poydras College in Pointe Coupee, Louisiana, read about the bloodshed and wrote "Maryland, My Maryland," a hymn to Southern resistance. Encouraged by what he believed to be indications that Maryland was about to join the Confederacy, Randall quickly submitted the work for publication in the April 26 edition of the New Orleans *Delta*. When introduced in Baltimore, the poem was set to the music of "Tannenbaum, O Tannenbaum" and distributed by pro-Confederate publishers with the Maryland state coat of arms on the cover. Though Maryland voted overwhelmingly to remain in the Union, the city of Baltimore remained firmly committed to Southern independence.

The despot's heel is on thy shore,
Maryland, my Maryland!
His torch is at thy temple door,
Maryland, my Maryland!
Avenge the patriotic gore
That flecked the streets of Baltimore,
And be the battle queen of yore,
Maryland, my Maryland!

Hark to an exiled son's appeal,
Maryland, my Maryland!
My mother state, to thee I kneel,
Maryland, my Maryland!
For life or death, for woe or weal,
Thy peerless chivalry reveal,
And gird thy beauteous limbs with steel,
Maryland, my Maryland!

Thou wilt not cower in the dust,
Maryland, my Maryland!
Thy beaming sword shall never rust,
Maryland, my Maryland!
Remember Carroll's sacred trust,
Remember Howard's warlike thrust,
And all thy slumberers with the just,
Maryland, my Maryland!

Come! 'Tis the red dawn of the day,
Maryland, my Maryland!
Come with thy panoplied array,
Maryland, my Maryland!
With Ringgold's spirit for the fray,
With Watson's blood at Monterey,
With fearless Lowe and dashing May,
Maryland, my Maryland!

Dear mother, burst the tyrant's chain,
Maryland, my Maryland!
Virginia should not call in vain,
Maryland, my Maryland!
She meets her sisters on the plain,
"Sic temper," 'tis the proud refrain
That baffles minion's back amain,
Maryland, my Maryland!

Come! for thy shield is bright and strong,
Maryland, my Maryland!
Come! for thy dalliance does thee wrong,
Maryland, my Maryland!
Come to thine own heroic throng,
Stalking with liberty along,
And chant thy dauntless slogan-song,
Maryland, my Maryland!

I see the blush upon thy cheek,
Maryland, my Maryland!
But thou wast ever bravely meek,
Maryland, my Maryland!
But lo! there surges forth a shriek,
From hill to hill, from creek to creek,
Potomac calls to Chesapeake,
Maryland, my Maryland!

Thou wilt not yield the vandal toll,
Maryland, my Maryland!
Thou wilt not crook to his control,
Maryland, my Maryland!
Better the fire upon the roll,
Better the shot, the blade, the bowl,
Than crucifixion of the soul,
Maryland, my Maryland!

I hear the distant thunder-hum,
Maryland, my Maryland!
The "Old Line's" bugle, fife and drum,
Maryland, my Maryland!
She is not dead, nor deaf nor dumb,
Huzza! she spurns the Northern scum—
She breathes! She burns! She'll come! She'll come!
Maryland, my Maryland!

John Brown's Body

First published under the title "Glory Hallelujah!," the original version of this song was written by members of the Second Battalion of Massachusetts Infantry, stationed at Fort Warren in Boston. It was intended as a parody of their own sergeant, John Brown. The music was borrowed from a popular song by William Steffe of South Carolina. As the abolition of slavery became a goal of the Civil War, the lyrics were rewritten to pay homage to John Brown, the martyr of Harpers Ferry, whose fervent opposition to slavery and incredible courage and intelligence facing death made him the hero of many.

Old John Brown's body lies a-mouldering in the grave,
While weep the sons of bondage whom he ventured all to save;
His truth is marching on.

Chorus:
    Glory, glory, Hallelujah!
    Glory, glory, Hallelujah!
    Glory, glory, Hallelujah!
    His truth is marching on.

John Brown was a hero, undaunted, true, and brave;
Kansas knew his valor when he fought her rights to save;
And now though the grass grows green above his grave,
His truth is marching on.

He captured Harpers Ferry with his nineteen men so few,
And he frightened "Old Virginny" till she trembled through and through,
They hung him for a traitor, themselves a traitor crew,
But his truth is marching on.

John Brown was John the Baptist for the Christ we are to see,
Christ who of the bondsman shall the Liberator be;
And soon throughout the sunny South the slaves shall all be free.
For his truth is marching on.

The conflict that he heralded, he looks from heaven to view,
On the army of the Union with its flag, red, white, and blue,
And heaven shall ring with anthems o'er the deeds they mean to do,
For his truth is marching on.

Oh, soldiers of freedom, then strike while strike you may
The deathblow of oppression in a better time and way;
For the dawn of old John Brown has brightened into day,
And his truth is marching on.

President Lincoln visits General George B. McClellan and his staff near Sharpsburg, Maryland, on October 3, 1862, a few weeks after the Battle of Antietam. Lincoln was there to try to persuade McClellan to pursue the retreating forces of Robert E. Lee into Virginia. McClellan, who regularly overestimated enemy troop strength, declined to press the advantage. This led to his dismissal as commander of the Army of the Potomac.

JULIA WARD HOWE

Battle Hymn of the Republic

Julia Ward Howe (1819-1910), one of the most well-known women of her era, was born into a prominent New York City family. She was a distinguished writer, editor, and lecturer who became further known as a leading abolitionist and suffragist. She is best remembered, however, for introducing the idea of Mother's Day and for writing one of America's most endearing hymns.

In November of 1861, Mrs. Howe visited Union Army camps near the Potomac with her husband, Dr. Samuel Gridley Howe, a member of President Lincoln's Military Sanitary Commission. With them was Reverend James Freeman Clarke. During the course of their visit, the group began to sing some of the more popular war songs of the day, among them "John Brown's Body." Reverend Clarke, familiar with Mrs. Howe's literary talents, suggested that she write new lyrics to the well-known tune. The following morning, as Mrs. Howe later described it, she "awoke … in the gray of the early dawn, and to my astonishment found that the wished-for lines were arranging themselves in my brain. I lay quite still until the last verse had completed itself in my thoughts, then hastily arose, saying to myself, 'I shall lose this if I don't write it down immediately.'"

The religious and patriotic verses that Mrs. Howe applied to paper that morning were those to "Battle Hymn of the Republic." Published anonymously in the *Atlantic Monthly* in 1862, the song was immediately embraced by the Union and remained popular with American soldiers during the Spanish-American War, World War I, and World War II.

Mine eyes have seen the glory of the coming of the Lord;
He is trampling out the vintage where the grapes of wrath are stored;
He hath loosed the fateful lightning of His terrible swift sword:
His truth is marching on.

I have seen Him in the watch-fires of a hundred circling camps;
They have builded Him an alter in the evening dews and damps;
I can read His righteous sentence by the dim and flaring lamps:
His day is marching on.

I have read a fiery gospel, writ in burnished rows of steel:
"As ye deal with my contemners, so with you my grace shall deal;
Let the Hero, born of woman, crush the serpent with his heel,
Since God is marching on."

He has sounded forth the trumpet that shall never call retreat;
He is sifting out the hearts of men before His judgment-seat:
Oh, be swift, my soul to answer Him! be jubilant, my feet!
Our God is marching on.

In the beauty of the lilies Christ was born across the sea,
With a glory in his bosom that transfigures you and me:
As He died to make men holy, let us die to make men free,
While God is marching on.

He is coming like the glory of the morning on the wave,
He is wisdom to the mighty, He is honor to the brave,
So the world shall be His footstool, and the soul of wrong His slave,
Our God is marching on!

WALTER KITTREDGE

Tenting on the Old Camp Ground

Walter Kittredge (1834-1905), a professional singer, was drafted into the Union Army but rejected for military service due to ill health. In 1863, Kittredge wrote the words and music for "Tenting on the Old Camp Ground," one of the most popular camp songs of the war. Union officers discouraged its singing, however, because it aroused feelings of homesickness, which led to desertions.

We're tenting to-night on the old camp-ground,
Give us a song to cheer
Our weary hearts, a song of home
And friends we love so dear.

Chorus:
    Many are the hearts that are weary to-night,
    Wishing for the war to cease;
    Many are the hearts looking for the right,
    To see the dawn of peace.
    Tenting to-night, tenting to-night,
    Tenting on the old camp-ground.

We've been tenting to-night on the old camp-ground,
Thinking of days gone by,
Of the loved ones at home that gave us the hand,
And the tear that said, "Good-bye!"

We are weary of war on the old camp-ground,
Many are the dead and gone
Of the brave and true who have left their homes,
Others wounded long.

We've been fighting to-day on the old camp-ground,
Many are lying near;
Some are dead-and dying are some,
Many a one in tears.

Alternate Chorus:
    Many are the hearts that are weary to-night,
    Wishing for the war to cease;
    Many are the hearts that are looking for the right,
    To see the dawn of peace.
    Dying to-night, dying to-night,
    Dying on the old camp-ground.

When Johnny Comes Marching Home

Patrick Sarsfield Gilmore (1829-1892) was born in Ireland and emigrated to America in the 1840s, one step ahead of the potato famine. He was serving as bandmaster for the U.S. Army when the Civil War broke out and he remained loyal to the Union. In 1863, anticipating a return to peaceful times, Gilmore wrote the lyrics to "When Johnny Comes Marching Home" and set them to the Irish tune "Johnny I Hardly Knew Ye." The song has since been a favorite of Americans welcoming home returning soldiers and survives alongside "Battle Hymn of the Republic" as the only Civil War-era songs to rise above sectionalism and become truly national in their appeal.

When Johnny comes marching home again,
Hurrah! hurrah!
We'll give him a hearty welcome then,
Hurrah! hurrah!
The men will cheer, and the boys will shout,
The ladies, they will all turn out,
And we'll all feel gay,
When Johnny comes marching home.

The old church-bell will peal with joy,
Hurrah! hurrah!
To welcome home our darling boy,
Hurrah! hurrah!
The village lads and lasses say,
With roses they will strew the way;
And we'll all feel gay,
When Johnny comes marching home.

Get ready for the Jubilee,
Hurrah! hurrah!
We'll give the hero three times three,
Hurrah! hurrah!
The laurel wreath is ready now
To place upon his loyal brow,
And we'll all feel gay,
When Johnny comes marching home.

Let love and friendship on that day,
Hurrah! hurrah!
Their choicest treasures then display,
Hurrah! hurrah!
And let each one perform some part,
To fill with joy the warrior's heart;
And we'll all feel gay,
When Johnny comes marching home.

ABRAHAM LINCOLN

Emancipation Proclamation

All persons held as slaves within any State or designated part of a State, the people whereof shall then be in rebellion against the United States, shall be then, thenceforward, and forever free.

On September 22, 1862, less than one week after the Union victory at Antietam, President Lincoln issued a preliminary decree stating that, unless those areas still in rebellion returned to the Union within one hundred days, freedom would be granted to slaves within those areas. Lincoln also advocated national legislation similar to the District of Columbia Compensated Emancipation Act, which ended slavery in Washington, D.C., by paying slaveowners for releasing their slaves. The Confederate States of America ignored these proposals and, on January 1, 1863, the Emancipation Proclamation went into effect.

Despite its expansive wording, Lincoln's proclamation was quite limited. It applied only to states that had seceded from the Union, leaving slavery intact in the loyal border states of Kentucky, Missouri, Delaware, and Maryland. It also expressly exempted parts of the Confederacy that had already come under Northern control. Most significant, the freedom it promised depended upon Union military victory. Secretary of State William H. Seward commented, "We show our sympathy with slavery by emancipating slaves where we cannot reach them and holding them in bondage where we can set them free." Lincoln recognized the irony, but he did not want to antagonize those regions that permitted slavery while remaining loyal to the Union.

The Emancipation Proclamation fundamentally transformed the character of the war from a fight for national preservation to a fight for freedom. This was particularly significant because many foreign powers sympathized with the South, but dared not support the Confederacy only because they condemned slavery as evil. The proclamation announced the acceptance of black men "into the armed service of the United States," thus enabling the liberated to become liberators. By war's end, almost 200,000 black soldiers and sailors had fought for the Union. The Emancipation Proclamation, therefore, served both a political and military purpose and paved the way for the greater moral purpose—the Thirteenth Amendment, which was finally ratified in December 1865.

Whereas, on the twenty-second day of September, in the year of our Lord one thousand eight hundred and sixty-two, a proclamation was issued by the President of the United States, containing, among other things, the following, to wit:

"That on the first day of January, in the year of our Lord one thousand eight hundred and sixty-three, all persons held as slaves within any State or designated part of a State, the people whereof shall then be in rebellion against the United States, shall be then, thenceforward, and forever free; and the Executive Government of the United States, including the military and naval authority thereof, will recognize and maintain the freedom of such persons, and will do no act or acts to repress such persons, or any of them, in any efforts they may make for their actual freedom.

"That the Executive will, on the first day of January aforesaid, by proclamation, designate the States and parts of States, if any, in which the people thereof, respectively, shall then be in rebellion against the United States; and the fact that any State, or the people thereof, shall on that day be, in good faith, represented in the Congress of the United States by members chosen thereto at elections wherein a majority of the qualified voters of such State shall have participated, shall, in the absence of strong countervailing testimony, be deemed conclusive evidence that such State, and the people thereof, are not then in rebellion against the United States."

Now, therefore I, Abraham Lincoln, President of the United States, by virtue of the power in me vested as Commander-in-Chief of the Army and Navy of the United States in time of actual armed rebellion against the authority and government of the United States, and as a fit and necessary war measure for suppressing said rebellion, do, on this first day of January, in the year of our Lord one thousand eight hundred and sixty-three, and in accordance with my purpose so to do, publicly proclaimed for the full period of one hundred days, from the day first above mentioned, order and designate as the States and parts of States wherein the people thereof respectively, are this day in rebellion against the United States, the following, to wit:

Arkansas, Texas, Louisiana (except the Parishes of St. Bernard, Plaquemines, Jefferson, St. John, St. Charles, St. James Ascension, Assumption, Terrebonne, Lafourche, St. Mary, St. Martin, and Orleans, including the City of New Orleans) Mississippi, Alabama, Florida, Georgia, South Carolina, North Carolina, and Virginia, (except the forty-eight counties designated as West Virginia, and also the counties of Berkley, Accomac, Northampton, Elizabeth City, York, Princess Ann, and Norfolk, including the cities of Norfolk and Portsmouth[)], and which excepted parts, are for the present, left precisely as if this proclamation were not issued.

And by virtue of the power, and for the purpose aforesaid, I do order and declare that all persons held as slaves within said designated States, and parts of States, are, and henceforward shall be free; and that the Executive government of the United States, including the military and naval authorities thereof, will recognize and maintain the freedom of said persons.

And I hereby enjoin upon the people so declared to be free to abstain from all violence, unless in necessary self-defence; and I recommend to them that, in all cases when allowed, they labor faithfully for reasonable wages.

And I further declare and make known, that such persons of suitable condition, will be received into the armed service of the United States to garrison forts, positions, stations, and other places, and to man vessels of all sorts in said service.

And upon this act, sincerely believed to be an act of justice, warranted by the Constitution, upon military necessity, I invoke the considerate judgment of mankind, and the gracious favor of Almighty God.

In witness whereof, I have hereunto set my hand and caused the seal of the United States to be affixed.

Done at the City of Washington, this first day of January, in the year of our Lord one thousand eight hundred and sixty-three, and of the Independence of the United States of America the eighty-seventh.

By the President: Abraham Lincoln
William H. Seward, Secretary of State.

JOHN GREENLEAF WHITTIER

Stanzas for the Times, Maud Muller, and Barbara Frietchie

John Greenleaf Whittier (1807-1892), the son of Quaker farmers, was born in Haverhill, Massachusetts. An ardent abolitionist, Whittier worked closely with William Lloyd Garrison and was a leading founder of the Republican Party.

Known as the "Quaker poet," Whittier's work usually reflected either a disgust for slavery or a love of New England country life. In "Stanzas for the Times," a poem written in reaction to pro-slavery forces who had sought to restrict free speech in order to hinder the abolitionist cause, Whittier attacked the hypocrisy of those who claimed to cherish freedom yet defended slavery. "Maud Muller," one of Whittier's best-loved poems, contains the famous couplet, "For of all sad words of tongue or pen / The saddest are these: 'It might have been!'"

"Barbara Frietchie," a departure from his usual body of work, is perhaps Whittier's most widely anthologized poem. Its patriotic sentiment appealed even to those who were turned off by Whittier's "extremist" social reform goals. The poem was written in honor of Barbara Frietchie of Frederick, Maryland, a friend of Francis Scott Key, who supposedly waved the Stars and Stripes to spite the advancing Confederate Army.

Stanzas for the Times

Is this the land our fathers loved,
The freedom which they toiled to win?
Is this the soil whereon they moved?
Are these the graves they slumber in?
Are we the sons by whom are borne
The mantles which the dead have worn?

And shall we crouch above these graves,
With craven soul and fettered lip?
Yoke in with marked and branded slaves,
And tremble at the driver's whip?
Bend to the earth our pliant knees,
And speak but as our masters please?

Shall outraged Nature cease to feel?
Shall Mercy's tears no longer flow?
Shall ruffian threats of cord and steel,
The dungeon's gloom, the assassin's blow,
Turn back the spirit roused to save
The Truth, our Country, and the slave?

Of human skulls that shrine was made,
Round which the priests of Mexico
Before their loathsome idol prayed;
Is Freedom's altar fashioned so?
And must we yield to Freedom's God,
As offering meet, the negro's blood?

Shall tongue be mute, when deeds are wrought
Which well might shame extremest hell?
Shall freemen lock the indignant thought?
Shall Pity's bosom cease to swell?
Shall honor bleed?—shall Truth succumb?
Shall pen, and press, and soul be dumb?

No; by each spot of haunted ground,
Where Freedom weeps her children's fall;
By Plymouth's rock, and Bunker's mound;
By Griswold's stained and shattered wall;
By Warren's ghost, by Langdon's shade;
By all the memories of our dead!

By their enlarging souls, which burst
The bands and fetters round them set;
By the free Pilgrim spirit nursed
Within our inmost bosoms, yet,
By all above, around, below,
Be ours the indignant answer,—No!

No; guided by our country's laws,
For truth, and right, and suffering man,
Be ours to strive in Freedom's cause,
As Christians may, as freemen can!
Still pouring on unwilling ears
That truth oppression only fears.

What! shall we guard our neighbor still,
While woman shrieks beneath his rod,
And while he tramples down at will
The image of a common God?
Shall watch and ward be round him set,
Of Northern nerve and bayonet?

And shall we know and share with him
The danger and the growing shame?
And see our Freedom's light grow dim,
Which should have filled the world with flame?
And, writhing, feel, where'er we turn,
A world's reproach around us burn?

Is't not enough that this is borne?
And asks our haughty neighbor more?
Must fetters which his slaves have worn
Clank round the Yankee farmer's door?
Must he be told, beside his plough,
What he must speak, and when, and how?

Must he be told his freedom stands
On Slavery's dark foundations strong;
On breaking hearts and fettered hands,
On robbery, and crime, and wrong?
That all his fathers taught is vain,—
That Freedom's emblem is the chain?

Its life, its soul, from slavery drawn!
False, foul, profane! Go, teach as well
Of holy Truth from Falsehood born!
Of Heaven refreshed by airs from Hell!
Of Virtue in the arms of Vice!
Of Demons planting Paradise!

Rail on, then, brethren of the South,
Ye shall not hear the truth the less;
No seal is on the Yankee's mouth,
No fetter on the Yankee's press!
From our Green Mountains to the sea,
One voice shall thunder, We are free!

Maud Muller

Maud Muller on a summer's day
Raked the meadow sweet with hay.

Beneath her torn hat glowed the wealth
Of simple beauty and rustic health.

Singing, she wrought, and her merry glee
The mock-bird echoed from his tree.

But when she glanced to the far-off town
White from its hill-slope looking down,

The sweet song died, and a vague unrest
And a nameless longing filled her breast,—

A wish that she hardly dared to own,
For something better than she had known.

The Judge rode slowly down the lane,
Smoothing his horse's chestnut mane.

He drew his bridle in the shade
Of the apple-trees, to greet the maid,

And asked a draught from the spring that flowed
Through the meadow across the road.

She stooped where the cool spring bubbled up,
And filled for him her small tin cup,

And blushed as she gave it, looking down
On her feet so bare, and her tattered gown.

"Thanks!" said the Judge; "a sweeter draught
From a fairer hand was never quaffed."

He spoke of the grass and flowers and trees,
Of the singing birds and the humming bees;

Then talked of the haying, and wondered whether
The cloud in the west would bring foul weather.

And Maud forgot her brier-torn gown
And her graceful ankles bare and brown;

And listened, while a pleased surprise
Looked from her long-lashed hazel eyes.

At last, like one who for delay
Seeks a vain excuse, he rode away.

Maud Muller looked and sighed: "Ah me!
That I the Judge's bride might be!

"He would dress me up in silks so fine,
And praise and toast me at his wine.

"My father should wear a broadcloth coat;
My brother should sail a pointed boat.

"I'd dress my mother so grand and gay,
And the baby should have a new toy each day.

"And I'd feed the hungry and clothe the poor,
And all should bless me who left our door."

The Judge looked back as he climbed the hill,
And saw Maud Muller standing still.

"A form more fair, a face more sweet,
Ne'er hath it been my lot to meet.

"And her modest answer and graceful air
Show her wise and good as she is fair.

"Would she were mine, and I to-day,
Like her, a harvester of hay.

"No doubtful balance of rights and wrongs,
Nor weary lawyers with endless tongues,

"But low of cattle and song of birds,
And health and quiet and loving words."

But he thought of his sisters, proud and cold,
And his mother, vain of her rank and gold.

So, closing his heart, the Judge rode on,
And Maud was left in the field alone.

But the lawyers smiled that afternoon,
When he hummed in court an old love-tune;

And the young girl mused beside the well
Till the rain on the unraked clover fell.

He wedded a wife of richest dower,
Who lived for fashion, as he for power.

Yet oft, in his marble hearth's bright glow,
He watched a picture come and go;

And sweet Maud Muller's hazel eyes
Looked out in their innocent surprise.

Oft, when the wine in his glass was red,
He longed for the wayside well instead;

And closed his eyes on his garnished rooms
To dream of meadows and clover-blooms.

And the proud man sighed, and with a secret pain,
"Ah, that I were free again!

"Free as when I rode that day,
Where the barefoot maiden raked her hay."

She wedded a man unlearned and poor,
And many children played round her door.

But care and sorrow, and childbirth pain,
Left their traces on heart and brain.

And oft, when the summer sun shone hot
On the new-mown hay in the meadow lot,

And she heard the little spring brook fall
Over the roadside, through a wall,

In the shade of the apple-tree again
She saw a rider draw his rein;

And, gazing down with timid grace,
She felt his pleased eyes read her face.

Sometimes her narrow kitchen walls
Stretched away into stately halls;

The weary wheel to a spinet turned,
The tallow candle an astral burned,

And for him who sat by the chimney lug,
Dozing and grumbling o'er pipe and mug,

A manly form at her side she saw,
And joy was duty and love was law.

Then she took up her burden of life again,
Saying only, "It might have been."

Alas for the maiden, alas for the Judge,
For rich repiner and household drudge!

God pity them both and pity us all,
Who vainly the dreams of youth recall.

For of all sad words of tongue or pen,
The saddest are these: "It might have been!"

Ah, well! for us all some sweet hope lies
Deeply buried from human eyes;

And, in the hereafter, angels may
Roll the stone from its grave away!

Barbara Frietchie

Up from the meadows rich with corn,
Clear in the cool September morn,

The clustered spires of Frederick stand
Green-walled by the hills of Maryland.

Round about them orchards sweep,
Apple and peach tree fruited deep,

Fair as the garden of the Lord
To the eyes of the famished rebel horde,

On that pleasant morn of the early fall
When Lee marched over the mountain-wall;

Over the mountains winding down,
Horse and foot, into Frederick town.

Forty flags with their silver stars,
Forty flags with their crimson bars,

Flapped in the morning wind: the sun
Of noon looked down, and saw not one.

Up rose old Barbara Frietchie then,
Bowed with her fourscore years and ten;

Bravest of all in Frederick town,
She took up the flag the men hauled down;

In her attic window the staff she set,
To show that one heart was loyal yet.

Up the street came the rebel tread,
Stonewall Jackson riding ahead.

Under his slouched hat left and right
He glanced; the old flag met his sight.

"Halt!"—the dust-brown ranks stood fast.
"Fire!"—out blazed the rifle-blast.

It shivered the window, pane and sash;
It rent the banner with seam and gash.

Quick as it fell, from the broken staff
Dame Barbara snatched the silken scarf.

She leaned far out on the window-sill,
And shook it forth with a royal will.

"Shoot, if you must, this old gray head,
But spare your country's flag," she said.

A shade of sadness, a blush of shame,
Over the face of the leader came;

The nobler nature within him stirred
To life at that woman's deed and word;

"Who touches a hair on yon gray head
Dies like a dog! March on!" he said.

All day long through Frederick street
Sounded the tread of marching feet:

All day long that free flag tost
Over the heads of the rebel host.

Ever its torn folds rose and fell
On the loyal winds that loved it well;

And through the hill-gaps sunset light
Shone over it with a warm good-night.

Barbara Frietchie's work is o'er,
And the Rebel rides on his raids no more.

Honor to her! and let a tear
Fall, for her sake, on Stonewall's bier.

Over Barbara Frietchie's grave
Flag of Freedom and Union, wave!

Peace and order and beauty draw
Round thy symbol of light and law;

And ever the stars above look down
On thy stars below in Frederick town!

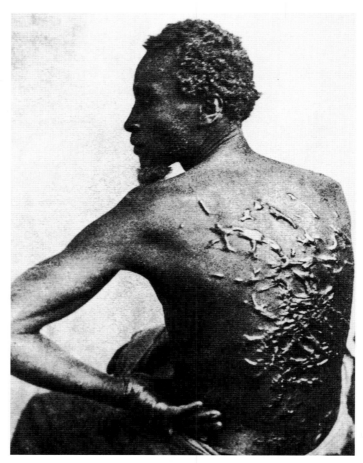

Rear view of a former slave revealing scars on his back from a savage whipping. This 1863 photo was taken after he escaped to become a Union soldier during the Civil War.

ABRAHAM LINCOLN

The Gettysburg Address

Four score and seven years ago …

The Union victory at Gettysburg, Pennsylvania, on July 3, 1863, was the bloodiest battle of the Civil War. General Meade's Union Army suffered 23,000 casualties, while 28,000 of the badly outnumbered Confederates under the command of Robert E. Lee were killed, wounded, or listed as missing.

On November 19, 1863, a ceremony was held in order to dedicate a cemetery on the Gettysburg battlefield. The principal speaker at that ceremony was Edward Everett, a great orator of the day. Everett spoke for nearly two hours and was followed by President Lincoln, who gave a brief address that survives to this day as perhaps the pinnacle of human eloquence—a poetic tribute to those who made the ultimate sacrifice. The power of Lincoln's words was recognized immediately. Edward Everett later wrote a letter to the President in which he said, "I should be glad if I could flatter myself that I came as near to the central occasion in two hours as you did in two minutes."

Four score and seven years ago, our fathers brought forth on this continent a new nation, conceived in liberty, and dedicated to the proposition that all men are created equal.

Now we are engaged in a great civil war, testing whether that nation, or any nation so conceived and so dedicated, can long endure. We are met on a great battlefield of that war. We have come to dedicate a portion of that field as a final resting place for those who here gave their lives that that nation might live. It is altogether fitting and proper that we should do this.

But in a larger sense we cannot dedicate—we cannot consecrate—we cannot hallow—this ground. The brave men, living and dead, who struggled here have consecrated it far above our poor power to add or detract. The world will little note, nor long remember, what we say here, but it can never forget what they did here. It is for us the living, rather, to be dedicated here to the unfinished work which they who fought here have thus far so nobly advanced. It is rather for us to be here dedicated to the great task remaining before us—that from these honored dead we take increased devotion to that cause for which they gave the last full measure of devotion, that we here highly resolve that these dead shall not have died in vain, that this nation, under God, shall have a new birth of freedom, and that government of the people, by the people, for the people, shall not perish from the earth.

NATHANIEL GRAHAM SHEPHERD

Roll-Call

Born in New York City, Nathaniel Graham Shepherd (1835-1869) worked as a correspondent for his hometown newspaper during the Civil War. A talented and diverse writer, Shepherd gained nationwide fame for his poems, the best known of which were "The Dead Drummer-Boy" and "Roll-Call," which also became a popular song.

"Corporal Green!" the Orderly cried;
"Here!" was the answer loud and clear,
From the lips of a soldier standing near,—
And "Here!" was the word the next replied.

"Cyrus Drew!"—then a silence fell;
This time no answer followed the call;
Only his rear-man had seen him fall:
Killed or wounded—he could not tell.

There they stood in the failing light,
These men of battle, with grave, dark looks,
As plain to be read as open books,
While slowly gathered the shades of night.

The fern on the hill-sides was splashed with blood,
And down in the corn, where the poppies grew,
Were redder stains than the poppies knew,
And crimson-dyed was the river's flood.

For the foe had crossed from the other side,
That day, in the face of a murderous fire
That swept them down in its terrible ire;
And their life-blood went to color the tide.

"Herbert Cline!"—At the call there came
Two stalwart soldiers into the line,
Bearing between them this Herbert Cline,
Wounded and bleeding, to answer his name.

"Ezra Kerr!"—and a voice answered "Here!"
"Hiram Kerr!"—but no man replied.
They were brothers, these two; the sad wind sighed,
And a shudder crept through the cornfield near.

"Ephraim Deane!"—then a soldier spoke:
"Dean carried our regiment's colors," he said,
"When our ensign was shot; I left him dead
Just after the enemy wavered and broke.

"Close to the roadside his body lies;
I paused a moment and gave him to drink;
He murmured his mother's name, I think,
And Death came with it and closed his eyes."

'Twas a victory,—yes; but it cost us dear:
For that company's roll, when called at night,
Of a hundred men who went into the fight,
Numbered but twenty that answered *"Here!"*

ABRAHAM LINCOLN

Second Inaugural Address

With malice toward none, with charity for all …

In the election of 1864, Lincoln was opposed by General George B. McClellan, who had gained the Democratic Party's nomination. The Democrats were willing to negotiate away emancipation in exchange for peace. Lincoln, whose popularity was suffering from a drawn-out war, feared defeat saying, "It seems exceedingly probable that this administration will not be re-elected."

Union military breakthroughs in late summer, such as General Sherman's capture of Atlanta, however, turned the military tide in the Union's favor and, with it, the political tide in Lincoln's. The president was re-elected and, with the end of the war in sight, used the occasion of his second inaugural to speak—not of vengeance on the South—but of liberty and Union.

Fellow Countrymen:

At this second appearing to take the oath of the Presidential office there is less occasion for an extended address than there was at the first. Then a statement somewhat in detail of a course to be pursued seemed fitting and proper. Now, at the expiration of four years, during which public declarations have been constantly called forth on every point and phase of the great contest which still absorbs the attention and engrosses the energies of the nation, little that is new could be presented. The progress of our arms, upon which all else chiefly depends, is as well known to the public as to myself, and it is, I trust, reasonably satisfactory and encouraging to all. With high hope for the future, no prediction in regard to it is ventured.

On the occasion corresponding to this four years ago all thoughts were anxiously directed to an impending civil war. All dreaded it, all sought to avert it. While the inaugural address was being delivered from this place, devoted altogether to *saving* the Union without war, insurgent agents were in the city seeking to *destroy* it without war—seeking to dissolve the Union and divide effects by negotiation. Both parties deprecated war, but one of them would *make* war rather than let the nation survive, and the other would *accept* war rather than let it perish, and the war came.

One-eighth of the whole population were colored slaves, not distributed generally over the Union, but localized in the southern part of it. These slaves constituted a peculiar and powerful interest. All knew that this interest was somehow the cause of war. To strengthen, perpetuate, and extend this interest was the object for which the insurgents would rend the Union even by war, while the Government claimed no right to do more than to restrict the territorial enlargement of it. Neither party expected for the war the magnitude or the duration which it has already attained. Neither anticipated that the *cause* of the conflict might cease with or even before the conflict itself should cease. Each looked for an easier triumph, and a result less fundamental and astounding. Both read the same Bible and pray to the same God, and each invokes His aid against the other. It may seem strange that any men should dare to ask a just God's assistance in wringing their bread from the sweat of other men's faces, but let us judge not, that we be not judged. The prayers of both could not be answered. That of neither has been answered fully. The Almighty has His own purposes. "Woe unto the world because of offenses; for it must needs be that offenses come, but woe to that man by whom the offense cometh." If we shall suppose that American slavery is one of those offenses which, in the providence of God, must needs come, but which, having continued through His appointed time,

He now wills to remove, and that He gives to both North and South this terrible war as the woe due to those by whom the offense came, shall we discern therein any departure from those divine attributes which the believers in a living God always ascribe to Him? Fondly do we hope, fervently do we pray, that this mighty scourge of war may speedily pass away. Yet, if God wills that it continue until all the wealth piled by the bondsman's two hundred and fifty years of unrequited toil shall be sunk, and until every drop of blood drawn with the lash shall be paid by another drawn with the sword, as was said three thousand years ago, so still it must be said "the judgments of the Lord are true and righteous altogether."

With malice toward none, with charity for all, with firmness in the right as God gives us to see the right, let us strive on to finish the work we are in, to bind up the nation's wounds, to care for him who shall have borne the battle and for his widow and his orphan, to do all which may achieve and cherish a just and lasting peace among ourselves and with all nations.

FREDERICK DOUGLASS

Speech to the American Anti-Slavery Society

Slavery is not abolished until the black man has the ballot.

Frederick Douglass addressed the Thirty-Second Annual Meeting of the American Anti-Slavery Society on May 10, 1865. The purpose of the address was to emphasize that the Society, and indeed the entire abolitionist machinery, need not disband simply because Congress had passed the Thirteenth Amendment. Douglass knew that the abolition of slavery did not signify the abolition of racial discrimination. He recognized that the subordination of blacks would continue until they were able to enjoy all the rights of citizenship without oppression and under the full protection of the law.

… I do not wish to appear here in any fault-finding spirit, or as an impugner of the motives of those who believe that the time has come for this Society to disband. I am conscious of no suspicion of the purity and excellence of the motives that animate the President of this Society [William Lloyd Garrison], and other gentlemen who are in favor of its disbandment. I take this ground; whether this Constitutional Amendment [the thirteenth] is law or not, whether it has been ratified by a sufficient number of States to make it law or not, I hold that the work of Abolitionists is not done. Even if every State in the Union had ratified that Amendment, while the black man is confronted in the legislation of the South by the word "white," our work as Abolitionists, as I conceive it, is not done. I took the ground, last night, that the South, by unfriendly legislation, could make our liberty, under that provision, a delusion, a mockery, and a snare, and I hold that ground now. What advantage is a provision like this Amendment to the black man, if the Legislature of any State can to-morrow declare that no black man's testimony shall be received in a court of law? Where are we then? Any wretch may enter the house of a black man, and commit any violence he pleases; if he happens to do it only in the presence of black persons, he goes unwhipt of justice. And don't tell me that those people down there have become so just and honest all at once that they will not pass laws denying to black men the right to testify against white men in the courts of law. Why, our Northern States have done it. Illinois, Indiana and Ohio have done it. Here, in the midst of institutions that have gone forth from old Plymouth Rock, the black man has been excluded from testifying in the courts of law; and if the Legislature of every Southern State to-morrow pass a law, declaring that no Negro shall testify in any courts of law, they will not violate that provision of the Constitution. Such laws exist now at the South. The next day, the Legislatures may pass a law that any black man who shall lift his arm in self-defence, even, against a white man, shall have that arm severed from his body, and may be hanged and quartered, and his head and quarters set up in the most public parts of the district where the crime shall have been committed. Such laws now exist at the South, and they might exist under this provision of the Constitution, that there shall be neither slavery not involuntary servitude in any State of the Union. …

Slavery is not abolished until the black man has the ballot. While the Legislatures of the South retain the right to pass laws making any discrimination between black and white, slavery still lives there. As Edmund Quincy once said, "While the word 'white' is on the statute-book of Massachusetts, Massachusetts is a slave state. While a black man can be turned out of a car in Massachusetts, Massachusetts is a slave state. While a slave can be taken from old Massachusetts, Massachusetts is a slave state." That is what I heard Edmund Quincy say twenty-three or twenty-four years ago. I never forget such a thing. Now, while the black man can be denied a vote, while the Legislatures of the South can take from him the right to keep and bear arms, as they can—they would not allow a Negro to walk with a cane where I came from, they would not allow five of them to assemble together—the work of the Abolitionists is not finished. Notwithstanding the provision in the Constitution of the United States, that the right to keep and bear arms shall not be abridged, the black man has never had the right either to keep or bear arms; and the Legislatures of the States will still have the power to forbid it, under this Amendment. They can carry on a system of unfriendly legislation, and will they not do it? Have they not got prejudice there to do it with? Think you, that because they are for the moment in the talons and beak of our glorious eagle, instead of the slave being there, as formerly, that they are converted? I hear of the loyalty at Wilmington, the loyalty at South Carolina—what is it worth?

["Not a straw."]

Not a straw. I thank my friend for admitting it. They are loyal while they see 200,000 sable soldiers, with glistening bayonets, walking in their midst. But let the civil power of the South be restored, and the old prejudices and hostility to the Negro will revive. Aye, the very fact that the Negro has been used to defeat this rebellion and strike down the standards of the Confederacy will be a stimulus to all their hatred, to all their malice, and lead them to legislate with greater stringency towards this class than ever before. The American people are bound—bound by their sense of honor (I hope by their sense of honor, at least, by a just sense of honor), to extend the franchise to the Negro; and I was going to say, that the Abolitionists of the American Anti-Slavery Society were bound to "stand still, and see the salvation of God," until that work is done. Where shall the black man look for support, my friends, if the American Anti-Slavery Society fails him? From whence shall we expect a certain sound from the trumpet of freedom, when the old pioneer, when this Society that has survived mobs, and martyrdom, and the combined efforts of priest-craft and state-craft to suppress it, shall at once subside, on the mere intimation that the Constitution has been amended, so that neither slavery nor involuntary servitude shall hereafter be allowed in this land? What did the slaveholders of Richmond say to those who objected to arming the Negro, on the ground that it would make him a freeman? Why, they said, "The argument is absurd. We may make these Negroes fight for us; but while we retain the political power of the South, we can keep them in their subordinate positions." That was the argument; and they were right. They might have employed the Negro to fight for them, and while they retained in their hands power to exclude him from political rights, they could have reduced him to a condition similar to slavery. They would not call it slavery, but some other name. Slavery has been fruitful in giving itself names. It has been called "the peculiar institution," "the social system," and the "impediment," as it was called by the General Conference of the Methodist Episcopal Church. It has been called by a great many names, and it will call itself by yet another name; and you and I and all of us had better wait and see what new form this old monster will assume, in what new skin this old snake will come forth next.

ULYSSES S. GRANT

Appomattox

I felt like anything rather than rejoicing at the downfall of a foe who had fought so long and valiantly.

Born in Point Pleasant, Ohio, Hiram Ulysses Grant (1822-1885) entered the United States Military Academy at West Point in 1839. His congressman made the appointment to *Ulysses S. Grant,* however, confusing the young man's first name and assuming his middle name was Simpson (his mother's maiden name). Grant chose to accept the name change and, after graduating, joined the Army, where he fought in the Mexican-American War and eventually rose in rank to captain. In 1854, he resigned to civilian life with his wife and son.

With the outbreak of war in 1861, Grant re-enlisted in the Army and was soon appointed brigadier general. A decisive leader, he won numerous victories over Confederate forces and was steadily promoted. President Lincoln, desperate for aggressive military leadership, named him commander of all Union armies in early 1864. While many objected to the heavy casualties suffered under his command, claiming his initials stood for "Unspeakable Slaughter," admirers hailed him as "Unconditional Surrender" Grant. President Lincoln was among his defenders, saying, "I can spare this man—he fights!"

When the war came to a conclusion, Grant briefly supported Andrew Johnson, who had become president upon Lincoln's assassination. He soon became frustrated, however, with what he viewed as Johnson's mild Reconstruction policies which failed to protect Negro rights. Grant became the Republican nominee for President in 1868 and easily defeated the Democratic nominee, Horatio Seymour. He was re-elected in 1872.

In 1884, as he was dying of cancer, Grant began writing his memoirs, which were published by Mark Twain. The following excerpt from those memoirs is a reflection on General Lee's surrender at Appomattox.

I had known General Lee in the old army, and had served with him in the Mexican War; but did not suppose, owing to the difference in our age and rank, that he would remember me; while I would more naturally remember him distinctly, because he was the chief of staff of General Scott in the Mexican War.

When I left camp that morning I had not expected so soon the result that was then taking place, and consequently was in rough garb. I was without a sword, as I usually was when on horseback on the field, and wore a soldier's blouse for a coat, with the shoulder straps of my rank to indicate to the army who I was. When I went into the house I found General Lee. We greeted each other, and after shaking hands took our seats. I had my staff with me, a good portion of whom were in the room during the whole of the interview.

What General Lee's feelings were I do not know. As he was a man of much dignity, with an impassible face, it was impossible to say whether he felt inwardly glad that the end had finally come, or felt sad over the result, and was too manly to show it. Whatever his feelings, they were entirely concealed from my observation; but my own feelings, which had been quite jubilant on the receipt of his letter, were sad and depressed. I felt like anything rather than rejoicing at the downfall of a foe who had fought so long and valiantly. …

ROBERT E. LEE

Farewell to His Army

You will take with you the satisfaction that proceeds from the consciousness of duty faithfully performed.

A relative of Revolutionary statesmen Francis Lightfoot Lee and Richard Henry Lee, and son of famed cavalry commander Henry "Light-Horse Harry" Lee, Robert Edward Lee (1807-1870) carried on his family's proud tradition. He graduated with honors from West Point, fought in the Mexican-American War, served as superintendent of West Point, and later protected settlers from Apache and Comanche Indians on the Texas frontier.

When the Civil War erupted, President Lincoln offered Lee command of the United States Army. Though conflicted over slavery—calling it sinful and therefore "a greater evil to the white man than to the colored race"—and not wishing to see the nation divided, Lee nonetheless held a greater allegiance to his own state of Virginia. He wrote: "With all my devotion to the Union, and the feeling of loyalty and duty of an American citizen, I have not been able to make up my mind to raise my hand against my relatives, my children, my home. I have therefore resigned my commission in the army, and, save in defense of my native state—with the sincere hope that my poor services may never be needed—I hope I may never be called upon to draw my sword."

Once the fighting between the states began, Lee joined the Confederate Army as an adviser to Jefferson Davis and was soon appointed general. His brilliant leadership proved to be the South's greatest asset, but the Confederacy nonetheless succumbed to "overwhelming numbers and resources." After surrendering to Grant, Lee bid farewell to his army. His voting rights were restored via a general amnesty granted in 1868, and Lee then applied for a complete individual pardon. His application, however, lacked the required oath of allegiance to the United States. He signed an oath and sent it to Washington, but it became lost or, more likely, intentionally misplaced. Lee's oath was found in a desk drawer in 1970 by an employee of the National Archives. It reads: "I Robert E. Lee of Lexington, Virginia, do solemnly swear, in the presence of Almighty God, that I will henceforth support, protect and defend the Constitution of the United States, and the Union of the States thereunder, and that I will, in like manner, abide by and faithfully support all laws and proclamations which have been made during the existing rebellion with reference to the emancipation of slaves, so help me God."

In 1975, the United States Congress restored Robert E. Lee's American citizenship. "Recollect that we form one country now," the general had long ago admonished. "Abandon all these local animosities, and make your sons Americans."

After four years of arduous service, marked by unsurpassed courage and fortitude, the Army of Northern Virginia has been compelled to yield to overwhelming numbers and resources.

I need not tell the survivors of so many hard-fought battles, who have remained steadfast to the last, that I have consented to this result from no distrust of them. But, feeling that valour and devotion could accomplish nothing that could compensate for the loss that would have attended the continuation of the contest, I have determined to avoid the useless sacrifice of those whose past services have endeared them to their countrymen.

By the terms of the agreement, officers and men can return to their homes and remain there until exchanged. You will take with you the satisfaction that proceeds from the consciousness of duty faithfully performed; and I earnestly pray that a merciful God will extend to you His blessing and protection.

With an increasing admiration of your constancy and devotion to your country, and a grateful remembrance of your kind and generous consideration of myself, I bid you an affectionate farewell.

Union soldiers at the old Appomattox County Courthouse, April 1865. The first major land battle of the Civil War took place in Manassas, Virginia, on July 18, 1861, in what would become known as the First Battle of Bull Run. In the lead-up to that battle, Union artillery fired at Wilmer McLean's house, headquarters for Confederate Brigadier General P.G.T. Beauregard. In 1863, seeking to escape the war, McLean moved his family 120 miles south to Appomattox County, Virginia, near the town of Appomattox Court House. On April 9, 1865, the war came back to Wilmer McLean when Confederate General Robert E. Lee surrendered to General Ulysses S. Grant in the parlor of McLean's house following the Battle of Appomattox Court House, effectively ending the Civil War. McLean, a wholesale grocer who made his living supplying the Confederate Army throughout the war, was fond of saying, "The war began in my front yard and ended in my front parlor."

FREDERICK DOUGLASS

In Memory of Abraham Lincoln

Viewed from the genuine abolition ground, Mr. Lincoln seemed tardy, cold, dull, and indifferent; but measuring him by the sentiment he was bound as a statesman to consult, he was swift, zealous, radical, and determined.

On April 14, 1865, President Lincoln and the First Lady attended a performance of *Our American Cousin* at Ford's Theatre. There, Abraham Lincoln suffered a fatal shot to the back of his head delivered by John Wilkes Booth, a famous actor and Southern sympathizer.

In April 1876, at the dedication of the Freedmen's Memorial Monument to Lincoln in Washington, D.C., Frederick Douglass eulogized the slain president in the following manner. Douglass had many criticisms of the president during the war, but viewed Lincoln as a truly great man and one of his heroes.

... Though the Union was more to him than our freedom or our future, under his wise and beneficent rule we saw ourselves gradually lifted from the depths of slavery to the heights of liberty and manhood; under his wise and beneficent rule, and by measures approved and vigorously pressed by him, we saw that the handwriting of ages, in the form of prejudice and proscription, was rapidly fading away from the face of our whole country; under his rule, and in due time, about as soon after all as the country could tolerate the strange spectacle, we saw our brave sons and brothers laying off the rags of bondage and being clothed all over in the blue uniforms of the soldiers of the United States; under his rule we saw two hundred thousand of our dark and dusky people responding to the call of Abraham Lincoln and, with muskets on their shoulders and eagles on their buttons, timing their high footsteps to liberty and union under the national flag; under his rule we saw the independence of the black republic of Haiti, the special object of slaveholding aversion and horror, fully recognized, and her minister, a colored gentleman, duly received here in the city of Washington; under his rule we saw the internal slave trade, which so long disgraced the nation, abolished, and slavery abolished in the District of Columbia; under his rule we saw for the first time the law enforced against the foreign slave trade, and the first slave trader hanged like any other pirate or murderer; under his rule, assisted by the greatest captain of our age, and his inspiration, we saw the Confederate States, based upon the idea that our race must be slaves, and slaves forever, battered to pieces and scattered to the four winds; under his rule, and in the fullness of time, we saw Abraham Lincoln, after giving the slaveholders three months' grace in which to save their hateful slave system, penning the immortal paper, which, though special in its language, was general in its principles and effect, making slavery forever impossible in the United States. Though we waited long, we saw all this and more.

Can any colored man, or any white man friendly to the freedom of all men, ever forget the night which followed the first day of January 1863, when the world was to see if Abraham Lincoln would prove to be as good as his word? I shall never forget that memorable night, when in a distant city I waited and watched at a public meeting with three thousand others not less anxious than myself, for the word of deliverance which we have heard read today. Nor shall I ever forget the outburst of joy and thanksgiving that rent the air when the lightning brought to us the Emancipation Proclamation. In the happy hour we forgot all delay, and forgot all tardiness, forgot that the president had bribed the rebels to lay down their arms by a promise to withhold the bolt which would smite the slave system with destruction; and we were thenceforward willing to allow the president all the latitude of time, phraseology, and every honorable device that statesmanship might require for the achievement of a great and beneficent measure of liberty and progress. ...

His great mission was to accomplish two things: first, to save his country from dismemberment and ruin; and, second, to free his country from the great crime of slavery. To do one or the other, or both, he must have the earnest sympathy and the powerful cooperation of his loyal fellow countrymen. Without this primary and essential condition to success, his efforts must have been vain and utterly fruitless. Had he put the abolition of slavery before the salvation of the Union, he would have inevitably driven from him a powerful class of the American people and rendered resistance to rebellion impossible. Viewed from the genuine abolition ground, Mr. Lincoln seemed tardy, cold, dull, and indifferent; but measuring him by the sentiment he was bound as a statesman to consult, he was swift, zealous, radical, and determined. ...

The judgment of the present hour is, that taking him for all in all, measuring the tremendous magnitude of the work before him, considering the necessary means to ends, and surveying the end from the beginning, infinite wisdom has seldom sent any man into the world better fitted for his mission than Abraham Lincoln. His birth, his training, and his natural endowments, both mental and physical, were strongly in his favor. Born and reared among the lowly, a stranger to wealth and luxury, compelled to grapple single-handed with the flintiest hardships of life, from tender youth to sturdy manhood, he grew strong in the manly and heroic qualities demanded by the great mission to which he was called by the votes of his countrymen. The hard condition of his early life, which would have depressed and broken down weaker men, only gave greater life, vigor, and buoyancy to the heroic spirit of Abraham Lincoln. ...

Had Abraham Lincoln died from any of the numerous ills to which flesh is heir; had he reached that good old age of which his vigorous constitution and his temperate habits gave promise; had he been permitted to see the end of his great work; had the solemn curtain of death come down but gradually—we should still have been smitten with a heavy grief and treasured his name lovingly. But dying as he did die, by the red hand of violence, killed, assassinated, taken off without warning, not because of personal hate— for no man who knew Abraham Lincoln could hate him— but because of his fidelity to union and liberty, he is doubly dear to us, and his memory will be precious forever. …

I Hear America Singing and O Captain! My Captain!

Walt Whitman (1819-1892), one of the world's great poets, was born in Long Island, New York, and grew up in Brooklyn. He worked as a printer and journalist in New York City and, in 1848, began working on *Leaves of Grass*, a collection of his poetry. He tried to have the work published in 1855 but couldn't find a publisher willing to take a chance on the rather unusual form and content. As a result, Whitman published the work at his own expense. His poems, which praised the ideas of democracy, were a tribute to the United States. In the preface, Whitman wrote: "The United States themselves are essentially the greatest poem." *Leaves of Grass* was expanded and periodically revised throughout Whitman's life and, though initially dismissed, is now considered one of the world's great literary works.

"I Hear America Singing," published in 1860, represents the poet's lifelong fascination with both the diversity and the vitality of those who make America work. "O Captain! My Captain!," Whitman's most popular poem and a departure from his usual rhythm, mourns the death of Abraham Lincoln.

I Hear America Singing

I hear America singing, the varied carols I hear,
Those of mechanics, each one singing his as it should be blithe and strong,
The carpenter singing his as he measures his plank or beam,
The mason singing his as he makes ready for work, or leaves off work,
The boatman singing what belongs to him in his boat, the deck-hand singing on
the steamboat deck,
The shoemaker singing as he sits on his bench, the hatter singing as he stands,
The wood-cutter's song, the ploughboy's on his way in the morning, or at
noon intermission or at sundown,
The delicious singing of the mother, or of the young wife at work, or of the
girl sewing or washing,
Each singing what belongs to him or her and to none else,
The day what belongs to the day—at night the party of young fellows, robust, friendly,
Singing with open mouths their strong melodious songs.

O Captain! My Captain!

O Captain! my Captain! our fearful trip is done,
The ship has weather'd every rack, the prize we sought is won,
The port is near, the bells I hear, the people all exulting,
While follow eyes the steady keel, the vessel grim and daring;
But O heart! heart! heart!
O the bleeding drops of red,
Where on the deck my Captain lies,
Fallen cold and dead.

O Captain! my Captain! rise up and hear the bells;
Rise up—for you the flag is flung—for you the bugle trills,
For you bouquets and ribbon'd wreaths—for you the shores a-crowding,
For you they call, the swaying mass, their eager faces turning;
Here Captain! dear father!
This arm beneath your head!
It is some dream that on the deck,
You've fallen cold and dead.

My Captain does not answer, his lips are pale and still,
My father does not feel my arm, he has no pulse nor will,
The ship is anchor'd safe and sound, its voyage closed and done,
From fearful trip the victor ship comes in with object won;
Exult, O shores! and ring, O bells!
But I with mournful tread,
Walk the deck my Captain lies,
Fallen cold and dead.

The Blue and the Gray

"The Blue and the Gray," by Francis Miles Finch, was first printed in 1867 in the *Atlantic Monthly*. The inspiration for this poem comes from the women of Columbus, Mississippi, who placed flowers on the graves of both Union and Confederate dead.

By the flow of the inland river,
Whence the fleets of iron have fled,
Where the blades of the grave grass quiver,
Asleep are the ranks of the dead;—
Under the sod and the dew,
Waiting the judgment day;—
Under the one, the Blue;
Under the other, the Gray.

These in the robings of glory,
Those in the gloom of defeat,
All with the battle blood gory,
In the dusk of eternity meet;—
Under the sod and the dew,
Waiting the judgment day;—
Under the laurel, the Blue;
Under the willow, the Gray.

From the silence of sorrowful hours
The desolate mourners go,
Lovingly laden with flowers
Alike for the friend and the foe,—
Under the sod and the dew,
Waiting the judgment day;—
Under the roses, the Blue;
Under the lilies, the Gray.

So with an equal splender
The morning sun rays fall,
With a touch, impartially tender,
On the blossoms blooming for all;—
Under the sod and the dew,
Waiting the judgment day;—
'Broidered with gold, the Blue;
Mellowed with gold, the Gray.

So, when the summer calleth,
On forest and field of grain
With an equal murmur falleth
The cooling drip of the rain;—
Under the sod and the dew,
Waiting the judgment day;—
Wet with the rain, the Blue;
Wet with the rain, the Gray.

Sadly, but not with upbraiding,
The generous deed was done;
In the storm of the years that are fading,
No braver battle was won;—
Under the sod and the dew,
Waiting the judgment day;—
Under the blossoms, the Blue;
Under the garlands, the Gray

No more shall the war cry sever,
Or the winding rivers be red;
They banish our anger forever
When they laurel the graves of our dead!
Under the sod and the dew,
Waiting the judgment day;—
Love and tears for the Blue,
Tears and love for the Gray.

* * *

The ceremony for the driving of the golden spike at Promontory Summit, Utah, on May 10, 1869. Here, marking completion of the United States' first Transcontinental Railroad, the railheads of the Union Pacific and Central Pacific railroads finally met.

Postwar Society: The Progressive Age

The Ballad of John Henry

The continued expansion of the nation's railroads was a key component of the post Civil War industry. During this time, many former slaves found work laying track, blasting tunnels, and constructing bridges. "The Ballad of John Henry," one of the many rhythmic songs produced to accompany the often backbreaking work, tells the legend of a black steel driver who pitted himself against a newly introduced mechanical steam drill, winning the contest, but dying in the effort. The legend of John Henry, like that of Paul Bunyan, serves as a tribute to the spirit of man against machine. The U.S. Postal Service paid homage to that indomitable spirit in 1997, issuing a commemorative John Henry stamp.

John Henry was a little baby boy
You could hold him in the palm of your hand.
He gave a long and lonesome cry,
"Gonna be a steel-drivin' man, Lawd, Lawd,
Gonna be a steel-drivin' man."

They took John Henry to the tunnel,
Put him in the lead to drive,
The rock was so tall, John Henry so small,
That he laid down his hammer and he cried, "Lawd, Lawd,"
Laid down his hammer and he cried.

John Henry started on the right hand,
The steam drill started on the left,
"Fo' I'd let that steamdrill beat me down,
I'd hammer my fool self to death, Lawd, Lawd,
Hammer my fool self to death."

John Henry told his captain,
"A man ain't nothin' but a man,
Fo' I let your steamdrill beat me down
I'll die with this hammer in my hand, Lawd, Lawd,
Die with this hammer in my hand."

Now the Captain told John Henry,
"I believe my tunnel's sinkin' in."
"Stand back, Captain, and doncha be afraid,
That's nothing but my hammer catchin' wind, Lawd, Lawd,
That's nothing but my hammer catchin' wind."

John Henry told his Cap'n,
"Look yonder, boy, what do I see?
Your drill's done broke and your hole's done choke,
And you can't drive steel like me, Lawd, Lawd,
You can't drive steel like me."

John Henry hammerin' in the mountain,
Til the handle of his hammer caught on fire,
He drove so hard till he broke his po' heart,
Then he laid down his hammer and he died, Lawd, Lawd,
He laid down his hammer and he died.

They took John Henry to the tunnel,
And they buried him in the sand,
An' every locomotive come rollin' by
Say, "There lies a steel-drivin' man, Lawd, Lawd,
There lies a steel-drivin' man."

The signing of the Alaska Treaty of Cessation on March 30, 1867, as depicted by Emanuel Leutze. Russia, lacking resources to establish permanent settlements and further weakened by the Crimean War, first offered to sell Alaska to the United States in 1859. With the threat of civil war looming, the United States was forced to decline. After the war, Secretary of State William H. Seward (second from left), a strong proponent of expansion, reopened talks with Russia and agreed to buy Alaska for $7.2 million—less than two cents per acre. Incredibly, the Senate passed the treaty to buy Alaska by just one vote. Critics lambasted the "exorbitant" price, referring to Alaska as "Seward's icebox" or President Andrew Johnson's "polar bear garden." The Alaskan territory was officially transferred to the U.S. on October 18, 1867, and was recognized as the 49th state in 1959.

HIRAM R. REVELS

On Readmission of Georgia to the Union

I protest in the name of truth and human rights against any and every attempt to fetter the hands of one hundred thousand white and colored citizens of the state of Georgia.

With the end of the Civil War and the coming of Reconstruction, the former Confederate states were re-admitted to the Union only after ratifying the Thirteenth and Fourteenth Amendments to the Constitution. A key factor in limiting the political influence of ex-Confederates was the "Ironclad Oath," which required a person to swear he had never borne arms against the Union or supported the Confederacy. Consequently, a minority coalition of freedmen, northern carpetbaggers, and southern Unionist whites helped the Republican Party became dominant in the South.

With ratification of the Fifteenth Amendment in 1870, the stage was set for the election of the first African Americans to the federal legislature. On February 23, 1870, Hiram Rhodes Revels (1827-1901), Republican of Mississippi, was sworn in as the first African American member of the U.S. Senate. He was followed in December of that year by Republican Joseph H. Rainey of South Carolina, the first African American member of the House of Representatives.

The son of free blacks, Revels was born in Fayetteville, North Carolina, and moved throughout the North in search of educational and professional opportunities. Ordained as a minister in the African Methodist Episcopal Church, he helped organize African American volunteer regiments for the Union Army. After the war, he moved to Natchez, Mississippi, and was elected state senator. In 1870, once Mississippi was re-admitted to the Union, the legislature elected him to fill the fourteen months remaining in the unexpired Senate term of Jefferson Davis. Upon arriving in Washington, several Democratic senators attempted to prevent Revels from being seated, charging that he could not have been a citizen for the nine years required by the Constitution since even free blacks were not considered citizens before 1866. Revels countered that he had been a voter many years earlier in Ohio and was, therefore, a citizen. Republicans prevailed, with the Senate voting forty-eight to eight to seat Revels.

On March 16, 1870, Revels delivered the following speech on the Senate floor. At issue was a bill re-admitting Georgia to the Union with a House amendment that could be used to prevent blacks from holding state office. Revels stressed the responsible behavior of most slaves during the war and declared that black citizens "ask but the rights which are theirs by God's universal law." A vigorous advocate of racial equality, Revels pled to reinstate the black legislators of the Georgia General Assembly who had been illegally ousted by white representatives. He likewise argued for amnesty and a restoration of full citizenship for all ex-Confederates, provided they swore an oath of loyalty to the United States.

The Senate did not heed Revels's plea, however, and retained the objectionable amendment when it passed the bill. Revels resigned two months before his term expired and was appointed the first president of Alcorn Agricultural and Mechanical College (now Alcorn State University) in Claiborne County, Mississippi.

I rise at this particular juncture in the discussion of the Georgia bill with feelings which perhaps never before entered into the experience of any member of this body. I rise, too, with misgivings as to the propriety of lifting my voice at this early period after my admission into the Senate. Perhaps it were wiser for me, so inexperienced in the details of senatorial duties, to have remained a passive listener in the progress of this debate; but when I remember that my term is short, and that the issues with which this bill is fraught are momentous in their present and future influence upon the well-being of my race, I would seem indifferent to the importance of the hour and recreant to the high trust imposed upon me if I hesitated to lend my voice on behalf of the loyal people of the South. ...

I stand today on this floor to appeal for protection from the strong arm of the government for her loyal children, irrespective of color and race, who are citizens of the southern states, and particularly of the state of Georgia. ...

While the confederate army pressed into its ranks every white male capable of bearing arms, the mothers, wives, daughters, and sisters of the southern soldiers were left defenseless and in the power of the blacks, upon whom the chains of slavery were still riveted; and to bind those chains the closer was the real issue for which so much life and property was sacrificed.

And now, sir, I ask, how did the race act? Did they in those days of confederate weakness and impotence evince the malignity of which we hear so much? Granting, for the sake of argument, that they were ignorant and besotted, which I do not believe, yet with all their supposed ignorance and credulity they in their way understood as fully as you or I the awful import of the contest. They knew if the gallant corps of national soldiers were beaten back and their flag trailed in the dust that it was the presage of still heavier bondage. They longed, too, as their fathers did before them, for the advent of that epoch over which was shed the hallowed light of inspiration itself. They desired, too, with their fathers, to welcome the feet of the stranger shod with the peaceful preparation of good news.... Think, Sir, for a moment, what the condition of this land would be today if the slave population had risen in servile insurrection against those who month by month were fighting to perpetuate that institution which brought to them all the evils of which they complained. ...

I maintain that the past record of my race is a true index of the feelings which today animate them. They bear toward their former masters no revengeful thoughts, no hatreds, no animosities. They aim not to elevate themselves by sacrificing one single interest of their white fellow-citizens. They ask but the rights which are theirs by God's universal law, and which are the natural outgrowth, the logical sequence of the condition in which the legislative enactments of this nation have placed them. They appeal to you and to me to see that they receive that protection which alone will enable them to pursue their daily avocations with success and enjoy the liberties of citizenship on the same footing with their white neighbors and friends. ...

The taunt is frequently flung at us that a Nemesis more terrible than the Greek personation of the anger of the gods awaits her hour of direful retribution. We are told that at no distant day a great uprising of the American people will demand that the Reconstruction acts of Congress be undone and blotted forever from the annals of legislative enactment. I inquire, Sir, if this delay in affording protection to the loyalists of the state of Georgia does not lend an uncomfortable significancy to this boasting sneer with which we so often meet? Delay is perilous at best; for it is as true in legislation as in physic, that the longer we

procrastinate to apply the proper remedies the more chronic becomes the malady that we seek to heal. ...

I favor the motion to strike out so much of the bill under debate as tends to abridge the term of the existing legislature of Georgia. Let me, then, as briefly as possible, review the history of the case which so urgently claims our prompt action. In the month of November 1867, an election was held by the authority of the reconstruction policy of this Congress in the state of Georgia. Its object was to settle by the ballot of her whole people, white and colored, whether it was expedient to summon a convention which should frame a constitution for civil government in that state. A certain class of the population declined to take any part in the election. The vote cast at that election represented thirty thousand white and eighty thousand colored citizens of the state. It was a majority, too, of the registered vote, and in consequence a convention was called. A number of the delegates who formed that convention were colored. By its authority a constitution was framed just and equitable in all its provisions. Race, color, or former condition of servitude found no barrier in any of its ample enactments, and it extended to those lately in armed rebellion all the privileges of its impartial requirements. This constitution was submitted to the people of the state for ratification. Every effort which human ingenuity could call into requisition to defeat its adoption was resorted to. The loyal population of the state was victorious; and notwithstanding the determination of some to defeat the constitution that same class sought under its provisions to procure the nomination for all the offices within the gift of the people. A number were declared elected as county officers and members of the general assembly.

Under the authority given by the act of Congress of June 25, 1868, the legislature thus elected convened on the Fourth of July of the same year in Atlanta. The act of Congress to which I refer reaffirmed certain qualifications which were demanded from all persons who were to hold office in the reconstructed states. After some delay a resolution was adopted by the legislature of Georgia declaring that the body was duly qualified, and thus began the civil government in the state. Peace and harmony seemed at last to have met together, truth and justice to have kissed each other. But their reign was of short duration. By and by the Reconstruction acts of Congress began to be questioned, and it was alleged that they were unconstitutional; and the legislature which was elected under the constitution framed and supported by colored men declared that a man having more than an eighth of African blood in his veins was ineligible to office or a seat in the legislature of the state of Georgia. These very men, to whom the Republican party extended all the rights and privileges of citizenship, whom they were empowered, if deemed expedient, to cut off forever from such beneficent grants, were the men to deny political equality to a large majority of their fellow-citizens. In the month of September 1868, twenty-eight members of the legislature were expelled from that body, and upon the assumption of the strange and startling hypothesis just mentioned they continued to legislate in open violation of the constitution. That constitution is required by its provisions the establishment of a system of free schools. Such provisions were wholly abortive, indeed a dead letter, for none were established. The courts of law, at least so far as colored men were regarded, were a shameless mockery of justice. And here an illustration, perhaps, will the better give point to my last remark. A case in which was involved the question whether or not a colored man was eligible to one of the county offices was taken before the superior court, and the judge upon the bench rendered as his judicial opinion that a man of color was not entitled to hold office. I am told, sir, that the colored man in question is a graduate of Oberlin, Ohio, and served with honor as a commissioned officer in the Union army during the late war. Is any comment needed in this body upon such a condition of affairs in the state of Georgia? Sir, I trust not. ...

The present legislature of Georgia has adopted the Fourteenth and Fifteenth Amendments to the Constitution of the United States and the fundamental conditions required by the act of June 25, 1868. The reconstructed state of Georgia now offers herself, through the constitutionally

elected senators, as meet and fit for the recognition and admission by this Congress.

I have thus rapidly gone over the history of the events which have transpired in the state of Georgia till I have come to the legislation of the present time. The Committee on Reconstruction in the other house prepared and presented a bill providing for the admission of the state on similar grounds to those on which my own state and Virginia were allowed to take their places in the Union. An amendment, however, was proposed in the House and adopted, the aim and purport of which is to legalize the organization of 1868, and declare that the terms of the members of the legislature, who have so recently qualified for a fair and just recognition by Congress, shall expire before they have completed their full term of two years under the constitution. Again, this amendment seeks to retain in office, whether approved by the legislature of the state or not, the judges who have declared, in opposition to the constitution and the law, that in the state of Georgia at least there exists a distinction as to race and color, so far as civil and political rights are concerned. If there be any meaning in the words of the constitution of that state no such class distinction as this exists. ...

I protest in the name of truth and human rights against any and every attempt to fetter the hands of one hundred thousand white and colored citizens of the state of Georgia. Sir, I now leave this question to the consideration of this body, and I wish my last words upon the great issues involved in the bill before us to be my solemn and earnest demand for full and prompt protection for the helpless loyal people of Georgia.

I appeal to the legislative enactments of this Congress, and ask if now, in the hour when a reconstructed state most needs support, this Senate, which hitherto has done so nobly, will not give it such legislation as it needs.

I've Been Working on the Railroad

By 1880, nearly 100,000 miles of railroad track had been laid by men of differing races and national origins. "I've Been Working on the Railroad," one of the most popular folk songs of the day, soon became identified with the mostly Irish laborers building rail lines west of the Mississippi. First known as "The Levee Song," the tune is believed to have originated with black workers building levees on the Mississippi River during the 1830s. Another version of this song, "The Eyes of Texas," was adopted as the official song of the University of Texas at Austin, which opened in 1883.

I've been working on the railroad,
All the live-long day,
I've been working on the railroad,
Just to pass the time away.
Don't you hear the whistle blowing,
Rise up so early in the morn;
Don't you hear the captain shouting,
"Dinah, blow your horn!"

Dinah, won't you blow,
Dinah, won't you blow,
Dinah, won't you blow your horn?
Dinah, won't you blow
Dinah, won't you blow,
Dinah, won't you blow your horn?

Someone's in the kitchen with Dinah,
Someone's in the kitchen I know,
Someone's in the kitchen with Dinah,
Strummin' on the old banjo, and singin':
Fee-fi-fidd-lee-i-o
Fee-fi-fidd-lee-i-o
Fee-fi-fidd-lee-i-o
Strummin' on the old banjo.

Home on the Range

"Home on the Range," known as the "cowboy's national anthem," was written in the 1870s. The song was never copyrighted despite the best attempts of several individuals to claim authorship. Some historians attribute the words and music to Brewster Higley and Dan Kelley, two Kansas homesteaders. "Home on the Range" has been the official state song of Kansas since 1947.

Oh, give me a home,
Where the buffalo roam,
Where the deer and the antelope play;
Where seldom is heard a discouraging word,
And the skies are not cloudy all day.

Chorus:
> Home, home on the range,
> Where the deer and the antelope play;
> Where seldom is heard a discouraging word,
> And the skies are not cloudy all day.

How often at night when the heavens are bright
With the lights of the glittering stars,
Have I stood there amazed and asked as I gazed
If their glory exceeds that of ours.

Oh, give me a land where the bright diamond sand
Flows leisurely down the stream;
Where the graceful white swan goes gliding along
Like a maid in a heavenly dream.

Where the air is so pure, the Zephyrs so free,
The breezes so balmy and light,
That I would not exchange my home on the range,
For all the cities so bright.

Clementine

Originating in the 1880s, "Clementine" is another popular song which bears no copyright. Its authorship, therefore, cannot be substantiated although some attribute the music and at least one set of lyrics to Percy Montross. Whatever its origin, the humorous story of Clementine has been a favorite inclusion in songbooks for decades and will likely be for decades to come.

In a cavern, in a canyon
Excavating for a mine
Lived a miner, forty-niner
And his daughter Clementine.

Chorus:
    Oh my darling, O my darling, O my darling Clementine!
    You are lost and gone forever, Dreadful sorry, Clementine!

Light she was and like a fairy
And her shoes were number nine
Herring boxes, without topses
Sandals were for Clementine

Drove she ducklings to the water
Every morning just at nine,
Hit her foot against a splinter
Fell into the foaming brine

Ruby lips above the water
Blowing bubbles soft and fine
Alas, for me! I was no swimmer
So I lost my Clementine

In a churchyard, near the cavern
Where the myrtle doth entwine
There grow roses and other posies
Fertilized by Clementine.

Then the miner, forty-niner
Soon began to peak and pine
Thought he ought-er join his daughter
Now he's with his Clementine.

In my dreams she oft doth haunt me
With her garments soaked in brine
Though in life I used to hug her
Now she's dead, I'll draw the line.

How I missed her, how I missed her,
How I missed my Clementine
Then I kissed her little sister
And forgot my Clementine

Photograph of Thomas Edison with his phonograph, taken by Mathew Brady in 1877. Edison was invited to the White House in April 1878 to demonstrate the device for President Rutherford B. Hayes. One of the most prolific inventors in history, Edison held a record 1,093 U.S. patents while describing genius as "one percent inspiration, ninety-nine percent perspiration." Perhaps most significant among his many achievements, Edison originated the concept and implementation of electric power generation and distribution to homes, businesses, and factories. This was instrumental in the development of the modern industrialized world.

Women's Right to Vote

It was we, the people, not we, the white male citizens, nor we, the male citizens; but we, the whole people, who formed this Union.

Susan Brownell Anthony (1820-1906) was born into a Quaker family in Adams, Massachusetts, and taught school as an unmarried woman. She worked in the abolitionist and temperance movements and, in 1851, joined with Elizabeth Cady Stanton in the women's rights movement.

On Thanksgiving Day, 1872, Anthony was arrested for having "knowingly voted without having a lawful right to vote." She spent the rest of the year traveling throughout New York state, giving the following speech about the injustice of being denied the right to participate in elections. Despite her claim that women's suffrage was guaranteed by the Fourteenth and Fifteenth Amendments, she was nonetheless indicted. Without benefit of a jury trial, the presiding judge declared her guilty and imposed a one-hundred-dollar fine. He then asked Anthony if she had anything to say.

"Yes," she replied. "I have many things to say; for in your ordered verdict of guilty, you have trampled under foot every vital principle of our government. My natural rights, my civil rights, my political rights, my judicial rights, are all ignored. Robbed of the fundamental privilege of citizenship, I am degraded from the status of a citizen to that of a subject; and not only myself individually, but all of my sex, are, by your honor's verdict, doomed to political subjection under this, so-called, form of government."

Susan B. Anthony died in 1906, fourteen years before the passage of the Nineteenth Amendment granting women the right to vote. In 1979, Anthony became the first woman to be pictured on U.S. currency when the government began minting one-dollar coins with her likeness.

Friends and fellow citizens: I stand before you under indictment for the alleged crime of having voted at the last presidential election, without having a lawful right to vote. It shall be my work this evening to prove to you that in thus doing, I not only committed no crime, but instead simply exercised my citizen's rights, guaranteed to me and all United States citizens by the National Constitution beyond the power of any State to deny.

Our democratic-republican government is based on the idea of the natural right of every individual member thereof to a voice and a vote in making and executing the laws. We assert the province of government to be to secure the people in the enjoyment of their inalienable rights. We throw to the winds the old dogma that government can give rights. No one denies that before governments were organized each individual possessed the right to protect his own life, liberty and property. When 100 to 1,000,000 people enter into a free government, they do not barter away their natural rights; they simply pledge themselves to protect each other in the enjoyment of them through prescribed judicial and legislative tribunals. They agree to abandon the methods of brute force in the adjustment of their differences and adopt those of civilization.... The Declaration of Independence,

the United States Constitution, the constitutions of the several States and the organic laws of the Territories, all alike propose to *protect* the people in the exercise of their God-given rights. Not one of them pretends to bestow rights.

> All men are created equal, and endowed by their Creator with certain inalienable rights. Among these are life, liberty and the pursuit of happiness. To secure these, governments are instituted among men, deriving their just powers from the consent of the governed.

Here is no shadow of government authority over rights, or exclusion of any class from their full and equal enjoyment. Here is pronounced the right of all men, and "consequently," as the Quaker preacher said, "of all women," to a voice in the government. And here, in this first paragraph of the Declaration, is the assertion of the natural right of all to the ballot; for how can "the consent of the governed" be given, if the right to vote be denied?... The women, dissatisfied as they are with this form of government, that enforces taxation without representation—that compels them to obey laws to which they never have given their consent—that imprisons and hangs them without a trial by a jury of their peers—and robs them, in marriage, of the custody of their own persons, wages, and children—are this half of the people who are left wholly at the mercy of the other half, in direct violation of the spirit and letter of the declarations of the framers of this government, every one of which was based on the immutable principle of equal rights to all. By these declarations, kings, popes, priests, aristocrats, all were alike dethroned and placed on a common level, politically, with the lowliest born subject or serf. By them, too, men, as such, were deprived of their divine right to rule and placed on a political level with women. By the practice of these declarations all class and caste distinctions would be abolished, and slave, serf, plebeian, wife, woman, all alike rise from their subject position to the broader platform of equality.

The preamble of the Federal Constitution says:

We, the People of the United States, in order to form a more perfect union, establish justice, insure domestic tranquility, provide for the common defense, promote the general welfare and secure the blessings of liberty to ourselves and our posterity, do ordain and establish this Constitution for the United States of America.

It was we, the people, not we, the white male citizens, nor we, the male citizens; but we, the whole people, who formed this Union. We formed it not to give the blessings of liberty but to secure them; not to the half of ourselves and the half of our posterity, but to the whole people—women as well as men. It is downright mockery to talk to women of their enjoyment of the blessings of liberty while they are denied the only means of securing them provided by this democratic-republican government—the ballot....

When, in 1871, I asked [Senator Charles Sumner] to declare the power of the United States Constitution to protect women in their right to vote—as he had done for black men—he handed me a copy of all his speeches during that reconstruction period, and said:

Put "sex" where I have "race" or "color," and you have here the best and strongest argument I can make for woman. There is not a doubt but women have the constitutional right to vote, and I will never vote for a Sixteenth Amendment to guarantee it to them. I voted for both the Fourteenth and Fifteenth under protest; would never have done it but for the pressing emergency of that hour; would have insisted that the power of the original Constitution to protect all citizens in the equal enjoyment of their rights should have been vindicated through the courts. But the newly-made freedmen had neither the intelligence, wealth nor time to await that slow process. Women do possess all these in an eminent degree, and I insist that they shall appeal to the courts and through them establish the powers of our American magna charta to protect every citizen of the republic.

But, friends, when in accordance with Senator Sumner's counsel I went to the ballot-box, last November, and exercised my citizen's right to vote, the courts did not wait for me to appeal to them—they appealed to me, and indicted me on the charge of having voted illegally. ...

For any State to make sex a qualification, which must ever result in the disfranchisement of one entire half of the people, is to pass a bill of attainder, an ex post facto law, and is therefore a violation of the supreme law of the land. By it the blessings of liberty are forever withheld from women and their female posterity. For them, this government has no just powers derived from the consent of the governed. For them this government is not a democracy; it is not a republic. It is the most odious aristocracy ever established on the face of the globe. An oligarchy of wealth, where the rich govern the poor; an oligarchy of learning, where the educated govern the ignorant; or even an oligarchy of race, where the Saxon rules the African, might be endured; but this oligarchy of sex which makes father, brothers, husband, sons, the oligarchs over the mother and sisters, the wife and daughters of every household; which ordains all men sovereigns, all women subjects—carries discord and rebellion into every home of the nation. ...

It is urged that the use of the masculine pronouns *he*, *his*, and *him* in all the constitutions and laws, is proof that only men were meant to be included in their provisions. If you insist on this version of the letter of the law, we shall insist that you be consistent and accept the other horn of the dilemma, which would compel you to exempt women from taxation for the support of the government and from penalties for the violation of laws. There is no *she* or *her* or *hers* in the tax laws, and this is equally true of all the criminal laws.

Take for example, the civil rights law which I am charged with having violated; not only are all the pronouns in it masculine, but everybody knows that it was intended expressly to hinder the rebel men from voting. It reads,

"If any person shall knowingly vote without *his* having a lawful right." … I insist if government officials may thus manipulate the pronouns to tax, fine, imprison and hang women, it is their duty to thus change them in order to protect us in our right to vote. …

Though the words persons, people, inhabitants, electors, citizens, are all used indiscriminately in the national and State constitutions, there was always a conflict of opinion, prior to the war, as to whether they were synonymous terms, but whatever room there was for doubt, under the old regime, the adoption of the Fourteenth Amendment settled that question forever in its first sentence:

All persons born or naturalized in the United States, and subject to the jurisdiction thereof, are citizens of the United States, and of the State wherein they reside.

The second settles the equal status of all citizens:

No State shall make or enforce any law which shall abridge the privileges or immunities of citizens of the United States; nor shall any State deprive any person of life, liberty or property without due process of law, or deny to any person within its jurisdiction the equal protection of the laws.

The only question left to be settled now is: Are women persons? I scarcely believe any of our opponents will have the hardihood to say they are not. Being persons, then, women are citizens, and no State has a right to make any new law, or to enforce any old law, which shall abridge their privileges or immunities. Hence, every discrimination against women in the constitutions and laws of the several States is today null and void, precisely as is every one against negroes.

Is the right to vote one of the privileges or immunities of citizens? I think the disfranchised ex-rebels and ex-State prisoners all will agree that it is not only one of them, but the one without which all the others are nothing. Seek first the kingdom of the ballot and all things else shall be added, is the political injunction. …

However much the doctors of the law may disagree as to whether people and citizens, in the original Constitution, were one and the same, or whether the privileges and immunities in the Fourteenth Amendment include the right of suffrage, the question of the citizen's right to vote is forever settled by the Fifteenth Amendment. "The right of

citizens of the United States to vote shall not be denied or abridged by the United States, or by any State, on account of race, color or previous condition of servitude." How can the State deny or abridge the right of the citizen, if the citizen does not possess it? There is no escape from the conclusion that to vote is the citizen's right, and the specifications of race, color or previous condition of servitude can in no way impair the force of that emphatic assertion that the citizen's right to vote shall not be denied or abridged. …

If, however, you will insist that the Fifteenth Amendment's emphatic interdiction against robbing United States citizens of their suffrage "on account of race, color or previous condition of servitude," is a recognition of the right of either the United States or any State to deprive them of the ballot for any or all other reasons, I will prove to you that the class of citizens for whom I now plead are, by all the principles of our government and many of the laws of the States, included under the term "previous conditions of servitude."

Consider first married women and their legal status. What is servitude? "The condition of a slave." What is a slave? "A person who is robbed of the proceeds of his labor; a person who is subject to the will of another." By the laws of Georgia, South Carolina, and all the States of the South, the negro had no right to the custody and control of his person. He belonged to his master. If he were disobedient, the master had the right to use correction. If the negro did not like the correction and ran away, the master had the right to use coercion to bring him back. By the laws of almost every State in this Union today, North as well as South, the married woman has no right to the custody and control of her person. The wife belongs to the husband; and if she refuses obedience he may use moderate correction, and if she do not like his moderate correction and leave his "bed and board," the husband may use moderate coercion to bring her back. The little word "moderate," you see, is the saving clause for the wife, and would doubtless be overstepped should her offended husband administer his correction with the "cat-o'-nine-tails," or accomplish his coercion with blood-hounds.

Again the slave had no right to the earnings of his hands, they belonged to his master; no right to the custody of his children, they belonged to his master; no right to sue or be sued, or to testify in the courts. If he committed a crime, it was the master who must sue or be sued. In many of the States there has been special legislation, giving married women the right to property inherited or received by bequest, or earned by the pursuit of any avocation outside the home; also giving them the right to sue and be sued in matters pertaining to such separate property; but not a single State of this Union has ever secured the wife in the enjoyment of her right to equal ownership of the joint earnings of the marriage copartnership. And since, in the nature of things, the vast majority of married women never earn a dollar by work outside their families, or inherit a dollar from their fathers, it follows that from the day of their marriage to the day of the death of their husbands not one of them ever has a dollar, except it shall please her husband to let her have it. ...

Is anything further needed to prove woman's condition of servitude sufficient to entitle her to the guarantees of the Fifteenth Amendment? Is there a man who will not agree with me that to talk of freedom without the ballot is mockery to the women of this republic, precisely as New England's orator, Wendell Phillips, at the close of the late war declared it to be to the newly emancipated black man? I admit that, prior to the rebellion, by common consent, the right to enslave, as well as to disfranchise both native and foreign born persons, was conceded to the States. But the one grand principle settled by the war and the reconstruction legislation, is the supremacy of the national government to protect the citizens of the United States in their right to freedom and the elective franchise, against any and every interference on the part of the several States; and again and again have the American people asserted the triumph of this principle by their overwhelming majorities for Lincoln and Grant.

The one issue of the last two presidential elections was whether the Fourteenth and Fifteenth Amendments should be considered the irrevocable will of the people; and the decision was that they should be, and that it is not only the right, but the duty of the national government to protect all United States citizens in the full enjoyment and free exercise of their privileges and immunities against the attempt of any State to deny or abridge. ...

It is upon this just interpretation of the United States Constitution that our National Woman Suffrage Association, which celebrates the twenty-fifth anniversary of the woman's rights movement next May in New York City, has based all its arguments and action since the passage of these amendments. We no longer petition legislature or Congress to give us the right to vote, but appeal to women everywhere to exercise their too long neglected "citizen's right." We appeal to the inspectors of election to receive the votes of all United States citizens, as it is their duty to do. We appeal to the United States commissioners and marshals to arrest, as is their duty, the inspectors who reject the votes of United States citizens, and leave alone those who perform their duties and accept these votes. We ask the juries to return verdicts of "not guilty" in the cases of law-abiding United States citizens who cast their votes, and inspectors of election who receive and count them.

We ask the judges to render unprejudiced opinions of the law, and wherever there is room for doubt to give the benefit to the side of liberty and equal rights for women, remembering that, as Sumner says, "The true rule of interpretation under our National Constitution, especially since its amendments, is that anything *for* human rights is constitutional, everything *against* human rights unconstitutional." It is on this line that we propose to fight our battle for the ballot—peaceably but nevertheless persistently—until we achieve complete triumph and all United States citizens, men and women alike, are recognized as equals in the government.

CHIEF JOSEPH

Speech of Surrender

I will fight no more forever.

Chief Joseph (1840-1904), known to his people as "Thunder Rolling in the Mountains," led the Nez Percé in armed conflict against the U.S. government in 1877. The fighting began when a group of young warriors, angry that the government had ordered the Indians out of Oregon's Wallowa Valley to an Idaho reservation, massacred a group of white settlers. Joseph, who had sought to avoid war, led his people on a 1,700-mile retreat in a desperate attempt to join forces with Sioux Indians in Canada. Though not a war chief, Joseph was able to consistently outmaneuver the Army while inflicting substantial casualties. Relentlessly pursued by General Howard, who had assisted in planning Union strategy at Gettysburg, Joseph's defeat was, nevertheless, a foregone conclusion. On October 5, mourning the deaths of fellow chiefs Tuhulkutsut and Looking Glass, and his brother Alokut ("He Who Led the Young Men"), the "Red Napoleon of the West" surrendered to General Nelson A. Miles and delivered the following address to the soldiers.

Tell General Howard I know his heart. What he told me before I have in my heart. I am tired of fighting. Our chiefs are killed. Looking Glass is dead. Tuhulkutsut is dead. The old men are all dead. He Who Led the Young Men is dead. It is cold and we have no blankets. The little children are freezing to death. My people, some of them, have run away to the hills, and have no blankets, no food. No one knows where they are, perhaps freezing to death. I want to have time to look for my children and see how many I can find. Maybe I shall find them among the dead.

Hear me, my chiefs! I am tired. My heart is sick and sad. From where the sun now stands, I will fight no more forever.

Black fabric drapes the White House in 1881 to express a nation in mourning for President James Garfield, assassinated by a political supporter upset over rejection of his repeated attempts to be appointed as the United States consul in Paris—a position for which he was not qualified. Garfield's assassination led to passage of the Pendleton Civil Service Reform Act, which established the United States Civil Service Commission. This act placed most federal government employees on the merit system and marked the end of the so-called spoils system.

FREDERICK DOUGLASS

Speech to the National Convention of Colored Men

Who would be free, themselves must strike the blow.

On September 25, 1883, Frederick Douglass gave the following speech to the National Convention of Colored Men in Louisville, Kentucky. Here, he explained why blacks must be vigilant in securing their rights. Weeks later, the United States Supreme Court threw out the Civil Rights Act of 1875, which had banned racial discrimination in public places, claiming that such discrimination did not violate the Constitution.

… With apparent surprise, astonishment and impatience we have been asked: "What more can the colored people of this country want than they now have, and what more is possible to them?" It is said they were once slaves, they are now free; they were once subjects, they are now sovereigns; they were once outside of all American institutions, they are now inside of all and are a recognized part of the whole American people. Why, then, do they hold Colored National Conventions and thus insist upon keeping up the color line between themselves and their white fellow countrymen? We do not deny the pertinence and plausibility of these questions, nor do we shrink from a candid answer to the argument which they are supposed to contain. For we do not forget that they are not only put to us by those who have no sympathy with us, but by many who wish us well, and that in any case they deserve an answer. …

If liberty, with us, is yet but a name, our citizenship is but a sham, and our suffrage thus far only a cruel mockery, we may yet congratulate ourselves upon the fact, that the laws and institutions of the country are sound, just and liberal. There is hope for a people when their laws are righteous, whether for the moment they conform to their requirements or not. But until this nation shall make its practice accord with its Constitution and its righteous laws, it will not do to reproach the colored people of this country with keeping up the color line—for that people would prove themselves scarcely worthy of even theoretical freedom, to say nothing of practical freedom, if they settled down in silent, servile and cowardly submission to their wrongs, from fear of making their color visible. They are bound by every element of manhood to hold conventions, in their own name, and on their own behalf, to keep their grievances before the people and make every organized protest against the wrongs inflicted upon them within their power. They should scorn the counsels of cowards, and hang their banner on the outer wall. Who would be free, themselves must strike the blow. We do not believe, as we are often told, that the Negro is the ugly child of the National family, and the more he is kept out of sight the better it will be for him. You know that liberty given is never so precious as liberty sought for and fought for. The man outraged is the man to make the outcry. Depend upon it, men will not care much for people who do not care for themselves. …

If the six millions of colored people of this country, armed with the Constitution of the United States, with a million votes of their own to lean upon, and millions of white men at their back, whose hearts are responsive to the claims of humanity, have not sufficient spirit and wisdom to organize and combine to defend themselves from outrage, discrimination and oppression, it will be idle for them to expect that the Republican party or any other political party will organize and combine for them or care what becomes of them. Men may combine to prevent cruelty to animals, for they are dumb and cannot speak for themselves; but we are men and must speak for ourselves, or we shall not be spoken for at all. We have conventions in America for Ireland, but we should have none if Ireland did not speak for herself. It is because she makes a noise and keeps her cause before the people that other people go to her help. It was the sword of Washington that gave Independence the sword of Lafayette. In conclusion upon this color objection, we have to say that we meet here in open daylight. There is nothing sinister about us. The eyes of the nation are upon us. Ten thousand newspapers may tell if they choose of whatever is said and done here. They may commend our wisdom or condemn our folly, precisely as we shall be wise or foolish.

We put ourselves before them as honest men, and ask their judgment upon our work.

Not the least important among the subjects to which we invite your earnest attention is the condition of the laboring class at the South. Their cause is one with the laboring classes all over the world. The labor unions of the country should not throw away this colored element of strength. …

What labor everywhere wants, what it ought to have and will some day demand and receive, is an honest day's pay for an honest day's work. As the laborer becomes more intelligent he will develop what capital already possess— that is the power to organize and combine for its own protection. Experience demonstrates that there may be a wages of slavery only a little less galling and crushing in its effects than chattel slavery, and that this slavery of wages must go down with the other. …

No more crafty effective device for defrauding the Southern laborer could be adopted than the one that substitutes orders upon shopkeepers for currency in payment of wages. It has the merit of a show of honesty, while it puts the laborer completely at the mercy of the landowner and the shop-keeper. He is between the upper and the nether millstones and is hence ground to dust. It gives the shop-keeper a customer who can trade with no other storekeeper, and thus leaves the latter no motive for fair dealing except his own moral sense, which is never too strong. While the laborer holding the orders is tempted by their worthlessness as a circulating medium, to get rid of them at any sacrifice, and hence is led into extravagance and consequent destitution.

The merchant puts him off with his poorest commodities at highest prices, and can say to him take those or nothing. Worse still. By this means the laborer is brought into debt, and hence is kept always in the power of the landowner. When this system is not pursued and land is rented to the freedman, he is charged more for the use of an acre of land for a single year than the land would bring in the market if offered for sale. On such a system of fraud and wrong one might well invoke a bolt from heaven—red with uncommon wrath. …

Flagrant as have been the outrages committed upon colored citizens in respect to their civil rights, more flagrant, shocking and scandalous still have been the outrages committed upon our political rights, by means of bull-dozing and Kukluxing, Mississippi plans, fraudulent counts, tissue ballots and like devices. Three states in which the colored people outnumber the white population are without colored representation and their political voice suppressed. The colored citizens in those States are virtually disfranchised, the Constitution held in utter contempt and its provisions nullified. This has been done in the face of the Republican party and successive Republican Administrations.

It was once said by the great O'Connell that the history of Ireland might be traced like a wounded man through a crowd by the blood, and the same may be truly said of the history of the colored voters of the South.

They have marched to the ballot-box in face of gleaming weapons, wounds and death. They have been abandoned by the Government and left to the laws of nature. So far as they are concerned, there is no Government or Constitution of the United States.

They are under control of a foul, haggard and damning conspiracy against reason, law and constitution. How you can be indifferent, how any leading colored men can allow themselves to be silent in the presence of this state of things we cannot see. …

This is no question of party. It is a question of law and government. It is a question whether men shall be protected by law or be left to the mercy of cyclones of anarchy and bloodshed. It is whether the Government or the mob shall rule this land; whether the promises solemnly made to us in the Constitution be manfully kept or meanly and flagrantly broken. Upon this vital point we ask the whole people of the United States to take notice that whatever of political power we have shall be exerted for no man of any party who will not in advance of election promise to use every power given him by the Government, State or National, to make the black man's path to the ballot-box as straight, smooth and safe as that of any other American citizen. …

We hold it to be self-evident that no class or color should be the exclusive rulers of this country. If there is such a ruling class, there must of course be a subject class, and when this condition is once established this Government of the people, by the people and for the people will have perished from the earth.

EMMA LAZARUS

The New Colossus

The Statue of Liberty, properly known as "Liberty Enlightening the World," was given to the United States by the people of France in 1884 as a token of friendship. Standing on Liberty Island in New York Harbor, the statue represents a woman dressed in a loose robe lifting a torch in the air with her right hand while her left hand holds a tablet bearing the date of the Declaration of Independence. At the feet of the statue is a broken shackle symbolizing the overthrow of tyranny.

In 1883, as a fundraising campaign was underway to pay for construction of the statue's pedestal, a New York poet named Emma Lazarus (1849-1887) wrote "The New Colossus." Lazarus, who viewed Lady Liberty as the "Mother of Exiles," looked upon this "New Colossus" as the antithesis of the Colossus of Rhodes—one of the Seven Ancient Wonders of the world, built in honor of the sun god Helios after the people of Rhodes successfully repelled a year-long siege by the Macedonians. Lazarus's poem was not immediately associated with the Statue of Liberty, however. In fact, the poem gained little notice until 1903, when it was placed on a bronze plaque inside the statue. It then took another thirty years before that plaque was moved to the main entrance.

The lack of affection for Lazarus's poem was the result of many Americans unenthusiastic welcome to the "huddled masses," "the wretched refuse," and "the homeless, tempest-tost." Public pressure to restrict immigration eventually brought an end to the mass European exodus in the early 1920s, but Lazarus's words were not without later appeal, however—particularly in the 1930s, when many Jews fleeing Nazi Germany sought refuge in the United States. Lazarus, herself a member of a wealthy Jewish family, had worked as a philanthropist aiding persecuted Jews fleeing Europe and Russia in the late 1800s.

Not like the brazen giant of Greek fame,
With conquering limbs astride from land to land;
Here at our sea-washed, sunset gates shall stand
A mighty woman with a torch, whose flame
Is the imprisoned lightning, and her name
Mother of Exiles. From her beacon-hand
Glows world-wide welcome; her mild eyes command
The air-bridged harbor that twin cities frame.

"Keep, ancient lands, your storied pomp!" cries she
With silent lips. "Give me your tired, your poor,
Your huddled masses yearning to breathe free,
The wretched refuse of your teeming shore.
Send these, the homeless, tempest-tost to me,
I lift my lamp beside the golden door!"

FREDERICK DOUGLASS

I Have No Apology

As men choose wives from friends and associates, it is not strange that I have so chosen my wife and that she has chosen me.

In August 1882, Frederick Douglass lost his wife of nearly forty-four years, Anna Murray Douglass. On January 24, 1884, Douglass married Helen Pitts, a white woman twenty-one years his junior. As news of their interracial marriage spread, Douglass became the recipient of severe criticism from "false friends of both colors." He was pleased, therefore, to receive a congratulatory note from Elizabeth Cady Stanton. In his reply letter, dated May 30, 1884, Douglass asserted that his marriage was a private matter and condemned racial exclusivity as detrimental to the continued progress of civilization.

I am very glad to find, as I do find by your kind good letter, that I have made no mistake in respect of your feeling concerning my marriage. I have known you and your love of liberty so long and well that, without one word from you on the subject, I had recorded your word and vote against the clamor raised against my marriage to a white woman. To those who find fault with me on this account, I have no apology to make. My wife and I have simply obeyed the convictions of our own minds and hearts in a matter wherein we alone were concerned and about which nobody has any right to interfere. I could never have been at peace with my own soul or held up my head among men had I allowed the fear of popular clamor to deter me from following my convictions as to this marriage. I should have gone to my grave a self-accused and a self-convicted moral coward. Much as I respect the good opinion of my fellow men, I do not wish it at expense of my own self-respect.

Circumstances have, during the last forty years, thrown me much more into white society than in that of colored people. While true to the rights of the colored race, my nearest personal friends, owing to association and common sympathy and aims, have been white people, and as men choose wives from friends and associates, it is not strange that I have so chosen my wife and that she has chosen me. You, Dear Mrs. Stanton, could have found a straight, smooth, and pleasant road through the world had you allowed the world to decide for you your sphere in life, that is, had you allowed it to sink your moral and intellectual individuality into nonentity. But you have nobly asserted your own and the rights of your sex, and the world will know hereafter that you have lived and worked beneficently in the world.

You have made both Mrs. Douglass and myself very glad and happy by your letter, and we both give you our warmest thanks for it. Helen is a braver woman than I am a man and bears the assaults of popular prejudice more serenely than I do. No sigh or complaint escapes her. She is steady, firm, and strong and meets the gaze of the world with a tranquil heart and unruffled brow. I am amazed by her heroic bearing, and I am greatly strengthened by it. She has sometimes said she would not regret though the storm of opposition were ten times greater. …

ERNEST LAWRENCE THAYER

Casey at the Bat

Ernest Lawrence Thayer (1863-1940) published "Casey at the Bat" in the *San Francisco Examiner* on June 3, 1888. It is the poem most closely associated with America's national pastime, and is loved for that reason and for its anti-heroic ending. Although multiple versions with minor changes have since been produced, the following is the complete poem as it originally appeared.

The Outlook wasn't brilliant for the Mudville nine that day;
The score stood four to two with but one inning more to play.
And then when Cooney died at first, and Barrows did the same,
A sickly silence fell upon the patrons of the game.

A straggling few got up to go in deep despair. The rest
Clung to that hope which springs eternal in the human breast;
They thought, if only Casey could get but a whack at that—
We'd put up even money now with Casey at the bat.

But Flynn preceded Casey, as did also Jimmy Blake,
And the former was a lulu and the latter was a cake;
So upon that stricken multitude grim melancholy sat,
For there seemed but little chance of Casey's getting to the bat.

But Flynn let drive a single, to the wonderment of all,
And Blake, the much despise-ed, tore the cover off the ball;
And when the dust had lifted, and the men saw what had occurred,
There was Jimmy safe at second and Flynn a-hugging third.

Then from 5,000 throats and more there rose a lusty yell;
It rumbled through the valley, it rattled in the dell;
It knocked upon the mountain and recoiled upon the flat,
For Casey, mighty Casey, was advancing to the bat.

There was ease in Casey's manner as he stepped into his place;
There was pride in Casey's bearing and a smile on Casey's face.
And when, responding to the cheers, he lightly doffed his hat,
No stranger in the crowd could doubt 'twas Casey at the bat.

Ten thousand eyes were on him as he rubbed his hands with dirt;
Five thousand tongues applauded when he wiped them on his shirt.
Then while the writhing pitcher ground the ball into his hip,
Defiance gleamed in Casey's eye, a sneer curled Casey's lip.

And now the leather-covered sphere came hurtling through the air,
And Casey stood a-watching it in haughty grandeur there.
Close by the sturdy batsman the ball unheeded sped—
"That ain't my style," said Casey. "Strike one," the umpire said.

From the benches, black with people, there went up a muffled roar,
Like the beating of the storm-waves on a stern and distant shore.
"Kill him! Kill the umpire!" shouted some one on the stand;
And its likely they'd have killed him had not Casey raised his hand.

With a smile of Christian charity great Casey's visage shone;
He stilled the rising tumult; he bade the game go on;
He signaled to the pitcher, and once more the spheroid flew;
But Casey still ignored it, and the umpire said, "Strike two."

"Fraud!" cried the maddened thousands, and echo answered fraud;
But one scornful look from Casey and the audience was awed.
They saw his face grow stern and cold, they saw his muscles strain,
And they knew that Casey wouldn't let that ball go by again.

The sneer is gone from Casey's lip, his teeth are clenched in hate;
He pounds with cruel violence his bat upon the plate.
And now the pitcher holds the ball, and now he lets it go,
And now the air is shattered by the force of Casey's blow.

Oh, somewhere in this favored land the sun is shining bright;
The band is playing somewhere, and somewhere hearts are light,
And somewhere men are laughing, and somewhere children shout;
But there is no joy in Mudville—mighty Casey has struck out.

BENJAMIN HARRISON

True Patriotism

Let those who would die for the flag on the field of battle, give a better proof of their patriotism and a higher glory to their country by promoting fraternity and justice.

President Benjamin Harrison (1833-1901) was the grandson of President William Henry Harrison, the famed Indian fighter and hero of the Battle of Tippecanoe who died of pneumonia only thirty days after his inauguration, and the great-grandson of Benjamin Harrison (1726?-1791), a signer of the Declaration of Independence. As president, Benjamin Harrison did more than any other chief executive to encourage respect for the American flag. He ordered it flown above the White House and all federal buildings, and urged that it be flown over every school in the nation. In 1892, as part of the 400th anniversary celebration of Christopher Columbus's discovery of America, Harrison called for patriotic exercises in the schools. This was the first time students recited the Pledge of Allegiance, a promise of loyalty to the United States written by Francis Bellamy of Boston, an associate editor of the *Youth's Companion*. The following are the concluding remarks from Benjamin Harrison's inaugural address, delivered on March 4, 1889.

... Let us exalt patriotism and moderate our party contentions. Let those who would die for the flag on the field of battle, give a better proof of their patriotism and a higher glory to their country by promoting fraternity and justice. A party success that is achieved by unfair methods or by practices that partake of revolution, is hurtful and evanescent, even from a party standpoint. We should hold our different opinions in mutual respect; and, having submitted them to the arbitrament of the ballot, should accept an adverse judgment with the same respect that we would have demanded of our opponents if the decision had been more in our favor.

No other people have a government more worthy of their respect and love, or a land so magnificent in extent, so pleasant to look upon, and so full of generous suggestion to enterprise and labor. God has placed upon our head a diadem, and has laid at our feet power and wealth beyond definition or calculation. But we must not forget that we take these gifts upon the condition that justice and mercy shall hold the reigns of power, and that the upward avenues of hope shall be free for all the people.

I do not mistrust the future. Dangers have been in frequent ambush along our path, but we have uncovered and vanquished them all. Passion has swept some of our communities, but only to give us a new demonstration that the great body of our people are stable, patriotic, and law-abiding. No political party can long pursue advantage at the expense of public honor, or by rude and indecent methods, without protest and fatal disaffection in its own body. The peaceful agencies of commerce are more fully revealing the necessary unity of all our communities, and the increasing intercourse of our people in promoting mutual respect. We shall find unalloyed pleasure in the revelation which our census will make of the swift development of the great resources of some of the states. Each state will bring its generous contributions to the great aggregate of the nation's increase. And when the harvests from the fields, the cattle from the hills, and the ores from the earth, shall have been weighed, counted, and valued, we will turn from all to crown with the highest honor the state that has most promoted education, virtue, justice and patriotism among its people.

SAMUEL GOMPERS

What Does the Working Man Want?

We want eight hours and nothing less. We have been accused of being selfish, and it has been said that we will want more; that last year we got an advance of ten cents and now we want more. We do want more.

Samuel Gompers (1850-1924) was born in London and emigrated to the United States with his family in 1863, where he followed in his father's footsteps as a cigar maker. He became the first registered member of the Cigar-Makers' International Union and, in 1886, established the American Federation of Labor. He served as president of that organization for the rest of his life, save for one year—his sabbatical in 1895. As head of the AFL, Gompers campaigned for shorter hours, higher wages, safe and sanitary working conditions, child labor laws, and collective bargaining, and was instrumental in the creation of the U.S. Department of Labor. Gompers's aim was to counter the radical image that employers tried to associate with organized labor and demonstrate that workers simply wanted what everyone else wanted: a better quality of life.

The following speech was delivered by Gompers on May 1, 1890, in Louisville, Kentucky, when he was campaigning to establish the eight-hour workday.

... My friends, we have met here today to celebrate the idea that has prompted thousands of working-people of Louisville and New Albany to parade the streets of y[our] city; that prompts the toilers of Chicago to turn out by their fifty or hundred thousand of men; that prompts the vast army of wage-workers in New York to demonstrate their enthusiasm and appreciation of the importance of this idea; that prompts the toilers of England, Ireland, Germany, France, Italy, Spain, and Austria to defy the manifestos of the autocrats of the world and say that on May the first, 1890, the wage-workers of the world will lay down their tools in sympathy with the wage-workers of America, to establish a principle of limitations of hours of labor to eight hours for sleep, eight hours for work, and eight hours for what we will.

It has been charged time and time again that were we to have more hours of leisure we would merely devote it to debauchery, to the cultivation of vicious habits—in other words, that we would get drunk. I desire to say this in answer to that charge: As a rule, there are two classes in society who get drunk. One is the class who has no work to do in consequence of too much money; the other class, who also has no work to do, because it can't get any, and gets drunk on its face. I maintain that that class in our social life that exhibits the greatest degree of sobriety is that class who are able, by a fair number of hours of day's work to earn fair wages—not overworked. The man who works twelve, fourteen, and sixteen hours a day requires some artificial stimulant to restore the life ground out of him in the drudgery of the day. ...

We ought to be able to discuss this question on a higher ground, and I am pleased to say that the movement in which we are engaged will stimulate us to it. They tell us that the eight-hour movement can not be enforced, for the reason that it must check industrial and commercial progress. I say that the history of this country, in its industrial and commercial relations, shows the reverse. I say that is the plane on which this question ought to be discussed—that is the social question. As long as they make this question an economic one, I am willing to discuss it with them. I would retrace every step I have taken to advance this movement did it mean industrial and commercial stagnation. But it does not mean that. It means greater prosperity; it means a greater degree of progress for the whole people; it means more advancement and intelligence, and a nobler race of people. ...

They say they can't afford it. Is that true? Let us see for one moment. If a reduction in the hours of labor causes industrial and commercial ruination, it would naturally follow increased hours of labor would increase the prosperity, commercial and industrial. If that were true, England and America ought to be at the tail end, and China at the head of civilization.

Is it not a fact that we find laborers in England and the United States, where the hours are eight, nine and ten hours a day—do we not find that the employers and laborers are more successful? Don't we find them selling articles cheaper? We do not need to trust the modern moralist to tell us those things. In all industries where the hours of labor are long, there you will find the least development of the power of invention. Where the hours of labor are long, men are cheap, and where men are cheap there is no necessity for invention. How can you expect a man to work ten or twelve or fourteen hours at his calling and then devote any time to the invention of a machine or discovery of a new principle or force? If he be so fortunate as to be able to read a paper he will fall asleep before he has read through the second or third line.

Why, when you reduce the hours of labor, say an hour a day, just think what it means. Suppose men who work ten hours a day had the time lessened to nine, or men who work nine hours a day have it reduced to eight hours; what does it mean? It means millions of golden hours and opportunities for thought. Some men might say you will go to sleep. Well, some men might sleep sixteen hours a day; the ordinary man might try that, but he would soon find he could not do it long. He would have to do something. He would probably go to the theater one night, to a concert another night, but he could not do that every night. He would probably become interested in some study and the hours that have been taken from manual labor are devoted to mental labor, and the mental labor of one hour will produce for him more wealth than the physical labor of a dozen hours.

I maintain that this is a true proposition—that men under the short-hour system not only have opportunity to improve themselves, but to make a greater degree of prosperity for their employers. Why, my friends, how is it in China, how is it in Spain, how is it in India and Russia, how is it in Italy? Cast your eye throughout the universe and observe the industry that forces nature to yield up its fruits to man's necessities, and you will find that where the hours of labor are the shortest the progress of invention in machinery and the prosperity of the people are the greatest. It is the greatest impediment to progress to hire men cheaply. Wherever men are cheap, there you find the least degree of progress. It has only been under the great influence of our great republic, where our people have exhibited their great senses, that we can move forward, upward and onward, and are watched with interest in our movements of progress and reform. …

The man who works the long hours has no necessities except the barest to keep body and soul together, so he can work. He goes to sleep and dreams of work; he rises in the morning to go to work; he takes his frugal lunch to work; he comes home again to throw himself down on a miserable apology for a bed so that he can get that little rest that he may be able to go to work again. He is nothing but a veritable machine. He lives to work instead of working to live.

My friends, the only thing the working people need besides the necessities of life, is time. Time. Time with which our lives begin; time with which our lives close; time to cultivate the better nature within us; time to brighten our homes. Time, which brings us from the lowest condition up to the highest civilization; time, so that we can raise men to a higher plane.

My friends, you will find that it has been ascertained that there is more than a million of our brothers and sisters—able-bodied men and women—on the streets, and on the highways and byways of our country willing to work but who cannot find it. You know that it is the theory of our government that we can work or cease to work at will. It is only a theory. You know that it is only a theory and not a fact. It is true that we can cease to work when we want to, but I deny that we can work when we will, so long as there are a million idle men and women tramping the streets of our cities, searching for work. The theory that we can work or cease to work when we will is a delusion and a snare. It is a lie.

What we want to consider is, first, to make our employment more secure, and, secondly, to make wages more permanent, and, thirdly, to give these poor people a chance to work. The laborer has been regarded as a mere producing machine...but back of labor is the soul of man and honesty of purpose and aspiration. No you can not, as the political economists and college professors, say that labor is a commodity to be bought and sold. I say we are American citizens with the heritage of all the great men who have stood before us; men who have sacrificed all in the cause except honor. Our enemies would like to see this movement thrust into hades, they would like to see it in a warmer climate, but I say to you that this labor movement has come to stay. Like Banquo's ghost, it will not down. I say the labor movement is a fixed fact. It has grown out of the necessities of the people, and, although some may desire to see it fail, still the labor movement will be found to have a strong lodgment in the hearts of the people, and we will go on until success has been achieved.

We want eight hours and nothing less. We have been accused of being selfish, and it has been said that we will want more; that last year we got an advance of ten cents and now we want more. We do want more. You will find that a man generally wants more. Go and ask a tramp what he wants, and if he doesn't want a drink he will want a good, square meal. You ask a workingman, who is getting two dollars a day, and he will say that he wants ten cents more. Ask a man who gets five dollars a day and he will want fifty cents more. The man who receives five thousand dollars a year wants six thousand dollars a year, and the man who owns eight or nine hundred thousand dollars will want a hundred thousand dollars more to make it a million, while the man who has his millions will want every thing he can lay his hands on and then raise his voice against the poor devil who wants ten cents more a day. We live in the latter part of the Nineteenth century. In the age of electricity and steam that has produced wealth a hundred fold, we insist that it has been brought about by the intelligence and energy of the workingmen, and while we find that it is now easier to produce it is harder to live. We do want more, and when it becomes more, we shall still want more. And we shall never cease to demand more until we have received the results of our labor. …

ELIZABETH CADY STANTON

The Solitude of Self

The talk of sheltering woman from the fierce storms of life is the sheerest mockery, for they beat on her from every point of the compass, just as they do on man, and with more fatal results, for he has been trained to protect himself, to resist, and to conquer.

Elizabeth Cady Stanton (1815-1902), the leading figure of the women's rights movement, was born in Johnstown, New York. She graduated from the Troy Female Seminary and, in 1840, married Henry B. Stanton, an abolitionist leader with whom she would have seven children. In addition to organizing the Seneca Falls convention, Stanton also founded and served as president of the National Woman Suffrage Association; in 1878, she initiated the legislation that eventually passed as the Nineteenth Amendment. "The Solitude of Self," perhaps the best expression of early feminist ideology, was first delivered by Stanton in 1892.

The point I wish plainly to bring before you on this occasion is the individuality of each human soul; our Protestant idea, the right of individual conscience and judgment; our republican idea, individual citizenship. In discussing the rights of woman, we are to consider, first, what belongs to her as an individual, in a world of her own, the arbiter of her own destiny, an imaginary Robinson Crusoe with her woman, Friday, on a solitary island. Her rights under such circumstances are to use all her faculties for her own safety and happiness.

Secondly, if we consider her as a citizen, as a member of a great nation, she must have the same rights as all other members, according to the fundamental principles of our government.

Thirdly, viewed as a woman, an equal factor in civilization, her rights and duties are still the same—individual happiness and development.

Fourthly, it is only the incidental relations of life, such as mother, wife, sister, daughter, which may involve some special duties and training. …

The strongest reason for giving woman all the opportunities for higher education, for the full development of her faculties, her forces of mind and body; for giving her the most enlarged freedom of thought and action; a complete emancipation from all forms of bondage, of custom, dependence, superstition; from all the crippling influences of fear—is the solitude and personal responsibility of her own individual life. The strongest reason why we ask for woman a voice in the government under which she lives; in the religion she is asked to believe; equality in social life, where she is the chief factor; a place in the trades and professions, where she may earn her bread, is because of her birthright to self-sovereignty; because, as an individual, she must rely on herself. No matter how much women prefer to lean, to be protected and supported, nor how much men desire to have them do so, they must make the voyage of life alone, and for safety in an emergency, they must know something of the laws of navigation. To guide our own craft, we must be captain, pilot, engineer; with chart and compass to stand at the wheel; to watch the winds and waves, and know when to take in the sail, and to read the signs in the firmament over all. It matters not whether the solitary voyager is man or woman; nature, having endowed them equally, leaves them to their own skill and judgment in the hour of danger, and, if not equal to the occasion, alike they perish.

To appreciate the importance of fitting every human soul for independent action, think for a moment of the immeasurable solitude of self. We come into the world alone, unlike all who have gone before us, we leave it alone, under circumstances peculiar to ourselves. No mortal ever has been, no mortal ever will be like the soul just launched on the sea of life. There can never again be just such a combination of prenatal influences; never again just such environments as make up the infancy, youth and manhood of this one. Nature never repeats herself, and the possibilities of one human soul will never be found in another. No one has ever found two blades of ribbon grass alike, and no one will ever find two human beings alike. Seeing, then, that what must be the infinite diversity in human character, we can in a measure appreciate the loss to a nation when any class of the people is uneducated and unrepresented in the government.

We ask for the complete development of every individual, first, for his own benefit and happiness. In fitting out an army, we give each soldier his own knapsack, arms, powder, his blanket, cup, knife, fork and spoon. We provide alike for all their individual necessities; then each man bears his own burden.

Again, we ask complete individual development for the general good; for the consensus of the competent on the whole round of human interests, on all questions of national life; and here each man must bear his share of the general burden. It is sad to see how soon friendless children are left to bear their own burdens, before they can analyze their feelings; before they can even tell their joys and sorrows, they are thrown on their own resources. The great lesson that nature seems to teach us at all ages is self-dependence, self-protection, self-support. ...

We ask no sympathy from others in the anxiety and agony of a broken friendship or shattered love. When death sunders our nearest ties, alone we sit in the shadow of our affliction. Alike amid the greatest triumphs and darkest tragedies of life, we walk alone. On the divine heights of human attainment, eulogized and worshipped as a hero or saint, we stand alone. In ignorance, poverty and vice, as a pauper or criminal, alone we starve or steal; alone we suffer the sneers and rebuffs of our fellows; alone we are hunted and hounded through dark courts and alleys, in by-ways and high-ways; alone we stand in the judgment seat; alone in the prison cell we lament our crimes and misfortunes; alone we expiate them on the gallows. In hours like these we realize the awful solitude of individual life, its pains, its penalties, its responsibilities, hours in which the youngest and most helpless are thrown on their own resources for guidance and consolation. Seeing, then, that life must ever be a march and a battle that each soldier must be equipped for his own protection, it is the height of cruelty to rob the individual of a single natural right.

To throw obstacles in the way of a complete education is like putting out the eyes; to deny the rights of property is like cutting off the hands. To refuse political equality is to rob the ostracized of all self-respect; of credit in the market place; of recompense in the world of work, of a voice in choosing those who make and administer the law, a choice in the jury before whom they are tried, and in the judge who decides their punishment. [Think of]...woman's position! Robbed of her natural rights, handicapped by law and custom at every turn, yet compelled to fight her own battles, and in the emergencies of life to fall back on herself for protection. ...

The young wife and mother, at the head of some establishment, with a kind husband to shield her from the adverse winds of life, with wealth, fortune and position, has a certain harbor of safety, secure against the ordinary ills of life. But to manage a household, have a desirable influence in society, keep her friends and the affections of her husband, train her children and servants well, she must have rare common sense, wisdom, diplomacy, and a knowledge of human nature. To do all this, she needs the cardinal virtues and the strong points of character that the most successful statesman possesses. An uneducated woman trained to dependence, with no resources in herself, must make a failure of any position in life. But society says women do not need a knowledge of the world, the liberal training that experience in public life must give, all the advantages of collegiate education; but when for the lack of all this, the woman's happiness is wrecked, alone she bears her humiliation; and the solitude of the weak and ignorant is indeed pitiable. In the wild chase for the prizes of life, they are ground to powder.

In age, when the pleasures of youth are passed, children grown up, married and gone, the hurry and bustle of life in a measure over, when the hands are weary of active service, when the old arm chair and the fireside are the chosen resorts, then men and women alike must fall back on their own resources. If they cannot find companionship in books, if they have no interest in the vital questions of the hour, no interest in watching the consummation of reforms with which they might have been identified, they soon pass into their dotage. The more fully the faculties of the mind are developed and kept in use, the longer the period of vigor and active interest in all around us continues. If, from a life-long participation in public affairs, a woman feels responsible for the laws regulating our system of education, the discipline of our jails and prisons, the sanitary condition of our private homes, public building and thoroughfares, an interest in commerce, finance, our foreign relations, in any or all these questions, her solitude will at least be respectable, and she will not be driven to gossip or scandal for entertainment.

The chief reason for opening to every soul the doors to the whole round of human duties and pleasures is the individual development thus attained, the resources thus provided under all circumstances to mitigate the solitude that at times must come to everyone. ...

Inasmuch, then, as woman shares equally the joys and sorrows of time and eternity, is it not the height of presumption in man to propose to represent her at the ballot box and the throne of grace, to do her voting in the state, her praying in the church, and to assume the position of high priest at the family altar?

Nothing strengthens the judgment and quickens the conscience like individual responsibility. Nothing adds such dignity to character as the recognition of one's self-sovereignty; the right to an equal place, everywhere conceded—a place earned by personal merit, not an artificial attainment by inheritance, wealth, family and position. Conceding, then, that the responsibility of life rest equally on man and woman, that their destiny is the same, they need the same preparation for time and eternity. The talk of sheltering woman from the fierce storms of life is the sheerest mockery, for they beat on her from every point of the compass, just as they do on man, and with more fatal results, for he has been trained to protect himself, to resist, and to conquer. Such are the facts in human experience, the responsibilities of individual sovereignty. Rich and poor, intelligent and ignorant, wise and foolish, virtuous and vicious, man and woman; it is ever the same, each soul must depend wholly on itself.

Whatever the theories may be of woman's dependence on man, in the supreme moments of her life, he cannot bear her burdens. Alone she goes to the gates of death to give life to every man that is born into the world; no one can share her fears, no one can mitigate her pangs; and if her sorrow is greater than she can bear, alone she passes beyond the gates into the vast unknown. ...

So it ever must be in the conflicting scenes of life, in the long, weary march, each one walks alone. We may have many friends, love, kindness, sympathy and charity, to smooth our pathway in everyday life, but in the tragedies and triumphs of human experience, each mortal stands alone. ...

Women are already the equals of men in the whole realm of thought, in art, science, literature and government. With telescopic vision they explore the starry firmament and bring back the history of the planetary spheres. With chart and compass they pilot ships across the mighty deep, and with skillful fingers send electric messages around the world. In galleries of art the beauties of nature and the virtues of humanity are immortalized by them on canvas, and by their inspired touch dull block of marble are transformed into angels of light. In music they speak again the language of Mendelssohn, Beethoven, Chopin, Schumann, and are worthy interpreters of their great thoughts. The poetry and novels of the century are theirs, and they have touched the keynote of reform, in religion, politics and social life. They fill the editor's and professor's chair, plead at the bar of justice, walk the wards of the hospital, speak from the pulpit and the platform. Such is the type of womanhood that an enlightened public sentiment welcomes today, and such the triumph of the facts of life over the false theories of the past.

Is it, then, consistent to hold the developed woman of this day within the same narrow political limits as the dame with the spinning wheel and knitting needles occupied in the past? No, no! Machinery has taken the labors of woman as well as man on its tireless shoulders; the loom and the spinning wheel are but dreams of the past; the pen, the brush, the easel, the chisel, have taken their places, while the hopes and ambitions of women are essentially changed.

We see reason sufficient in the outer conditions of human beings for individual liberty and development, but when we consider the self-dependence of every human soul, we see the need of courage, judgment and the exercise of every faculty of mind and body, strengthened and developed by use, in woman as well as man.

Whatever may be said of man's protecting power in ordinary conditions, amid all the terrible disasters by land and sea, in the supreme moments of danger, alone woman must ever meet the horrors of the situation. The Angel of Death even makes no royal pathway for her. Man's love and sympathy enter only into the sunshine of our lives. In that solemn solitude of self, that links us with the immeasurable and the eternal, each soul lives alone forever. …

And yet, there is a solitude which each and every one of us has always carried with him, more inaccessible than the ice-cold mountains, more profound than the midnight sea; the solitude of self. Our inner being which we call ourself, no eye nor touch of man or angel has ever pierced. It is more hidden than the caves of the gnome; the sacred adytum of the oracle; the hidden chamber of Eleusinian mystery, for to it only omniscience is permitted to enter.

Such is individual life. Who, I ask you, can take, dare take, on himself the rights, the duties, the responsibilities of another human soul?

At precisely noon on September 16, 1893, a cannon's boom signaled the largest land rush in American history. An estimated 100,000 people raced to claim plots of land in an area of the Oklahoma Territory known as the Cherokee Outlet. Those who had waited for the signaled start before rushing into the land claim were discouraged to see that many prime parcels had already been claimed by settlers in covered wagons and even on foot. Despite enforcement efforts by two regiments of U.S. Army cavalry troops, as many as nine out of ten of these settlers had jumped the gun, thus earning the nickname "Sooners." (The "sooner clause" of the Indian Appropriations Bill of 1889, which preceded the first Oklahoma land run, stated that no one should be allowed to enter and occupy the land prior to the opening time.) Land runs such as these were made possible by the original Homestead Act of 1862, signed by President Lincoln, which allowed settlers to claim unappropriated federal lands in lots up to 160 acres in size. Provided a settler lived on the land for five years and made improvements, the settler could then receive the title to the land. Homesteading was discontinued in 1976, except in Alaska, where it continued for another decade.

KATHARINE LEE BATES
America the Beautiful

Katharine Lee Bates (1859-1929) was born in Falmouth, Massachusetts, and taught at her alma mater, Wellesley College, from 1885 to 1925. She also wrote several short stories, children's books, and collections of poetry. "America the Beautiful," found in her *Selected Poems* (1930), was first published in *The Congregationalist* in 1895. Set to the music of Samuel Ward, the song is often suggested as a substitute for "The Star-Spangled Banner" as the national anthem, and is the work for which she is best remembered.

O beautiful for spacious skies,
For amber waves of grain,
For purple mountain majesties
Above the fruited plain!
America! America!
God shed his grace on thee
And crown thy good with brotherhood
From sea to shining sea!

O beautiful for pilgrim feet,
Whose stern, impassioned stress
A thoroughfare for freedom beat
Across the wilderness!
America! America!
God mend thine every flaw,
Confirm thy soul in self-control,
Thy liberty in law!

O beautiful for heroes proved
In liberating strife,
Who more than self their country loved,
And mercy more than life!
America! America!
May God thy gold refine,
Till all success be nobleness
And every gain divine!

O beautiful for patriot dream
That sees beyond the years
Thine alabaster cities gleam
Undimmed by human tears!
America! America!
God shed His grace on thee,
And crown thy good with brotherhood
From sea to shining sea!

BOOKER T. WASHINGTON
The Atlanta Exposition Address

In all things that are purely social we can be separate as the fingers, yet one as the hand in all things essential to mutual progress.

Booker Taliaferro Washington (1856-1915) was born a slave in Hales Ford, Virginia. After being freed by the Thirteenth Amendment, he attended the Hampton Institute and returned to the school in 1879 as a teacher. He later founded Tuskegee Institute, which focused on vocational courses such as carpentry and mechanics. Emphasizing industrial education at the expense of a traditional college curriculum, Washington's view was that blacks were best served by acquiring a trade, working hard, and obtaining property. Rather than concern themselves with immediate equality, Washington believed that blacks should seek to cultivate friendly relations with their white neighbors and resign themselves to begin "at the bottom of life," not the top. By the same token, he encouraged whites to give better jobs to blacks and lobbied wealthy individuals for contributions to black organizations. Washington also owned several newspapers, advised Presidents Theodore Roosevelt and William Howard Taft on racial problems, and was instrumental in the appointment of several black leaders to government positions.

In his speech to a white audience at the Atlanta Exposition on September 18, 1895, Washington spoke of patience and moderation in the pursuit of racial justice. His views were also expressed in several books he wrote, including his autobiography, *Up From Slavery*.

One-third of the population of the South is of the Negro race. No enterprise seeking the material, civil, or moral welfare of this section can disregard this element of our population and reach the highest success. I but convey to you, Mr. President and Directors, the sentiment of the masses of my race when I say that in no way have the value and manhood of the American Negro been more fittingly and generously recognized than by the managers of this magnificent Exposition at every stage of its progress. It is a recognition that will do more to cement the friendship of the two races than any occurrence since the dawn of our freedom.

Not only this, but the opportunity here afforded will awaken among us a new era of industrial progress. Ignorant and inexperienced, it is not strange that in the first years of our new life we began at the top instead of at the bottom; that a seat in Congress or the State Legislature was more sought than real estate or industrial skill; that the political convention or stump speaking had more attractions than starting a dairy farm or truck garden.

A ship lost at sea for many days suddenly sighted a friendly vessel. From the mast of the unfortunate vessel was seen a signal: "Water, water, we die of thirst." The answer from the friendly vessel at once came back, "Cast down your bucket where you are." A second time the signal, "Water, water, send us water," ran up from the distressed vessel and was answered, "Cast down your bucket where you are." And a third and fourth signal for water was answered "Cast down your bucket where you are." The captain of the distressed vessel, at last heeding the injunction, cast down his bucket and it came up full of fresh, sparkling water from the mouth of the Amazon River. To those of my race who depend on bettering their condition in a foreign land, or who underestimate the importance of cultivating friendly relations with the Southern white man who is their next-door neighbor, I would say: "Cast down your bucket where you are" —cast it down in making friends, in every manly way, of the people of all races by whom we are surrounded.

Cast it down in agriculture, mechanics, in commerce, in domestic service, and in the professions. And in this connection it is well to bear in mind that whatever other sins the South may be called upon to bear, when it comes to business pure and simple, it is in the South that the Negro is given a man's chance in the commercial world, and in nothing is this Exposition more eloquent than in emphasizing this chance. Our greatest danger is that, in the great leap from slavery to freedom, we may overlook the fact that the masses of us are to live by the productions of our hands and fail to keep in mind that we shall prosper in the proportion as we learn to dignify and glorify common labor, and put brains and skill into the common occupations of life; shall prosper in proportion as we learn to draw the line between the superficial and the substantial, the ornamental gewgaws of life and the useful. No race can prosper till it learns that there is as much dignity in tilling a field as in writing a poem. It is at the bottom of life we must begin, and not at the top. Nor should we permit our grievances to overshadow our opportunities.

To those of the white race who look to the incoming of those of foreign birth and strange tongue and habits for the prosperity of the South, were I permitted I would repeat what I say to my own race, "Cast down your bucket where you are." Cast it down among the 8,000,000 Negroes whose habits you know, whose fidelity and love you have tested in days when to have proved treacherous meant the ruin of your firesides. Cast down your bucket among these people who have, without strikes and labor wars, tilled your fields, cleared your forests, builded your railroads and cities, and brought forth treasures from the bowels of the earth and helped make possible this magnificent representation of the progress of the South. Casting down your bucket among my people, helping them and encouraging them as you are doing on these grounds, and, with education of head, hand and heart, you will find that they will buy your surplus land, make blossom the waste places in your fields, and run your factories. While doing this, you can be sure in the future, as in the past, that you and your families will be surrounded by the most patient, faithful, law-abiding, and unresentful people that the world has seen. As we have proved our loyalty to you in the past, in nursing your children, watching by the sick-bed of your mothers and fathers, and often following them with tear-dimmed eyes to their graves, so in the future, in our humble way, we shall stand by you with a devotion that no foreigner can approach, ready to lay down our lives, if need be, in defense of yours; interlacing our industrial, commercial, civil, and religious life with yours in a way that shall make the interests of both races one. In all things that are purely social we can be separate as the fingers, yet one as the hand in all things essential to mutual progress.

There is no defense or security for any of us except in the highest intelligence and development of all. If anywhere there are efforts tending to curtail the fullest growth of the Negro, let these efforts be turned into stimulating, encouraging and making him the most useful and intelligent citizen. Effort or means so invested will pay a thousand per cent interest. These efforts will be twice blessed—blessing him that gives and him that takes.

There is no escape, through law of man or God, from the inevitable:

"The laws of changeless justice bind
  Oppressor with oppressed;
And close as sin and suffering joined
  We march to fate abreast."

Nearly sixteen million hands will aid you in pulling the load upward, or they will pull against you the load downward. We shall constitute one-third and more of the ignorance and crime of the South, or one-third its intelligence and progress; we shall contribute one-third to the business and industrial prosperity of the South, or we shall prove a veritable body of death, stagnating, depressing, retarding every effort to advance the body politic.

Gentlemen of the Exposition: As we present to you our humble effort at an exhibition of our progress, you must not expect over much. Starting thirty years ago with ownership here and there in a few quilts and pumpkins and chickens (gathered from miscellaneous sources), remember: the path that has led us from these to the invention and production of agricultural implements, buggies, steam engines, newspapers, books, statuary, carving, paintings, the management of drugstores and banks, has not been trodden without contact with thorns and thistles. While we take pride in what we exhibit as a result of our independent efforts, we do not for a moment forget that our part in this exhibition would fall far short of your expectations but for the constant help that has come to our educational life, not only from the Southern states, but especially from Northern philanthropists who have made their gifts a constant stream of blessing and encouragement.

The wisest among my race understand that the agitation of questions of social equality is the extremest folly, and that progress in the enjoyment of all the privileges that will come to us must be the result of severe and constant struggle rather than of artificial forcing. No race that has anything to contribute to the markets of the world is long in any degree ostracized. It is important and right that all privileges of the law be ours, but it is vastly more important that we be prepared for the exercise of those privileges. The opportunity to earn a dollar in a factory just now is worth infinitely more than the opportunity to spend a dollar in an opera house.

In conclusion, may I repeat that nothing in thirty years has given us more hope and encouragement and drawn us so near to you of the white race as this opportunity offered by the Exposition; and here bending, as it were, over the altar that represents the results of the struggles of your race and mine, both starting practically empty-handed three decades ago, I pledge that, in your effort to work out the great and intricate problem which God has laid at the doors of the South, you shall have at all times the patient, sympathetic help of my race. Only let this be constantly in mind that, while from representations in these buildings of the product of field, of forest, of mine, of factory, letters and art, much good will come—yet far above and beyond material benefits, will be that higher good, that let us pray God will come, in a blotting out of sectional differences and racial animosities and suspicions, in a determination to administer absolute justice, in a willing obedience among all classes to the mandates of law. This, coupled with material prosperity, will bring into our beloved South a new heaven and a new earth.

The Cross of Gold

You shall not press down upon the brow of labor this crown of thorns; you shall not crucify mankind upon a cross of gold.

William Jennings Bryan (1860-1925) served in the U.S. House of Representatives from 1891 to 1895. He adamantly opposed the gold standard, whereby the price of gold was fixed and money could, in theory at least, be exchanged for its face value in gold. Bryan argued against the "sound money" theory, saying that the supply of money should be increased at a fixed rate in the form of silver coinage as a means of reflation. As the nominee of the Democratic Party for president in 1896, Bryan gave the following speech, in various forms, more than 600 times. Despite the popularity of Bryan's "Cross of Gold" speech, however, he lost the presidency to William McKinley and the argument over free coinage. The United States applied the gold standard on and off again until 1971.

Bryan twice more sought the presidency, but was unsuccessful in both attempts. He later served as secretary of state to Woodrow Wilson and retired soon after to a life of public speaking. In 1925, Bryan became involved in the famed "Scopes Monkey Trial," resulting from the teaching of Charles Darwin's theory of evolution in a Tennessee public school by John Scopes, who did so in violation of state law. Taking the stand in defense of the Bible's authority, Bryan was subjected to a withering cross-examination by famed defense attorney Clarence Darrow. Their exchange typified the divide between fundamentalists and modernists and may have contributed to Bryan's demise. He died suddenly on July 26 in Dayton, Tennessee, just five days after the trial's conclusion.

I would be presumptuous, indeed, to present myself against the distinguished gentlemen to whom you have listened if this were a mere measuring of abilities; but this is not a contest between persons. The humblest citizen in all the land, when clad in the armor of a righteous cause, is stronger than all the hosts of error. I come to speak to you in defense of a cause as holy as the cause of liberty—the cause of humanity. ...

When you [turning to the gold delegates] come before us and tell us that we are about to disturb your business interests, we reply that you have disturbed our business interests by your course.

We say to you that you have made the definition of a business man too limited in its application. The man who is employed for wages is as much a business man as his employer, the attorney in a country town is as much as business man as the corporation counsel in a great metropolis; the merchant at the cross-roads store is as much a business man as the merchant of New York; the farmer who goes forth in the morning and toils all day—who begins in the spring and toils all summer—and who by the application of brain and muscle to the natural resources of the country creates wealth, is as much a business man as the man who goes upon the board of trade and bets upon the price of grain; the miners who go down a thousand feet into the earth, or climb two thousand feet upon the cliffs, and bring forth from their hiding places the precious metals to be poured into the channels of trade are as much business men as the few financial magnates who, in a back room, corner the money of the world. We come to speak for this broader class of business men.

Ah, my friends, we say not one word against those who live upon the Atlantic coast, but the hardy pioneers who have braved all the dangers of the wilderness, who have made the desert to blossom as the rose—the pioneers away out there [pointing to West], who rear their children near to nature's heart, where they can mingle their voices with the voices of the birds—out there where they have erected schoolhouses for the education of their young, churches where they praise the Creator, and cemeteries where rest the ashes of their dead—these people, we say, are as deserving of the consideration of our party as any people in this country. It is for these that we speak. We do not come as aggressors. Our war is not a war of conquest; we are fighting in the defense of our homes, our families, and posterity. We have petitioned, and our petitions have been scorned; we have entreated, and our entreaties have been disregarded; we have begged, and they have mocked when our calamity came. We beg no longer; we entreat no more; we petition no more. We defy them! ...

And now, my friends, let me come to the paramount issue. If they ask us why it is that we say more on the money question than we say upon the tariff question, I reply that, if protection has slain its thousands, the gold standard has slain its ten of thousands. If they ask why we do not embody in our platform all the things that we believe in, we reply that when we have restored the money of the Constitution all other necessary reforms will be possible; but that until this is done there is no other reform that can be accomplished.

Why is it that within three months such a change has come over the country? Three months ago, when it was confidently asserted that those who believe in the gold standard would frame our platform and nominate our candidates, even the advocates of the gold standard did not think that we could elect a President. And they had good reason for their doubt, because there is scarcely a state here today asking for the gold standard which is not in the absolute control of the Republican party. But note the change. Mr. McKinley was nominated at St. Louis upon a platform which declared for the maintenance of the gold standard until it can be changed into bimetallism by international agreement. Mr. McKinley was the most popular man among the Republicans, and three months ago everybody in the Republican party prophesied his election. How is it today? Why, the man who was once pleased to think that he looked like Napoleon—that man shudders today when he remembers that he was nominated on the anniversary of the battle of Waterloo. Not only that, but as he listens he can hear with ever-increasing distinctness the sound of the waves as they beat upon the lonely shores of St. Helena.

Why this change? Ah, my friends, is not the reason for the change evident to any one who will look at the matter? No private character, however pure, no personal popularity, however great, can protect from the avenging wrath of an indignant people a man who will declare that he is in favor of fastening the gold standard upon this country, or who is willing to surrender the right of self-government and place the legislative control of our affairs in the hands of foreign potentates and powers.

We go forth confident that we shall win. Why? Because upon the paramount issue of this campaign there is not a spot of ground upon which the enemy will dare to challenge battle. If they tell us that the gold standard is a good thing, we shall point to their platform and tell them that their platform pledges the party to get rid of the gold standard and substitute bimetallism. If the gold standard is a good thing, why try to get rid of it? I call your attention to the fact that some of the very people who are in this convention today and who tell us that we ought to declare in favor of international bimetallism—thereby declaring that the gold standard is wrong and that the principle of bimetallism is better—these very people four months ago were open and avowed advocates of the gold standard, and were then telling us that we could not legislate two metals together, even with the aid of all the world. If the gold standard is a good thing, we ought to declare in favor of its retention and not in favor of abandoning it; and if the gold standard is a bad thing why should we wait until other nations are willing to help us to let go? Here is the line of battle, and we care not upon which issue they force the fight; we are prepared to meet them on either issue or on both. If they tell us that the gold standard is the standard of civilization, we reply to them that this, the most enlightened of all the nations of the earth, has never declared for a gold standard and that both the great parties this year are declaring against it. If the gold standard is the standard of civilization, why my friends, should we not have it? If they come to meet us on that issue we can present the history of our nation. More than that; we can tell them that they will search the pages of history in vain to find a single instance where the common people of any land have ever declared themselves in favor of the gold standard. They can find where the holders of fixed investments have declared for a gold standard, but not where the masses have.

Mr. Carlisle said in 1878 that this was a struggle between "the idle holders of idle capital" and "the struggling masses, who produce the wealth and pay the taxes of the country;" and, my friends, the question we are to decide is: Upon which side will the Democratic party fight; upon the side of "the idle holders of idle capital" or upon the side of "the struggling masses"? That is the question which the party must answer first, and then it must be answered by each individual hereafter. The sympathies of the Democratic party, as shown by the platform, are on the side of the struggling masses who have ever been the foundation of the Democratic party. There are two ideas of government. There are those who believe that, if you will only legislate to make the well-to-do prosperous, their prosperity will leak through on those below. The Democratic idea, however, has been that if you legislate to make the masses prosperous, their prosperity will find its way up through every class which rests upon them.

You come to us and tell us that the great cities are in favor of the gold standard; we reply that the great cities rest upon our broad and fertile prairies. Burn down your cities and leave our farms, and your cities will spring up again as if by magic; but destroy our farms and the grass will grow in the streets of every city in the country.

My friends, we declare that this nation is able to legislate for its own people on every question, without waiting for the aid or consent of any other nation on earth; and upon that issue we expect to carry every state in the Union. I shall not slander the inhabitants of the fair state of Massachusetts nor the inhabitants of the state of New York by saying that, when they are confronted with the proposition, they will declare that this nation is not able to attend to its own business. It is the issue of 1776 over again. Our ancestors, when but three millions in number, had the courage to declare their political independence of every other nation; shall we, their descendants, when we have grown to seventy millions, declare that we are less independent than our forefathers? No, my friends, that will never be the verdict of our people. Therefore, we care not upon what lines the battle is fought. If they say bimetallism is good, but that we cannot have it until other nations help us, we reply that, instead of having a gold standard because England has, we will restore bimetallism, and then let England have bimetallism because the United States has it. If they dare to come out in the open field and defend the gold standard as a good thing, we will fight them to the uttermost. Having behind us the producing masses of this nation and the world, supported by the commercial interests, the laboring interests, and the toilers everywhere, we will answer their demand for a gold standard by saying to them: You shall not press down upon the brow of labor this crown of thorns; you shall not crucify mankind upon a cross of gold.

JOHN MARSHALL HARLAN

Dissent from *Plessy v. Ferguson*

Our Constitution is color-blind, and neither knows nor tolerates classes among citizens.

John Marshall Harlan (1833-1911) was born in Boyle County, Kentucky, and educated at Centre College and Transylvania University. He came from a large slaveholding family and initially defended the institution of slavery as an exercise in private property rights. During the Civil War, Harlan served in the U.S. Army, placing greater value on the survival of the Union, but he opposed Abraham Lincoln's Emancipation Proclamation, declaring it "unconstitutional and null and void."

Harlan was a man of constant political evolution during his youth. He started out a Whig, then briefly espoused the anti-foreigner and anti-Catholic doctrines of the Know-Nothings, and then joined several other parties before his most astonishing political conversion—joining the Republican Party in 1868 and becoming a proponent of the policies he had once criticized. "I have," said Harlan, "lived long enough to feel and declare that...the most perfect despotism that ever existed on this earth was the institution of African slavery.... With slavery it was death or tribute.... It knew no compromise, it tolerated no middle course. I rejoice that it is gone." Harlan defended his conversion thusly: "Let it be said that I am right rather than consistent."

In 1877, after spending many years as a Republican leader in Kentucky and the state's attorney general, Harlan was appointed to the United States Supreme Court. There, he distinguished himself as a champion of legal equality, offering dissenting opinions in such cases as the 1883 ruling that declared the Civil Rights Act of 1875 unconstitutional. In the landmark case of *Plessy v. Ferguson* (1896), a Louisianan of mixed race, Homer Plessy, was arrested for sitting in the whites-only section of a train car. Plessy argued that "separate but equal" violated the principle of legal equality. The court, in a majority decision, disagreed. Harlan was the lone dissenter, writing, "The arbitrary separation of citizens, on the basis of race, while they are on a public highway, is a badge of servitude wholly inconsistent with the civil freedom and the equality before the law established by the Constitution." The doctrine of "separate but equal" continued until *Brown v. Board of Education* (1954) ended the legality of Jim Crow discrimination. Harlan was, as Supreme Court Justice Thurgood Marshall would say generations later, "a solitary and lonely figure writing for posterity."

John Marshall Harlan's grandson, also named John Marshall Harlan (1899-1971), served as an associate justice of the Supreme Court from 1955 to 1971.

... In respect of civil rights, common to all citizens, the Constitution of the United States does not, I think, permit any public authority to know the race of those entitled to be protected in the enjoyment of such rights. Every true man has pride of race, and under appropriate circumstances when the rights of others, his equals before the law, are not to be affected, it is his privilege to express such pride and to take such action based upon it as to him seems proper. But I deny that any legislative body or judicial tribunal may have regard to the race of citizens when the civil rights of those citizens are involved. Indeed, such legislation, as that here in question, is inconsistent not only with that equality of rights which pertains to citizenship, National and State, but with the personal liberty enjoyed by every one within the United States.

The Thirteenth Amendment does not permit the withholding or the deprivation of any right necessarily inhering in freedom. It not only struck down the institution of slavery as previously existing in the United States, but it prevents the imposition of any burdens or disabilities that constitute badges of slavery or servitude. It decreed universal civil freedom in this country. This court has so adjudged. But that amendment having been found inadequate to the protection of the rights of those who had been in slavery, it was followed by the Fourteenth Amendment, which added greatly to the dignity and glory of American citizenship, and to the security of personal liberty, by declaring that "all persons born or naturalized in the United States, and subject to the jurisdiction thereof, are citizens of the United States and of the State wherein they reside," and that "no State shall make or enforce any law which shall abridge the privileges or immunities of citizens of the United States; nor shall any State deprive any person of life, liberty or property without due process of law, nor deny to any person within its jurisdiction the equal protection of the laws." These two amendments, if enforced according to their true intent and meaning, will protect all the civil rights that pertain to freedom and citizenship. Finally, and to the end that no citizen should be denied, on account of his race, the privilege of participating in the political control of his country, it was declared by the Fifteenth Amendment that "the right of citizens of the United States to vote shall not be denied or abridged by the United States or by any State on account of race, color or previous condition of servitude."

These notable additions to the fundamental law were welcomed by the friends of liberty throughout the world. They removed the race line from our governmental systems. They had, as this court has said, a common purpose, namely, to secure "to a race recently emancipated, a race that through many generations have been held in slavery, all the civil rights that the superior race enjoy." They declared, in legal effect, this court has further said, "that the law in the States shall be the same for the black as for the white; that all persons, whether colored or white, shall stand equal before the laws of the States, and, in regard to the colored race, for whose protection the amendment was primarily designed, that no discrimination shall be made against them by law because of their color." We also said: "The words of the amendment, it is true, are prohibitory, but they contain a necessary implication of a positive immunity, or right, most valuable to the colored race—the right to exemption from unfriendly legislation against them distinctively as colored—exemption from legal discriminations, implying inferiority in civil society, lessening the security of their enjoyment of the rights which others enjoy, and discriminations which are steps towards reducing them to the condition of a subject race." It was, consequently, adjudged that a state law that excluded citizens of the colored race from juries, because of their race and however well qualified in other respects to discharge the duties of jurymen, was repugnant to the Fourteenth Amendment. …

The white race deems itself to be the dominant race in this country. And so it is, in prestige, in achievements, in education, in wealth and in power. So, I doubt not, it will continue to be for all time, if it remains true to its great heritage and holds fast to the principles of constitutional liberty. But in view of the Constitution, in the eye of the law, there is in this country no superior, dominant, ruling class of citizens. There is no caste here. Our Constitution is color-blind, and neither knows nor tolerates classes among citizens. In respect of civil rights, all citizens are equal before the law. The humblest is the peer of the most powerful. The law regards man as man, and takes no account of his surroundings or of his color when his civil rights as guaranteed by the supreme law of the land are involved. It is, therefore, to be regretted that this high tribunal, the final expositor of the fundamental law of the land, has reached the conclusion that it is competent for a State to regulate the enjoyment by citizens of their civil rights solely upon the basis of race.

In my opinion, the judgment this day rendered will, in time, prove to be quite as pernicious as the decision made by this tribunal in the Dred Scott case. It was adjudged in that case that the descendants of Africans who were imported into this country and sold as slaves were not included nor intended to be included under the word "citizens" in the Constitution, and could not claim any of the rights and privileges which that instrument provided for and secured to citizens of the United States; that at the time of the adoption of the Constitution they were "considered as a subordinate and inferior class of beings, who had been subjugated by the dominant race, and, whether emancipated or not, yet remained subject to their authority, and had no rights or privileges but such as those who held the power and the government might choose to grant them." The recent amendments of the Constitution, it was supposed, had eradicated these principles from our institutions. But it seems that we have yet, in some of the States, a dominant race—a superior class of citizens, which assumes to regulate the enjoyment of civil rights, common to all citizens, upon the basis of race. The present decision, it may well be apprehended, will not only stimulate aggressions, more or less brutal and irritating, upon the admitted rights of colored citizens, but will encourage the belief that it is possible, by means of state enactments, to defeat the beneficent purposes which the people of the United States had in view when they adopted the recent amendments of the Constitution, by one of which the blacks of this country were made citizens of the United States and of the States in which they respectively reside, and whose privileges and immunities, as citizens, the States are forbidden to abridge. Sixty millions of whites are in no danger from the presence here of eight millions of blacks. The destinies of the two races, in this country, are indissolubly linked together, and the interests of both require that the common government of all shall not permit the seeds of race hate to be planted under the sanction of law. What can more certainly arouse race hate, what can more certainly create and perpetuate a feeling of distrust between these races, than state enactments, which, in fact, proceed on the ground that colored citizens are so inferior and degraded that they cannot be allowed to sit in public coaches occupied by white citizens? That, as all will admit, is the real meaning of such legislation as was enacted in Louisiana. …

The arbitrary separation of citizens, on the basis of race, while they are on a public highway, is a badge of servitude wholly inconsistent with the civil freedom and the equality before the law established by the Constitution. It cannot be justified upon any legal grounds.

If evils will result from the commingling of the two races upon public highways established for the benefit of all, they will be infinitely less than those that will surely come from state legislation regulating the enjoyment of civil rights upon the basis of race. We boast of the freedom enjoyed by our people above all other peoples. But it is difficult to reconcile that boast with a state of the law which, practically, puts the brand of servitude and degradation upon a large class of our fellow-citizens, our equals before the law. The thin disguise of "equal" accommodations for passengers in railroad coaches will not mislead any one, nor atone for the wrong this day done. …

For the reasons stated, I am constrained to withhold my assent from the opinion and judgment of the majority.

The Duties of American Citizenship

The first duty of an American citizen, then, is that he shall work in politics; his second duty is that he shall do that work in a practical manner; and his third is that it shall be done in accord with the highest principles of honor and justice.

His biography reads like a work of fiction. The improbable life of Theodore Roosevelt (1858-1919) was one of constant activity, seemingly boundless energy, and daring adventure. Possessed of an iron will and great determination, Roosevelt was a relentless overachiever who overcame a sickly childhood and personal setbacks by leading what he called the "strenuous life." He lifted weights, became a vigorous outdoorsman and rancher, and expressed great enthusiasm for something by referring to it as "bully." He studied under the guidance of a tutor, graduated from Harvard University, attended Columbia Law School, and became a prolific writer of historical works.

Roosevelt saw politics as a means of public service and utilized his engaging personality to pursue public office. Always eager to assume center stage, it was said that Roosevelt wanted to be "the bride at every wedding and the corpse at every funeral." He held office in the state legislature, served as police commissioner in New York City, and was assistant secretary of the navy in the McKinley administration. He resigned the latter position in 1898 to become commander of the fearless Rough Riders during the Spanish-American War. Consisting mostly of former college athletes and western cowboys, the volunteer cavalry regiment played a prominent role in the capture of San Juan Hill. Having worked diligently to strengthen America's naval force, Roosevelt earned additional praise due to the success of the U.S. Navy in the battles of Manila Bay and Santiago.

The fame he earned in Cuba propelled Roosevelt into the governorship of New York. Describing his policy as, "Speak softly and carry a big stick," he soon alienated party leaders. The Republican machinery, fearing Roosevelt's independence and originality, decided to get rid of him by securing his nomination as vice president on McKinley's re-election ticket in 1900, thus taking advantage of Roosevelt's popularity while relegating him to the political sidelines. The plan backfired, however, when President McKinley was assassinated only six months into his second term. Roosevelt, at the age of forty-two, became the youngest man ever to be president of the United States and, in 1904, was elected in his own right. As chief executive, he became the first president to visit a foreign country while in office, began construction of the Panama Canal, established the U.S. Forest Service, served as the chief nemesis of the corporate trusts that threatened to monopolize entire industries at the start of the century, and became the first American to win a Nobel prize—the Peace Prize, for successfully mediating the Russo-Japanese War.

In the following speech, delivered on January 26, 1883, in Buffalo, New York, Roosevelt spoke of "The Duties of American Citizenship."

Of course, in one sense, the first essential for a man's being a good citizen is his possession of the home virtues of which we think when we call a man by the emphatic adjective of manly. No man can be a good citizen who is not a good husband and a good father, who is not honest in his dealings with other men and women, faithful to his friends and fearless in the presence of his foes, who has not got a sound heart, a sound mind, and a sound body; exactly as no amount of attention to civil duties will save a nation if the domestic life is undermined, or there is lack of the rude military virtues which alone can assure a country's position in the world. In a free republic the ideal citizen must be one willing and able to take arms for the defense of the flag, exactly as the ideal citizen must be the father of many healthy children. A race must be strong and vigorous; it must be a race of good fighters and good breeders, else its wisdom will come to naught and its virtue be ineffective; and no sweetness and delicacy, no love for and appreciation of beauty in art or literature, no capacity for building up material prosperity can possibly atone for the lack of the great virile virtues.

But this is aside from my subject, for what I wish to talk of is the attitude of the American citizen in civic life. It ought to be axiomatic in this country that every man must devote a reasonable share of his time to doing his duty in the Political life of the community. No man has a right to shirk his political duties under whatever plea of pleasure or business; and while such shirking may be pardoned in those of small means it is entirely unpardonable in those among whom it is most common—in the people whose circumstances give them freedom in the struggle for life. In so far as the community grows to think rightly, it will likewise grow to regard the young man of means who shirks his duty to the State in time of peace as being only one degree worse than the man who thus shirks it in time of war. A great many of our men in business, or of our young men who are bent on enjoying life (as they have a perfect right to do if only they do not sacrifice other things to enjoyment), rather plume themselves upon being good citizens if they even vote; yet voting is the very least of their duties. Nothing worth gaining is ever gained without effort. You can no more have freedom without striving and suffering for it than you can win success as a banker or a lawyer without labor and effort, without self-denial in youth and the display of a ready and alert intelligence in middle age. The people who say that they have not time to attend to politics are simply saying that they are unfit to live in a free community. Their place is under a despotism. …

The first duty of an American citizen, then, is that he shall work in politics; his second duty is that he shall do that work in a practical manner; and his third is that it shall be done in accord with the highest principles of honor and justice. …

One seemingly very necessary caution to utter is, that a man who goes into politics should not expect to reform everything right off, with a jump. I know many excellent young men who, when awakened to the fact that they have neglected their political duties, feel an immediate impulse to form themselves into an organization which shall forthwith purify politics everywhere, national, State, and city alike; and I know of a man who having gone round once to a primary, and having, of course, been unable to accomplish anything in a place where he knew no one and could not combine with anyone, returned saying it was quite useless for a good citizen to try to accomplish anything in such a manner. To these too hopeful or too easily discouraged people I always feel like reading Artemus Ward's article upon the people of his town who came together in a meeting to resolve that the town should support the Union and the Civil War, but were unwilling to take any part in putting down the rebellion

unless they could go as brigadier-generals. After the battle of Bull Run there were a good many hundreds of thousands of young men in the North who felt it to be their duty to enter the Northern armies; but no one of them who possessed much intelligence expected to take high place at the outset, or anticipated that individual action would be of decisive importance in any given campaign. He went in as private or sergeant, lieutenant or captain, as the case might be, and did his duty in his company, in his regiment, after a while in his brigade. When Ball's Bluff and Bull Run succeeded the utter failure of the Peninsular campaign, when the terrible defeat of Fredericksburg was followed by the scarcely less disastrous day at Chancellorsville he did not announce (if he had any pluck or manliness about him) that he considered it quite useless for any self-respecting citizen to enter the Army of the Potomac, because he really was not of much weight in its councils, and did not approve of its management; he simply gritted his teeth and went doggedly on with his duty, grieving over, but not disheartened at the innumerable shortcomings and follies committed by those who helped to guide the destinies of the army, recognizing also the bravery, the patience, intelligence, and resolution with which other men in high places offset the follies and shortcomings and persevering with equal mind through triumph and defeat until finally he saw the tide of failure turn at Gettysburg and the full flood of victory come with Appomattox.

I do wish that more of our good citizens would go into politics, and would do it in the same spirit with which their fathers went into the Federal armies. Begin with the little thing, and do not expect to accomplish anything without an effort. Of course, if you go to a primary just once, never having taken the trouble to know any of the other people who go there you will find yourself wholly out of place; but if you keep on attending and try to form associations with other men whom you meet at the political gatherings, or whom you can persuade to attend them, you will very soon find yourself a weight. In the same way, if a man feels that the politics of his city, for instance, are very corrupt and wants to reform them, it would be an excellent idea for him to begin with his district. If he joins with other people who think as he does to form a club where abstract political virtue will be discussed, he may do a great deal of good. We need such clubs; but he must also get to know his own ward or his own district, put himself in communication with the decent people in that district, of whom we may rest assured there will be many, willing and able to do something practical for the procurance of better government. Let him set to work to procure a better assemblyman or better alderman before he tries his hand at making a mayor, a governor, or a president. If he begins at the top he may make a brilliant temporary success, but the chances are a thousand to one that he will only be defeated eventually; and in no event will the good he does stand on the same broad and permanent foundation as if he had begun at the bottom. Of course, one or two of his efforts may be failures; but if he has the right stuff in him he will go ahead and do his duty irrespective of whether he meets with success or defeat. …

But in advising you to be practical and to work hard, I must not for one moment be understood as advising you to abandon one iota of your self-respect and devotion to principle. It is a bad sign for the country to see one class of our citizens sneer at practical politicians, and another at Sunday-school politics. No man can do both effective and decent work in public life unless he is a practical politician on the one hand, and a sturdy believer in Sunday-school politics on the other. He must always strive manfully for the best, and yet, like Abraham Lincoln, must often resign himself to accept the best possible. Of course when a man verges on to the higher ground of statesmanship, when he becomes a leader, he must very often consult with others and defer to their opinion, and must be continually settling in his mind how far he can go in just deference to the wishes and prejudices of others while yet adhering to his own moral standards: but I speak not so much of men of this stamp as I do of the ordinary citizen, who wants to do his duty as a member of the commonwealth in its civic life; and for this man I feel that the one quality which he ought always to hold most essential is that of disinterestedness. If he once begins to feel that he wants office himself, with a willingness to get it at the cost of his convictions, or to keep it when gotten, at the cost of his convictions, his usefulness is gone. Let him make up his mind to do his duty in politics without regard to holding office at all, and let him know that often the men in this country who have done the best work for our public life have not been the men in office. If, on the other hand, he attains public position, let him not strive to plan out for himself a career. I do not think that any man should let himself regard his political career as a means of livelihood, or as his sole occupation in life; for if he does he immediately becomes most seriously handicapped. The moment that he begins to think how such and such an act will affect the voters in his district, or will affect some great political leader who will have an influence over his destiny, he is hampered and his hands are bound. Not only may it be his duty often to disregard the wishes of politicians, but it may be his clear duty at times to disregard the wishes of the people. The voice of the people is not always the voice of God; and when it happens to be the voice of the devil, then it is a man's clear duty to defy its behests.

Different political conditions breed different dangers. The demagogue is as unlovely a creature as the courtier, though one is fostered under republican and the other under monarchical institutions. There is every reason why a man should have an honorable ambition to enter public life, and an honorable ambition to stay there when he is in; but he ought to make up his mind that he cares for it only as long as he can stay in it on his own terms, without sacrifice of his own principles; and if he does thus make up his mind he can really accomplish twice as much for the nation, and can reflect a hundredfold greater honor upon himself, in a short term of service, than can the man who grows gray in the public employment at the cost of sacrificing what he believes to be true and honest. And moreover, when a public servant has definitely made up his mind that he will pay no heed to his own future, but will do what he honestly deems best for the community, without regard to how his actions may affect his prospects, not only does he become infinitely more useful as a public servant, but he has a far better time. He is freed from the harassing care which is inevitably the portion of him who is trying to shape his sails to catch every gust of the wind of political favor.

But let me reiterate, that in being virtuous he must not become ineffective, and that he must not excuse himself for shirking his duties by any false plea that he cannot do his duties and retain his self-respect. This is nonsense, he can; and when he urges such a plea it is a mark of mere laziness and self-indulgence. And again, he should beware how he becomes a critic of the actions of others, rather than a doer of deeds himself; and in so far as he does act as a critic (and of course the critic has a great and necessary function) he must beware of indiscriminate censure even more than of indiscriminate praise. The screaming vulgarity of the foolish spread-eagle orator who is continually yelling defiance at Europe, praising everything American, good and bad, and resenting the introduction of any reform because it has previously been tried successfully abroad, is offensive and contemptible to the last degree; but after all it is scarcely as harmful as the peevish, fretful, sneering, and continual faultfinding of the refined, well-educated man, who is always attacking good and bad alike, who genuinely distrusts America, and in the true spirit of servile colonialism considers us inferior to the people across the water. It may be taken for granted that the man who is always sneering at our public life and our public men is a thoroughly bad citizen, and that what little influence he wields in the community is wielded for evil. The public speaker or the editorial writer who teaches men of education that their proper attitude toward American politics should be one of dislike or indifference is doing all he can to perpetuate and aggravate the very evils of which he is ostensibly complaining. Exactly as it is generally the case that when a man bewails the decadence of our civilization he is himself physically, mentally, and morally a first-class type of the decadent, so it is usually the case that when a man is perpetually sneering at American politicians, whether worthy or unworthy, he himself is a poor citizen and a friend of the very forces of evil against which he professes to contend. Too often these men seem to care less for attacking bad men, than for ruining the characters of good men with whom they disagree on some pubic question. ...

It is the duty of all citizens, irrespective of party, to denounce, and, so far as may be, to punish crimes against the public on the part of politicians or officials. But exactly as the public man who commits a crime against the public is one of the worst of criminals, so, close on his heels in the race for iniquitous distinction, comes the man who falsely charges the public servant with outrageous wrongdoing; whether it is done with foul-mouthed and foolish directness in the vulgar and violent party organ, or with sarcasm, innuendo, and the half-truths that are worse than lies, in some professed organ of independence. Not only should criticism be honest, but it should be intelligent, in order to be effective. ...

Congressmen are very often demagogues; they are very often blind partisans; they are often exceedingly short-sighted, narrow-minded, and bigoted; but they are not usually corrupt; and to accuse a narrow-minded demagogue of corruption when he is perfectly honest, is merely to set him more firmly in his evil course and to help him with his constituents, who recognize that the charge is entirely unjust, and in repelling it lose sight of the man's real shortcomings. ...

Finally, the man who wishes to do his duty as a citizen in our country must be imbued through and through with

the spirit of Americanism. I am not saying this as a matter of spread-eagle rhetoric: I am saying it quite soberly as a piece of matter-of-fact common-sense advice, derived from my own experience of others. Of course, the question of Americanism has several sides. If a man is an educated man, he must show his Americanism by not getting misled into following out and trying to apply all the theories of the political thinkers of other countries, such as Germany and France, to our own entirely different conditions. He must not get a fad, for instance, about responsible government; and above all things he must not, merely because he is intelligent, or a college professor well read in political literature, try to discuss our institutions when he has had no practical knowledge of how they are worked. Again, if he is a wealthy man, a man of means and standing, he must really feel, not merely affect to feel, that no social differences obtain save such as a man can in some way himself make by his own actions. People sometimes ask me if there is not a prejudice against a man of wealth and education in ward politics. I do not think that there is, unless the man in turn shows that he regards the facts of his having wealth and education as giving him a claim to superiority aside from the merit he is able to prove himself to have in actual service. Of course, if he feels that he ought to have a little better treatment than a carpenter, a plumber, or a butcher, who happens to stand beside him, he is going to be thrown out of the race very quickly, and probably quite roughly; and if he starts in to patronize and elaborately condescend to these men he will find that they resent this attitude even more. Do not let him think about the matter at all. Let him go into the political contest with no more thought of such matters than a college boy gives to the social standing of the members of his own and rival teams in a hotly contested football match. As soon as he begins to take an interest in politics (and he will speedily not only get interested for the sake of politics, but also take a good healthy interest in playing the game itself—an interest which is perfectly normal and praise-worthy, and to which only a prig would object), he will begin to work up the organization in the way that will be most effective, and he won't care a rap about who is put to work with him, save in so far as he is a good fellow and an efficient worker. ...

In facing the future and in striving, each according to the measure of his individual capacity, to work out the salvation of our land, we should be neither timid pessimists nor foolish optimists. We should recognize the dangers that exist and that threaten us: we should neither overestimate them nor shrink from them, but steadily fronting them should set to work to overcome and beat them down. Grave perils are yet to be encountered in the stormy course of the Republic—perils from political corruption, perils from individual laziness, indolence and timidity, perils springing from the greed of the unscrupulous rich, and from the anarchic violence of the thriftless and turbulent poor. There is every reason why we should recognize them, but there is no reason why we should fear them or doubt our capacity to overcome them, if only each will, according to the measure of his ability, do his full duty, and endeavor so to live as to deserve the high praise of being called a good American citizen.

The Rough Riders, standing with their leader, Colonel Theodore Roosevelt (center, with glasses) at the top of a hill they captured in the battle of San Juan during the Spanish-American War.

True Americanism

From his own standpoint, it is beyond all question the wise thing for the immigrant to become thoroughly Americanized. Moreover, from our standpoint, we have a right to demand it.

Roosevelt could almost certainly have won re-election to the presidency in 1908, but he honored an earlier pledge not to seek a third term. William Howard Taft, a member of his cabinet, had won Roosevelt's full confidence as a loyal and competent supporter of his ideas. Roosevelt, therefore, strongly and effectively backed Taft for the Republican nomination and subsequently saw him elected to the presidency. After leaving the White House, Roosevelt went on extended safari in Africa where he brought down nearly 300 big-game animals and continued his writing pursuits.

Upon returning to the United States, Roosevelt found himself the focus of national attention. Progressive Republicans felt betrayed by Taft's increasingly conservative positions and ultimately convinced Roosevelt to re-enter politics in search of a third term. Roosevelt entered and won several primaries, proving to be the popular choice, but Taft controlled the party machinery and was re-nominated by the Republican National Convention. Claiming fraud, Roosevelt's supporters formed the Progressive Party, or *Bull Moose* party as it was colloquially known. "I feel as strong as a bull moose," Roosevelt had said in response to a reporter's question about his health. On October 14, 1912, while campaigning in Milwaukee, Roosevelt survived an assassination attempt when a glasses case in his pocket partially deflected a bullet fired by a deranged saloonkeeper. With the bullet lodged in his chest, Roosevelt continued, saying, "I will deliver this speech or die."

The split in the Republican Party resulted in the election of New Jersey Governor Woodrow Wilson, for whom Roosevelt would develop an intense dislike due to Wilson's reluctance to enter World War I. All of Roosevelt's sons fought in the Great War, and his youngest, Quentin, was killed in an aerial dogfight with a German pilot. Roosevelt, himself, wanted to raise a division of troops to fight in France, but his request was refused.

Prior to America's involvement in the war, Roosevelt had traveled throughout South America. While exploring the River of Doubt in the Brazilian jungle, he contracted a form of jungle fever and returned to the United States, his health compromised. In 1918, Roosevelt underwent operations to remove abscesses in his ears—the result of his illness. He had lost all hearing in his left ear, and it was then that Roosevelt revealed he had been blind in his left eye since a 1904 boxing bout with a professional fighter.

Staunchly opposed to American membership in the League of Nations, Roosevelt seemed the probable Republican nominee for president in 1920, but he died suddenly of a blood clot in the heart on January 6, 1919.

"True Americanism," like all of Teddy Roosevelt's speeches and writings, is characteristic of a leader who was, in the words of Elihu Root, T.R.'s former secretary of war and secretary of state, "the greatest teacher of the essentials of popular self-government the world has ever known." For this reason, and for his many enduring accomplishments, the most charismatic leader of the first half of the twentieth century is forever immortalized alongside Washington, Lincoln, and Jefferson on Mount Rushmore in the Black Hills of South Dakota.

This selection, which deals primarily with the issue of immigration and assimilation, first appeared in a magazine called the *Forum* in April 1894.

… We Americans have many grave problems to solve, many threatening evils to fight, and many deeds to do, if, as we hope and believe, we have the wisdom, the strength, the courage, and the virtue to do them. But we must face facts as they are. We must neither surrender ourselves to a foolish optimism, nor succumb to a timid and ignoble pessimism. Our nation is that one among all the nations of the earth which holds in its hands the fate of the coming years. We enjoy exceptional advantages, and are menaced by exceptional dangers; and all signs indicate that we shall either fail greatly or succeed greatly. I firmly believe that we shall succeed; but we must not foolishly blink from the dangers by which we are threatened, for that is the way to fail. On the contrary, we must soberly set to work to find out all we can about the existence and the extent of every evil, must acknowledge it to be such, and must then attack it with unyielding resolution. There are many such evils, and each must be fought after a fashion; yet there is one quality which we must bring to the solution of every problem—that is, an intense and fervid Americanism. We shall never be successful over the dangers that confront us; we shall never achieve true greatness, nor reach the lofty ideal which the founders and preservers of our mighty federal Republic have set before us, unless we are Americans in heart and soul, in spirit and purpose, keenly alive to the responsibility implied in the very name of American, and proud beyond measure of the glorious privilege of bearing it.

There are two or three sides to the question of Americanism, and two or three senses in which the word "Americanism" can be used to express the antithesis of what is unwholesome and undesirable. In the first place we wish to be broadly American and national, as opposed to being local or sectional. We do not wish, in politics, in literature, or in art, to develop that unwholesome parochial spirit, that over-exaltation of the little community at the expense of the great nation, which produces what has been described as the patriotism of the village, the patriotism of the belfry.... The patriotism of the village or belfry is bad, but the lack of all patriotism is even worse. There are philosophers who assure us that, in the future, patriotism will be regarded not as a virtue at all, but merely as a mental stage in the journey toward a state of feeling when our patriotism will include the whole human race and all the world. This may be so; but the age of which these philosophers speak is still several eons distant. In fact, philosophers of this type are so very advanced that they are of no practical service to the present generation. It may be, that in ages so remote that we cannot now understand any of the feelings of those who will dwell in them, patriotism will no longer be regarded as a virtue, exactly as it may be that in those remote ages people will look down upon and disregard monogamic marriage; but as things now are and have been for two or three thousand years past, and are likely to be for two or three thousand years to come, the words home and country mean a great deal. Nor do they show any tendency to lose their significance. At present, treason, like adultery, ranks as one of the worst of all possible crimes.

One may fall very far short of treason and yet be an undesirable citizen in the community. The man who becomes Europeanized, who loses his power of doing good work on this side of the water, and who loses his love for his native land, is not a traitor; but he is a silly and undesirable citizen. He is as emphatically a noxious element in our body politic as is the man who comes here from abroad and remains a foreigner. Nothing will more quickly or more surely disqualify a man from doing good work in the world than the acquirement of that flaccid habit of mind which its possessors style cosmopolitanism.

It is not only necessary to Americanize the immigrants of foreign birth who settle among us, but it is even more necessary for those among us who are by birth and descent already Americans not to throw away our birthright, and, with incredible and contemptible folly, wander back to bow down before the alien gods whom our forefathers forsook. It is hard to believe that there is any necessity to warn Americans that, when they seek to model themselves on the lines of other civilizations, they make themselves the butts of all right-thinking men; and yet the necessity certainly exists to give this warning to many of our citizens who pride themselves on their standing in the world of arts and letters, or perchance, on what they would style their social leadership in the community. It is always better to be an original than an imitation, even when the imitation is of something better than the original; But what shall we say of the fool who is content to be an imitation of something worse? Even if the weaklings who seek to be other than Americans were right in deeming other nations to be better than their own, the fact yet remains that to be a first-class American is fiftyfold better than to be a second-class imitation of a Frenchman or Englishman. As a matter of fact, however, those of our countrymen who do believe in American inferiority are always individuals who, however cultivated, have some organic weakness in their moral or mental makeup; and the great mass of our people, who are robustly patriotic, and who have sound, healthy minds, are justified in regarding these feeble renegades with a half-impatient and half-amused scorn. ...

It remains true that, in spite of all our faults and shortcomings, no other land offers such glorious possibilities to the man able to take advantage of them, as does ours; it remains true that no one of our people can do any work really worth doing unless he does it primarily as an American. It is because certain classes of our people retain their spirit of colonial dependence on, and exaggerated deference to, European opinion, that they fail to accomplish what they ought to. It is precisely along the lines where we have worked most independently that we have accomplished the greatest results; and it is in those professions where there has been no servility to, but merely a wise profiting by foreign experience, that we have produced our greatest men. Our soldiers and statesmen and orators; our explorers, our wilderness-winners, and commonwealth builders; the men who have made our laws and seen that they were executed; and the other men whose energy and ingenuity have created our marvelous material prosperity—all these have been men who have drawn wisdom from the experience of every age and nation, but who have nevertheless thought, and worked, and conquered, and lived, and died, purely as Americans; and on the whole they have done better work than has been done in any other country during the short period of our national life. ...

We must Americanize [the newcomers to our shores] in every way, in speech, in political ideas and principles, and in their way of looking at the relations between church and state. We welcome the German or the Irishman who becomes an American. We have no use for the German or the Irishman who remains such. We do not wish German-Americans or Irish-Americans who figure as such in our social and political life; we want only Americans, and provided they are such, we do not care whether they are of native or of German or of Irish ancestry. We have no room in any healthy American community for a German-American vote or an Irish-American vote, and it is contemptible demagogy to put planks into any party platform with the purpose of catching such a vote. We have no room for any people who do not act and vote simply as Americans, and as nothing else. ...

The mighty tide of immigration to our shores has brought in its train much of good and much of evil; and whether the good or the evil shall predominate depends on whether these newcomers do or do not throw themselves heartily into our national life, cease to be Europeans, and become Americans like the rest of us.... An immense number of them have become Americanized, and these stand on exactly the same plane as the descendants of any Puritan, Cavalier, or Knickerbocker among us, and do their full and honorable share of the nation's work. But where immigrants, or the sons of immigrants, do not heartily and in good faith throw in their lot with us, but cling to the speech, the customs, the ways of life, and the habits of thought of the Old World

which they have left, they thereby harm both themselves and us. If they remain alien elements, unassimilated, and with interests separate from ours, they are mere obstructions to the current of our national life, and, moreover, can get no good from it themselves. In fact, though we ourselves also suffer from their perversity, it is they who really suffer most. It is an immense benefit to the European immigrant to change him into an American citizen. To bear the name of American is to bear the most honorable titles; and whoever does not so believe has no business to bear the name at all, and, if he comes from Europe, the sooner he goes back there the better. Besides, the man who does not become Americanized nevertheless fails to remain a European, and becomes nothing at all. The immigrant cannot possibly remain what he was, or continue to be a member of the old-world society. If he tries to retain his old language, in a few generations it becomes a barbarous jargon; if he tries to retain his old customs and ways of life, in a few generations he becomes an uncouth boor. He has cut himself off from the Old World, and cannot retain his connection with it; and if he wishes ever to amount to anything he must throw himself heart and soul, and without reservation, into the new life to which he has come. ...

From his own standpoint, it is beyond all question the wise thing for the immigrant to become thoroughly Americanized. Moreover, from our standpoint, we have a right to demand it. We freely extend the hand of welcome and of good-fellowship to every man, no matter what his creed or birthplace, who comes here honestly intent on becoming a good United States citizen like the rest of us; but we have a right, and it is our duty, to demand that he shall indeed become so and shall not confuse the issues with which we are struggling by introducing among us old-world quarrels and prejudices. There are certain ideas which he must give up. For instance, he must learn that American life is incompatible with the existence of any form of anarchy, or of any secret society having murder for its aim, whether at home or abroad; and he must learn that we exact full religious toleration and the complete separation of church and state. Moreover, he must not bring in his old-world religious race and national antipathies, but must merge them into love for our common country, and must take pride in the things which we can all take pride in. He must revere only our flag; not only must it come first, but no other flag should even come second. ... Above all, the immigrant must learn to talk and think and be the United States. ...

Americanism is a question of spirit, conviction, and purpose, not of creed or birthplace. The politician who bids for the Irish or German vote, or the Irishman or German who votes as an Irishman or German, is despicable, for all citizens of this commonwealth should vote solely as Americans; but he is not a whit less despicable than the voter who votes against a good American, merely because that American happens to have been born in Ireland or Germany.... It is a base outrage to oppose a man because of his religion or birthplace, and all good citizens will hold any such effort in abhorrence. A Scandinavian, a German, or an Irishman who has really become an American has the right to stand on exactly the same footing as any native-born citizen in the land, and is just as much entitled to the friendship and support, social and political, of his neighbors. ...

In closing, I cannot better express the ideal attitude that should be taken by our fellow citizens of foreign birth than by quoting the words of a representative American, born in Germany, the Honorable Richard Guenther, of Wisconsin. ...

"We know as well as any other class of American citizens where our duties belong. We will work for our country in time of peace and fight for it in time of war, if a time of war should ever come. When I say our country, I mean, of course, our adopted country. I mean the United States of America. After passing through the crucible of naturalization, we are no longer Germans; we are Americans. Our attachment to America cannot be measured by the length of our residence here. We are Americans from the moment we touch the American shore until we are laid in American graves. We will fight for America whenever necessary. America, first, last, and all the time. America against Germany, America against the world; America, right or wrong; always America. We are Americans."

All honor to the man who spoke such words as those; and I believe they express the feelings of the great majority of those among our fellow American citizens who were born abroad. We Americans can only do our allotted task well if we face it steadily and bravely, seeing but not fearing the dangers. Above all we must stand shoulder to shoulder, not asking as to the ancestry or creed of our comrades, but only demanding that they be in very truth Americans, and that we will all work together, heart, hand, and head, for the honor and the greatness of our common country.

THEODORE ROOSEVELT

The Strenuous Life

Far better it is to dare mighty things, to win glorious triumphs, even though checkered by failure, than to take rank with those poor spirits who neither enjoy much nor suffer much, because they live in the gray twilight that knows not victory nor defeat.

"The Strenuous Life," Roosevelt's most popular speech and the title of a 1901 collection of his essays and addresses, was delivered on April 10, 1899, in Chicago. Responding to William Jennings Bryan, who had appeared in the Windy City six weeks prior denouncing imperialism, Roosevelt combined his personal views of life as a constant struggle with his conception of what America's role in the world should be. He pointed out that "while a nation's first duty is within its own borders, it is not thereby absolved from facing its duties in the world."

A proponent of righteous war, Roosevelt believed in securing peace through strength. As president, he maintained that America had a duty to serve as "the world's policeman" and, in 1907, as part of his "big stick diplomacy," sent sixteen battleships known as the *Great White Fleet* on a goodwill tour of the world. His assertion that the United States might be forced "in flagrant cases of ... wrongdoing or impotence, to the exercise of an international police power" is known as the *Roosevelt Corollary* of the Monroe Doctrine.

"No triumph of peace is quite so great as the supreme triumphs of war," said T.R. While agreeing that diplomacy has its place in world affairs, Roosevelt maintained that "the diplomat is the servant, not the master, of the soldier."

In speaking to you, men of the greatest city of the West, men of the State which gave to the country Lincoln and Grant, men who preeminently and distinctly embody all that is most American in the American character, I wish to preach, not the doctrine of ignoble ease, but the doctrine of the strenuous life; the life of toil and effort, of labor and strife; to preach that highest form of success which comes, not to the man who desires mere easy peace, but to the man who does not shrink from danger, from hardship or from bitter toil, and who out of these wins the splendid ultimate triumph.

A life of slothful ease, a life of that peace which springs merely from lack either of desire or of power to strive after great things, is as little worthy of a nation as of an individual. I ask only that what every self-respecting American demands from himself and from his sons shall be demanded of the American nation as a whole. Who among you would teach your boys that ease, that peace, is to be the first consideration in their eyes—to be the ultimate goal after which they strive? You men of Chicago have made this city great, you men of Illinois have done your share, and more than your share, in making America great, because you neither preach nor practice such a doctrine. You work yourselves, and you bring up your sons to work. If you are rich and are worth your salt, you will teach your sons that though they may have leisure, it is not to be spent in idleness; for wisely used leisure merely means that those who possess it, being free from the necessity of working for their livelihood, are all the more bound to carry on some kind of non-remunerative work in science, in letters, in art, in exploration, in historical research—work of the type we most need in this country, the successful carrying out of which reflects most honor upon the nation. We do not admire the man of timid peace. We admire the man who embodies victorious effort; the man who never wrongs his neighbor, who is prompt to help a friend, but who has those virile qualities necessary to win in the stern strife of actual life. It is hard to fail, but it is worse never to have tried to succeed. In this life we get nothing save by effort. Freedom from effort in the present merely means that there has been stored up effort in the past. A man can be freed from the necessity of work only by the fact that he or his fathers before him have worked to good purpose. If the freedom thus purchased is used aright, and the man still does actual work, though of a different kind, whether as a writer or a general, whether in the field of politics or in the field of exploration and adventure, he shows he deserves his good fortune. But if he treats this period of freedom from the need of actual labor as a period, not of preparation, but of mere enjoyment, even though perhaps not of vicious enjoyment, he shows that he is simply a cumberer of the earth's surface, and he surely unfits himself to hold his own with his fellows if the need to do so should again arise. A mere life of ease is not in the end a very satisfactory life, and, above all, it is a life which ultimately unfits those who follow it for serious work in the world. ...

As it is with the individual, so it is with the nation. It is a base untruth to say that happy is the nation that has no history. Thrice happy is the nation that has a glorious history. Far better it is to dare mighty things, to win glorious triumphs, even though checkered by failure, than to take rank with those poor spirits who neither enjoy much nor suffer much, because they live in the gray twilight that knows not victory nor defeat. If in 1861 the men who loved the Union had believed that peace was the end of all things, and war and strife the worst of all things, and had acted up to their belief, we would have saved hundreds of thousands of lives, we would have saved hundreds of millions of dollars. Moreover, besides saving all the blood and treasure we then lavished, we would have prevented the heartbreak of many women, the dissolution of many homes, and we would have spared the country those months of gloom and shame when it seemed as if our armies marched only to defeat. We could have avoided all this suffering simply by shrinking from strife. And if we had thus avoided it, we would have shown that we were weaklings, and that we were unfit to stand among the great nations of the earth. Thank God for the iron in the blood of our fathers, the men who upheld the wisdom of Lincoln, and bore sword or rifle in the armies of Grant! Let us, the children of the men who proved themselves equal to the mighty days, let us, the children of the men who carried the great Civil War to a triumphant conclusion, praise the God of our fathers that the ignoble counsels of peace were rejected; that the suffering and loss, the blackness of sorrow and despair, were unflinchingly faced, and the years of strife endured; for in the end the slave was freed, the Union restored, and the mighty American republic placed once more as a helmeted queen among nations.

We of this generation do not have to face a task such as that our fathers faced, but we have our tasks, and woe to us if we fail to perform them! We cannot, if we would, play the part of China, and be content to rot by inches in ignoble ease within our borders, taking no interest in what goes on beyond them, sunk in a scrambling commercialism; heedless of the higher life, the life of aspiration, of toil and risk, busying ourselves only with the wants of our bodies for the day, until suddenly we should find, beyond a shadow of question, what China has already found, that in this world the nation that has trained itself to a career of unwarlike and isolated ease is bound, in the end, to go down before other nations which have not lost the manly and adventurous qualities. If we are to be a really great people, we must strive in good faith to play a great part in the world. We cannot avoid meeting great issues. All that we can determine for ourselves is whether we shall meet them well or ill. In 1898 we could not help being brought face to face with the problem of war with Spain. All we could decide was whether we should shrink like cowards from the contest, or enter into it as beseemed a brave and high-spirited people; and, once in, whether failure or success should crown our banners. So it is now. We cannot avoid the responsibilities that confront us in Hawaii, Cuba, Puerto Rico, and the Philippines. All we can decide is whether we shall meet them in a way that will redound to the national credit, or whether we shall make of our dealings with these new problems a dark and shameful page in our history. To refuse to deal with them at all merely amounts to dealing with them badly. We have a given problem to solve. If we undertake the solution, there is, of course, always danger that we may not solve it aright; but to refuse to undertake the solution simply renders it certain that we cannot possibly solve it aright.

The timid man, the lazy man, the man who distrusts his country, the over-civilized man, who has lost the great fighting, masterful virtues, the ignorant man, and the man of dull mind, whose soul is incapable of feeling the mighty lift that thrills "stern men with empires in their brains"—all these, of course, shrink from seeing the nation undertake its new duties; shrink from seeing us build a navy and an army adequate to our needs; shrink from seeing us do our share of the world's work, by bringing order out of chaos in the great, fair tropic islands from which the valor of our soldiers and sailors has driven the Spanish flag. These are the men who fear the strenuous life, who fear the only national life which is really worth leading. They believe in that cloistered life which saps the hardy virtues in a nation, as it saps them in the individual; or else they are wedded to that base spirit of gain and greed which recognizes in commercialism the

be-all and end-all of national life, instead of realizing that, though an indispensable element, it is, after all, but one of the many elements that go to make up true national greatness. No country can long endure if its foundations are not laid deep in the material prosperity which comes from thrift, from business energy and enterprise, from hard, unsparing effort in the fields of industrial activity; but neither was any nation ever yet truly great if it relied upon material prosperity alone. All honor must lie paid to the architects of our material prosperity, to the great captains of industry who have built our factories and our railroads, to the strong men who toil for wealth with brain or hand; for great is the debt of the nation to these and their kind. But our debt is yet greater to the men whose highest type is to be found in a statesman like Lincoln, a soldier like Grant. They showed by their lives that they recognized the law of work, the law of strife; they toiled to win a competence for themselves and those dependent upon them; but they recognized that there were yet other and even loftier duties—duties to the nation and duties to the race.

We cannot sit huddled within our own borders and avow ourselves merely an assemblage of well-to-do hucksters who care nothing for what happens beyond. Such a policy would defeat even its own end; for as the nations grow to have ever wider and wider interests, and are brought into closer and closer contact, if we are to hold our own in the struggle for naval and commercial supremacy, we must build up our power without our own borders. We must build the isthmian canal, and we must grasp the points of vantage which will enable us to have our say in deciding the destiny of the oceans of the East and the West. …

Of course we are bound to handle the affairs of our own household well. We must see that there is civic honesty, civic cleanliness, civic good sense in our home administration of city, State, and nation. We must strive for honesty in office, for honesty toward the creditors of the nation and of the individual; for the widest freedom of individual initiative where possible, and for the wisest control of individual initiative where it is hostile to the welfare of the many. But because we set our own household in order we are not thereby excused from playing our part in the great affairs of the world. A man's first duty is to his own home, but he is not thereby excused from doing his duty to the State; for if he fails in this second duty it is under the penalty of ceasing to be a freeman. In the same way, while a nation's first duty is within its own borders, it is not thereby absolved from facing its duties in the world as a whole; and if it refuses to do so, it merely forfeits its right to struggle for a place among the peoples that shape the destiny of mankind. ...

But to do this work, keep ever in mind that we must show in a very high degree the qualities of courage, of honesty, and of good judgment. Resistance must be stamped out. The first and all-important work to be done is to establish the supremacy of our flag. We must put down armed resistance before we can accomplish anything else, and there should be no parleying, no faltering, in dealing with our foe. As for those in our own country who encourage the foe, we can afford contemptuously to disregard them; but it must be remembered that their utterances are not saved from being treasonable merely by the fact that they are despicable. ...

I preach to you, then, my countrymen, that our country calls not for the life of ease but for the life of strenuous endeavor. The twentieth century looms before us big with the fate of many nations. If we stand idly by, if we seek merely swollen, slothful ease and ignoble peace, if we shrink from the hard contests where men must win at hazard of their lives and at the risk of all they hold dear, then the bolder and stronger peoples will pass us by, and will win for themselves the domination of the world. Let us therefore boldly face the life of strife, resolute to do our duty well and manfully; resolute to uphold righteousness by deed and by word; resolute to be both honest and brave, to serve high ideals, yet to use practical methods. Above all, let us shrink from no strife, moral or physical, within or without the nation, provided we are certain that the strife is justified, for it is only through strife, through hard and dangerous endeavor, that we shall ultimately win the goal of true national greatness.

A crowd overflows the playing field prior to Game 3 of the 1903 World Series, the first to be played in modern Major League Baseball. The Boston Americans prevailed five games to three over the Pittsburg Pirates in the best-of-nine series.

The Talented Tenth

I insist that the object of all true education is not to make men carpenters, it is to make carpenters men.

William Edward Burghardt Du Bois (1868-1963) was born in Great Barrington, Massachusetts. He graduated from Fisk University and earned his Ph.D. at Harvard. The most recognized black leader of the first half of the twentieth century, Du Bois founded the Niagara Movement and was a leading founder of the NAACP. He also wrote several books, including *Black Reconstruction*, *The Autobiography of W. E. B. Du Bois*, and *The Souls of Black Folk*.

A critic of the views of Booker T. Washington, Du Bois believed that equality should be the primary goal of blacks. This was best achieved, he argued, by promoting the development of higher education. As such, he scorned Washington's reliance on industrial education for blacks, writing, in *The Negro Problem* (1903), "The Talented Tenth of the Negro race must be made leaders of thought and missionaries of culture among their people."

Disenchanted with the slow progress of the struggle for equality, Du Bois moved to Ghana in 1961 and lived there the remainder of his life. In *The Souls of Black Folk*, he wrote, "One ever feels his twoness—an American, a Negro; two souls, two thoughts, two unreconciled strivings; two warring ideals in one dark body."

The Negro race, like all races, is going to be saved by its exceptional men. The problem of education, then, among Negroes must first of all deal with the Talented Tenth; it is the problem of developing the best of this race that they may guide the mass away from the contamination and death of the worst, in their own and other races. Now the training of men is a difficult and intricate task. Its technique is a matter for educational experts, but its object is for the vision of seers. If we make money the object of mantraining, we shall develop money-makers but not necessarily men; if we make technical skill the object of education, we may possess artisans but not, in nature, men. Men we shall have only as we make manhood the object of the work of the schools—intelligence, broad sympathy, knowledge of the world that was and is, and of the relation of men to it—this is the curriculum of that Higher Education which must underlie true life.... From the very first it has been the educated and intelligent of the Negro people that have led and elevated the mass, and the sole obstacles that nullified and retarded their efforts were slavery and race prejudice; for what is slavery but the legalized survival of the unfit and the nullification of the work of natural internal leadership? ...

It is the fashion of today to...say that with freedom Negro leadership should have begun at the plow and not in the Senate—a foolish and mischievous lie; two hundred and fifty years that black serf toiled at the plow and yet that toiling was in vain till the Senate passed the war amendments; and two hundred and fifty years more the half-free serf of today may toil at his plow, but unless he have political rights and righteously guarded civic status, he will still remain the poverty-stricken and ignorant plaything of rascals, that he now is. This all sane men know even if they dare not say it. ...

How then shall the leaders of a struggling people be trained and the hands of the risen few strengthened? There can be but one answer: The best and most capable of their youth must be schooled in the colleges and universities of the land. We will not quarrel as to just what the university of the Negro should teach or how it should teach it—I willingly admit that each soul and each race-soul needs its own peculiar curriculum. But this is true: A university is a human invention for the transmission of knowledge and culture from generation to generation, through the training of quick minds and pure hearts, and for this work no other human invention will suffice, not even trade and industrial schools.

All men cannot go to college but some men must; every isolated group or nation must have its yeast, must have for the talented few centers of training where men are not so mystified and befuddled by the hard and necessary toil of earning a living, as to have no aims higher than their bellies, and no God greater than Gold. This is true training, and thus in the beginning were the favored sons of the freedmen trained. ... Where ought they to have begun to build? At the bottom, of course, quibbles the mole with his eyes in the earth. Aye! truly at the bottom, at the very bottom; at the bottom of knowledge, down in the very depths of knowledge there where the roots of justice strike into the lowest soil of Truth. And so they did begin; they founded colleges, and up from the colleges shot normal schools, and out from the normal schools went teachers, and around the normal teachers clustered other teachers to teach the public schools; the college trained in Greek and Latin and mathematics, 2,000 men; and these men trained full 50,000 others in morals and manners, and they in turn taught thrift and the alphabet to nine millions of men, who today hold $300,000,000 of property. It was a miracle—the most wonderful peace-battle of the nineteenth century, and yet today men smile at it, and in fine superiority tell us that it was all a strange mistake; that a proper way to found a system of education is first to gather the children and buy them spelling books and hoes; afterward men may look about for teachers, if haply they may find them; or again they would teach men work, but as for life—why, what has work to do with life, they ask vacantly. …

The college-bred Negro … is, as he ought to be, the group leader, the man who sets the ideals of the community where he lives, directs its thoughts, and heads its social movements. It need hardly be argued that the Negro people need social leadership more than most groups; that they have no traditions to fall back upon, no long-established customs, no strong family ties, no well-defined social classes. All these things must be slowly and painfully evolved. The preacher was, even before the war, the group leader of the Negroes, and the church their greatest social institution. Naturally this preacher was ignorant and often immoral, and the problem of replacing the older type by better educated men has been a difficult one. Both by direct work and by direct influence on other preachers, and on congregations, the collegebred preacher has an opportunity for reformatory work and moral inspiration, the value of which cannot be overestimated.

It has, however, been in the furnishing of teachers that the Negro college has found its peculiar function. Few persons realize how vast a work, how mighty a revolution has been thus accomplished. To furnish five millions and more of ignorant people with teachers of their own race and blood, in one generation, was not only a very difficult undertaking, but a very important one, in that it placed before the eyes of almost every Negro child an attainable ideal. It brought the masses of the blacks in contact with modern civilization,

made black men the leaders of their communities and trainers of the new generation. In this work college-bred Negroes were first teachers, and then teachers of teachers. And here it is that the broad culture of college work has been of peculiar value. Knowledge of life and its wider meaning has been the point of the Negro's deepest ignorance, and the sending out of teachers whose training has not been simply for breadwinning, but also for human culture, has been of inestimable value in the training of these men. …

The main question, so far as the Southern Negro is concerned, is: What, under the present circumstance, must a system of education do in order to raise the Negro as quickly as possible in the scale of civilization? The answer to this question seems to me clear: It must strengthen the Negro's character, increase his knowledge, and teach him to earn a living. Now it goes without saying, that it is hard to do all these things simultaneously or suddenly, and that at the same time it will not do to give all the attention to one and neglect the others; we could give black boys trades, but that alone will not civilize a race of ex-slaves; we might simply increase their knowledge of the world, but this would not necessarily make them wish to use this knowledge honestly; we might seek to strengthen character and purpose, but to what end if this people have nothing to eat or to wear?… Schoolhouses do not teach themselves—piles of brick and mortar and machinery do not send out men. It is the trained, living human soul, cultivated and strengthened by long study and thought, that breathes the real breath of life into boys and girls and makes them human, whether they be black or white, Greek, Russian, or American. …

I would not deny, or for a moment seem to deny, the paramount necessity of teaching the Negro to work, and to work steadily and skillfully; or seem to depreciate in the slightest degree the important part industrial schools must play in the accomplishment of these ends, but I do say, and insist upon it, that it is industrialism drunk with its vision of success to imagine that its work can be accomplished without providing for the training of broadly cultured men and women to teach its own teachers, and to teach the teachers of the public schools. …

I am an earnest advocate of manual training and trade teaching for black boys, and for white boys, too. I believe that next to the founding of Negro colleges the most valuable addition to Negro education since the war has been industrial training for black boys. Nevertheless, I insist that the object of all true education is not to make men carpenters, it is to make carpenters men; there are two means of making the carpenter a man, each equally important; the first is to give the group and community in which he works liberally trained teachers and leaders to teach him and his family what life means; the second is to give him sufficient intelligence and technical skill to make him an efficient workman; the first object demands the Negro college and college-bred men—not a quantity of such colleges, but a few of excellent quality; not too many college-bred men, but enough to leaven the lump, to inspire the masses, to raise the Talented Tenth to leadership; the second object demands a good system of common schools, well-taught, conveniently located, and properly equipped. ...

Men of America, the problem is plain before you. Here is a race transplanted through the criminal foolishness of your fathers. Whether you like it or not the millions are here, and here they will remain. If you do not lift them up, they will pull you down. Education and work are the levers to uplift a people. Work alone will not do it unless inspired by the right ideals and guided by intelligence. Education must not simply teach work—it must teach life. The Talented Tenth of the Negro race must be made leaders of thought and missionaries of culture among their people. No others can do this work and Negro colleges must train men for it. The Negro race, like all other races, is going to be saved by its exceptional men.

W. E. B. DU BOIS

Advice to a Student

Ignorance is a cure for nothing.

In 1905, a white school teacher in Pennsylvania wrote to Du Bois about a black student who was academically gifted, but refused to apply herself as she believed there would never be an opportunity to put her knowledge to use. Du Bois responded with the following letter to the student, Vernealia Fareira.

I wonder if you will let a stranger say a word to you about yourself? I have heard that you are a young woman of some ability but that you are neglecting your school work because you have become hopeless of trying to do anything in the world. I am very sorry for this. How any human being whose wonderful fortune it is to live in the 20th century should under ordinarily fair advantages despair of life is almost unbelievable. And if in addition to this that person is, as I am, of Negro lineage with all the hopes and yearnings of hundreds of millions of human souls dependent in some degree on her striving, then her bitterness amounts to crime.

There are in the U.S. today tens of thousands of colored girls who would be happy beyond measure to have the chance of educating themselves that you are neglecting. If you train yourself as you easily can, there are wonderful chances of usefulness before you: you can join the ranks of 15,000 Negro women teachers, of hundreds of nurses and physicians, of the growing number of clerks and stenographers, and above all of the host of homemakers. Ignorance is a cure for nothing. Get the very best training possible & the doors of opportunity will fly open before you as they are flying before thousands of your fellows. On the other hand every time a colored person neglects an opportunity, it makes it more difficult for others of the race to get such an opportunity. Do you want to cut off the chances of the boys and girls of tomorrow?

HENRY HOLCOMB BENNETT

The Flag Goes By

Born in Chillicothe, Ohio, Henry Holcomb Bennett (1863-1924) was an ornithologist who also illustrated books, composed short stories about Army life, and wrote numerous poems, including "The Flag Goes By," first published in 1904.

Hats off!
Along the street there comes
A blare of bugles, a ruffle of drums,
A flash of color beneath the sky:
Hats off!
The flag is passing by!

Blue and crimson and white it shines,
Over the steel-tipped, ordered lines.
Hats off!
The colors before us fly;
But more than the flag is passing by.

Sea-fights and land-fights, grim and great,
Fought to make and to save the State:
Weary marches and sinking ships;
Cheers of victory on dying lips;

Days of plenty and years of peace;
March of a strong land's swift increase;
Equal justice, right and law,
Stately honor and reverend awe;

Sign of a nation, great and strong
To ward her people from foreign wrong:
Pride and glory and honor—all
Live in the colors to stand or fall.

Hats off!
Along the street there comes
A blare of bugles, a ruffle of drums;
And loyal hearts are beating high:
Hats off!
The flag is passing by!

A view of San Francisco in ruins after the earthquake of April 18, 1906. Tremors were felt from Oregon to Los Angeles and as far inland as central Nevada. The earthquake and resulting fire, which claimed 3,000 lives and destroyed more than 25,000 buildings, are remembered as the worst natural disaster in the history of the United States alongside the Galveston Hurricane of 1900.

Patriotism and Holidays

Our country is infinitely more than a domain affording to those who dwell upon it immense material advantages and opportunities.

Grover Cleveland (1837-1908), the only American president to serve two nonconsecutive terms, became the only president to be married in the White House when he exchanged vows in the Blue Room with his twenty-one-year-old bride, Frances Folsom, the nation's youngest First Lady.

Speaking before the Union League Club of Chicago on February 22, 1907, on occasion of George Washington's 175th birthday, the former president put forth the expectations of all those who would be worthy citizens of the republic.

… The commemoration of the day on which American independence was born has been allowed to lose much of its significance as a reminder of Providential favor and the inflexible patriotism of the fathers of the republic, and has nearly degenerated to a revel of senseless noise and dangerous explosion, leaving in its train far more of mishap and accident than lessons of good citizenship or pride of country. The observance of Thanksgiving is kept alive through its annual designation by Federal and State authority. But it is worth our while to inquire whether its original meaning, as a day of united praise and gratitude to God for the blessings bestowed upon us as a people and as individuals, is not smothered in feasting and social indulgence. We, in common with Christian nations everywhere, celebrate Christmas—but, how much less as a day of commemorating the birth of the Redeemer of mankind, than as a day of hilarity and the exchange of gifts.

I will not, without decided protest, be accused of antagonizing or deprecating light-hearted mirth and jollity. On the contrary, I am an earnest advocate of every kind of sane, decent, social enjoyment, and all sorts of recreation. But, nevertheless, I feel that the allowance of an incongruous possession by them of our commemorative days is evidence of a certain condition, and is symptomatic of a popular tendency which are by no means reassuring. …

Beyond all doubt, the commemorations of the birth of American heroes and statesmen who have rendered redemptive service to their country in emergencies of peace and war should be rescued from entire neglect and from fitful and dislocated remembrance. And, while it would be more gratifying to know that throughout our country there was such a spontaneous appreciation of this need, that in no part of our domain would there be a necessity of urging such commemorations by self-constituted organizations, yet it is

comforting to know that, in the midst of prevailing apathy, there are those among us who have determined that the memory of the events and lives we should commemorate shall not be smothered in the dust and smoke of sordidness, nor crushed out by ruthless materialism.…

I deem it a great privilege to be allowed to participate with the League in a commemoration so exactly designed, not only to remind those of mature years, of the duty exacted by their heirship in American free institutions, but to teach children the inestimable value of those institutions, to inspire them to emulation of the virtues in which our nation had its birth, and to lead them to know the nobility of patriotic citizenship. …

It would have been impossible to select for observance any other civic holiday having as broad and fitting a significance as this. It memorizes the birth of one whose glorious deeds are transcendently above all others recorded in our national annals; and, in memorizing the birth of Washington, it commemorates the incarnation of all the virtues and all the ideals that made our nationality possible, and gave it promise of growth and strength. It is a holiday that belongs exclusively to the American people. All that Washington did was bound up in our national life, and became interwoven with the warp of our national destiny. The battles he fought were fought for American liberty, and the victories he won gave us national independence. His example of unselfish consecration and lofty patriotism made manifest, as in an open book, that those virtues were conditions not more vital to our nation's beginning than to its development and durability. His faith in God, and the fortitude of his faith, taught those for whom he wrought that the surest strength of nations comes from the support of God's almighty arm. His universal and unaffected sympathy with those in every sphere of American life, his thorough knowledge of existing American conditions, and his wonderful foresight of those yet to be, coupled with his powerful influence in the counsels of those who were to make or mar the fate of an infant nation, made him a tremendous factor in the construction and adoption of the constitutional chart by which the course of the newly launched republic could be safely sailed. And it was he who first took the helm, and demonstrated for the guidance of all who might succeed him, how and in what spirit and intent the responsibilities of our chief magistracy should be discharged. …

The American people need today the example and teachings of Washington no less than those who fashioned our nation needed his labors and guidance; and only so far as we commemorate his birth with a sincere and unreserved recognition of this need can our commemoration be useful to the present generation. …

The question presses upon us with a demand for reply that will not be denied: "Who among us all, if our hearts are purged of misleading impulses and our minds freed from perverting pride, can be sure that today the posture of affairs and the prevailing disposition of our countrymen, cooperate in the establishment and promotion of harmony, honesty, industry, and frugality?"

When Washington wrote that nothing but these were necessary to make us a great and happy people, he had in mind the harmony of American brotherhood and unenvious good will, the honesty that insures against the betrayal of public trust and hates devious ways and conscienceless practices, the industry that recognizes in faithful work and intelligent endeavor abundant promise of well-earned competence and provident accumulation, and the frugality which outlaws waste and extravagant display as plunderers of thrift and promoters of covetous discontent.

The self-examination invited by this day's commemoration will be incomplete and superficial if we are not thereby forced to the confession that there are signs of the times which indicate a weakness and relaxation of our hold upon these saving virtues. When thus forewarned, it is the height of recreancy for us obstinately to close our eyes to the needs of the situation, and refuse admission to the thought that evil can overtake us. If we are to deserve security, and make good our claims to sensible, patriotic Americanism, we will carefully and dutifully take our bearings, and discover, if we can, how far wind and tide have carried us away from safe waters.

If we find that the wickedness of destructive agitators and the selfish depravity of demagogues have stirred up discontent and strife where there should be peace and harmony, and have arrayed against each other interests which should dwell together in hearty cooperation; if we find that the old standards of sturdy, uncompromising American honesty have become so corroded and weakened by a sordid atmosphere that our people are hardly startled by crime in high places and shameful betrayals of trust everywhere; if we find a sadly prevalent disposition among us to turn from the highway of honorable industry into shorter crossroads leading to irresponsible and worthless ease; if we find that widespread wastefulness and extravagance have discredited the wholesome frugality which was once the pride of Americanism, we should recall Washington's admonition that harmony, industry, and frugality are "essential pillars of public felicity," and forthwith endeavor to change our course. …

I protest that I have not spoken in a spirit of pessimism. I have and enjoy my full share of the pride and exultation which our country's material advancement so fully justifies. Its limitless resources, its astonishing growth, its unapproachable industrial development and its irrepressible inventive genius have made it the wonder of the centuries.

Nevertheless, these things do not complete the story of a people truly great. Our country is infinitely more than a domain affording to those who dwell upon it immense material advantages and opportunities. In such a country we live. But I love to think of a glorious nation built upon the will of free men, set apart for the propagation and cultivation of humanity's best ideal of a free government, and made ready for the growth and fruitage of the highest aspirations of patriotism. This is the country that lives in us. I indulge in no mere figure of speech when I say that our nation—the immortal spirit of our domain, lives in us—in our hearts, and minds, and consciences. There it must find its nutriment or die. This thought more than any other presents to our minds the impressiveness and responsibility of American citizenship. The land we live in seems to be strong and active. But how fares the land that lives in us? Are we sure that we are doing all we ought to keep it in vigor and health? Are we keeping its roots well surrounded by the fertile soil of loving allegiance, and are we furnishing them the invigorating moisture of unselfish fidelity? Are we as diligent as we ought to be to protect this precious growth against the poison that must arise from the decay of harmony and honesty and industry and frugality; and are we sufficiently watchful against the deadly, burrowing pests of consuming greed and cankerous cupidity? Our answers to these questions make up the account of our stewardship as keepers of a sacred trust. …

ALBERT VON TILZER AND JACK NORWORTH

Take Me Out to the Ball Game

In the 1989 film, *Field of Dreams*, actor James Earl Jones, portraying the character Terence Mann, explained baseball's prominence in American life thusly:

"The one constant through all the years has been baseball. America has rolled by like an army of steamrollers. It has been erased like a blackboard, rebuilt, and erased again. But baseball has marked the time. This field, this game, is a part of our past. It reminds us of all that once was good, and that could be again."

Known as the national anthem of the national pastime, "Take Me Out to the Ball Game" was written in 1908 by Albert Von Tilzer (who had never been to a baseball game) and Jack Norworth, two veteran songwriters and lyricists who were responsible for some of the most popular songs of their day. The chorus of "Take Me Out to the Ball Game" is usually sung during "the seventh inning stretch."

Katie Casey was baseball mad,
Had the fever and had it bad;
Just to root for the hometown crew,
Ev'ry sou, Katie blew.
On a Saturday, her young beau
Called to see if she'd like to go,
To see a show but Miss Kate said, "No,
I'll tell you what you can do":

Chorus:
    Take me out to the ball game,
    Take me out with the crowd
    Buy me some peanuts and crackerjack,
    I don't care if I never get back,
    Let me root, root, root for the home team,
    If they don't win it's a shame
    For it's one, two, three strikes you're out,
    At the old ball game.

Katie Casey saw all the games,
Knew the players by their first names;
Told the umpire he was wrong,
All along, good and strong.
When the score was just two and two,
Katie Casey knew just what to do,
Just to cheer up the boys she knew,
She made the gang sing this song:

ALICE DUER MILLER

Evolution

Alice Duer Miller (1874-1942) was born in New York City and, in 1899, graduated from Barnard College. A dedicated suffragist, she contributed to the women's rights movement in poetic form. "Evolution" is taken from her 1915 collection, *Are Women People? A Book of Rhymes for Suffrage Times.*

Said Mr. Jones in 1910:
"Women, subject yourselves to men."
Nineteen-Eleven heard him quote:
"They rule the world without the vote."
By Nineteen-Twelve, he would submit
"When all the women wanted it."
By Nineteen-Thirteen, looking glum,
He said that it was bound to come.
This year I heard him say with pride:
"No reasons on the other side!"
By Nineteen-Fifteen, he'll insist
He's always been a suffragist.
And what is really stranger, too,
He'll think that what he says is true.

Suffragettes keeping warm beside a bonfire while protesting along the north fenceline of the White House during the winter of 1917-18.

MARGARET SANGER

Woman and the New Race

No woman can call herself free who does not own and control her body. No woman can call herself free until she can choose consciously whether she will or will not be a mother.

Margaret Sanger (1879-1966), the co-founder of what became Planned Parenthood, was born the sixth of eleven children in Corning, New York. She worked as a nurse in the poor neighborhoods of New York City, where she was exposed to women suffering the effects of self-induced abortions. Believing that women should have options other than pregnancy or abstinence, she started writing a column for the *New York Call* entitled, "What Every Girl Should Know." She also caused scandal and risked imprisonment by acting in defiance of the Comstock Law of 1873, which outlawed as obscene the dissemination of contraceptive information and devices. In 1914, she launched *The Woman Rebel*, a monthly newsletter further promoting contraception. Coining the term "birth control," Sanger argued that women should be able to enjoy sexual relations without fear of unwanted pregnancy. That same year, she was indicted for violating postal obscenity laws, but jumped bail and fled to England under an alias. Sanger returned to the United States in 1915 to face the charges, but the case was dismissed when her five-year-old daughter died suddenly of pneumonia. She then began smuggling diaphragms illegally into the country and, in 1916, opened the nation's first birth control clinic in the Brownsville neighborhood of Brooklyn. When the clinic was raided by police, she served thirty days in jail.

In 1918, the New York Court of Appeals issued a ruling allowing doctors to prescribe contraception. Sanger continued lecturing on birth control and, following World War I, traveled and lectured throughout Asia and Europe. Shortly before Sanger's death, the Supreme Court ruled, in *Griswold v. Connecticut* (1965), that the private use of contraceptives was a constitutional right. In the landmark 1973 case, *Roe v. Wade*, the Supreme Court ruled that a woman may abort her pregnancy at any time for any reason up until the "point at which the fetus becomes viable." This ruling sparked an ongoing debate over what remains the most divisive and hotly contested national issue since slavery.

The following excerpt is from Sanger's 1920 book, *Woman and the New Race*. She also published *The Pivot of Civilization* (1922), *Happiness in Marriage* (1926), and *My Fight For Birth Control* (1931).

The problem of birth control has arisen directly from the effort of the feminine spirit to free itself from bondage. Woman herself has wrought that bondage through her reproductive powers and while enslaving herself has enslaved the world. The physical suffering to be relieved is chiefly woman's. Hers, too, is the love life that dies first under the blight of too prolific breeding. Within her is wrapped up the future of the race—it is hers to make or mar. All of these considerations point unmistakably to one fact—it is woman's duty as well as her privilege to lay hold of the means of freedom. Whatever men may do, she cannot escape the responsibility. For ages she has been deprived of the opportunity to meet this obligation. She is now emerging from her helplessness. Even as no one can share the suffering of the overburdened mother, so no one can do this work for her. Others may help, but she and she alone can free herself.

The basic freedom of the world is woman's freedom.

A free race cannot be born of slave mothers. A woman enchained cannot choose but give a measure of that bondage to her sons and daughters. No woman can call herself free who does not own and control her body. No woman can call herself free until she can choose consciously whether she will or will not be a mother.

It does not greatly alter the case that some women call themselves free because they earn their own livings, while others profess freedom because they defy the conventions of sex relationship. She who earns her own living gains a sort of freedom that is not to be undervalued, but in quality and in quantity it is of little account beside the untrammeled choice of mating or not mating, or being a mother or not being a mother. She gains food and clothing and shelter, at least, without submitting to the charity of her companion, but the earning of her own living does not give her the development of her inner sex urge, far deeper and more powerful in its outworkings than any of these externals. In order to have that development, she must still meet and solve the problem of motherhood.

With the so-called "free" woman, who chooses a mate in defiance of convention, freedom is largely a question of character and audacity. If she does attain to an unrestricted choice of a mate, she is still in a position to be enslaved through her reproductive powers. Indeed, the pressure of law and custom upon the woman not legally married is likely to make her more of a slave than the woman fortunate enough to marry the man of her choice.

Look at it from any standpoint you will, suggest any solution you will, conventional or un- conventional, sanctioned by law or in defiance of law, woman is in the same position, fundamentally, until she is able to determine for herself whether she will be a mother and to fix the number of her offspring. This unavoidable situation is alone enough to make birth control, first of all, a woman's problem. On the very face of the matter, voluntary motherhood is chiefly the concern of the woman.

It is persistently urged, however, that since sex expression is the act of two, the responsibility of controlling the results should not be placed upon woman alone. Is it fair, it is asked, to give her, instead of the man, the task of protecting herself when she is, perhaps, less rugged in physique than her mate, and has, at all events, the normal, periodic inconveniences of her sex?

We must examine this phase of her problem in two lights—that of the ideal, and of the conditions working toward the ideal. In an ideal society, no doubt, birth control would become the concern of the man as well as the woman. The hard, inescapable fact which we encounter to-day is that man has not only refused any such responsibility, but has individually and collectively sought to prevent woman from obtaining knowledge by which she could assume this responsibility for herself. She is still in the position of a dependent to-day because her mate has refused to consider her as an individual apart from his needs. She is still bound because she has in the past left the solution of the problem to him. Having left it to him, she finds that instead of rights, she has only such privileges as she has gained by petitioning, coaxing and cozening. Having left it to him, she is exploited, driven and enslaved to his desires.

While it is true that he suffers many evils as the consequence of this situation, she suffers vastly more. While it is true that he should be awakened to the cause of these evils, we know that they come home to her with crushing force every day. It is she who has the long burden of carrying, bearing and rearing the unwanted children. It is she who must watch beside the beds of pain where lie the babies who suffer because they have come into overcrowded homes. It is her heart that the sight of the deformed, the subnormal, the undernourished, the overworked child smites first and oftenest and hardest. It is her love life that dies first in the fear of undesired pregnancy. It is her opportunity for self expression that perishes first and most hopelessly because of it.

Conditions, rather than theories, facts, rather than dreams, govern the problem. They place it squarely upon the shoulders of woman. She has learned that whatever the moral responsibility of the man in this direction may be, he does not discharge it. She has learned that, lovable and considerate as the individual husband may be, she has nothing to expect from men in the mass, when they make laws and decree customs. She knows that regardless of what ought to be, the brutal, unavoidable fact is that she will never receive her freedom until she takes it for herself.

Having learned this much, she has yet something more to learn. Women are too much inclined to follow in the footsteps of men, to try to think as men think, to try to solve the general problems of life as men solve them. If after attaining their freedom, women accept conditions in the spheres of government, industry, art, morals and religion as they find them, they will be but taking a leaf out of man's book. The woman is not needed to do man's work. She is not needed to think man's thoughts. She need not fear that the masculine mind, almost universally dominant, will fail to take care of its own. Her mission is not to enhance the masculine spirit, but to express the feminine; hers is not to preserve a man-made world, but to create a human world by the infusion of the feminine element into all of its activities.

Woman must not accept; she must challenge. She must not be awed by that which has been built up around her; she must reverence that within her which struggles for expression. Her eyes must be less upon what is and more clearly upon what should be. She must listen only with a frankly questioning attitude to the dogmatized opinions of man-made society. When she chooses her new, free course of action, it must be in the light of her own opinion—of her own intuition. Only so can she give play to the feminine spirit. Only thus can she free her mate from the bondage which he wrought for himself when he wrought hers. Only thus can she restore to him that of which he robbed himself in restricting her. Only thus can she remake the world. …

Against Prohibition

The way to get rid of a bad law, which means a law obnoxious to large masses of people, is not by trying to keep it alive, but by letting it die a natural death.

Clarence Seward Darrow (1857-1938) was born in Kinsman, Ohio, and studied at Allegheny College in Meadville, Pennsylvania, and the University of Michigan Law School. After apprenticing to a local lawyer, he was admitted to the Ohio bar in 1878. Seeking more interesting cases than those available to a small-town lawyer, Darrow moved to Chicago in 1887 and immediately joined the effort to free anarchists charged with murder in the "Haymarket Riot"—named for Haymarket Square, rally point for striking workers participating in a nationwide campaign for the establishment of an eight-hour workday. Darrow went on to serve as a Chicago city attorney and corporate counsel for the Chicago and North Western Railway. He resigned from the railroad in 1894 in order to defend Eugene V. Debs, leader of the American Railway Union and antagonist in the Pullman Strike, thus establishing his reputation as a union and criminal trial lawyer. He also represented striking United Mine Workers of America in Pennsylvania, the first case in which the federal government intervened as a neutral arbitrator in a labor dispute. Darrow then became involved in several other high-profile cases: He secured the acquittal of William Haywood, co-founder of the Industrial Workers of the World, in the assassination of former Idaho Governor Frank Steunenberg; he defended the McNamara brothers, accused of bombing the *Los Angeles Times* building in 1911; he saved Richard Loeb and Nathan Leopold from a death sentence for the much publicized thrill killing of a young boy; and he won acquittal from an all-white jury for members of an African American family who, acting in self defense, killed a white man who was part of a mob trying to expel them from their home in a white Detroit neighborhood.

Perhaps Darrow's most famous case, as noted earlier in this work, was the 1925 "Scopes Monkey Trial." Darrow and his opponent in the trial, Democratic politician William Jennings Bryan, were two of the most prominent public figures of the early twentieth century. Their contrasting views typified the cultural divide of the 1910s and 1920s. Darrow stood for civil liberties, reason, and modernism. Bryan symbolized rural America, Christian evangelicalism, and traditionalism. These two noted orators opposed each other in another arena as well—the public debate over Prohibition. Bryan, raised in a "dry" family, was a leading advocate of Prohibition. His popular speeches in favor of temperance proved very effective during the campaign for passage of the Eighteenth Amendment and the accompanying Volstead Act. Clarence Darrow, on the other hand, was a high-profile opponent of the temperance movement. The following article, "The Ordeal of Prohibition," was published in *American Mercury* magazine in 1924. Darrow's argument against the increasingly unpopular Prohibition contributed to its eventual repeal.

It took many months for the inhabitants of the United States to realize that (at least theoretically) the country had gone dry. The Eighteenth Amendment and the Volstead Act were passed without submission to the people, who had been educated for nearly a century and a half to believe that they were the supreme power in the government of the land. A radical and revolutionary change in policy was made as a war measure, at a time when the great majority of citizens were engrossed in graver matters, and when none but a few zealots considered Prohibition important. While the legislation designed to put it into effect was pending, a large number of our young men were fighting in France and the whole country had its thoughts on the war. It was a favorable time for zealots to do their work.

But all that is now past. By whatever means it was done, and however slight may have been the understanding of the people, the fact is that Prohibition is entrenched today in the fundamental law of the nation, and, what is more important, that there are many men and powerful organizations who feel it to be their duty to enforce it. The impossibility of its complete repeal has only slowly dawned upon the American people. Even to modify the Volstead Act would require a political revolution; to repeal the Eighteenth Amendment is well-nigh inconceivable. Eleven or twelve million voters, properly distributed amongst the States that naturally support Prohibition, will suffice to keep it on the books. But does this mean that it will remain in force forever? Does it mean that millions of people who have no sense of wrong in making, selling or using intoxicating liquors will be subject for all time to drastic penalties and tyrannical judgments?

The question can be best answered by a glance at the history of the methods by which laws have been made and repealed in the past. Against the rash doctrine of the unthinking, so often heard today, that so long as a law is on the books it must and shall be enforced, stands the almost universal experience of mankind. Probably no one who ever actually studied the growth and change of law and understood the true nature of government has ever held that so long as a statute is on the books it should be enforced. All such students know that it is an idle statement, made by men who are ignorant of history, or who are excessively eager to enforce some particular law.

Most laws grow out of the habits and customs of the people. These customs grow into mores and are finally embodied in laws. Long before statutes are passed, the great mass of men have formed their attitudes and ways of living and the statutes are simply codifications of existing folkways. Now and then, however, this natural process is changed. Some active minority, moved by religious zeal, political intolerance or special interest, finds itself able to pass a law that has not originated like the others in the customs and habits of the people. Such laws are often extremely arrogant and oppressive; they violate the conscience, the practice and the beliefs of a large number of the citizens of the state. No better illustration can be found than the body of statutes which shaped and directed the Inquisition. These were laws meant to enforce religious doctrines; they were passed alternately by Catholics and Protestants, depending upon which was in power at the time. During the three or four hundred years of violence and bloodshed that followed, many millions of human beings were directly put to death by execution or indirectly by war, and they comprised many of the best, the most intelligent, and the noblest people of the earth. The reign of terror devastated large portions of Europe and threatened completely to destroy freedom of thought and speech. Very few people in any country today would advocate the revival of any of those fierce and bloody laws. Civilization looks back upon them in amazement and horror. It feels a deep relief that the Inquisition is dead. But it forgets the method by which the laws underlying the Inquisition were got rid of.

It took religious persecution more than a hundreds years to die in Europe. It lingered in some countries long after it was dead in others. It was not disposed of at last by repealing the various civil and canonical laws under which hundreds of thousands had been burned at the stake and tortured in the most horrible ways; it perished through the growth of scientific knowledge and rationalism in the churches and out. ...

Along with these laws, and really a part of them, was the code which punished the crime of witchcraft. This, like the code of the Inquisition, was a part of both the civil and the canonical law. The statutes were numerous and brutal in the extreme. They provided for torture, for burning, and for even more horrible modes of killing. After the death of the witch, his or her estate was confiscated. These cruel and barbarous laws were in effect all over Europe and spread to America; they were in force, at one place or another, for three hundred years. Now and then some judge or ecclesiastic who was more enlightened and humane than the others refused to put witches to death, and so prosecutions would tend to fall off. But at some subsequent time they would be resumed again by a sudden flaming of religious fanaticism. Joan of Arc was one of the noblest victims of fanaticism. Would our modern Prohibitions have approved of her death on the ground that the law was on the books? Would they have solemnly mouthed the foolish phrase that "the best way to get rid of a bad law is to enforce it?"...

The long code of laws in America which have passed into history under the name of the Blue Laws furnish another illustration of the way in which fanaticism burdens the statute-books with oppressive legislation, and also of the way in which the common sense of the people finally disposes of it. It would be hard to find a variety of conduct that the Blue Laws did not attempt to regulate or any expression of pleasure that was not frowned upon or forbidden. They forbade women to dress their hair in a way that would attract attention, or to wear ribbons or silks. They forbade attending theatres; all kinds of travel on Sunday, except going to and from church; sleeping in church, not attending church, and the playing of any game of any sort on Sunday. They regulated the diet of the people, and of course regulated it so that they could eat nothing which tasted good or was expensive. They constituted, in brief, a desperate crusade against joy. Their theory was that good people would have pleasures after death, and the less joy they indulged in on earth the more they would get in the hereafter. ...

Politicians, Better Government Associations and Law Enforcement Leagues loudly proclaimed that all these laws must be observed; that so long as they were on the books they must be enforced. They are, however, not enforced today—even though many of them have not been repealed. Theatres were forbidden in Boson, but there were plenty of playhouses in New York and the well-to-do who lived in Boston and believed in enforcing the law went to New York and attended the theatre there, just as they now go to Havana, Canada, Mexico and England for a drink. Later, theatres were built in Boston, at first under the pretense that they were not theatres at all, but only lecture-halls. In them songs were sung and women walked on tight ropes. The people grew bolder and bolder as their natural impulses asserted themselves. The performances were prosecuted, but the juries acquitted them and judges began distinguishing what the law meant until it finally meant nothing.

Most of the other Blue Laws died the same way. The law compelled going to church on Sunday, but many people would not go. The law forbade sleeping in church, but they slept. Women wore ribbons and silks and curled their hair in spite of the law. Children were children, and played on Sunday. Occasionally, after they had been long ignored, under the impetus of a general housecleaning, some of the old statutes were repealed. But many remain on the books today; they are not worth repealing, for they are dead. ...

The history of the past is carried into the present. All of our codes are filled with obsolete laws. The Fugitive Slave Law was never obeyed in the North; it took more than a law to compel a humane white man to send a black man back to slavery. The Sunday laws today in many states of the Union forbid the publication of newspapers, the running of trains and street cars, riding and driving for pleasure, attending moving picture shows, playing any game, the starting out of boats on voyages, or the doing of any work except works of necessity. Nearly all these laws are dead, though they still remain on the books. They are dead because they do not fit the age. They are not now a part of the customs, habits and mores of the people. They could not be enforced ... No one even quotes the foolish statement of General Grant that the "best way to repeal a bad law is to enforce it." No doubt Grant was a good soldier, but he was never suspected of being a philosopher or an historian. The way to get rid of

a bad law, which means a law obnoxious to large masses of people, is not by trying to keep it alive, but by letting it die a natural death. This is the way that society has always followed in dealing with unjust laws. The tax laws are a part of our civil and criminal codes, yet those who shout the loudest for enforcing Prohibition never pretend to obey them. When a man argues that a law must be enforced so long as it is a law, or that the best way to repeal a bad law is to enforce it, he is talking about some law he wants enforced and not about a law that he believes is tyrannical and unjust. ...

It is much easier to pass a new law than to repeal an old one. Legislation which represents special interests or is demanded by organized associations which make a great show of power before law-making bodies is seldom met by strong opposition. The force which demands the law is active and persistent; its insistence leads politicians to believe that a large mass of men is behind it. But when the statute goes into effect it may create serious oppression and violent disorder; it may come into conflict with the desires and prejudices of the majority of the people affected by it. But, once it is on the books, an active minority can easily prevent its repeal. It is only by the steady resistance of the people that it is eventually destroyed.

In spite of the common opinion, this method has always been the ruling one in getting rid of bad laws. It is Nature's way of letting the old die by opposition, neglect and disuse. If it were not in operation there could be no real progress in the law. If history were not replete with illustrations, if philosophy did not plainly show that this must be the method of society's growth, it would be easier to understand the people who so glibly argue that, whatever the cruelty or the hardship, the law must be enforced while it is on the books. A law cannot be taken off the books while it is complacently obeyed. Constant protest is the only manner that history offers the common people of having their way in the making and administration of the law.

All this, of course, does not mean that all laws are or should be habitually violated. The larger part of criminal code represents the ideas of right and wrong of nearly all our people. But the sumptuary laws that regulate individual conduct and custom are never believed in by the great mass of the people. Men, unfortunately, are in the habit of being influenced by aphorisms and catchwords. We continually hear of "Law and Order," as if they always went together and law came first. As a matter of fact, order is the mother of law, and the law which seriously overturns habits and customs does not promote order, but interferes with it instead. The enforcement of an unpopular law by drastic threats, by increasing penalties, by more cruelty, is not the administration of justice; it is tyranny under the form of law. ...

All laws are made, altered and amended in the same way. When a large class does not respect them, but believes them to be tyrannical, unjust or oppressive, they cannot be enforced. It is a popular idea that the majority should rule. But this does not mean that the people should vote on every question affecting human life, and that the majority should then pass penal statutes to make the rest conform. No society can hold together that does not have a broad toleration for minorities. To enforce the obedience of minorities by criminal statute because a mere majority is found to have certain views is tyranny and must result in endless disorder and suffering.

When the advocates of Prohibition urge that all laws must be enforced, they really refer only to the Prohibition laws. They do not refer to the numerous other laws in every State in the Union that have never been enforced. Even the drastic Volstead Act has not prevented and cannot prevent the use of alcoholic beverages. The acreage of grapes has rapidly increased since it was passed and the price gone up with the demand. The government is afraid to interfere with the farmer's cider. The fruit grower is making money. The dandelion is now the national flower. Everyone who wants alcoholic beverages is fast learning how to make them at home. In the old days the housewife's education was not complete unless she had learned how to brew. She lost the art because it became cheaper to buy beer. She has lost the art of making bread in the same way, for she can now buy bread at the store. But she can learn to make bread again, for she has already learned to brew. It is evident that no law can now be passed to prevent her. Even should Congress pass such a law, it would be impossible to find enough Prohibition agents to enforce it, or to get the taxes to pay them. The folly of the attempt must soon convince even the more intelligent Prohibitionists that all this legislation is both a tragedy and a hoax.

A wise ruler studies the customs and habits of his people and tries to fit laws and institutions to their folk ways, knowing perfectly well that any other method will cause violence and evil; he knows that fitting laws to men is like fitting clothes to men. The man comes first and both the laws and the clothes should be fitted to him. Instead of increasing penalties, stimulating cruelty, and redoubling the search for violators, he should take a lesson from Trajan, the Roman Emperor, as shown by his correspondence with Pliny. About the year 112, when the campaign against the Christians was in full sway in the Empire, Pliny, who was the governor of a province, wrote to Trajan for instructions as to how to carry on the prosecutions. The Emperor replied: "Do not go out of your way to look for them."

Temperance advocate Carry A. Nation with her weapons of choice—her Bible and her hatchet. Born Carrie Amelia Moore in Garrard County, Kentucky, Nation got her myth-making last name from her second husband, Dr. David Nation. Her first husband was an alcoholic, which contributed to the dissolution of their marriage and his early death. Due to this experience, Nation became a crusader and leader of the Woman's Christian Temperance Movement. Expressing her viewpoint through vandalism, the six-foot-tall, 175-pound Nation would enter saloons and begin smashing the bar. Nation did not live to see prohibition become the law of the United States, which occurred eight years after her death.

ROBERT FROST

The Road Not Taken, Stopping by Woods on a Snowy Evening, and The Gift Outright

Born in San Francisco, Robert Lee Frost (1874-1963) lived most of his life in New England. He went to high school in Lawrence, Massachusetts, and briefly attended college at Dartmouth and Harvard. Before gaining fame as a poet, he worked as a farmer and schoolteacher, providing the experiences that would serve as themes for many of his greatest works.

The most popular poet of his era, Robert Frost won the Pulitzer Prize for poetry in 1924, 1931, 1937, and 1943. In 1960, he was awarded a gold medal by Congress in recognition of his poetry which "enriched the culture of the United States and the philosophy of the world." His two most famous poems—"The Road Not Taken" (1915) and "Stopping by Woods on a Snowy Evening" (1923)—were, like most of his writings, inspired by New England landscapes and crafted in plain language that made his works easily accessible. "The Gift Outright," representing the climax of Frost's public career, was read by the poet himself at the inauguration of President Kennedy in 1961.

The Road Not Taken

Two roads diverged in a yellow wood,
And sorry I could not travel both
And be one traveler, long I stood
And looked down one as far as I could
To where it bent in the undergrowth;

Then took the other, as just as fair,
And having perhaps the better claim,
Because it was grassy and wanted wear;
Though as for that, the passing there
Had worn them really about the same,

And both that morning equally lay
In leaves no step had trodden black.
Oh, I kept the first for another day!
Yet knowing how way leads on to way,
I doubted if I should ever come back.

I shall be telling this with a sigh
Somewhere ages and ages hence;
Two roads diverged in a wood, and I—
I took the one less traveled by,
And that has made all the difference.

Stopping by Woods on a Snowy Evening

Whose woods these are I think I know.
His house is in the village though;
He will not see me stopping here
To watch his woods fill up with snow.

My little horse must think it queer
To stop without a farmhouse near
Between the woods and frozen lake
The darkest evening of the year.

He gives his harness bells a shake
To ask if there is some mistake.
The only other sound's the sweep
Of easy wind and downy flake.

The woods are lovely, dark and deep,
But I have promises to keep,
And miles to go before I sleep,
And miles to go before I sleep.

The Gift Outright

The land was ours before we were the land's.
She was our land more than a hundred years
Before we were her people. She was ours
In Massachusetts, in Virginia,
But we were England's, still colonials,
Possessing what we still were unpossessed by,
Possessed by what we now no more possessed.
Something we were withholding made us weak
Until we found out that it was ourselves
We were withholding from our land of living,
And forthwith found salvation in surrender.
Such as we were we gave ourselves outright
(The deed of gift was many deeds of war)
To the land vaguely realizing westward,
But still unstoried, artless, unenhanced,
Such as she was, such as she would become.

* * *

Upon entry of the United States into World War I, it became apparent that large expenditures would be needed both to support European allies and to conduct the war activities of the nation. To obtain the necessary funds, the Treasury resorted to borrowing through a series of bond issues. The first four issues were known as liberty loans; the fifth and last was called the victory loan. This 1919 poster by artist Howard Chandler Christy, supporting that fundraising effort, depicts the allegorical female figure of America, standing in front of the American flag and holding a wreath over an "Honor Roll" consisting of last names from different ethnic groups.

The Great War

VACHEL LINDSAY

Abraham Lincoln Walks at Midnight

Born in Springfield, Illinois, Vachel Lindsay (1879-1931) was a failed artist who found success as a poet, publishing his first volume, *General William Booth Enters into Heaven*, in 1913. Believing poems should be performed, not simply read, Lindsay often included stage directions in his works and routinely invited audiences to join in the refrain. Always sympathetic to the plight of the common man, many of Lindsay's poems paid tribute to the leaders he most admired. It was said that "Lincoln was Lindsay's god; William Jennings Bryan one of his prophets."

"Abraham Lincoln Walks at Midnight" was written in 1914 as the Great War was breaking out in Europe.

It is portentous, and a thing of state
That here at midnight, in our little town
A mourning figure walks, and will not rest,
Near the old court-house pacing up and down,

Or by his homestead, or in shadowed yards
He lingers where his children used to play,
Or through the market, on the well-worn stones
He stalks until the dawn-stars burn away.

A bronzed, lank man! His suit of ancient black,
A famous high-top hat and plain worn shawl
Make him the quaint great figure that men love,
The prairie lawyer, master of us all.

He cannot sleep upon his hillside now.
He is among us:—as in times before!
And we who toss and lie awake for long
Breathe deep, and start, to see him pass the door.

His head is bowed. He thinks on men and kings.
Yea, when the sick world cries, how can he sleep?
Too many peasants fight, they know not why,
Too many homesteads in black terror weep.

The sins of all the war-lords burn his heart.
He sees the dreadnaughts scouring every main.
He carries on his shawl-wrapped shoulders now
The bitterness, the folly and the pain.

He cannot rest until a spirit-dawn
Shall come;—the shining hope of Europe free:
The league of sober folk, the Workers' Earth,
Bringing long peace to Cornland, Alp and Sea.

It breaks his heart that kings must murder still,
That all his hours of travail here for men
Seem yet in vain. And who will bring white peace
That he may sleep upon his hill again?

ALFRED BRYAN AND AL PIANTADOSI

I Didn't Raise My Boy to Be a Soldier

Alfred Bryan was a successful lyricist whose works include "Come Josephine in My Flying Machine," "Peg 'o My Heart," and "Daddy, You've Been a Mother to Me." Al Piantadosi, an accomplished songwriter in his own right, played piano in New York saloons and often accompanied traveling vaudeville performers. The two men collaborated to write the most popular song of 1915, "I Didn't Raise My Boy to Be a Soldier," which represented the desire of most Americans to stay out of the war in Europe.

Ten million soldiers to the war have gone,
Who may never return again.
Ten million mothers' hearts must break
For the ones who died in vain.
Head bowed down in sorrow
In her lonely years,
I heard a mother murmur thru' her tears:

Chorus:

    I didn't raise my boy to be a soldier,
    I brought him up to be my pride and joy,
    Who dares to put a musket on his shoulder,
    To shoot some other mother's darling boy?
    Let nations arbitrate their future troubles,
    It's time to lay the sword and gun away,
    There'd be no war today,
    If mothers all would say,
    "I didn't raise my boy to be a soldier."

What victory can cheer a mother's heart,
When she looks at her blighted home?
What victory can bring her back
All she cared to call her own?
Let each mother answer
In the year to be,
Remember that my boy belongs to me!

WOODROW WILSON

War Message to Congress

The world must be made safe for democracy.

In August 1914, World War I—the "Great War," as it was then called—erupted in Europe between the Entente Powers (Britain, France, and Russia) and the Central Powers (Germany and Austria-Hungary). President Woodrow Wilson (1856-1924) expressed the will of the American people, saying, the nation "must be neutral in fact as well as in name...impartial in thought as well as in action." The desire of many Americans for neutrality changed on May 7, 1915, however, when a German submarine sank the Lusitania, a British passenger liner (which was also carrying munitions to be used against German soldiers). More than 1,200 people were killed, including 128 Americans. With many Americans clamoring for vengeance, Wilson opted for diplomacy and secured a German pledge not to attack neutral or passenger ships.

Wilson won a narrow re-election victory in 1916, campaigning on the slogan, "He kept us out of war." The president had hoped to bring the warring sides together and secure a "peace without victory," but Germany, in early 1917, resumed its practice of unrestricted submarine warfare. Shortly thereafter, British agents intercepted a message written by German Foreign Secretary Arthur Zimmerman proposing "an alliance on the following basis with Mexico: That we shall make war together and together make peace. We shall give general financial support, and it is understood that Mexico is to reconquer the lost territory in New Mexico, Texas, and Arizona."

This threat to American sovereignty was the decisive act. On April 2, 1917, President Wilson asked Congress for a formal declaration of war against Germany.

… On the third of February last, I officially laid before you the extraordinary announcement of the Imperial German government that on and after the first day of February it was its purpose to put aside all restraints of law or of humanity and use its submarines to sink every vessel that sought to approach either the ports of Great Britain and Ireland or the western coasts of Europe or any of the ports controlled by the enemies of Germany within the Mediterranean.

That had seemed to be the object of the German submarine warfare earlier in the war, but since April of last year the Imperial government had somewhat restrained the commanders of its undersea craft in conformity with its promise then given to us that passenger boats should not be sunk and that due warning would be given to all other vessels which its submarines might seek to destroy, when no resistance was offered or escape attempted, and care taken that their crews were given at least a fair chance to save their lives in their open boats. The precautions taken were meager and haphazard enough, as was proved in distressing instance after instance in the progress of the cruel and unmanly business, but a certain degree of restraint was observed.

The new policy has swept every restriction aside. Vessels of every kind, whatever their flag, their character, their cargo, their destination, their errand, have been ruthlessly sent to the bottom without warning and without thought of help or mercy for those on board, the vessels of friendly neutrals along with those of belligerents. Even hospital ships and ships carrying relief to the sorely bereaved and stricken people of Belgium, though the latter were provided with safe conduct through the proscribed areas by the German government itself and were distinguished by unmistakable marks of identity, have been sunk with the same reckless lack of compassion or of principle.

I was for a little while unable to believe that such things would in fact be done by any government that had hitherto subscribed to the humane practices of civilized nations. International law had its origin in the attempt to set up some law which would be respected and observed upon the seas, where no nation had right of dominion and where lay the free highways of the world. By painful stage after stage has that law been built up, with meager enough results, indeed, after all was accomplished that could be accomplished, but always with a clear view, at least, of what the heart and conscience of mankind demanded.

This minimum of right the German government has swept aside under the plea of retaliation and necessity and because it had no weapons which it could use at sea except these which it is impossible to employ as it is employing them without throwing to the winds all scruples of humanity or of respect for the understandings that were supposed to underlie the intercourse of the world. I am not now thinking of the loss of property involved, immense and serious as that is, but only of the wanton and wholesale destruction of the lives of noncombatants, men, women, and children, engaged in pursuits which have always, even in the darkest periods of modern history, been deemed innocent and legitimate. Property can be paid for; the lives of peaceful and innocent people cannot be.

The present German submarine warfare against commerce is a warfare against mankind. It is a war against all nations. American ships have been sunk, American lives taken in ways which it has stirred us very deeply to learn of; but the ships and people of other neutral and friendly nations have been sunk and overwhelmed in the waters in the same way. There has been no discrimination. The challenge is to all mankind.

Each nation must decide for itself how it will meet it. The choice we make for ourselves must be made with a moderation of counsel and a temperateness of judgment befitting our character and our motives as a nation. We must put excited feeling away. Our motive will not be revenge or the victorious assertion of the physical might of the nation, but only the vindication of right, of human right, of which we are only a single champion. …

Armed neutrality is ineffectual enough at best; in such circumstances and in the face of such pretensions it is worse than ineffectual: it is likely only to produce what it was meant to prevent; it is practically certain to draw us into the war without either the rights or the effectiveness of belligerents. There is one choice we cannot make, we are incapable of making: we will not choose the path of submission and suffer the most sacred rights of our nation and our people to be ignored or violated. The wrongs against which we now array ourselves are no common wrongs; they cut to the very roots of human life.

With a profound sense of the solemn and even tragical character of the step I am taking and of the grave responsibilities which it involves, but in unhesitating obedience to what I deem my constitutional duty, I advise that the Congress declare the recent course of the Imperial German government to be in fact nothing less than war against the government and people of the United States;

that it formally accept the status of belligerent which has thus been thrust upon it; and that it take immediate steps, not only to put the country in a more thorough state of defense but also to exert all its power and employ all its resources to bring the government of the German Empire to terms and end the war. ...

Our object now, as then, is to vindicate the principles of peace and justice in the life of the world as against selfish and autocratic power and to set up among the really free and self-governed peoples of the world such a concert of purpose and of action as will henceforth ensure the observance of those principles. Neutrality is no longer feasible or desirable where the peace of the world is involved and the freedom of its peoples, and the menace to that peace and freedom lies in the existence of autocratic governments backed by organized force which is controlled wholly by their will, not by the will of their people. We have seen the last of neutrality in such circumstances. We are at the beginning of an age in which it will be insisted that the same standards of conduct and of responsibility for wrong done shall be observed among nations and their governments that are observed among the individual citizens of civilized states.

We have no quarrel with the German people. We have no feeling toward them but one of sympathy and friendship. It was not upon their impulse that their government acted in entering this war. It was not with their previous knowledge or approval. It was a war determined upon as wars used to be determined upon in the old, unhappy days when peoples were nowhere consulted by their rulers and wars were provoked and waged in the interest of dynasties or of little groups of ambitious men who were accustomed to use their fellowmen as pawns and tools. ...

A steadfast concert for peace can never be maintained except by a partnership of democratic nations. No autocratic government could be trusted to keep faith within it or observe its covenants. It must be a league of honor, a partnership of opinion. Intrigue would eat its vitals away; the plottings of inner circles who could plan what they would and render account to no one would be a corruption seated at its very heart. Only free peoples can hold their purpose and their honor steady to a common end and prefer the interests of mankind to any narrow interest of their own. ...

Even in checking these things and trying to extirpate them, we have sought to put the most generous interpretation possible upon them because we knew that their source lay, not in any hostile feeling or purpose of the German people toward us (who were no doubt as ignorant of them as we ourselves were) but only in the selfish designs of a government that did what it pleased and told its people nothing. But they have played their part in serving to convince us at last that that government entertains no real friendship for us and means to act against our peace and security at its convenience. That it means to stir up enemies against us at our very doors the intercepted note to the German minister at Mexico City is eloquent evidence.

We are accepting this challenge of hostile purpose because we know that in such a government, following such methods, we can never have a friend; and that in the presence of its organized power, always lying in wait to accomplish we know not what purpose, there can be no assured security for the democratic governments of the world. We are now about to accept gauge of battle with this natural foe to liberty and shall, if necessary, spend the whole force of the nation to check and nullify its pretensions and its power. We are glad, now that we see the facts with no veil of false pretense about them, to fight thus for the ultimate peace of the world and for the liberation of its peoples, the German peoples included: for the rights of nations great and small and the privilege of men everywhere to choose their way of life and of obedience.

The world must be made safe for democracy. Its peace must be planted upon the tested foundations of political liberty. We have no selfish ends to serve. We desire no conquest, no dominion. We seek no indemnities for ourselves, no material compensation for the sacrifices we shall freely make. We are but one of the champions of the rights of mankind. We shall be satisfied when those rights have been made as secure as the faith and the freedom of nations can make them.

Just because we fight without rancor and without selfish object, seeking nothing for ourselves but what we shall wish to share with all free peoples, we shall, I feel confident, conduct our operations as belligerents without passion and ourselves observe with proud punctilio the principles of right and of fair play we profess to be fighting for. ...

It will be all the easier for us to conduct ourselves as belligerents in a high spirit of right and fairness because we act without animus, not in enmity toward a people or with the desire to bring any injury or disadvantage upon them, but only in armed opposition to an irresponsible government which has thrown aside all considerations of humanity and of right and is running amuck. We are, let me say again, the sincere friends of the German people, and shall desire nothing so much as the early re-establishment of intimate relations of mutual advantage between us—however hard it may be for them, for the time being, to believe that this is spoken from our hearts.

We have borne with their present government through all these bitter months because of that friendship—exercising a patience and forbearance which would otherwise have been impossible. We shall, happily, still have an opportunity to prove that friendship in our daily attitude and actions toward the millions of men and women of German birth and native sympathy who live among us and share our life, and we shall be proud to prove it toward all who are in fact loyal to their neighbors and to the government in the hour of test. They are, most of them, as true and loyal Americans as if they had never known any other fealty or allegiance. They will be prompt to stand with us in rebuking and restraining the few who may be of a different mind and purpose. If there should be disloyalty, it will be dealt with a firm hand of stern repression; but, if it lifts its head at all, it will lift it only here and there and without countenance except from a lawless and malignant few.

It is a distressing and oppressive duty, gentlemen of the Congress, which I have performed in thus addressing you. There are, it may be, many months of fiery trial and sacrifice ahead of us. It is a fearful thing to lead this great peaceful people into war, into the most terrible and disastrous of all wars, civilization itself seeming to be in the balance. But the right is more precious than peace, and we shall fight for the things which we have always carried nearest our hearts—for democracy, for the right of those who submit to authority to have a voice in their own governments, for the rights and liberties of small nations, for a universal dominion of right by such a concert of free peoples as shall bring peace and safety to all nations and make the world itself at last free.

To such a task we can dedicate our lives and our fortunes, everything that we are and everything that we have, with the pride of those who know that the day has come when America is privileged to spend her blood and her might for the principles that gave her birth and happiness and the peace which she has treasured. God helping her, she can do no other.

GEORGE NORRIS

Against the War in Europe

We are going to run the risk of sacrificing millions of our countrymen's lives in order that other countrymen may coin their lifeblood into money.

A leading voice of opposition to American involvement in World War I was Senator George William Norris (1861–1944), Republican from Nebraska. An advocate of progressive and liberal causes, Norris served five terms in the House and five terms in the Senate. Although he supported some of Wilson's programs, Norris became a firm isolationist and expressed concern that monetary interests were manipulating the country into war. He believed that the government wanted to take part in this war only because the wealthy had already aided the British financially and therefore had a stake in the outcome.

Within two months of the conflict's August 1914 beginning, Bethlehem Steel, an arms merchant headed by Charles Schwab, secured orders from the British government for millions of artillery shells and nearly a dozen submarines. Circumventing American neutrality laws by routing goods through Canada, the company's earnings in 1916 alone were more than its combined gross revenues for the previous eight years. The international banking firm of J. P. Morgan in New York loaned the Allies more than $2 billion and served as the official purchasing agent of the British government, reaping millions in profit.

In the face of enormous pressure from the media and the Wilson administration, Norris was one of the few to vote against the declaration of war on Germany. He outlined his objections in the following speech, delivered April 4, 1917.

The short term result of the war was a victory for the Entente Powers. The longer term effects are more difficult to gauge, with unresolved issues contributing to a second global conflict. Millions of Americans were mobilized for the war effort in Europe, with U.S. casualties exceeding 100,000. Despite this sacrifice, there is currently no national memorial to the first generation of Americans to go abroad to defend foreign soil against aggression. The last surviving American veteran of World War I, Frank Woodruff Buckles, passed away on February 27, 2011, at the age of 110 years, lamenting this very fact.

... No close student of recent history will deny that both Great Britain and Germany have, on numerous occasions since the beginning of the war, flagrantly violated in the most serious manner the rights of neutral vessels and neutral nations under existing international law as recognized up to the beginning of this war by the civilized world.

The reason given by the President in asking Congress to declare war against Germany is that the German Government has declared certain war zones, within which, by the use of submarines, she sinks, without notice, American ships and destroys American lives.

Let us trace briefly the origin and history of these so-called war zones. The first war zone was declared by Great Britain. She gave us and the world notice of it on the 4th day of November, 1914. The zone became effective November 5, 1914, the next day after the notice was given. This zone so declared by Great Britain covered the whole of the North Sea. The order establishing it sought to close the north of Scotland route around the British Isles to

Denmark, Holland, Norway, Sweden, and the Baltic Sea. The decree of establishment drew an arbitrary line from the Hebrides Islands along the Scottish coast to Iceland, and warned neutral shipping that it would cross those lines at its peril, and ordered that ships might go to Holland and other neutral nations by taking the English Channel route through the Strait of Dover.

The first German war zone was declared on the 4th day of February, 1915, just three months after the British war zone was declared. Germany gave 15 days' notice of the establishment of her zone, which became effective on the 18th day of February, 1915. The German war zone covered the English Channel and the high sea waters around the British Isles. It sought to close the English Channel route around the British Isles to Holland, Norway, Sweden, Denmark, and the Baltic Sea. The German war zone decreed that neutral vessels would be exposed to danger in the English Channel route, but that the route around the north of Scotland and in the eastern part of the North

Sea, in a strip 30 miles wide along the Dutch coast, would be free from danger. It will thus be seen that the British Government declared the north of Scotland route into the Baltic Sea as dangerous and the English Channel route into the Baltic Sea as safe.

The German Government in its order did exactly the reverse. It declared the north of Scotland route into the Baltic Sea as safe and the English Channel route into the Baltic Sea as dangerous. …

Thus we have the two declarations of the two Governments, each declaring a military zone and warning neutral shipping from going into the prohibited area. England sought to make her order effective by the use of submerged mines. Germany sought to make her order effective by the use of submarines. Both of these orders were illegal and contrary to all international law as well as the principles of humanity. Under international law no belligerent Government has the right to place submerged mines in the high seas. Neither has it any right to take human life without notice by the use of submarines. If there is any difference on the ground of humanity between these two instrumentalities, it is certainly in favor of the submarines. The submarine can exercise some degree of discretion and judgment. The submerged mine always destroys without notice, friend and foe alike, guilty and innocent the same. In carrying out these two policies, both Great Britain and Germany have sunk American ships and destroyed American lives without provocation and without notice. There have been more ships sunk and more American lives lost from the action of submarines than from English mines in the North Sea: for the simple reason that we finally acquiesced in the British war zone and kept our ships out of it, while in the German war zone we have refused to recognize its legality and have not kept either our ships or our citizens out of its area. If American ships had gone into the British war zone in defiance of Great Britain's order, as they have gone into the German war zone in defiance of the German Governments order, there would have been many more American lives lost and many more American ships sunk by the instrumentality of the mines than the instrumentality of the submarines.

A Neutral America?

… There are a great many American citizens who feel that we owe it as a duty to humanity to take part in this war. Many instances of cruelty and inhumanity can be found on both sides. Men are often biased in their judgment on account of their sympathy and their interests. To my mind, what we ought to have maintained from the beginning was the strictest neutrality. If we had done this I do not believe we would have been on the verge of war at the present time. We had a right as a nation, if we desired, to cease at any time to be neutral. We had a technical right to respect the English war zone and to disregard the German war zone, but we could not do that and be neutral. I have no quarrel to find with the man who does not desire our country to remain neutral. While many such people are moved by selfish motives and hopes of gain, I have no doubt but that in a great many instances, through what I believe to be a misunderstanding of the real condition, there are many honest, patriotic citizens who think we ought to engage in this war and who are behind the President in his demand that we should declare war against Germany. I think such people err in judgment and to a great extent have been misled as to the real history and the true facts by the almost unanimous demand of the great combination of wealth that has a direct financial interest in our participation in the war. We have loaned many hundreds of millions of dollars to the allies in this controversy. While such action was legal and countenanced by international law, there is no doubt in my mind but the enormous amount of money loaned to the allies in this country has been instrumental in bringing about a public sentiment in favor of our country taking a course that would make every bond worth a hundred cents on the dollar and making the payment of every debt certain and sure. Through this instrumentality and also through the instrumentality of others who have not only made millions out of the war in the manufacture of munitions, etc., and who would expect to make millions more if our country can be drawn into the catastrophe, a large number of the great newspapers and news agencies of the country have been controlled and enlisted in the greatest propaganda that the world has ever known, to manufacture sentiment in favor of war. It is now demanded that the American citizens shall be used as insurance policies to guarantee the safe delivery of munitions of war to belligerent nations. The enormous profits of munition manufacturers, stockbrokers, and bond dealers must be still further increased by our entrance into the war. This has brought us to the present moment, when Congress, urged by the President and backed by the artificial sentiment, is about to declare war and engulf our country in the greatest holocaust that the world has ever known. …

"The troubles of Europe ought to be settled by Europe,

and … we ought to … permit them to settle their questions without our interference."

To whom does war bring prosperity? Not to the soldier who for the munificent compensation of $16 per month shoulders his musket and goes into the trench, there to shed his blood and to die if necessary; not to the broken-hearted widow who waits for the return of the mangled body of her husband; not to the mother who weeps at the death of her brave boy; not to the little children who shiver with cold; not to the babe who suffers from hunger; nor to the millions of mothers and daughters who carry broken hearts to their graves. War brings no prosperity to the great mass of common and patriotic citizens. It increases the cost of living of those who toil and those who already must strain every effort to keep soul and body together. War brings prosperity to the stock gambler on Wall Street—to those who are already in possession of more wealth than can be realized or enjoyed. …

Their object in having war and in preparing for war is to make money. Human suffering and the sacrifice of human life are necessary, but Wall Street considers only the dollars and the cents. The men who do the fighting, the people who make the sacrifices, are the ones who will not be counted in the measure of this great prosperity…. The stock brokers would not, of course, go to war, because the very object they have in bringing on the war is profit, and therefore they must remain in their Wall Street offices in order to share in that great prosperity which they say war will bring. The volunteer officer, even the drafting officer, will not find them. They will be concealed in their palatial offices on Wall Street, sitting behind mahogany desks, covered up with clipped coupons—coupons soiled with the sweat of honest toil, coupons stained with mothers' tears, coupons dyed in the lifeblood of their fellow men.

We are taking a step today that is fraught with untold danger. We are going into war upon the command of gold. We are going to run the risk of sacrificing millions of our countrymen's lives in order that other countrymen may coin their lifeblood into money. And even if we do not cross the Atlantic and go into the trenches, we are going to pile up a debt that the toiling masses that shall come many generations after us will have to pay. Unborn millions will bend their backs in toil in order to pay for the terrible step we are now about to take. We are about to do the bidding of wealth's terrible mandate. By our act we will make millions of our countrymen suffer, and the consequences of

it may well be that millions of our brethren must shed their lifeblood, millions of broken-hearted women must weep, millions of children must suffer with cold, and millions of babes must die from hunger, and all because we want to preserve the commercial right of American citizens to deliver munitions of war to belligerent nations. …

A Dollar Sign on the Flag

I know that I am powerless to stop it. I know that this war madness has taken possession of the financial and political powers of our country. I know that nothing I can say will stay the blow that is soon to fall. I feel that we are committing a sin against humanity and against our countrymen. I would like to say to this war god, "You shall not coin into gold the lifeblood of my brethren." I would like to prevent this terrible catastrophe from falling upon my people. I would be willing to surrender my own life if I could cause this awful cup to pass. I charge no man here with a wrong motive, but it seems to me that this war craze has robbed us of our judgment. I wish we might delay our action until reason could again be enthroned in the brain of man. I feel that we are about to put the dollar sign upon the American flag.

I have no sympathy with the military spirit that dominates the Kaiser and his advisers. I do not believe that they represent the heart of the great German people. I have no more sympathy with the submarine policy of Germany than I have with the mine-laying policy of England. I have heard with rejoicing of the overthrow of the Czar of Russia and the movement in that great country toward the establishment of a government where the common people will have their rights, liberty, and freedom respected. I hope and pray that a similar revolution may take place in Germany, that the Kaiser may be overthrown, and that on the ruins of his military despotism may be established a German republic, where the great German people may work out their world destiny. The working out of that problem is not an American burden. We ought to remember the advice of the Father of our Country and keep out of entangling alliances. Let Europe solve her problems as we have solved ours. Let Europe bear her burdens as we have borne ours. In the greatest war of our history and at the time it occurred, the greatest war in the world's history, we were engaged in solving an American problem. We settled the question of human slavery and washed our flag clean by the sacrifice of human blood. It was a great problem and a great burden, but we solved it ourselves. Never once did we think of asking Europe to take part in its solution. Never once did any European nation undertake to settle the great question. We solved it, and history has rendered a unanimous verdict that we solved it right. The troubles of Europe ought to be settled by Europe, and wherever our sympathies may lie, disagreeing as we do, we ought to remain absolutely neutral and permit them to settle their questions without our interference. We are now the greatest neutral nation. Upon the passage of this resolution we will have joined Europe in the great catastrophe and taken America into entanglements that will not end with this war, but will live and bring their evil influences upon many generations yet unborn.

ROBERT M. LA FOLLETTE, SR.

Free Speech in Wartime

If every preparation for war can be made the excuse for destroying free speech and a free press and the right of the people to assemble together for peaceful discussion, then we may well despair of ever again finding ourselves for a long period in a state of peace.

From the American Revolution forward, Americans of all varieties have objected to war. World War II and the military response to the attacks of September 11, 2001, were less controversial because of the initial attacks on the homeland, but even those conflicts had their conscientious objectors. Presidents Madison in 1812, Polk in 1846 and McKinley in 1898 all made the case that America's interests were being threatened, if not her actual soil. The case for war was a harder sell in 1917, as many Americans believed that the conflict in Europe, characterized by bloody trench warfare and the introduction of deadly chemical agents, was none of their business.

Another prominent critic of America's involvement in World War I was Senator Robert Marion La Follette, Sr. (1855-1925), Republican from Wisconsin. A former member of the U.S. House of Representatives and governor of the State of Wisconsin, La Follette resolutely opposed America's entry into World War I and thereafter opposed military conscription, the Espionage Act of 1917, President Wilson's efforts to finance the war, and the prosecution of Eugene V. Debs and others for their opposition to the war.

La Follette introduced a resolution calling on the Wilson administration to "declare definitely its strategic goals, to condemn the continuation of the war for the purposes of territorial annexation, and to demand that the Allies restate their peace terms immediately." Amidst calls for his arrest on espionage charges and petitions for his expulsion from the Senate, La Follette remained resolute. On October 6, 1917, he took to the Senate floor to defend the right of free speech for all "honest and law-abiding citizens of this country." His remarks, excerpted here, lasted three hours and included numerous citations from constitutional scholars and distinguished statesmen.

After the war, charges against La Follette were dismissed and he was awarded compensation for legal expenses incurred as a result of the investigation into his activities. La Follette ran for president of the United States as the nominee of his own Progressive Party in 1924, carrying Wisconsin and 17 percent of the overall national popular vote while coming in third behind incumbent President Calvin Coolidge and Democratic candidate John W. Davis. This represents the third highest showing for a third party candidate since the Civil War, surpassed only by Theodore Roosevelt's 27 percent in 1912 and Ross Perot's 19 percent in 1992.

… Six members of the Senate and 50 members of the House voted against the declaration of war. Immediately there was let loose upon those Senators and Representatives a flood of invective and abuse from newspapers and individuals who had been clamoring for war, unequaled, I believe, in the history of civilized society.

Prior to the declaration of war every man who had ventured to oppose our entrance into it had been condemned as a coward or worse, and even the President had by no means been immune from these attacks.

Since the declaration of war the triumphant war press has pursued those Senators and Representations who voted against war with malicious falsehood and recklessly libelous attacks, going to the extreme limit of charging them with treason against their country.

This campaign of libel and character assassination directed against the members of Congress who opposed our entrance into the war has been continued down to the present hour, and I have upon my desk newspaper clippings, some of them libels upon me alone, some directed as well against other Senators who voted in opposition to the declaration of war.

One of these newspaper reports most widely circulated represents a Federal judge in the State of Texas as saying, in a charge to a grand jury—I read the article as it appeared in the newspaper and the headline with which it is introduced:

DISTRICT JUDGE WOULD LIKE TO TAKE SHOT AT TRAITORS IN CONGRESS

(By Associated Press leased wire)

Houston, Texas. October 1, 1917

Judge Waller T. Burns, of the United States district court, in charging a Federal grand jury at the beginning of the October term today, after calling by name Senators STONE of Missouri, HARDWICK of Georgia, VARDAMAN of Mississippi, GRONNA of North Dakota, GORE of Oklahoma, and LAFOLLETTE of Wisconsin, said:

"If I had a wish, I would wish that you men had jurisdiction to return bills of indictment against these men. They ought to be tried promptly and fairly, and I believe this court could administer the law fairly; but I have a conviction, as strong as life, that this country should stand them up against an adobe wall tomorrow and give them what they deserve. If any man deserves death, it is a traitor. I wish that I could pay for the ammunition. I would like to attend the execution, and if I were in the firing squad I would not want to be the marksman who had the blank shell."

… If this newspaper clipping were a single or exceptional instance of lawless defamation, I should not trouble the Senate with a reference to it. But, Mr. President, it is not. …

I am aware, Mr. President, that in pursuance of this general campaign of vilification and attempted intimidation, requests from various individuals and certain organizations

have been submitted to the Senate for my expulsion from this body, and that such requests have been referred to and considered by one of the committees of the Senate.

If I alone had been made the victim of these attacks, I should not take one moment of the Senate's time for their consideration, and I believe that other Senators who have been unjustly and unfairly assailed, as I have been, hold the same attitude upon this that I do. Neither the clamor of the mob nor the voice of power will ever turn me by the breadth of a hair from the course I mark out for myself, guided by such knowledge as I can obtain and controlled and directed by a solemn conviction of right and duty.

But, sir, it is not alone members of Congress that the war party in this country has sought to intimidate. The mandate seems to have gone forth to the sovereign people of this country that they must be silent while those things are being done by their Government which most vitally concern their well-being, their happiness, and their lives. Today and for weeks past honest and law-abiding citizens of this country are being terrorized and outraged in their rights by those sworn to uphold the laws and protect the rights of the people. I have in my possession numerous affidavits establishing the fact that people are being unlawfully arrested, thrown into jail, held incommunicado for days, only to be eventually discharged without ever having been taken into court, because they have committed no crime. Private residences are being invaded, loyal citizens of undoubted integrity and probity arrested, cross-examined, and the most sacred constitutional rights guaranteed to every American citizen are being violated.

It appears to be the purpose of those conducting this campaign to throw the country into a state of terror, to coerce public opinion, to stifle criticism, and suppress discussion of the great issues involved in this war.

I think all men recognize that in time of war the citizen must surrender some rights for the common good which he is entitled to enjoy in time of peace. But sir, the right to control their own Government according to constitutional forms is not one of the rights that the citizens of this country are called upon to surrender in time of war.

Rather in time of war the citizen must be more alert to the preservation of his right to control his Government. He must be most watchful of the encroachment of the military upon the civil power. He must beware of those precedents in support of arbitrary action by administrative officials, which excused on the plea of necessity in war time, become the fixed rule when the necessity has passed and normal conditions have been restored.

More than all, the citizen and his representative in Congress in time of war must maintain his right of free speech. More than in times of peace it is necessary that the channels for free public discussion of governmental policies shall be open and unclogged. I believe, Mr. President, that I am now touching upon the most important question in this country today—and that is the right of the citizens of this country and their representatives in Congress to discuss in an orderly way frankly and publicly and without fear, from the platform and through the press, every important phase of this war; its causes, the manner in which it should be conducted, and the terms upon which peace should be made. The belief which is becoming wide spread in this land that this most fundamental right is being denied to the citizens of this country is a fact the tremendous significance of which, those in authority have not yet begun to appreciate. I am contending, Mr. President, for the great fundamental right of the sovereign people of this country to make their voice heard and have that voice heeded upon the great questions arising out of this war, including not only how the war shall be prosecuted but the conditions upon which it may be terminated with a due regard for the rights and the honor of this Nation and the interests of humanity.

I am contending for this right because the exercise of it is necessary to the welfare, to the existence of this Government, to the successful conduct of this war, and to a peace which shall be enduring and for the best interest of this country. ...

I say without fear of contradiction that there has never been a time for more than a century and a half when the right of free speech and free press and the right of the people to peaceably assemble for public discussion have been so violated among English-speaking people as they are violated today throughout the United States. Today, in the land we have been wont to call the free United States, governors, mayors, and policemen are preventing or breaking up peaceable meetings called to discuss the questions growing out of this war, and judges and courts, with some notable and worthy exceptions, are failing to protect the citizens in their rights.

It is no answer to say that when the war is over the citizen may once more resume his rights and feel some security in his liberty and his person. As I have already tried to point out, now is precisely the time when the country needs the counsel of all its citizens. In time of war even more than in time of peace, whether citizens happen to agree with the ruling administration or not, these precious fundamental personal rights—free speech, free press, and right of assemblage so explicitly and emphatically guaranteed by the Constitution should be maintained inviolable. There is no rebellion in the land, no martial law, no courts are closed, no legal processes suspended, and there is no threat even of invasion.

But more than this, if every preparation for war can be made the excuse for destroying free speech and a free press and the right of the people to assemble together for peaceful discussion, then we may well despair of ever again finding ourselves for a long period in a state of peace. With the possessions we already have in remote parts of the world, with the obligations we seem almost certain to assume as a result of the present war, a war can be made any time overnight and the destruction of personal rights now occurring will be pointed to then as precedents for a still further invasion of the rights of the citizen. This is the road which all free governments have heretofore traveled to their destruction, and how far we have progressed along it is shown when we compare the standard of liberty of Lincoln, Clay, and Webster with the standard of the present day....

Since the Constitution vests in Congress the supreme power to determine when and for what purposes the country will engage in war and the objects to attain which the war will be prosecuted, it seems to me to be an evasion of a solemn duty on the part of the Congress not to exercise that power at this critical time in the Nation's affairs. The Congress can no more avoid its responsibility in this matter than it can in any other. As the Nation's purposes in conducting this war are of supreme importance to the country, it is the supreme duty of Congress to exercise the function conferred upon it by the Constitution of guiding the foreign policy of the Nation in the present crisis....

We have been six months at war. We have incurred financial obligation and made expenditures of money in amounts already so large that the human mind can not comprehend them. The Government has drafted from the peaceful occupations of civil life a million of our finest young men—and more will be taken if necessary—to be transported 4,000 miles over the sea, with their equipment and supplies, to the trenches of Europe.

The first chill winds of autumn remind us that another winter is at hand. The imagination is paralyzed at the thought of the human misery, the indescribable suffering, which the winter months, with their cold and sleet and ice and snow, must bring to the war-swept lands, not alone to the soldiers at the front but to the noncombatants at home.

To such excesses of cruelty has this war descended that each nation is now, as a part of its strategy, planning to starve the women and children of the enemy countries. Each warring nation is carrying out the unspeakable plan of starving noncombatants. Each nurses the hope that it may break the spirit of the men of the enemy country at the front by starving the wives and babes at home, and woe be it that we have become partners in this awful business and are even cutting off food shipments from neutral countries in order to force them to help starve women and children of the country against whom we have declared war.

There may be some necessity overpowering enough to justify these things, but the people of America should demand to know what results are expected to satisfy the sacrifice of all that civilization holds dear upon the bloody altar of a conflict which employs such desperate methods of warfare. ...

CAMPAIGN SHOULD BE MADE ON CONSTITUTIONAL LINES

And, sir, this is the ground on which I stand. I maintain that Congress has the right and the duty to declare the objects of the war and the people have the right and the obligation to discuss it.

American citizens may hold all shades of opinion as to the war; one citizen may glory in it, another may deplore it, each has the same right to voice his judgment. An American citizen may think and say that we are not justified in prosecuting this war for the purpose of dictating the form of government which shall be maintained by our enemy or our ally, and not be subject to punishment at law. He may pray aloud that our boys shall not be sent to fight and die on European battle fields for the annexation of territory or the maintenance of trade agreements and be within his legal rights. He may express the hope that an early peace may be secured on the terms set forth by the new Russia and by President Wilson in his speech of January 22, 1917, and he can not lawfully be sent to jail for the expression of his convictions.

It is the citizen's duty to obey the law until it is repealed or declared unconstitutional. But he has the inalienable right to fight what he deems an obnoxious law or a wrong policy in the courts and at the ballot box.

It is the suppressed emotion of the masses that breeds revolution.

If the American people are to carry on this great war, if public opinion is to be enlightened and intelligent, there must be free discussion. ...

Permit me, sir, this word in conclusion. It is said by many persons for whose opinions I have profound respect and whose motives I know to be sincere that "we are in this war and must go through to the end." That is true. But it is not true that we must go through to the end to accomplish an undisclosed purpose, or to reach an unknown goal. ...

Shall we ask the people of this country to shut their eyes and take the entire war program on faith? There are no doubt many honest and well-meaning persons who are willing to answer that question in the affirmative rather than risk the dissensions which they fear may follow a free discussion of the issues of this war. With that position I do not—I can not agree. Have the people no intelligent contribution to make to the solution of the problems of this war? I believe that they have, and that in this matter, as in so many others, they may be wiser than their leaders, and that if left free to discuss the issues of the war they will find the correct settlement of these issues.

But it is said that Germany will fight with greater determination if her people believe that we are not in perfect agreement. Mr. President, that is the same worn-out pretext which has been used for three years to keep the plain people of Europe engaged in killing each other in this war. And, sir, as applied to this country, at least, it is a pretext with nothing to support it.

The way to paralyze the German arm, to weaken the German military force, in my opinion, is to declare our objects in this war, and show by that declaration to the German people that we are not seeking to dictate a form of government to Germany or to render more secure England's domination of the seas.

A declaration of our purposes in this war, so far from strengthening our enemy, I believe would immeasurably weaken her, for it would no longer be possible to misrepresent our purposes to the German people. Such a course on our part, so far from endangering the life of a single one of our boys, I believe would result in saving the lives of hundreds of thousands of them by bringing about an earlier and more lasting peace by intelligent negotiation, instead of securing a peace by the complete exhaustion of one or the other of the belligerents.

Such a course would also immeasurably, I believe, strengthen our military force in this country, because when the objects of this war are clearly stated and the people approve of those objects they will give to the war a popular support it will never otherwise receive. ...

General John "Black Jack" Pershing, the American commander in Europe during WWI, arrives in France with the first American soldiers sent to fight after the United States declared war on Germany.

JOYCE KILMER

Trees

Born in New Brunswick, New Jersey, Alfred Joyce Kilmer (1886-1918) published his first volume of poetry, *Summer of Love*, in 1911. "Trees," the work for which he is remembered, first appeared in *Poetry Magazine* in 1913 and was the title poem in his 1914 collection, *Trees and Other Poems*.

Often referred to as the "rainbow poet," Kilmer served in World War I as a member of the famed Rainbow Division. He was killed in action at the second Battle of the Marne and was posthumously awarded the Croix de Guerre, a French medal for bravery.

I think that I shall never see
A poem lovely as a tree.

A tree whose hungry mouth is prest
Against the earth's sweet flowing breast;

A tree that looks at God all day,
And lifts her leafy arms to pray;

A tree that may in Summer wear
A nest of robins in her hair;

Upon whose bosom snow has lain;
Who intimately lives with rain.

Poems are made by fools like me,
But only God can make a tree.

HUBBARD PARKER

Old Flag

Little is known of Hubbard Parker, but his poem "Old Flag" endures as a fitting legacy. Anthologized in a 1918 collection of patriotic writing, "Old Flag" was written as America entered the First World War.

What shall I say to you, Old Flag?
You are so grand in every fold,
So linked with mighty deeds of old,
So steeped in blood where heroes fell,
So torn and pierced by shot and shell,
So calm, so still, so firm, so true,
My throat swells at the sight of you,
Old Flag.

What of the men who lifted you, Old Flag,
Upon the top of Bunker's Hill;
Who crushed the Briton's cruel will,
'Mid shock and roar and crash and scream;
Who crossed the Delaware's frozen stream,
Who starved, who fought, who bled, who died,
That you might float in glorious pride,
Old Flag?

What of the women brave and true, Old Flag,
Who, while the cannon thundered wild,
Sent forth a husband, lover, child;
Who labored in the field by day;
Who, all the night long, knelt to pray,
And thought that God great mercy gave,
If only freely you might wave,
Old Flag?

What is your mission now, Old Flag?
What, but to set all people free,
To rid the world of misery,
To guard the right, avenge the wrong,
And gather in one joyful throng
Beneath your folds in close embrace
All burdened ones of every race,
Old Flag?

Right nobly do you lead the way, Old Flag,
Your stars shine out for liberty,
Your white stripes stand for purity,
Your crimson claims that courage high
For Honor's sake to fight and die.
Lead on against the alien shore!
We'll follow you e'en to Death's door,
Old Flag!

A Toast to the Flag

First published in 1917, "A Toast to the Flag" is the work which immortalized John Jay Daly (1888?-1976), a journalist, poet, and author who wrote several books and magazine articles and worked as a newspaper reporter and editor from 1911 until the mid-1940s.

Here's to the Red of it—
There's not a thread of it,
No, nor a shred of it
In all the spread of it
From foot to head,
But heroes bled for it,
Faced steel and lead for it,
Precious blood shed for it,
Bathing in Red!

Here's to the White of it—
Thrilled by the sight of it,
Who knows the right of it
But feels the might of it
Through day and night?
Womanhood's care for it
Made manhood dare for it;
Purity's pray'r for it
Keeps it so White!

Here's to the Blue of it—
Beauteous view of it,
Heavenly hue of it,
Star-spangled dew of it
Constant and true;
Diadems gleam for it,
States stand supreme for it,
Liberty's beam for it
Brightens the Blue!

Here's to the Whole of it—
Stars, stripes and pole of it,
Body and soul of it,
O, and the roll of it,
Sun shining through;
Hearts in accord for it
Swear by the sword for it,
Thanking the Lord for it,
Red, White and Blue!

Women making Browning machine guns at the Winchester Repeating Arms Company in New Haven, Connecticut. Prior to the outbreak of world war, a woman's role in the workplace was restricted mainly to domestic labor and such professions as nursing and teaching. The Great War forever changed the role of women in the workplace. As more and more young men volunteered or were conscripted into the armed forces, women were called upon to fill their roles in the factories, mines, and many other roles traditionally carried out by men.

ADRIAN EDWARDS

Letter to His Mother

Life is not the highest boon of existence.

Adrian Edwards, a lawyer from Carrollton, Illinois, volunteered for duty in World War I. In early May 1918, he wrote the following letter to his mother to be delivered in the event of his death. Tragically, Edwards was killed in battle only days later, making his sacrifice upon what Abraham Lincoln called "the altar of freedom."

My dear Mother:

I am about to go into battle and have instructed the company clerk to send you this letter in case I become a casualty, hence the receipt of this letter by you will indicate that I am either with God or a prisoner in the hands of the enemy.

Since I will never become a prisoner of the foe if I remain conscious and able to fight, it is doubtful if I will ever be an inmate of a German prison camp.

Do not grieve that I am among the missing, but rather rejoice that you have given a son in sacrifice to make the greatest military caste of all time lay down the sword— to save civilization, to prevent future wars, to punish the Germans, who have disregarded every law of God and mankind, whose only god is the god of war and military force—and to make the world safe for democracy.

I desire that you view the matter in the light and spirit of the Spartan mothers of old, who, when their sons went forth to battle for freedom and their native land, said to their sons: "Either come home proudly bearing your shield before you, or upon it."

War was absolutely necessary on the part of my country, and although I was thirty-four years old and nobody expected me to go, yet some one had to go; some one must make the sacrifice, some mother must lose her son.

In the light of these facts, and knowing our country's great need, I volunteered, and have never for one moment regretted my decision, and I will not, although my life and a useful career must end. Life is not the highest boon of existence. There are ideals that are superhuman, interests greater than life itself, for which it is worth while fighting, suffering, and dying.

If possible after the war, I would like for my remains to be brought to America and interred at White Hall. I have provided well for your support, as I have a $10,000 insurance policy with the Government and several thousand with the old-line companies. My friends, Thompson and Jess, have these policies and other valuable papers.

Good-bye, Mother; I will see you in the next world. You may know I died fighting for you, my country, and all that life holds dear.

Your son
Adrian

ELIAS LIEBERMAN

I Am an American

Every drop of blood in me holds a heritage of patriotism … Every drop of blood in me will keep that vow.

Elias Lieberman (1883-1969) emigrated to the United States from Russia when he was eight years old. Educated in the New York City public schools, he became an English teacher and principal of Thomas Jefferson High School. A noted magazine editor and poet, Lieberman also edited several texts for junior high school students and incorporated many of his own writings into those works, including the following two selections. "I Am an American," Lieberman's most widely disseminated work, first appeared in *Everybody's Weekly* in July 1916.

The Great War in Europe made a strong call for the exercise of American patriotism. And why should not Americans be patriotic? If the German believes that his Fatherland is of more value than life itself; if the Englishman thrills at the thought of the British Empire; if the Irishman knows no country as dear as the Emerald Isle; if the Frenchman's living and dying prayer is, *"Vive la France";* if the Chinaman pities everybody born outside the Flowery Kingdom, and the Japanese give their sole devotion to the Land of the Rising Sun—shall not we, in this land of glorious liberty, have some thought and love of country?

At a meeting of school children in Madison Square Garden, New York City, to celebrate the Fourth of July, one boy, a descendant of native Americans, spoke as follows:

"I am an American. My father belongs to the Sons of the Revolution; my mother, to the Colonial Dames. One of my ancestors pitched tea overboard in Boston Harbor; another stood his ground with Warren; another hungered with Washington at Valley Forge. My forefathers were American in the making: they spoke in her council halls; they died on her battlefields; they commanded her ships; they cleared her forests. Dawns reddened and paled. Stanch hearts of mine beat fast at each new star in the nation's flag. Keen eyes of mine foresaw her greater glory; the sweep of her seas, the plenty of her plains, the man-hives in her billion-wired cities. Every drop of blood in me holds a heritage of patriotism. I am proud of my past. I am an American."

Then a foreign-born boy arose and said:

"I am an American. My father was an atom of dust, my mother was a straw in the wind, to His Serene Majesty. One of my ancestors died in the mines of Siberia; another was crippled for life by twenty blows of the *knout;* another was killed defending his home during the massacres. The history of my ancestors is a trail of blood to the palace-gate of the Great White Czar. But then the dream came—the dream of America. In the light of the Liberty torch the atom of dust became a man and the straw in the wind became a woman for the first time. 'See,' said my father, pointing to the flag that fluttered near, 'that flag of stars and stripes is yours; it is the emblem of the promised land. It means, my son, the hope of humanity. Live for it...die for it!' Under the open sky of my new country I swore to do so; and every drop of blood in me will keep that vow. I am proud of my future. I am an American."

ELIAS LIEBERMAN

Credo

"Most men and women guide their lives by their beliefs," wrote Lieberman. "We call that a philosophy of life. We do the right and we avoid the wrong because of deep-seated principles which determine our actions. In this poem [I] attempted to state why [I] believe in our country and in loyalty to it which must be 'utter, irrevocable, inviolate.' The poem ends with a prayer for strength."

I believe
That there are greater things in life
Than life itself;
I believe
In climbing upward
Even when the spent and broken thing
I call my body
Cries "Halt!"
I believe
To the last breath
In the truths
Which God permits me to see.
I believe
In fighting for them;
In drawing,
If need be,
Not the bloody sword of man
Brutal with conquest
And drunk with power,
But the white sword of God,
Flaming with His truth
And healing while it slays.

I believe
In my country and her destiny,
In the great dream of her founders,
In her place among the nations,
In her ideals;
I believe
That her democracy must be protected,
Her privileges cherished,
Her freedom defended.
I believe
That, humbly before the Almighty,
But proudly before all mankind,
We must safeguard her standard,
The vision of her Washington,
The martyrdom of her Lincoln,
With the patriotic ardor
Of the minute men
And the boys in blue
Of her glorious past.
I believe
In loyalty to my country
Utter, irrevocable, inviolate.

Thou, in whose sight
A thousand years are but as yesterday
And as a watch in the night,
Help me
In my frailty
To make real
What I believe.

Some of the African American men of the 369th (15th New York), the "Harlem Hellfighters," who won the Croix de Guerre for gallantry in action.

WILLIAM TYLER PAGE

The American's Creed

It is my duty to my country to love it; to support its Constitution; to obey its laws; to respect its flag, and to defend it against all enemies.

"In 1917," wrote William Bennett in his best-selling *Book of Virtues*, "William Tyler Page of Maryland won a nationwide contest for 'the best summary of American political faith.' The U.S. House of Representatives accepted the statement as the American's Creed on April 3, 1918. Its two paragraphs remind us that responsibilities are the source of rights. It deserves to be read and recited. Today very few people have even heard of it.".

I believe in the United States of America as a government of the people, by the people, for the people; whose just powers are derived from the consent of the governed; a democracy in a republic; a sovereign Nation of many sovereign States; a perfect union, one and inseparable; established upon those principles of freedom, equality, justice, and humanity for which American patriots sacrificed their lives and fortunes.

I therefore believe it is my duty to my country to love it; to support its Constitution; to obey its laws; to respect its flag, and to defend it against all enemies.

HENRY VAN DYKE

America for Me

Born in Germantown, Pennsylvania, Henry Van Dyke (1852-1933) was a clergyman and educator who devoted his time to writing novels, poems, essays, and religious literature. From 1913 to 1916, Van Dyke served as minister to the Netherlands and Luxembourg and, during World War I, served in the U.S. Navy as a chaplain. "America for Me," lively and patriotic, is Van Dyke's poetic tribute to his country.

'Tis fine to see the Old World, and travel up and down
Among the famous palaces and cities of renown,
To admire the crumbly castles and the statues of the kings—
But now I think I've had enough of antiquated things.

So it's home again, and home again, America for me!
My heart is turning home again, and there I long to be
In the land of youth and freedom beyond the ocean bars,
Where the air is full of sunlight and the flag is full of stars.

Oh, London is a man's town, there's power in the air;
And Paris is a woman's town, with flowers in her hair;
And it's sweet to dream in Venice, and it's great to study Rome,
But when it comes to living, there is no place like home.

I like the German fir-woods, in green battalions drilled;
I like the gardens of Versailles with flashing fountains filled;
But, oh, to take your hand, my dear, and ramble for a day
In the friendly western woodland where Nature has her way!

I know that Europe's wonderful, yet something seems to lack!
The Past is too much with her, and the people looking back.
But the glory of the Present is to make the Future free,—
We love our land for what she is and what she is to be.

Oh, it's home again, and home again, America for me!
I want a ship that's westward bound to plow the rolling sea,
To the blessed Land of Room Enough beyond the ocean bars,
Where the air is full of sunlight and the flag is full of stars.

CHARLES EVANS HUGHES

National Symbol

You cannot be saved by the valor and devotion of your ancestors.

Charles Evans Hughes (1862-1948), one of the most distinguished yet overlooked figures in American history, was born in Glens Falls, New York. Having graduated from Brown University and Columbia Law School, he was twice elected governor of New York and, in 1910, was appointed by President Taft as an associate justice of the U.S. Supreme Court. In 1916, Hughes resigned from the court to run for president on the Republican ticket, losing to Woodrow Wilson by a narrow margin. On June 5 of that year, shortly before the Republican Convention in Chicago, Hughes delivered the following address to his daughter's graduating class during the presentation of the flag at the National Cathedral School in Washington, D.C.

Hughes went on to serve as secretary of state from 1921 to 1925 under Presidents Warren G. Harding and Calvin Coolidge and, in 1928, became a member of the Permanent Court of International Justice, also known as the World Court. In 1930, President Herbert Hoover reappointed Hughes to the Supreme Court, where he served as chief justice until 1941. During Franklin Roosevelt's administration, the Hughes Court ruled many of the New Deal programs unconstitutional. Hughes was also instrumental in defeating the 1937 court reorganization bill, which was an attempt by Roosevelt to "pack" the court with judges more favorable to his policies. Thought by many to have been the greatest chief justice of the United States since John Marshall, Hughes won recognition for his commitment to the Constitution and human liberties.

On this happy occasion, we meet to measure and reward achievement. In these last school days, your hearts are full of the perfect joy of friendship and the dominant thought is doubtless of the associations which have been more potent in their influence than either study or precept. The teachers you love mean more to you than the subjects they have taught. It is because of the winning power of their personality, and your response to the message of their lives, that memory will ever turn fondly to this spot. But while all this is implied, the ceremony of today has a distinctive significance in its recognition of scholarship. This is a place of serious intellectual discipline. Intellectual interests are not sacrificed to meet the whims of folly or the indifference of the thoughtless. We are the "heirs of all the ages in the foremost files of time," but this vast inheritance counts only as we actually possess it and use it. It is a miserable spectacle to see youth neglecting the lessons of science, the instruction of history, the resources of literature and art, and leading a life small and impoverished amid the opportunities of the Twentieth century. Peculiarly is it necessary for us to realize the need of thorough, well directed training. The school is the powerhouse of democracy. You cannot expect to make efficient men and women out of the ill-instructed and the undisciplined. I am glad that there is here the zest of a wholesome competition in school work. You have had a generous rivalry and you all rejoice in the success of those who have won. Their success takes from no one the fine results of her own endeavor. Each has her own prize in her own effort. And in the giving of this reward for distinguished excellence, you all recognize that the ideal of all is being honored.

It is a beautiful prize that I am privileged to give. It has floated over your heads during the past year and is associated with every activity of your school life. It means much to you in its association with this place. It will ever call to your memory the forms of teachers, classmates and friends, mingling in happy comradeship under these trees. It speaks to you of the days of serious toil, when determined to achieve you put forth all your powers and triumphed.

It means more than association and reward. It is the symbol of our National unity, our National endeavor, our National aspiration. It tells of the struggle for independence, of Union preserved, of liberty and Union one and inseparable, of the sacrifices of brave men and women to whom the ideals and honor of this Nation have been dearer than life. It means America first; it means an undivided allegiance. It means America united, strong, and efficient, equal to her tasks. It means that you cannot be saved by the valor and devotion of your ancestors; that to each generation comes its patriotic duty; and that upon your willingness to sacrifice and endure, as those before you have sacrificed and endured, rests the National hope. It speaks of equal rights; of the inspiration of free institutions exemplified and vindicated; of liberty under law intelligently conceived and impartially administered. There is not a thread in it but scorns self-indulgence, weakness, and rapacity. It is eloquent of our community interests, outweighing all divergences of opinion; and of our common destiny. Given as a prize to those who have the highest standing, it happily enforces the lesson that intelligence and zeal must go together; that discipline must accompany emotion; and that we must ultimately rely on enlightened opinion. …

"The Human U.S. Shield," comprised of 30,000 men at Camp Custer in Battle Creek, Michigan. Photographers Arthur Mole and John Thomas developed the technique of collective portraiture for religious and patriotic themes, to include the Liberty Bell and the Statue of Liberty. The Human Shield, organized in 1918, was their largest production.

Heaven

One step this side and you are paupers for eternity. One step on the other side and you are kings and queens for eternity.

Born in Ames, Iowa, William Ashley Sunday (1862-1935) was a professional baseball player who became the best-known evangelist of the first half of the twentieth century. Sunday played for major league teams in Chicago, Pittsburgh, and Philadelphia from 1883 to 1891, when he began working for the Young Men's Christian Association. Soon thereafter, he began traveling from town to town, holding revival meetings in temporary wooden tabernacles. Condemning liquor, birth control, and other "sins of the modern age," Sunday's popular "fire and brimstone" speaking style was a throwback to Jonathan Edwards, George Whitefield, and other leaders of the eighteenth century Great Awakening.

Sunday was described by Lyle Dorsett, in his biography of the preacher, as "a man with numerous flaws. He certainly overindulged his children, put enormous demands on his wife, sought the applause of the crowd, placed too much emphasis on money, and equated the gospel of Jesus Christ with special interests and American foreign policy...," but he was "a sincere man whose life was fundamentally changed by his response to an evangelist's call to repent of his sins, to believe that Jesus Christ died in his place for those sins, and to follow Christ in thanksgiving by worshiping and obeying him. ... Furthermore, Sunday was constrained by an obsession to tell others how he had finally found inner peace and a more purposeful life. This same gospel, he said, would similarly transform others. The evidence is overwhelming that it did."

The following is the complete text of one of Billy Sunday's most oft repeated sermons—*Heaven*. This sermon, as Dorsett said, "give[s] evidence of a preacher who was decidedly more complex and gifted than his many critics have claimed."

"Let not your heart be troubled: ye believe in God, believe also in me. In my Father's house are many mansions: if it were not so, I would have told you. I go to prepare a place for you. And if I go and prepare a place for you, I will come again, and receive you unto myself; that where I am, there ye may be also. And whither I go ye know, and the way ye know. Thomas saith unto him, Lord, we know not whither thou goest; and how can we know the way? Jesus saith unto him, I am the way, the truth, and the life: no man cometh unto the Father, but by me." —John 14: 1-6.

Everybody wants to go to Heaven.
We are all curious.
We want to know:
>Where heaven is,
>How it looks,
>Who are there,
>What they wear,
>And how to get there.

Some say: Heaven is a state or a condition. You are wrong. Your home is not a state or a condition. It is a place.

The penitentiary is not a state or a condition. It is a place.

Jesus said: "I go to prepare a place for you ... that where I am, there ye may be also."

The only source of information we have about Heaven is the Bible. It tells us that God's throne is in the heavens and that the earth is His footstool. And if our spiritual visions are not blinded, we believe it is true.

Enoch walked with God and was not—for God took him to Heaven. He left this earth at the behest of God and went to Heaven where God has His dwelling place.

Elijah, when his mission on earth was finished, in the providence of God, was wafted to Heaven in a chariot of fire. The former pupils went out to search for the translated prophet but they did not find him.

But it was the privilege of Peter, James, and John on the Mount of Transfiguration with Jesus to see the gates of Heaven open and two spirits jump down on the earth whom they recognized as Moses and Elijah, who so many years before had walked through Palestine and warned the people of their sins and who slew 450 of the false prophets of Baal.

When Jesus began His public ministry we are told the heavens opened and God stopped making worlds and said from Heaven: "This is My beloved Son. Hear ye Him."

Then Stephen, with his face lit up with the glories of the Celestial Kingdom as he looked steadfastly toward Heaven, saw it open. And Jesus Himself was standing at the right hand of God, the place He had designated before His crucifixion and resurrection would be His abiding place until the time of the Gentiles should be fulfilled, when He would leave Heaven with a shout of triumph and return to this earth in the clouds of Heaven.

Among the last declarations of Jesus, in which we all find so much comfort in the hour of bereavement, is: "In My Father's house are many mansions: if it were not so I would have told you."

When Heaven's music burst upon human ears that first Christmas morning while the shepherds guarded their flocks on the moonlit hills of Judea, as the angels sang: "On earth peace, good will toward men. For unto you is born this day in the City of David a Saviour which is Christ the Lord."

We have ample proof that Heaven is a real place.

When we've been there ten thousand years,
Bright shining as the sun,
We've no less days to sing God's praise,
Than when we first begun.

What a Wonderful Place!

Oh, what a place Heaven is! The Tuileries of the French, the Windsor Castle of the English, the Alhambra of the Spanish, the Schonbrunn of the Austrians, the White House of the United States—these are all dungeons compared with Heaven.

There are mansions there for all the redeemed—one for the martyrs with blood-red robes; one for you ransomed from sin; one for me plucked like a brand from the fire.

Look and see—who are climbing the golden stairs, who are walking the golden streets, who are looking out of the windows? Some whom we knew and loved here on earth. Yes, I know them.

My father and mother, blithe and young as they were on their wedding day. Our son and our daughter, sweet as they were when they cuddled down to sleep in our arms. My brother and sister, merrier than when we romped and roamed the fields and plucked wild flowers and listened to the whippoorwill as he sang his lonesome song away over

in Sleepy Hollow on the old farm in Iowa where we were born and reared.

Cough, gone—cancer, gone—consumption, gone—erysipelas, gone—blindness, gone—rheumatism, gone—asthma, gone—lameness, gone—tears, gone—groans, sighs, gone—sleepless nights, gone.

I think it will take some of us a long time to get used to Heaven.

Fruits without one speck upon them.

Pastures without one thistle or weed.

Orchestra without one discord.

Violin without a broken string.

Harps all in tune.

The river without a torn or overflowed bank.

The sunrise and sunset swallowed up in the Eternal Day. "For there shall be no night there."

Heaven will be free from all that curses us here. No sin—no sorrow—no poverty—no sickness—no pain—no want—no aching heads or hearts—no war—no death. No watching the undertaker screw the coffin-lid over our loved ones.

When I reach Heaven I won't stop to look for Abraham, Isaac, Jacob, Moses, Joseph, David, Daniel, Peter or Paul. I will rush past them all saying, "Where is Jesus? I want to see Jesus who saved my soul one dark stormy night in Chicago in 1887."

If we could get a real appreciation of what Heaven is we would all be so homesick for Heaven the Devil wouldn't have a friend left on earth.

The Bible's description of Heaven is: the length and the breadth and the height of it are equal. I sat down and took 12 inches for a foot, our standard. That would make it two thousand five hundred miles long, two thousand five hundred miles wide, two thousand five hundred miles high. Made of pure gold like glass. Twelve gates, each gate made of one pearl. The foundations are of precious stones. Imagine eight thousand miles of diamonds, rubies, sapphires, emeralds, topaz, amethysts, jade, garnets.

Someone may say: "Well, that will be pleasant, if true."

Another says: "I hope it's true";

"Perhaps it's true";

"I wish it were true."

It is true!

Heaven: Where There Is No More Death

The kiss of reunion at the gate of Heaven is as certain as the goodbye kiss when you drift out with the tide.

> God holds the key
> Of all unknown,
> And I am glad.
> If other hands should hold the key,
> Or if He trusted it to me,
> I might be sad.

Death is a cruel enemy. He robs the mother of her baby, the wife of her husband, the parents of their children, the lover of his intended wife. He robs the nation of its President.

Death is a rude enemy. He upsets our best plans without an apology. He enters the most exclusive circles without an invitation.

Death is an international enemy. There is no nation which he does not visit. The islands of the seas where the black skinned mothers rock their babies to sleep to the lullaby of the ocean's waves, the restless sea, the majestic mountains—all are his haunts.

Death is an untiring enemy. He continues his ghastly work spring, summer, autumn and winter. He never tires in his ceaseless rounds, gathering his spoils of human souls.

But Death is a vanquished enemy. Jesus arose from the dead and abolished death, although we may be called upon to die.

Death to the Christian is swinging open the door through which he passes into Heaven.

"Aren't you afraid?" said the wife to a dying miner.

"Afraid, Lassie. Why should I be? I know Jesus and Jesus knows me."

This house in which we live, "our body," is beginning to lean. The windows rattle. The glass is dim. The shingles are falling off.

> You will reach the river's brink,
> Some sweet day, by and by.
> You will clasp your broken link
> Some sweet day, by and by.

> There's a glorious kingdom waiting
> In the land beyond the sky,
> Where the Saints have been gathering
> Year by year.

> And the days are swiftly passing
> That shall bring the Kingdom nigh,
> For the coming of the Lord
> Draweth near.

Thank God for the rainbow of hope that bends above the graves of our loved ones.

We stand on this side of the grave and mourn as they go. They stand on the other side and rejoice as they come.

> On the Resurrection morning
> Soul and body meet again.
> No more sorrow, no more weeping,
> No more pain.

> Soul and body reunited.
> Thenceforth nothing can divide.
> Waking up in Christ's own likeness;
> Satisfied!

> On that happy Easter morning,
> All the graves their dead restore.
> Father, sister, child and mother,
> Meet once more.

> To that brightest of all meetings
> Brings us Jesus Christ, at last,
> By thy cross through death and judgment,
> Holding fast.

The Bible indicates that angels know each other. If they have the power to recognize each other, won't we?

The Bible describes Heaven as a great home circle. It would be a queer home circle if we did not know each other.

The Bible describes death as a sleep. Well, we know each other before we go to sleep and we know each other when we wake up. Do you imagine we will be bigger fools in Heaven than we are here on earth?

A woman lay dying. She had closed her eyes. Her sister, thinking her dead, commenced the wail of mourning. The dying woman raised her hand and said: "Hush! Hush! I am listening to the breezes waving the branches in the trees of life."

You will be through with your back-biting enemies. They will call you vile names no more. They will no longer misrepresent your good deeds. Broken hearts will be bound up. Wounds will be healed. Sorrows ended.

The comfort of God is greater than the sorrows of men. I've thanked God a thousand times for the roses but never for the thorns, but now I have learned to thank Him for the thorns.

You will never be sick again; never be tired again; never weep again.

What's the use of fretting when we are on our way to such a coronation.

Jesus, the Only Way to Heaven

You must know the password if you ever enter Heaven. Jesus said, "I am the way, the truth and the life: no man cometh unto the Father but by me."

Here comes a crowd. They cry: "Let me in. I was very useful on earth. I built churches. I endowed colleges. I was famous for my charities. I have done many wonderful things."

"I never knew you."

Another crowd shouts: "We were highly honored on earth. The world bowed very low before us. Now we have come to get our honors in Heaven."

"We never knew you."

Another crowd shouts: "We were very moral. We never lied, swore or got drunk."

"We never knew you."

Another crowd approaches and says: "We were sinners, wanderers from God. We have come up, not because we deserve Heaven, but because we heard of the saving power of Jesus, and we have accepted Him as our Saviour."

They all cry, "Jesus, Jesus. Thou Son of God, open to us."

They all pass through the pearly gates.

One step this side and you are paupers for eternity. One step on the other side and you are kings and queens for eternity. When I think of Heaven and my entering it I feel awkward.

Sometimes when I have been exposed to the weather, shoes covered with mud, coat wet and soiled with mud and rain, hair disheveled, I feel I am not fit to go in and sit among the well-dressed guests.

So I feel that way about Heaven. I need to be washed in the blood of the Lamb and clothed in the robe of Christ's righteousness. I need the pardoning waves of God's mercy to roll over my soul. And thank God, they have.

If you go first will you come down half way and meet me between the willow banks of earth and the palm groves of Heaven? You who have loved ones in Heaven, will you take a pledge with me to meet them when the day dawns and the shadows flee away?

Some who read this are sadly marching into the face of the setting sun. You are sitting by the window of your soul looking out toward the twilight of life's purple glow. You are listening to the music of the breaking waves of life's ebbing tide and longing for the sight of faces and the sound of voices loved and lost a while.

But if you are true to God and have accepted Jesus as your Saviour at last you will hail the coming morning radiant and glorious when the waves of the sea will become crystal chords in the grand organ of Eternity.

A saint lay dying. She said: "My faith is being tried. The brightness of which you speak I do not have. But I have accepted Jesus as my Saviour and if God wishes to put me to sleep in the dark His will be done."

Blessed Hope for the Christian

Sorrow sometimes plays strange dirges on the heartstrings of life before they break but the music always has a message of hope.

Should You Go First

Should you go first, and I remain
To walk the road alone,
I'll live in memory's garden, dear,
With happy days we've known.
In spring I'll watch for roses red,
When fade the lilacs blue;
In early fall, when brown leaves fall,
I'll catch a breath of you.

Should you go first, and I remain
For battles to be fought,
Each thing you've touched along the way
Will be a hallowed spot.
I'll hear your voice, I'll see you smile,
Though blindly I may grope;
The memory of your helping hand
Will buoy me on with hope.

Should you go first, and I remain
To finish with the scroll,
No length'ning shadows shall creep in
To make this life seem droll.
We've known so much of happiness,
We've had our cup of joy;
Ah, memory is one gift of God
That death cannot destroy.

Should you go first, and I remain,
One thing I'd have you do;
Walk slowly down the path of death,
For soon I'll follow you.
I'll want to know each step you take,
That I may walk the same;
For some day—down that lonely road—
You'll hear me call your name.

A. K. Rowswell (Rosey)

One day when the children were young I was romping and playing with them and I grew tired and lay down to rest. Half asleep and half awake I dreamed I journeyed to a far-off land.

It was not Persia, although the oriental beauty and splendor were there.

It was not India, although the coral strands were there.

It was not Ceylon, although the beauty and spicy perfume of that famous island paradise were there.

It was not Italy, although the dreamy haze of the blue Italian sky beat above me.

It was not California nor Florida, although the soft flower-ladened breezes of the Pacific and the Atlantic were there.

I looked for weeds, briars, thorns and thistles, but I found none.

I saw the sun in all his meridian glory. I asked "When will the sun set and it grow dark?"

They said: "Oh, it never grows dark in this land. There is no night here. Jesus is the light."

I saw the people all clothed in holiday attire with faces wreathed in smiles and halos of glory about their heads.

I asked: "When will the working men go by with calloused hands and empty dinner buckets and faces grimed with dust and toil?"

They said: "Oh, we toil not, neither do we sow nor reap in this land."

I strolled out into the suburbs and the hills which would be a fit resting place for the dead to sleep. I looked for monuments, mausoleums, marble slabs, tombs and graves, but I saw none. I did see towers, spires and minarets.

I asked: "Where do you bury the dead of this great city? Where are the grave-diggers? Where are the hearses that haul the dead to their graves?"

They said: "Oh, we never die in this land."

I asked: "Where are the hospitals where you take the sick? Where are the doctors with scalpel and trocar? Where are the nurses with panacea and opiates to ease the pain?"

They said: "Oh, we are never sick. None ever die in this land."

I asked: "Where do the poor people live? Where are the homes of penury and want?"

They said: "Oh, there are no poor in this land. There is no want here. None are ever hungry here."

I was puzzled.

I looked and saw a river. Its waves were breaking against golden and jewel-strewn beaches.

I saw ships with sails of pure silk, bows covered with gold, oars tipped with silver.

I looked and saw a great multitude no man could number, rushing out of jungles of roses, down banks of violets, redolent of eternal spring, pulsing with bird song and the voices of angels.

I realized Time had ended and Eternity had dawned.

I cried: "Are all here?"

They echoed: "Yes, all here."

And tower and spire and minaret all caroled my welcome home. And we all went leaping and singing and shouting the eternal praises of
God the Father,
God the Son,
God the Holy Spirit.
Home, home, at last!

Here's to you, my friends.
May you live a hundred years,
Just to help us
Through this vale of tears.

May I live a hundred years
Short just one day,
Because I don't want to be here
After all my friends have gone away.

GEORGE M. COHAN

Yankee Doodle Boy and Over There

Born in Providence, Rhode Island, George Michael Cohan (1878-1942) performed in a vaudeville act as a child with his parents and sister. "The Four Cohans," as they were called, wrote songs and performed sketches. George began to write independently as a teenager and, during the early 1900s, wrote more than forty plays and musicals and played an active role in their production, often directing and even starring in them. "Yankee Doodle Boy," perhaps his best-loved song, appeared in the 1942 film loosely based on his own life, *Yankee Doodle Dandy* starring James Cagney. Cohan, in fact, always claimed to be "born on the fourth of July" although his birth certificate shows his birth to be July 3.

Other timeless compositions by Cohan include "You're a Grand Old Flag," "Give My Regards to Broadway," "Mary's a Grand Old Name," and "Harrigan." Cohan also wrote the most popular patriotic song of World War I, "Over There," receiving a Congressional Gold Medal for his contributions to morale. Known as "Mr. Broadway" for his preeminent role in American musical theater, Cohan is immortalized by a statue in Times Square in New York City.

Yankee Doodle Boy

I'm the kid that's all the candy, I'm a Yankee Doodle Dandy
I'm glad I am, So's Uncle Sam
I'm a real live Yankee Doodle, Made my name and fame and boodle
Just like Mister Doodle did by riding on a pony
I love to listen to the Dixie strain, "I long to see the girl I left behind me"
And that ain't a josh, she's a Yankee, by gosh
Oh, say can you see
Anything about a Yankee that's a phoney?

Chorus:

    I'm a Yankee Doodle Dandy
    A Yankee Doodle, do or die
    A real live nephew of my uncle Sam's
    Born on the Fourth of July
    I've got a Yankee Doodle sweetheart
    She's my Yankee Doodle joy
    Yankee Doodle came to London just to ride the ponies
    I am a Yankee Doodle boy

Father's name was Hezikiah, Mother's name was Ann Maria
Yanks through and through, red, white and blue
Father was so Yankee hearted when the Spanish War was started
He slipped upon his uniform and hopped up on a pony
My mother's mother was a Yankee true, my father's father was a Yankee too
And that's going some for the Yankees, by gum
Oh, say can you see
Anything about my pedigree that's phoney?

Over There

Johnnie get your gun, get your gun, get your gun,
Take it on the run, on the run, on the run;
Hear them calling you and me;
Ev'ry son of liberty.
Hurry right away, no delay, go today,
Make your daddy glad, to have had such a lad,
Tell your sweetheart not to pine,
To be proud of her boy's in line.

Chorus:
    Over there, over there,
    Send the word, send the word over there,
    That the Yanks are coming,
    The drums rum-tumming ev'ry where—
    So prepare, say a pray'r,
    Send the word, send the word to beware,
    We'll be over, we're coming over,
    And we won't come back till it's over over there.

Johnnie get your gun, get your gun, get your gun,
Johnnie show the Hun, you're a son-of-a-gun,
Hoist the flag and let her fly,
Like true heroes, do or die.
Pack your little kit, show your grit, do your bit,
Soldiers to the ranks from the towns and the tanks,
Make your mother proud of you,
And to liberty be true.

EDMUND L. GRUBER

The Caisson Song

"The Caisson Song," also known as "The Field Artillery Song" and "The Army Goes Rolling Along," was originally written by Lieutenant (later Brigadier General) Edmund L. Gruber (1879-1941) in 1908, while he was stationed in the Philippines. The noted composer and conductor John Philip Sousa produced an instrumental version of the song in 1918, helping to popularize it on the home front and among the troops during World War I. An alternate version of the lyrics printed here was adopted in 1956 as the official song of the U.S. Army.

Over hill, over dale, we have hit the dusty trail,
And those caissons go rolling along.
In and out, hear them shout, "Counter march and right about!"
And those caissons go rolling along.

Chorus:
    Then it's hi! hi! hee! in the field artillery,
    Sound off your numbers loud and strong.
    Where e'er you go you will always know
    That those caissons are rolling along.
    Keep them rolling! And those caissons go rolling along.
    Then it's Battery Halt!

Through the storm, through the night, up to where the doughboys fight,
All our caissons go rolling along.
At Zero we'll be there, answering every call and flare,
While our caissons go rolling along.

Cavalry, boot to boot, we will join in the pursuit,
While the caissons go rolling along.
Action front, at a trot; volley fire with shell and shot,
While those caissons go rolling along.

But if fate me should call, and in action I should fall,
And those caissons go rolling along.
Fire at will, lay 'em low, never stop for any foe,
While those caissons go rolling along.

But if fate me should call, and in action I should fall,
Keep those caissons a-rolling along.
Then in peace I'll abide when I take my final stride
On a caisson that's rolling along.

The Marines' Hymn

The music to "The Marines' Hymn" comes from "Couplets des deux hommes d'armes," a song from an 1868 opera called *Geneviève de Brabant*. The authorship of the lyrics, however, is unknown since no one holds a copyright. The words first appeared in the *National Police Gazette* in 1917. The Marine Corps itself printed the lyrics a year later in the *Quantico Leatherneck*.

From the halls of Montezuma
To the shores of Tripoli;
We fight our country's battles
In the air, on land and sea;
First to fight for right and freedom
And to keep our honor clean;
We are proud to claim the title
Of United States Marine.

Our flag's unfurled to ev'ry breeze
From dawn to setting sun;
We have fought in ev'ry clime and place
Where we could take a gun;
In the snow of far-off Northern lands
And in sunny tropic scenes;
You will find us always on the job—
The United States Marines.

Here's health to you and to our Corps
Which we are proud to serve;
In many a strife we've fought for life
And never lost our nerve;
If the Army and the Navy
Ever look on Heaven's scenes;
They will find the streets are guarded
By United States Marines

CARL SANDBURG

Grass

Born in Galesburg, Illinois, Carl Sandburg (1878-1967) was a noted poet, journalist, and historian. Having dropped out of school as a teenager, he worked as a day laborer for several years and then traveled across the country as a hobo. He briefly served in the U.S. Army in 1898 during the Spanish-American War and returned to Galesburg that same year, renewing his education at Lombard College.

Sandburg's first collection of poetry, *Chicago Poems*, was published in 1916 and included one of his most famous works, "Chicago," a poem deploring the violence of American cities while praising their vitality. Sandburg's "Grass," one of the most memorable poems about the Great War, is taken from his collection *Cornhuskers* and represents the poet's respect for the sanctity of life and disdain for armed conflict. Carl Sandburg was awarded the Pulitzer Prize for poetry in 1919 and again in 1951 for his *Complete Poems*. His greatest literary achievement, however, was the 1940 Pulitzer Prize for history, awarded for his massive, six-volume biography of Abraham Lincoln. Sandburg's autobiography, *Always the Young Strangers*, was published in 1953.

Pile the bodies high at Austerlitz and Waterloo.
Shovel them under and let me work—
I am the grass; I cover all.

And pile them high at Gettysburg
And pile them high at Ypres and Verdun.
Shovel them under and let me work.

Two years, ten years, and passengers ask the conductor:
What place is this?
Where are we now?

I am the grass.
Let me work.

Preamble to the American Legion Constitution

We associate ourselves together … to foster and perpetuate a one hundred percent Americanism.

During World War I, a group of twenty officers of the American Expeditionary Forces serving in France began working on ways to improve the morale of American troops. One of those officers, Lieutenant Colonel Theodore Roosevelt, Jr., son of the twenty-sixth president of the United States, suggested an organization of veterans. The American Legion, as it would be called, held its first meeting in February 1919 and, in September, was granted a national charter by Congress.

The nation's largest veterans' organization, the American Legion has thousands of posts throughout the country dedicated to the support of wounded and disabled veterans. The Legion works to obtain compensation and medical care and, at the conclusion of World War II, helped draft the GI Bill of Rights. The Legion also sponsors youth athletic teams, awards scholarships, and constructs community centers and parks. The American Legion advocates a state of military preparedness and strongly opposes Communism, Socialism, Fascism, and all ideologies contrary to traditional American ideals.

For God and Country, we associate ourselves together for the following purposes:

To uphold and defend the Constitution of the United States of America; to maintain law and order; to foster and perpetuate a one hundred percent Americanism; to preserve the memories and incidents of our associations in the great wars; to inculcate a sense of individual obligation to the community, state and nation; to combat the autocracy of both the classes and the masses; to make right the master of might; to promote peace and goodwill on earth; to safeguard and transmit to posterity the principles of justice, freedom and democracy; to consecrate and sanctify our comradeship by our devotion to mutual helpfulness.

American troops parading through Vladivostok in 1918 while Japanese marines stand at attention. The U.S. Army entered Siberia during the tail end of World War I, intervening in the Russian Civil War, in order to protect military supplies and rescue Czechoslovak Legions who were being held up by Bolshevik forces as they attempted to make their way to the Western Front.

American Sovereignty

An American I was born, an American I have remained all my life. I can never be anything else but an American ...

In 1918, Woodrow Wilson gave a speech in which he highlighted "Fourteen Points" to be used as a basis for peace at the war's conclusion. Many of the points were general in principle while others dealt with immediate territorial disputes. The fourteenth point called for the establishment of a "general association of nations"—what Wilson viewed as an instrument for "affording mutual guarantees of political independence and territorial integrity to great and small states alike." At the 1919 peace talks in Paris, most of Wilson's points were sacrificed by allied leaders intent on pursuing their own national interests, but the negotiated Treaty of Versailles did include a charter for the League of Nations—for which Wilson was awarded the 1919 Nobel Peace Prize.

The United States, however, never joined the league. This was due in large part to the efforts of Senator Henry Cabot Lodge (1850-1924) who, as chairman of the Senate Foreign Relations Committee, led Republicans in opposition. Lodge feared that membership in the league would involve the United States in the "entangling alliances" George Washington had warned against and was unwilling to accept the league without significantly reducing America's obligations to it. His August 12, 1919, speech on the floor of the U.S. Senate, excerpted here, was a patriotic appeal to Americans to reject internationalism. Lodge argued that America best served the world by solving its own problems, "for if the United States fails the best hopes of mankind fail with it."

When the League of Nations dissolved in 1946, the United States became a charter member of the newly formed United Nations. Lodge's grandson, Henry Cabot Lodge, Jr. (1902-1985), later became U.S. ambassador to the UN and defended his grandfather's efforts, saying, "He simply preserved the power of Congress—a power which is jealously guarded today, which is completely safeguarded both in the United Nations Charter and the Atlantic Pact, and which President Wilson was unwilling categorically to express at that time."

... The independence of the United States is not only more precious to ourselves but to the world than any single possession. Look at the United States today. We have made mistakes in the past. We have had shortcomings. We shall make mistakes in the future and fall short of our own best hopes. But none the less is there any country today on the face of the earth which can compare with this in ordered liberty, in peace, and in the largest freedom? I feel that I can say this without being accused of undue boastfulness, for it is the simple fact, and in making this treaty and taking on these obligations all that we do is in a spirit of unselfishness and in a desire for the good of mankind. But it is well to remember that we are dealing with nations every one of which has a direct individual interest to serve, and there is grave danger in an unshared idealism. Contrast the United States with any country on the face of the earth today and ask yourself whether the situation of the United States is not the best to be found. I will go as far as anyone in world service, but the first step to world service is the maintenance of the United States.

You may call me selfish if you will, conservative or reactionary, or use any other harsh adjective you see fit to apply, but an American I was born, an American I have remained all my life. I can never be anything else but an American, and I must think of the United States first, and when I think of the United States first in an arrangement like this I am thinking of what is best for the world, for if the United States fails the best hopes of mankind fail with it. I have never had but one allegiance—I cannot divide it now. I have loved but one flag and I cannot share that devotion and give affection to the mongrel banner invented for a league. Internationalism, illustrated by the Bolshevik and by the men to whom all countries are alike provided they can make money out of them, is to me repulsive. National I must remain, and in that way I like all other Americans can render the amplest service to the world. The United States is the world's best hope, but if you fetter her in the interests and quarrels of other nations, if you tangle her in the intrigues of Europe, you will destroy her power for good and endanger her very existence. Leave her to march freely through the centuries to come as in the years that have gone. Strong, generous, and confident, she has nobly served mankind. Beware how you trifle with your marvelous inheritance, this great land of ordered liberty, for if we stumble and fall freedom and civilization everywhere will go down in ruin.

We are told that we shall "break the heart of the world" if we do not take this league just as it stands. I fear that the hearts of the vast majority of mankind would beat on strongly and steadily and without any quickening if the league were to perish altogether. If it should be effectively and beneficently changed the people who would lie awake in sorrow for a single night could be easily gathered in one not very large room, but those who would draw a long breath of relief would reach to millions.

We hear much of visions and I trust we shall continue to have visions and dream dreams of a fairer future for the race. But visions are one thing and visionaries are another, and the mechanical appliances of the rhetorician designed to give a picture of a present which does not exist and of a future which no man can predict are as unreal and short-lived as the steam or canvas clouds, the angels suspended on wires, and the artificial lights of the stage. They pass with the moment of effect and are shabby and tawdry in the daylight. Let us at least be real. Washington's entire honesty of mind and his fearless look into the face of all facts are qualities which can never go out of fashion and which we should all do well to imitate.

Ideals have been thrust upon us as an argument for the league until the healthy mind, which rejects cant, revolts from them. Are ideals confined to this deformed experiment upon a noble purpose, tainted as it is with bargains, and tied to a peace treaty which might have been disposed of long ago to the great benefit of the world if it had not been compelled to carry this rider on its back? "*Post equitem sedet atra cura*," Horace tells us, but no blacker care ever sat behind any rider than we shall find in this covenant of doubtful and disputed interpretation as it now perches upon the treaty of peace.

No doubt many excellent and patriotic people see a coming fulfillment of noble ideals in the words "league for peace." We all respect and share these aspirations and desires, but some of us see no hope, but rather defeat, for them in this murky covenant. For we, too, have our ideals, even if we differ from those who have tried to establish a monopoly of idealism. Our first ideal is our country, and we see her in the future, as in the past, giving service to all her people and to the world. Our ideal of the future is that she should continue to render that service of her own free will. She has great problems of her own to solve, very grim and perilous problems, and a right solution, if we can attain to it, would largely benefit mankind. We would have our country strong to resist a peril from the West, as she has flung back the German menace from the East. We would not have our politics distracted and embittered by the dissensions of other lands. We would not have our country's vigor exhausted or her moral force abated by everlasting meddling and muddling in every quarrel, great and small, which afflicts the world. Our ideal is to make her ever stronger and better and finer, because in that way alone, as we believe, can she be of the greatest service to the world's peace and to the welfare of mankind.

BILLY ROSE

The Unknown Soldier

After World War I had concluded, the governments of Great Britain, France, Italy, Belgium, and the United States all buried the remains of an unknown soldier near their national capitals. The Unknown Soldier of the United States was one of the war dead taken from American cemeteries in Europe. The remains were brought to the United States Capitol to lie in state, and on Armistice Day (now Veterans Day—November 11) 1921, were buried in Arlington National Cemetery. Ten years later, a tomb was completed with a white marble sarcophagus bearing the inscription, "Here rests in honored glory an American soldier known but to God." The east side of the tomb, opposite the inscription, contains a scene depicting three figures: Peace, holding a dove; Victory, holding a palm branch; Valor, holding a sword—Peace through Victory by Valor. On the north and south faces of the tomb are a total of six wreaths, inverted as a sign of mourning, which represent the six major campaigns of World War I: Château-Thierry, Ardennes, Oise-Aisne, Meuse- Argonne, Belleau Wood, and the Somme.

In 1958, Congress directed that an unidentifiable American soldier from both World War II and the Korean War be chosen to lie in state at the Capitol and then be buried in marble-capped crypts at the head of the Tomb of the Unknown Soldier. The double interment took place on May 30, 1958. The Vietnam Unknown was interred on May 28, 1984, but disinterred on May 14, 1998, when DNA tests identified the remains as those of U.S. Air Force pilot Lieutenant Michael Joseph Blassie of St. Louis, Missouri. A memorial amphitheater, built in honor of all members of the armed forces killed in battle, stands near the tomb and is the site of Memorial Day services. An armed sentinel guards the Tomb of the Unknown(s) at all times.

"The Unknown Soldier" was written by Billy Rose (1899-1966), a New York-born showman who began his career as a lyricist and later owned several popular night clubs and ran "Aquacades" at the New York and San Francisco World's Fairs.

There's a graveyard near the White House
Where the Unknown Soldier lies,
And the flowers there are sprinkled
With the tears from mother's eyes.

I stood there not so long ago
With roses for the brave,
And suddenly I heard a voice
Speak from out the grave:

"I am the Unknown Soldier,"
The spirit voice began,
"And I think I have the right
To ask some questions man to man.

"Are my buddies taken care of?
Was their victory so sweet?
Is that big reward you offered
Selling pencils on the street?

"Did they really win the freedom
They battled to achieve?
Do you still respect that Croix de Guerre
Above that empty sleeve?

"Does a gold star in the window
Now mean anything at all?
I wonder how my old girl feels
When she hears a bugle call.

"And that baby who sang
'Hello, Central, give me no man's land'—
Can they replace her daddy
With a military band?

"I wonder if the profiteers
Have satisfied their greed?
I wonder if a soldier's mother
Ever is in need?

"I wonder if the kings, who planned it all
Are really satisfied?
They played their game of checkers
And eleven million died.

"I am the Unknown Soldier
And maybe I died in vain,
But if I were alive and my country called,
I'd do it all over again."

* * *

Five U.S. Marines and a U.S. Navy Corpsman raising the American flag atop Mount Suribachi during the Battle of Iwo Jima on February 23, 1945. Three of the six would be killed during the battle. This photograph was later used by Felix de Weldon to sculpt the USMC War Memorial, located adjacent to Arlington National Cemetery.

Depression
and
World War II

MILTON AGER AND JACK YELLEN

Happy Days Are Here Again

"Happy Days Are Here Again" was composed by Milton Ager, with words by Jack Yellen. Ironically, the song debuted on the eve of the stock market crash in October 1929, which plunged the nation into the Great Depression. With "Happy Days" nowhere on the horizon, the American people were in desperate need of cheering up. As the nation struggled through one of the most severe crises in its history, this song gained notoriety as the theme song of Franklin Roosevelt's presidential campaigns. It has since been a standard at national conventions of the Democratic Party..

So long, sad times;
Go 'long, bad times!
We are rid of you at last.
Howdy, gay times!
Cloudy gray times,
You are a thing of the past.

'Cause happy days are here again!
The skies above are clear again.
Let us sing a song of cheer again
Happy days are here again!
Altogether shout it now!
There's no one who can doubt it now,
So let's tell the world about it now
Happy days are here again!

Your cares and troubles are gone;
There'll be no more from now on.
Happy days are here again,
The skies above are clear again;
Let us sing a song of cheer again
Happy days are here again!

CLAUDE MCKAY

America and If We Must Die

Born in Jamaica, Claude McKay (1890-1948) moved to the United States in 1912 and studied at Tuskegee Institute and Kansas State University. During the late 1920s, he became known as one of the most radical voices of the Harlem Renaissance, a period of enormous creativity among black American writers, musicians, and artists—many of whom lived and worked in the Harlem neighborhood of New York City. McKay's four novels and several collections of poetry challenged the notion that any group of people have the right to suppress another. Early in life, McKay embraced Communism and, at one time, was an editor of a Socialist newspaper. After spending time in Europe and the Soviet Union, however, he became disillusioned with the ideologies he had once embraced. McKay returned to the United States in 1934 and published his autobiography, *A Long Way from Home*, in 1937.

America

Although she feeds me bread of bitterness,
And sinks into my throat her tiger's tooth,
Stealing my breath of life, I will confess
I love this cultured hell that tests my youth!
Her vigor flows like tide into my blood,
Giving me strength erect against her hate.
Her bigness sweeps my being like a flood.
Yet as a rebel fronts a king in state,
I stand within her walls with not a shred
Of terror, malice, not a word of jeer.
Darkly I gaze into the days ahead,
And see her mite and granite wonders there,
Beneath the touch of Time's unerring hand,
Like priceless treasures sinking in the sand.

If We Must Die

If we must die, let it not be like hogs
Hunted and penned in an inglorious spot,
While round us bark the mad and hungry dogs,
Making their mock at our accursed lot.
If we must die, O let us nobly die,
So that our precious blood may not be shed
In vain; then even the monsters we defy
Shall be constrained to honor us though dead!
O kinsmen! we must meet the common foe!
Though far outnumbered let us show us brave,
And for their thousand blows deal one deathblow!
What though before us lies the open grave?
Like men we'll face the murderous, cowardly pack,
Pressed to the wall, dying, but fighting back!

JAY GORNEY AND E. Y. HARBURG

Brother, Can You Spare a Dime?

E. Y. Harburg wrote the lyrics, and Jay Gorney composed the music to "Brother, Can You Spare a Dime?" A popular anthem of the Great Depression, this song was first introduced in 1932 at the Shubert Theatre in New York as part of the musical revue *Americana*. Harburg also wrote the lyrics to "Over the Rainbow," made famous by Judy Garland in *The Wizard of Oz* (1939).

They used to tell me I was building a dream,
And so I followed the mob
When there was earth to plough or guns to bear
I was always there right there on the job.

They used to tell me I was building a dream
With peace and glory ahead
Why should I be standing in line
Just waiting for bread?

Once I built a railroad, made it run,
Made it race against time.
Once I built a railroad,
Now it's done
Brother, can you spare a dime?

Once I built a tower, to the sun,
Brick and rivet and lime,
Once I built a tower,
Now it's done,
Brother, can you spare a dime?

Once in khaki suits
Gee, we looked swell
Full of that Yankee Doodle-de-dum.
Half a million boots went sloggin' thru Hell,
And I was the kid with the drum.

Say, don't you remember, they called me Al
It was Al all the time
Say, don't you remember, I'm your Pal!
Buddy, can you spare a dime?

FRANKLIN D. ROOSEVELT

First Inaugural Address

The only thing we have to fear is fear itself—nameless, unreasoning, unjustified terror which paralyzes needed efforts to convert retreat into advance.

Franklin Delano Roosevelt (1882-1945), one of the most beloved and charismatic leaders in history, led the United States through two major traumas—the Great Depression and World War II. His unprecedented election to four terms in office will probably never be repeated; the Twenty-second Amendment to the Constitution, passed after his death, prevents any person from being elected president more than twice.

An only child, FDR was born into a wealthy family in Hyde Park, New York. He graduated from Harvard College, married his distant cousin Eleanor Roosevelt, and studied at Columbia University Law School. He began his political career as a state senator and, in 1913, was appointed assistant secretary of the navy by President Wilson, whom Roosevelt had backed against his cousin Theodore. Despite being crippled by polio in 1921, Roosevelt was elected governor of New York in 1928. In 1932, he was elected to the presidency, defeating the incumbent Republican, Herbert Hoover.

When Roosevelt was sworn in, on March 4, 1933, the Great Depression was at its worst. A quarter of the nation's work force was unemployed—many of them had been out of work for a year or even longer—and the nation's banking system had collapsed. Although the American depression had been signaled by the stock market crash in New York City in 1929, it had since become part of a worldwide economic collapse. Whether the American people would be satisfied with the change in administration depended, in large part, on the president's success in bringing aid to those in despair. Toward that end, Roosevelt first sought to help people regain faith in themselves. His first inaugural address, like his "fireside chats," displayed the president's ability to lift the spirits of the American people by portraying a confident outlook of the future.

I am certain that my fellow Americans expect that on my induction into the Presidency I will address them with a candor and a decision which the present situation of our Nation impels. This is preeminently the time to speak the truth, the whole truth, frankly and boldly. Nor need we shrink from honestly facing conditions in our country today. This great Nation will endure as it has endured, will revive and will prosper. So, first of all, let me assert my firm belief that the only thing we have to fear is fear itself—nameless, unreasoning, unjustified terror which paralyzes needed efforts to convert retreat into advance. In every dark hour of our national life a leadership of frankness and vigor has met with that understanding and support of the people themselves which is essential to victory. I am convinced that you will again give that support to leadership in these critical days.

In such a spirit on my part and on yours we face our common difficulties. They concern, thank God, only material things. Values have shrunken to fantastic levels; taxes have risen; our ability to pay has fallen; government of all kinds is faced by serious curtailment of income; the means of exchange are frozen in the currents of trade; the withered leaves of industrial enterprise lie on every side; farmers find no markets for their produce; the savings of many years in thousands of families are gone.

More important, a host of unemployed citizens face the grim problem of existence, and an equally great number toil with little return. Only a foolish optimist can deny the dark realities of the moment.

Yet our distress comes from no failure of substance. We are stricken by no plague of locusts. Compared with the perils which our forefathers conquered because they believed and were not afraid, we have still much to be thankful for. Nature still offers her bounty and human efforts have multiplied it. Plenty is at our doorstep, but a generous use of it languishes in the very sight of the supply. Primarily this is because the rulers of the exchange of mankind's goods have failed, through their own stubbornness and their own incompetence, have admitted their failure, and abdicated. Practices of the unscrupulous money changers stand indicted in the court of public opinion, rejected by the hearts and minds of men. ...

Happiness lies not in the mere possession of money; it lies in the joy of achievement, in the thrill of creative effort. The joy and moral stimulation of work no longer must be forgotten in the mad chase of evanescent profits. These dark days will be worth all they cost us if they teach us that our true destiny is not to be ministered unto but to minister to ourselves and to our fellow men. ...

Our greatest primary task is to put people to work. This is no unsolvable problem if we face it wisely and courageously. It can be accomplished in part by direct recruiting by the Government itself, treating the task as we would treat the emergency of a war, but at the same time, through this employment, accomplishing greatly needed projects to stimulate and reorganize the use of our natural resources.

Hand in hand with this we must frankly recognize the overbalance of population in our industrial centers and, by engaging on a national scale in a redistribution, endeavor to provide a better use of the land for those best fitted for the land. The task can be helped by definite efforts to raise the values of agricultural products and with this the power to purchase the output of our cities. It can be helped by preventing realistically the tragedy of the growing loss through foreclosure of our small homes and our farms. It can be helped by insistence that the Federal, State, and local governments act forthwith on the demand that their cost be drastically reduced. It can be helped by the unifying of relief activities which today are often scattered, uneconomical, and unequal. It can be helped by national planning for and supervision of all forms of transportation and of communications and other utilities which have a definitely public character. There are many ways in which it can be helped, but it can never be helped merely by talking about it. We must act and act quickly.

Finally, in our progress toward a resumption of work we require two safeguards against a return of the evils of the old order; there must be a strict supervision of all banking and credits and investments; there must be an end to speculation with other people's money, and there must be provision for an adequate but sound currency.

There are the lines of attack. I shall presently urge upon a new Congress in special session detailed measures for their fulfillment, and I shall seek the immediate assistance of the several States.

Through this program of action we address ourselves to putting our own national house in order and making income balance outgo. ...

In the field of world policy I would dedicate this nation to the policy of the good neighbor—the neighbor who resolutely respects himself and, because he does so, respects the rights of others—the neighbor who respects his obligations and respects the sanctity of his agreements in and with a world of neighbors.

If I read the temper of our people correctly, we now realize, as we have never realized before, our interdependence on each other; that we cannot merely take, but we must give as well; that if we are to go forward we must move as a trained and loyal army willing to sacrifice for the good of a common discipline, because without such discipline no progress is made, no leadership becomes effective. We are, I know, ready and willing to submit our lives and property to such discipline because it makes possible a leadership which aims at a larger good. This I propose to offer, pledging that the larger purposes will bind upon us all as a sacred obligation with a unity of duty hitherto evoked only in time of armed strife.

With this pledge taken, I assume unhesitatingly the leadership of this great army of our people, dedicated to a disciplined attack upon our common problems.

Action in this image and to this end is feasible under the form of government which we have inherited from our ancestors. Our Constitution is so simple and practical that it is possible always to meet extraordinary needs by changes in emphasis and arrangement without loss of essential form. That is why our constitutional system has proved itself the most superbly enduring political mechanism the modern world has produced. It has met every stress of vast expansion of territory, of foreign wars, of bitter internal strife, of world relations.

It is to be hoped that the normal balance of executive and legislative authority may be wholly adequate to meet the unprecedented task before us. But it may be that an unprecedented demand and need for undelayed action may call for temporary departure from that normal balance of public procedure.

I am prepared under my constitutional duty to recommend the measures that a stricken nation in the midst of a stricken world may require. These measures, or such other measures as the Congress may build out of its experience and wisdom, I shall seek, within my constitutional authority, to bring to speedy adoption.

But in the event that the Congress shall fail to take one of these courses, and in the event that the national emergency is still critical, I shall not evade the clear course of duty that will then confront me. I shall ask the Congress for the one remaining instrument to meet the crisis—broad executive power to wage a war against the emergency as great as the power that would be given to me if we were in fact invaded by a foreign foe.

For the trust reposed in me I will return the courage and the devotion that befit the time. I can do no less.

We face the arduous days that lie before us in the warm courage of national unity, with the clear consciousness of seeking old and precious moral values, with the clean satisfaction that comes from the stern performance of

duty by old and young alike. We aim at the assurance of a rounded and permanent national life.

We do not distrust the future of essential democracy. The people of the United States have not failed. In their need they have registered a mandate that they want direct, vigorous action. They have asked for discipline and direction under leadership. They have made me the present instrument of their wishes. In the spirit of the gift I take it.

In this dedication of a nation we humbly ask the blessing of God. May He protect each and every one of us. May He guide me in the days to come.

Bonus Marchers, 1932. The self-named Bonus Expeditionary Force was an assemblage of some 43,000 veterans and their supporters who protested in Washington, D.C., in the spring and summer of 1932. The veterans, many of whom had been out of work since the beginning of the Great Depression, sought immediate cash payment of Service Certificates granted to them eight years earlier via the Adjusted Service Certificate Law of 1924. Each Service Certificate, issued to a qualified veteran soldier, bore a face value equal to the soldier's promised payment, plus compound interest. The problem was that the certificates matured twenty years from the date of original issuance and could not be redeemed until 1945. On July 28, U.S. Attorney General Mitchell ordered the veterans removed from all government property. Washington police met with resistance, and two veterans were killed. President Hoover then ordered the Army to clear out the veterans. In 1936, Congress overrode a veto by President Roosevelt to give the veterans their bonus ten years early.

FRANKLIN D. ROOSEVELT

Second Inaugural Address

I see one-third of a nation ill-housed, ill-clad, ill-nourished.

Bewildered by the continuing failure of the U.S. economy, Roosevelt promoted an array of social spending and public works projects known as the "New Deal." In so doing, he set aside earlier pledges that he would reduce spending and balance the federal budget. His landslide re-election in 1936 reflected the fact that most Americans felt more comfortable with the leadership of a man pledged to experiment than they did with seemingly inflexible Republican alternatives. Roosevelt described his reform program as the "use of the authority of government as an organized form of self-help for all classes and groups and sections of our country." In his second inaugural address, for example, the president spoke of "the need to find through government the instrument of our united purpose to solve for the individual the ever-rising problems of a complex civilization." Throughout his entire second term and until the beginning of World War II, which actually brought America out of the Great Depression, Roosevelt engaged in protracted battles with the courts to create new executive agencies to provide such things as social security for the aged, price supports for agricultural products, and work for the unemployed. His introduction of far-reaching reforms within the free enterprise system prepared the way for what is often called the welfare state.

When four years ago we met to inaugurate a President, the Republic, single-minded in anxiety, stood in spirit here. We dedicated ourselves to the fulfillment of a vision—to speed the time when there would be for all the people that security and peace essential to the pursuit of happiness. We of the Republic pledged ourselves to drive from the temple of our ancient faith those who had profaned it; to end by action, tireless and unafraid, the stagnation and despair of that day. We did those first things first.

Our covenant with ourselves did not stop there. Instinctively we recognized a deeper need—the need to find through government the instrument of our united purpose to solve for the individual the ever-rising problems of a complex civilization. Repeated attempts at their solution without the aid of government had left us baffled and bewildered. For, without that aid, we had been unable to create those moral controls over the services of science which are necessary to make science a useful servant instead of a ruthless master of mankind. To do this we knew that we must find practical controls over blind economic forces and blindly selfish men.

We of the Republic sensed the truth that democratic government has innate capacity to protect its people against disasters once considered inevitable, to solve problems once considered unsolvable. We would not admit that we could not find a way to master economic epidemics just as,

after centuries of fatalistic suffering, we had found a way to master epidemics of disease. We refused to leave the problems of our common welfare to be solved by the winds of chance and the hurricanes of disaster. ...

Four years of new experience have not belied our historic instinct. They hold out the clear hope that government within communities, government within the separate States, and government of the United States can do the things the times require, without yielding its democracy. Our tasks in the last four years did not force democracy to take a holiday.

Nearly all of us recognize that as intricacies of human relationships increase, so power to govern them also must increase—power to stop evil; power to do good. The essential democracy of our Nation and the safety of our people depend not upon the absence of power, but upon lodging it with those whom the people can change or continue at stated intervals through an honest and free system of elections. The Constitution of 1787 did not make our democracy impotent.

In fact, in these last four years, we have made the exercise of all power more democratic; for we have begun to bring private autocratic powers into their proper subordination to the public's government. The legend that they were invincible—above and beyond the processes of a democracy—has been shattered. They have been challenged and beaten.

Our progress out of the depression is obvious. But that is not all that you and I mean by the new order of things. Our pledge was not merely to do a patchwork job with secondhand materials. By using the new materials of social justice we have undertaken to erect on the old foundations a more enduring structure for the better use of future generations.

In that purpose we have been helped by achievements of mind and spirit. Old truths have been relearned; untruths have been unlearned. We have always known that heedless self-interest was bad morals; we know now that it is bad economics. Out of the collapse of a prosperity whose builders boasted their practicality has come the conviction that in the long run economic morality pays. We are beginning to wipe out the line that divides the practical from the ideal; and in so doing we are fashioning an instrument of unimagined power for the establishment of a morally better world.

This new understanding undermines the old admiration of worldly success as such. We are beginning to abandon our tolerance of the abuse of power by those who betray for profit the elementary decencies of life.

In this process evil things formerly accepted will not be so easily condoned. Hard-headedness will not so easily excuse hardheartedness. We are moving toward an era of good feeling. But we realize that there can be no era of good feeling save among men of good will. For these reasons I am justified in believing that the greatest change we have witnessed has been the change in the moral climate of America.

Among men of good will, science and democracy together offer an ever-richer life and ever-larger satisfaction to the individual. With this change in our moral climate and our rediscovered ability to improve our economic order, we have set our feet upon the road of enduring progress. Shall we pause now and turn our back upon the road that lies ahead? Shall we call this the promised land? Or, shall we continue on our way? For "each age is a dream that is dying, or one that is coming to birth."

Many voices are heard as we face a great decision. Comfort says, "Tarry a while." Opportunism says, "This is a good spot." Timidity asks, "How difficult is the road ahead?"

True, we have come far from the days of stagnation and despair. Vitality has been preserved. Courage and confidence have been restored. Mental and moral horizons have been extended. But our present gains were won under the pressure of more than ordinary circumstances. Advance became imperative under the goad of fear and suffering. The times were on the side of progress.

To hold to progress today, however, is more difficult. Dulled conscience, irresponsibility, and ruthless self-interest already reappear. Such symptoms of prosperity may become portents of disaster! Prosperity already tests the persistence of our progressive purpose. Let us ask again: Have we reached the goal of our vision of that fourth day of March 1933? Have we found our happy valley?

I see a great nation, upon a great continent, blessed with a great wealth of natural resources. Its hundred and thirty million people are at peace among themselves; they are making their country a good neighbor among the nations. I see a United States which can demonstrate that, under democratic methods of government, national wealth can be translated into a spreading volume of human comforts hitherto unknown, and the lowest standard of living can be raised far above the level of mere subsistence.

But here is the challenge to our democracy: In this nation I see tens of millions of its citizens—a substantial part of its whole population—who at this very moment are denied the greater part of what the very lowest standards of today call the necessities of life.

I see millions of families trying to live on incomes so meager that the pall of family disaster hangs over them day by day.

I see millions whose daily lives in city and on farm continue under conditions labeled indecent by a so-called polite society half a century ago.

I see millions denied education, recreation, and the opportunity to better their lot and the lot of their children.

I see millions lacking the means to buy the products of farm and factory and by their poverty denying work and productiveness to many other millions.

I see one-third of a nation ill-housed, ill-clad, ill-nourished.

It is not in despair that I paint you that picture. I paint it for you in hope—because the Nation, seeing and understanding the injustice in it, proposes to paint it out. We are determined to make every American citizen the subject of his country's interest and concern; and we will never regard any faithful law-abiding group within our borders as superfluous. The test of our progress is not whether we add more to the abundance of those who have much; it is whether we provide enough for those who have too little.

If I know aught of the spirit and purpose of our Nation, we will not listen to Comfort, Opportunism, and Timidity. We will carry on. …

Today we reconsecrate our country to long-cherished ideals in a suddenly changed civilization. In every land there are always at work forces that drive men apart and forces that draw men together. In our personal ambitions we are individualists. But in our seeking for economic and political progress as a nation, we all go up, or else we all go down, as one people. …

Man selling apples on 8th Avenue, New York City in 1930. One of the many finding another means of support after losing his job, he is also displaying a sign asking for information as to the whereabouts of his missing wife.

The Court-Packing Plan

Why should we not quit legislating by pious preambles and conform our enactments to the requirements of the Constitution and thus put upon notice the cabal of amateur experimenters that we will have no more of their trash?

The makeup of the Supreme Court when Franklin Roosevelt took office was relatively balanced. Of the nine justices, the conservative coalition of James Clark McReynolds, Willis Van Devanter, George Sutherland, and Pierce Butler—"The Four Horsemen," as they were known—generally clashed with liberal justices Louis Brandeis, Harlan Stone, and Benjamin Cardozo. Justice Owen Roberts and Chief Justice Charles Evans Hughes remained more or less moderate. While the court initially accepted most of Roosevelt's programs, it had more recently ruled that the executive branch had unconstitutionally assumed powers reserved for the legislature or the states. The president was further shocked, on May 27, 1935, when the court delivered three unanimous opinions that struck down key provisions of the New Deal.

Frustrated with what he perceived as a court intent on slowing down the progress of his recovery program, Roosevelt made a bold and controversial decision. Since the U.S. Constitution does not limit the size of the Supreme Court, Roosevelt sought to counter this entrenched opposition to his political agenda by expanding the number of justices in order to create a pro-New Deal majority on the bench. On February 5, 1937, he submitted to Congress his "Judiciary Reorganization Bill" and made it the subject of his March 9, 1937, fireside chat. Dubbed the "court-packing" plan by its opponents, the bill would have allowed Roosevelt to appoint one new judge to match every sitting judge that had served at least ten years and hadn't retired or resigned within six months of turning seventy years of age. Under the plan, Roosevelt could add dozens of new federal judges and, most importantly, up to six new Supreme Court justices.

Validating the concerns of many who felt that Roosevelt was intent on one-man rule, the judicial reorganization plan sparked intense opposition and mobilized conservative foes of the New Deal. Chief Justice Hughes likewise entered the political fray, providing court records as evidence to debunk Roosevelt's allegations of inefficiency from "aged, overworked justices." Most significantly, the court-packing plan met fierce opposition from the president's own party, especially Senator Burton Wheeler of Montana, who declared, "Every despot has usurped the power of the legislative and judicial branches in the name of the necessity for haste to promote the general welfare of the masses— and then proceeded to reduce them to servitude."

On March 29, 1937, Democratic Senator Carter Glass of Virginia delivered the following radio address from Washington, in which he, too, vehemently attacked the president's "attempt to replace representative government with an autocracy." On the same day, however, just as the opposition was running strong, an unexpected turn of events took place. The Supreme Court reversed itself and upheld a state minimum-wage law very similar to laws the court had previously struck down. Shortly thereafter, the court upheld as constitutional both the National Labor Relations Act and the Social Security Act. For reasons unknown, Justice Owen Roberts decided to switch sides in these cases, thus providing the three liberal justices along with Chief Justice Hughes a 5-4 majority. Just weeks later, the court having clearly altered course, Justice Van Devanter announced his intention to retire, thus giving FDR his first opportunity to make a Supreme Court appointment.

The Senate rejected Roosevelt's court-packing plan by a vote of 70-20, causing him to abandon the legislation. However, the president would eventually appoint eight justices while in office and effectively "pack" the court with men of his choosing. Though Roosevelt remained popular, the protracted legislative battle over the court-packing bill divided the New Deal coalition and heralded an end to the social and economic reforms he had begun.

… This entire nation is aroused over the many definite proposals to reverse the deliberate judgments of an independent court and to substitute for them the previously pledged opinions of judicial subalterns. With men of this undisguised radical type campaigning the country, freely applying their wretched opprobriums to the Supreme Court,

Forward America. But which way is forward? Surely we have been going forward during the last one hundred and fifty years towards a goal which the Pilgrims established in 1620 and which was carried on by the founders of our nation. That goal was increased individual freedom, with more material welfare to enjoy it. Surely we went forward in spite of this talk about financial feudalism. Men were more free in 1932, *before* the New Deal, then they were in any other country in the world. Their material welfare had steadily increased until the average workman had a standard of living three times as high as it was in 1820. The average New Dealer seems to think that because 1933 represented the bottom of a financial depression there was no democracy or prosperity in the United States before Franklin D. Roosevelt. Surely a majority of the people decided every four years what kind of government they wished, and surely the Congresses then as now voted the way they thought their constituents wanted them to vote.

It is the New Dealers who no longer wish to go forward along our well-marked path. They started along that path in 1933 for a few years, but they have wandered farther and farther into the forest of Government regimentation until, in complete darkness, they are moving back in the direction of the Middle Ages. …

Many of the New Dealers have no concern whatever for individual freedom. They are collectivists, like Marx and Lenin and Mussolini. They believe in planned economy; that the Government should regulate every detail of industrial and commercial and agricultural life. They are willing to sacrifice individual freedom in order supposedly to improve the conditions of the poor and increase their material welfare. But in this purpose the policy has completely failed. There are more than ten million people unemployed today, and the largest relief expense this year, ten years after the depression, than any in the history of the United States. Farm prices are lower than they have been for six years. Business men are discouraged and indignant. Deposits have piled up in the banks because rich and poor alike are afraid to put their time or money into private enterprise, because they fear that Government regulation will prevent success, and Government taxation will take whatever profit there might be. The New Deal policy is the only one which has ever plunged us into a second depression before we were out of the first. If any policy leads backward and not forward, it is the policy of spending billions of borrowed money and piling up a

tremendous debt for future generations to pay. A policy which inevitably leads to bankruptcy and inflation of the currency will not only make the poor people poorer but is likely to force a socialism which will utterly deprive them of individual freedom. …

Instead of throwing away all past experience and embarking on uncharted seas, we would keep the good things which the American system produced, encourage the principles which produced them, and correct the abuses which crept into it as they will creep into any system. Let us remember that conditions in the twenties in many ways were better than they ever have been since. Farm prices were more than twice what they are today. Unemployment practically did not exist. Men were eager to engage in new industries, expand old industries, and build up both production and employment. If we had the same national per capita income today as we had then, we would have ninety billion dollars instead of sixty-seven, and if we had this thirty-five per cent more income than we actually have today, we could put most of the unemployed men back to work. We must restore conditions in which thousands of men and women every year were willing to invest their time and money in building up the United States and the prosperity of the people of the United States.

Representative Smith says that Republicans wish the many well through the assured welfare of the few. Of course this is not true. No one has ever *assured* the welfare of any business enterprise until the New Dealers tried to do it under the N.R.A. [National Recovery Administration]. It is said that two out of every three new businesses fail. It is not the assurance of success; it is the existence of conditions which make it likely that a man of exceptional ability or ingenuity, who is willing to work hard, shall have a chance to obtain exceptional rewards for himself or his family, a chance which shall not be destroyed by Government regulation and interference. This, says Representative Smith, is the "seepage" theory of welfare. As a matter of fact, the men who are put to work in new jobs by new enterprise get their living and their purchasing power many months and often many years before the men who started the enterprises receive their reward, if they do receive it.

We have tried the alternative theory of producing prosperity based on dishing out Government funds to great classes of people, and, while such action has been necessary, it has certainly failed completely to produce general prosperity and has not even restored those men who receive it to the material welfare they enjoyed in the twenties.

What were the abuses to be corrected in the system of the twenties? There were too many people rich beyond their deserts. I thoroughly approve of the New Deal measures to prevent fraud and sharp practice through the sale of securities, which was one of the principal methods of undeserved wealth. There were undoubtedly some monopolies whose owners received profits greater than they deserved. I may say, however, that the monopolies before 1932 were nothing to the monopolies fostered and built up by the New Deal under the N.R.A. For a number of years the New Deal was dominated by the theory that all business should consist of Government-controlled monopolies. Undoubtedly the Government should keep competition free and open, so that men may not make profits which they do not deserve, but I feel that the existence of business monopoly has been exaggerated. In practically all of the articles which average people buy, there exists today, and existed in 1928, the most intense competition, notably in foodstuffs and clothing and automobiles. …

Another abuse of the system of the twenties was that the distribution of income was not sufficient for a decent living for the poorer groups. I might point out that this condition has always existed under every system and certainly exists in Russia under communism today. To increase the condition of the poor has been the earnest desire of every public-spirited statesman in either party. The question is not one of purpose; the question is what method will improve that condition. The Republican party thoroughly approves of old age pensions, unemployment insurance, relief when necessary, and subsidized housing, but all of these together have not improved the conditions of the poor over what it was in the twenties. There are more underprivileged today than there were in the twenties. There are more people wholly unemployed, and many more earning a bare subsistence on relief. If we could restore the economic and business activity of 1928, we could add twenty-three billion to the national income, most of it to the relief classes. Relief and old age pensions together do not add more than four billion at a maximum.

Finally, in the twenties it is probable that the laboring groups and the farm groups were at a disadvantage in dealing with individual employers and individual buyers of farm products. The Wagner Act, to promote collective bargaining in the labor field, and the farm coöperative acts, to encourage collective bargaining on the part of the farmer, are sound measures, if properly administered, to see that oppression does not arise in the normal processes of bargaining and competition. But Representative Smith wholly fails to distinguish between measures designed to assist coöperative organization and measures proposing that the Government regulate agriculture and labor and industry. He confuses self-organization with governmental bureaucratic organizations. It is no slight confusion. It is the difference between freedom and slavery. In the Guffey Coal Act to regulate prices and wages in the coal industry, in the wage-hour act, except to the extent that it is a real minimum wage law, in the agricultural acts which practically fix the prices of agricultural products, in the administration of the Wagner Act, which goes far beyond the purpose of that act to tell employers how they shall run their business, in the power sought to make arbitrary changes in the value of the dollar and the currency to effect some individual's idea of what prices should be, we see being worked out a complete Government-controlled economy. In order to allow the farmer to organize, it is not necessary for the Government to pay out eight hundred and fifty million dollars in benefits, or loan money on cotton and wheat in excess of the value of cotton and wheat. These measures, like the N.R.A. and the A.A.A. [Agricultural Adjustment Administration], lead backward. If we ever get to the point where the Government fixes the price of all basic commodities, we cannot stop short of complete regimentation. There is a fundamental distinction between measures intended to keep the course of competition and investment and individual incentive open and those measures intended to direct the activities of the men who engage in that competition and industry. Above all, we have the entire Government regulation process stimulated by the theory that Government spending can produce prosperity, a theory utterly disproved by our actual experience and by every sound economic principle. The New Dealers today no longer go forward along the path which this country pursued for one hundred and fifty years. They admit it. They say that everything is changed; a new era has come, requiring new methods. I don't believe it. Americans are still American. They have the same basic ideals which they have had for hundreds of years. They are just as eager for individual freedom. They are just as anxious to be let alone by Government agents. They are just as anxious to run their owl local affairs and their own schools. They don't like relief, and they know that a reasonable prosperity can do away with the necessity for relief. They know that thrift and ability and hard work ought to bring rewards today, as they did in the horse and buggy days, if it were not for Government interference. They know that only the Republican party can avert the disaster which will inevitably result from deficit spending, arbitrary price-fixing, excessive taxation, and Government regulation of everything and everybody.

We have heard a good deal about the depression of 1933 and the terrific condition left by the Republicans. But the depression of 1933 existed throughout the entire world, while the depression of 1937 was a special American depression, created by New Deal policies. ...

IRVING BERLIN

Oh, How I Hate to Get Up in the Morning and God Bless America

Israel Baline (1888-1989) was born in Russia and emigrated to the United States with his family in 1893. He left school at the age of eight when his father died and went to work selling newspapers and singing in local bars for tip money. When he published his first song at nineteen, his name was mistakenly printed as "I. Berlin." Changing his first name and assuming the new surname, Berlin achieved his first hit in 1911 with "Alexander's Ragtime Band." Despite an inability to read or write music, Berlin was recognized, by the age of thirty, as one of the greatest songwriters in American history.

During World War I, while serving as an Army sergeant, Berlin staged a show called *Yip, Yip, Yaphank* for the purpose of boosting morale. The show included "Oh, How I Hate to Get Up in the Morning," which Berlin also included in his 1942 musical, *This is the Army*. "God Bless America" was originally written for the Army musical, but Berlin tucked the song away and did not use it until 1938 when Kate Smith, a popular singer, asked the songwriter for a patriotic song she could use for a national radio broadcast. Having already donated the more than ten million dollars generated by *This is the Army* to the government, Berlin gave the royalties from "God Bless America" to the Boy Scouts and Girl Scouts. Berlin's legacy includes numerous musicals and more than 1,500 songs, including such additional hits as, "There's No Business Like Show Business," "Blue Skies," "Easter Parade," "Puttin' on the Ritz," and the classic "White Christmas."

Oh, How I Hate to Get Up in the Morning

The other day I chanced to meet
A soldier friend of mine;
He'd been in camp for sev'ral weeks,
And he was looking fine.
His muscles had developed,
And his cheeks were rosy red,
I asked him how he liked the life,
And this is what he said:

Chorus:
  "Oh! How I hate to get up in the morning!
  Oh! how I'd love to remain in bed!
  For the hardest blow of all
  Is to hear the bugler call:
  'You've got to get up,
  You've got to get up,
  You've got to get up this morning!'
  Someday I'm going to murder the bugler;
  Someday they're going to find him dead –
  I'll amputate his reveille,
  And step upon it heavily,
  And spend the rest of my life in bed."

A bugler in the army
Is the luckiest of men:
He wakes the boys at five and then
Goes back to bed again.
He doesn't have to blow again
Until the afternoon;
If ev'rything goes well with me,
I'll be a bugler soon.

"Oh, boy! the minute the battle is over,
Oh, boy! the minute the foe is dead,
I'll put my uniform away
And move to Philadelph-I-A
And spend the rest of my life in bed."

God Bless America

While the storm clouds gather
Far across the sea,
Let us swear allegiance
To a land that's free;
Let us all be grateful
For a land so fair,
As we raise our voices
In a solemn prayer.

God bless America,
Land that I love,
Stand beside her and guide her
Through the night with the light from above.
From the mountains, to the prairies,
To the oceans white with foam,
God bless America,
My home sweet home.

LOU GEHRIG

Farewell

Today I consider myself the luckiest man on the face of this earth.

Henry Louis Gehrig (1903-1941) was one the greatest baseball players and all-around athletes in history. He had a lifetime batting average of .340, hitting 493 home runs—including twenty-three grand slams—and batting in one hundred or more runs for thirteen consecutive years—including 150 or more runs in seven of those seasons. Known as the "Iron Horse," Gehrig played in 2,130 consecutive games during fourteen seasons with the New York Yankees. His record for durability, broken in 1995 by Cal Ripken, Jr. of the Baltimore Orioles, came to an end only when Gehrig benched himself because his play began to suffer from the effects of amyotrophic lateral sclerosis. The rare degenerative nerve disease, for which there is still no known cure, is now commonly referred to as *Lou Gehrig's Disease.*

On July 4, 1939, fans packed Yankee Stadium for "Gehrig Appreciation Day." Surrounded by his teammates, city officials, and former Yankee greats, including Babe Ruth, Gehrig bid farewell to baseball and gave the nation a lesson in courage. The Yankees retired his number (#4), the first time a player in any sport had ever been honored in such a manner and, before his death, Lou Gehrig was inducted into the Baseball Hall of Fame.

Fans, for the past two weeks you have been reading about the bad break I got. Yet today I consider myself the luckiest man on the face of this earth. I have been in ballparks for seventeen years and have never received anything but kindness and encouragement from you fans. Look at these grand men. Which of you wouldn't consider it the highlight of his career just to associate with them for even one day? Sure I'm lucky. Who wouldn't consider it an honor to have known Jacob Ruppert? Also, the builder of baseball's greatest empire, Ed Barrow? To have spent six years with that wonderful little fellow, Miller Huggins? Then to have spent the next nine years with that outstanding leader, that smart student of psychology, the best manager in baseball today, Joe McCarthy? Sure I'm lucky. When the New York Giants, a team you would give your right arm to beat, and vice versa, sends you a gift—*that's* something. When everybody down to the groundskeepers and those boys in white coats remember you with trophies—that's something. When you have a wonderful mother-in-law who takes sides with you in squabbles with her own daughter—that's something. When you have a father and a mother who work all their lives so you can have an education and build your body—it's a blessing. When you have a wife who has been a tower of strength and shown more courage than you dreamed existed—that's the finest I know. So I close in saying that I may have had a tough break, but I have an awful lot to live for.

Flag Day

We love our country because there was a little tree on a hill, and grass thereon, and a sweet valley below.

Flag Day was observed for the first time in 1877, the one hundredth anniversary of the adoption of America's red-white-and-blue banner. On May 30, 1916, President Woodrow Wilson officially established Flag Day by proclamation. Though the event was celebrated in communities for decades thereafter, it was not until August 3, 1949, when President Harry Truman signed an Act of Congress, that June 14 of each year became National Flag Day.

The following tribute to America's national symbol was published anonymously in *The New York Times* in 1940. "Flag Day" speaks of America's rich national heritage and the love Americans have for their country as a whole, as well as for their own "little corners of the land." As President Wilson once remarked, "The things that the flag stands for were created by the experiences of a great people. Everything that it stands for was written by their lives. The flag is the embodiment, not of sentiment, but of history. It represents the experiences made by men and women, the experiences of those who do and live under the flag."

What's a flag? What's the love of country for which it stands? Maybe it begins with love of the land itself. It is the fog rolling in with the tide at Eastport, or through the Golden Gate and among the towers of San Francisco. It is the sun coming up behind the White Mountains, over the Green, throwing a shining glory on Lake Champlain and above the Adirondacks. It is the storied Mississippi rolling swift and muddy past St. Louis, rolling past Cairo, pouring down past the levees of New Orleans. It is lazy noontide in the pines of Carolina, it is a sea of wheat rippling in Western Kansas, it is the San Francisco peaks far north across the glowing nakedness of Arizona, it is the Grand Canyon and a little stream coming down out of a New England ridge, in which are trout.

It is men at work. It is the storm-tossed fishermen coming into Gloucester and Providence and Astoria. It is the farmer riding his great machine in the dust of harvest, the dairyman going to the barn before sunrise, the lineman mending the broken wire, the miner drilling for the blast. It is the servants of fire in the murky splendor of Pittsburgh, between the Allegheny and the Monongahela, the trucks rumbling through the night, the locomotive engineer bringing the train in on time, the pilot in the clouds, the riveter running along the beam a hundred feet in air. It is the clerk in the office, the housewife doing the dishes and sending the children off to school. It is the teacher, doctor and parson tending and helping, body and soul, for small reward.

It is small things remembered, the little corners of the land, the houses, the people that each one loves. We love our country because there was a little tree on a hill, and grass thereon, and a sweet valley below; because the hurdy-gurdy man came along on a sunny morning in a city street; because a beach or a farm or a lane or a house that might not seem much to others were once, for each of us, made magic. It is voices that are remembered only, no longer heard. It is parents, friends, the lazy chat of street and store and office, and the ease of mind that makes life tranquil. It is Summer and Winter, rain and sun and storm. These are flesh of our flesh, bone of our bone, blood of our blood, a lasting part of what we are, each of us and all of us together.

It is stories told. It is the Pilgrims dying in their first dreadful Winter. It is the minute man standing his ground at Concord Bridge, and dying there. It is the army in rags, sick, freezing, starving at Valley Forge. It is the wagons and the men on foot going westward over Cumberland Gap, floating down the great rivers, rolling over the great plains. It is the settler hacking fiercely at the primeval forest on his new, his own lands. It is Thoreau at Walden Pond, Lincoln at Cooper Union, and Lee riding home from Appomattox.

It is corruption and disgrace, answered always by men who would not let the flag lie in the dust, who have stood up in every generation to fight for the old ideals and the old rights, at risk of ruin or of life itself.

It is a great multitude of people on pilgrimage, common and ordinary people, charged with the usual human failings, yet filled with such a hope as never caught the imaginations and the hearts of any nation on earth before. The hope of liberty. The hope of justice. The hope of a land in which a man can stand straight, without fear, without rancor.

The land and the people and the flag—the land a continent, the people of every race, the flag a symbol of what humanity may aspire to when the wars are over and the barriers are down; to these each generation must be dedicated and consecrated anew, to defend with life itself, if need be, but, above all, in friendliness, in hope, in courage, to live for.

WOODY GUTHRIE

This Land Is Your Land

Woody Guthrie (1912-1967) is remembered as an influential singer-songwriter and folk musician whose legacy includes an estimated 1,000 songs covering a multitude of subjects. Born in Okemah, Oklahoma, a small agricultural and railroad town, Guthrie was forced to become self-sufficient at an early age due to a series of family tragedies. At the age of nineteen, he relocated to Pampa, Texas, where he met and ultimately married his first wife.

When the Great Depression deepened and drought turned a large section of the Great Plains into the Dust Bowl, making it impossible for Guthrie to support his growing family, he took to the road in search of work—riding in freight trains, hitchhiking, and living in hobo camps. Much of his time was spent following the Okies, a term used by many to disparage the poor, mostly white migrant workers and their families who traveled in search of jobs, land, dignity, and a future. The term became well-known nationwide with the publication of John Steinbeck's novel, *The Grapes of Wrath*.

Guthrie's exposure to both the effects of the Great Depression on peoples' lives and the beauty of the American landscape served as the basis for many of his songs, the most popular of which was "This Land Is Your Land" (1940). Guthrie died in 1967 from Huntington's disease, a degenerative nerve disorder he had been battling for thirteen years. His autobiography, *Bound for Glory*, was published in 1943.

This land is your land, this land is my land
From California to the New York island;
From the red wood forest to the Gulf Stream waters
This land was made for you and me.

As I was walking that ribbon of highway,
I saw above me that endless skyway:
I saw below me that golden valley:
This land was made for you and me.

I've roamed and rambled and I followed my footsteps
To the sparkling sands of her diamond deserts;
And all around me a voice was sounding:
This land was made for you and me.

When the sun came shining, and I was strolling,
And the wheat fields waving and the dust clouds rolling,
As the fog was lifting a voice was chanting:
This land was made for you and me.

As I went walking I saw a sign there
And on the sign it said "No Trespassing."
But on the other side it didn't say nothing,
That side was made for you and me.

In the shadow of the steeple I saw my people,
By the relief office I seen my people;
As they stood there hungry, I stood there asking
Is this land made for you and me?

Nobody living can ever stop me,
As I go walking that freedom highway;
Nobody living can ever make me turn back
This land was made for you and me.

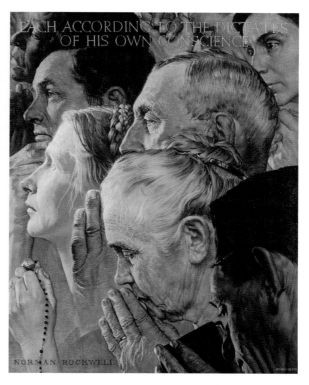

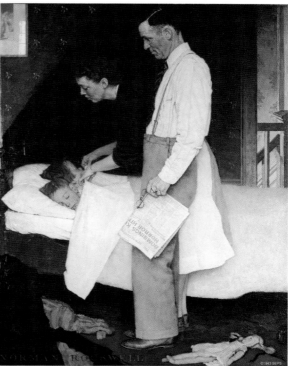

The Four Freedoms, *a series of oil paintings produced by Norman Rockwell and inspired by President Franklin Roosevelt's 1941 State of the Union speech. The paintings appeared on the cover of* The Saturday Evening Post *over the course of four consecutive weeks in 1943 alongside essays by prominent thinkers of the day. Later, they served as the highlight of a touring exhibition sponsored by the Department of the Treasury to help finance the war effort through the sale of war bonds. (Clockwise from upper left: Freedom of Speech; Freedom of Worship; Freedom From Fear; Freedom From Want)*

FRANKLIN D. ROOSEVELT

The Four Freedoms

We look forward to a world founded upon four essential human freedoms. The first is freedom of speech and expression … The second is freedom of every person to worship God in his own way … The third is freedom from want … The fourth is freedom from fear.

World War II began in 1939 with Germany's invasion of Poland and the subsequent declarations of war on Germany by Great Britain and France. Through a series of neutrality acts passed in the 1930s, the United States made clear its intention of remaining isolated from world affairs. By 1940, however, the U.S. was giving all aid to Great Britain short of direct military involvement. In his 1941 State of the Union speech, fearing the possible military collapse of Great Britain, President Roosevelt prepared the American public for increased participation in the war effort. He also outlined the four basic freedoms he felt should be pursued on behalf of all mankind at the war's conclusion. Two months later, Congress passed the Lend-Lease Act authorizing the provision of supplies to any nation at war with the Axis powers.

I address you, the members of this new Congress, at a moment unprecedented in the history of the union. I use the word "unprecedented" because at no previous time has American security been as seriously threatened from without as it is today.

Since the permanent formation of our government under the Constitution in 1789, most of the periods of crisis in our history have related to our domestic affairs. And, fortunately, only one of these—the four-year war between the States—ever threatened our national unity. Today, thank God, 130,000,000 Americans in forty-eight States have forgotten points of the compass in our national unity. …

Every realist knows that the democratic way of life is at this moment being directly assailed in every part of the world—assailed either by arms or by secret spreading of poisonous propaganda by those who seek to destroy unity and promote discord in nations still at peace. During sixteen months this assault has blotted out the whole pattern of democratic life in an appalling number of independent nations, great and small. And the assailants are still on the march, threatening other nations, great and small.

Therefore, as your President, performing my constitutional duty to "give to the Congress information of the state of the union," I find it unhappily necessary to report that the future and the safety of our country and of our democracy are overwhelmingly involved in events far beyond our borders.

Armed defense of democratic existence is now being gallantly waged in four continents. If that defense fails, all the population and all the resources of Europe and Asia, Africa and Australia will be dominated by conquerors. And let us remember that the total of those populations in those four continents, the total of those populations and their resources greatly exceeds the sum total of the population and the resources of the whole of the Western Hemisphere—many times over.

In times like these it is immature—and incidentally untrue—for anybody to brag that an unprepared America, single-handed, and with one hand tied behind its back, can hold off the whole world.

No realistic American can expect from a dictator's peace international generosity, or return of true independence, or world disarmament, or freedom of expression, or freedom of religion—or even good business. Such a peace would bring no security for us or for our neighbors. "Those who would give up essential liberty to purchase a little temporary safety deserve neither liberty nor safety."

As a nation we may take pride in the fact that we are soft-hearted; but we cannot afford to be soft-headed. We must always be wary of those who with sounding brass and a tinkling cymbal preach the "ism" of appeasement. We must especially beware of that small group of selfish men who would clip the wings of the American eagle in order to feather their own nests.

I have recently pointed out how quickly the tempo of modern warfare could bring into our very midst the physical attack which we must eventually expect if the dictator nations win this war.

There is much loose talk of our immunity from immediate and direct invasion from across the seas. Obviously, as long as the British Navy retains its power, no such danger exists. Even if there were no British Navy, it is not probable that any enemy would be stupid enough to attack us by landing troops in the United States from across thousands of miles of ocean, until it had acquired strategic bases from which to operate.

But we learn much from the lessons of the past years in Europe—particularly the lesson of Norway, whose essential seaports were captured by treachery and surprise built up over a series of years. The first phase of the invasion of this hemisphere would not be the landing of regular troops. The necessary strategic points would be occupied by secret agents and by their dupes—and great numbers of them are already here and in Latin America. As long as the aggressor nations maintain the offensive they, not we, will choose the time and the place and the method of their attack.

That is why the future of all the American Republics is today in serious danger. That is why this annual message to the Congress is unique in our history. That is why every member of the executive branch of the government and every member of the Congress face great responsibility— great accountability. The need of the moment is that our actions and our policy should be devoted primarily— almost exclusively—to meeting this foreign peril. For all our domestic problems are now a part of the great emergency.

Just as our national policy in internal affairs has been based upon a decent respect for the rights and the dignity of all of our fellow men within our gates, so our national policy in foreign affairs has been based on a decent respect for the rights and the dignity of all nations, large and small. And the justice of morality must and will win in the end.

Our national policy is this:

First, by an impressive expression of the public will and without regard to partisanship, we are committed to all-inclusive national defense.

Second, by an impressive expression of the public will and without regard to partisanship, we are committed to full support of all those resolute people everywhere who are resisting aggression and are thereby keeping war away from our hemisphere. By this support we express our determination that the democratic cause shall prevail, and we strengthen the defense and the security of our own nation.

Third, by an impressive expression of the public will and without regard to partisanship, we are committed to the proposition that principles of morality and considerations for our own security will never permit us to acquiesce in a peace dictated by aggressors and sponsored by appeasers.

We know that enduring peace cannot be bought at the cost of other people's freedom. ...

Therefore, the immediate need is a swift and driving increase in our armament production. ...

To change a whole nation from a basis of peacetime production of implements of peace to a basis of wartime production of implements of war is no small task. The greatest difficulty comes at the beginning of the program, when new tools, new plant facilities, new assembly lines, new shipways must first be constructed before the actual material begins to flow steadily and speedily from them.

The Congress, of course, must rightly keep itself informed at all times of the progress of the program. However, there is certain information, as the Congress itself will readily recognize, which, in the interests of our own security and those of the nations that we are supporting, must of needs be kept in confidence.

New circumstances are constantly begetting new needs for our safety. I shall ask this Congress for greatly increased new appropriations and authorizations to carry on what we have begun.

I also ask this Congress for authority and for funds sufficient to manufacture additional munitions and war supplies of many kinds, to be turned over to those nations which are now in actual war with aggressor nations. Our most useful and immediate role is to act as an arsenal for them as well as for ourselves. They do not need manpower, but they do need billions of dollars' worth of the weapons of defense.

The time is near when they will not be able to pay for them all in ready cash. We cannot, and we will not, tell them that they must surrender merely because of present inability to pay for the weapons which we know they must have.

I do not recommend that we make them a loan of dollars with which to pay for these weapons—a loan to be repaid in dollars. I recommend that we make it possible for those nations to continue to obtain war materials in the United States, fitting their orders into our own program. And nearly all of their material would, if the time ever came, be useful in our own defense.

Taking counsel of expert military and naval authorities, considering what is best for our own security, we are free to decide how much should be kept here and how much should be sent abroad to our friends who, by their determined and heroic resistance, are giving us time in which to make ready our own defense.

For what we send abroad we shall be repaid, repaid within a reasonable time following the close of hostilities, repaid in similar materials, or at our option in other goods of many kinds which they can produce and which we need.

Let us say to the democracies: "We Americans are vitally concerned in your defense of freedom. We are putting forth our energies, our resources and our organizing powers to give you the strength to regain and maintain a free world. We shall send you in ever-increasing numbers, ships, planes, tanks, guns. That is our purpose and our pledge."

In fulfillment of this purpose we will not be intimidated by the threats of dictators that they will regard as a breach of international law and as an act of war our aid to the democracies which dare to resist their aggression. Such aid is not an act of war, even if a dictator should unilaterally proclaim it so to be.

When the dictators are ready to make war upon us, they will not wait for an act of war on our part.

They did not wait for Norway or Belgium or the Netherlands to commit an act of war. Their only interest is in a new one-way international law which lacks mutuality in its observance, and, therefore, becomes an instrument of oppression. The happiness of future generations of Americans may well depend on how effective and how immediate we can make our aid felt. No one can tell the exact character of the emergency situations that we may be called upon to meet. The nation's hands must not be tied when the nation's life is in danger.

We must prepare to make the sacrifices that the emergency—as serious as war itself—demands. Whatever stands in the way of speed and efficiency in defense preparations must give way to the national need.

A free nation has the right to expect full cooperation from all groups. A free nation has the right to look to the leaders of business, of labor and of agriculture to take the lead in stimulating effort, not among other groups but within their own groups.

The best way of dealing with the few slackers or trouble-makers in our midst is, first, to shame them by patriotic example, and if that fails, to use the sovereignty of government to save government.

As men do not live by bread alone, they do not fight by armaments alone. Those who man our defenses and those behind them who build our defenses must have the stamina and the courage which come from an unshakable belief in the manner of life which they are defending. The mighty action that we are calling for cannot be based on a disregard of all the things worth fighting for.

The nation takes great satisfaction and much strength from the things which have been done to make its people conscious of their individual stake in the preservation of democratic life in America. Those things have toughened the fiber of our people, have renewed their faith and strengthened their devotion to the institutions we make ready to protect. ...

In the future days, which we seek to make secure, we look forward to a world founded upon four essential human freedoms.

The first is freedom of speech and expression—everywhere in the world.

The second is freedom of every person to worship God in his own way—everywhere in the world.

The third is freedom from want, which, translated into world terms, means economic understandings which will secure to every nation a healthy peacetime life for its inhabitants—everywhere in the world.

The fourth is freedom from fear, which, translated into world terms, means a world-wide reduction of armaments to such a point and in such a thorough fashion that no nation will be in a position to commit an act of physical aggression against any neighbor—anywhere in the world.

That is no vision of a distant millennium. It is a definite basis for a kind of world attainable in our own time and generation. That kind of world is the very antithesis of the so-called new order of tyranny which the dictators seek to create with the crash of a bomb.

To that new order we oppose the greater conception—the moral order. A good society is able to face schemes of world domination and foreign revolutions alike without fear.

Since the beginning of our American history we have been engaged in change, in a perpetual, peaceful revolution, a revolution which goes on steadily, quietly adjusting itself to changing conditions—without the concentration camp or the quick-lime in the ditch. The world order which we seek is the cooperation of free countries, working together in a friendly, civilized society.

This nation has placed its destiny in the hands, heads and hearts of its millions of free men and women, and its faith in freedom under the guidance of God. Freedom means the supremacy of human rights everywhere. Our support goes to those who struggle to gain those rights and keep them. Our strength is our unity of purpose.

To that high concept there can be no end save victory.

A draftee gets simultaneous smallpox and typhoid injections from medical officers at Fort Dix, New Jersey. The Selective Training and Service Act of 1940 became the first peacetime conscription in U.S. history. This Act required men between the ages of twenty-one and thirty-five to register with local draft boards. Later, when the U.S. entered World War II, all men aged eighteen to forty-five were made liable for military service, and all men aged eighteen to sixty-five were required to register.

FRANKLIN D. ROOSEVELT

War Message to Congress

December 7, 1941—a date which will live in infamy.

The premeditated and unprovoked Japanese attack on the U.S. Pacific fleet at Pearl Harbor resulted in the deaths of more than 2,300 American servicemen and 1,400 additional casualties; the sinking of eight battleships, three destroyers, and seven additional vessels; and the destruction of roughly 170 American planes. Japan then officially declared war on both the United States and Great Britain. President Roosevelt responded by delivering the following address to Congress, in which he asked for a formal declaration of war against Japan. The Congress obliged with only one dissenting vote— Congresswoman Jeannette Rankin of Montana, a pacifist Republican.

Yesterday, December 7, 1941—a date which will live in infamy—the United States of America was suddenly and deliberately attacked by naval and air forces of the empire of Japan.

The United States was at peace with that nation and, at the solicitation of Japan, was still in conversation with its government and its emperor looking toward the maintenance of peace in the Pacific.

Indeed, one hour after Japanese air squadrons had commenced bombing in the American Island of Oahu, the Japanese Ambassador to the United States and his colleague delivered to our Secretary of State a formal reply to a recent American message. And, while this reply stated that it seemed useless to continue the existing diplomatic negotiations, it contained no threat or hint of war or of armed attack.

It will be recorded that the distance of Hawaii from Japan makes it obvious that the attack was deliberately planned many days or even weeks ago. During the intervening time the Japanese Government has deliberately sought to deceive the United States by false statements and expressions of hope for continued peace.

The attack yesterday on the Hawaiian Islands has caused severe damage to American naval and military forces. I regret to tell you that very many American lives have been lost. In addition, American ships have been reported torpedoed on the high seas between San Francisco and Honolulu.

Yesterday the Japanese Government also launched an attack against Malaya.

Last night Japanese forces attacked Hong Kong.

Last night Japanese forces attacked Guam.

Last night Japanese forces attacked the Philippine Islands.

Last night the Japanese attacked Wake Island.

And this morning the Japanese attacked Midway Island.

Japan has therefore undertaken a surprise offensive extending throughout the Pacific area. The facts of yesterday and today speak for themselves. The people of the United States have already formed their opinions and well understand the implications to the very life and safety of our nation.

As Commander in Chief of the Army and Navy I have directed that all measures be taken for our defense.

Always will our whole nation remember the character of the onslaught against us.

No matter how long it may take us to overcome this premeditated invasion, the American people, in their righteous might, will win through to absolute victory.

I believe that I interpret the will of the Congress and of the people when I assert that we will not only defend ourselves to the uttermost but will make it very certain that this form of treachery shall never again endanger us.

Hostilities exist. There is no blinking at the fact that our people, our territory and our interests are in grave danger.

With confidence in our armed forces, with the unbounding determination of our people, we will gain the inevitable triumph. So help us God.

I ask that the Congress declare that since the unprovoked and dastardly attack by Japan on Sunday, December 7, 1941, a state of war has existed between the United States and the Japanese Empire.

On April 18, 1942, Lt. Colonel James Doolittle, center right with members of his flight crew and Chinese officials, led the first air attack on the Japanese home islands during World War II. The plan called for sixteen B-25 bombers, launched from the aircraft carrier USS Hornet, *to strike military targets in Japan and continue westward to land in China. Because the raid had to be launched earlier than planned, fifteen of the aircraft ran out of fuel and crash landed in the Chinese provinces of Zhejiang and Jiangxi. One of the B-25s landed in the Soviet Union at Vladivostok, where it was confiscated and its crew interned for more than a year. Eleven crewmen were either killed or captured, with three of the captured men executed by the Japanese Army in China. Most of the B-25 crews, after parachuting into China, eventually made it to safety with assistance from Chinese soldiers and civilians. The Japanese responded in brutal fashion, killing an estimated 250,000 Chinese civilians while searching for Doolittle's men. The Doolittle Raid caused negligible material damage to Japan, but it succeeded in its goal of helping boost American morale while simultaneously forcing the Japanese to redeploy assets and alter their war strategy. The Doolittle Raid was the subject of the 1944 feature film,* Thirty Seconds Over Tokyo, *based on a book of the same title by Doolittle Raider Captain Ted W. Lawson.*

ROBERT CRAWFORD

The U.S. Air Force

Robert Crawford (1899-1961) was born in the Yukon Territory and educated at Princeton University and the Juilliard School of Music. In 1939, *Liberty* magazine offered a prize for "a spirited, enduring musical composition to become the official Army Air Corps song." Crawford, then a civilian pilot, responded with the winning entry and later served as a major in the Air Corps during the Second World War. Originally titled "The Army Air Corps," the song was later retitled "The U.S. Air Force." The original version by Crawford includes the verse "A Toast to the Host," which commemorates those who have fallen in the service of the nation—thus, the change in melody.

Off we go, into the wild blue yonder,
Climbing high, into the sun;
Here they come, zooming to meet our thunder,
At 'em, boys, Give'er the gun!
Down we dive, spouting our flame from under,
Off with one helluva roar!
We live in fame, or go down in flame—hey!
NOTHING'LL STOP THE ARMY AIR CORPS!

Minds of men fashioned a crate of thunder,
Sent it high into the blue,
Hands of men blasted the world asunder;
How they lived, God only knew!
Souls of men dreaming of skies to conquer
Gave us wings, ever to soar!
With scouts before and bombers galore—hey!
NOTHING'LL STOP THE ARMY AIR CORPS!

Here's a toast to the host
Of those who love the vastness of the sky,
To a friend we send a message of his brother men who fly,
We drink to those who gave their all of old,
Then down we roar to score the rainbow's pot of gold.
A toast to the host of men we boast, the Army Air Corps!

Off we go into the wild sky yonder,
Keep the wings level and true;
If you'd live to be a gray-haired wonder
Keep the nose out of the blue!
Flying men, guarding the nation's border,
We'll be there, followed by more!
In echelon, we carry on—hey!
NOTHING'LL STOP THE ARMY AIR CORPS!

CHARLES A. ZIMMERMAN AND ALFRED H. MILES

Anchors Aweigh

Navy Lieutenant Charles A. Zimmerman, a graduate of the Peabody Conservatory in Baltimore, became bandmaster of the United States Naval Academy in 1887. "Zimmy," as he was affectionately known by the midshipmen, started the practice of composing a marching song for each graduating class. In 1906, Lieutenant Zimmerman was approached with a special request from Midshipman First Class Alfred Hart Miles. As a member of the Class of 1907, Miles wanted a lively piece of music that could be used as a football marching song—one so spirited that it would "live forever."

Working together at the Naval Academy Chapel organ, Zimmerman composed the music and Miles wrote the lyrics to "Anchors Aweigh." The song debuted at the 1906 Army-Navy football game and served as the football marching song until 1926, when it was published in a collection of navy songs and became nationally known as the theme song of the U.S. Navy. Many different lyrics have been written over the years, often including disparaging remarks about the nation's enemies. The last stanza of the version printed here was one of those originally written by Midshipman Miles.

Stand Navy out to sea,
Fight our battle cry;
We'll never change our course,
So vicious foe steer shy-y-y-y.
Roll out the TNT,
Anchors Aweigh.
Sail on to victory
And sink their bones to Davy Jones, hooray!

Anchors Aweigh, my boys,
Anchors Aweigh.
Farewell to foreign shores,
We sail at break of day-ay-ay-ay.
Through our last night ashore,
Drink to the foam,
Until we meet once more.
Here's wishing you a happy voyage home.

Blue of the mighty deep:
Gold of God's great sun.
Let these our colors be
Till all of time be done, done, done, done.
On seven seas we learn
Navy's stern call:
Faith, courage, service true,
With honor, over honor, over all.

Stand Navy down the field,
Sail set to the sky;
We'll never change our course,
So Army you steer shy-y-y-y.
Roll up the score, Navy
Anchors Aweigh.
Sail Navy down the field
And sink the Army, sink the Army grey!

Members of a farm family board an evacuation bus for housing in a War Relocation Authority center in 1942. In the wake of Imperial Japan's attack on the United States, President Franklin Roosevelt signed Executive Order 9066 authorizing military commanders to establish "exclusion zones" from which "any or all persons may be excluded." This power was used to declare that all people of Japanese ancestry were excluded from the entire Pacific coast, including all of California and most of Oregon and Washington, except for those in internment camps. The United States Census Bureau assisted the internment efforts by providing confidential neighborhood information on Japanese Americans. In 1988, Congress passed and President Ronald Reagan signed legislation which apologized for the internment on behalf of the U.S. government and authorized reparations. The legislation stated that government actions were based on "race prejudice, war hysteria, and a failure of political leadership."

LEARNED HAND

The Spirit of Liberty

Liberty lies in the hearts of men and women; when it dies there, no constitution, no law, no court can save it.

Although never appointed to the Supreme Court, Learned Hand (1872-1961) is among the most respected jurists in American history. Born in Albany, New York, he received his law degree from Harvard in 1896 and was first appointed to the federal bench in 1909. He was later elevated to the Second Circuit Court of Appeals and served as chief judge of that court from 1939 to 1951. Often referred to as the "tenth justice of the Supreme Court," Judge Hand received praise for his eloquent and thoughtfully worded rulings which upheld the freedom of individuals and the principles of democracy.

On May 21, 1944, Judge Hand was invited to speak at a gathering in New York's Central Park to honor "I Am An American Day." He concluded his remarks with the Pledge of Allegiance—minus the phrase "under God," which was not officially incorporated into the pledge until 1954. The popularity of this speech, delivered during the critical days of the war, earned him a repeat invitation on the same occasion the following year. In 1952, Judge Hand published a collection of his papers and addresses, also titled "The Spirit of Liberty."

We have gathered here to affirm a faith, a faith in a common purpose, a common conviction, a common devotion. Some of us have chosen America as the land of our adoption; the rest have come from those who did the same. For this reason we have some right to consider ourselves a picked group, a group of those who had the courage to break from the past and brave the dangers and the loneliness of a strange land. What was the object that nerved us, or those who went before us, to this choice? We sought liberty—freedom from oppression, freedom from want, freedom to be ourselves. This we then sought; this we now believe that we are by way of winning. What do we mean when we say that first of all we seek liberty? I often wonder whether we do not rest our hopes too much upon constitutions, upon laws, and upon courts. These are false hopes; believe me, these are false hopes. Liberty lies in the hearts of men and women; when it dies there, no constitution, no law, no court can save it; no constitution, no law, no court can even do much to help it. While it lies there, it needs no constitution, no law, no court to save it. And what is this liberty which must lie in the hearts of men and women? It is not the ruthless, the unbridled will; it is not freedom to do as one likes. That is the denial of liberty, and leads straight to its overthrow. A society in which men recognize no check upon their freedom soon becomes a society where freedom is the possession of only a savage few—as we have learned to our sorrow.

What, then, is the spirit of liberty? I cannot define it; I can only tell you my own faith. The spirit of liberty is the spirit which is not too sure that it is right; the spirit of liberty is the spirit which seeks to understand the minds of other men and women; the spirit of liberty is the spirit which weighs their interests alongside its own without bias; the spirit of liberty remembers that not even a sparrow falls to earth unheeded; the spirit of liberty is the spirit of Him who, near two thousand years ago, taught mankind that lesson it has never learned, but has never quite forgotten—that there may be a kingdom where the least shall be heard and considered side by side with the greatest. And now in that spirit, that spirit of an America which has never been, and which may never be—nay, which never will be except as the conscience and courage of Americans create it—yet in the spirit of that America which lies hidden in some form in the aspirations of us all; in the spirit of that America for which our young men are at this moment fighting and dying; in that spirit of liberty and of America so prosperous, and safe, and contented, we shall have failed to grasp its meaning, and shall have been truant to its promise, except as we strive to make it a signal, a beacon, a standard, to which the best hopes of mankind will ever turn; In confidence that you share that belief, I now ask you to raise your hands and repeat with me this pledge:

I pledge allegiance to the flag of the United States of America, and to the Republic for which it stands—one nation, indivisible, with liberty and justice for all.

Letter from a Navy Pilot

If our country takes these sacrifices with indifference it will be the cruelest ingratitude the world has ever known.

Printed here is the quintessential tribute to American youth, its idealism and its ingenuity, embodied in the person of an unknown U.S. Navy pilot who fought in the Battle of Midway. This letter is indicative of the courage and self-sacrifice of the World War II generation.

The Fates have been kind to me. When you hear people saying harsh things about American youth, you will know how wrong they all are. So many times that now they have become commonplace, I've seen incidents that make me know that we were never soft, never weak.

Many of my friends are now dead. To a man, each died with a nonchalance that each would have denied was courage, but simply called a lack of fear and forgot the triumph. If anything great or good has been born of this war, it should be valued in the youth of our country, who were never trained for war, who almost never believed in war, but who have, from some hidden source, brought forth a gallantry which is homespun, it is so real.

Out here between the spaceless sea and sky, American youth has found itself, and given of itself, so that a spark may catch, burst into flame, and burn high. If our country takes these sacrifices with indifference it will be the cruelest ingratitude the world has ever known.

You will, I know, do all in your power to help others keep the faith. My luck can't last much longer. But the flame goes on and only that is important.

The five Sullivan brothers of Waterloo, Iowa—from left to right: Joseph, Francis, Albert, Madison, and George. The Sullivans enlisted in the U.S. Navy on January 3, 1942, with the stipulation that they serve together. The Navy policy of separating siblings was not strictly enforced, and all five were assigned to the light cruiser USS Juneau. Their ship was sunk by Japanese submarines during the Battle of Guadalcanal, ultimately killing all five brothers and the entire crew save ten survivors. The brothers' story was immortalized in the 1944 movie, The Fighting Sullivans. The Navy named two destroyers in their honor. The motto for both ships: "We Stick Together."

GEORGE S. PATTON, JR.

Speech to the Third Army

Thirty years from now when you are sitting by the fireplace with your grandson on your knee and he asks you what you did in the great World War II, you won't have to cough, shift him to the other knee and say, "Well, your Granddaddy shoveled shit in Louisiana."

Known as "Old Blood and Guts," George Smith Patton, Jr. (1885-1945) was, in his own words, "the best damned ass-kicker in the U.S. Army." Born in San Gabriel, California, Patton graduated from the U.S. Military Academy at West Point, joined the cavalry, and competed in the 1912 Olympics, placing fifth in the pentathlon. He served in the 1916 Mexican expedition under the command of General John J. Pershing in pursuit of the Mexican bandit chieftain, Pancho Villa; during World War I, he served in France as commander of the first-ever American tank brigade.

Patton's most significant leadership role of World War II came in January 1944 when he took command of the Third Army, which stormed across France and, in December of 1944, fought in the famous Battle of the Bulge. Perhaps the greatest achievement in military history, Patton's Third Army liberated 81,500 square miles and inflicted 1.5 million enemy casualties. As commander of the Third Army, Patton became a full general and held a large portion of what would become the American occupation zone of Germany.

A man of abrupt speech and daring, reckless behavior, Patton earned great praise, but also suffered criticism and professional setbacks for his often heavy-handed methods and indiscreet political statements. Motivated by apprehensions of Communist takeovers in Europe, Patton publicly criticized the post-war denazification program in occupied Germany and argued for a combined Allied-German campaign against the Soviet Union. His support for keeping former Nazis in administrative and other positions led to his being transferred in October 1945 from command of the Third Army and the military governorship of Bavaria to command of a largely bureaucratic Fifteenth Army, set up to interview captured Germans and prepare an official history of the war. Shortly thereafter, in December of 1945, Patton died a rather inglorious death from injuries suffered in an automobile accident; he was buried in a Third Army cemetery in Luxembourg.

The following is a compilation of several short, morale-boosting speeches delivered by Patton over the course of the war and is believed to be reflective of an address delivered by "America's Fightingest General" to the soldiers and officers of the Third Army on June 5, 1944. A much sanitized version of this speech served as the basis for one of the most memorable scenes in cinematic history—the commencement of the 1970 film, *Patton*. "When I want my men to remember something important, to really make it stick," said Patton, "I give it to them double dirty. It may not sound nice to some bunch of little old ladies at an afternoon tea party, but it helps my soldiers to remember. You can't run an army without profanity; and it has to be eloquent profanity. An army without profanity couldn't fight its way out of a piss-soaked paper bag."

Be seated.

Now I want you to remember that no bastard ever won a war by dying for his country. You won it by making the other poor dumb bastard die for his country. Men, this stuff that some sources sling around about America wanting out of this war, not wanting to fight, is a crock of bullshit. Americans love to fight, traditionally. All REAL AMERICANS love the sting and clash of battle. You are here today for three reasons. First, because you are here to defend your homes and your loved ones. Second, you are here for your own self respect, because you would not want to be anywhere else. Third, you are here because you are real men and all real men like to fight. When you, here, every one of you, were kids, you all admired the champion marble player, the fastest runner, the toughest boxer, the big league ball players, and the All-American football players. Americans love a winner. Americans will not tolerate a loser. Americans despise cowards. Americans play to win all of the time. I wouldn't give a hoot in hell for a man who lost and laughed. That's why Americans have never lost nor will ever lose a war; for the very idea of losing is hateful to an American.

You are not all going to die. Only two percent of you right here today would die in a major battle. Death must not be feared. Death, in time, comes to all men. Yes, every man is scared in his first battle. If he says he's not, he's a liar. Some men are cowards but they fight the same as the brave men or they get the hell slammed out of them watching men fight who are just as scared as they are. The real hero is the man who fights even though he is scared. Some men get over their fright in a minute under fire. For some, it takes an hour. For some, it takes days. But a real man will never let his fear of death overpower his honor, his sense of duty to his country, and his innate manhood. Battle is the most magnificent competition in which a human being can indulge. It brings out all that is best and it removes all that is base. Americans pride themselves on being he-men and they ARE he-men. Remember that the enemy is just as frightened as you are, and probably more so. They are not supermen.

All through your Army careers, you men have bitched about what you call "chicken shit drilling." That, like everything else in this Army, has a definite purpose. That purpose is alertness. Alertness must be bred into every soldier. I don't give a fuck for a man who's not always on his toes. You men are veterans or you wouldn't be here. You are ready for what's to come. A man must be alert at all times if he expects to stay alive. If you're not alert, sometime, a German son-of-an-asshole-bitch is going to sneak up behind you and beat you to death with a sock full of shit!

There are four hundred neatly marked graves somewhere in Sicily, all because ONE MAN went to sleep on the job. But they are GERMAN graves, because we caught the bastard asleep before they did. An Army is a team. It lives, sleeps, eats, and fights as a team. This individual heroic stuff is pure horse shit. The bilious bastards who write that kind of stuff for the *Saturday Evening Post* don't know any more about real fighting under fire than they know about fucking!

We have the finest food, the finest equipment, the best spirit, and the best men in the world. Why, by God, I actually pity those poor sons-of-bitches we're going up against. By God, I do.

My men don't surrender. I don't want to hear of any soldier under my command being captured unless he has been hit. Even if you are hit, you can still fight back. That's not just bull shit either. The kind of man that I want in my command is just like the lieutenant in Libya, who, with a Luger against his chest, jerked off his helmet, swept the gun aside with one hand, and busted the hell out of the Kraut

with his helmet. Then he jumped on the gun and went out and killed another German before they knew what the hell was coming off. And, all of that time, this man had a bullet through a lung. There was a real man!

All of the real heroes are not storybook combat fighters, either. Every single man in this Army plays a vital role. Don't ever let up. Don't ever think that your job is unimportant. Every man has a job to do and he must do it. Every man is a vital link in the great chain. What if every truck driver suddenly decided that he didn't like the whine of those shells overhead, turned yellow, and jumped headlong into a ditch? The cowardly bastard could say, "Hell, they won't miss me, just one man in thousands." But, what if every man thought that way? Where in the hell would we be now? What would our country, our loved ones, our homes, even the world, be like? No, Goddamnit, Americans don't think like that. Every man does his job. Every man serves the whole. Every department, every unit, is important in the vast scheme of this war. The ordnance men are needed to supply the guns and machinery of war to keep us rolling. The Quartermaster is needed to bring up food and clothes because where we are going there isn't a hell of a lot to steal. Every last man on K.P. has a job to do, even the one who heats our water to keep us from getting the "G.I. Shits." Even the Chaplain is important, for if we get killed and he is not there to bury us we would all go to hell.

Each man must not think only of himself, but also of his buddy fighting beside him. We don't want yellow cowards in this Army. They should be killed off like rats. If not, they will go home after this war and breed more cowards. The brave men will breed more brave men. Kill off the Goddamned cowards and we will have a nation of brave men. One of the bravest men that I ever saw was a fellow on top of a telegraph pole in the midst of a furious fire fight in Tunisia. I stopped and asked what the hell he was doing up there at a time like that. He answered, "Fixing the wire, Sir." I asked, "Isn't that a little unhealthy right about now?" He answered, "Yes Sir, but the Goddamned wire has to be fixed." I asked, "Don't those planes strafing the road bother you?" And he answered, "No, Sir, but you sure as hell do!" Now, there was a real man. A real soldier. There was a man who devoted all he had to his duty, no matter how seemingly insignificant his duty might appear at the time, no matter how great the odds. And you should have seen those trucks on the road to Tunisia. Those drivers were magnificent. All day and all night they rolled over those son-of-a-bitching roads, never stopping, never faltering from their course, with shells bursting all around them all of the time. We got through on good old American guts. Many of those men drove for over forty consecutive hours. These men weren't combat men, but they were soldiers with a job to do. They did it, and in one hell of a way they did it. They were part of a team. Without team effort, without them, the fight would have been lost. All of the links in the chain pulled together and the chain became unbreakable.

Don't forget, you men don't know that I'm here. No mention of that fact is to be made in any letters. The world is not supposed to know what the hell happened to me. I'm not supposed to be commanding this Army. I'm not even supposed to be here in England. Let the first bastards to find out be the Goddamned Germans. Some day I want to see them raise up on their piss-soaked hind legs and howl, "Jesus Christ, it's the Goddamned Third Army again and that son-of-a-fucking-bitch Patton."

We want to get the hell over there. The quicker we clean up this Goddamned mess, the quicker we can take a little jaunt against the purple-pissing Japs and clean out their nest too, before the Marines get in and claim all the Goddamned credit.

Sure, we want to go home. We want this war over with. The quickest way to get it over with is to go get the bastards who started it. The quicker they are whipped, the quicker we can go home. The shortest way home is through Berlin and Tokyo. And when we get to Berlin, I am personally going to shoot that paper hanging son-of-a-bitch Hitler. Just like I'd shoot a snake!

When a man is lying in a shell hole, if he just stays there all day, a German will get to him eventually. The hell with that idea. The hell with taking it. My men don't dig foxholes. I don't want them to. Foxholes only slow up an offensive. Keep moving. And don't give the enemy time to dig one either. We'll win this war, but we'll win it only by fighting and by showing the Germans that we've got more guts than they have; or ever will have. We're not going to just shoot the sons-of-bitches, we're going to rip out their living Goddamned guts and use them to grease the treads of our tanks. We're going to murder those lousy Hun cocksuckers by the bushel-fucking-basket. War is a bloody, killing business. You've got to spill their blood, or they will spill yours. Rip them up the belly. Shoot them in the guts. When shells are hitting all around you and you wipe the dirt off your face and realize that instead of dirt it's the blood and guts of what once was your best friend beside you, you'll know what to do!

From time to time there will be some complaints that we are pushing our people too hard. I don't give a good Goddamn about such complaints. I believe in the old and sound rule that an ounce of sweat will save a gallon of blood. The harder we push, the more Germans we will kill. The more Germans we kill, the fewer of our men will be killed. Pushing means fewer casualties. I want you all to remember that.

There is another thing I want you to remember. Forget this Goddamn business of worrying about our flanks. We must guard our flanks, but not to the extent that we don't do anything else.

Some Goddamned fool once said that flanks must be secured, and since then sons-of-bitches all over the world have been going crazy guarding their flanks. Flanks are something for the enemy to worry about, not us.

Also, I don't want to get any messages saying, "I am holding my position." We are not holding a Goddamned thing. Let the Hun do that. We are advancing constantly and we are not interested in holding onto anything except the enemy. We're going to hold onto him by the nose, and we're going to kick him in the ass. We are going to twist his balls and kick the living shit out of him all of the time. Our basic plan of operation is to advance and to keep on advancing regardless of whether we have to go over, under, or through the enemy. We are going to go through him like crap through a goose; like shit through a tin horn! We have one motto, *"L'audace, l'audace, tojours l'audace!"* Remember that. From here on out, until we win or die in the attempt, we will always be audacious.

There is one great thing that you men will all be able to say after this war is over and you are home once again, and you may thank God for it. You may be thankful that thirty years from now when you are sitting by the fireplace with your grandson on your knee and he asks you what you did in the great World War II, you won't have to cough, shift him to the other knee and say, "Well, your Granddaddy shoveled shit in Louisiana." No, Sir, you can look him straight in the eye and say, "Son, your Granddaddy rode with the Great Third Army and a Son-of-a-Goddamned-Bitch named Georgie Patton!"

Alright now, you sons-of-bitches, you know how I feel. I will be proud to lead you wonderful guys into battle anytime, anywhere.

That is all.

President Franklin Roosevelt, center, with British Prime Minister Winston Churchill and Soviet leader Joseph Stalin at the Livadia Palace in Yalta in 1945. The leaders met to establish an agenda for governing post-war Germany.

GEORGE S. PATTON, JR.

Through a Glass, Darkly

General Patton was a study in contrasts. The foul-mouthed, pistol-packing warrior was also a highly educated, Bible-quoting military historian. The following is a selection, not of his military theories or battle plans, but of his poetry. Many of Patton's poems were crude, both in form and language, but they are each entertaining and offer insight into the mind of one of America's purest fighting men and greatest of patriots.

Through the travail of the ages,
Midst the pomp and toil of war,
Have I fought and strove and perished
Countless times upon this star.

In the form of many people
In all panoplies of time
Have I seen the luring vision
Of the Victory Maid, sublime.

I have battled for fresh mammoth,
I have warred for pastures new,
I have listed to the whispers
When the race trek instinct grew.

I have known the call to battle
In each changeless changing shape
From the high souled voice of conscience
To the beastly lust for rape.

I have sinned and I have suffered,
Played the hero and the knave;
Fought for belly, shame, or country,
And for each have found a grave.

I cannot name my battles
For the visions are not clear,
Yet, I see the twisted faces
And I feel the rending spear.

Perhaps I stabbed our Savior
In His sacred helpless side.
Yet, I've called His name in blessing
When after times I died.

In the dimness of the shadows
Where we hairy heathens warred,
I can taste in thought the lifeblood;
We used teeth before the sword.

While in later clearer vision
I can sense the coppery sweat,
Feel the pikes grow wet and slippery
When our Phalanx, Cyrus met.

Hear the rattle of the harness
Where the Persian darts bounced clear,
See their chariots wheel in panic
From the Hoplite's leveled spear.

See the goal grow monthly longer,
Reaching for the walls of Tyre.
Hear the crash of tons of granite,
Smell the quenchless eastern fire.

Still more clearly as a Roman,
Can I see the legions close,
As our third rank moved in forward
And the short sword found our foes.

Once again I feel the anguish
Of that blistering treeless plain
When the Parthian showered death bolts,
And our discipline was in vain.

I remember all the suffering
Of those arrows in my neck.
Yet, I stabbed a grinning savage
As I died upon my back.

Once again I smell the heat sparks
When my Flemish plate gave way
And the lance ripped through my entrails
As on Crecy's field I lay.

In the windless, blinding stillness
Of the glittering tropic sea
I can see the bubbles rising
Where we set the captives free.

Midst the spume of half a tempest
I have heard the bulwarks go
When the crashing, point blank round shot
Sent destruction to our foe.

I have fought with gun and cutlass
On the red and slippery deck
With all Hell aflame within me
And a rope around my neck.

And still later as a General
Have I galloped with Murat
When we laughed at death and numbers
Trusting in the Emperor's Star.

Till at last our star faded,
And we shouted to our doom
Where the sunken road of Ohein
Closed us in it's quivering gloom.

So but now with Tanks a'clatter
Have I waddled on the foe
Belching death at twenty paces,
By the star shell's ghastly glow.

So as through a glass, and darkly
The age long strife I see
Where I fought in many guises,
Many names, but always me.

And I see not in my blindness
What the objects were I wrought,
But as God rules o'er our bickerings
It was through His will I fought.

So forever in the future,
Shall I battle as of yore,
Dying to be borne a fighter,
But to die again, once more.

FRANK LOESSER

Praise the Lord and Pass the Ammunition

Frank Loesser (1910-1969) was born in New York City and worked as a cartoonist, reporter, and press agent. He went to Hollywood in 1931 as a songwriter for Universal Pictures and produced a number of memorable works, including the music and lyrics for *Guys and Dolls*, one of the most successful Broadway productions ever. Loesser won the 1949 Academy Award for his song "Baby, It's Cold Outside" and, in 1962, shared the Pulitzer Prize for drama with Abe Burrows for their musical comedy *How to Succeed in Business Without Really Trying*. Loesser also wrote "Praise the Lord and Pass the Ammunition," one of the surprisingly few militaristic songs of the Second World War.

Down went the gunner, a bullet was his fate,
Down went the gunner, and then the gunner's mate.
Up jumped the sky pilot, gave the boys a look.
And manned the gun himself as he laid aside The Book,
Shouting

Chorus:
    "Praise the Lord, and pass the ammunition!
    Praise the Lord, and pass the ammunition!
    Praise the Lord , and pass the ammunition
    And we'll stay free!
    Praise the Lord, and swing into position.
    Can't afford to sit around a-wishin'.
    Praise the Lord, we're all between perdition
    And the deep blue sea!"

Yes, the sky pilot said it,
You've got to give him credit
For a son-of-a gun of a gunner was he,
Shouting

"Praise the Lord, we're on a mighty mission!
All aboard! We're not a-goin' fishin'.
Praise the Lord, and pass the ammunition
And we'll all stay free!"

General Douglas MacArthur, Supreme Commander for the Allied Powers, signs the Instrument of Surrender following the signature of the Japanese foreign minister on deck of the USS Missouri, anchored in Tokyo Bay, September 2, 1945. The Allied Powers had previously called upon Japan to surrender or face "prompt and utter destruction." Japan's rejection of this ultimatum and public pledge to fight "to the bitter end" led to President Truman's decision to drop atomic bombs on Hiroshima and Nagasaki, respectively.

KARL SHAPIRO

Elegy for a Dead Soldier

Karl Shapiro (1913-2000) was born in Baltimore and served as a soldier in the South Pacific during World War II. He began publishing his poetry in 1935 and later served as editor of the *Prairie Schooner* and *Poetry* magazine. In 1945, Shapiro received the Pulitzer Prize for *V-Letter and Other Poems*, which contained the following selection.

A white sheet on the tail-gate of a truck
Becomes an altar; two small candlesticks
Sputter at each side of the crucifix
Laid round with flowers brighter than the blood,
Red as the red of our apocalypse,
Hibiscus that a marching man will pluck
To stick into his rifle or his hat,
And great blue morning-glories pale as lips
That shall no longer taste or kiss or swear.
The wind begins a low magnificat,
The chaplain chats, the palmtrees swirl their hair,
The columns come together through the mud.

II
We too are ashes as we watch and hear
The psalm, the sorrow, and the simple praise
Of one whose promised thoughts of other days
Were such as ours, but now wholly destroyed,
The service record of his youth wiped out,
His dream dispersed by shot, must disappear.
What can we feel but wonder at a loss
That seems to point at nothing but the doubt
Which flirts our sense of luck into the ditch?
Reader of Paul who prays beside this fosse,
Shall we believe our eyes or legends rich
With glory and rebirth beyond the void?

III

For this comrade is dead, dead in the war,
A young man out of millions yet to live,
One cut away from all that war can give,
Freedom of self and peace to wander free.
Who mourns in all this sober multitude
Who did not feel the bite of it before
The bullet found its aim? This worthy flesh,
This boy laid in a coffin and reviewed—
Who has not wrapped himself in this same flag,
Heard the light fall of dirt, his wound still fresh,
Felt his eyes closed, and heard the distant brag
Of the last volley of humanity?

IV

By chance I saw him die, stretched on the ground,
A tattooed arm lifted to take the blood
Of someone else sealed in a tin. I stood
During the last delirium that stays
The intelligence a tiny moment more,
And then the strangulation, the last sound.
The end was sudden, like a foolish play,
A stupid fool slamming a foolish door,
The absurd catastrophe, half-prearranged,
And all the decisive things still left to say.
So we disbanded, angrier and unchanged,
Sick with the utter silence of dispraise.

V

We ask for no statistics of the killed,
For nothing political impinges on
This single casualty, or all those gone,
Missing or healing, sinking or dispersed,
Hundreds of thousands counted, millions lost.
More than an accident and less than willed
Is every fall, and this one like the rest.
However others calculate the cost,
To us the final aggregate is *one*,
One with a name, one transferred to the blest;
And though another stoops and takes the gun,
We cannot add the second to the first.

VI

I would not speak for him who could not speak
Unless my fear were true: he was not wronged,
He knew to which decision he belonged
But let it choose itself. Ripe in instinct,
Neither the victim nor the volunteer,
He followed, and the leaders could not seek
Beyond the followers. Much of this he knew;
The journey was a detour that would steer
Into the Lincoln Highway of a land
Remorselessly improved, excited, new,
And that was what he wanted. He had planned
To earn and drive. He and the world had winked.

VII

No history deceived him, for he knew
Little of times and armies not his own;
He never felt that peace was but a loan,
Had never questioned the idea of gain.
Beyond the headlines once or twice he saw
The gathering of a power by the few
But could not tell their names; he cast his vote,
Distrusting all the elected but not law.
He laughed at socialism; *on mourrait*
Pour les industriels? He shed his coat
And not for brotherhood, but for his pay.
To him the red flag marked the sewer main.

VIII

Above all else he loathed the homily,
The slogan and the ad. He paid his bill
But not for Congressmen at Bunker Hill.
Ideals were few and those there were not made
For conversation. He belonged to church
But never spoke of God. The Christmas tree,
The Easter egg, baptism, he observed,
Never denied the preacher on his perch,
And would not sign Resolved That or Whereas.
Softness he had and hours and nights reserved
For thinking, dressing, dancing to the jazz.
His laugh was real, his manners were homemade.

IX

Of all men poverty pursued him least;
He was ashamed of all the down and out,
Spurned the panhandler like an uneasy doubt,
And saw the unemployed as a vague mass
Incapable of hunger or revolt.
He hated other races, south or east,
And shoved them to the margin of his mind.
He could recall the justice of the Colt,
Take interest in a gang-war like a game.
His ancestry was somewhere far behind
And left him only his peculiar name.
Doors opened, and he recognized no class.

X

His children would have known a heritage,
Just or unjust, the richest in the world,
The quantum of all art and science curled
In the horn of plenty, bursting from the horn,
A people bathed in honey, Paris come,
Vienna transferred with the highest wage,
A World's Fair spread to Phoenix, Jacksonville,
Earth's capitol, the new Byzantium,
Kingdom of man—who knows? Hollow or firm,
No man can ever prophesy until
Out of our death some undiscovered germ,
Whole toleration or pure peace is born.

XI

The time to mourn is short that best becomes
The military dead. We lift and fold the flag,
Lay bare the coffin with its written tag,
And march away. Behind, four others wait
To lift the box, the heaviest of loads.
The anesthetic afternoon benumbs,
Sickens our senses, forces back our talk.
We know that others on tomorrow's roads
Will fall, ourselves perhaps, the man beside,
Over the world the threatened, all who walk:
And could we mark the grave of him who died
We would write this beneath his name and date:

EPITAPH

Underneath this wooden cross there lies
A Christian killed in battle. You who read,
Remember that this stranger died in pain;
And passing here, if you can lift your eyes
Upon a peace kept by a human creed,
Know that one soldier has not died in vain.

ROSEMARY AND STEPHEN VINCENT BENÉT

U.S.A.

Stephen Vincent Benét (1898-1943) and his brother, William, and sister, Laura, were well-known writers whose works were influenced by a love of American history and folklore. Born in Bethlehem, Pennsylvania, Benét received the Pulitzer Prize in 1928 for *John Brown's Body* and again, in 1943, for *Western Star*. "U.S.A.," which adds a touch of humility to all partisans of democratic ideas, was written by Benét in collaboration with his wife, Rosemary Carr, a contributing author to numerous magazines.

So we march into the present
And it's always rather pleasant
To speculate on what the years ahead of us will see,
For our words and thoughts and attitudes,
All our novelties and platitudes,
Will be Rather Ancient History in 2033.

Will they find us wise—or silly?
Looking backwards, willy-nilly,
At our queer old-fashioned costumes and our quaint old-fashioned ways?
When our doings face the ages,
Printed down on textbook pages,
Will they cry, "This Savage Era"? Will they sigh, "Those were the days!"?

I don't know—you may be wiser.
Time's a curious capsizer
Of a lot of reputations that seemed certain to endure,
While he'll sometimes make his heroes
Out of people, once thought zeroes,
For the most well-grounded reasons, by the solemnly cocksure.

So, instead of prophesying
(Which is fun, but rather trying)
Who they'll pick to be our great ones when the books are on the shelves,
Here's the marching panorama
Of our past and present drama
—And we shan't know all the answers till we're history ourselves.

* * *

Moving day in a California suburb. Newly-built houses jammed side-by-side, divided by a street clogged with moving vans. The 1950s marked the rise of consumerism, whereby Americans bought big houses in newly constructed suburbs along with new time-saving household appliances. This buying trend was aided by the G.I. Bill, officially titled the Servicemen's Readjustment Act of 1944, which provided college or vocational education for returning World War II veterans. It also provided many different types of loans for returning veterans to buy homes and start businesses. This buying trend took place amidst fears of the growing "red menace."

Cold War Conflict

BERNARD BARUCH

The Baruch Plan for Control of Atomic Energy

We are here to make a choice between the quick and the dead.

Born in Camden, South Carolina, Bernard Mannes Baruch (1870-1965) was a wealthy financier who owned a seat on the Stock Exchange. He volunteered as an adviser for five presidents, including Harry Truman, who appointed him U.S. representative to the United Nations Atomic Energy Commission. In 1946, Baruch presented a U.S. plan to place atomic energy under international control. The United States had a monopoly on knowledge of the atomic bomb at that time, but the plan was rejected because Soviet dictator Joseph Stalin would not agree to a provision that called for inspections. In their quest for "mutual assured destruction," the Soviet Union's position prevented an international agreement until 1963, when the U.S., Great Britain, and the U.S.S.R. signed the Nuclear Test Ban Treaty, which banned atomic testing in the atmosphere, under water, and in outer space. The arms race, however, was well under way.

We are here to make a choice between the quick and the dead. That is our business.

Behind the black portent of the new atomic age lies a hope which, seized upon with faith, can work our salvation. If we fail, then we have damned every man to be the slave of fear. Let us not deceive ourselves: We must elect world peace or world destruction.

Science has torn from nature a secret so vast in its potentialities that our minds cower from the terror it creates. Yet terror is not enough to inhibit the use of the atomic bomb. The terror created by weapons has never stopped man from employing them, for each new weapon a defense has been produced, in time. But now we face a condition in which adequate defense does not exist.

Science, which gave us the dread power, shows that it *can* be made a giant help to humanity, but science does *not* show us how to prevent its baleful use. So we have been appointed to obviate that peril by finding a meeting of the minds and the hearts of our peoples. Only in the will of mankind lies the answer.

It is to express this will and make it effective that we have been assembled. We must provide the mechanism to assure that atomic energy is used for peaceful purposes and preclude its use in war. To that end, we must provide immediate, swift, and sure punishment of those who violate the agreements that are reached by the nations. Penalization is essential if peace is to be more than a feverish interlude between wars. And, too, the United Nations can prescribe individual responsibility and punishment on the principles applied at Nuremberg by the Union of Soviet Socialist Republics, the United

Kingdom, France, and the United States—a formula certain to benefit the world's future.

In this crisis, we represent not only our governments but, in a larger way, we represent the peoples of the world. We must remember that the peoples do not belong to th-e governments but that the governments belong to the peoples. We must answer their demands; we must answer the world's longing for peace and security.

In that desire, the United States shares ardently and hopefully. The search of science for the absolute weapon has reached fruition in this country. But she stands ready to proscribe and destroy this instrument—to lift its use from death to life—if the world will join in a pact to that end. ...

Now, if ever, is the time to act for the common good. Public opinion supports the world movement toward security. If I read the sign aright, the peoples want a program not composed merely of pious thoughts but of enforceable sanctions—an international law with teeth in it.

We of this nation, desirous of helping to bring peace to the world and realizing the heavy obligations upon us arising from our possession of the means of producing the bomb and from the fact that it is a part of our armament, are prepared to make our full contribution toward effective control of atomic energy. ...

But before a country is ready to relinquish any winning weapons, it must have more than words to reassure it. It must have a guarantee of safety, not only against the offenders in the atomic area but against the illegal users of other weapons—bacteriological, biological, gas—perhaps—and why not?—against war itself.

In the elimination of war lies our solution, for only

then will nations cease to compete with one another in the production and use of dread "secret" weapons which are evaluated solely by their capacity to kill. This devilish program takes us back, not merely to the Dark Ages but from cosmos to chaos. If we succeed in finding a suitable way to control atomic weapons, it is reasonable to hope that we may also preclude the use of other weapons adaptable to mass destruction. When a man learns to say "A" he can, if he chooses, learn the rest of the alphabet, too.

Let this be anchored in our minds: Peace is never long preserved by weight of metal or by an armament race. Peace can be made tranquil and secure only by understanding and agreement fortified by sanctions. We must embrace international cooperation or international disintegration …

GEORGE C. MARSHALL

The Marshall Plan Speech

Our policy is directed not against any country or doctrine but against hunger, poverty, desperation, and chaos.

George Catlett Marshall (1880-1959), one of America's greatest soldiers and statesmen, was born in Uniontown, Pennsylvania. His father was a distant cousin of John Marshall, the former Chief Justice of the Supreme Court. In 1901, George graduated from the Virginia Military Institute and began his career as a professional soldier. During World War II, he served as chief of staff of the U.S. Army and was responsible for planning the overall strategy of the war. He later served as secretary of state from 1947 to 1949, president of the American Red Cross in 1949 and 1950, and secretary of defense from 1950 to 1951.

In his commencement address at Harvard University on June 5, 1947, Marshall laid the basis for what would become the European Recovery Program, also called the Marshall Plan, a program of economic assistance to war-torn Europe. Under this plan, one of the most generous and effective foreign policy initiatives in world history, the United States spent billions of dollars to rebuild western Europe in order to check the spread of Communism. For his role in European reconstruction, Marshall was awarded the 1953 Nobel Peace Prize.

… In considering the requirements for the rehabilitation of Europe, the physical loss of life, the visible destruction of cities, factories, mines, and railroads was correctly estimated, but it has become obvious during recent months that this visible destruction was probably less serious than the dislocation of the entire fabric of European economy. For the past ten years conditions have been abnormal. The feverish preparation for war and the more feverish maintenance of the war effort engulfed all aspects of national economies. Machinery has fallen into disrepair or is entirely obsolete. Under the arbitrary and destructive Nazi rule, virtually every possible enterprise was geared into the German war machine. Long-standing commercial ties, private institutions, banks, insurance companies, and shipping companies disappeared through loss of capital, absorption through nationalization, or by simple destruction. In many countries, confidence in the local currency has been severely shaken. The breakdown of the business structure of Europe during the war was complete. Recovery has been seriously retarded by the fact that two years after the close of hostilities a peace settlement with Germany and Austria has not been agreed upon. But even given a more prompt solution of these difficult problems, the rehabilitation of the economic structure of Europe quite evidently will require a much longer time and greater effort than has been foreseen.

There is a phase of this matter which is both interesting and serious. The farmer has always produced the foodstuffs to exchange with the city dweller for the other necessities of life. This division of labor is the basis of modern civilization. At the present time it is threatened with breakdown. The town and city industries are not producing adequate goods to exchange with the food-producing farmer. Raw materials and fuel are in short supply. Machinery is lacking or worn out. The farmer or the peasant cannot find the goods for sale which he desires to purchase. So the sale of his farm produce for money which he cannot use seems to him an unprofitable transaction. He, therefore, has withdrawn many fields from crop cultivation and is using them for grazing. He feeds more grain to stock and finds for himself and his family an ample supply of food, however short he may be on clothing and the other ordinary gadgets of civilization. Meanwhile, people in the cities are short of food and fuel, and in some places approaching the starvation levels. So the governments are forced to use their foreign money and credits to procure these necessities abroad. This process exhausts funds which are urgently needed for reconstruction. Thus a very serious situation is rapidly developing which bodes no good for the world. The modern system of the division of labor upon which the exchange of products is based is in danger of breaking down.

The truth of the matter is that Europe's requirements for the next three or four years of foreign food and other essential products—principally from America—are so much greater than her present ability to pay that she must have substantial additional help or face economic, social, and political deterioration of a very grave character.

The remedy lies in breaking the vicious circle and restoring the confidence of the European people in the economic future of their own countries and of Europe as a whole. The manufacturer and the farmer throughout wide areas must be able and willing to exchange their product for currencies, the continuing value of which is not open to question.

Aside from the demoralizing effect on the world at large and the possibilities of disturbances arising as a result of the desperation of the people concerned, the consequences to the economy of the United States should be apparent to all. It is logical that the United States should do whatever it is able to do to assist in the return of normal economic health in the world, without which there can be no political stability and no assured peace. Our policy is directed not against any country or doctrine but against hunger, poverty, desperation, and chaos. Its purpose should be the revival of a working economy in the world so as to permit the emergence of political and social conditions in which free institutions can exist. Such assistance, I am convinced, must not be on a piecemeal basis as various crises develop. Any assistance that this Government may render in the future should provide a cure rather than a mere palliative. Any government that is willing to assist in the task of recovery will find full cooperation, I am sure, on the part of the United States Government. Any government which maneuvers to block the recovery of other countries cannot expect help from us. Furthermore, governments, political parties, or groups which seek to perpetuate human misery in order to profit therefrom politically or otherwise will encounter the opposition of the United States.

It is already evident that, before the United States Government can proceed much further in its efforts to alleviate the situation and help start the European world on its way to recovery, there must be some agreement among the countries of Europe as to the requirements of the situation and the part those countries themselves will take in order to give proper effect to whatever action might be undertaken by this Government. It would be neither fitting nor efficacious for this Government to undertake to draw up unilaterally a program designed to place Europe on its feet economically. This is the business of the Europeans. The initiative, I think, must come from Europe. The role of this country should consist of friendly aid in the drafting of a European program and of later support of such a program so far as it may be practical for us to do so. The program should be a joint one, agreed to by a number, if not all, European nations.

An essential part of any successful action on the part of the United States is an understanding on the part of the people of America of the character of the problem and the remedies to be applied. Political passion and prejudice should have no part. With foresight, and a willingness on the part of our people to face up to the vast responsibility which history has clearly placed upon our country, the difficulties I have outlined can and will be overcome. …

President Harry S. Truman gleefully displays a premature early edition of the Chicago Daily Tribune *from his train in St. Louis, Missouri, after his defeat of Thomas E. Dewey in the 1948 presidential election.*

HARRY S. TRUMAN

Inaugural Address

What we have achieved in liberty, we will surpass in greater liberty.

The son of a Missouri farm family, Harry S. Truman (1884-1972) finished high school but could not afford to go to college. He tried his hand at farming and several other business ventures, served with distinction in World War I, then succeeded in local politics. He was elected to the U.S. Senate in 1934 and was chosen vice president in 1944. He became president upon the death of Franklin Roosevelt on April 12, 1945.

On May 7 of that year, Germany formally surrendered and Truman responded by declaring May 8, his sixty-first birthday, as Victory-In-Europe Day (V-E Day). While attending the Potsdam Conference in Germany with British Prime Minister Winston Churchill and Russian Premier Joseph Stalin to discuss the continuing war in the Pacific, Truman received word that American scientists of the Manhattan Project had successfully tested the world's first atomic bomb. Realizing that the planned invasion of the Japanese home island would result in tremendous casualties, Truman ordered an atomic bomb dropped on the city of Hiroshima. Three days later, following Japan's refusal to surrender, a second atomic bomb was dropped on Nagasaki. Japan opened peace negotiations the very next day and, on September 2, 1945, offered its unconditional surrender (V-J Day). "I realize the tragic significance of the atomic bomb," said Truman, "but we have used it in order to shorten the agony of war; in order to save the lives of thousands and thousands of young Americans."

The election of 1948 appeared a probable victory for the Republican Party, which had gained control of both houses of Congress in the 1946 elections. In perhaps the greatest upset in political history, Truman overcame a resurgent opposition party and a deep split within his own party to defeat the Republican nominee, Thomas E. Dewey, who was well respected for his successful prosecution of organized crime.

Truman's inaugural address marked the heightening of Cold War hostilities. He singled out Communism as the next great threat to freedom and presented a four point program that embarked the United States on a new, more prominent role in world affairs. Shortly thereafter, in June of 1950, Truman committed American forces to war in Korea.

... Each period of our national history has had its special challenges. Those that confront us now are as momentous as any in the past. Today marks the beginning not only of a new administration, but of a period that will be eventful, perhaps decisive, for us and for the world.

It may be our lot to experience, and in large measure to bring about, a major turning point in the long history of the human race. The first half of this century has been marked by unprecedented and brutal attacks on the rights of man, and by the two most frightful wars in history. The supreme need of our time is for men to learn to live together in peace and harmony.

The peoples of the earth face the future with grave uncertainty, composed almost equally of great hopes and great fears. In this time of doubt, they look to the United States as never before for good will, strength, and wise leadership.

It is fitting, therefore, that we take this occasion to proclaim to the world the essential principles of the faith by which we live, and to declare our aims to all peoples.

The American people stand firm in the faith which has inspired this Nation from the beginning. We believe that all men have a right to equal justice under law and equal opportunity to share in the common good. We believe that all men have the right to freedom of thought and expression. We believe that all men are created equal because they are created in the image of God.

From this faith we will not be moved.

The American people desire, and are determined to work for, a world in which all nations and all peoples are free to govern themselves as they see fit, and to achieve a decent and satisfying life. Above all else, our people desire, and are determined to work for, peace on earth—a just and lasting peace—based on genuine agreement freely arrived at by equals.

In the pursuit of these aims, the United States and other like-minded nations find themselves directly opposed by a regime with contrary aims and a totally different concept of life.

That regime adheres to a false philosophy which purports to offer freedom, security, and greater opportunity to mankind. Misled by this philosophy, many peoples have sacrificed their liberties only to learn to their sorrow that deceit and mockery, poverty and tyranny, are their reward.

That false philosophy is communism.

Communism is based on the belief that man is so weak and inadequate that he is unable to govern himself, and therefore requires the rule of strong masters.

Democracy is based on the conviction that man has the moral and intellectual capacity, as well as the inalienable right, to govern himself with reason and justice.

Communism subjects the individual to arrest without lawful cause, punishment without trial, and forced labor as the chattel of the state. It decrees what information he shall receive, what art he shall produce, what leaders he shall follow, and what thoughts he shall think.

Democracy maintains that government is established for the benefit of the individual, and is charged with the responsibility of protecting the rights of the individual and his freedom in the exercise of his abilities.

Communism maintains that social wrongs can be corrected only by violence.

Democracy has proved that social justice can be achieved through peaceful change.

Communism holds that the world is so deeply divided into opposing classes that war is inevitable.

Democracy holds that free nations can settle differences justly and maintain lasting peace.

These differences between communism and democracy do not concern the United States alone. People everywhere are coming to realize that what is involved is material well-being, human dignity, and the right to believe in and worship God.

I state these differences, not to draw issues of belief as such, but because the actions resulting from the Communist philosophy are a threat to the efforts of free nations to bring about world recovery and lasting peace.

Since the end of hostilities, the United States has invested its substance and its energy in a great constructive effort to restore peace, stability, and freedom to the world.

We have sought no territory and we have imposed our will on none. We have asked for no privileges we would not extend to others.

We have constantly and vigorously supported the United Nations and related agencies as a means of applying democratic principles to international relations. We have consistently advocated and relied upon peaceful settlement of disputes among nations.

We have made every effort to secure agreement on effective international control of our most powerful weapon, and we have worked steadily for the limitation and control of all armaments.

We have encouraged, by precept and example, the expansion of world trade on a sound and fair basis.

Almost a year ago, in company with 16 free nations of Europe, we launched the greatest cooperative economic program in history. The purpose of that unprecedented effort is to invigorate and strengthen democracy in Europe, so that the free people of that continent can resume their rightful place in the forefront of civilization and can contribute once more to the security and welfare of the world.

Our efforts have brought new hope to all mankind. We have beaten back despair and defeatism. We have saved a number of countries from losing their liberty. Hundreds of millions of people all over the world now agree with us, that we need not have war—that we can have peace. …

In the coming years, our program for peace and freedom will emphasize four major courses of action.

First, we will continue to give unfaltering support to the United Nations and related agencies, and we will continue to search for ways to strengthen their authority and increase their effectiveness. We believe that the United Nations will be strengthened by the new nations which are being formed in lands now advancing toward self-government under democratic principles.

Second, we will continue our programs for world economic recovery.

This means, first of all, that we must keep our full weight behind the European recovery program. We are confident of the success of this major venture in world recovery. We believe that our partners in this effort will achieve the status of self-supporting nations once again.

In addition, we must carry out our plans for reducing the barriers to world trade and increasing its volume. Economic recovery and peace itself depend on increased world trade.

Third, we will strengthen freedom-loving nations against the dangers of aggression. We are now working out with a number of countries a joint agreement designed to strengthen the security of the North Atlantic area. Such an agreement would take the form of a collective defense arrangement within the terms of the United Nations Charter. …

Fourth, we must embark on a bold new program for making the benefits of our scientific advances and industrial progress available for the improvement and growth of underdeveloped areas.

More than half the people of the world are living in conditions approaching misery. Their food is inadequate. They are victims of disease. Their economic life is primitive and stagnant. Their poverty is a handicap and a threat both to them and to more prosperous areas.

For the first time in history, humanity possesses the knowledge and the skill to relieve the suffering of these people.

The United States is pre-eminent among nations in the development of industrial and scientific techniques. The material resources which we can afford to use for the assistance of other peoples are limited. But our imponderable resources in technical knowledge are constantly growing and are inexhaustible.

I believe that we should make available to peace-loving peoples the benefits of our store of technical knowledge in order to help them realize their aspirations for a better life. And, in cooperation with other nations, we should foster capital investment in areas needing development.

Our aim should be to help the free peoples of the world, through their own efforts, to produce more food, more clothing, more materials for housing, and more mechanical power to lighten their burdens.

We invite other countries to pool their technological resources in this undertaking. Their contributions will be warmly welcomed. This should be a cooperative enterprise in which all nations work together through the United Nations and its specialized agencies wherever practicable. It must be a worldwide effort for the achievement of peace, plenty, and freedom.

With the cooperation of business, private capital, agriculture, and labor in this country, this program can greatly increase the industrial activity in other nations and can raise substantially their standards of living. Such new economic developments must be devised and controlled to benefit the peoples of the areas in which they are established. Guarantees to the investor must be balanced by guarantees in the interest of the people whose resources and whose labor go into these developments.

The old imperialism—exploitation for foreign profit—has no place in our plans. What we envisage is a program of development based on the concepts of democratic fair-dealing.

All countries, including our own, will greatly benefit from a constructive program for the better use of the world's human and natural resources. Experience shows that our commerce with other countries expands as they progress industrially and economically.

Greater production is the key to prosperity and peace. And the key to greater production is a wider and more vigorous application of modern scientific and technical knowledge.

Only by helping the least fortunate of its members to help themselves can the human family achieve the decent, satisfying life that is the right of all people.

Democracy alone can supply the vitalizing force to stir the peoples of the world into triumphant action, not only against their human oppressors, but also against their ancient enemies—hunger, misery, and despair.

On the basis of these four major courses of action we hope to help create the conditions that will lead eventually to personal freedom and happiness for all mankind.

If we are to be successful in carrying out these policies, it is clear that we must have continued prosperity in this country and we must keep ourselves strong.

Slowly but surely we are weaving a world fabric of international security and growing prosperity.

We are aided by all who wish to live in freedom from fear—even by those who live today in fear under their own governments.

We are aided by all who want relief from the lies of propaganda—who desire truth and sincerity.

We are aided by all who desire self-government and a voice in deciding their own affairs.

We are aided by all who long for economic security—for the security and abundance that men in free societies can enjoy.

We are aided by all who desire freedom of speech, freedom of religion, and freedom to live their own lives for useful ends.

Our allies are the millions who hunger and thirst after righteousness.

In due time, as our stability becomes manifest, as more and more nations come to know the benefits of democracy and to participate in growing abundance, I believe that those countries which now oppose us will abandon their delusions and join with the free nations of the world in a just settlement of international differences.

Events have brought our American democracy to new influence and new responsibilities. They will test our courage, our devotion to duty, and our concept of liberty. But I say to all men, what we have achieved in liberty, we will surpass in greater liberty. Steadfast in our faith in the Almighty, we will advance toward a world where man's freedom is secure.

To that end we will devote our strength, our resources, and our firmness of resolve. With God's help, the future of mankind will be assured in a world of justice, harmony, and peace.

MARGARET CHASE SMITH

Declaration of Conscience

I don't want to see the Republican Party ride to political victory on the Four Horsemen of Calumny—Fear, Ignorance, Bigotry, and Smear.

Post World War II Communist gains caused deep division within the United States as conservatives assigned blame to the Roosevelt and Truman administrations and claimed that Communists were influencing U.S. foreign policy. These concerns received widespread public support because of frustration over the war in Korea, an exposed plot by left-wing subversives to take over the film industry, and the arrest and conviction of several Americans accused of spying for the Soviet Union.

In Hollywood, movie star John Wayne led the fight against the "red menace" as president of the Motion Picture Alliance for the Preservation of American Ideals. At the same time, a young Richard Nixon campaigned for the Senate, accusing his opponent of being "pink ... right down to her underwear." On Capitol Hill, Republican Senator Joseph R. McCarthy of Wisconsin led the crusade to rid the government of suspected Communists. Through a series of public investigations, McCarthy repeatedly asserted that the Truman administration was "soft on Communism" and later accused the Eisenhower administration of treason. From 1950 to December 1954, when finally condemned by his Senate colleagues, McCarthy and the feared House Un-American Activities Committee recklessly destroyed people's careers and reputations on the basis of little more than rumor and innuendo.

Margaret Chase Smith (1897-1995), a Republican from Maine and the first woman elected to both houses of Congress, was among the early opponents of "McCarthyism." Supported by six other Republican Senators—Charles Tobey of New Hampshire, George Aiken of Vermont, Wayne Morse of Oregon, Edward Thye of Minnesota, Irving Ives of New York, and Robert Hendrickson of New Jersey—she outlined her objections in the following "Declaration of Conscience" and presented it to the Senate on June 1, 1950.

Mr. President, I would like to speak briefly and simply about a serious national condition. It is a national feeling of fear and frustration that could result in national suicide and the end of everything that we Americans hold dear. It is a condition that comes from the lack of effective leadership in either the Legislative Branch or the Executive Branch of our Government.

That leadership is so lacking that serious and responsible proposals are being made that national advisory commissions be appointed to provide such critically needed leadership.

I speak as briefly as possible because too much harm has already been done with irresponsible words of bitterness and selfish political opportunism. I speak as simply as possible because the issue is too great to be obscured by eloquence. I speak simply and briefly in the hope that my words will be taken to heart.

I speak as a Republican. I speak as a woman. I speak as a United States Senator. I speak as an American.

The United States Senate has long enjoyed worldwide respect as the greatest deliberative body in the world. But recently that deliberative character has too often been debased to the level of a forum of hate and character assassination sheltered by the shield of congressional immunity.

It is ironical that we Senators can in debate in the Senate, directly or indirectly, by any form of words, impute to any American who is not a Senator any conduct or motive unworthy or unbecoming an American—and without that non-Senator American having any legal redress against us—yet if we say the same thing in the Senate about our colleagues we can be stopped on the grounds of being out of order.

It is strange that we can verbally attack anyone else without restraint and with full protection and yet we hold ourselves above the same type of criticism here on the Senate Floor. Surely the United States Senate is big enough to take self-criticism and self-appraisal. Surely we should be able to take the same kind of character attacks that we "dish out" to outsiders.

I think that it is high time for the United States Senate and its members to do some soul searching—for us to weigh our consciences—on the manner in which we are performing our duty to the people of America—on the manner in which we are using or abusing our individual powers and privileges.

I think that it is high time that we remembered that we have sworn to uphold and defend the Constitution. I think that it is high time that we remembered that the Constitution, as amended, speaks not only of the freedom of speech but also of trial by jury instead of trial by accusation.

Whether it be a criminal prosecution in court or a character prosecution in the Senate, there is little practical distinction when the life of a person has been ruined.

Those of us who shout the loudest about Americanism in making character assassinations are all too frequently those who, by our own words and acts, ignore some of the basic principles of Americanism:

The right to criticize;

The right to hold unpopular beliefs;

The right to protest;

The right of independent thought.

The exercise of these rights should not cost one single American citizen his reputation or his right to a livelihood nor should he be in danger of losing his reputation or livelihood merely because he happens to know someone who holds unpopular beliefs. Who of us doesn't? Otherwise none of us could call our souls our own. Otherwise thought control would have set in.

The American people are sick and tired of being afraid to speak their minds lest they be politically smeared as "Communists" or "Fascists" by their opponents. Freedom of speech is not what it used to be in America. It has been so abused by some that it is not exercised by others.

The American people are sick and tired of seeing innocent people smeared and guilty people whitewashed. But there have been enough proved cases, such as the Amerasia case, the Hiss case, the Coplon case, the Gold case, to cause nationwide distrust and strong suspicion that there may be something to the unproved, sensational accusations.

As a Republican, I say to my colleagues on this side of the aisle that the Republican Party faces a challenge today that is not unlike the challenge that it faced back in Lincoln's day. The Republican Party so successfully met that challenge that it emerged from the Civil War as the champion of a united nation—in addition to being a Party that unrelentingly fought loose spending and loose programs.

Today our country is being psychologically divided by the confusion and the suspicions that are bred in the United States Senate to spread like cancerous tentacles of "know nothing, suspect everything" attitudes. Today we have a Democratic Administration that has developed a mania for loose spending and loose programs. History is repeating itself—and the Republican Party again has the opportunity to emerge as the champion of unity and prudence.

The record of the present Democratic Administration has provided us with sufficient campaign issues without the necessity of resorting to political smears. America is rapidly losing its position as leader of the world simply because the Democratic Administration has pitifully failed to provide effective leadership.

The Democratic Administration has completely confused the American people by its daily contradictory grave warnings and optimistic assurances—that show the people that our Democratic Administration has no idea of where it is going.

The Democratic Administration has greatly lost the confidence of the American people by its complacency to the threat of communism here at home and the leak of vital secrets to Russia through key officials of the Democratic Administration. There are enough proved cases to make this point without diluting our criticism with unproved charges.

Surely these are sufficient reasons to make it clear to the American people that it is time for a change and that a Republican victory is necessary to the security of this country. Surely it is clear that this nation will continue to suffer as long as it is governed by the present ineffective Democratic Administration.

Yet to displace it with a Republican regime embracing a philosophy that lacks political integrity or intellectual honesty would prove equally disastrous to this nation. The nation sorely needs a Republican victory. But I don't want to see the Republican Party ride to political victory on the Four Horsemen of Calumny—Fear, Ignorance, Bigotry, and Smear.

I doubt if the Republican Party could—simply because I don't believe the American people will uphold any political party that puts political exploitation above national interest. Surely we Republicans aren't that desperate for victory.

I don't want to see the Republican Party win that way. While it might be a fleeting victory for the Republican Party, it would be a more lasting defeat for the American people. Surely it would ultimately be suicide for the Republican Party and the two-party system that has protected our American liberties from the dictatorship of a one party system.

As members of the Minority Party, we do not have the primary authority to formulate the policy of our Government. But we do have the responsibility of rendering constructive criticism, of clarifying issues, of allaying fears by acting as responsible citizens.

As a woman, I wonder how the mothers, wives, sisters, and daughters feel about the way in which members of their families have been politically mangled in Senate debate—and I use the word "debate" advisedly.

As a United States Senator, I am not proud of the way in which the Senate has been made a publicity platform for irresponsible sensationalism. I am not proud of the reckless abandon in which unproved charges have been hurled from this side of the aisle. I am not proud of the obviously staged, undignified countercharges that have been attempted in retaliation from the other side of the aisle.

I don't like the way the Senate has been made a rendezvous for vilification, for selfish political gain at the sacrifice of individual reputations and national unity. I am not proud of the way we smear outsiders from the Floor of the Senate and hide behind the cloak of congressional immunity and still place ourselves beyond criticism on the Floor of the Senate.

As an American, I am shocked at the way Republicans and Democrats alike are playing directly into the Communist design of "confuse, divide and conquer." As an American, I don't want a Democratic Administration "whitewash" or "cover-up" any more than I want a Republican smear or witch hunt.

As an American, I condemn a Republican "Fascist" just as much as I condemn a Democrat "Communist." I condemn a Democrat "Fascist" just as much as I condemn a Republican "Communist." They are equally dangerous to you and me and to our country. As an American, I want to see our nation recapture the strength and unity it once had when we fought the enemy instead of ourselves. ...

The Berlin Airlift brings supplies to the blockaded city as German children eagerly await. At the end of WW II, Berlin was divided into American, British, French, and Soviet sectors. Supplies for western sectors had to pass through the Soviet-controlled zone. As friction between the USSR and the West widened, the Soviets stopped all incoming traffic and cut off supplies from eastern power stations. Allied leaders considered a variety of plans ranging from withdrawal to military action. Rather than abandon the city's more than two million residents, President Truman ordered an aerial supply effort beginning in June of 1948. The Berlin Airlift carried over two million tons of supplies in 270,000 flights. The blockade of Berlin was finally lifted by the Soviets on May 12, 1949. Berlin became a symbol of the United States resolve to stand up to the Soviet threat without being forced into a direct conflict.

LANGSTON HUGHES

Dark Youth of the U.S.A., Let America Be America Again, and Refugee in America

James Mercer Langston Hughes (1902-1967), one of the great poets and short story writers of the twentieth century, was born in Joplin, Missouri, and educated at Lincoln University in Pennsylvania. He also studied at Columbia University for a year while working odd jobs to support his writing habits. He published his first poem, "The Negro Speaks of Rivers," in Crisis magazine in 1921; his first volume of poetry, *The Weary Blues*, appeared in 1926. Hughes wrote, often in an angry voice, of the despair blacks felt over social and economic conditions, but frowned on violence, advocating instead self-control. The following three selections are representative of his writing in that they examine the hardships of being black in America while nonetheless extolling the virtues of being an American.

Dark Youth of the U.S.A.

(A recitation to be delivered by a Negro boy, bright, clean, and neatly dressed, carrying his books to school.)

Sturdy I stand, books in my hand—
Today's dark child, tomorrow's strong man:
The hope of my race
To mould a place
In America's magic land.

American am I, none can deny:
He who oppresses me, him I defy!
I am Dark Youth
Seeking the truth
Of a free life beneath our great sky.

Long a part of the Union's heart—
Years ago at the nation's start
Attucks died
That right might abide
And strength to our land impart.

To be wise and strong, then, studying long,
Seeking the knowledge that rights all wrong—
That is my mission.
Lifting my race to its rightful place
Till beauty and pride fills each dark face
Is my ambition.

So I climb toward tomorrow, out of past sorrow,
Treading the modern way
With the White and the Black whom nothing holds back—
The American Youth of today.

Let America Be America Again

Let America be America again.
Let it be the dream it used to be.
Let it be the pioneer on the plain
Seeking a home where he himself is free.

(America never was America to me.)

Let America be the dream the dreamers dreamed—
Let it be that great strong land of love
Where never kings connive nor tyrants scheme
That any man be crushed by one above.

(It never was America to me.)

O, let my land be a land where Liberty
Is crowned with no false patriotic wreath,
But opportunity is real, and life is free,
Equality is in the air we breathe.

(There's never been equality for me,
Nor freedom in this "homeland of the free.")

Say who are you that mumbles in the dark?
And who are you that draws your veil across the stars?

I am the poor white, fooled and pushed apart,
I am the Negro bearing slavery's scars.
I am the red man driven from the land,
I am the immigrant clutching the hope I seek—
And finding only the same old stupid plan.
Of dog eat dog, of mighty crush the weak.

I am the young man, full of strength and hope,
Tangled in that ancient endless chain
Of profit, power, gain, of grab the land!
Of grab the gold! Of grab the ways of satisfying need!
Of work the men! Of take the pay!
Of owning everything for one's own greed!

I am the farmer, bondsman to the soil,
I am the worker sold to the machine.
I am the Negro, servant to you all.
I am the people, humble, hungry, mean—
Hungry yet today despite the dream.
Beaten yet today—O, Pioneers!
I am the man who never got ahead,
The poorest worker bartered through the years.

Yet I'm the one who dreamt our basic dream
In that Old World while still a serf of kings,
Who dreamt a dream so strong, so brave, so true,
That even yet its mighty daring sings
In every brick and stone, in every furrow turned
That's made America the land it has become.
O, I'm the man who sailed those early seas
In search of what I meant to be my home—
For I'm the one who left dark Ireland's shore,
And Poland's plain, and England's grassy lea,
And torn from Black Africa's strand I came
To build a "homeland of the free."

The free?

Who said the free? Not me?
Surely not me? The millions on relief today?
The millions shot down when we strike?
The millions who have nothing for our pay?
For all the dreams we've dreamed
And all the songs we've sung
And all the hopes we've held
And all the flags we've hung,
The millions who have nothing for our pay—
Except the dream that's almost dead today.

O, let America be America again—
The land that never has been yet—
And yet must be—the land where *every* man is free.
The land that's mine—the poor man's, Indian's, Negro's,
ME—
Who made America,
Whose sweat and blood, whose faith and pain,
Whose hand at the foundry, whose plow in the rain,
Must bring back our mighty dream again.

Sure, call me any ugly name you choose—
The steel of freedom does not stain.
From those who live like leeches on the people's lives,
We must take back our land again,
America!

O, yes,
I say it plain,
America never was America to me,
And yet I swear this oath—
America will be!

Out of the rack and ruin of our gangster death,
The rape and rot of graft, and stealth, and lies,
We, the people, must redeem
The land, the mines, the plants, the rivers,
The mountains and the endless plain—
All, all the stretch of these great green states—
And make America again!

Refugee in America

There are words like *Freedom*
Sweet and wonderful to say.
On my heartstrings freedom sings
All day everyday.

There are words like *Liberty*
That almost make me cry.
If you had known what I knew
You would know why.

GWENDOLYN BROOKS

The Mother

Gwendolyn Elizabeth Brooks (1917-2000) was born in Topeka, Kansas, and raised in the slums of Chicago. Her first collection of poetry, modeled after her childhood surroundings, was titled *A Street in Bronzeville*. In 1950, Brooks became the first black American to win a Pulitzer Prize, receiving the award for her second collection of poetry, *Annie Allen*. Additional collections include *The Bean Eaters* (1960), *Selected Poems* (1963), *In the Mecca* (1968), *Riot* (1969), *Family Pictures* (1970), *Aloneness* (1971), *To Disembark* (1981), *The Near-Johannesburg Boy* (1987), *Blacks* (1987), *Gottschalk and the Grande Tarantelle* (1989), and *Children Coming Home* (1992).

Abortions will not let you forget.
You remember the children you got that you did not get,
The damp small pulps with a little or with no hair,
The singers and workers that never handled the air.
You will never neglect or beat them,
Or silence or buy with a sweet.
You will never wind up the sucking-thumb
Or scuttle off ghosts that come.
You will never leave them, controlling your luscious sigh,
Return for a snack of them, with gobbling mother-eye.

I have heard in the voices of the wind the voices of my dim killed children.
I have contracted. I have eased my dim dears at the breasts they could never suck.
I have said, Sweets, if I sinned, if I seized Your Luck
And your lives from your unfinished reach,
If I stole your births and your names,
Your straight baby tears and your games,
Your stilted or lovely loves, your tumults, your marriages, aches, and your deaths,
If I poisoned the beginnings of your breaths,
Believe that even in my deliberateness I was not deliberate.
Though why should I whine,
Whine that the crime was other than mine?—
Since anyhow you are dead.
Or rather, or instead,
You were never made.
But that too, I am afraid,
Is faulty: oh, what shall I say, how is the truth to be said?
You were born, you had body, you died.
It is just that you never giggled or planned or cried.

Believe me, I loved you all.
Believe me, I knew you, though faintly, and I loved, I loved you
All.

STAN JONES

Riders in the Sky

Stan Jones (1914-1963) was born in Douglas, Arizona, and served in the U.S. Navy during World War II. He earned his degree in zoology from the University of California and gained employment as a park ranger in Death Valley.

In 1949, Jones assisted Hollywood filmmakers in scouting locations for the filming of *Three Godfathers*, starring John Wayne. During the filming, Jones entertained the cast and crew with some of his own music, including "Riders in the Sky," which would bring him nationwide fame; that same year, he appeared in the Gene Autry movie *Riders in the Sky*. Jones went on to write compositions for various Walt Disney productions and Western genre movies, including the title song to another John Wayne film, *The Searchers*.

An old cow poke went riding out one dark and windy day,
Upon a ridge he rested as he went along his way,
When all at once a mighty herd of red-eyed cows he saw
A ploughin' thru the ragged skies and up a cloudy draw.
Yi-pi-yi-ay, Yi-pi-yi-oh, the ghost herd in the sky.

Their brands were still on fire and their hooves wuz made of steel,
Their horns wuz black and shiny and their hot breath he could feel,
A bolt of fear went through him as they thundered thru the sky,
For he saw the riders comin' hard and he heard their mournful cry.
Yi-pi-yi-ay, Yi-pi-yi-oh, Ghost Riders in the sky.

Their faces gaunt, their eyes were blurred, and shirts all soaked with sweat,
They're ridin' hard to catch that herd but they ain't caught them yet,
'Cause they've got to ride forever on that range up in the sky,
On horses snortin' fire, as they ride on hear their cry.
Yi-pi-yi-ay, Yi-pi-yi-oh, Ghost Riders in the sky.

The riders loped on by him and he heard one call his name,
"If you want to save your soul from hell a-ridin' on our range,
Then cowboy change your ways today or with us you will ride,
A-try'n to catch the devil's herd across these endless skies."
Yi-pi-yi-ay, Yi-pi-yi-oh, Ghost Riders in the sky.

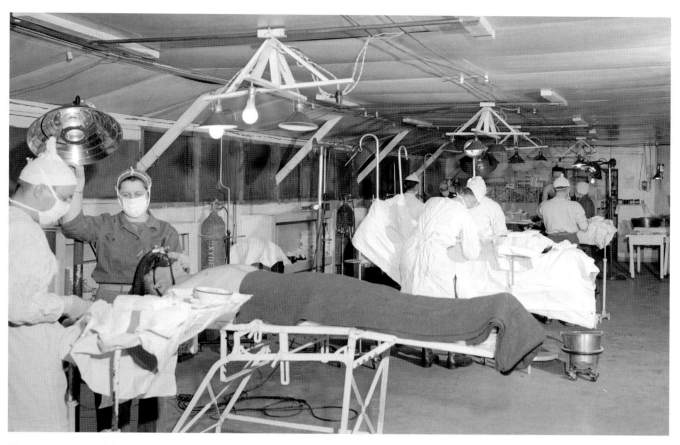

The operating room of the 44th Mobile Army Surgical Hospital in Korea, 1954. MASH units, as they were known, were deployed to forward locations just out of enemy artillery range. Intended to be truly mobile, each truck-borne MASH was fully staffed with surgical and medical personnel, and equipped to provide life-saving surgery to casualties that could not otherwise survive transportation to rear medical facilities. In 1968, Dr. Richard Hornberger, using the alias Richard Hooker, published a fictional account of his years at the 8055 Mobile Army Surgical Hospital in Korea. Hornberger based the lead character, Hawkeye, on himself and later wrote additional novels featuring the same characters. A movie based on Hornberger's novel was released in the fall of 1970 when opposition to the Vietnam War was at its peak. The film's success led to a television series of the same name.

ROY ROGERS AND DALE EVANS

Happy Trails

Born Leonard Franklin Slye near Cincinnati, Ohio, Roy Rogers (1911-1998) began his career as a singer and helped found the *Sons of the Pioneers* singing group. In 1938, Rogers earned his first starring film role in *Under Western Skies* and, upon retiring from the movies in the 1950s, had appeared in more than eighty films for Republic Studios. Like Gene Autry, Rogers was a singing cowboy whose films were "formula westerns." Rogers often co-starred with his palomino horse, Trigger, comedic sidekick George "Gabby" Hayes, and heroine, Dale Evans (born Frances Octavia Smith, 1912-2001), whom Rogers married in 1947.

Known as the "King of the Cowboys" and the "Queen of the West," Rogers and Evans also starred together in numerous television specials, including *The Roy Rogers Show* (1951-1956), the signature song of which was "Happy Trails." Rogers later founded a chain of restaurants that bear his name, and he and Dale maintained a museum dedicated to the Old West and served as co-chairpersons of the Happy Trails Children's Foundation.

Happy trails to you until we meet again.
Happy trails to you, keep smilin' until then.
Who cares about the clouds when we're together?
Just sing a song and bring the sunny weather.
Happy trails to you 'till we meet again.

Some trails are happy ones,
Others are blue.
It's the way you ride the trail that counts;
Here's a happy one for you.

Happy trails to you until we meet again.
Happy trails to you, keep smilin' until then.
Who cares about the clouds when we're together?
Just sing a song and bring the sunny weather.
Happy trails to you 'till we meet again.

ADLAI E. STEVENSON

The Nature of Patriotism

I venture to suggest that ... patriotism ... is not short, frenzied outbursts of emotion, but the tranquil and steady dedication of a lifetime.

Adlai Ewing Stevenson (1900-1965) was the presidential nominee of the Democratic Party in 1952 and 1956. He was the grandson of Adlai Ewing Stevenson (1835-1914), vice president of the United States from 1893 to 1897 in the administration of Grover Cleveland.

Born in Los Angeles, California, Stevenson graduated from Princeton University after a brief enlistment in the U.S. Navy and later studied at Harvard and Northwestern. He went to work for his family-owned newspaper in Illinois and, beginning in 1933, held a variety of public positions. In 1948, Stevenson was elected governor of Illinois by the largest majority in state history; he won his party's 1952 presidential nomination even though he had not actively campaigned for it. In truth, the Democratic Party was floundering due to the War in Korea and the effective, although often erroneous charges of Republican Senator Joseph McCarthy, who constantly ridiculed the Democratic Party as being soft on Communism.

On August 27, in his campaign against the immensely popular Republican nominee, General Eisenhower, Stevenson addressed the American Legion Convention in Madison Square Garden.

... I have no claim, as many of you do, to the honored title of old soldier. Nor have I risen to high rank in the armed services. The fact that a great general and I are competing candidates for the presidency will not diminish my warm respect for his military achievements. Nor will that respect keep me from using every honest effort to defeat him in November! ...

We talk a great deal about patriotism. What do we mean by "patriotism" in the context of our times? I venture to suggest that what we mean is a sense of national responsibility which will enable America to remain master of her power—to walk with it in serenity and wisdom, with self-respect and the respect of all mankind; a patriotism that puts country ahead of self; a patriotism which is not short,

frenzied outbursts of emotion, but the tranquil and steady dedication of a lifetime. The dedication of a lifetime—these are words that are easy to utter, but this is a mighty assignment. For it is often easier to fight for principles than to live up to them.

Patriotism, I have said, means putting country before self. This is no abstract phrase, and unhappily, we find some things in American life today of which we cannot be proud.

Consider the groups who seek to identify their special interests with the general welfare. I find it sobering to think that their pressures might one day be focused on me. I have resisted them before, and I hope the Almighty will give me the strength to do so again and again. And I should tell you—my fellow Legionnaires—as I would tell all other organized groups, that I intend to resist pressures from veterans, too, if I think their demands are excessive or in conflict with the public interest, which must always be the paramount interest.

Let me suggest, incidentally, that we are rapidly becoming a nation of veterans. If we were all to claim a special reward for our service, beyond that to which specific disability or sacrifice has created a just claim, who would be left to pay the bill? After all, we are Americans first and veterans second, and the best maxim for any administration is still Jefferson's: "Equal rights for all, special privileges for none."

True patriotism, it seems to me, is based on tolerance and a large measure of humility.

There are men among us who use "patriotism" as a club for attacking other Americans. What can we say for the self-styled patriot who thinks that a Negro, a Jew, a Catholic, or a Japanese-American is less an American than he? That betrays the deepest article of our faith, the belief in individual liberty and equality which has always been the heart and soul of the American idea.

What can we say for the man who proclaims himself a patriot—and then for political or personal reasons attacks the patriotism of faithful public servants? I give you, as a shocking example, the attacks which have been made on the loyalty and the motives of our great wartime chief of staff, General Marshall. To me this is the type of "patriotism" which is, in Dr. Johnson's phrase, "the last refuge of scoundrels."

The anatomy of patriotism is complex. But surely intolerance and public irresponsibility cannot be cloaked in the shining armor of rectitude and righteousness. Nor can the denial of the right to hold ideas that are different—the freedom of man to think as he pleases. To strike freedom of the mind with the fist of patriotism is an old and ugly subtlety.

And the freedom of the mind, my friends, has served America well. The vigor of our political life, our capacity for change, our cultural, scientific, and industrial achievements, all derive from free inquiry, from the free mind—from the imagination, resourcefulness, and daring of men who are not afraid of new ideas. Most all of us favor free enterprise for business. Let us also favor free enterprise for the mind. For, in the last analysis, we would fight to the death to protect it. Why is it, then, that

we are sometimes slow to detect, or are indifferent to, the dangers that beset it?

Many of the threats to our cherished freedoms in these anxious, troubled times arise, it seems to me, from a healthy apprehension about the Communist menace within our country. Communism is abhorrent. It is strangulation of the individual; it is death for the soul. Americans who have surrendered to this misbegotten idol have surrendered their right to our trust. And there can be no secure place for them in our public life.

Yet, as I have said before, we must take care not to burn down the barn to kill the rats. All of us, and especially patriotic organizations of enormous influence like the American Legion, must be vigilant in protecting our birthright from its too zealous friends while protecting it from its evil enemies.

The tragedy of our day is the climate of fear in which we live, and fear breeds repression. Too often sinister threats to the Bill of Rights, to freedom of the mind, are concealed under the patriotic cloak of anticommunism.

I could add, from my own experience, that it is never necessary to call a man a Communist to make political capital. Those of us who have undertaken to practice the ancient but imperfect art of government will always make enough mistakes to keep our critics well supplied with standard ammunition. There is no need for poison gas ... .

Let me now, in my concluding words, inquire with you how we may affirm our patriotism in the troubled yet hopeful years that are ahead.

The central concern of the American Legion—the ideal which holds it together—the vitality which animates it—is patriotism. And those voices which we have heard most clearly and which are best remembered in our public life have always had the accent of patriotism.

It was always accounted a virtue in man to love his country. With us it is now something more than a virtue. It is a necessity, a condition of survival. When an American says that he loves his country, he means not only that he loves the New England hills, the prairies glistening in the sun, the wide and rising plains, the great mountains, and the sea. He means that he loves an inner air, an inner light in which freedom lives and in which a man can draw the breath of self-respect.

Men who have offered their lives for their country know that patriotism is not the *fear* of something; it is the *love* of something. Patriotism with us is not the hatred of

Russia; it is the love of this Republic and of the ideal of liberty of man and mind in which it was born, and to which this Republic is dedicated.

With this patriotism—patriotism in its large and wholesome meaning—America can master its power and turn it to the noble cause of peace. We can maintain military power without militarism; political power without oppression; and moral power without compulsion or complacency.

The road we travel is long, but at the end lies the grail of peace. And in the valley of peace we see the faint outlines of a new world, fertile and strong. It is odd that one of the keys to abundance should have been handed to civilization on a platter of destruction. But the power of the atom to work evil gives only the merest hint of its power for good.

I believe that man stands on the eve of his greatest day. I know, too, that that day is not a gift but a prize—that we shall not reach it until we have won it.

Legionnaires are united by memories of war. Therefore, no group is more devoted to peace. I say to you now that there is work to be done, that the difficulties and dangers that beset our path at home and abroad are incalculable. There is sweat and sacrifice; there is much of patience and quiet persistence in our horoscope. Perhaps the goal is not even for us to see in our lifetime.

But we are embarked on a great adventure. Let us proclaim our faith in the future of man. Of good heart and good cheer, faithful to ourselves and our traditions, we can lift the cause of freedom, the cause of free men, so high no power on earth can tear it down. We can pluck this flower, safety, from this nettle, danger. Living, speaking, like men—like Americans—we can lead the way to our rendezvous in a happy, peaceful world.

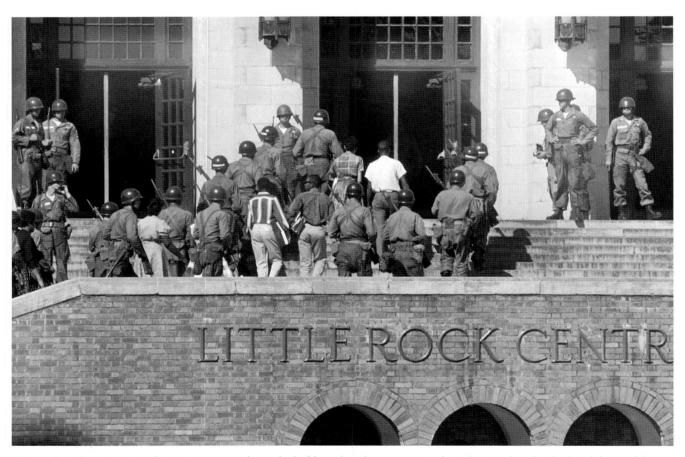

The "Little Rock Nine," nine African American students who had been denied entrance to Little Rock Central High School in defiance of the 1954 Supreme Court ruling ordering integration of the public schools, walk up the steps of the school entrance under protection of the U.S. Army. President Eisenhower used the military to enforce the federal court ruling and simultaneously federalized the entire 10,000-man Arkansas National Guard, thus removing them from control of Governor Orval Faubus.

DOUGLAS MACARTHUR

Farewell Address at West Point

The long gray line has never failed us. Were you to do so, a million ghosts in olive drab, in brown khaki, in blue and gray, would rise from their white crosses, thundering those magic words: Duty, Honor, Country.

Excepting George Washington's leadership of the Continental Army, Douglas MacArthur (1880-1964) is perhaps the most significant military figure in American history. His father, General Arthur MacArthur, was a hero of the Civil War and Congressional Medal of Honor recipient who later served as military governor of the Philippines. Born in Little Rock, Arkansas, in 1903, young Douglas graduated with highest honors from the United States Military Academy at West Point and later served as an aide to President Theodore Roosevelt. During World War I, he obtained the rank of general and won numerous honors for his heroism and leadership of the 42nd (Rainbow) Division. From 1919 to 1922, he served as superintendent of West Point and later became chief of staff of the U.S. Army. In 1932, during the Great Depression, he provoked much criticism by personally commanding troop action against the "Bonus Expeditionary Force," a group of World War I veterans seeking immediate cashing of adjusted compensation certificates, driving them from Washington, D.C.

From 1935 to 1941, mirroring his father's travels, MacArthur was military adviser to the Philippine Commonwealth and, in July of 1941, was appointed by President Franklin Roosevelt as commander of U.S. Army Forces Far East. For his defense of the Philippine Islands during World War II, he was awarded the Medal of Honor—thus making the MacArthurs the first father and son to both receive the nation's highest military award. With the war's conclusion, MacArthur presided over the formal surrender of Japan aboard the USS *Missouri* in Tokyo Bay. He was then appointed supreme commander of Allied forces in the Pacific and placed in charge of the occupation of Japan.

On June 25, 1950, the Korean War broke out when the Communist forces of North Korea crossed the demilitarized thirty-eighth parallel into South Korea. Appointed head of military forces of the United Nations, MacArthur successfully turned back the incursion and actually invaded North Korea. The United Nations were driven back south of the thirty-eighth parallel, however, when Communist Chinese forces entered the war on the side of the North. MacArthur wanted to extend the war into China. When President Truman refused, fearing the possible outbreak of a third world war, MacArthur criticized the president in a letter that was made public by a congressman and even went so far as to send an unauthorized message demanding the surrender of the Chinese. Willing to accept nothing less than absolute victory, MacArthur had become frustrated by the policy of mere Communist containment. With the development of the atomic bomb, however, the concept of total victory had been overshadowed by the fear of nuclear annihilation. For his unwillingness to "give his wholehearted support" to the policies of the U.S. government and the United Nations, MacArthur was relieved of all commands.

He returned to the United States for the first time in fourteen years to a hero's welcome. Shortly thereafter, on April 19, 1951, he addressed a joint session of Congress, before which he publicized his views on foreign policy. He closed that speech with what has become his most frequently quoted public statement, saying:

"The world has turned over many times since I took the oath on the plain at West Point, and the hopes and dreams have long since vanished. But I still remember the refrain of one of the most popular barrack ballads of that day which proclaimed most proudly that—'Old soldiers never die; they just fade away.' And like the old soldier of that ballad, I now close my military career and just fade away—an old soldier who tried to do his duty as God gave him the light to see that duty."

On May 12, 1962, MacArthur visited West Point to receive the *Sylvanus Thayer Award*. His farewell address to the cadets was delivered extemporaneously and endures as one of the most eloquent orations in American history.

No human being could fail to be deeply moved by such a tribute as this, coming from a profession I have served so long and a people I have loved so well. It fills me with an emotion I cannot express. But this award is not intended primarily for a personality, but to symbolize a great moral code—the code of conduct and chivalry of those who guard this beloved land of culture and ancient descent. ...

"Duty," "Honor," "Country"—those three hallowed words reverently dictate what you want to be, what you can be, what you will be. They are your rallying point to build courage when courage seems to fail, to regain faith when there seems to be little cause for faith, to create hope when hope becomes forlorn.

Unhappily, I possess neither that eloquence of diction, that poetry of imagination, nor that brilliance of metaphor to tell you all that they mean.

The unbelievers will say they are but words, but a slogan, but a flamboyant phrase. Every pedant, every demagogue, every cynic, every hypocrite, every troublemaker, and, I am sorry to say, some others of an entirely different character, will try to downgrade them even to the extent of mockery and ridicule.

But these are some of the things they build. They build your basic character. They mold you for your future roles as the custodians of the nation's defense. They make you strong enough to know when you are weak, and brave enough to face yourself when you are afraid.

They teach you to be proud and unbending in honest failure, but humble and gentle in success; not to substitute words for action; not to seek the path of comfort, but to face the stress and spur of difficulty and challenge; to learn to stand up in the storm, but to have compassion on those who fall; to master yourself before you seek to master others; to have a heart that is clean, a goal that is high; to learn to laugh, yet never forget how to weep; to reach into the future, yet never neglect the past; to be serious, yet never take yourself too seriously; to be modest so that you will remember the simplicity of true greatness, the open mind of true wisdom, the meekness of true strength.

They give you a temperate will, a quality of imagination, a vigor of the emotions, a freshness of the deep springs of life, a temperamental predominance of courage over timidity, an appetite for adventure over love of ease.

They create in your heart the sense of wonder, the unfailing hope of what next, and the joy and inspiration of life. They teach you in this way to be an officer and a gentleman.

And what sort of soldiers are those you are to lead? Are they reliable? Are they brave? Are they capable of victory?

Their story is known to all of you. It is the story of the American man at arms. My estimate of him was formed on the battle-fields many, many years ago, and has never changed.

I regarded him then, as I regard him now, as one of the world's noblest figures; not only as one of the finest military characters, but also as one of the most stainless.

His name and fame are the birthright of every American citizen. In his youth and strength, his love and loyalty, he gave all that mortality can give. He needs no eulogy from me, or from any other man. He has written his own history and written it in red on his enemy's breast. ...

In twenty campaigns, on a hundred battlefields, around a thousand campfires, I have witnessed that enduring fortitude, that patriotic self-abnegation, and that invincible determination which have carved his statue in the hearts of his people. From one end of the world to the other, he has drained deep the chalice of courage.

As I listened to those songs in memory's eye I could see those staggering columns of the First World War, bending under soggy packs on many a weary march, from dripping dusk to drizzling dawn, slogging ankle deep through mire of shell-pocked roads; to form grimly for the attack, blue-lipped, covered with sludge and mud, chilled by the wind and rain, driving home to their objective, and for many, to the judgment seat of God.

I do not know the dignity of their birth, but I do know the glory of their death. They died unquestioning, uncomplaining, with faith in their hearts, and on their lips the hope that we would go on to victory.

Always for them: Duty, Honor, Country. Always their blood, and sweat, and tears, as they saw the way and the light. And twenty years after, on the other side of the globe, against the filth of dirty foxholes, the strength stench of ghostly trenches, the slime of dripping dugouts, those boiling suns of the relentless heat, those torrential rains of devastating storms, the loneliness and utter desolation of jungle trails, the bitterness of long separation of those they loved and cherished, the deadly pestilence of tropic disease, the horror of stricken areas of war.

Their resolute and determined defense, their swift and sure attack, their indomitable purpose, their complete and decisive victory—always victory, always through the bloody haze of their last reverberating shot, the vision of gaunt, ghastly men, reverently following your password of Duty, Honor, Country. ...

You now face a new world, a world of change. The thrust into outer space of the satellite spheres and missiles marks a beginning of another epoch in the long story of mankind. In the five or more billions of years the scientists tell us it has taken to form the earth, in the three or more billion years of development of the human race, there has never been a more abrupt or staggering evolution.

We deal now, not with things of this world alone, but with the illimitable distances and yet unfathomed mysteries of the universe.

We are reaching out for a new and boundless frontier. We speak in strange terms of harnessing the cosmic energy, of making winds and tides work for us, of creating unheard of synthetic materials to supplement or even replace our old standard basics; to purify sea water for our drink; of mining ocean floors for new fields of wealth and food; of disease preventatives to expand life into the hundred of years; of controlling the weather for a more equitable distribution of heat and cold, of rain and shine; of spaceships to the moon; of the primary target in war, no longer limited to the armed forces of an enemy, but instead to include his civil population; of ultimate conflict between a united human race and the sinister forces of some other planetary galaxy; such dreams and fantasies as to make life the most exciting of all times.

And through all this welter of change and development your mission remains fixed, determined, inviolable. It is to win our wars. Everything else in your professional career is but corollary to this vital dedication. All other public purpose, all other public projects, all other public needs, great or small, will find others for their accomplishments; but you are the ones who are trained to fight.

Yours is the profession of arms, the will to win, the sure knowledge that in war there is no substitute for victory, that if you lose, the Nation will be destroyed, that the very obsession of your public service must be Duty, Honor, Country.

Others will debate the controversial issues, national and international, which divide men's minds. But serene, calm, aloof, you stand as the Nation's war guardians, as its lifeguards from the raging tides of international conflict, as its gladiators in the arena of battle. For a century and a half you have defended, guarded and protected its hallowed traditions of liberty and freedom of right and justice.

Let civilian voices argue the merits or demerits of our processes of government; whether strength is being sapped by deficit financing indulged in too long, by federal paternalism grown too mighty, by power groups grown too arrogant, by politics grown too corrupt, by crime grown too rampant, by morals grown too low, by taxes grown too high, by extremists grown too violent; whether our personal liberties are as firm and complete as they should be.

These great national problems are not for your professional participation or military solution. Your guidepost stands out like a tenfold beacon in the night: Duty, Honor, Country.

You are the leaven which binds together the entire fabric of our national system of defense. From your ranks come the great captains who hold the Nation's destiny in their hands the moment the war tocsin sounds.

The long gray line has never failed us. Were you to do so, a million ghosts in olive drab, in brown khaki, in blue and gray, would rise from their white crosses, thundering those magic words: Duty, Honor, Country.

This does not mean that you are warmongers. On the contrary, the soldier above all other people prays for peace, for he must suffer and bear the deepest wounds and scars of war. But always in our ears ring the ominous words of Plato, that wisest of all philosophers: "Only the dead have seen the end of war."

The shadows are lengthening for me. The twilight is here. My days of old have vanished—tone and tints. They have gone glimmering through the dreams of things that were. Their memory is one of wondrous beauty, watered by tears and coaxed and caressed by the smiles of yesterday. I listen then, but with thirsty ear, for the witching melody of faint bugles blowing reveille, of far drums beating the long roll.

In my dreams I hear again the crash of guns, the rattle of musketry, the strange, mournful mutter of the battlefield. But in the evening of my memory I come back to West Point. Always there echoes and re-echoes: Duty, Honor, Country.

Today marks my final roll call with you. But I want you to know that when I cross the river, my last conscious thoughts will be of the corps, and the corps, and the corps.

I bid you farewell.

DWIGHT D. EISENHOWER

Farewell Address

We must guard against the acquisition of unwarranted influence, whether sought or unsought, by the military-industrial complex.

Dwight David Eisenhower (1890-1969) was born in Denison, Texas, and raised in Abilene, Kansas. A graduate of West Point, he trained tank battalions during World War I and, in 1933, became an aide to Army Chief of Staff Douglas MacArthur. During World War II, Eisenhower was MacArthur's counterpart in the European theater of operations, serving as supreme commander of Allied forces. Eisenhower was responsible for implementing *Operation Overlord*, the June 6, 1944 (D-Day) invasion of Normandy.

At the war's conclusion, "Ike" replaced George Marshall as Army chief of staff. He later served as president of Columbia University, wrote a best-selling book about his war time experiences and, in 1950, returned to active duty as supreme commander in Europe of the newly formed North Atlantic Treaty Organization.

Beginning in 1943, both the Democratic and Republican parties tried to recruit Eisenhower to run for president. Asking that he be left alone to perform his duties as a soldier, the general resisted their efforts until 1952, when he successfully campaigned for the Republican nomination and was elected in a landslide to the first of two terms.

In his farewell address, delivered on January 17, 1961, Eisenhower upheld the wisdom of Washington—"remembering ... that timely disbursements to prepare for danger frequently prevent much greater disbursements to repel it"—arguing the need for a "permanent armaments industry." But Eisenhower warned against the amassing of power by "a scientific-technological elite." Pundit Walter Lippmann characterized Eisenhower's farewell as being "in the great tradition" of presidential farewell addresses. "Washington made the theme of his Farewell Address a warning against allowing the influence of foreign governments to invade our political life. That was then the menace to the civilian power. Now Eisenhower, speaking from his experience and looking ahead, is concerned with a contemporary threat to the supremacy of the civilian power."

... We now stand ten years past the midpoint of a century that has witnessed four major wars among great nations. Three of these involved our own country. Despite these holocausts America is today the strongest, the most influential and most productive nation in the world. Understandably proud of this pre-eminence, we yet realize that America's leadership and prestige depend, not merely upon our unmatched material progress, riches and military strength, but on how we use our power in the interests of world peace and human betterment.

Throughout America's adventure in free government, our basic purposes have been to keep the peace; to foster progress in human achievement, and to enhance liberty, dignity and integrity among peoples and among nations.

To strive for less would be unworthy of a free and religious people. Any failure traceable to arrogance, or our lack of comprehension or readiness to sacrifice would inflict upon us grievous hurt both at home and abroad.

Progress toward these noble goals is persistently threatened by the conflict now engulfing the world. It commands our whole attention, absorbs our very beings.

We face a hostile ideology—global in scope, atheistic in character, ruthless in purpose, and insidious in method. Unhappily, the danger it poses promises to be of indefinite duration. To meet it successfully, there is called for, not so much the emotional and transitory sacrifices of crisis, but rather those which enable us to carry forward steadily, surely, and without complaint the burdens of a prolonged and complex struggle—with liberty the stake. Only thus shall we remain, despite every provocation, on our chartered course toward permanent peace and human betterment ... .

A vital element in keeping the peace is our military establishment. Our arms must be mighty, ready for instant action, so that no potential aggressor may be tempted to risk his own destruction.

Our military organization today bears little relation to that known by any of my predecessors in peacetime, or indeed by the fighting men of World War II or Korea. Until the latest of our world conflicts, the United States had no armaments industry. American makers of plowshares could, with time and as required, make swords as well. But now we can no longer risk emergency improvisation of national defense; we have been compelled to create a permanent armaments industry of vast proportions. Added to this, three and a half million men and women are directly engaged in the defense establishment. We annually spend on military security more than the net income of all United States corporations.

This conjunction of an immense military establishment and a large arms industry is new in the American experience. The total influence—economic, political, even spiritual—is felt in every city, every Statehouse, every office of the Federal government. We recognize the imperative need for this development. Yet we must not fail to comprehend its grave implications. Our toil, resources and livelihood are all involved; so is the very structure of our society.

In the councils of government, we must guard against the acquisition of unwarranted influence, whether sought or unsought, by the military-industrial complex. The potential for the disastrous rise of misplaced power exists and will persist.

We must never let the weight of this combination endanger our liberties or democratic processes. We should take nothing for granted. Only an alert and knowledgeable citizenry can compel the proper meshing of the huge industrial and military machinery of defense with our peaceful methods and goals, so that security and liberty may prosper together.

Akin to, and largely responsible for the sweeping changes in our industrial-military posture, has been the technological revolution during recent decades.

In this revolution, research has become central; it also becomes more formalized, complex, and costly. A steadily increasing share is conducted for, by, or at the direction of, the Federal government.

Today, the solitary inventor, tinkering in his shop, has been overshadowed by task forces of scientists in laboratories and testing fields. In the same fashion, the free university, historically the fountainhead of free ideas and scientific discovery, has experienced a revolution in the conduct of research. Partly because of the huge costs involved, a government contract becomes virtually a substitute for intellectual curiosity. For every old blackboard there are now hundreds of new electronic computers.

The prospect of domination of the nation's scholars by Federal employment, project allocations, and the power of money is ever present—and is gravely to be regarded.

Yet, in holding scientific research and discovery in respect, as we should, we must also be alert to the equal and opposite danger that public policy could itself become the captive of a scientific-technological elite.

It is the task of statesmanship to mold, to balance, and to integrate these and other forces, new and old, within the principles of our democratic system—ever aiming toward the supreme goals of our free society.

Another factor in maintaining balance involves the element of time. As we peer into society's future, we—you and I, and our government—must avoid the impulse to live only for today, plundering, for our own ease and convenience, the precious resources of tomorrow. We cannot mortgage the material assets of our grandchildren without asking the loss also of their political and spiritual heritage. We want democracy to survive for all generations to come, not to become the insolvent phantom of tomorrow.

Down the long lane of the history yet to be written America knows that this world of ours, ever growing smaller, must avoid becoming a community of dreadful fear and hate, and be, instead, a proud confederation of mutual trust and respect.

Such a confederation must be one of equals. The weakest must come to the conference table with the same confidence as do we, protected as we are by our moral, economic, and military strength. That table, though scarred by many past frustrations, cannot be abandoned for the certain agony of the battlefield.

Disarmament, with mutual honor and confidence, is a continuing imperative. Together we must learn how to compose differences, not with arms, but with intellect and decent purpose. Because this need is so sharp and apparent, I confess that I lay down my official responsibilities in this field with a definite sense of disappointment. As one who has witnessed the horror and the lingering sadness of war—as one who knows that another war could utterly destroy this civilization which has been so slowly and painfully built over thousands of years—I wish I could say tonight that a lasting peace is in sight.

Happily, I can say that war has been avoided. Steady progress toward our ultimate goal has been made. But, so much remains to be done. As a private citizen, I shall never cease to do what little I can to help the world advance along that road.

So, in this, my last "good night" to you as your President, I thank you for the many opportunities you have given me for public service in war and peace. I trust that in that service you find some things worthy; as for the rest of it, I know you will find ways to improve performance in the future.

You and I—my fellow citizens—need to be strong in our faith that all nations, under God, will reach the goal of peace with justice. May we be ever unswerving in devotion to principle, confident but humble with power, diligent in pursuit of the Nations' great goals.

To all the peoples of the world, I once more give expression to America's prayerful and continuing aspiration:

We pray that peoples of all faiths, all races, all nations, may have their great human needs satisfied; that those now denied opportunity shall come to enjoy it to the full; that all who yearn for freedom may experience its spiritual blessings; that those who have freedom will understand, also, its heavy responsibilities; that all who are insensitive to the needs of others will learn charity; that the scourges of poverty, disease and ignorance will be made to disappear from the earth, and that, in the goodness of time, all peoples will come to live together in a peace guaranteed by the binding force of mutual respect and love.

Now, on Friday noon, I am to become a private citizen. I am proud to do so. I look forward to it.

* * *

A protestor shoving carnations into the gun barrels of MPs during an anti-Vietnam War protest at the Pentagon in 1967.

Troubled Times

JOHN F. KENNEDY

Speech to the Greater Houston Ministerial Association

If this election is decided on the basis that forty million Americans lost their chance of being President on the day they were baptized, then it is the whole nation that will be the loser in the eyes of Catholics and non-Catholics around the world, in the eyes of history, and in the eyes of our own people.

John Fitzgerald Kennedy (1917-1963) was born into a distinguished family in Brookline, Massachusetts, and educated at Harvard University. He served in the U.S. Navy during World War II, seeing combat in the Pacific, and then pursued a career in politics. He was elected to the U.S. House of Representatives in 1946, where he served three terms, and then, in 1952, to the first of two terms in the U.S. Senate. Having unsuccessfully lobbied for the Democratic nomination for vice president in 1956 on the Adlai Stevenson ticket, Kennedy threw his hat in the ring for the presidency in 1960.

As a candidate for the nation's highest office, John Kennedy faced numerous drawbacks. Many people felt uncomfortable with his youth, his lack of experience in foreign affairs, and many members of his own party opposed Kennedy because they considered him to be too conservative. His biggest obstacle, however, occurred when religion became a central issue in the campaign. Many Americans believed that, as a Roman Catholic, Kennedy would be under the influence of the Vatican. Before Kennedy, only one other Roman Catholic—Alfred E. Smith, who was badly defeated by Herbert Hoover in 1928—had ever been nominated for president by a major political party.

Speaking to the Greater Houston Ministerial Association on September 12, 1960, Kennedy addressed the religious issue.

I am grateful for your generous invitation to state my views. While the so-called religious issue is necessarily and properly the chief topic here tonight, I want to emphasize from the outset that I believe that we have far more critical issues in the 1960 campaign: the spread of Communist influence, until it now festers only ninety miles from the coast of Florida—the humiliating treatment of our President and Vice President by those who no longer respect our power—the hungry children I saw in West Virginia, the old people who cannot pay their doctor's bills, the families forced to give up their farms—an America with too many slums, with too few schools, and too late to the moon and outer space.

These are the real issues which should decide this campaign. And they are not religious issues—for war and hunger and ignorance and despair know no religious barriers.

But because I am a Catholic, and no Catholic has ever been elected President, the real issues in this campaign have been obscured—perhaps deliberately—in some quarters less responsible than this. So it is apparently necessary for me to state once again—not what kind of church I believe in, for that should be important only to me, but what kind of America I believe in.

I believe in an America where the separation of church and state is absolute—where no Catholic prelate would tell the President (should he be Catholic) how to act and no Protestant minister would tell his parishioners for whom to vote—where no church or church school is granted any public funds or political preference—and where no man is denied public office merely because his religion differs from the President who might appoint him or the people who might elect him.

I believe in an America that is officially neither Catholic, Protestant nor Jewish—where no public official either requests or accepts instructions on public policy from the Pope, the National Council of Churches or any other ecclesiastical source—where no religious body seeks to impose its will directly or indirectly upon the general populace or the public acts of its officials—and where religious liberty is so indivisible that an act against one church is treated as an act against all.

For, while this year it may be a Catholic against whom the finger of suspicion is pointed, in other years it has been, and may someday be again, a Jew—or a Quaker—or a Unitarian—or a Baptist. It was Virginia's harassment of Baptist preachers, for example, that led to Jefferson's statute of religious freedom. Today, I may be the victim—but tomorrow it may be you—until the whole fabric of our harmonious society is ripped apart at a time of great national peril.

Finally, I believe in an America where religious intolerance will someday end—where all men and all churches are treated as equal—where every man has the same right to attend or not to attend the church of his choice—where there is no Catholic vote, no anti-Catholic vote, no bloc voting of any kind—and where Catholics, Protestants and Jews, at both the lay and the pastoral level, will refrain from those attitudes of disdain and division which have so often marred their works in the past, and promote instead the American ideal of brotherhood.

That is the kind of America in which I believe. And it represents the kind of Presidency in which I believe—a great office that must be neither humbled by making it the instrument of any religious group, nor tarnished by arbitrarily withholding its occupancy from the members of any one religious group. I believe in a President whose views on religion are his own private affair, neither imposed by him upon the nation nor imposed by the nation upon him as a condition to holding that office.

I would not look with favor upon a President working to subvert the First Amendment's guarantees of religious liberty (nor would our system of checks and balances permit him to do so). And neither do I look with favor upon those who would work to subvert Article VI of the Constitution by requiring a religious test—even by indirection—for if they disagree with that safeguard, they should be openly working to repeal it.

I want a chief executive whose public acts are responsible to all and obligated to none, who can attend any ceremony, service or dinner his office may appropriately require him to fulfill, and whose fulfillment of his Presidential office is not limited or conditioned by any religious oath, ritual or obligation.

This is the kind of America I believe in, and this is the kind of America I fought for in the South Pacific and the kind my brother died for in Europe. No one suggested then that we might have a "divided loyalty," that we did "not believe in liberty" or that we belonged to a disloyal group that threatened "the freedoms for which our forefathers died."

And in fact this is the kind of America for which our forefathers did die when they fled here to escape religious test oaths that denied office to members of less favored churches—when they fought for the Constitution, the Bill of Rights, the Virginia Statute of Religious Freedom—and when they fought at the shrine I visited today, the Alamo. For side by side with Bowie and Crockett died Fuentes, and McCafferty, and Bailey, and Badillo, and Carey—but no one knows whether they were Catholics or not. For there was no religious test there.

I ask you tonight to follow in that tradition, to judge me on the basis of fourteen years in the Congress—on my declared stands against an ambassador to the Vatican, against unconstitutional aid to parochial schools, and against any boycott of the public schools (which I attended myself)—instead of judging me on the basis of these pamphlets and publications we all have seen that carefully select quotations out of context from the statements of Catholic church leaders, usually in other countries, frequently in other centuries, and rarely relevant to any situation here—and always omitting, of course, the statement of the American Bishops in 1948 which strongly endorsed church-state separation, and which more nearly reflects the views of almost every American Catholic.

I do not consider these other quotations binding upon my public acts—why should you? But let me say, with respect to other countries, that I am wholly opposed to the state being used by any religious group, Catholic or Protestant, to compel, prohibit or prosecute the free exercise of any other religion. And that goes for any persecution at any time, by anyone, in any country. …

But let me stress again that these are my views—for, contrary to common newspaper usage, I am not the Catholic candidate for President. I am the Democratic party's candidate for President who happens also to be a Catholic.

I do not speak for my church on public matters—and the church does not speak for me. Whatever issue may come before me as President, if I should be elected—on birth control, divorce, censorship, gambling, or any other subject—I will make my decision in accordance with these views, in accordance with what my conscience tells me to be in the national interest, and without regard to outside religious pressure or dictate. And no power or threat of punishment could cause me to decide otherwise.

But if the time should ever come—and I do not concede any conflict to be remotely possible—when my office would require me to either violate my conscience, or violate the national interest, then I would resign the office, and I hope any other conscientious public servant would do likewise.

But I do not intend to apologize for these views to my

critics of either Catholic or Protestant faith, nor do I intend to disavow either my views or my church in order to win this election. If I should lose on the real issues, I shall return to my seat in the Senate satisfied that I tried my best and was fairly judged.

But if this election is decided on the basis that forty million Americans lost their chance of being President on the day they were baptized, then it is the whole nation that will be the loser in the eyes of Catholics and non-Catholics around the world, in the eyes of history, and in the eyes of our own people.

But if, on the other hand, I should win this election, then I shall devote every effort of mind and spirit to fulfilling the oath of the Presidency—practically identical, I might add, with the oath I have taken for fourteen years in the Congress. For, without reservation, I can, and I quote "solemnly swear that I will faithfully execute the office of President of the United States and will to the best of my ability preserve, protect and defend the Constitution, so help me God."

Senator John F. Kennedy (left) and Vice President Richard Nixon shake hands in the TV studio on September 26, 1960, after meeting in the first of their nationally televised "Great Debate" series. Howard K. Smith, moderator, is in the center. These were the first presidential debates held on television, and thus attracted enormous publicity. Nixon infamously refused makeup and had campaigned right up until the debate. Kennedy, by contrast, appeared tan and rested. Most people who watched the debate on TV believed Kennedy had won while radio listeners, a smaller audience, believed Nixon had won. After it had ended, polls showed Kennedy moving from a slight deficit into a slight lead over Nixon.

JOHN F. KENNEDY

Inaugural Address

Ask not what your country can do for you—ask what you can do for your country.

John Kennedy was the youngest man ever elected president, defeating incumbent Vice President Richard Nixon by fewer than 120,000 popular votes. JFK took charge of a nation suffering from increased racial tensions and the continuing spread of Communism amidst the threat of nuclear war. Kennedy addressed these and other issues, such as his commitment to space exploration, in his inaugural address—the most eloquent and oft quoted of the twentieth century.

… We observe today not a victory of party but a celebration of freedom—symbolizing an end as well as a beginning—signifying renewal as well as change. For I have sworn before you and Almighty God the same solemn oath our forebears prescribed nearly a century and three quarters ago.

The world is very different now. For man holds in his mortal hands the power to abolish all forms of human poverty and all forms of human life. And yet the same revolutionary beliefs for which our forbears fought are still at issue around the globe—the belief that the rights of man come not from the generosity of the state but from the hand of God.

We dare not forget today that we are the heirs of that first revolution. Let the word go forth from this time and place, to friend and foe alike, that the torch has been passed to a new generation of Americans—born in this century, tempered by war, disciplined by a hard and bitter peace, proud of our ancient heritage—and unwilling to witness or permit the slow undoing of those human rights to which this nation has always been committed, and to which we are committed today at home and around the world.

Let every nation know, whether it wishes us well or ill, that we shall pay any price, bear any burden, meet any hardship, support any friend, oppose any foe to assure the survival and the success of liberty.

This much we pledge—and more.

To those old allies whose cultural and spiritual origins we share, we pledge the loyalty of faithful friends. United, there is little we cannot do in a host of co-operative ventures. Divided, there is little we can do—for we dare not meet a powerful challenge at odds and split asunder.

To those new states whom we welcome to the ranks of the free, we pledge our word that one form of colonial control shall not have passed away merely to be replaced by a far more iron tyranny. We shall not always expect to find them supporting our view. But we shall always hope to find them strongly supporting their own freedom—and to remember that, in the past, those who foolishly sought power by riding the back of the tiger ended up inside.

To those people in the huts and villages of half the globe struggling to break the bonds of mass misery, we pledge our best efforts to help them help themselves, for whatever period is required—not because the Communists may be doing it, not because we seek their votes, but because it is right. If a free society cannot help the many who are poor, it cannot save the few who are rich.

To our sister republics south of the border, we offer a special pledge—to convert our good words into good deeds—in a new alliance for progress—to assist free men and free governments in casting off the chains of poverty. But this peaceful revolution of hope cannot become the prey of hostile powers. Let all our neighbors know that we shall join with them to oppose aggression or subversion anywhere in the Americas. And let every other power know that this hemisphere intends to remain the master of its own house.

To that world assembly of sovereign states, the United Nations, our last best hope in an age where the instruments of war have far outpaced the instruments of peace, we renew our pledge of support—to prevent it from becoming merely a forum for invective—to strengthen its shield of the new and the weak—and to enlarge the area in which its writ may run.

Finally, to those nations who would make themselves our adversary, we offer not a pledge but a request: that both sides begin anew the quest for peace, before the dark powers of destruction unleashed by science engulf all humanity in planned or accidental self-destruction.

We dare not tempt them with weakness. For only when our arms are sufficient beyond doubt can we be certain beyond doubt that they will never be employed.

But neither can two great and powerful groups of nations take comfort from our present course—both sides overburdened by the cost of modern weapons, both rightly alarmed by the steady spread of the deadly atom, yet both racing to alter that uncertain balance of terror that stays the hand of mankind's final war.

So let us begin anew—remembering on both sides that civility is not a sign of weakness, and sincerity is always subject to proof. Let us never negotiate out of fear. But let us never fear to negotiate.

Let both sides explore what problems unite us instead of belaboring those problems which divide us.

Let both sides, for the first time, formulate serious and precise proposals for the inspection and control of arms—and bring the absolute power to destroy other nations under the absolute control of all nations.

Let both sides seek to invoke the wonders of science instead of its terrors. Together let us explore the stars, conquer the deserts, eradicate disease, tap the ocean depths, and encourage the arts and commerce.

Let both sides unite to heed in all corners of the earth the command of Isaiah—to "undo the heavy burdens and let the oppressed go free."

And if a beachhead of co-operation may push back the jungle of suspicion, let both sides join in creating a new endeavor, not a new balance of power, but a new world of law, where the strong are just and the weak secure and the peace preserved.

All this will not be finished in the first one hundred days. Nor will it be finished in the first one thousand days, nor in the life of this administration, nor even perhaps in our lifetime on this planet. But let us begin.

In your hands, my fellow citizens, more than mine, will rest the final success or failure of our course. Since this country was founded, each generation of Americans has been summoned to give testimony to its national loyalty. The graves of young Americans who answered the call to service surround the globe.

Now the trumpet summons us again—not as a call to bear arms, though arms we need; not as a call to battle, though embattled we are; but a call to bear the burden of a long twilight struggle, year in and year out, "rejoicing in hope, patient in tribulation"—a struggle against the common enemies of man: tyranny, poverty, disease, and war itself.

Can we forge against these enemies a grand and global alliance, North and South, East and West, that can assure a more fruitful life for all mankind? Will you join in that historic effort?

In the long history of the world, only a few generations have been granted the role of defending freedom in its hour of maximum danger. I do not shrink from this responsibility—I welcome it. I do not believe that any of us would exchange places with any other people or any other generation. The energy, the faith, the devotion which we bring to this endeavor will light our country and all who serve it—and the glow from that fire can truly light the world.

And so, my fellow Americans: ask not what your country can do for you—ask what you can do for your country.

My fellow citizens of the world: ask not what America will do for you, but what together we can do for the freedom of man.

Finally, whether you are citizens of America or citizens of the world, ask of us here the same high standards of strength and sacrifice which we ask of you. With a good conscience our only sure reward, with history the final judge of our deeds, let us go forth to lead the land we love, asking His blessing and His help, but knowing that here on earth, God's work must truly be our own.

PETE SEEGER

Where Have All the Flowers Gone?

Pete Seeger, the son of a violinist and a distinguished musicologist, was born in New York City in 1919. He briefly attended Harvard but left to travel throughout the United States—playing his banjo, singing, and collecting songs. In 1940, Seeger joined with Woody Guthrie in forming the *Almanac Singers*. Eight years later, after a short stint in the U.S. Army, he discovered commercial success with another group, the *Weavers*. The group disbanded in 1952, however, when the entertainment industry began blacklisting performers who had been involved in left-wing politics. Seeger, in fact, was investigated by the House Un-American Activities Committee, but charges against him were dismissed. Ever active in politics, Seeger used song to rally support for the civil rights movement, the anti-war movement, and environmental causes.

"Where Have All the Flowers Gone?" (1961), one of his best-known compositions, was inspired by lines from *And Quiet Flows the Don*, a Soviet novel by Mikhail Sholokhov.

Where have all the flowers gone?
Long time passing.
Where have all the flowers gone?
Long time ago.
Where have all the flowers gone?
The girls have picked them ev'ry one.
Oh, when will you ever learn?
Oh, when will you ever learn?

Where have all the young girls gone?
Long time passing.
Where have all the young girls gone?
Long time ago.
Where have all the young girls gone?
They've taken husbands, every one.
Oh, when will you ever learn?
Oh, when will you ever learn?

Where have all the young men gone?
Long time passing.
Where have all the young men gone?
Long time ago.
Where have all the young men gone?
They're all in uniform.
Oh, when will you ever learn?
Oh, when will you ever learn?

Where have all the soldiers gone?
Long time passing.
Where have all the soldiers gone?
Long time ago.
Where have all the soldiers gone?
They've gone to graveyards, every one.
Oh, when will they ever learn?
Oh, when will they ever learn?

Where have all the graveyards gone?
Long time passing.
Where have all the graveyards gone?
Long time ago.
Where have all the graveyards gone?
They're covered with flowers, every one.
Oh, when will they ever learn?
Oh, when will they ever learn?

Where have all the flowers gone?
Long time passing.
Where have all the flowers gone?
Long time ago.
Where have all the flowers gone?
Young girls picked them, every one.
Oh, when will they ever learn?
Oh, when will they ever learn?

MARTIN LUTHER KING, JR.

Letter from Birmingham City Jail

Injustice anywhere is a threat to justice everywhere.

Michael Luther King, Jr. (1929-1968), the son and grandson of Baptist ministers, was born in Atlanta, Georgia. At the age of six, his father had both their first names legally changed in honor of the German religious figure, Martin Luther, leader of the sixteenth century Protestant Reformation. A gifted student, King entered Morehouse College at the age of fifteen, then earned a divinity degree at Crozer Theological Seminary in Chester, Pennsylvania, and a doctorate in philosophy from Boston University. Ordained as a minister in 1947, he became pastor of the Dexter Avenue Baptist Church in Montgomery, Alabama, in 1954. As the leading figure of the civil rights movement, King preached the doctrine of non-violent civil disobedience, although he himself was often a target of violence.

In addition to serving as first president of the Southern Christian Leadership Conference, King routinely organized and participated in sit-ins, boycotts, and marches. During a march through Birmingham, Alabama, in 1963, he was arrested and placed in solitary confinement for refusing to obey a court order to end the demonstrations. While in jail, he received a letter from eight white clergymen who wanted him to focus less on acts of civil disobedience and more on negotiations and the courts. King spent Easter weekend drafting the following response, which was then turned over to his assistants and widely disseminated as an "open letter" in order to generate public support. He later published a second, more polished version of this letter with numerous minor changes.

My dear Fellow Clergymen: While confined here in the Birmingham City Jail, I came across your recent statement calling our present activities "unwise and untimely." Seldom, if ever, do I pause to answer criticism of my work and ideas. If I sought to answer all the criticisms that cross my desk, my secretaries would be engaged in little else in the course of the day and I would have no time for constructive work. But since I feel that you are men of genuine goodwill and your criticisms are sincerely set forth, I would like to answer your statement in what I hope will be patient and reasonable terms.

I think I should give the reason for my being in Birmingham, since you have been influenced by the argument of "outsiders coming in." ...

I am in Birmingham because injustice is here. Just as the eighth century prophets left their little villages and carried their "thus saith the Lord" far beyond the boundaries of their home town, and just as the Apostle Paul left his little village of Tarsus and carried the gospel of Jesus Christ to practically every hamlet and city of the Graeco-Roman world, I too am compelled to carry the gospel of freedom beyond my particular home town. Like Paul, I must constantly respond to the Macedonian call for aid.

Moreover, I am cognizant of the interrelatedness of all communities and states. I cannot sit idly by in Atlanta and not be concerned about what happens in Birmingham. Injustice anywhere is a threat to justice everywhere. We are caught in an inescapable network of mutuality tied in a single garment of destiny. Whatever affects one directly affects all indirectly. Never again can we afford to live with the narrow, provincial "outside agitator" idea. Anyone who lives inside the United States can never be considered an outsider anywhere in this country.

You deplore the demonstrations that are presently taking place in Birmingham. But I am sorry that your statement did not express a similar concern for the conditions that brought the demonstrations into being. I am sure that each of you would want to go beyond the superficial social analyst who looks merely at effects, and does not grapple with underlying causes. I would not hesitate to say that it is unfortunate that so-called demonstrations are taking place in Birmingham at this time, but I would say in more emphatic terms that it is even more unfortunate that the white power structure of this city left the Negro community with no other alternative.

In any nonviolent campaign there are four basic steps: (1) Collection of the facts to determine whether injustices are alive; (2) Negotiation; (3) Self-purification; and (4) Direct action. We have gone through all of these steps in Birmingham. There can be no gainsaying of the fact that racial injustice engulfs this community. Birmingham is probably the most thoroughly segregated city in the United States. Its ugly record of police brutality is known in every section of this country. Its unjust treatment of Negroes in the courts is a notorious reality. There have been more unsolved bombings of Negro homes and churches in Birmingham than any city in this nation. These are the hard, brutal, and unbelievable facts. ...

We know through painful experience that freedom is never voluntarily given by the oppressor; it must be demanded by the oppressed. Frankly I have never yet engaged in a direct action movement that was "well timed," according to the timetable of those who have not suffered unduly from the disease of segregation. For years now I have heard the word "Wait!" It rings in the ear of every Negro with a piercing familiarity. This "wait" has almost always meant "never." It has been a tranquilizing thalidomide, relieving the emotional stress for a moment, only to give birth to an ill-formed infant of frustration. We must come to see with the distinguished jurist of yesterday that "justice too long delayed is justice denied."

We have waited for more than three hundred and forty years for our constitutional and God-given rights. The nations of Asia and Africa are moving with jet-like speed toward the goal of political independence, and we still creep at horse and buggy pace toward the gaining of a cup of coffee at a lunch counter. ...

You express a great deal of anxiety over our willingness to break laws. This is certainly a legitimate concern. Since we so diligently urge people to obey the Supreme Court's decision of 1954 outlawing segregation in the public schools, it is rather strange and paradoxical to find us consciously breaking laws. One may well ask: "How can you advocate breaking some laws and obeying others?" The answer is found in the fact that there are two types of laws: There are just laws and there are unjust laws. I would be the first to advocate obeying just laws. One has not only a legal but moral responsibility to obey just laws. Conversely, one has a moral responsibility to disobey unjust laws. I would agree with Saint Augustine that "An unjust law is no law at all."

Now what is the difference between the two? How does one determine when a law is just or unjust? A just law is a man-made code that squares with the moral law or the law of God. An unjust law is a code that is out of harmony with the moral law. To put it in the terms of Saint Thomas Aquinas, an unjust law is a human law that is not rooted in eternal and natural law. Any law that uplifts human personality is just. Any law that degrades human personality is unjust.

All segregation statutes are unjust because segregation distorts the soul and damages the personality. It gives the segregator a false sense of superiority and the segregated a false sense of inferiority. To use the words of Martin Buber, the great Jewish philosopher, segregation substitutes an "I-it" relationship for an "I-thou" relationship, and ends up relegating persons to the status of things. So segregation is not only politically, economically, and sociologically unsound, but it is morally wrong and sinful. Paul Tillich has said that sin is separation. Isn't segregation an existential expression of man's tragic separation, an expression of his awful estrangement, his terrible sinfulness? So I can urge men to obey the1954 decision of the Supreme Court because it is morally right, and I can urge them to disobey segregation ordinances because they are morally wrong. ...

There are some instances when a law is just on its face but unjust in its application. For instance, I was arrested Friday on a charge of parading without a permit. Now there is nothing wrong with an ordinance which requires a permit for a parade, but when the ordinance is used to preserve segregation and to deny citizens the First Amendment privilege of peaceful assembly and peaceful protest, then it becomes unjust.

I hope you can see the distinction I am trying to point out. In no sense do I advocate evading or defying the law as the rabid segregationist would do. This would lead to anarchy. One who breaks an unjust law must do it openly, lovingly ... and with a willingness to accept the penalty. I submit that an individual who breaks a law that conscience tells him is unjust, and willingly accepts the penalty by staying in jail to arouse the conscience of the community over its injustice, is in reality expressing the very highest respect for law.

Of course there is nothing new about this kind of civil disobedience. It was seen sublimely in the refusal of Shadrach, Meshach, and Abednego to obey the laws of Nebuchadnezzar because a higher moral law was involved. It was practiced superbly by the early Christians who were willing to face hungry lions and the excruciating pain of chopping blocks, before submitting to certain unjust laws of the Roman Empire. To a degree academic freedom is a reality today because Socrates practiced civil disobedience.

We can never forget that everything Hitler did in Germany was "legal" and everything the Hungarian freedom fighters did in Hungary was "illegal." It was "illegal" to aid and comfort a Jew in Hitler's Germany. But I am sure that, if I had lived in Germany during that time, I would have aided and comforted my Jewish brothers even though it was illegal. If I lived in a communist country today where certain principles dear to the Christian faith are suppressed, I believe I would openly advocate disobeying these anti-religious laws.

I must make two honest confessions to you, my Christian and Jewish brothers. First, I must confess that over the last few years I have been gravely disappointed with the white moderate. I have almost reached the regrettable conclusion that the Negroes' great stumbling block in the stride toward freedom is not the White Citizen's "Councilor" or the Ku Klux Klanner, but the white moderate who is more devoted to "order" than to justice; who prefers a negative peace which is the absence of tension to a positive peace which is the presence of justice; who constantly says "I agree with you in the goal you seek, but I can't agree with your methods of direct action"; who paternalistically feels that he can set the timetable for another man's freedom; who lives by the myth of time and who constantly advises the Negro to wait until a "more convenient season." Shallow understanding from people of good will is more frustrating than absolute misunderstanding from people of ill will. Lukewarm acceptance is much more bewildering than outright rejection. ...

In your statement you asserted that our actions, even though peaceful, must be condemned because they precipitate violence. But can this assertion be logically made? Isn't this like condemning the robbed man because his possession of money precipitated the evil act of robbery? Isn't this like condemning Socrates because his unswerving commitment to truth and his philosophical delvings precipitated the misguided popular mind to make him drink the hemlock? Isn't this like condemning Jesus because His unique God consciousness and never-ceasing devotion to His will precipitated the evil act of crucifixion? We must come to see, as federal courts have consistently affirmed, that it is immoral to urge an individual to withdraw his efforts to gain his basic constitutional rights because the quest precipitates violence. Society must protect the robbed and punish the robber. ...

We will have to repent in this generation not merely for the vitriolic words and actions of the bad people, but for the appalling silence of the good people. We must come to see that human progress never rolls in on wheels of inevitability. It comes through the tireless efforts and persistent work of men willing to be co-workers with God, and without this hard work time itself becomes an ally of the forces of social stagnation. We must use time creatively, and forever realize that the time is always ripe to do right. Now is the time to make real the promise of democracy, and transform our pending national elegy into a creative psalm of brotherhood. Now is the time to lift our national policy from the quicksand of racial injustice to the solid rock of human dignity.

You spoke of our activity in Birmingham as extreme. At first I was rather disappointed that fellow clergymen would see my nonviolent efforts as those of the extremist. ... But as I continued to think about the matter I gradually gained a bit of satisfaction from being considered an extremist. Was not Jesus an extremist in love? "Love your enemies, bless them that curse you, pray for them that despitefully use you." Was not Amos an extremist for justice—"Let justice roll down like waters and righteousness like a mighty stream." Was not Paul an extremist for the gospel of Jesus Christ—"I bear in my body the marks of the Lord Jesus." Was not Martin Luther an extremist—"Here I stand; I can do none other so help me God." Was not John Bunyan an extremist—"I will stay in jail to the end of my days before I make a butchery of my conscience." Was not Abraham Lincoln an extremist—"This nation cannot survive half slave and half free." Was not Thomas Jefferson an extremist—"We hold these truths to be self-evident, that all men are created equal."

So the question is not whether we will be extremist but what kind of extremist will we be. Will we be extremists for hate or will we be extremists for love? Will we be extremists for the preservation of injustice—or will we be extremists for the cause of justice? In that dramatic scene on Calvary's hill three men were crucified. We must never forget that all three were crucified for the same crime—the crime of extremism. Two were extremists for immorality, and thus fell below their environment. The other, Jesus Christ, was an extremist for love, truth, and goodness, and thereby rose above His environment. So, after all, maybe the South, the nation, and the world are in dire need of creative extremists. ...

In deep disappointment, I have wept over the laxity of the church. But be assured that my tears have been tears of love. There can be no deep disappointment where there is not deep love. Yes, I love the Church; I love her sacred walls.

How could I do otherwise? I am in the rather unique position of being the son, the grandson, and the great-grandson of preachers. Yes, I see the Church as the body of Christ. But, oh! How we have blemished and scarred that body through social neglect and fear of being nonconformist.

There was a time when the Church was very powerful. It was during that period when the early Christians rejoiced when they were deemed worthy to suffer for what they believed. In those days the Church was not merely a thermometer that recorded the ideas and principles of popular opinion; it was a thermostat that transformed the mores of society. Wherever the early Christians entered a town the power structure got disturbed and immediately sought to convict them for being "disturbers of the peace" and "outside agitators." But they went on with the conviction that they were "a colony of heaven" and had to obey God rather than man. They were small in number but big in commitment. They were too God-intoxicated to be "astronomically intimidated." They brought an end to such ancient evils as infanticide and gladiatorial contest.

Things are different now. The contemporary Church is so often a weak, ineffectual voice with an uncertain sound. It is so often the arch-supporter of the status quo. Far from being disturbed by the presence of the Church, the power structure of the average community is consoled by the Church's silent and often vocal sanction of things as they are.

But the judgment of God is upon the Church as never before. If the Church of today does not recapture the sacrificial spirit of the early Church, it will lose its authentic ring, forfeit the loyalty of millions, and be dismissed as an irrelevant social club with no meaning for the twentieth century. … I am thankful to God that some noble souls from the ranks of organized religion have broken loose from the paralyzing chains of conformity and joined us as active partners in the struggle for freedom. They have left their secure congregations and walked the streets of Albany, Georgia, with us. They have gone through the highways of the South on torturous rides for freedom. Yes, they have gone to jail with us. Some have been kicked out of their churches and lost the support of their bishops and fellow ministers. But they have gone with the faith that right defeated is stronger than evil triumphant. These men have been the leaven in the lump of the race. Their witness has been the spiritual salt that has preserved the true meaning of the Gospel in these troubled times. They have carved a tunnel of hope through the dark mountain of disappointment.

I hope the Church as a whole will meet the challenge of this decisive hour. But even if the Church does not come to the aid of justice, I have no despair about the future. I have no fear about the outcome of our struggle in Birmingham, even if our motives are presently misunderstood. We will reach the goal of freedom in Birmingham and all over the nation, because the goal of America is freedom. Abused and scorned though we may be, our destiny is tied up with the destiny of America. …

One day the South will recognize its real heroes. They will be the James Merediths, courageously and with a majestic sense of purpose, facing jeering and hostile mobs and the agonizing loneliness that characterizes the life of the pioneer. They will be old, oppressed, battered Negro women, symbolized in a seventy-two year old woman of Montgomery, Alabama, who rose up with a sense of dignity and with her people decided not to ride the segregated buses, and responded to one who inquired about her tiredness with ungrammatical profundity: "My feets is tired, but my soul is rested." They will be the young high school and college students, young ministers of the gospel and a host of their elders courageously and nonviolently sitting-in at lunch counters and willingly going to jail for conscience sake. One day the South will know that when these disinherited children of God sat down at lunch counters they were in reality standing up for the best in the American dream and the most sacred values in our Judaeo-Christian heritage, and thus carrying our whole nation back to those great wells of democracy which were dug deep by the founding fathers in the formulation of the Constitution and the Declaration of Independence.

Never before have I written a letter this long (or should I say a book?). I'm afraid it is much too long to take your precious time. I can assure you that it would have been much shorter if I had been writing from a comfortable desk, but what else is there to do when you are alone for days in the dull monotony of a narrow jail cell other than write long letters, think strange thoughts, and pray long prayers?

If I have said anything in this letter that is an overstatement of the truth and is indicative of an unreasonable impatience, I beg you to forgive me. If I have said anything in this letter that is an understatement of the truth and is indicative of my having a patience that makes me patient with anything less than brotherhood, I beg God to forgive me.

I hope this letter finds you strong in the faith. I also hope that circumstances will soon make it possible for me to meet each of you, not as an integrationist or a civil rights leader, but as a fellow clergyman and a Christian brother. Let us all hope that the dark clouds of racial prejudice will soon pass away and the deep fog of misunderstanding will be lifted from our fear-drenched communities and in some not too distant tomorrow the radiant stars of love and brotherhood will shine over our great nation with all their scintillating beauty.

JOHN F. KENNEDY

Speech at the Berlin Wall

Ich bin ein Berliner.

John Kennedy was president during the height of the Cold War, presiding over such trying events as the "Bay of Pigs," a failed attempt by Cuban rebels, backed by the United States, to overthrow the Communist dictator Fidel Castro. The failed coup was followed eighteen months later by the Cuban Missile Crisis, the result of a Soviet plan to establish on the island nation missile delivery systems capable of reaching U.S. cities. Kennedy ordered a naval blockade of Cuba and, for more than a week, war seemed probable. The crisis was resolved when Soviet Premier Nikita Khrushchev removed all Soviet missiles in exchange for a U.S. agreement to remove its offensive missiles from Turkey and a promise not to invade Cuba.

In August 1961, the Communist East German government erected a barricade to divide East and West Berlin. The Soviets had, in 1948, cut off supply routes through East Germany into West Berlin, hoping the city would succumb to Communism. The western nations, however, responded by airlifting supplies into the city and the blockade was broken. The purpose of the newly built barricade, which was soon replaced with a massive concrete wall patrolled by armed guards, was to stop the mass exodus of East Germans fleeing into the non-Communist West.

On a visit to Europe in 1963, President Kennedy stood before the Berlin Wall and declared: "Ich bin ein Berliner"—"I am a Berliner." This speech served to bolster the morale and strengthen the resolve of those living under the oppression of Communism. Five months later, when Kennedy was assassinated in Dallas, Texas, the square in front of City Hall in West Berlin was renamed in his memory.

... Two thousand years ago the proudest boast was "civis Romanus sum." Today, in the world of freedom, the proudest boast is "Ich bin ein Berliner."

I appreciate my interpreter translating my German.

There are many people in the world who really don't understand, or say they don't, what is the great issue between the free world and the Communist world. Let them come to Berlin. There are some who say that Communism is the wave of the future. Let them come to Berlin. And there are some who say, in Europe and elsewhere, we can work with the Communists. Let them come to Berlin. And there are even a few who say that it is true that Communism is an evil system, but it permits us to make economic progress. Lass' sie nach Berlin kommen. Let them come to Berlin!

Freedom has many difficulties and democracy is not perfect, but we have never had to put a wall up to keep our people in, to prevent them from leaving us. I want to say, on behalf of my countrymen, who live many miles away on the other side of the Atlantic, who are far distant from you, that they take the greatest pride that they have been able to share with you, even from a distance, the story of the last eighteen years. I know of no town, no city, that has been besieged for eighteen years that still lives with the vitality and the force, and the hope and the determination of the city of West Berlin. While the wall is the most obvious and vivid demonstration of the failures of the Communist system, for all the world to see, we take no satisfaction in it, for it is an offense not only against history but an offense against humanity, separating families, dividing husbands and wives and brothers and sisters, and dividing a people who wish to be joined together.

What is true of this city is true of Germany—real, lasting peace in Europe can never be assured as long as one German out of four is denied the elementary right of free men, and that is to make a free choice. In eighteen years of peace and good faith, this generation of Germans has earned the right to be free, including the right to unite their families and their nation in lasting peace with good will to all people. You live in a defended island of freedom, but your life is part of the main. So let me ask you, as I close, to lift your eyes beyond the dangers of today to the hopes of tomorrow, beyond the freedom merely of this city of Berlin, or your country of Germany, to the advance of freedom everywhere, beyond the wall to the day of peace with justice, beyond yourselves and ourselves to all mankind. Freedom is indivisible, and when one man is enslaved, all are not free. When all are free, then we can look forward to that day when this city will be joined as one—and this country, and this great continent of Europe—in a peaceful and hopeful glow. When that day finally comes, as it will, the people of West Berlin can take sober satisfaction in the fact that they were in the front lines for almost two decades.

All free men, wherever they may live, are citizens of Berlin, and, therefore, as a free man, I take pride in the words "Ich bin ein Berliner."

Dr. Martin Luther King, Jr. delivers his famous "I Have a Dream" speech in front of the Lincoln Memorial during the Freedom March on Washington on August 28, 1963.

MARTIN LUTHER KING, JR.

March on Washington Address

I have a dream that my four little children will one day live in a nation where they will not be judged by the color of their skin but by the content of their character.

On August 28, 1963, Martin Luther King, Jr. delivered the following address to a crowd of more than 200,000 people, both black and white, who had come to the nation's capital to demand an end to racial segregation. The March on Washington represented the apex of the civil rights movement and the embodiment of King's vision for America. King also expounded on his beliefs in a series of books written between 1958 and 1968. They are: *Stride Toward Freedom, Strength to Love, Why We Can't Wait, Where Do We Go From Here: Chaos or Community?,* and *The Trumpet of Conscience.*

On April 3, 1968, King addressed a congregation in Memphis, Tennessee, saying, in his closing remarks, "We've got some difficult days ahead. But it doesn't matter with me now. Because I've been to the mountaintop. And I don't mind. Like anybody, I would like to live a long life. Longevity has its place. But I'm not concerned about that now. I just want to do God's will. And He's allowed me to go up to the mountain. And I've looked over. And I've seen the promised land. I may not get there with you. But I want you to know tonight that we, as a people, will get to the promised land. And I'm happy, tonight. I'm not worried about anything. I'm not fearing any man. Mine eyes have seen the glory of the coming of the Lord."

King's words proved prophetic. He was assassinated the following day by a white escaped convict named James Earl Ray, who confessed to the crime, but later recanted after his conviction. In 1974, King's mother, Alberta King, was murdered during services at Ebenezer Baptist Church by a black university student.

For his leadership in the civil rights movement, King was awarded the Nobel Peace Prize in 1964. In 1983, President Reagan signed into law the creation of a federal holiday in the slain civil rights leader's honor.

... Five score years ago, a great American, in whose symbolic shadow we stand today, signed the Emancipation Proclamation. This momentous decree came as a great beacon light of hope to millions of Negro slaves who had been seared in the flames of withering injustice. It came as a joyous daybreak to end the long night of their captivity.

But one hundred years later, the Negro still is not free. One hundred years later, the life of the Negro is still sadly crippled by the manacles of segregation and the chains of discrimination. One hundred years later, the Negro lives on a lonely island of poverty in the midst of a vast ocean of material prosperity. One hundred years later, the Negro is still languished in the corners of American society and finds himself in exile in his own land. And so we've come here today to dramatize a shameful condition.

In a sense we've come to our nation's Capital to cash a check. When the architects of our republic wrote the magnificent words of the Constitution and the Declaration of Independence, they were signing a promissory note to which every American was to fall heir. This note was a promise that all men, yes, black men as well as white men, would be guaranteed the "unalienable Rights" of "Life, Liberty, and the pursuit of Happiness." It is obvious today that America has defaulted on this promissory note insofar as her citizens of color are concerned. Instead of honoring this sacred obligation, America has given the Negro people a bad check, a check which has come back marked "insufficient funds."

But we refuse to believe that the bank of justice is bankrupt. We refuse to believe that there are insufficient funds in the great vaults of opportunity of this nation. And so, we've come to cash this check—a check that will give us upon demand the riches of freedom and the security of justice.

We have also come to this hallowed spot to remind America of the fierce urgency of *now.* This is no time to engage in the luxury of cooling off or to take the tranquilizing drug of gradualism. *Now* is the time to make real the promises of democracy. *Now* is the time to rise from the dark and desolate valley of segregation to the sunlit path of racial justice. *Now* is the time to lift our nation from the quicksands of racial injustice to the solid rock of brotherhood. *Now* is the time to make justice a reality for all God's children.

It would be fatal for the nation to overlook the urgency of the moment. This sweltering summer of the Negro's legitimate discontent will not pass until there is an invigorating autumn of freedom and equality. Nineteen sixty-three is not an end, but a beginning. Those who hope that the Negro needed to blow off steam and will now be content will have a rude awakening if the nation returns to business as usual. There will be neither rest nor tranquility in America until the Negro is granted his citizenship rights. The whirlwinds of revolt will continue to shake the foundations of our nation until the bright day of justice emerges.

But there is something that I must say to my people who stand on the warm threshold which leads into the palace of justice. In the process of gaining our rightful place, we must not be guilty of wrongful deeds. Let us not seek to satisfy our thirst for freedom by drinking from the cup of bitterness and hatred. We must forever conduct our struggle on the high plane of dignity and discipline. We must not allow our creative protest to degenerate into physical violence. Again and again, we must rise to the majestic heights of meeting physical force with soul force.

The marvelous new militancy which has engulfed the Negro community must not lead us to a distrust of all white people, for many of our white brothers, as evidenced by their presence here today, have come to realize that their destiny is tied up with our destiny, and they have come to realize that their freedom is inextricably bound to our freedom. We cannot walk alone.

And as we walk, we must make the pledge that we shall always march ahead. We cannot turn back.

There are those who are asking the devotees of civil rights, "When will you be satisfied?"

We can never be satisfied as long as the Negro is the victim of the unspeakable horrors of police brutality.

We can never be satisfied as long as our bodies, heavy with the fatigue of travel, cannot gain lodging in the motels of the highways and the hotels of the cities.

We cannot be satisfied as long as the Negro's basic mobility is from a smaller ghetto to a larger one.

We can never be satisfied as long as our children are stripped of their self-hood and robbed of their dignity by signs stating "For Whites only."

We cannot be satisfied as long as a Negro in Mississippi cannot vote and a Negro in New York believes he has nothing for which to vote.

No, no, we are not satisfied, and we will not be satisfied until "justice rolls down like waters and righteousness like a mighty stream."

I am not unmindful that some of you have come here out of great trials and tribulations. Some of you have come fresh from narrow jail cells. Some of you have come from areas where your quest for freedom left you battered by the storms of persecution and staggered by the winds of police brutality. You have been the veterans of creative suffering. Continue to work with the faith that unearned suffering is redemptive.

Go back to Mississippi; go back to Alabama; go back to South Carolina; go back to Georgia; go back to Louisiana; go back to the slums and ghettos of our northern cities, knowing that somehow this situation can and will be changed. Let us not wallow in the valley of despair.

I say to you today, my friends, that even though we must face the difficulties of today and tomorrow, I still have a dream. It is a dream deeply rooted in the American dream.

I have a dream that one day this nation will rise up and live out the true meaning of its creed—"We hold these truths to be self-evident, that all men are created equal."

I have a dream that one day on the red hills of Georgia, the sons of former slaves and the sons of former slave owners will be able to sit down together at the table of brotherhood.

I have a dream that one day even the state of Mississippi, a state sweltering with the heat of injustice, sweltering with the heat of oppression, will be transformed into an oasis of freedom and justice.

I have a dream that my four little children will one day live in a nation where they will not be judged by the color of their skin but by the content of their character.

I have a dream today!

I have a dream that one day, down in Alabama, with its vicious racists, with its governor having his lips dripping with the words of "interposition" and "nullification," that one day, right there in Alabama, little black boys and black girls will be able to join hands with little white boys and white girls as sisters and brothers. I have a dream today!

I have a dream that one day every valley shall be exalted, every hill and mountain shall be made low, the rough places will be made plain, and the crooked places will be made straight, "and the glory of the Lord shall be revealed, and all flesh shall see it together."

This is our hope, and this is the faith that I go back to the South with.

With this faith, we will be able to hew out of the mountain of despair a stone of hope. With this faith we will be able to transform the jangling discords of our nation into a beautiful symphony of brotherhood. With this faith, we will be able to work together, to pray together, to struggle together, to go to jail together, to stand up for freedom together, knowing that we will be free one day.

This will be the day when all of God's children will be able to sing with new meaning—"My country, 'tis of thee, sweet land of liberty, of thee I sing. Land where my fathers died, land of the pilgrim's pride, from every mountainside, let freedom ring."

And if America is to be a great nation, this must become true.

So let freedom ring from the prodigious hilltops of New Hampshire.

Let freedom ring from the mighty mountains of New York.

Let freedom ring from the heightening Alleghenies of Pennsylvania!

Let freedom ring from the snow-capped Rockies of Colorado!

Let freedom ring from the curvaceous slopes of California!

But not only that.

Let freedom ring from Stone Mountain of Georgia!

Let freedom ring from Lookout Mountain of Tennessee!

Let freedom ring from every hill and molehill of Mississippi.

From every mountainside, let freedom ring.

And when this happens, when we allow freedom to ring, when we let it ring from every village and every hamlet, from every state and every city, we will be able to speed up that day when all of God's children—black men and white men, Jews and Gentiles, Protestants and Catholics—will be able to join hands and sing in the words of the old Negro spiritual: "Free at last! Free at last! Thank God Almighty, we are free at last!"

We Shall Overcome

The signature song of the civil rights movement, "We Shall Overcome," was sung at nearly all public gatherings and demonstrations, including the 1963 March on Washington. The song originated in the 1800s as a Negro spiritual and has since been popular, in various forms, as a means of social protest.

We shall overcome,
We shall overcome,
We shall overcome,
Someday.
Oh, deep in my heart,
I do believe, that
We shall overcome
Someday.

We'll walk hand in hand,
We'll walk hand in hand,
We'll walk hand in hand,
Someday.
Oh, deep in my heart,
I do believe, that
We shall overcome
Someday.

We are not afraid,
We are not afraid,
We are not afraid,
Oh, no, no, no,
'Cause, deep in my heart,
I do believe, that
We shall overcome,
Someday.

DUDLEY RANDALL

Ballad of Birmingham

Dudley Randall (1914-2000) was born in Washington, D.C., and raised in Detroit. He received his bachelor's degree in English from Wayne State University and his master's degree in library science from the University of Michigan. As the founder and editor of the Broadside Press, a leading publisher of black poetry, Randall edited several collections and also published numerous volumes of his own work.

"Ballad of Birmingham" was written in response to the bombing of a black church in Birmingham, Alabama, on September 15, 1963, which killed four young girls. Many civil rights leaders blamed George Wallace, governor of Alabama, for fanning the flames of racial animus. Just months earlier, the Democrat governor took the oath of office and infamously declared: "In the name of the greatest people that have ever trod this earth, I draw the line in the dust and toss the gauntlet before the feet of tyranny, and I say segregation now, segregation tomorrow, segregation forever." The white supremacists who carried out the church bombing had hoped to impede the desegregation campaign in Birmingham. Instead, they succeeded in mobilizing national opinion on behalf of the civil rights movement.

"Mother dear, may I go downtown
instead of out to play,
and march the streets of Birmingham
in a freedom march today?"

"No, baby, no, you may not go,
for the dogs are fierce and wild,
and clubs and hoses, guns and jails
ain't good for a little child."

"But, mother, I won't go alone.
Other children will go with me,
and march the streets of Birmingham
to make our country free."

"No, baby, no, you may not go,
for I fear those guns will fire.
But you may go to church instead,
and sing in the children's choir."

She has combed and brushed her nightdark hair,
and bathed rose petal sweet,
and drawn white gloves on her small brown hands,
and white shoes on her feet.

The mother smiled to know her child
was in the sacred place,
but that smile was the last smile
to come upon her face.

For when she heard the explosion,
her eyes grew wet and wild.
She raced through the streets of Birmingham
calling for her child.

She clawed through bits of glass and brick,
then lifted out a shoe.
"O, here's the shoe my baby wore,
but, baby, where are you?"

Blowin' in the Wind

Robert Allan Zimmerman was born in 1941 in Duluth, Minnesota. Leaving college after one year, he changed his name to Bob Dylan and began traveling across the country as a folk singer-composer. He became noted for such social protest songs as "Like A Rolling Stone," "A Hard Rain's A-Gonna Fall," and "The Times They Are A-Changin'." Inducting Dylan into the Rock and Roll Hall of Fame, Bruce Springsteen said, "Bob freed the mind the way Elvis freed the body. He showed us that just because the music was innately physical did not mean that it was anti-intellectual."

"Blowin' in the Wind," featured on the 1963 album *The Freewheelin' Bob Dylan*, was embraced as the unofficial anthem of the civil rights movement and later became identified with the anti-war movement.

How many roads must a man walk down
Before you call him a man?
Yes, 'n' how many seas must a white dove sail
Before she sleeps in the sand?
Yes, 'n' how many times must the cannonballs fly
Before they're forever banned?
The answer, my friend, is blowin' in the wind
The answer is blowin' in the wind

How many years can a mountain exist
Before it's washed to the sea?
Yes, 'n' how many years can some people exist
Before they're allowed to be free?
Yes, 'n' how many times can a man turn his head
Pretending he just doesn't see?
The answer, my friend, is blowin' in the wind
The answer is blowin' in the wind

How many times must a man look up
Before he can see the sky?
Yes, 'n' how many ears must one man have
Before he can hear people cry?
Yes, 'n' how many deaths will it take till he knows
That too many people have died?
The answer, my friend, is blowin' in the wind
The answer is blowin' in the wind

Lyndon B. Johnson being sworn in as president aboard Air Force One by Federal Judge Sarah T. Hughes, following the assassination of John F. Kennedy. To Johnson's left is Jacqueline Kennedy, widow of the slain president; to his right is Mrs. Lady Bird Johnson. Assistant Press Secretary Malcolm Kilduff, at bottom left, records the event with a dictaphone.

LYNDON B. JOHNSON

The American Promise

Those who appeal to you to hold on to the past do so at the cost of denying you your future.

Lyndon Baines Johnson (1908-1973) became the thirty-sixth president of the United States, sworn in aboard Air Force One just one hour and thirty-nine minutes after President Kennedy was assassinated. As president, Johnson advocated a domestic legislation program he called "The Great Society." At his urging, Congress increased federal funding for education, created new housing laws, passed a civil rights act and expanded protection of voting rights, including the Twenty-fourth Amendment, which eliminated poll taxes.

On March 15, 1965, after being elected to a full term as president, Johnson delivered a special message to a joint session of Congress. In this speech, which was broadcast nationally, he stressed the need for racial equality and successfully prevailed on Congress to pass the National Voting Rights Act of 1965 which, in that year alone, resulted in the first-time voter registration of more than 250,000 African Americans.

Johnson also expressed his desire to be remembered as a president committed to the education, health, and welfare of the American people. Unfortunately, his administration got bogged down by the Vietnam War, which consumed his time and much of the federal budget. He finished his only full term in office, saying, "I shall not seek, and I will not accept, the nomination of my party for another term as your president."

I speak tonight for the dignity of man and the destiny of democracy. I urge every member of both parties, Americans of all religions and of all colors, from every section of this country, to join me in that cause.

At times history and fate meet at a single time in a single place to shape a turning point in man's unending search for freedom. So it was at Lexington and Concord. So it was a century ago at Appomattox. So it was last week in Selma, Alabama.

There, long-suffering men and women peacefully protested the denial of their rights as Americans. Many were brutally assaulted. One good man, a man of God, was killed.

There is no cause for pride in what has happened in Selma. There is no cause for self-satisfaction in the long denial of equal rights of millions of Americans. But there is cause for hope and for faith in our democracy in what is happening here tonight.

For the cries of pain and the hymns and protests of oppressed people have summoned into convocation all the majesty of this great Government—the Government of the greatest Nation on earth.

Our mission is at once the oldest and the most basic of this country: to right wrong, to do justice, to serve man.

In our time we have come to live with moments of great crisis. Our lives have been marked with debate about great issues; issues of war and peace, issues of prosperity and depression. But rarely in any time does an issue lay bare the secret heart of America itself. Rarely are we met with a challenge, not to our growth or abundance, our welfare or our security, but rather to the values and the purposes and the meaning of our beloved Nation.

The issue of equal rights for American Negroes is such an issue. And should we defeat every enemy, should we double our wealth and conquer the stars, and still be unequal to this issue, then we will have failed as a people and as a nation.

For with a country as with a person, "What is a man profited, if he shall gain the whole world, and lose his own soul?" …

To deny a man his hopes because of his color or race, his religion or the place of his birth—is not only to do injustice, it is to deny America and to dishonor the dead who gave their lives for American freedom.

Our fathers believed that if this noble view of the rights of man was to flourish, it must be rooted in democracy. The most basic right of all was the right to choose your own leaders. The history of this country, in large measure, is the history of the expansion of that right to all of our people.

Many of the issues of civil rights are very complex and most difficult. But about this there can and should be no argument. Every American citizen must have an equal right to vote. There is no reason which can excuse the denial of that right. There is no duty which weighs more heavily on us than the duty we have to ensure that right.

Yet the harsh fact is that in many places in this country men and women are kept from voting simply because they are Negroes.

Every device of which human ingenuity is capable has been used to deny this right. The Negro citizen may go to register only to be told that the day is wrong, or the hour is late, or the official in charge is absent. And if he persists, and if he manages to present himself to the registrar, he may be disqualified because he did not spell out his middle name or because he abbreviated a word on the application.

And if he manages to fill out an application he is given a test. The registrar is the sole judge of whether he passes this test. He may be asked to recite the entire Constitution, or explain the most complex provisions of State law. And even a college degree cannot be used to prove that he can read and write.

For the fact is that the only way to pass these barriers is to show a white skin. …

As a man whose roots go deeply into Southern soil I know how agonizing racial feelings are. I know how difficult it is to reshape the attitudes and the structure of our society.

But a century has passed, more than a hundred years, since the Negro was freed. And he is not fully free tonight.

It was more than a hundred years ago that Abraham Lincoln, a great President of another party, signed the Emancipation Proclamation, but emancipation is a proclamation and not a fact.

A century has passed, more than a hundred years, since equality was promised. And yet the Negro is not equal.

A century has passed since the day of promise. And the promise is un-kept.

The time of justice has now come. I tell you that I believe sincerely that no force can hold it back. It is right in the eyes of man and God that it should come. And when it does, I think that day will brighten the lives of every American.

For Negroes are not the only victims. How many white children have gone uneducated? How many white families have lived in stark poverty? How many white lives have been scarred by fear, because we have wasted our energy and our substance to maintain the barriers of hatred and terror?

So I say to all of you here, and to all in the Nation tonight, that those who appeal to you to hold on to the past do so at the cost of denying you your future.

This great, rich, restless country can offer opportunity and education and hope to all: black and white, North and South, sharecropper and city dweller. These are the enemies: poverty, ignorance, disease. They are the enemies and not our fellow man, not our neighbor. And these enemies too—poverty, disease and ignorance: we shall overcome.

Now let none of us in any section look with prideful righteousness on the troubles in another section, or on the problems of our neighbors. There is really no part of America where the promise of equality has been fully kept. In Buffalo as well as in Birmingham, in Philadelphia as well as in Selma, Americans are struggling for the fruits of freedom. …

As we meet here in this peaceful, historic chamber tonight, men from the South, some of whom were at Iwo Jima; men from the North, who have carried Old Glory to far corners of the world and brought it back without a stain on it; men from the East and from the West—are all fighting together without regard to religion, or color, or region, in Vietnam. Men from every region fought for us across the world twenty years ago.

And in these common dangers and these common sacrifices the South made its contribution of honor and gallantry no less than any other region of the great Republic—and in some instances, a great many of them, more.

And I have not the slightest doubt that good men from everywhere in this country, from the Great Lakes to the Gulf of Mexico, from the Golden Gate to the harbors along the Atlantic, will rally together now in this cause to vindicate the freedom of all Americans. For all of us owe this duty; and I believe that all of us will respond to it.

Your President makes that request of every American.

The real hero of this struggle is the American Negro. His actions and protests, his courage to risk safety and even to risk his life, have awakened the conscience of this Nation. His demonstrations have been designed to call attention to injustice, designed to provoke change, designed to stir reform.

He has called upon us to make good the promise of America. And who among us can say that we would have made the same progress were it not for his persistent bravery, and his faith in American democracy.

For at the real heart of battle for equality is a deep-seated belief in the democratic process. Equality depends not on the force of arms or tear gas but upon the force of moral right; not on recourse to violence but on respect for law and order.

There have been many pressures upon your President and there will be others as the days come and go. But I pledge to you tonight that we intend to fight this battle where it should be fought: in the courts, and in the Congress, and in the hearts of men.

We must preserve the right of free speech and the right of free assembly. But the right of free speech does not carry with it, as has been said, the right to holler fire in a crowded theater. We must preserve the right to free assembly, but free assembly does not carry with it the right to block public thoroughfares to traffic.

We do have a right to protest, and a right to march under conditions that do not infringe upon the constitutional rights of our neighbors. And I intend to protect all those rights as long as I am permitted to serve in this office.

We will guard against violence, knowing it strikes from our hands the very weapons which we seek—progress, obedience to law, and belief in American values.

In Selma as elsewhere we seek and pray for peace. We seek order. We seek unity. But we will not accept the peace of stifled rights, or the order imposed by fear, or the unity that stifles protest. For peace cannot be purchased at the cost of liberty. …

All Americans must have the right to vote. And we are going to give them that right.

All Americans must have the privileges of citizenship regardless of race. And they are going to have those privileges of citizenship regardless of race.

But I would like to caution you and remind you that to exercise these privileges takes much more than just legal right. It requires a trained mind and a healthy body. It requires a decent home, and the chance to find a job, and the opportunity to escape from the clutches of poverty.

Of course, people cannot contribute to the Nation if they are never taught to read or write, if their bodies are stunted from hunger, if their sickness goes untended, if their life is spent in hopeless poverty just drawing a welfare check.

So we want to open the gates to opportunity. But we are also going to give all our people, black and white, the help that they need to walk through those gates. …

This is the richest and most powerful country which ever occupied the globe. The might of past empires is little compared to ours. But I do not want to be the President who built empires, or sought grandeur, or extended dominion.

I want to be the President who educated young children to the wonders of their world. I want to be the President who helped to feed the hungry and to prepare them to be taxpayers instead of taxeaters.

I want to be the President who helped the poor to find their own way and who protected the right of every citizen to vote in every election.

I want to be the President who helped to end hatred among his fellow men and who promoted love among the people of all races and all regions and all parties.

I want to be the President who helped to end war among the brothers of this earth ... .

Beyond this great chamber, out yonder in 50 States, are the people we serve. Who can tell what deep and unspoken hopes are in their hearts tonight as they sit there and listen. We all can guess, from our own lives, how difficult they often find their own pursuit of happiness, how many problems each little family has. They look most of all to themselves for their futures. But I think that they also look to each of us.

Above the pyramid on the great seal of the United States it says—in Latin—"God has favored our undertaking."

God will not favor everything that we do. It is rather our duty to divine His will. But I cannot help believing that He truly understands and that He really favors the undertaking that we begin here tonight.

ROBERT F. KENNEDY

Ending the War in Vietnam

At the end of it all, there will only be more Americans killed ... so that they may say, as Tacitus said of Rome: "They made a desert, and called it peace."

From the 1800s until the 1940s, France controlled the Indochina colony composed of Vietnam, Laos, and Kampuchea (Cambodia). With France's defeat by Germany in World War II, control of French Indochina was assumed by the Japanese. France tried to reestablish control of the colony following Japan's surrender in 1945, but that effort was thwarted by Ho Chi Minh, a Vietnamese Communist who led a three-year war against the French—the result of which was a division of the country into North and South Vietnam with an agreement to reunify the country through elections in 1956.

The United States, which was surprised by the 1949 Communist takeover of China, had contributed more than two billion dollars in military equipment to the French during this war and was engaged in its own anti-Communist struggle in Korea. These policies reflected President Truman's commitment to aid any nation threatened by Communists. President Eisenhower upheld the Truman Doctrine, urging the South Vietnam government not to participate in the agreed-upon 1956 national election for fear that Communists in the North would corrupt the democratic process. Eisenhower sent civilian and military advisers to South Vietnam, and President John Kennedy continued that policy in his administration while expanding economic aid as well. In 1965, President Lyndon Johnson committed the first combat soldiers and, by 1969, American troop strength in South Vietnam had grown to more than 540,000.

The war in Vietnam, from the beginning, was a point of strife in the United States. Some felt that American involvement was a necessary check on Communist expansion. Others viewed U.S. involvement as unimportant to American security and an unwise limited engagement against an enemy heavily supplied by both China and the Soviet Union. One of the most outspoken critics of the war was Senator Robert Kennedy (1925-1968), who was seeking the Democratic nomination for president. Speaking at Kansas State University on March 18, 1968, Kennedy emphasized his commitment to the withdrawal of American forces from Southeast Asia.

... This is a year of choice—a year when we choose not simply who will lead us, but where we wish to be led; the country we want for ourselves, and the kind we want for our children. If in this year of choice we fashion new policies out of old illusions, we ensure for ourselves nothing but crisis for the future, and we bequeath to our children the bitter harvest of those crises.

For with all we have done, with all our immense power and richness, our problems seem to grow not less, but greater. We are in a time of unprecedented turbulence, of danger and questioning. It is at its root a question of the national soul. The President calls it restlessness, while cabinet officers and commentators tell us that America is deep in a malaise of the spirit—discouraging initiative, paralyzing will and action, dividing Americans from one another by their age, their views, and the color of their skins.

There are many causes. Some are in the failed promise of America itself. ... Another cause is in our inaction in the face of danger. We seem equally unable to control the violent disorder within our cities, or the pollution and destruction of the country, of the water and land that we use and our children inherit. And a third great cause of discontent is the course we are following in Vietnam, in a war which has divided Americans as they have not been divided since your state was called Bloody Kansas.

All this—questioning and uncertainty at home, divisive war abroad—has led us to a deep crisis of confidence: in our leadership, in each other, and in our very self as a nation.

Today I would speak to you of the third of those great crises: of the war in Vietnam. I come here, to this serious forum in the heart of the nation to discuss this war with you; not on the basis of emotion, but fact; not, I hope, in clichés, but with a clear and discriminating sense of where the national interest lies.

I do not want—as I believe most Americans do not want—to sell out American interests, to simply withdraw, to raise the white flag of surrender. That would be unacceptable to us as a country and as a people. But, I am concerned—as I believe most Americans are concerned—that the course we are following at the present time is deeply wrong. I am concerned—as I believe most Americans are concerned—that we are acting as if no other nations existed, against the judgment and desires of neutrals and our historic allies alike. I am concerned—as I believe most Americans are concerned—that our present course will not bring victory; will not bring peace; will not stop the bloodshed; and will

not advance the interests of the United States or the cause of peace in the world.

I am concerned that, at the end of it all, there will only be more Americans killed; more of our treasure spilled out; and because of the bitterness and hatred on every side of this war, more hundreds of thousands of Vietnamese slaughtered; so that they may say, as Tacitus said of Rome: "They made a desert, and called it peace."

And I do not think that is what the American spirit is really all about.

Let me begin this discussion with a note both personal and public. I was involved in many of the early decisions of Vietnam, decisions which helped set us on our present path. It may be that effort was doomed from the start; that it was never really possible to bring all the people of South Vietnam under the rule of the successive governments we supported—governments, one after another, riddled with corruption, inefficiency, and greed; governments which did not and could not successfully capture and energize the national feeling of their people. If that is the case, as it well may be, then I am willing to bear my share of the responsibility, before history and before my fellow citizens. But past error is no excuse for its own perpetuation. Tragedy is a tool for the living to gain wisdom, not a guide by which to live. Now, as ever, we do ourselves best justice when we measure ourselves against ancient tests, as in the Antigone of Sophocles: "All men make mistakes, but a good man yields when he knows his course is wrong, and repairs the evil. The only sin is pride." ...

It is becoming more evident with every passing day that the victories we achieve will only come at the cost of destruction for the nation we once hoped to help. ...

An American commander said of the town of Ben Tre, "It became necessary to destroy the town in order to save it." It is difficult to quarrel with the decision of American commanders to use air power and artillery to save the lives of their men; if American troops are to fight for Vietnamese cities, they deserve protection. What I cannot understand is why the responsibility for the recapture and attendant destruction of Hue, and Ben Tre and the others, should fall to American troops in the first place.

If Communist insurgents or invaders held New York or Washington or San Francisco, we would not leave it to foreigners to take them back, and destroy them and their people in the process. ...

If the government's troops will not or cannot carry the fight for their cities, we cannot ourselves destroy them. That kind of salvation is not an act we can presume to perform for them. For we must ask our government—we must ask ourselves: Where does such logic end? If it becomes "necessary" to destroy all of South Vietnam in order to "save" it, will we do that, too? And if we care so little about South Vietnam that we are willing to see the land destroyed and its people dead, then why are we there in the first place?

Can we ordain to ourselves the awful majesty of God—to decide what cities and villages are to be destroyed, who will live and who will die, and who will join refugees wandering in a desert of our own creation? If it is true that we have a commitment to the South Vietnamese people, we must ask, are they being consulted? …

Let us have no misunderstanding. The Viet Cong are a brutal enemy indeed. Time and time again, they have shown their willingness to sacrifice innocent civilians, to engage in torture and murder and despicable terror to achieve their ends. …

We set out to prove our willingness to keep commitments everywhere in the world. What we are ensuring, instead, is that it is most unlikely that the American people would ever again be willing to … engage in this kind of struggle. Meanwhile, our oldest and strongest allies pull back to their own shores, leaving us alone to police all of Asia. …

Higher yet is the price we pay in our own innermost lives, and in the spirit of our country. For the first time in a century, we have open resistance to service in the cause of the nation. For the first time perhaps in our history, we have desertions from our army on political and moral grounds. The front pages of our newspapers show photographs of American soldiers torturing prisoners. Every night we watch horror on the evening news. Violence spreads inexorably across the nation, filling our streets and crippling our lives.

And whatever the costs to us, let us think of the young men we have sent there: not just the killed, but those who have to kill; not just the maimed, but also those who must look upon the results of what they do.

It may be asked: Is not such degradation the cost of all wars? Of course it is. That is why war is not an enterprise lightly to be undertaken, nor prolonged one moment past its absolute necessity. All this—the destruction of Vietnam, the cost to ourselves, the danger to the world—all this we would stand, willingly, if it seemed to serve some worthwhile end. But the costs of the war's present course far outweigh anything we can reasonably hope to gain by it, for ourselves or for the people of Vietnam. It must be ended, and it can be ended in a peace for brave men who have fought each other with a terrible fury, each believing that he alone was in the right. We have prayed to different gods, and the prayers of neither have been answered fully. Now, while there is still time for some of them to be partly answered, now is the time to stop. …

A young girl kneels over the body of a student shot dead by the Ohio National Guard on the campus of Kent State University on May 4, 1970. Students, and others, were protesting President Nixon's announced expansion of the Vietnam War into Cambodia. Amidst calls to "bring the war home," many protestors engaged in vandalism and looting. The campus Reserve Officer Training Corps (ROTC) building at Kent State was set ablaze, and responding firemen and police officers were assaulted with rocks and bottles. The National Guard was called in and, after issuing lawful orders to disperse, was also assaulted by protestors. The guardsmen indiscriminately opened fire, killing four students and wounding nine others, one of whom suffered permanent paralysis. Two of the four shot dead were not participants in the protest, and were simply walking between classes. In response to the shootings, hundreds of schools across the country closed due to a strike of more than four million students. This event further affected public opinion over the role of the United States in Vietnam.

Kilroy

The phrase "Kilroy was here," accompanied by a cartoon character with an elongated nose peering over a wall, has been found inscribed atop the torch of the Statue of Liberty, on the dome of the U.S. Capitol, on the girders of New York's George Washington Bridge, atop Mt. Everest, the underside of the Arc De Triomphe, and was even found scrawled in dust on the moon.

As an unknown author writing for the bi-monthly publication *Off Duty* explains, the legend of Kilroy began during World War II where, in the most remote regions of the earth, his name greeted GIs. "Kilroy was here" adorned every surface from Adolf Hitler's "Eagle's Nest" at Berchtesgaden to the battleship *Pennsylvania* on which the prankish words were found after it had been blasted by the atomic bomb test at Bikini Atoll. When infantry stormed Utah Beach at Normandy, they found Kilroy's name emblazoned on a German pillbox. One recon unit, in fact, presumably the first Americans ashore, reported seeing enemy soldiers painting over Kilroy's logo. Beside the mess tent at a naval base in the Philippines was inscribed: "Kilroy starved to death waiting in this line." At Canton Island Airfield, way out in the Pacific waters, a pilot scribbled a triumphant, "I was here before Kilroy" on the flight tower. After returning from his next flight, however, the following retort awaited him: "Like hell you were, I was here when this was only a gleam in the CO's eye—Kilroy." And on Kwajalein Atoll, newcomers read: "No grass atoll, no trees atoll, no water atoll, no women atoll, no liquor atoll, no fun atoll. I just didn't pause atoll—Kilroy." At an American air base in Japan, the grizzled veteran had the last say there as well. On a barracks wall, someone had written: "Slap your hands and jump for joy, for you were here before Kilroy." Beneath this quickly appeared: "Sorry to spoil your little joke. I was here but my pencil broke—Kilroy." Even the walls of a top-security washroom being used by President Truman, Soviet leader Joseph Stalin, and Clement Attlee (who had replaced Churchill as British prime minister) during the Potsdam Conference in 1945 were not safe from the omnipresent GI and his marker. The first person inside was Stalin, who emerged and asked his aide, "Who is Kilroy?"

In seeking an answer to that question, the U.S. Army's Adjutant General in Washington searched the Army's files on ten million ex-GIs, only to conclude: "As far as we're concerned, Kilroy doesn't exist." There is, however, one piece of factual evidence. In 1941, a shipyard inspector at the Fore River Shipyard in Quincy, Massachusetts, whose job it was to check on the number of rivets completed by the riveters, chalked his name on the side of all the war materials that were his responsibility. All of this war material, bearing the autograph of James J. Kilroy of Halifax, Massachusetts, found its way to every corner of the earth and American soldiers, in turn, did their best to promulgate the catchy signature.

Although Kilroy continues to live on in the armed forces, America's most famous GI was not always so glib. When American troops combed through the ruins of Hiroshima after the war, for example, they discovered several signs proclaiming "Kilroy doesn't want to be here!" And in Vietnam, Kilroy was noticeably absent from what would have been familiar haunts had morale not been so low.

Aware of Kilroy's absence, Senator Eugene McCarthy (1916-2005) of Minnesota wrote the following poem about the legendary veteran's MIA status. In 1968, McCarthy sought the Democratic nomination for president, campaigning on a pledge to end the Vietnam War.

Kilroy is gone,
the word is out,
absent without leave,
from Vietnam.

Kilroy
who wrote his name
in every can
from Poland to Japan
and places in between
like Sheboygan and Racine
is gone
absent without leave
from Vietnam.

Kilroy
who kept the dice
and stole the ice
out of the BOQ
Kilroy
whose name was good
on every IOU
in World War II
and even in Korea
is gone
absent without leave
from Vietnam.

Kilroy
the unknown soldier
who was the first to land
the last to leave,
with his own hand
has taken his good name
from all the walls
and toilet stalls.
Kilroy
whose name around the world
was like the flag unfurled
has run it down
and left Saigon
and the Mekong
without a hero or a song
and gone
absent without leave
from Vietnam.

Hollywood legend Bob Hope joins the famed Nicholas brothers, Harold and Fayard, in a dance step aboard the aircraft carrier USS Ticonderoga *in 1965. The United Service Organizations (USO), a private, nonprofit organization supported by private citizens and corporations, was formed in 1941 at the behest of President Franklin Roosevelt who determined it would be best if private organizations handled the recreation needs of the rapidly growing U.S. armed forces. That same year, Bob Hope began his nearly six decades of unwavering commitment to the morale of America's servicemen and women. In 1997, both houses of Congress unanimously passed a resolution making Hope an honorary veteran—the first individual so honored in the history of the United States.*

ROBERT F. KENNEDY

On the Death of Martin Luther King, Jr.

We can move in that direction as a country ... filled with hatred toward one another ... Or we can make an effort ... to understand with compassion and love.

While campaigning in Indiana during 1968, Robert Kennedy received word of Martin Luther King's assassination. Speaking in a ghetto of Indianapolis, Kennedy shared the news of King's death, which had not yet reached the community. In trying to calm the anger and hurt, he spoke publicly for the first time of his own brother's assassination. While rioting broke out in cities all across America, Indianapolis remained quiet.

On June 4, 1968, after addressing supporters in Los Angeles's Ambassador Hotel, Kennedy exited through the hotel kitchen where he was shot in the head by a Jordanian-born Arab. He died two days later at the age of forty-two.

I have bad news for you, for all of our fellow citizens, and people who love peace all over the world, and that is that Martin Luther King was shot and killed tonight.

Martin Luther King dedicated his life to love and to justice for his fellow human beings, and he died because of that effort.

In this difficult day, in this difficult time for the United States, it is perhaps well to ask what kind of a nation we are and what direction we want to move in. For those of you who are black—considering the evidence there evidently is that there were white people who were responsible—you can be filled with bitterness, with hatred, and a desire for revenge. We can move in that direction as a country, in great polarization—black people amongst black, white people amongst white, filled with hatred toward one another.

Or we can make an effort, as Martin Luther King did, to understand and to comprehend, and to replace that violence, that stain of bloodshed that has spread across our land, with an effort to understand with compassion and love.

For those of you who are black and are tempted to be filled with hatred and distrust at the injustice of such an act, against all white people, I can only say that I feel in my own heart the same kind of feeling. I had a member of my family killed, but he was killed by a white man. But we have to make an effort in the United States. We have to make an effort to understand, to go beyond these rather difficult times.

My favorite poet was Aeschylus. He wrote: "In our sleep, pain which cannot forget falls drop by drop upon the heart until, in our own despair, against our will, comes wisdom through the awful grace of God."

What we need in the United States is not division; what we need in the United States is not hatred; what we need in the United States is not violence or lawlessness, but love and wisdom, and compassion toward one another, and a feeling of justice towards those who still suffer within our country, whether they be white or they be black.

So I shall ask you tonight to return home, to say a prayer for the family of Martin Luther King, that's true, but more importantly to say a prayer for our own country, which all of us love—a prayer for understanding and that compassion of which I spoke.

We can do well in this country. We will have difficult times. We've had difficult times in the past. We will have difficult times in the future. It is not the end of violence; it is not the end of lawlessness; it is not the end of disorder.

But the vast majority of white people and the vast majority of black people in this country want to live together, want to improve the quality of our life, and want justice for all human beings who abide in our land.

Let us dedicate ourselves to what the Greeks wrote so many years ago: to tame the savageness of man and to make gentle the life of this world.

Let us dedicate ourselves to that, and say a prayer for our country and for our people.

BARRY SADLER AND ROBERT L. MOORE

Ballad of the Green Berets

Born in New Mexico, Barry Sadler (1940-1989) served as a combat soldier with the Green Berets in Vietnam. A medic in his Special Forces unit, Sadler's tour ended when he stepped on a Vietcong-planted punji stick. While recuperating from the leg wound, he wrote "Ballad of the Green Berets," the U.S. Army's answer to the folk-rock anti-war ballads of the Vietnam era. Robert "Robin" Moore, who wrote a book of the same title, contributed to the lyrics. Sadler later sang the tune on a record that became the nation's number one hit for five weeks in 1966 and eventually sold nine million singles and albums. The song also served as the theme song for the 1968 John Wayne film, *The Green Berets*, and it was the featured work on an album titled *Ballad of the Green Berets and Songs of America's Fighting Men*, sung by Roger Dewey. After the war, Sadler became a best-selling author and served as a contributing editor to *Soldier of Fortune* magazine.

Fighting soldiers from the sky,
Fearless men who jump and die,
Men who mean just what they say
The brave men of the Green Beret.

Chorus:
    Silver wings upon their chests,
    These are men, America's best,
    One hundred men we'll test today,
    But only three win the Green Beret.

Trained to live off nature's land,
Trained in combat, hand to hand,
Men who fight by night and day,
Courage take from the Green Beret.

Back at home a young wife waits,
Her Green Beret has met his fate,
He has died for those oppressed,
Leaving her this last request:

Put silver wings on my son's chest,
Make him one of America's best,
He'll be a man they'll test one day,
Have him win the Green Beret.

THOMAS B. ALLEN

A Place for Memories

"When we touch the Wall we know that you are there."

In January 1973, the United States, South Vietnam, and the Communist North signed a cease-fire agreement, and the U.S. withdrew all ground forces from South Vietnam. By year's end, however, the Communists launched another offensive on the South and, by 1976, had successfully unified the country. Saigon was renamed Ho Chi Minh City and hundreds of thousands of Vietnamese became refugees. The Vietnam "conflict" (war was never actually declared) was the longest American military involvement to date and the only time that the United States failed to achieve its military objective. That failure was the result of the United States committing itself to a limited war, underestimating Communist sympathies in South Vietnam, and failing to win the full support of Americans on the home front.

More than 2,700,000 Americans fought in Vietnam and more than 58,000 Americans were killed, while thousands more were subjected to brutal torture in prison camps. The names of all those killed and missing in action are engraved on the Vietnam Wall in Washington, D.C. "A Place for Memories" is an excellent portrayal of the history behind the memorial wall and the wide range of emotions it generates. Thomas Allen's book, *Offerings at the Wall*, from which this selection is taken, is a compilation of artifacts from the Vietnam Veterans Memorial Collection. One such artifact included in that collection is a letter addressed to "Timothy, Christopher, Frank & John," which reads: "It is always difficult to obviously determine how the conditions concerning the deaths and injury of so many can affect the current state of consciousness of a new generation. Whether directly or indirectly your passing has had significant affect on our culture today. I know that as time travels forward the effects are less and less apparent, but future youth will experience similar traumas distinctive to their own generation. In their own painful realities perhaps your conditions will not be forgotten."

They come to the wall silently, passing along the walkway where the black stone slabs rise. They walk slowly, seeing their faces mirrored and mingled in the rows of names … Freddie A. Blackburn … Daniel Diaz … Bobby Ray Jones … Hallie W. Smith—those 58,196 names. Usually they stop and run their fingers along the names, touching a war that this memorial keeps forever unforgotten. For those moments, they are not mere tourists who have arrived at the Vietnam Veterans Memorial while making the rounds of Washington's monuments. They are pilgrims who have journeyed to a place that has become a national shrine and an honored repository for keepsakes of grief.

A few stoop and leave an offering—a note hastily written, a flag, a single rose, a burnished plaque, a teddy bear brought from a faraway time. A hat was left with a poem that said, "When we touch the Wall we know that you are there." There are those who prefer the night. They walk past the veterans who are always there and, stepping into the shadows of the Wall, leave a piece of memory to the darkness. People usually leave ordinary things. The toys of sons and brothers. The badges and the dog tags

and the medals of warriors who are parting at last with the past. Birthday cards from mothers. Notes from girlfriends growing old: Linda writes to Gary, Doug, and Billy, high school boyfriends who became names on the Wall—"Well, that time has rolled around and the Class of '65 is having its 20-year reunion. Cheers, cheers for old Orchard Park high school. … After you all died … I pretty much screwed up for ten years. … Now I'm much better, more responsible. I learned that the pain and loss never goes away. It just changes. … I'm still mad." A man who had been in the 101st Airborne left a photo of a North Vietnamese man posed with a young girl and wrote a letter:

"Dear Sir, For twenty-two years I have carried your picture in my wallet. I was only eighteen years old that day that we faced one another on that trail in Chu Lai, Vietnam. Why you did not take my life I'll never know. You stared at me for so long, armed with your AK-47, and yet you did not fire. Forgive me for taking your life. I was reacting just the way I was trained, to kill V.C. … So many times over the years I have stared at your picture and your daughter, I suspect. Each time my heart and guts would burn with the pain of guilt. I have two daughters myself now. ... I perceive you as a brave soldier defending his homeland. Above all else, I can now respect the importance that life held for you. I suppose that is why I am able to be here today. ... It is time for me to continue the life process and release my pain and guilt. Forgive me, Sir."

A man left a coin and ring showing membership in Narcotics Anonymous, and with them he spilled these words: "I learned fear. I learned to be ALONE—NEVER let ANYONE in. I learned to be an animal—to take what I wanted, when I wanted. I learned to kill—no—learned it was OK to kill. ... I came home and nothing worked—my family did not want me—they were—ARE—afraid of me. I am afraid of me. I pray for your forgiveness for my life/lies. ... " He ended with the words, "No more hurt."

They come with burdens and they lay them down at the Wall. They come with words of rage and despair and leave the words at the Wall. But most of the words and the objects come from hearts scarred by loss. There is a watch, stopped at 10:03, and with it a letter to a dead comrade: "When I held you in my arms you felt cold. I would not let them take you from me for as long as I could. And then you were gone." There are two wedding rings that had been placed on a coffin by the widow of a man killed in Vietnam. A friend visiting the grave much later saw the rings, which had somehow worked their way to the surface. He brought his comrade's ring to the Wall—"where his spirit now resides."

There is a box of cookies from home addressed on its brown paper wrapper to a name that matches a name on the Wall—returned as undeliverable and still unopened. "Mom & Dad want you to have these cookies & Kool Aid," reads a note. "It's time they gave these to you. ... " A man who lost thirteen friends left a dozen cans of beer and a packet of Kool Aid for the kid who never drank.

Men pay off debts, leaving a promised dollar or can of beer or pack of cigarettes. A Special Forces soldier, long ago desperate for a smoke, had broken into a friend's foot locker and snatched a carton, intending to pay for it with two cans of sardines. But before he could do so the friend was killed. After keeping the sardines for twenty years, the borrower sought out his friend's name on the Wall and finally gave him the cans.

On September 23, 1970, a mother wrote a letter to her son in Vietnam: "Dear Al, Everytime we hear the news on the TV or radio, we wonder if you are one of those that are being shot down. ... " She got the letter back, undelivered.

On September 20 her son had been killed when his helicopter was shot down. For years, she held on to those tragically prophetic words. Then one day Al's cousin left the letter at the Wall, with a note, "We thought you should still have it."

Someone else had carried around the stained and creased roster of Alpha Company. Most of the names were typed in capital letters. A few names—newcomers added to the list of "Personnel in Field"—were written in a shaky hand on May 6, 1966, when Alpha Company went into battle. When it was over, name after name was circled. Written after the names was KIA for killed in action, or WIA for wounded in action. The man who held on to the roster for twenty-four years came to the Wall and finally gave it up, writing along the bottom, "Rest in Peace, Gentlemen."

People come to terms with what they have lost. A young woman left two sonograms and a framed note addressed to a name on the Wall: "I don't know if it's a boy or a girl—if the baby is a boy—he'll be named after you. Dad—this child will know you. Just how I have grown to know and love you—even though the last time I saw you I was only 4 mo. old. ... "

Many letters begin with Dad. "I know you would like Lisa," one says. "You could not ask for a better wife. Dad, you have a granddaughter. Her name is Meghan and when she sees your picture she says, 'That's my pa pa.'" To another Dad: "I've always been told I look like you ... how I wish I could remember you. I was four when you were killed but all I have are visions and childhood dreams of what you were. ... "

No one expected the Wall to become the country's most visited monument. Nor did anyone expect it to become a pilgrimage site or a shrine of loving words and cherished objects. The Vietnam Veterans Memorial was envisioned to be a place of remembrance and reflection, a way to remember not the Vietnam War but the men and women who died in it. The memorial was the idea of Jan Scruggs, who went to war as a teenage infantryman and came home a wounded man. He wanted his fellow veterans to "have a place to confront and perhaps make peace with the ghosts of their past." The place, he decided, would be a memorial that listed the names of everyone killed in America's longest and most wrenching war. "We'll accept no money from the government," he vowed. "Dollars will come from the American people." A comedian mocked him later on a television show after he had collected only $144.50 from his fund-raising effort. But Scruggs labored on, working with others to create the nonprofit Vietnam Veterans Memorial Fund. Eventually, more than 650,000 people contributed over $5,000,000 and Congress authorized a site, two acres near the Lincoln Memorial.

The veterans group launched a design competition, setting three requirements: The memorial must contain the names of all the dead and missing, not make any political statement, and be harmonious with the site. Maya Ying Lin, a twenty-year-old senior at Yale, won the competition with her vision of a V of black granite rising out of the earth, its gleaming surface reflecting the images of the living, uniting them with the names of the dead. "I had an impulse to cut open the earth," she later wrote, "an initial violence that in time would heal." Her design was denounced as a "black gash of shame," a tombstone to death and defeat. In a compromise with traditional-minded critics, a flagpole and a representational sculpture group were added to the site. Sculptor Frederick Hart's bronze statue of three young soldiers was placed so that they seem to be looking at the Wall, perhaps searching it for their own names.

In the summer of 1982, a U.S. Navy officer walked up to the trench where the concrete for the foundation of the Wall was being poured. He stood over the trench for a moment, then tossed something into it and saluted. When a workman asked him what he was doing, he said he was giving his dead brother's Purple Heart to the Wall. That was the first offering.

Since then, more than 30,000 objects and letters have been left at the Wall. As it became a shrine, it also became a place to confront futures that could not be. Tucked into a wreath are the things of an imagined life: new baby shoes for a baby who never would be, pencils and crayons for a first day of kindergarten that never would be, champagne glasses to toast a wedding anniversary that never would be, ornaments for a Christmas tree that never would be. Others have left a birthday card for a fortieth birthday that never would come, a royal flush in spades for a poker game that never would be played.

There are autographed baseballs and marijuana joints and bottles of whiskey. There is a plastic bag with a note that begins: "This is to tell my brothers on the Wall, I know you wanted to grow your beard." The writer of this note had shaved off his own beard and left it as a memento for the dead who "never got your chance."

At first, National Park Service rangers gathered up the objects and the pieces of paper and put them in boxes that were kept at a maintenance yard. The rangers and the volunteers at the Wall knew, instinctively, that everything—the baseballs, the envelope of whiskers, the letters to the dead—had to be saved. Just as instinctively, they knew that sealed letters given to the Wall should never be opened. Soon the accumulation of unexpected artifacts became the Vietnam Veterans Memorial Collection, an official national heritage with the Park Service as its steward. Twice a day volunteers collect the offerings, but there are a few exceptions to the collect-everything rule. Flowers and floral wreaths are not preserved, but their ribbons and messages are. American flags without messages written on them are given to the Boy Scouts and Girl Scouts and other patriotic organizations. Drugs and drug paraphernalia are routinely confiscated as contraband. However, at least one joint and one roach clip somehow made it into the collection.

Each artifact is tagged with the date it was left and given a reference number. Also recorded is beneath which of the 140 panels of names the object was left, for it probably relates to someone listed on that panel. The day's objects are taken to a storage space in the nearby Lincoln Memorial. Later they are transferred to a huge repository, the Museum and Archaeological Regional Storage Facility (MARS), in Lanham, Maryland, about twelve miles from the Wall. There the artifacts are preserved for posterity, alongside such historic items as weapons from the Battle of Antietam and a life mask of Abraham Lincoln.

From a computerized list of the collection, a sampler: armband (MP's), berets, Bible, boots, bottles (Jack Daniel's and Budweiser are the leading brands of libation), buttons, can openers, flags in funeral fold, fishing float, foodstuffs (including walnuts, Spam, fruit cocktail, and M&Ms), hats (10-gallon with black band, bush, Australian), insignia, name tapes (Morrison, Murphy, Zepeda, Coveny, Petshke, Despins, Koger), service ribbons, a sock for an amputee's stump, a popsicle stick with writing on it, four mortarboard tassels, a golf trophy, the foil wrapper from a Hershey's kiss. Many of the objects were not easy to label. They puzzled the white-gloved Park Service employees who handled them, and Vietnam veterans volunteered to help. One of them was Duery Felton, Jr., a black, wounded ex-infantryman. Drafted at nineteen and sent to Vietnam, he was grievously wounded in a battle that he will not describe. He recovered at Walter Reed Army Hospital in Washington, which was and is his hometown. He will not talk about the way he earned his Purple Heart, but he does say, "I was almost a name on the Wall." He still has a look that warns off questions and keeps memories locked, but it was the unlocking and tapping of those memories that gave Duery Felton a new mission in life.

Shown the graffiti on a helmet cover ("Don't shoot, I'm short"), Felton explains that the words were about time, not height. The message indicated that the soldier was a short-timer, having safely reached the last month of his tour in Vietnam. Shown a photo of soldiers facing three rifles hung with helmets and stuck upright in the ground by their bayonets, Felton says, "Memorial service. Lots of times the body hadn't been brought in yet." And, with white-gloved hands, he turns the photo over. On it are written two names and, simply, "new guy." Felton reflects that sometimes a new guy would arrive "and be gone before you knew his name."

Looking at a Bazooka bubble gum wrapper left at the Wall, Felton says, "Maybe it was for a guy nicknamed Bazooka. Maybe somebody was remembering how they would take a ditty bag full of trash with them into the field, and how they'd throw the trash around in a wide area when they were being pursued, so the enemy would think there were more men than there actually were." Or he reads words printed on a cigarette—"It ain't broke and it ain't wet"—and explains that a dry, intact cigarette was a prize during monsoon months in Vietnam. Felton might pick up a smooth stone and speculate that it came from the favorite trout stream of someone on the Wall. His intuition, his lore, his deeply etched memories became so valuable that by 1986 he had been hired as a temporary museum technician.

Now he is curator of the collection, and he treats his job as a sacred trust. The artifacts, he hopes, will help people understand a terrible war and cherish those who died in it. A note, addressed to "Viet Vets," says it well: "Prayerfully we will come to realize your sacrifice. Forgive please our lack of support and understanding. May your healing come soon." Many notes like this one address both the dead and the living. Other objects and notes—many marked "please do not open"—are what Felton calls direct communication between the donor and the dead: a nursing mother's breast pad stained by her milk … a pacifier … three ancient Roman coins … the model airplanes … the two lollipop trees … the two pink washcloths folded in the shape of a rabbit … the bicycle fender. Trying to fathom them is like staring at rows of votive candles placed before an altar and trying to grasp the prayers flickering within those flames. Was the lollipop tree a family rite at birthday parties? And

why two? Felton has examined so many offerings that he often seems able to tug meaning from them. Or, aided by a network of volunteers, he finds ways to reach a donor and gently ask questions. It turns out that the folded washcloths were "Boo-boo Bunnies" that a mother used in treating her dead son's cuts and scratches when he was a little boy. The man who left the bicycle fender explained that a friend of his younger brother, who used to ride a bike without fenders, was killed in Vietnam. "In remembrance of his brother's friend," Felton says, "the donor removed the fenders from his own bicycle and left one at the memorial. Without that information, it was just a fender. Now it has meaning."

The bicycle fender, along with hundreds of other items, became part of a Smithsonian Institution exhibit of the collection. But the overwhelming majority of the artifacts will never be seen in public. They will remain in the chill, windowless repository in Lanham, a hangar-size building that workers call MARS, as much for its location as for its acronym. Objects that are small enough lie in plastic bags in multidrawer cabinets. Bigger ones—such as the lollipop trees and the painting on a door—stand on platforms in the dimly lit building. Because of the sacred nature of many Native American artifacts in the collection, tribal leaders dispatched a shaman to MARS, instructing him to bless both the objects and the curators. The blessing sanctioned the handling of sacred objects by curators and their viewing by non-Native Americans.

When the Vietnam Women's Memorial was built near the Wall in 1993, the tradition of offering continued. Among the objects left there were eight gold bracelets, each placed on a branch of a tree growing beside a sculptural grouping by Glenna Goodacre that shows three women caring for a wounded soldier. And each bracelet carries the name of one of the eight women who are remembered on the Wall. Flowers and flags, the most frequently found offerings, often appear at the two nearby statuary groups. But it is the Wall that remains the focus of remembrance.

"The objects are primary sources, giving validity to a historic event," says David Guynes, site manager of MARS and an authority on the preservation of objects of the past. "People who ordinarily would not be articulate are telling us about an era. They are choosing the things to keep, not a museum curator." Analysts of the collection have discovered, for example, that the higher a unit's casualty count the higher the number of objects associated with that unit. Guynes says that this helps in the understanding of long-term grief.

Through the years, the collection has been changing. At first what was typically left was something personal or a few words spontaneously jotted down on a piece of paper, often the stationary of a Washington hotel. Gradually, as donors became aware of the collection, they carefully prepared their letters or objects, preserving them in advance by enclosing them in plastic or by engraving their words on metal plaques. Felton sees 1988 as a year of change, following President Reagan's visit to the memorial, where he left a note to "Our young friends … . in our hearts you will always be young, full of the love that is youth, love of life … ." After that, Felton says, "There was a validation, as if America was saying, 'It's OK to be a vet.' The letters began saying, 'I've got on with my life.'"

Toys and other objects of the 1950s and early 1960s are now appearing more frequently. Intuitively, Felton senses the effects of a generation passing: The parents of the Vietnam dead are themselves dying. From their attics and closets come the keepsakes of dead children that now pass to brothers and sisters, who bring them to the Wall. They are also bringing their own children, the nieces and nephews who are told of an uncle or an aunt they will never meet. One such brother was a teacher, who brought his fifth graders to see the Wall and show them his older brother's name. He touched the name and began to cry, and then he wrote a letter, which seemed to help. "I'm alright and doing fine," he wrote. "I will love you always."

The memorial is also a rallying point for demonstrators who come to Washington for a cause. A Medal of Honor became an offering in 1986 when a recipient renounced his medal, the nation's highest award for valor, and left it, with a letter to President Reagan, as "my strongest public expression of opposition to U.S. military policies in Central America."

The Wall has become a permanent site for those who keep alive the prisoners of war issue. When the memorial was built, about 1,150 names were marked with a cross to indicate that the person was missing in action or known to be a prisoner at the end of the war. For the kin of those declared missing in action, the Wall has become a rendezvous of rage and memory. To remind visitors of the unknown fate of these men, MIA-POW organizations keep vigil there.

Long before the Wall, people began wearing bracelets engraved with names of men declared missing in action. They were modeled after the plain brass bracelets given to U.S. servicemen by their Montagnard allies. These bracelets bound their wearers to the hope that the MIAs were still alive somewhere as prisoners of war. Over the years, more than 1,500 people have come to the memorial and relinquished their bracelets, apparently satisfied that the Wall is now custodian of their hopes.

Words and objects supporting or protesting many issues are left at the Wall, which has become a kind of bulletin board for whatever it is visitors need to communicate. Veterans of the Persian Gulf War came and left remembrances of their battles. But it remains, most of all, the place where people leave their thoughts about the Vietnam War. A few come again and again. One mother leaves a decorated Christmas tree every year. Another first brought her son a simple message. Then, year by year, she has brought more and more elaborate collages of words and Xeroxed photos. She is what the volunteers call a repeater.

The Wall draws many visitors on holidays, and year after year more Christmas cards and Easter baskets are added to the collection. So are Father's Day cards; an estimated four of every ten men on the Wall was a father—or about to become one—when he died. Some offerings are even for people not on the Wall. Gail walked along the Wall and left a letter three days after Jim died. "Although you did not die in Vietnam, a part of you remained there," she wrote. "You were too young to die. This walk was for you."

Others come to mark deaths from causes they attribute to the war, especially to the effects of the herbicide known as Agent Orange. A widow left a model of the Wall and a photograph of her husband, who died in 1985. "My son asked if his Dad's name would be carved on your beautiful face," she wrote. "I had to tell him that it would not, because he did not die *in* Vietnam but from *being* in Vietnam. … " Like so many who come to the Wall, she addresses it directly, as if within its stone lies an understanding that can come from no other source. This is a place where memories weave, where hearts heal. This is a place where people can feel what Lincoln called the mystic chords of memory, "stretching from every battle-field and patriot grave, to every living heart and hearthstone, all over this broad land. … "

RICHARD NIXON

Final Remarks at the White House

Always remember, others may hate you, but those who hate you don't win unless you hate them, and then you destroy yourself.

On June 17, 1972, members of President Richard Nixon's "Committee to Re-elect the President" were caught in an attempted burglary of the Democratic National Committee headquarters in the Watergate building in Washington, D.C. In early 1973, investigators linked the break-in and ensuing cover-up with top White House aides. President Nixon (1913-1994) claimed he had no knowledge of the break-in, took no part in the cover-up, and he promised a full investigation of the incident. After learning of the president's penchant for taping conversations in the White House, the Senate investigating committee requested certain recordings. Nixon refused, however, citing "executive privilege." He later offered to provide summaries of taped conversations, but Archibald Cox, who had been appointed to head the investigation, insisted on the actual tapes. Nixon had Cox fired, which led to the first move for impeachment.

Matters were further complicated in October 1973 when Vice President Spiro T. Agnew, who was under investigation for allegedly accepting bribes as governor of Maryland and vice president, resigned his office. Under the guidelines set by the Twenty-fifth Amendment, Nixon named House minority leader Gerald R. Ford vice president. In the months to come, the House Judiciary Committee issued subpoenas for the White House tapes, but Nixon again refused, only to submit when the committee recommended articles of impeachment. The tapes provided did not indicate that Nixon had any prior knowledge of the burglary, but showed he had approved a Watergate cover-up less than a week after the break-in. Republican congressmen warned the president that he faced probable impeachment by the House and removal from office by the Senate.

On August 8, 1974, President Nixon announced his resignation during a nationwide television appearance, bringing to an abrupt end one of the most active administrations of the twentieth century—"high purpose diminished by low politics." On August 9, he submitted his resignation to Congress and made his final remarks at the White House. Vice President Ford assumed the presidency, declaring, "Our long national nightmare is over. Our constitution works. Our great republic is a government of laws and not of men." One month later, seeking to move the nation forward, Ford granted the ex-president a pardon for any and all crimes he may have committed.

Members of the Cabinet, members of the White House Staff, all of our friends here:

I think the record should show that this is one of those spontaneous things that we always arrange whenever the President comes in to speak [laughter], and it will be so reported in the press, and we don't mind because they've got to call it as they see it.

But on our part, believe me, it is spontaneous.

You are here to say good-bye to us, and we don't have a good word for it in English—the best is au revoir. We'll see you again.

I just met with the members of the White House staff, you know, those who serve here in the White House day in and day out, and I asked them to do what I ask all of you to do to the extent that you can and, of course, are requested to do so: to serve our next President as you have served me and previous Presidents—because many of you have been here for many years—with devotion and dedication, because this office, great as it is, can only be as great as the men and women who work for and with the President.

This house, for example—I was thinking of it as we walked down this hall, and I was comparing it to some of the great houses of the world that I have been in. This isn't the biggest house. Many, and most, in even smaller countries, are much bigger. This isn't the finest house. Many in Europe, particularly, and in China, Asia, have paintings of great, great value, things that we just don't have here and, probably, will never have until we are 1,000 years old or older.

But this is the best house. It is the best house, because it has something far more important than numbers of people who serve, far more important than numbers of rooms or how big it is, far more important than numbers of magnificent pieces of art.

This house has a great heart, and that heart comes from those who serve. I was rather sorry they didn't come down. We said good-bye to them upstairs. But they are really great. And I recall after so many times I have made speeches, and some of them pretty tough, yet, I always come back, or after a hard day—and my days usually have run rather long—I would always get a lift from them, because I might be a little down but they always smiled.

And so it is with you. I look around here, and I see so many on this staff that, you know, I should have been by your offices and shaken hands, and I would love to have talked to you and found out how to run the world—everybody wants to tell the President what to do, and boy, he needs to be told many times—but I just haven't had the time. But I want you to know that each and every one of you, I know, is indispensable to this Government.

I am proud of this Cabinet. I am proud of all the members who have served in our Cabinet. I am proud of our sub-Cabinet. I am proud of our White House Staff. As I pointed out last night, sure, we have done some things wrong in this Administration, and the top man always takes the responsibility, and I have never ducked it. But I want to say one thing: We can be proud of it—5 1/2 years. No man or no woman came into this Administration and left it with more of this world's goods than when he came in. No man or no woman ever profited at the public expense or the public till. That tells something about you.

Mistakes, yes. But for personal gain, never. You did what you believed in. Sometimes right, sometimes wrong. And I only wish that I were a wealthy man—at the present time, I have got to find a way to pay my taxes—and if I were, I would like to recompense you for the sacrifices that all of you have made to serve in government.

But you are getting something in government—and I want you to tell this to your children, and I hope the Nation's children will hear it, too—something in government service that is far more important than money. It is a cause bigger than yourself. It is the cause of making this the greatest nation in the world, the leader of the world, because without our leadership, the world will know nothing but war, possibly starvation or worse, in the years ahead. With our leadership it will know peace, it will know plenty.

We have been generous, and we will be more generous in the future as we are able to. But most important, we must be strong here, strong in our hearts, strong in our souls, strong in our belief, and strong in our willingness to sacrifice, as you have been willing to sacrifice, in a pecuniary way, to serve in government.

There is something else I would like for you to tell your young people. You know, people often come in and say, "What will I tell my kids?" They look at government and see sort of a rugged life, and they see the mistakes that are made. They get the impression that everybody is here for the purpose of feathering his nest. That is why I made this earlier point—not in this Administration, not one single man or woman.

And I say to them, there are many fine careers. This country needs good farmers, good businessmen, good plumbers, good carpenters.

I remember my old man. I think that they would have called him sort of a little man, common man. He didn't consider himself that way. You know what he was? He was a streetcar motorman first, and then he was a farmer, and then he had a lemon ranch. It was the poorest lemon ranch in California, I can assure you. He sold it before they found oil on it. And then he was a grocer. But he was a great man, because he did his job, and every job counts up to the hilt, regardless of what happens.

Nobody will ever write a book, probably, about my mother. Well, I guess all of you would say this about your mother—my mother was a saint. And I think of her, two boys dying of tuberculosis, nursing four others in order that she could take care of my older brother for three years in Arizona, and seeing each of them die, and when they died, it was like one of her own. Yes, she will have no books written about her. But she was a saint.

Now, however, we look to the future. I had a little quote in the speech last night from T.R. As you know, I kind of like to read books. I am not educated, but I do read books—and the T.R. quote was a pretty good one. Here is another one I found as I was reading, my last night in the White House, and this quote is about a young man. He was a young lawyer in New York. He had married a beautiful girl, and they had a lovely daughter, and then suddenly she died, and this is what he wrote. This was in his diary.

He said, "She was beautiful in face and form and lovelier still in spirit. As a flower she grew and as a fair young flower she died. Her life had been always in the sunshine. There had never come to her a single great sorrow. None ever knew her who did not love and revere her for her bright and sunny temper and her saintly unselfishness. Fair, pure and joyous as a maiden, loving, tender and happy as a young wife. When she had just become a mother, when her life seemed to be just begun and when the years seemed so bright before her, then by a strange and terrible fate death came to her. And when my heart's dearest died, the light went from my life forever."

That was T.R. in his twenties. He thought the light had gone from his life forever—but he went on. And he not only became President but, as an ex-President, he served his country, always in the arena, tempestuous, strong, sometimes wrong, sometimes right, but he was a man.

And as I leave, let me say, that is an example I think all of us should remember. We think sometimes when things happen that don't go the right way; we think that when you don't pass the bar exam the first time—I happened to, but I was just lucky; I mean, my writing was so poor the bar examiner said, "We have just got to let the guy through." We think that when someone dear to us dies, we think that when we lose an election, we think that when we suffer a defeat that all is ended. We think, as T.R. said, that the light had left his life forever.

Not true. It is only a beginning, always. The young must know it; the old must know it. It must always sustain us, because the greatness comes not when things go always good for you, but the greatness comes when you are really tested, when you take some knocks, some disappointments, when sadness comes; because only if you've been in the deepest valley can you ever know how magnificent it is to be on the highest mountain.

And so I say to you on this occasion, as we leave, we leave proud of the people who have stood by us and worked for us and served this country.

We want you to be proud of what you have done. We want you to continue to serve in government, if that is your wish. Always give your best, never get discouraged, never be petty; always remember, others may hate you, but those who hate you don't win unless you hate them, and then you destroy yourself.

And so, we leave with high hopes, in good spirit, and with deep humility, and with very much gratefulness in our hearts. I can only say to each and every one of you, we come from many faiths, we pray perhaps to different gods—but really the same God in a sense—but I want to say for each and every one of you, not only will we always remember you, not only will we always be grateful to you but always you will be in our hearts and you will be in our prayers.

JOHNNY CASH

Ragged Old Flag

Born in Kingsland, Arkansas, John R. "Johnny" Cash (1932-2003) is one of the most celebrated artists in music history. An inductee into both the Country Music Hall of Fame and the Rock and Roll Hall of Fame, "The Man in Black" is known for such hits as "Folsom Prison Blues," "Ring of Fire," "I Walk the Line," "Delia's Gone," and "A Boy Named Sue."

The son of a World War I veteran, Johnny himself served in the U.S. Air Force during the early 1950s. "My daddy was proud of me for enlisting," wrote Cash. "Service in America's military had been a duty the Cash men performed for years. Maybe that's one reason why I love my country so much and believe in it so strongly. A lot of family blood has been shed for it. It's that American heritage which compelled me to write 'Ragged Old Flag' (1974)."

I walked through a county courthouse square,
On a park bench an old man was sitting there.
I said, "Your old courthouse is kinda run down,"
He said, "Naw, it'll do for our little town."
I said, "Your flagpole has leaned a bit,
And that's a RAGGED OLD FLAG you got hanging on it."

He said, "Have a seat," and I sat down.
"Is this the first time you've been to our little town?"
I said, "I think it is." He said, "I don't like to brag,
But we're kinda proud of that RAGGED OLD FLAG.

"You see, we got a little hole in that flag there
When Washington took it across the Delaware.
And it got powder-burned the night Francis Scott Key
Sat watching it writing 'Oh Say San You See.'
And it got a bad rip in New Orleans
With Packingham and Jackson tuggin' at its seams.

"And it almost fell at the Alamo
 Beside the Texas flag, but she waved on through.
 She got cut with a sword at Chancellorsville
 And she got cut again at Shiloh Hill.
 There was Robert E. Lee, Beauregard, and Bragg,
 And the south wind blew hard on that RAGGED OLD FLAG.

"On Flanders Field in World War I
 She got a big hole from a Bertha gun.
 She turned blood red in World War II.
 She hung limp and low by the time it was through.
 She was in Korea and Vietnam.
 She went where she was sent by her Uncle Sam.

"She waved from our ships upon the briny foam,
 And now they've about quit waving her back here at home.
 In her own good land here she's been abused—
 She's been burned, dishonored, denied and refused.

"And the government for which she stands
 is scandalized throughout the land.
 And she's getting threadbare and wearing thin,
 But she's in good shape for the shape she's in.
 'Cause she's been through the fire before
 and I believe she can take a whole lot more.

"So we raise her up every morning,
 Take her down every night.
 We don't let her touch the ground
 And we fold her up right.
 On second thought I do like to brag,
 'Cause I'm mighty proud of that RAGGED OLD FLAG."

* * *

President Ronald Reagan at work in the Oval Office.

The Shining City

RONALD REAGAN

First Inaugural Address

In this present crisis, government is not the solution to our problem; government is the problem.

Ronald Wilson Reagan (1911-2004), the son of a shoe salesman, was born into poverty in Tampico, Illinois. He graduated from Eureka College and worked as a radio announcer from 1932 to 1937, when he made a screen test for Warner Brothers and was signed to an acting contract. Between 1937 and 1964, he appeared in more than fifty films, served six terms as president of the Screen Actors Guild, and spent eight years as host of *The General Electric Theater*. Divorced from actress Jane Wyman in 1948, Reagan married actress Nancy Davis in 1952.

A registered Democrat, Reagan was active in politics and campaigned tirelessly for Harry Truman in 1948 and later for Republicans Dwight Eisenhower and Richard Nixon. In 1962, he switched parties and supported Arizona Senator Barry Goldwater's unsuccessful presidential campaign. Four years later, Reagan was elected to the first of two terms as governor of California. In July of 1980, he secured the Republican presidential nomination and easily defeated President Jimmy Carter in the general election, becoming the oldest man ever elected to the presidency.

In his first inaugural address, delivered on January 20, 1981, Reagan set forth the goals of his administration— less government regulation, lower taxes, increased military spending, a balanced federal budget, and a tougher stance towards the expansionist-minded Soviet Union. Just two months into his presidency, the ambitious Reagan agenda was nearly derailed when a mentally ill man shot the president and three other individuals, including Press Secretary James Brady. The attempt on Reagan's life was the ninth on an American president. With a bullet lodged in his left lung only a few inches from his heart, the grandfatherly president retained his sense of humor. "Honey, I forgot to duck," Reagan told his wife as he was wheeled into surgery. The president made a full recovery and the attempt on his life, as he later wrote, "allowed the pressure for change to build, so that when I was back in the fray I had momentum on my side."

... To a few of us here today this is a solemn and most momentous occasion, and yet in the history of our nation it is a commonplace occurrence. The orderly transfer of authority as called for in the Constitution routinely takes place, as it has for almost two centuries, and few of us stop to think how unique we really are. In the eyes of many in the world, this every-four-year-ceremony we accept as normal is nothing less than a miracle.

Mr. President, I want our fellow citizens to know how much you did to carry on this tradition. By your gracious cooperation in the transition process, you have shown a watching world that we are a united people pledged to maintaining a political system which guarantees individual liberty to a greater degree than any other, and I thank you and your people for all your help in maintaining the continuity which is the bulwark of our Republic.

The business of our nation goes forward. These United States are confronted with an economic affliction of great proportions. We suffer from the longest and one of the worst sustained inflations in our national history. It distorts our economic decisions, penalizes thrift, and crushes the struggling young and the fixed-income elderly alike. It threatens to shatter the lives of millions of our people.

Idle industries have cast workers into unemployment, human misery, and personal indignity. Those who do work are denied a fair return for their labor by a tax system which penalizes successful achievement and keeps us from maintaining full productivity.

But great as our tax burden is, it has not kept pace with public spending. For decades we have piled deficit upon deficit, mortgaging our future and our children's future for the temporary convenience of the present. To continue this long trend is to guarantee tremendous social, cultural, political, and economic upheavals.

You and I, as individuals, can, by borrowing, live beyond our means, but for only a limited period of time. Why, then, should we think that collectively, as a nation, we're not bound by that same limitation? We must act today in order to preserve tomorrow. And let there be no misunderstanding: We are going to begin to act, beginning today.

The economic ills we suffer have come upon us over several decades. They will not go away in days, weeks, or months, but they will go away. They will go away because we as Americans have the capacity now, as we've had in the past, to do whatever needs to be done to preserve this last and greatest bastion of freedom.

In this present crisis, government is not the solution to our problem; government is the problem. From time to time we've been tempted to believe that society has become too complex to be managed by self-rule, that government by an elite group is superior to government for, by, and of the people. Well, if no one among us is capable of governing himself, then who among us has the capacity to govern someone else? All of us together, in and out of government, must bear the burden. The solutions we seek must be equitable, with no one group singled out to pay a higher price.

We hear much of special interest groups. Well, our concern must be for a special interest group that has been too long neglected. It knows no sectional boundaries or ethnic and racial divisions, and it crosses political party lines. It is made up of men and women who raise our food, patrol our streets, man our mines and factories, teach our children, keep our homes, and heal us when we're sick—professionals, industrialists, shopkeepers, clerks, cabbies, and truck-drivers. They are, in short, "We the people," this breed called Americans.

Well, this administration's objective will be a healthy, vigorous, growing economy that provides equal opportunities for all Americans, with no barriers born of bigotry or discrimination. Putting America back to work means putting all Americans back to work. Ending inflation means freeing all Americans from the terror of runaway living costs. All must share in the productive work of this "new beginning," and all must share in the bounty of a revived economy. With the idealism and fair play which are the core of our system and our strength, we can have a strong and prosperous America, at peace with itself and the world.

So, as we begin, let us take inventory. We are a nation that has a government—not the other way around. And this makes us special among the nations of the earth. Our government has no power except that granted it by the people. It is time to check and reverse the growth of government, which shows signs of having grown beyond the consent of the governed.

It is my intention to curb the size and influence of the federal establishment and to demand recognition of the distinction between the powers granted to the federal government and those reserved to the states or to the people. All of us need to be reminded that the federal government did not create the states; the states created the federal government.

Now, so there will be no misunderstanding, it's not my intention to do away with government. It is rather to make it work—work with us, not over us; to stand by our side, not ride on our back. Government can and must provide opportunity, not smother it; foster productivity, not stifle it.

If we look to the answer as to why for so many years we achieved so much, prospered as no other people on earth, it was because here in this land we unleashed the energy and individual genius of man to a greater extent than has ever been done before. Freedom and the dignity of the individual have been more available and assured here than in any other place on earth. The price for this freedom at times has been high, but we have never been unwilling to pay that price.

It is no coincidence that our present troubles parallel and are proportionate to the intervention and intrusion in our lives that result from unnecessary and excessive growth of government. It is time for us to realize that we're too great a nation to limit ourselves to small dreams. We're not, as some would have us believe, doomed to an inevitable decline. I do not believe in a fate that will fall on us no matter what we do. I believe in a fate that will fall on us if we do nothing. So, with all the creative energy at our command, let us begin an era of national renewal. Let us renew our determination, our courage, and our strength. And let us renew our faith and our hope.

We have every right to dream heroic dreams. Those who say that we're in a time when there are not heroes, they just don't know where to look. You can see heroes every day going in and out of factory gates. Others, a handful in number, produce enough food to feed all of us and then the world beyond. You meet heroes across a counter, and they're on both sides of that counter. There are entrepreneurs, with faith in themselves and faith in an idea, who create new jobs, new wealth and opportunity. They're individuals and families whose taxes support the government and whose voluntary gifts support church, charity, culture, art, and education. Their patriotism is quiet, but deep. Their values sustain our national life.

Now, I have used the words "they" and "their" in speaking of these heroes. I could say "you" and "your" because I'm addressing the heroes of whom I speak—you, the citizens of this blessed land. Your dreams, your hopes, your goals are going to be the dreams, the hopes, and the goals of this administration, so help me God.

We shall reflect the compassion that is so much a part of your makeup. How can we love our country and not love our countrymen; and loving them, reach out a hand when they fall, heal them when they're sick, and provide opportunity to make them self-sufficient so they will be equal in fact and not just in theory?

Can we solve the problems confronting us? Well, the answer is an unequivocal and emphatic "yes." To paraphrase Winston Churchill, I did not take the oath I've just taken with the intention of presiding over the dissolution of the world's strongest economy.

In the days ahead I will propose removing the roadblocks that have slowed our economy and reduced productivity. Steps will be taken aimed at restoring the balance between the various levels of government. Progress may be slow, measured in inches and feet, not miles, but we will progress. It is time to reawaken this industrial giant, to get government back within its means, and to lighten our punitive tax burden. And these will be our first priorities, and on these principles there will be no compromise.

On the eve of our struggle for independence a man who might have been one of the greatest among the Founding Fathers, Dr. Joseph Warren, president of the Massachusetts Congress, said to his fellow Americans:

> "Our country is in danger, but not to be despaired of. … On you depend the fortunes of America. You are to decide the important questions upon which rests the happiness and the liberty of millions yet unborn. Act worthy of yourselves."

Well, I believe we, the Americans of today, are ready to act worthy of ourselves, ready to do what must be done to ensure happiness and liberty for ourselves, our children, and our children's children.

And as we renew ourselves here in our own land, we will be seen as having greater strength throughout the world. We will again be the exemplar of freedom and a beacon of hope for those who do not now have freedom.

To those neighbors and allies who share our freedom, we will strengthen our historic ties and assure them of our support and firm commitment. We will match loyalty with loyalty. We will strive for mutually beneficial relations. We will not use our friendship to impose on their sovereignty, for our own sovereignty is not for sale.

As for the enemies of freedom, those who are potential adversaries, they will be reminded that peace is the highest aspiration of the American people. We will negotiate for it, sacrifice for it; we will not surrender for it, now or ever.

Our forbearance should never be misunderstood. Our reluctance for conflict should not be misjudged as a failure of will. When action is required to preserve our national security, we will act. We will maintain sufficient strength to prevail if need be, knowing that if we do so we have the best chance of never having to use that strength.

Above all, we must realize that no arsenal or no weapon in the arsenals of the world is so formidable as the will and moral courage of free men and women. It is a weapon our adversaries in today's world do not have. It is a weapon that we as Americans do have. Let that be understood by those who practice terrorism and prey upon their neighbors.

I'm told that tens of thousands of prayer meetings are being held on this day, and for that I'm deeply grateful. We are a nation under God, and I believe God intended for us to be free. It would be fitting and good, I think, if on each Inaugural Day in future years it should be declared a day of prayer.

This is the first time in our history that this ceremony has been held, as you've been told, on this West Front of the Capitol. Standing here, one faces a magnificent vista, opening up on this city's special beauty and history. At the end of this open mall are those shrines to the giants on whose shoulders we stand.

Directly in front of me, the monument to a monumental man, George Washington, father of our country. A man of humility who came to greatness reluctantly. He led America out of revolutionary victory into infant nationhood. Off to one side, the stately memorial to Thomas Jefferson. The Declaration of Independence flames with his eloquence.

And then, beyond the Reflecting Pool, the dignified columns of the Lincoln Memorial. Whoever would understand in his heart the meaning of America will find it in the life of Abraham Lincoln.

Beyond those monuments to heroism is the Potomac River, and on the far shore the sloping hills of Arlington National Cemetery, with its row upon row of simple white markers bearing crosses or Stars of David. They add up to only a tiny fraction of the price that has been paid for our freedom.

Each one of those markers is a monument to the kind of hero I spoke of earlier. Their lives ended in places called Belleau Wood, the Argonne, Omaha Beach, Salerno, and halfway around the world on Guadalcanal, Tarawa, Pork Chop Hill, the Chosin Reservoir, and in a hundred rice paddies and jungles of a place called Vietnam.

Under one such marker lies a young man, Martin Treptow, who left his job in a small town barbershop in 1917 to go to France with the famed Rainbow Division. There, on the western front, he was killed trying to carry a message between battalions under heavy artillery fire.

We're told that on his body was found a diary. On the flyleaf under the heading, "My Pledge," he had written these words:

"America must win this war. Therefore I will work, I will save, I will sacrifice, I will endure, I will fight cheerfully and do my utmost, as if the issue of the whole struggle depended on me alone."

The crisis we are facing today does not require of us the kind of sacrifice that Martin Treptow and so many thousands of others were called upon to make. It does require, however, our best effort, and our willingness to believe in ourselves and to believe in our capacity to perform great deeds; to believe that together with God's help we can and will resolve the problems which now confront us.

And after all, why shouldn't we believe that? We are Americans.

MILTON AND ROSE FRIEDMAN

Free to Choose

Economic freedom is an essential requisite for political freedom.

Born in New York City, Milton Friedman (1912-2006) earned his Bachelor of Arts degree from Rutgers University, his AM from Chicago, and his PhD from Columbia. A recipient of the Nobel Prize for Economic Science and the author of such books as *An Economist's Protest, Dollars and Deficits*, and *Inflation: Causes and Consequences*, Friedman was perhaps the best-known economist in the world. An opponent of government intervention in the economy and adamant supporter of Adam Smith's economic philosophies, his theories directly influenced the policies of President Ronald Reagan, who presided over one of the greatest economic booms in history while describing government's often counterproductive view of the economy thusly: "If it moves, tax it. If it keeps moving, regulate it. And if it stops moving, subsidize it."

Rose Friedman (1910-2009), wife of Milton and herself an economist, collaborated with her husband on several books, including *Capitalism and Freedom, Tyranny of the Status Quo, Two Lucky People: Memoirs*, and *Free to Choose: A Personal Statement* (1980), excerpted here.

Ever since the first settlement of Europeans in the New World—at Jamestown in 1607 and at Plymouth in 1620—America has been a magnet for people seeking adventure, fleeing from tyranny, or simply trying to make a better life for themselves and their children.

An initial trickle swelled after the American Revolution and the establishment of the United States of America and became a flood in the nineteenth century, when millions of people streamed across the Atlantic, and a smaller number across the Pacific, driven by misery and tyranny, and attracted by the promise of freedom and affluence.

When they arrived, they did not find streets paved with gold; they did not find an easy life. They did find freedom

and an opportunity to make the most of their talents. Through hard work, ingenuity, thrift, and luck, most of them succeeded in realizing enough of their hopes and dreams to encourage friends and relatives to join them.

The story of the United States is the story of an economic miracle and a political miracle that was made possible by the translation into practice of two sets of ideas—both, by a curious coincidence, formulated in documents published in the same year, 1776.

One set of ideas was embodied in *The Wealth of Nations*, the masterpiece that established the Scotsman Adam Smith as the father of modern economics. It analyzed the way in which a market system could combine the freedom of individuals to pursue their own objectives with the extensive cooperation and collaboration needed in the economic field to produce our food, our clothing, our housing. Adam Smith's key insight was that both parties to an exchange can benefit and that, so *long as cooperation is strictly voluntary,* no exchange will take place unless both parties do benefit. No external force, no coercion, no violation of freedom is necessary to produce cooperation among individuals all of whom can benefit. That is why, as Adam Smith put it, an individual who "intends only his own gain" is "led by an invisible hand to promote an end which was no part of his intention. Nor is it always the worse for the society that it was no part of it. By pursuing his own interest he frequently promotes that of the society more effectually than when he really intends to promote it. I have never known much good done by those who affected to trade for the public good."

The second set of ideas was embodied in the Declaration of Independence, drafted by Thomas Jefferson to express the general sense of his fellow countrymen. It proclaimed a new nation, the first in history established on the principle that every person is entitled to pursue his own values: "We hold these truths to be self-evident, that all men are created equal, that they are endowed by their Creator with certain unalienable Rights; that among these are Life, Liberty, and the pursuit of Happiness."

Or, as stated in more extreme and unqualified form nearly a century later by John Stuart Mill:

The sole end for which mankind are warranted, individually or collectively, in interfering with the liberty of action of any of their number, is self protection. … [T]he only purpose for which power can be rightfully exercised over any member of a civilized community, against his will, is to prevent harm to others. His own good, either physical or moral, is not a sufficient warrant. … The only part of the conduct of any one, for which he is amenable to society, is that which concerns others. In the part which merely concerns himself, his independence is, of right, absolute. Over himself, over his own body and mind, the individual is sovereign.

Much of the history of the United States revolves about the attempt to translate the principles of the Declaration of Independence into practice—from the struggle over slavery, finally settled by a bloody civil war, to the subsequent attempt to promote equality of opportunity, to the more recent attempt to achieve equality of results.

Economic freedom is an essential requisite for political freedom. By enabling people to cooperate with one another without coercion or central direction, it reduces the area over which political power is exercised. In addition, by dispersing power, the free market provides an offset to whatever concentration of political power may arise. The combination of economic and political *power* in the same hands is a sure recipe for tyranny.

The combination of economic and political *freedom* produced a golden age in both Great Britain and the United States in the nineteenth century. The United States prospered even more than Britain. It started with a clean slate: fewer vestiges of class and status; fewer government restraints; a more fertile field for energy, drive, and innovation; and an empty continent to conquer.

The fecundity of freedom is demonstrated most dramatically and clearly in agriculture. When the Declaration of Independence was enacted, fewer than 3 million persons of European and African origin (i.e., omitting the native Indians) occupied a narrow fringe along the eastern coast. Agriculture was the main economic activity. It took nineteen out of twenty workers to feed the country's inhabitants and provide a surplus for export in exchange for foreign goods. Today it takes fewer than one out of twenty workers to feed the 220 million inhabitants and provide a surplus that makes the United States the largest single exporter of food in the world.

What produced this miracle? Clearly not central direction by government—nations like Russia and its satellites, mainland China, Yugoslavia, and India that today rely on central direction employ from one-quarter to one-half of their workers in agriculture, yet frequently rely on U.S. agriculture to avoid mass starvation. During most of the period of rapid agricultural expansion in the United States the government played a negligible role. Land was made available—but it was land that had been unproductive before. After the middle of the nineteenth century land-grant colleges were established, and they disseminated information and technology through governmentally financed extension services. Unquestionably, however, the main source of the agricultural revolution was private initiative operating in a free market open to all—the shame of slavery only excepted. And the most rapid growth came after slavery was abolished. The millions of immigrants from all over the world were free to work for themselves, as independent farmers or businessmen, or to work for others, at terms mutually agreed. They were free to experiment with new techniques—at their risk if the experiment failed, and to their profit if it succeeded. They got little assistance from government. Even more important, they encountered little interference from government. ...

Smith and Jefferson alike had seen concentrated government power as a great danger to the ordinary man; they saw the protection of the citizen against the tyranny of government as the perpetual need. ... To Smith and Jefferson, government's role was as an umpire, not a participant. Jefferson's ideal, as he expressed it in his first inaugural address (1801), was "[a] wise and frugal government, which shall restrain men from injuring one another, which shall leave them otherwise free to regulate their own pursuits of industry and improvement."

Ironically, the very success of economic and political freedom reduced its appeal to later thinkers. The narrowly limited government of the late nineteenth century possessed little concentrated power that endangered the ordinary man. The other side of that coin was that it possessed little power that would enable good people to do good. And in an imperfect world there were still many evils. Indeed, the very progress of society made the residual evils seem all the more objectionable. As always, people took the favorable developments for granted. They forgot the danger to freedom from a strong government. Instead, they were attracted by the good that a stronger government could achieve—if only government power were in the "right" hands.

These ideas began to influence government policy in Great Britain by the beginning of the twentieth century. They gained increasing acceptance among intellectuals in the United States but had little effect on government policy until the Great Depression of the early 1930s. ... Government's responsibility for the depression was not recognized—either then or now. Instead, the depression was widely interpreted as a failure of free market capitalism. That myth led the public to join the intellectuals in a changed view of the relative responsibilities of individuals and government. Emphasis on the responsibility of the individual for his own fate was replaced by emphasis on the individual as a pawn buffeted by forces beyond his control. The view that government's role is to serve as an umpire to prevent individuals from coercing one another was replaced by the view that government's role is to serve as a parent charged with the duty of coercing some to aid others.

These views have dominated developments in the United States during the past half-century. They have led to a growth in government at all levels, as well as to a transfer of power from local government and local control to central government and central control. The government has increasingly undertaken the task of taking from some to give to others in the name of security and equality. One government policy after another has been set up to "regulate" our "pursuits of industry and improvement," standing Jefferson's dictum on its head. ...

The experience of recent years—slowing growth and declining productivity—raises a doubt whether private ingenuity can continue to overcome the deadening effects of government control if we continue to grant ever more power to government, to authorize a "new class" of civil servants to spend ever larger fractions of our income supposedly on our behalf. Sooner or later—and perhaps sooner than many of us expect—an ever bigger government would destroy both the prosperity that we owe to the free market and the human freedom proclaimed so eloquently in the Declaration of Independence.

We have not yet reached the point of no return. We are still free as a people to choose whether we shall continue speeding down the "road to serfdom," as Friedrich Hayek entitled his profound and influential book, or whether we shall set tighter limits on government and rely more heavily on voluntary cooperation among free individuals to achieve our several objectives. Will our golden age come to an end in a relapse into the tyranny and misery that has always been, and remains today, the state of most of mankind? Or shall we have the wisdom, the foresight, and the courage to change our course, to learn from experience, and to benefit from a "rebirth of freedom"? ...

A Nation at Risk

If an unfriendly foreign power had attempted to impose on America the mediocre educational performance that exists today, we might well have viewed it as an act of war.

In 1983, the National Commission on Excellence in Education released a report titled *A Nation at Risk*. Appointed by Secretary of Education Terrell Bell (1921-1996), the commission sought to call public attention to declining academic standards. Its findings, which were featured on national television and in the daily press, caused many state legislatures and local school boards to take action to improve their schools. Despite a flurry of activity, however, classroom conditions steadily worsened while the overall curriculum was consistently "dumbed down." Noting the continued poor performance of American students and the resulting record numbers of children being home schooled, Ron Robinson, president of the Young America's Foundation, writes: "America's public schools and colleges have relinquished their role of defending and transmitting our history, religious heritage, and culture. Schools are hotbeds of violence, disrespect and failure. … Most of us know there is a problem, but we are tempted to underestimate how bad or how damaging it is. Abraham Lincoln expressed it best, 'The philosophy of the school room in one generation will be the philosophy of government in the next.'"

Our nation is at risk. Our once unchallenged preeminence in commerce, industry, science, and technological innovation is being overtaken by competitors throughout the world. This report is concerned with only one of the many causes and dimensions of the problem, but it is the one that undergirds American prosperity, security, and civility. We report to the American people that while we can take justifiable pride in what our schools and colleges have historically accomplished and contributed to the United States and the well-being of its people, the educational foundations of our society are presently being eroded by a rising tide of mediocrity that threatens our very future as a Nation and a people. What was unimaginable a generation ago has begun to occur—others are matching and surpassing our educational attainments.

If an unfriendly foreign power had attempted to impose on America the mediocre educational performance that exists today, we might well have viewed it as an act of war. As it stands, we have allowed this to happen to ourselves. We have even squandered the gains in student achievement made in the wake of the Sputnik challenge. Moreover, we have dismantled essential support systems which helped make those gains possible. We have, in effect, been committing an act of unthinking, unilateral educational disarmament.

Our society and its educational institutions seem to have lost sight of the basic purposes of schooling, and of the high expectations and disciplined effort needed to attain them.

This report, the result of 18 months of study, seeks to generate reform of our educational system in fundamental ways and to renew the Nation's commitment to schools and colleges of high quality throughout the length and breadth of our land.

That we have compromised this commitment is, upon reflection, hardly surprising, given the multitude of often conflicting demands we have placed on our Nation's schools and colleges. They are routinely called on to provide solutions to personal, social, and political problems that the home and other institutions either will not or cannot resolve. We must understand that these demands on our schools and colleges often exact an educational cost as well as a financial one. …

History is not kind to idlers. The time is long past when America's destiny was assured simply by an abundance of national resources and inexhaustible human enthusiasm, and by our relative isolation from the malignant problems of older civilizations. The world is indeed one global village. We live among determined, well-educated, and strongly motivated competitors. We compete with them for international standing and markets, not only with products but also with the ideas of our laboratories and neighborhood workshops. America's position in the world may once have been reasonably secure with only a few exceptionally well-trained men and women. It is no longer.

The risk is not only that the Japanese make automobiles more efficiently than Americans and have government subsidies for development and export. It is not just that the South Koreans recently built the world's most efficient steel mill, or that American machine tools, once the pride of the world, are being displaced by German products. It is also that these developments signify a redistribution of trained capability throughout the globe. Knowledge, learning, information, and skilled intelligence are the new raw materials of international commerce and are today spreading throughout the world as vigorously as miracle drugs, synthetic fertilizers, and blue jeans did earlier. If only to keep and improve on the slim competitive edge we still retain in world markets, we must dedicate ourselves to the reform of our educational system for the benefit of all—old and young alike, affluent and poor, majority and minority. Learning is the indispensable investment required for success in the "information age" we are entering.

Our concern, however, goes well beyond matters such as industry and commerce. It also includes the intellectual, moral, and spiritual strengths of our people which knit together the very fabric of our society. The people of the United States need to know that individuals in our society who do not possess the levels of skill, literacy, and training essential to this new era will be effectively disenfranchised, not simply from the material rewards that accompany competent performance, but also from the chance to participate fully in our national life. A high level of shared education is essential to a free, democratic society and to the fostering of a common culture, especially in a country that prides itself on pluralism and individual freedom.

For our country to function, citizens must be able to reach some common understandings on complex issues, often on short notice and on the basis of conflicting or incomplete evidence. Education helps form these common understandings, a point Thomas Jefferson made long ago in his justly famous dictum: "I know no safe depository of the ultimate powers of the society but the people themselves; and if we think them not enlightened enough to exercise their control with a wholesome discretion, the remedy is not to take it from them but to inform their discretion." ...

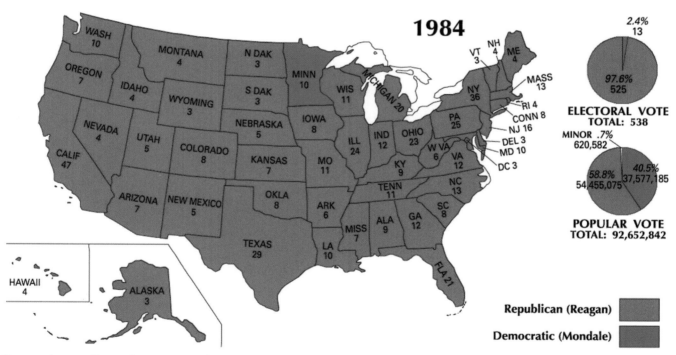

"Are you better off now than you were four years ago?" Ronald Reagan asked that question of the American people in the election of 1980, winning a landslide victory over incumbent President Jimmy Carter. Confidently posing the same question in his 1984 re-election effort against former Vice President Walter Mondale, Reagan carried 49 of the 50 states, becoming only the second presidential candidate to do so after Richard Nixon's victory in the 1972 presidential election. Mondale's only electoral votes came from the District of Columbia, long considered a Democratic guarantee, and his home state of Minnesota—which he won by fewer than 4,000 votes. Reagan's 525 electoral votes (out of 538) is the highest total ever received by a presidential candidate.

RONALD REAGAN

Speech on the *Challenger* Disaster

We will never forget them, nor the last time we saw them, this morning, as they prepared for the journey and waved goodbye and "slipped the surly bonds of earth" to "touch the face of God."

On January 28, 1986, the United States suffered the worst disaster in the history of its space program. As millions of Americans, including the nation's schoolchildren, watched on live television, the space shuttle *Challenger* exploded approximately seventy seconds after lift-off. Its entire seven member crew was killed. Among the dead—New Hampshire schoolteacher Christa McAuliffe, who was to be the first civilian in space. Before this disaster, NASA's first high-profile loss of life took place in 1967 when three astronauts were killed in a fire on the launching pad during the original Apollo mission. With Apollo 11's successful landing on the moon, people soon forgot about this tragedy and faith in NASA was quickly renewed. The *Challenger* disaster, however, set the U.S. space program back almost three years. Space exploration did not resume until September 29, 1988, when the space shuttle *Discovery* blasted off from Cape Canaveral, Florida.

Speaking from the Oval Office—and borrowing lines from the poem "High Flight" by John Gillespie Magee, Jr., a young American pilot who died defending England from the German Luftwaffe prior to America's involvement in World War II—Reagan sought to comfort a shocked and grieving nation. Days later, the president attended a memorial service in Houston where Jane Smith, wife of crewman Michael Smith, shared with the President a note her husband had written before the flight and left on their bedroom dresser. Quoting H. G. Wells, the note read: "For man, there is no rest and no ending. He must go on—conquest beyond conquest; This little planet, and its winds and ways, and all the laws of mind and matter that restrain him. Then the planets about him, and, at last out across the immensity to the stars. And when he has conquered all the depths of space and all the mysteries of time ... still he will be but beginning."

NASA went on to successfully complete eighty-seven space shuttle missions until 2003, when tragedy again struck the space program. On February 1, 2003, the space shuttle *Columbia* disintegrated over Texas during re-entry into the Earth's atmosphere, killing all seven crew members.

... Nineteen years ago, almost to the day, we lost three astronauts in a terrible accident on the ground. But, we've never lost an astronaut in flight; we've never had a tragedy like this. And perhaps we've forgotten the courage it took for the crew of the shuttle; but they, the *Challenger* Seven, were aware of the dangers, but overcame them and did their jobs brilliantly. We mourn seven heroes: Michael Smith, Dick Scobee, Judith Resnik, Ronald McNair, Ellison Onizuka, Gregory Jarvis, and Christa McAuliffe. We mourn their loss as a nation together.

For the families of the seven, we cannot bear, as you do, the full impact of this tragedy. But we feel the loss, and we're thinking about you so very much. Your loved ones were daring and brave, and they had that special grace, that special spirit that says, "Give me a challenge and I'll meet it with joy." They had a hunger to explore the universe and discover its truths. They wished to serve, and they did. They served all of us.

We've grown used to wonders in this century. It's hard to dazzle us. But for twenty-five years the United States space program has been doing just that. We've grown used to the idea of space, and perhaps we forget that we've only just begun. We're still pioneers. They, the members of the *Challenger* crew, were pioneers.

And I want to say something to the schoolchildren of America who were watching the live coverage of the shuttle's takeoff. I know it is hard to understand, but sometimes painful things like this happen. It's all part of the process of exploration and discovery. It's all part of taking a chance and expanding man's horizons. The future doesn't belong to the fainthearted; it belongs to the brave. The *Challenger* crew was pulling us into the future, and we'll continue to follow them. ...

There's a coincidence today. On this day 390 years ago, the great explorer Sir Francis Drake died aboard ship off the coast of Panama. In his lifetime the great frontiers were the oceans, and a historian later said, "He lived by the sea, died on it, and was buried in it." Well, today we can say of the *Challenger* crew: Their dedication was, like Drake's, complete.

The crew of the space shuttle *Challenger* honored us by the manner in which they lived their lives. We will never forget them, nor the last time we saw them, this morning, as they prepared for the journey and waved goodbye and "slipped the surly bonds of earth" to "touch the face of God."

Apollo I *prime crew: Edward H. White II, Virgil I. "Gus" Grissom, and Roger Bruce Chaffee, killed January 27, 1967, when fire swept through their command module.*

Crew of Space Shuttle Challenger *(STS-51L), eulogized by President Reagan: (L-R front row) Michael J. Smith, Francis R. Scobee, Ronald E. McNair and (L-R rear) Ellison Onizuka, Sharon Christa McAuliffe, Gregory Jarvis, and Judith A. Resnik.*

Crew of Space Shuttle Columbia *(STS-107), killed February 1, 2003: (L-R) David M. Brown, Rick D. Husband, Laurel Clark, Kalpana Chawla, Michael P. Anderson, William C. McCool, and Israeli astronaut Ilan Ramon.*

RONALD REAGAN

Brandenburg Gate Speech

Mr. Gorbachev, open this gate! Mr. Gorbachev, tear down this wall!

On June 12, 1987, President Reagan delivered the following address at the Brandenburg Gate in West Berlin, Germany. Commemorating the 750th anniversary of Berlin, Reagan articulated his abhorrence for the Berlin Wall and the totalitarian system it symbolized.

On November 9, 1989, following the erosion of political power in the pro-Soviet governments of Poland and Hungary, the East German government announced that all citizens of the German Democratic Republic could visit West Germany and West Berlin. Massive crowds of East Germans passed through or climbed over the wall, met by their countrymen on the other side in a celebratory atmosphere. The wall was dismantled in the coming weeks—first by souvenir hunters and, ultimately, with heavy equipment. The tearing down of the Berlin Wall paved the way for German reunification, which was formally achieved on October 3, 1990. The collapse of the Berlin Wall foreshadowed the political and economic collapse of the Soviet Union two years later.

... Twenty-four years ago, President John F. Kennedy visited Berlin, speaking to the people of this city and the world at the city hall. Well, since then two other presidents have come, each in his turn, to Berlin. And today I, myself, make my second visit to your city.

We come to Berlin, we American Presidents, because it's our duty to speak, in this place of freedom. But I must confess, we're drawn here by other things as well: by the feeling of history in this city, more than five hundred years older than our own nation; by the beauty of the

Grunewald and the Tiergarten; most of all, by your courage and determination. Perhaps the composer, Paul Lance, understood something about American Presidents. You see, like so many Presidents before me, I come here today because wherever I go, whatever I do: "Ich hab noch einen Koffer in Berlin." [I still have a suitcase in Berlin.]

Our gathering today is being broadcast throughout Western Europe and North America. I understand that it is being seen and heard as well in the East. To those listening throughout Eastern Europe, I extend my warmest greetings and the good will of the American people. To those listening in East Berlin, a special word: Although I cannot be with you, I address my remarks to you just as surely as to those standing here before me. For I join you, as I join your fellow countrymen in the West, in this firm, this unalterable belief: Es gibt nur ein Berlin. [There is only one Berlin.]

Behind me stands a wall that encircles the free sectors of this city, part of a vast system of barriers that divides the entire continent of Europe. From the Baltic, south, those barriers cut across Germany in a gash of barbed wire, concrete, dog runs, and guard towers. Farther south, there may be no visible, no obvious wall. But there remain armed guards and checkpoints all the same—still a restriction on the right to travel, still an instrument to impose upon ordinary men and women the will of a totalitarian state. Yet it is here in Berlin where the wall emerges most clearly; here, cutting across your city, where the news photo and the television screen have imprinted this brutal division of a continent upon the mind of the world. Standing before the Brandenburg Gate, every man is a German, separated from his fellow men. Every man is a Berliner, forced to look upon a scar.

President von Weizsacker has said: "The German question is open as long as the Brandenburg Gate is closed." Today I say: As long as this gate is closed, as long as this scar of a wall is permitted to stand, it is not the German question alone that remains open, but the question of freedom for all mankind. Yet I do not come here to lament. For I find in Berlin a message of hope, even in the shadow of this wall, a message of triumph.

In this season of spring in 1945, the people of Berlin emerged from their air-raid shelters to find devastation. Thousands of miles away, the people of the United States reached out to help. And in 1947, Secretary of State—as you've been told—George Marshall announced the creation of what would become known as the Marshall plan. Speaking precisely forty years ago this month, he said: "Our policy is directed not against any country or doctrine, but against hunger, poverty, desperation, and chaos."

In the Reichstag a few moments ago, I saw a display commemorating this 40th anniversary of the Marshall plan. I was struck by the sign on a burnt-out, gutted structure that was being rebuilt. I understand that Berliners of my own generation can remember seeing signs like it dotted throughout the Western sectors of the city. The sign read simply: "The Marshall plan is helping here to strengthen the free world." A strong, free world in the West, that dream became real. Japan rose from ruin to become an economic giant. Italy, France, Belgium—virtually every nation in Western Europe saw political and economic rebirth; the European Community was founded.

In West Germany and here in Berlin, there took place an economic miracle, the *Wirtschaftswunder*. Adenauer, Erhard, Reuter, and other leaders understood the practical importance of liberty—that just as truth can flourish only when the journalist is given freedom of speech, so prosperity can come about only when the farmer and businessman enjoy economic freedom. The German leaders reduced tariffs, expanded free trade, lowered taxes. From 1950 to 1960 alone, the standard of living in West Germany and Berlin doubled.

Where four decades ago there was rubble, today in West Berlin there is the greatest industrial output of any city in Germany—busy office blocks, fine homes and apartments, proud avenues, and the spreading lawns of park land. Where a city's culture seemed to have been destroyed, today there are two great universities, orchestras and an opera, countless theaters, and museums. Where there was want, today there's abundance—food, clothing, automobiles—the wonderful goods of the Ku'damm. From devastation, from utter ruin, you Berliners have, in freedom, rebuilt a city that once again ranks as one of the greatest on Earth. The Soviets may have had other plans. But, my friends, there were a few things the Soviets didn't count on—*Berliner herz, Berliner humor, ja, und Berliner schnauze.* [Berliner heart, Berliner humor, yes, and a Berliner *Schnauze.*]

In the 1950s, Khrushchev predicted: "We will bury you." But in the West today, we see a free world that has achieved a level of prosperity and well-being unprecedented in all human history. In the Communist world, we see failure, technological backwardness, declining standards of health, even want of the most basic kind—too little food.

Even today, the Soviet Union still cannot feed itself. After these four decades, then, there stands before the entire world one great and inescapable conclusion: Freedom leads to prosperity. Freedom replaces the ancient hatreds among the nations with comity and peace. Freedom is the victor.

And now the Soviets themselves may, in a limited way, be coming to understand the importance of freedom. We hear much from Moscow about a new policy of reform and openness. Some political prisoners have been released. Certain foreign news broadcasts are no longer being jammed. Some economic enterprises have been permitted to operate with greater freedom from state control.

Are these the beginnings of profound changes in the Soviet state? Or are they token gestures, intended to raise false hopes in the West, or to strengthen the Soviet system without changing it? We welcome change and openness; for we believe that freedom and security go together, that the advance of human liberty can only strengthen the cause of world peace. There is one sign the Soviets can make that would be unmistakable, that would advance dramatically the cause of freedom and peace.

General Secretary Gorbachev, if you seek peace, if you seek prosperity for the Soviet Union and Eastern Europe, if you seek liberalization: Come here to this gate! Mr. Gorbachev, open this gate! Mr. Gorbachev, tear down this wall!

I understand the fear of war and the pain of division that afflict this continent, and I pledge to you my country's efforts to help overcome these burdens. To be sure, we in the West must resist Soviet expansion. So we must maintain defenses of unassailable strength. Yet we seek peace; so we must strive to reduce arms on both sides.

Beginning ten years ago, the Soviets challenged the Western alliance with a grave new threat, hundreds of new and more deadly SS-20 nuclear missiles, capable of striking every capital in Europe. The Western alliance responded by committing itself to a counterdeployment unless the Soviets agreed to negotiate a better solution; namely, the elimination of such weapons on both sides. For many months, the Soviets refused to bargain in earnestness. As the alliance, in turn, prepared to go forward with its counterdeployment, there were difficult days—days of protests like those during my 1982 visit to this city—and the Soviets later walked away from the table.

But through it all, the alliance held firm. And I invite those who protested then—I invite those who protest today—to mark this fact: Because we remained strong, the Soviets came back to the table. And because we remained strong, today we have within reach the possibility, not merely of limiting the growth of arms, but of eliminating, for the first time, an entire class of nuclear weapons from the face of the Earth.

As I speak, NATO ministers are meeting in Iceland to review the progress of our proposals for eliminating these weapons. At the talks in Geneva, we have also proposed deep cuts in strategic offensive weapons. And the Western allies have likewise made far-reaching proposals to reduce the danger of conventional war and to place a total ban on chemical weapons.

While we pursue these arms reductions, I pledge to you that we will maintain the capacity to deter Soviet aggression at any level at which it might occur. And in cooperation with many of our allies, the United States is pursuing the Strategic Defense Initiative—research to base deterrence not on the threat of offensive retaliation, but on defenses that truly defend; on systems, in short, that will not target populations, but shield them. By these means we seek to increase the safety of Europe and all the world. But we must remember a crucial fact: East and West do not mistrust each other because we are armed; we are armed because we mistrust each other. And our differences are not about weapons but about liberty. When President Kennedy spoke at the City Hall those twenty-four years ago, freedom was encircled; Berlin was under siege. And today, despite all the pressures upon this city, Berlin stands secure in its liberty. And freedom itself is transforming the globe.

In the Philippines, in South and Central America, democracy has been given a rebirth. Throughout the Pacific, free markets are working miracle after miracle of economic growth. In the industrialized nations a technological revolution is taking place—a revolution marked by rapid, dramatic advances in computers and telecommunications.

In Europe, only one nation and those it controls refuse to join the community of freedom. Yet in this age of redoubled economic growth, of information and innovation, the Soviet Union faces a choice: It must make fundamental changes, or it will become obsolete. …

You Berliners have built a great city. You've done so in spite of threats—the Soviet attempts to impose the East-mark, the blockade. Today the city thrives in spite of the challenges implicit in the very presence of this wall. What keeps you here? Certainly there's a great deal to be said for your fortitude, for your defiant courage. But I believe there's something deeper, something that involves Berlin's whole look and feel and way of life—not mere sentiment. No one could live long in Berlin without being completely disabused of illusions. Something, instead, that has seen the difficulties of life in Berlin but chose to accept them, that continues to build this good and proud city in contrast to a surrounding totalitarian presence, that refuses to release human energies or aspirations, something that speaks with a powerful voice of affirmation, that says "yes" to this city, yes to the future, yes to freedom. In a word, I would submit that what keeps you in Berlin is "love"—love both profound and abiding.

Perhaps this gets to the root of the matter, to the most fundamental distinction of all between East and West. The totalitarian world produces backwardness because it does such violence to the spirit, thwarting the human impulse to create, to enjoy, to worship. The totalitarian world finds even symbols of love and of worship an affront.

Years ago, before the East Germans began rebuilding their churches, they erected a secular structure: the television tower at Alexander Platz. Virtually ever since, the authorities have been working to correct what they view as the tower's one major flaw, treating the glass sphere at the top with paints and chemicals of every kind. Yet even today when the Sun strikes that sphere—that sphere that towers over all Berlin—the light makes the sign of the cross. There in Berlin, like the city itself, symbols of love, symbols of worship, cannot be suppressed.

As I looked out a moment ago from the Reichstag, that embodiment of German unity, I noticed words crudely spray-painted upon the wall, perhaps by a young Berliner, "This wall will fall. Beliefs become reality." Yes, across Europe, this wall will fall. For it cannot withstand faith; it cannot withstand truth. The wall cannot withstand freedom. ...

GEORGE J. MITCHELL

The Iran-Contra Hearings

Although He is regularly asked to do so, God does not take sides in American politics.

The major foreign policy challenge of Reagan's second administration was the so-called "Iran-Contra scandal," resulting from the illegal sale of armaments to Iran, an enemy of the United States since the 1979 Iranian Revolution and subsequent seizure of the U.S. Embassy in Tehran. This arms sale, initiated by the National Security Council, was made specifically to Iran in exchange for an Iranian promise to help secure the release of American hostages being held by pro-Iranian terrorists. The proceeds from that sale were then used to fund the anti-Communist *Contras* rebelling against the Communist *Sandinistas*, who had taken control of the Nicaraguan government in 1979 and established a dictatorship. The clandestine Iran-Contra scheme came about after the U.S. Congress eliminated all funding for the Nicaraguan freedom fighters in 1984.

The point man for the operation was Marine Lieutenant Colonel Oliver North. In testifying before Congress in 1987, Colonel North defended his actions as those of a patriotic soldier motivated by a love of God and country. On July 13, 1987, Senator George Mitchell, Democrat from Maine, rendered his objections to the way in which Colonel North framed the debate and provided a defense of the rule of law.

The eight-year, $100-million investigation of Iran-Contra resulted in the convictions of Colonel North and National Security Adviser John Poindexter, but their convictions were later overturned on the grounds that they were based largely on testimony the two men had given before Congress—testimony for which they had been granted immunity. President Reagan, though deposed as a witness, was never personally implicated, thus contributing to his image as "the Teflon President."

Colonel North, you talked here often and eloquently about the need for a democratic outcome in Nicaragua. There is no disagreement on that. There is disagreement over how best to achieve that objective.

Many Americans agree with the President's policy. Many do not.

Many patriotic Americans, strongly anti-Communist, believe there's a better way to contain the Sandinistas, to bring about a democratic outcome in Nicaragua, and to bring peace to Central America.

And many patriotic Americans are concerned that in the pursuit of democracy abroad, we not compromise it in any way here at home.

You and others have urged consistency in our policies. You said that if we are not consistent, our allies and other nations will question our reliability.

That's a real concern. But, if it's bad to change policies, it's worse to have two different policies at the same time, one public policy and an opposite policy in private.

It's difficult to conceive of a greater inconsistency than that. It's hard to imagine anything that would give our allies more cause to consider us unreliable than that we say one thing in public and secretly do another.

And that's exactly what was done when arms were sold to Iran, and those arms were swapped for hostages.

Now, you've talked a lot about patriotism and the love of our country.

Most nations derive from a single tribe or a single race. They practice a single religion. Common racial, ethnic, and religious heritages are the glue of nationhood for many.

The United States is different. We have all races, all religions, a limited common heritage. The glue of nationhood for us is the American ideal of individual liberty and equal justice.

The rule of law is critical in our society. The law is the great equalizer, because in America everybody is equal before the law.

We must never allow the end to justify the means where the law is concerned. However important and noble an objective—and surely democracy abroad is important and noble—it cannot be achieved at the expense of the rule of law in our country.

You talked about your background and it was really very compelling. It's obviously one of the reasons why the American people are attracted to you.

Let me tell you a story from my background.

Before I entered the Senate, I had the great honor of serving as a Federal Judge. In that position I had great power. The one I most enjoyed exercising was the power to make people American citizens.

From time to time I presided at what we call naturalization ceremonies. They are citizenship ceremonies.

People came from all over the world, risked their lives, sometimes left their families and fortunes behind to come here. They had gone through the required procedures and I, in the final act, administered to them the oath of allegiance to the United States and I made them American citizens.

To this moment—to this moment it was the most exciting thing I have ever done in my life.

The ceremonies were always moving for me because my mother was an immigrant and my father was the orphan son of immigrants. Neither of them had any education and they worked at very menial tasks in our society. But because of opportunity and equal justice under law in America, I sit here today a United States Senator.

After every one of these ceremonies, I made it a point to speak to these new Americans. I asked them why they came, how they came to this country. Their stories, each of them, were inspiring. I think you would be interested and moved by them, given the views you have expressed on this country.

When I asked them why they came they said several things, mostly two. The first is that "We came because here in America everyone has a chance, an opportunity." They also said over and over again, particularly those from totalitarian societies, "We came here because in America you can criticize the government without looking over your shoulder." Here we have freedom to disagree with our government.

You have addressed several pleas to this Committee, none more forceful than when you asked that the Congress not cut off aid to the Contras, for the love of God and for the love of country.

Now I address a plea to you.

Of your qualities which the American people find compelling, none is more compelling than your obvious devotion to our country. Please remember that others share that devotion. And recognize that it is possible for an American to disagree with you on aid to the Contras, and still love God and still love this country as much as you do.

Although He is regularly asked to do so, God does not take sides in American politics.

And, in America, disagreement with the policies of the government is not evidence of a lack of patriotism. I want to repeat that. In America, disagreement with policies of the government is not evidence of a lack of patriotism. Indeed, it's the very fact that we can openly disagree with the government without fear of reprisal that is the essence of our freedom, and will keep us free.

I have one final plea. Debate this issue forcefully and vigorously, as you have and as you surely will. But, please, do it in a way that respects the patriotism and the motives of those who disagree with you, as you would have them respect yours.

JESSE JACKSON

Speech to the Democratic National Convention

Keep hope alive!

Jesse Jackson was born Jesse Louis Burns in 1941 in Greenville, South Carolina, to an un-wed sixteen-year-old mother. His biological father, married to another woman, was a professional boxer who took no part in Jesse's upbringing. Two years later, his mother married the man who would adopt Jesse and become his namesake.

Jackson studied at the University of Illinois before transferring to the Agricultural and Technical College of North Carolina. He became involved in the civil rights movement and, in 1965, began working for Martin Luther King Jr.'s Southern Christian Leadership Conference. Ordained as a Baptist minister in 1968, Jackson founded Operation PUSH (People United To Save Humanity) in 1971. This organization would later be combined with his Rainbow Coalition organization, formed in 1984. Jackson became active in electoral politics and led a voter registration drive in Chicago that helped elect the city's first African American mayor. In 1984 and 1988, Jackson entered the Democratic presidential primary, becoming the first African American to seriously contend for the presidency.

Jackson delivered the following speech at the Democratic National Convention on July 19, 1988. He arrived at the convention with over 1,200 delegates—second only to Massachusetts Governor Michael Dukakis, who would win the nomination, but lose the general election to Vice President George H. W. Bush. Jackson used this occasion to speak of his impoverished background and extol the virtues of his campaign.

… We meet tonight at the crossroads, a point of decision. Shall we expand, be inclusive, find unity and power; or suffer division and impotence?

We've come to Atlanta, the cradle of the Old South, the crucible of the New South. Tonight, there is a sense of celebration, because we are moved, fundamentally moved from racial battlegrounds by law, to economic common ground. Tomorrow we'll challenge to move to higher ground.

Common ground. Think of Jerusalem, the intersection where many trails met. A small village that became the birthplace for three great religions—Judaism, Christianity, and Islam. Why was this village so blessed? Because it provided a crossroads where different people met, different cultures, different civilizations could meet and find common ground. When people come together, flowers always flourish—the air is rich with the aroma of a new spring.

Take New York, the dynamic metropolis. What makes New York so special? It's the invitation at the Statue of Liberty, "Give me your tired, your poor, your huddled masses who yearn to breathe free." Not restricted to English only. Many people, many cultures, many languages with one thing in common: They yearn to breathe free. Common ground. …

That's the challenge of our party tonight—left wing, right wing. Progress will not come through boundless liberalism nor static conservatism, but at the critical mass of mutual survival. It takes two wings to fly. Whether you're a hawk or a dove, you're just a bird living in the same environment, in the same world.

The Bible teaches that when lions and lambs lie down together, none will be afraid, and there will be peace in the valley. It sounds impossible. Lions eat lambs. Lambs sensibly flee from lions. Yet even lions and lambs find common ground. Why? Because neither lions nor lambs want the forest to catch on fire. Neither lions nor lambs want acid rain to fall. Neither lions nor lambs can survive nuclear war. If lions and lambs can find common ground, surely we can as well, as civilized people. …

Common ground. America is not a blanket woven from one thread, one color, one cloth. When I was a child growing up in Greenville, South Carolina and grandmamma could not afford a blanket, she didn't complain and we did not freeze. Instead she took pieces of old cloth—patches, wool, silk, gabardine, crockersack—only patches, barely good enough to wipe off your shoes with. But they didn't stay that way very long. With sturdy hands and a strong cord, she sewed them together into a quilt, a thing of beauty and power and culture. Now, Democrats, we must build such a quilt.

Farmers, you seek fair prices and you are right—but you cannot stand alone. Your patch is not big enough.

Workers, you fight for fair wages, you are right—but your patch is not big enough.

Women, you seek comparable worth and pay equity, you are right—but your patch is not big enough.

Women, mothers, who seek Head Start, and day care and prenatal care on the front side of life, rather than jail care and welfare on the back side of life, you are right—but your patch is not big enough.

Students, you seek scholarships, you are right—but your patch is not big enough.

Blacks and Hispanics, when we fight for civil rights, we are right—but our patch is not big enough.

Gays and lesbians, when you fight against discrimination and a cure for AIDS, you are right—but your patch is not big enough.

Conservatives and progressives, when you fight for what you believe, right wing, left wing, hawk, dove, you are right from your point of view, but your point of view is not enough.

But don't despair. Be as wise as my grandmamma. Pull the patches and the pieces together, bound by a common thread. When we form a great quilt of unity and common ground, we'll have the power to bring about health care and housing and jobs and education and hope to our Nation.

We, the people, can win.

We stand at the end of a long dark night of reaction. We stand tonight united in the commitment to a new direction. For almost eight years we've been led by those who view social good coming from private interest, who view public life as a means to increase private wealth. They have been prepared to sacrifice the common good of the many to satisfy the private interests and the wealth of a few.

We believe in a government that's a tool of our democracy in service to the public, not an instrument of the aristocracy in search of private wealth. …

I just want to take common sense to high places. We're spending one hundred and fifty billion dollars a year defending Europe and Japan forty-three years after the war is over. We have more troops in Europe tonight than we had seven years ago. Yet the threat of war is ever more remote.

Germany and Japan are now creditor nations; that means they've got a surplus. We are a debtor nation—means we are in debt. Let them share more of the burden of their own defense. Use some of that money to build decent housing. Use some of that money to educate our children. Use some of that money for long-term health care. Use some of that money to wipe out these slums and put America back to work!

I just want to take common sense to high places. If we can bail out Europe and Japan; if we can bail out Continental Bank and Chrysler … we can bail out the family farmer.

I just want to make common sense. It does not make sense to close down six hundred and fifty thousand family farms in this country while importing food from abroad subsidized by the U.S. Government. Let's make sense.

It does not make sense to be escorting all our tankers up and down the Persian Gulf paying $2.50 for every one dollar worth of oil we bring out, while oil wells are capped in Texas, Oklahoma, and Louisiana. I just want to make sense.

Leadership must meet the moral challenge of its day. What's the moral challenge of our day? We have public accommodations. We have the right to vote. We have open housing. What's the fundamental challenge of our day? It is to end economic violence. Plant closings without notice—economic violence. Even the greedy do not profit long from greed—economic violence.

Most poor people are not lazy. They are not black. They are not brown. They are mostly White and female and young. But whether White, Black or Brown, a hungry baby's belly turned inside out is the same color—color it pain; color it hurt; color it agony.

Most poor people are not on welfare. Some of them are illiterate and can't read the want-ad sections. And when they can, they can't find a job that matches the address. They work hard everyday.

I know. I live amongst them. I'm one of them. I know they work. I'm a witness. They catch the early bus. They work every day.

They raise other people's children. They work everyday.

They clean the streets. They work everyday. They drive dangerous cabs. They work everyday. They change the beds you slept in in these hotels last night and can't get a union contract. They work everyday.

No, no, they are not lazy! Someone must defend them because it's right, and they cannot speak for themselves. They work in hospitals. I know they do. They wipe the bodies of those who are sick with fever and pain. They empty their bedpans. They clean out their commodes. No job is beneath them, and yet when they get sick they cannot lie in the bed they made up every day. America, that is not right. We are a better Nation than that. We are a better Nation than that. …

I'm often asked, "Jesse, why do you take on these tough issues? They're not very political. We can't win that way."

If an issue is morally right, it will eventually be political. It may be political and never be right. Fannie Lou Hamer didn't have the most votes in Atlantic City, but her principles have outlasted every delegate who voted to lock her out. Rosa Parks did not have the most votes, but she was morally right. Dr. King didn't have the most votes about the Vietnam War, but he was morally right. If we are principled first, our politics will fall in place.

"Jesse, why do you take these big bold initiatives?" A poem by an unknown author went something like this: "We mastered the air, we conquered the sea, annihilated distance and prolonged life, but we're not wise enough to live on this earth without war and without hate."

As for Jesse Jackson: "I'm tired of sailing my little boat, far inside the harbor bar. I want to go out where the big ships float, out on the deep where the great ones are. And should my frail craft prove too slight for waves that sweep those billows o'er, I'd rather go down in the stirring fight than drown to death at the sheltered shore."

We've got to go out, my friends, where the big boats are.

And then for our children. Young America, hold your head high now. We can win. We must not lose you to drugs and violence, premature pregnancy, suicide, cynicism, pessimism and despair. We can win. Wherever you are tonight, I challenge you to hope and to dream. Don't submerge your dreams. Exercise above all else, even on drugs, dream of the day you are drug free. Even in the gutter, dream of the day that you will be up on your feet again.

You must never stop dreaming. Face reality, yes, but don't stop with the way things are. Dream of things as they ought to be. Dream. Face pain, but love, hope, faith and dreams will help you rise above the pain. Use hope and imagination as weapons of survival and progress, but you keep on dreaming, young America. Dream of peace. Peace is rational and reasonable. War is irrational in this age, and unwinnable.

Dream of teachers who teach for life and not for a living. Dream of doctors who are concerned more about public health than private wealth. Dream of lawyers more concerned about justice than a judgeship. Dream of preachers who are concerned more about prophecy than profiteering. Dream on the high road with sound values. …

Do not surrender to drugs. The best drug policy is a "no first use." Don't surrender with needles and cynicism. Let's have "no first use" on the one hand, or clinics on the other. Never surrender, young America. Go forward.

America must never surrender to malnutrition. We can feed the hungry and clothe the naked. We must never surrender. We must go forward.

We must never surrender to illiteracy. Invest in our children. Never surrender; and go forward. We must never surrender to inequality. Women cannot compromise ERA or comparable worth. Women are making sixty cents on the dollar to what a man makes. Women cannot buy meat cheaper. Women cannot buy bread cheaper. Women cannot buy milk cheaper. Women deserve to get paid for the work that you do. It's right! And it's fair.

Don't surrender, my friends. Those who have AIDS tonight, you deserve our compassion. Even with AIDS you must not surrender.

In your wheelchairs. I see you sitting here tonight in those wheelchairs. I've stayed with you. I've reached out to you across our Nation. And don't you give up. I know it's tough sometimes. People look down on you. It took you a little more effort to get here tonight. And no one should look down on you, but sometimes mean people do. The only justification we have for looking down on someone is that we're going to stop and pick them up. …

Why I cannot challenge you this way? "Jesse Jackson, you don't understand my situation. You be on television. You don't understand. I see you with the big people. You don't understand my situation."

I understand. You see me on TV, but you don't know the me that makes me, me. They wonder, "Why does Jesse run?" because they see me running for the White House. They don't see the house I'm running from.

I have a story. I wasn't always on television. Writers were not always outside my door. When I was born late one afternoon, October 8th, in Greenville, South Carolina, no writers asked my mother her name. Nobody chose to write down our address. My mama was not supposed to make it, and I was not supposed to make it. You see, I was born of a teen-age mother, who was born of a teen-age mother.

I understand. I know abandonment, and people being mean to you, and saying you're nothing and nobody and can never be anything.

I understand. Jesse Jackson is my third name. I'm adopted. When I had no name, my grandmother gave me her name. My name was Jesse Burns 'til I was twelve. So I wouldn't have a blank space, she gave me a name to hold me over. I understand when nobody knows your name. I understand when you have no name.

I understand. I wasn't born in the hospital. Mama didn't have insurance. I was born in the bed at the house. I really do understand. Born in a three-room house, bathroom in the backyard, slop jar by the bed, no hot and cold running water. I understand. Wallpaper used for decoration? No. For a windbreaker. I understand. I'm a working person's person. That's why I understand you whether you're Black or White. I understand work. I was not born with a silver spoon in my mouth. I had a shovel programmed for my hand.

My mother, a working woman. So many of the days she went to work early, with runs in her stockings. She knew better, but she wore runs in her stockings so that my brother and I could have matching socks and not be laughed at, at school. I understand.

At 3 o'clock on Thanksgiving Day, we couldn't eat turkey because momma was preparing somebody else's turkey at 3 o'clock. We had to play football to entertain ourselves. And then around 6 o'clock she would get off the Alta Vista bus and we would bring up the leftovers and eat our turkey—leftovers, the carcass, the cranberries—around 8 o'clock at night. I really do understand.

Every one of these funny labels they put on you, those of you who are watching this broadcast tonight in the projects, on the corners, I understand. Call you outcast, low down, you can't make it, you're nothing, you're from nobody, subclass, underclass; when you see Jesse Jackson, when my name goes in nomination, your name goes in nomination.

I was born in the slum, but the slum was not born in me. And it wasn't born in you, and you can make it.

Wherever you are tonight, you can make it. Hold your head high; stick your chest out. You can make it. It gets dark sometimes, but the morning comes. Don't you surrender!

Suffering breeds character, character breeds faith. In the end faith will not disappoint.

You must not surrender! You may or may not get there but just know that you're qualified! And you hold on, and hold out! We must never surrender! America will get better and better.

Keep hope alive! Keep hope alive! Keep hope alive! On tomorrow night and beyond, keep hope alive!

RONALD REAGAN

Speech at Moscow State University

Democracy is less a system of government than it is a system to keep government limited, unintrusive; a system of constraints on power to keep politics and government secondary to the important things in life.

Ronald Reagan likened America to "a shining city upon a hill whose beacon light guides freedom-loving people everywhere." He borrowed the phrase "city on a hill" from John Winthrop, an early Puritan leader and first governor of the Massachusetts Bay Colony, who wrote it to describe the America he imagined. The phrase is originally derived from the Bible's Sermon on the Mount: *"You are the light of the world. A city that is set on a hill cannot be hidden."*

In 1988, Soviet leader Mikhail Gorbachev invited President Reagan to visit the Soviet Union—what Reagan viewed as the antithesis of that shining city. Reagan had described the Soviet Union as an "Evil Empire," one "destined for the ash heap of history." While there, Reagan addressed students at Moscow State University. Unbeknownst to the president, the Soviets only allowed students who were members of the Young Communist League into the auditorium. Standing beneath a portrait of Vladimir Lenin, Reagan described the democratic reforms that were sweeping the globe and made clear his view of Communism as a repressive and economically stagnant system. The response from the students was positive, and Reagan would later say, "I felt I could have been speaking to students anywhere. The coldness disappeared."

... Standing here before a mural of your revolution, I want to talk about a very different revolution that is taking place right now, quietly sweeping the globe, without bloodshed or conflict. Its effects are peaceful, but they will fundamentally alter our world, shatter old assumptions, and reshape our lives. It's easy to underestimate because it's not accompanied by banners or fanfare. It has been called the technological or information revolution, and as its emblem, one might take the tiny silicone chip, no bigger than a fingerprint. One of these chips has more computing power than a roomful of old-style computers.

As part of an exchange program, we now have an exhibition touring your country that shows how information technology is transforming our lives—replacing manual labor with robots, forecasting weather for farmers, or mapping the genetic code of DNA for medical researchers. These microcomputers today aid the design of everything from houses to cars to spacecraft; they even design better and faster computers. They can translate English into Russian or enable the blind to read or help Michael Jackson produce on one synthesizer the sounds of a whole orchestra. Linked by a network of satellites and fiber-optic cables, one individual with a desktop computer and a telephone commands resources unavailable to the largest governments just a few years ago.

Like a chrysalis, we're emerging from the economy of the Industrial Revolution—an economy confined to and limited by the Earth's physical resources—into, as one economist titled his book, *The Economy in Mind*, in which there are no bounds on human imagination and the freedom to create is the most precious natural resource. Think of that little computer chip. Its value isn't in the sand from which it is made, but in the microscopic architecture designed into it by ingenious human minds. Or take the example of the satellite relaying this broadcast around the world, which replaces thousands of tons of copper mined from the Earth and molded into wire. In the new economy, human invention increasingly makes physical resources obsolete. We're breaking through the material conditions of existence to a world where man creates his own destiny. Even as we explore the most advanced reaches of science, we're returning to the age-old wisdom of our culture, a wisdom contained in the book of Genesis in the Bible: In the beginning was the spirit, and it was from this spirit that the material abundance of creation issued forth.

But progress is not foreordained. The key is freedom—freedom of thought, freedom of information, freedom of communication. The renowned scientist, scholar, and founding father of this University, Mikhail Lomonosov, knew that. "It is common knowledge," he said, "that the achievements of science are considerable and rapid, particularly once the yoke of slavery is cast off and replaced by the freedom of philosophy." You know, one of the first contacts between your country and mine took place between Russian and American explorers. The Americans were members of Cook's last voyage on an expedition searching for an Artic passage; on the island of Unalaska, they came upon the Russians, who took them in, and together, with the native inhabitants, held a prayer service on the ice.

The explorers of the modern era are the entrepreneurs, men with vision, with the courage to take risks and faith enough to brave the unknown. These entrepreneurs and their small enterprises are responsible for almost all the economic growth in the United States. They are the prime movers of the technological revolution. In fact, one of the largest personal computer firms in the United States was started by two college students, no older than you, in the garage behind their home. Some people, even in my own country, look at the riot of experiment that is the free market and see only waste. What of all the entrepreneurs that fail? Well, many do, particularly the successful ones. Often several times. And if you ask them the secret of their success, they'll tell you, it's all they learned in their struggles along the way—yes, it's what they learned from failing. Like an athlete in competition, or a scholar in pursuit of the truth, experience is the greatest teacher.

And that's why it's so hard for government planners, no matter how sophisticated, to ever substitute for millions of individuals working night and day to make their dreams come true. The fact is, bureaucracies are a problem around the world. There's an old story about a town—it could be anywhere—with a bureaucrat who is known to be a good-for-nothing, but he somehow had always hung on to power. So one day, in a town meeting, an old woman got up and said to him: "There is a folk legend here where I come from that when a baby is born, an angel comes down from heaven and kisses it on one part of its body. If the angel kisses him on his hand, he becomes a handyman. If the angel kisses him on his forehead, he becomes bright and clever. And I've been trying to figure out where the angel kissed you so that you should sit there for so long and do nothing."

We are seeing the power of economic freedom spreading around the world. … Throughout the world, free markets are the model for growth. Democracy is the standard by which governments are measured.

We Americans make no secret of our belief in freedom. In fact, it's something of a national pastime. Every four years the American people choose a new president, and 1988 is one of those years. At one point there were thirteen major candidates running in the two major parties, not to mention all the others, including the Socialist and Libertarian candidates—all trying to get my job. About 1,000 local television stations, 8,500 radio stations, and 1,700 daily newspapers—each one an independent, private enterprise, fiercely independent of the government—report on the candidates, grill them in interviews, and bring them together for debates. In the end, the people vote; they decide who will be the next president.

But freedom doesn't begin or end with elections. Go to any American town, to take just an example, and you'll see dozens of churches, representing many different beliefs—in many places synagogues and mosques—and you'll see families of every conceivable nationality, worshipping together. Go into any schoolroom, and there you will see children being taught the Declaration of Independence, that they are endowed by their Creator with certain inalienable rights—among them life, liberty, and the pursuit of happiness—that no government can justly deny; the guarantees in their Constitution for freedom of speech, freedom of assembly, and freedom of religion.

Go into any courtroom and there will preside an independent judge, beholden to no government power. There every defendant has the right to a trial by a jury of his peers, usually twelve men and women—common citizens, they are the ones, the only ones, who weigh the evidence and decide on guilt or innocence. In that court, the accused is innocent until proven guilty, and the word of a policeman, or any official, has no greater legal standing than the word of the accused.

Go to any university campus, and there you'll find an open, sometimes heated discussion of the problems in American society and what can be done to correct them. Turn on the television, and you'll see the legislature conducting the business of government right there before the camera, debating and voting on the legislation that will become the law of the land. March in any demonstration, and there are many of them—the people's right of assembly is guaranteed in the Constitution and protected by the police. Go into any union hall, where the members know their right to strike is protected by law. As a matter of fact, one of the many jobs I had before this one was being president of a union, the Screen Actors Guild. I led my union out on strike, and I'm proud to say we won.

But freedom is more even than this: Freedom is the right to question, and change the established way of doing things. It is the continuing revolution of the marketplace. It is the understanding that allows us to recognize shortcomings and seek solutions. It is the right to put forth an idea, scoffed at by the experts, and watch it catch fire among the people. It is the right to dream—to follow your dream or stick to your conscience, even if you're the only one in a sea of doubters. Freedom is the recognition that no single person, no single authority or government has a monopoly on the truth, but that every individual life is infinitely precious, that every one of us put on this earth has been put here for a reason and has something to offer. ...

Freedom, it has been said, makes people selfish and materialistic, but Americans are one of the most religious peoples on earth. Because they know that liberty, just as life itself, is not earned but a gift from God, they seek to share that gift with the world. "Reason and experience," said George Washington in his farewell address, "both forbid us to expect that national morality can prevail in exclusion of religious principle. And it is substantially true, that virtue or morality is a necessary spring of popular government." Democracy is less a system of government than it is a system to keep government limited, unintrusive; a system of constraints on power to keep politics and government secondary to the important things in life, the true sources of value found only in family and faith.

But I hope you know I go on about these things not simply to extol the virtues of my own country, but to speak to the true greatness of the heart and soul of your land. Who, after all, needs to tell the land of Dostoevski about the quest for truth, the home of Kandinski and Scriabin about imagination, the rich and noble culture of the Uzbek man of letters, Alisher Navoi, about beauty and heart? The great culture of your diverse land speaks with a glowing passion to all humanity. Let me cite one of the most eloquent contemporary passages on human freedom. It comes, not from the literature of America, but from this country, from one of the greatest writers of the twentieth century, Boris Pasternak, in the novel *Dr. Zhivago*. He Writes, "I think that if the beast who sleeps in man could be held down by threats—any kind of threat, whether of jail or retribution after death—than the highest emblem of humanity would be the lion tamer in the circus with his whip, not the prophet who sacrificed himself. But this is just the point—what has for centuries raised man above the beast is not the cudgel, but an inward music—the irresistible power of unarmed truth."

The irresistible power of unarmed truth. Today the world looks expectantly to signs of change, steps toward greater freedom in the Soviet Union. ...

Americans seek always to make friends of old antagonists. After a colonial revolution with Britain, we have cemented for all ages the ties of kinship between our nations. After a terrible civil war between North and South, we healed our wounds and found true unity as a nation. We fought two world wars in my lifetime against Germany and one with Japan, but now the Federal Republic of Germany and Japan are two of our closest allies and friends.

Some people point to the trade disputes between us as a sign of strain, but they're the frictions of all families, and the family of free nations is a big and vital and sometimes boisterous one. I can tell you that nothing would please my heart more than in my lifetime to see American and Soviet diplomats grappling with the problem of trade disputes between America and a growing, exuberant, exporting Soviet Union that had opened up to economic freedom and growth. ...

Your generation is living in one of the most exciting, hopeful times in Soviet history. It is a time when the first breath of freedom stirs the air and the heart beats to the accelerated rhythm of hope, when the accumulated spiritual energies of a long silence yearn to break free. I am reminded of the famous passage near the end of Gogol's *Dead Souls*. Comparing his nation to a speeding troika, Gogol asks what will be its destination. But he writes, "There was no answer save the bell pouring forth marvelous sound."

We do not know what the conclusion of this journey will be, but we're hopeful that the promise of reform will be fulfilled. In this Moscow spring, this May 1988, we may be allowed that hope—that freedom, like the fresh green sapling planted over Tolstoi's grave, will blossom forth at last in the rich fertile soil of your people and culture. We may be allowed to hope that the marvelous sound of a new openness will keep rising through, ringing through, leading to a new world of reconciliation, friendship, and peace.

Thank you all very much, and *da blagoslovit vas gospod— God bless you.*

* * *

Firefighters George Johnson, Dan McWilliams, and Billy Eisengrein raising the flag amidst the ruins of the World Trade Center at Ground Zero in New York City on September 11, 2001.

Rendezvous with Destiny

NEWTON MINOW

Address to the Broadcasting Industry

I invite you to sit down in front of your television set ... I can assure you that you will observe a vast wasteland.

Newton Minow, former director of the Federal Communications Commission, was appointed to that position by President Kennedy. Speaking before the National Association of Broadcasters on May 9, 1961, Professor Minow indicted daily television programming as a "vast wasteland." His speech, excerpted here, launched a national debate that has not subsided.

Addressing the issue more than thirty years later, Professor Minow said of his original speech: "Almost overnight, those two words ['vast wasteland'] became television's first enduring sound bite. For decades, they have been used, over and over again, to describe what Americans find when they come home after work in the evenings and turn on their television sets, what our children find there after school or on Saturday morning. 'Vast wasteland' appears in newspaper headlines, in book titles, in magazine articles, in Bartlett's Familiar Quotations, even as the answer to a Trivial Pursuit question. ... The two words I wanted people to remember from that speech, however, were not 'vast wasteland.' The two words I cared about were 'public interest.' ... The law governing radio and television broadcasting, the Federal Communications Act of 1934, gives broadcasters free and exclusive use of broadcast channels on condition that they serve the 'public interest, convenience and necessity.' ... Because the act did not define what the public interest meant, Congress, the courts and the FCC have spent sixty frustrating years struggling to figure it out. ... To me the answer is clear. The public interest meant and still means what we should constantly ask: What can television do for our country, for the common good, for the American people?"

... Your industry possesses the most powerful voice in America. It has an inescapable duty to make that voice ring with intelligence and with leadership. In a few years this exciting industry has grown from a novelty to an instrument of overwhelming impact on the American people. It should be making ready for the kind of leadership that newspapers and magazines assumed years ago, to make our people aware of this world.

Ours has been called the jet age, the atomic age, the space age. It is also, I submit, the television age. And just as history will decide whether the leaders of today's world employed the atom to destroy the world or rebuild it for mankind's benefit, so will history decide whether today's broadcasters employed their powerful voice to enrich the people or debase them. ...

Like everybody, I wear more than one hat. I am the chairman of the FCC. I am also a television viewer and the husband and father of other television viewers. I have seen a great many television programs that seemed to me eminently worthwhile. ...

When television is good, nothing—not the theater, not the magazines or newspapers—nothing is better.

But when television is bad, nothing is worse. I invite you to sit down in front of your television set when your station goes on the air and stay there without a book, magazine, newspaper, profit-and-loss sheet, or rating book to distract you—and keep your eyes glued to that set until the station signs off. I can assure you that you will observe a vast wasteland.

You will see a procession of game shows, violence, audience participation shows, formula comedies about totally unbelievable families, blood and thunder, mayhem, violence, sadism, murder, Western badmen, Western good men, private eyes, gangsters, more violence and cartoons. And, endlessly, commercials—many screaming, cajoling, and offending. And, most of all, boredom. True, you will see a few things you will enjoy. But they will be very, very few. And if you think I exaggerate, try it.

Is there one person in this room who claims that broadcasting can't do better? ...

Why is so much of television so bad? I have heard many answers: demands of your advertisers; competition for even higher ratings; the need always to attract a mass audience; the high cost of television programs; the insatiable appetite for programming material—these are some of them. Unquestionably these are tough problems not susceptible to easy answers.

But I am not convinced that you have tried hard enough to solve them. I do not accept the idea that the present overall programming is aimed accurately at the public taste. The ratings tell us only that some people have their television sets turned on, and, of that number, so many are tuned to one channel and so many to another. They don't tell us what the public might watch if they were offered half a dozen additional choices. A rating, at best, is an indication of how many people saw what you gave them. Unfortunately it does not reveal the depth of the penetration or the intensity of reaction, and it never reveals what the acceptance would have been if what you gave them had been better—if all the forces of art and creativity and daring and imagination had been unleashed. I believe in the people's good sense and good taste, and I am not convinced that the people's taste is as low as some of you assume. ...

Certainly I hope you will agree that ratings should have little influence where children are concerned. The best estimates indicate that during the hours of 5 to 6 P.M., 60 percent of your audience is composed of children under twelve. And most young children today, believe it or not, spend as much time watching television as they do in the schoolroom. I repeat—let that sink in—most young children today spend as much time watching television as they do in the schoolroom. It used to be said that there were three great influences on a child: home, school, and church. Today there is a fourth great influence, and you ladies and gentlemen control it.

If parents, teachers, and ministers conducted their responsibilities by following the ratings, children would have a steady diet of ice cream, school holidays, and no Sunday school. What about your responsibilities? Is there no room on television to teach, to inform, to uplift, to stretch, to enlarge the capacities of our children? Is there no room for programs deepening their understanding of children in other lands? Is there no room for a children's news show explaining something about the world to them at their level of understanding? Is there no room for reading the great literature of the past, teaching them the great traditions of freedom? There are some fine children's shows, but they are drowned out in the massive doses of cartoons, violence, and more violence. Must these be your trademarks? Search your consciences and see if you cannot offer more to your young beneficiaries whose future you guide so many hours each and every day.

What about adult programming and ratings? You know, newspaper publishers take popularity ratings too. The answers are pretty clear; it is almost always the comics, followed by the advice-to-the-lovelorn columns. But, ladies and gentlemen, the news is still on the front page of all newspapers, the editorials are not replaced by more comics, the newspapers have not become one long collection of advice to the lovelorn. Yet newspapers do not need a license from the government to be in business—they do not use public property. But in television—where your responsibilities as public trustees are so plain—the moment that the ratings indicate that Westerns are popular, there are new imitations of Westerns on the air faster than the old coaxial cable could take us from Hollywood to New York. ...

Let me make clear that what I am talking about is balance. I believe that the public interest is made up of many interests. There are many people in this great country, and you must serve all of us. You will get no argument from me if you say that, given a choice between a Western and a symphony, more people will watch the Western. I like Westerns and private eyes too—but a steady diet for the whole country is obviously not in the public interest. We all know that people would more often prefer to be entertained than stimulated or informed. But your obligations are not satisfied if you look only to popularity as a test of what to broadcast. You are not only in show business; you are free to communicate ideas as well as relaxation. You must provide a wider range of choices, more diversity, more alternatives. It is not enough to cater to the nation's whims—you must also serve the nation's needs. ...

Let me address myself now to my role, not as a viewer but as chairman of the FCC. ... I want to make clear some of the fundamental principles which guide me.

First, the people own the air. They own it as much in prime evening time as they do at 6 o'clock Sunday morning. For every hour that the people give you, you owe them something. I intend to see that your debt is paid with service.

Second, I think it would be foolish and wasteful for us to continue any worn-out wrangle over the problems of payola, rigged quiz shows, and other mistakes of the past. ...

Third, I believe in the free enterprise system. I want to see broadcasting improved and I want you to do the job. ...

Fourth, I will do all I can to help educational television. There are still not enough educational stations, and major centers of the country still lack usable educational channels. ...

Fifth, I am unalterably opposed to governmental censorship. There will be no suppression of programming which does not meet with bureaucratic tastes. Censorship strikes at the taproot of our free society.

Sixth, I did not come to Washington to idly observe the squandering of the public's airwaves. The squandering of our airwaves is no less important than the lavish waste of any precious natural resource. ...

What you gentlemen broadcast through the people's air affects the people's taste, their knowledge, their opinions, their understanding of themselves and of their world. And their future. The power of instantaneous sight and sound is without precedent in mankind's history. This is an awesome power. It has limitless capabilities for good—and for evil. And it carries with it awesome responsibilities—responsibilities which you and I cannot escape. ...

HILLARY CLINTON

Women's Rights Are Human Rights

Women will never gain full dignity until their human rights are respected and protected.

Born in Chicago in 1947, Hillary Diane Rodham attended public schools before graduating from Wellesley College and Yale Law School, where she met Bill Clinton. She moved to Arkansas in 1974 and married Clinton the following year. As a working mother, Clinton served as an assistant professor at the University of Arkansas School of Law and went on to pursue a successful legal career while supporting her husband's political ambitions.

During her twelve years as First Lady of the State of Arkansas, Clinton became involved in a variety of public policy issues related to children and families. Following Governor Clinton's election as president of the United States in 1992, she became an advocate of health care reform and was heavily involved in numerous policy initiatives. In 2000, she became the first wife of a president to seek and win national office and the first woman to be elected to the U.S. Senate from New York. Following re-election in 2006, Clinton announced her plans to strive for another first—to become the nation's first female president. She offered her concession during the 2008 Democratic primaries, however, when it became apparent that fellow Senator Barack Obama held a majority of the delegates. Clinton went on to serve as secretary of state in the Obama administration.

Throughout her public life, Hillary Clinton has been a consistent and outspoken advocate of women's rights. On September 5, 1995, as First Lady of the United States, she delivered the following speech at the United Nations Fourth World Conference on Women in Beijing, China. Seeking to inspire women worldwide and help galvanize a global movement on behalf of women's rights, she catalogued a litany of abuses that afflicted women throughout the world and criticized the host nation for seeking to limit free and open discussion of women's issues at the conference.

This is truly a celebration—a celebration of the contributions women make in every aspect of life: in the home, on the job, in their communities, as mothers, wives, sisters, daughters, learners, workers, citizens and leaders.

It is also a coming together, much the way women come together every day in every country.

We come together in fields and in factories, in village markets and supermarkets, in living rooms and board rooms.

Whether it is while playing with our children in the park, or washing clothes in a river, or taking a break at the office water cooler, we come together and talk about our aspirations and concerns. And time and again, our talk turns to our children and our families. However different we may be, there is far more that unites us than divides us. We share a common future. And we are here to find common ground so that we may help bring new dignity and respect to women and girls all over the world—and in so doing, bring new strength and stability to families as well....

What we are learning around the world is that if women are healthy and educated, their families will flourish. If women are free from violence, their families will flourish. If women have a chance to work and earn as full and equal partners in society, their families will flourish.

And when families flourish, communities and nations will flourish....

The great challenge of this Conference is to give voice to women everywhere whose experiences go unnoticed, whose words go unheard.

Women comprise more than half the world's population. Women are 70 percent of the world's poor, and two-thirds of those who are not taught to read and write.

Women are the primary caretakers for most of the world's children and elderly. Yet much of the work we do is not valued—not by economists, not by historians, not by popular culture, not by government leaders.

At this very moment, as we sit here, women around the world are giving birth, raising children, cooking meals, washing clothes, cleaning houses, planting crops, working on assembly lines, running companies, and running countries.

Women also are dying from diseases that should have been prevented or treated; they are watching their children succumb to malnutrition caused by poverty and economic deprivation; they are being denied the right to go to school by their own fathers and brothers; they are being forced into prostitution, and they are being barred from the bank lending office and banned from the ballot box.

Those of us who have the opportunity to be here have the responsibility to speak for those who could not.

As an American, I want to speak up for women in my own country—women who are raising children on the minimum wage, women who can't afford health care or child care, women whose lives are threatened by violence, including violence in their own homes.

I want to speak up for mothers who are fighting for good schools, safe neighborhoods, clean air and clean airwaves; for older women, some of them widows, who have raised their families and now find that their skills and life experiences are not valued in the workplace; for women who are working all night as nurses, hotel clerks, and fast food cooks so that they can be at home during the day with their kids; and for women everywhere who simply don't have time to do everything they are called upon to do each day.

Speaking to you today, I speak for them, just as each of us speaks for women around the world who are denied the chance to go to school, or see a doctor, or own property, or have a say about the direction of their lives, simply because they are women. The truth is that most women around the world work both inside and outside the home, usually by necessity.

We need to understand that there is no formula for how women should lead their lives. That is why we must respect the choices that each woman makes for herself and her family. Every woman deserves the chance to realize her God-given potential.

We also must recognize that women will never gain full dignity until their human rights are respected and protected.

Our goals for this Conference, to strengthen families and societies by empowering women to take greater control over their own destinies, cannot be fully achieved unless all governments—here and around the world—accept their responsibility to protect and promote internationally recognized human rights.

The international community has long acknowledged— and recently affirmed at Vienna—that both women and men are entitled to a range of protections and personal freedoms, from the right of personal security to the right to determine freely the number and spacing of the children they bear.

No one should be forced to remain silent for fear of religious or political persecution, arrest, abuse or torture.

Tragically, women are most often the ones whose human rights are violated.

Even in the late 20th century, the rape of women continues to be used as an instrument of armed conflict. Women and children make up a large majority of the world's refugees. When women are excluded from the political process, they become even more vulnerable to abuse. I believe that, on the eve of a new millennium, it is time to break our silence. It is time for us to say here in Beijing, and the world to hear, that it is no longer acceptable to discuss women's rights as separate from human rights.

These abuses have continued because, for too long, the history of women has been a history of silence. Even today, there are those who are trying to silence our words.

The voices of this conference and of the women at Huairou must be heard loud and clear: It is a violation of human rights when babies are denied food, or drowned, or suffocated, or their spines broken, simply because they are born girls.

It is a violation of human rights when women and girls are sold into the slavery of prostitution.

It is a violation of human rights when women are doused with gasoline, set on fire and burned to death because their marriage dowries are deemed too small.

It is a violation of human rights when individual women are raped in their own communities and when thousands of women are subjected to rape as a tactic or prize of war.

It is a violation of human rights when a leading cause of death worldwide among women ages 14 to 44 is the violence they are subjected to in their own homes.

It is a violation of human rights when young girls

are brutalized by the painful and degrading practice of genital mutilation.

It is a violation of human rights when women are denied the right to plan their own families, and that includes being forced to have abortions or being sterilized against their will.

If there is one message that echoes forth from this conference, it is that human rights are women's rights—and women's rights are human rights. Let us not forget that among those rights are the right to speak freely—and the right to be heard.

Women must enjoy the right to participate fully in the social and political lives of their countries if we want freedom and democracy to thrive and endure.

It is indefensible that many women in nongovernmental organizations who wished to participate in this conference have not been able to attend—or have been prohibited from fully taking part.

Let me be clear. Freedom means the right of people to assemble, organize, and debate openly. It means respecting the views of those who may disagree with the views of their governments. It means not taking citizens away from their loved ones and jailing them, mistreating them, or denying them their freedom or dignity because of the peaceful expression of their ideas and opinions.

In my country, we recently celebrated the 75th anniversary of women's suffrage. It took 150 years after the signing of our Declaration of Independence for women to win the right to vote. It took 72 years of organized struggle on the part of many courageous women and men. It was one of America's most divisive philosophical wars. But it was also a bloodless war. Suffrage was achieved without a shot being fired.

We have also been reminded, in V-J Day observances last weekend, of the good that comes when men and women join together to combat the forces of tyranny and build a better world.

We have seen peace prevail in most places for a half century. We have avoided another world war.

But we have not solved older, deeply-rooted problems that continue to diminish the potential of half the world's population.

Now it is time to act on behalf of women everywhere. If we take bold steps to better the lives of women, we will be taking bold steps to better the lives of children and families too.

Families rely on mothers and wives for emotional support and care; families rely on women for labor in the home; and increasingly, families rely on women for income needed to raise healthy children and care for other relatives.

As long as discrimination and inequities remain so commonplace around the world—as long as girls and women are valued less, fed less, fed last, overworked, underpaid, not schooled and subjected to violence in and out of their homes—the potential of the human family to create a peaceful, prosperous world will not be realized.

Let this Conference be our—and the world's—call to action.

And let us heed the call so that we can create a world in which every woman is treated with respect and dignity, every boy and girl is loved and cared for equally, and every family has the hope of a strong and stable future.

CLARENCE THOMAS

Remarks to the National Bar Association

The tendency to personalize differences has grown to be an accepted way of doing business. One need not do the hard work of dissecting an argument. One need only attack and thus discredit the person making the argument.

Born in Pin Point, Georgia, in 1948, Clarence Thomas graduated from College of the Holy Cross and received his law degree from Yale University. He then held several government positions, including secretary for civil rights in the U.S. Department of Education. In 1982, he became chairman of the Equal Employment Opportunity Commission (EEOC) and, in 1990, was appointed by President George Herbert Walker Bush to the U.S. Court of Appeals for the District of Columbia. In 1991, Bush nominated Thomas to fill the vacancy on the Supreme Court created by the retirement of Thurgood Marshall.

The Senate confirmation hearings, many of which were televised, became the most bitter in history due to the testimony of Anita Hill, a law professor at the University of Oklahoma, who accused Thomas, in lurid detail, of having sexually harassed her while serving at the Department of Education and the EEOC. After more than three months of testimony, Thomas angrily lashed out at members of the Judiciary Committee, labeling the hearings "a circus," "a national disgrace," and "a high-tech lynching for uppity blacks who in any way deign to think for themselves, to do for themselves, to have different ideas." Reminding the committee that he had been a public figure for ten years, been confirmed four times, and had five FBI background checks, Thomas asserted that Ms. Hill's accusations were fabricated and claimed that she was motivated by his opposition to affirmative action programs. The Senate later confirmed Thomas by a vote of fifty-two to forty-eight—one of the narrowest margins in history.

Speaking in Memphis, Tennessee, on July 29, 1998, Justice Thomas addressed the National Bar Association, formed in 1925 by black lawyers who were precluded from joining the American Bar Association on account of their race.

Thirty years ago, we all focused intently on this city as the trauma of Dr. King's death first exploded, then sank into our lives. For so many of us who were trying hard to do what we thought was required of us in the process of integrating this society, the rush of hopelessness and isolation was immediate and overwhelming. It seemed that the whole world had gone mad.

I am certain that each of us has his or her memories of that terrible day in 1968. For me it was the final straw in the struggle to retain my vocation to become a Catholic priest. Suddenly, this cataclysmic event ripped me from the moorings of my grandparents, my youth and my faith and catapulted me headlong into the abyss that Richard Wright seemed to describe years earlier.

It was this event that shattered my faith in my religion and my country. I had spent the mid-'60s as a successful student in a virtually white environment. I had learned Latin, physics and chemistry. I had accepted the loneliness that came with being "the integrator," the first and the only. But this event, this trauma I could not take, especially when one of my fellow seminarians, not knowing that I was

standing behind him, declared that he hoped the S.O.B. died. This was a man of God, mortally stricken by an assassin's bullet, and one preparing for the priesthood had wished evil upon him.

The life I had dreamed of so often during those hot summers on the farm in Georgia or during what seemed like endless hours on the oil truck with my grandfather expired as Dr. King expired. As so many of you do, I still know exactly where I was when I heard the news. It was a low moment in our nation's history and a demarcation between hope and hopelessness for many of us.

But three decades have evaporated in our lives, too quickly and without sufficient residual evidence of their importance. But much has changed since then. The hope that there would be expeditious resolutions to our myriad problems has long since evaporated with those years. Many who debated and hoped then, now do neither. There now seems to be a broad acceptance of the racial divide as a permanent state. While we once celebrated those things that we had in common with our fellow citizens who did not share our race, so many now are triumphal about our differences, finding little, if anything, in common. Indeed, some go so far as to all but define each of us by our race and establish the range of our thinking and our opinions, if not our deeds, by our color.

I, for one, see this in much the same way I saw our denial of rights—as nothing short of a denial of our humanity. Not one of us has the gospel. Nor are our opinions based upon some revealed precepts to be taken as faith. As thinking, rational individuals, not one of us can claim infallibility, even from the overwhelming advantage of hindsight and Monday-morning quarterbacking.

This makes it all the more important that our fallible ideas be examined as all ideas are in the realm of reason, not as some doctrinal or racial heresy. None of us—none of us have been appointed by God or appointed God. And if any of us has, then my question is why hasn't he or she solved all these problems.

I make no apologies for this view now, nor do I intend to do so in the future. I have now been on the court for seven terms. For the most part, it has been much like other endeavors in life. It has its challenges and requires much of the individual to master the workings of the institution. We all know that. It is, I must say, quite different from what I might have anticipated if I had the opportunity to do so. Unlike the unfortunate practice or custom in Washington and in much of the country, the court is a model of civility. It's a wonderful place. Though there have been many contentious issues to come before the court during these initial years of my tenure, I have yet to hear the first unkind words exchanged among my colleagues. And quite frankly, I think that such civility is the sine qua non of conducting the affairs of the court and the business of the country.

As such, I think that it would be in derogation of our respective oaths and our institutional obligations to our country to engage in uncivil behavior. It would also be demeaning to any of us who engaged in such conduct. Having worn the robe, we have a lifetime obligation to conduct ourselves as having deserved to wear the robe in the first instance.

One of the interesting surprises is the virtual isolation, even within the court. It is quite rare that the members of the court see each other during those periods when we're not sitting or when we're not in conference. And the most regular contact beyond those two formal events are the lunches we have on conference and court days. Also, it is extraordinarily rare to have any discussions with the other members of the court before voting on petitions for certiorari or on the merits of the cases. And there is rarely extended debate during our conferences. For the most part, any debate about the cases is done in writing. It has struck me as odd that some think that there are cliques and cabals at the court. No such arrangements exist. Nor, contrary to suggestions otherwise, is there any intellectual or ideological pied piper on the court.

With respect to my following, or, more accurately, being led by other members of the court, that is silly, but expected since I couldn't possibly think for myself. And what else could possibly be the explanation when I fail to follow the jurisprudential, ideological and intellectual, if not anti-intellectual, prescription assigned to blacks. Since thinking beyond this prescription is presumptively beyond my abilities, obviously someone must be putting these strange ideas into my mind and my opinions.

Though being underestimated has its advantages, the stench of racial inferiority still confounds my olfactory nerves.

As Ralph Ellison wrote more than 35 years ago, "Why is it so often true that when critics confront the American as Negro, they suddenly drop their advance critical armament and revert with an air of confident superiority to quite primitive modes of analysis?" Those matters accomplished by whites are routinely subjected to sophisticated modes of analysis. But when the selfsame matters are accomplished by blacks, the opaque racial prism of analysis precludes such sophistication and all is seen in black and white. And some who would not venture onto the more sophisticated analytical turf are quite content to play in the minor leagues of primitive harping. The more things change, the more they remain the same.

Of course there is much criticism of the court by this group or that, depending on the court's decisions in various highly publicized cases. Some of the criticism is profoundly uninformed and unhelpful. And all too often, uncivil second-guessing is not encumbered by the constraints of facts, logic or reasoned analysis. On the other hand, the constructive and often scholarly criticism is almost always helpful in thinking about or rethinking decisions. It is my view that constructive criticism goes with the turf, especially when the stakes are so high and the cases arouse passions and emotions. And, in a free society, [where is found] the precious freedom of speech and the strength of ideas, we at the court could not possibly claim exemption from such criticism. Moreover, we are not infallible, just final.

As I have noted, I find a thoughtful, analytical criticism most helpful. I do not think any judge can address a vast array of cases and issues without testing and re-testing his or her reasoning and opinions in the crucible of debate. However, since we are quite limited in public debate about matters that may come before the court, such debate must, for the most part, occur intramurally, thus placing a premium on outside scholarship. Unfortunately, from time to time, the criticism of the court goes beyond the bounds of civil debate and discourse. Today it seems quite acceptable to attack the court and other institutions when one disagrees with an opinion or policy. I can still remember traveling along Highway 17 in south Georgia, the Coastal Highway, during the '50s and '60s and seeing the "Impeach Earl Warren" signs.

Clearly, heated reactions to the court or to its members are not unusual. Certainly, Justice Blackmun was attacked repeatedly because many disagreed, as I have, with the opinion he offered on behalf of the court in *Roe v. Wade*. Though I have joined opinions disagreeing with Justice Blackmun, I could not imagine ever being discourteous to him merely because we disagreed.

I have found during my almost 20 years in Washington that the tendency to personalize differences has grown to be an accepted way of doing business. One need not do the hard work of dissecting an argument. One need only attack and thus discredit the person making the argument. Though the matter being debated is not effectively resolved, the debate is reduced to unilateral pronouncements and glib but quotable clichés. I, for one, have been singled out for particularly bilious and venomous assaults. These criticisms, as near as I can tell, and I admit that it is rare that I take notice of this calumny, have little to do with any particular opinion, though each opinion does provide one more occasion to criticize. Rather, the principal problem seems to be a deeper antecedent offense.

I have no right to think the way I do because I'm black. Though the ideas and opinions themselves are not necessarily illegitimate if held by non-black individuals, they, and the person enunciating them, are illegitimate if that person happens to be black. Thus, there's a subset of criticism that must of necessity be reserved for me, even if every non-black member of the court agrees with the idea or the opinion. You see, they are exempt from this kind of criticism, precisely because they are not black. As noted earlier, they are more often than not subjected to the whites-only sophisticated analysis.

I will not catalogue my opinions to which there have been objections since they are a matter of public record. But I must note in passing that I can't help but wonder if some of my critics can read. One opinion that is trotted out for propaganda, for the propaganda parade, is my dissent in *Hudson v. McMillian*. The conclusion reached by the long arms of the critics is that I supported the beating of prisoners in that case. Well, one must either be illiterate or fraught with malice to reach that conclusion. Though one can disagree with my dissent, and certainly the majority of the court disagreed, no honest reading can reach such a conclusion. Indeed, we took the case to decide the quite narrow issue whether a prisoner's rights were violated under the "cruel and unusual punishment" clause of the Eighth Amendment as a result of a single incident of force by the prison guards which did not cause a significant injury. In the first section of my dissent, I stated the following. "In my view, a use of force that causes only insignificant harm to a prisoner may be immoral; it may be tortuous; it may be criminal, and it may even be remediable under other provisions of the Federal Constitution. But it is not cruel and unusual punishment."

Obviously, beating prisoners is bad. But we did not take the case to answer this larger moral question or a larger legal question of remedies under other statutes or provisions of the Constitution. How one can extrapolate these larger conclusions from the narrow question before the court is beyond me, unless, of course, there's a special segregated mode of analysis.

It should be obvious that the criticism of this opinion serves not to present counter-arguments, but to discredit and attack me because I've deviated from the prescribed path. In his intriguing and thoughtful essay on "My Race Problem and Ours," Harvard law professor Randall Kennedy, a self-described Social Democrat, correctly observes that "If racial loyalty is deemed essentially and morally virtuous, then a black person's adoption of positions that are deemed racially disloyal will be seen by racial loyalists as a supremely threatening sin, one warranting the harsh punishments that have historically been visited upon alleged traitors." Perhaps this is the defensive solidarity to which Richard Wright refers. If so, it is a reaction I understand, but resolutely decline to follow.

In the final weeks of my seminary days, shortly after Dr. King's death, I found myself becoming consumed by feelings of animosity and anger. I was disenchanted with my church and my country. I was tired of being in the minority, and I was tired of turning the other cheek. I, along with many blacks, found ways to protest and try to change the treatment we received in this country. Perhaps my passion for Richard Wright novels was affecting me. Perhaps I was being consumed by the circumstances in which I found myself, circumstances that I saw as responding only to race.

My feelings were reaffirmed during the summer of 1968 as a result of the lingering stench of racism in Savannah and the assassination of Bobby Kennedy. No matter what the reasons were, I closed out the '60s as one angry young man waiting on the revolution that I was certain would soon come. I saw no way out. I, like many others, felt the deep chronic agony of anomie and alienation. All seemed to be defined by race. We became a reaction to "the man," his ominous reflection.

The intensity of my feelings was reinforced by other events of the late '60s: the riots, the marches, the sense that something had to be done, done quickly to resolve the issue of race. In college there was an air of excitement, apprehension and anger. We started the Black Students Union. We protested. We worked in the Free Breakfast Program. We would walk out of school in the winter of 1969 in protest.

But the questioning for me started in the spring of 1970 after an unauthorized demonstration in Cambridge, Massachusetts to "free the political prisoners." Why was I doing this rather than using my intellect? Perhaps I was empowered by the anger and relieved that I could now strike back at the faceless oppressor. But why was I conceding my intellect and rather fighting much like a brute? This I could not answer, except to say that I was tired of being restrained. … It was intoxicating to act upon one's rage, to wear it on one's shoulder, to be defined by it. Yet, ultimately, it was destructive, and I knew it.

So in the spring of 1970 in a nihilistic fog, I prayed that I'd be relieved of the anger and the animosity that ate at my soul. I did not want to hate any more, and I had to stop before it totally consumed me. I had to make a fundamental choice. Do I believe in the principles of this country or not? After much angst, I concluded that I did. But the battle between passion and reason would continue, although abated, still intense.

Ironically, many of the people who are critics today were among those we called half-steppers, who had co-opted by "the man" because they were part of the system that oppressed us. When the revolution came, all of the so-called Negroes needed to be dealt with. It is interesting to remember that someone gave me a copy of Professor Thomas Sowell's book, *Education, Myths and Tragedies,* in which he predicted much of what has happened to blacks and education. I threw it in the trash, unread, declaring that he was not a black man since no black could take the positions that he had taken, whatever they were, since I had only heard his views were not those of a black man.

I was also upset to hear of a black conservative in Virginia named Jay Parker. How could a black man call himself a conservative? In a twist of fate, they both are dear friends today, and the youthful wrath I visited upon them is now being visited upon me, though without the youth. What goes around does indeed come around.

The summer of 1971 was perhaps one of the most difficult of my life. It was clear to me that the road to destruction was paved with anger, resentment and rage. But where were we to go? I would often spend hours in our small efficiency apartment in New Haven pondering this question and listening to Marvin Gaye's then new album, *What's Going On?* To say the least, it was a depressing summer.

As I think back on those years, I find it interesting that many people seemed to have trouble with their identities as black men. Having had to accept my blackness in the caldron of ridicule from some of my black schoolmates under segregation, then immediately thereafter remain secure in that identity during my years at an all-white seminary, I had few racial identity problems. I knew who I was and needed no gimmicks to affirm my identity. Nor, might I add, do I need anyone telling me who I am today. This is especially true of the psycho-silliness about forgetting my roots or self-hatred. If anything, this shows that some people have too much time on their hands.

There's a rush today to prescribe who is black, to prescribe our differences or to ignore what our differences are. Of course, those of us who came from the rural South were different from the blacks who came from the large northern cities, such as Philadelphia and New York. We were all black. But that similarity did not mask the richness of our differences. Indeed, one of the advantages of growing up in a black neighborhood was that we were richly blessed with the ability to see the individuality of each black person with all its fullness and complexity. We saw those differences at school, at home, at church, and definitely at the barbershop on Saturday morning.

Intra-racially, we consistently recognized our differences. It is quite counter-factual to suggest that such differences have not existed throughout our history. Indeed, when I was on the other side of the ideological divide, arguing strenuously with my grandfather that the revolution was imminent and that we all had to stick together as black people, he was quick to remind me that he had lived much longer than I had and during far more difficult times, and that, in any case, it took all kinds to make a world.

I agree with Ralph Ellison when he asked, perhaps rhetorically, why is it that so many of those who would tell us the meaning of "Negro," of Negro life, never bothered to learn how varied it really is. That is particularly true of many whites who have elevated condescension to an art form by advancing a monolithic view of blacks in much the same way that the mythic, disgusting image of the lazy, dumb black was advanced by open, rather than disguised, bigots. Today, of course, it is customary to collapse, if not overwrite, our individual characteristics into new, but now acceptable stereotypes. It no longer matters whether one is from urban New York City or rural Georgia. It doesn't matter whether we came from a highly educated family or a barely literate one. It does not matter if you are a Roman Catholic or a Southern Baptist. All of these differences are canceled by race, and a revised set of acceptable stereotypes has been put in place.

Long gone is the time when we opposed the notion that we all looked alike and talked alike. Somehow we have come to exalt the new black stereotype above all and to demand conformity to that norm. It is this notion that our race defines us that Ralph Ellison so eloquently rebuts in his essay, "The World and the Jug." He sees the lives of black people as more than a burden, but also a discipline, just as any human life which has endured so long is a discipline, teaching its own insights into the human condition, its own strategies of survival. There's a fullness and even a richness here. And here despite the realities of politics, perhaps, but nevertheless here and real because it is human life.

Despite some of the nonsense that has been said about me by those who should know better, and so much nonsense, the sum of which subtracts from the sum total of human knowledge, despite this all, I am a man, a black man, an American. And my history is not unlike that of many blacks from the deep South. And in many ways it is not that much different from that of many other Americans. It goes without saying that I understand the comforts and security of racial solidarity, defensive or otherwise. Only those who have not been set upon by hatred and repelled by rejection fail to understand its attraction. As I have suggested, I have been there.

The inverse relationship between the bold promises and the effectiveness of the proposed solutions, the frustrations with the so-called system, the subtle and not-so-subtle bigotry and animus towards members of my race made radicals and nationalists of many of us. Yes, I understand the reasons why this is attractive. But it is precisely this—in its historic form, not its present-day diluted form—that I have rejected. My question was whether as an individual I truly believed that I was the equal of individuals who were white. This I had answered with a resounding "yes" in 1964 during my sophomore year in the seminary. And that answer continues to be yes. Accordingly, my words and my deeds are consistent with this answer.

Any effort, policy or program that has as a prerequisite the acceptance of the notion that blacks are inferior is a non-starter with me. I do not believe that kneeling is a position of strength. Nor do I believe that begging is an effective tactic. I am confident that the individual approach, not the group approach, is the better, more acceptable, more supportable and less dangerous one. This approach is also consistent with the underlying principles of this country and the guarantees of freedom through government by consent. I, like Frederick Douglass, believe that whites and blacks can live together and be blended into a common nationality.

Do I believe that my views or opinions are perfect or infallible? No, I do not. But in admitting that I have no claim to perfection or infallibility, I am also asserting that competing or differing views similarly have no such claim. And they should not be accorded a status of infallibility or any status that suggests otherwise.

With differing, but equally fallible views, I think it is best that they be aired and sorted out in an environment of civility, consistent with the institutions in which we are involved. In this case, the judicial system.

It pains me deeply, more deeply than any of you can imagine, to be perceived by so many members of my race as doing them harm. All the sacrifice, all the long hours of preparation were to help, not to hurt. But what hurts more, much more, is the amount of time and attention spent on manufactured controversies and media sideshows when so many problems cry out for constructive attention.

I have come here today not in anger or to anger, though my mere presence has been sufficient, obviously, to anger some. Nor have I come to defend my views, but rather to assert my right to think for myself, to refuse to have my ideas assigned to me as though I was an intellectual slave because I'm black. I come to state that I'm a man, free to think for myself and do as I please.

I've come to assert that I am a judge and I will not be consigned the unquestioned opinions of others. But even more than that, I have come to say that isn't it time to move on? Isn't it time to realize that being angry with me solves no problems? Isn't it time to acknowledge that the problem of race has defied simple solutions and that not one of us, not a single one of us can lay claim to the solution? Isn't it time that we respect ourselves and each other as we have demanded respect from others? Isn't it time to ignore those whose sole occupation is sowing seeds of discord and animus? That is self-hatred.

Isn't it time to continue diligently to search for lasting solutions?

I believe that the time has come today. God bless each of you, and may God keep you.

HENRY HYDE

The Rule of Law

No man or woman, no matter how highly placed, no matter how effective a communicator, no matter how gifted a manipulator of opinion or winner of votes, can be above the law in a democracy.

On June 30, 1994, President Bill Clinton signed into law the Independent Counsel Act, calling it "a foundation stone for the trust between the Government and our citizens." Two months later, a former U.S. Court of Appeals judge named Kenneth Starr succeeded Robert B. Fiske, Jr. as Independent Counsel for the purpose of investigating the suicide death of Deputy White House Counsel Vince Foster and the Clintons' involvement in a fraudulent Arkansas land deal known as "Whitewater." Starr's investigation resulted in numerous felony convictions, including those of former Clinton business partners as well as Bill Clinton's successor as Arkansas governor, Jim Guy Tucker.

In September of 1998, after using the broad investigative powers of the Independent Counsel Act to expand his inquiry, Starr released his report to Congress citing eleven possible grounds for impeachment. The charges included perjury and obstruction of justice, resulting from the president lying under oath about a sexual affair he had with a twenty-one-year-old White House intern named Monica Lewinsky, who was listed as a witness in the case of *Jones v. Clinton*—a civilian lawsuit resulting from the president allegedly making unwanted sexual advances. The president's continued deception resulted in four articles of impeachment, two of which were passed by the House, making Bill Clinton the only elected president in American history to be impeached. Like Andrew Johnson 130 years earlier, Clinton would be acquitted by the Senate, the prosecution having failed to gain the two-thirds vote needed for removal from office.

The following speech by Illinois Republican Henry Hyde (1924-2007), chairman of the House Judiciary Committee, was delivered on the House floor during the debate of impeachment articles on December 18, 1998. Hyde presented the case for impeachment while rendering an eloquent explanation of the rule of law.

Mr. Speaker, my colleagues of the people's House, I wish to talk to you about the rule of law. After months of argument, hours of debate, there is no need for further complexity. The question before this House is rather simple. It's not a question of sex. Sexual misconduct and adultery are private acts and are none of Congress' business.

It's not even a question of lying about sex. The matter before the House is a question of lying under oath. This is a public act, not a private act. This is called perjury. The matter before the House is a question of the willful, premeditated, deliberate corruption of the nation's system of justice. Perjury and obstruction of justice cannot be reconciled with the office of the President of the United States.

The personal fate of the President is not the issue. The political fate of his party is not the issue. The Dow Jones Industrial Average is not the issue. The issue is perjury—

lying under oath. The issue is obstruction of justice, which the President has sworn the most solemn oath to uphold.

That oath constituted a compact between the President and the American people. That compact has been broken. The people's trust has been betrayed. The nation's chief executive has shown himself unwilling or incapable of enforcing its laws for he has corrupted the rule of law—the rule of law—by his perjury and his obstruction of justice.

That and nothing other than that is the issue before this House.

We have heard ceaselessly that, even if the President is guilty of the charges in the Starr referral, they don't rise to the level of an impeachable offense.

Well, just what is an impeachable offense?

One authority, Professor Stephen Presser of Northwestern University Law School said, and I quote, "Impeachable offenses are those which demonstrate a fundamental betrayal of public trust. They suggest the federal official has deliberately failed in his duty to uphold the Constitution and laws he was sworn to enforce."

And so we must decide if a President, the chief law enforcement officer of the land, the person who appoints the attorney general, the person who nominates every federal judge, the person who nominates to the Supreme Court and the only person with a constitutional obligation to take care that the laws be faithfully executed, can lie under oath repeatedly and maintain it is not a breach of trust sufficient for impeachment.

The President is the trustee of the nation's conscience and so are we here today. There have been many explosions in our committee hearings on the respective role of the House and Senate.

Under the Constitution, the House accuses and the Senate adjudicates.

True, the formula language of our articles recites the ultimate goal of removal from office, but this language doesn't trump the Constitution, which defines the separate functions, the different functions, of the House and the Senate.

Our Founding Fathers didn't want the body that accuses to be the same one that renders final judgment, and they set up an additional safeguard of a two-thirds vote for removal. So despite protests, our job is to decide if there is enough evidence to submit to the Senate for a trial.

That's what the Constitution says, no matter what the President's defenders say. When Ben Franklin, on September 18, 1787, told a Mrs. Powell that the founders and framers had given us a republic if you can keep it, perhaps he anticipated a future time when bedrock principles of our democracy would be mortally threatened as the rule of law stands in the line of fire today.

Nothing I can think of more clearly illustrates that America is a continuing experiment, never finished, that our democracy is always a work in progress, than this debate today for we sit here with the power to shape and reconfigure the charter of our freedom. Just as the founders and framers did, we can strengthen our Constitution by giving it content and meaning or we can weaken and wound it by tolerating and thus encouraging lies under oath and evasions and breaches of trust on the part of our chief executive.

The President's defenders in this House have rarely denied the facts. They have not seriously challenged the contention of the Independent Counsel that the President did not tell the truth in two sworn testimonies. They have not seriously attempted to discredit the facts brought before the committee by the Independent Counsel. They've admitted in effect—He did it. But then they've argued this does not rise to the level of an impeachable offense. This is the "so what" defense whereby a chief executive, a successor to George Washington, can cheapen the oath and it really doesn't matter.

They suggest that to impeach the President is to reverse the result of a national election, as though Senator Dole would become President.

They propose novel remedies like a congressional censure that may appease some constituents and certainly mollify the press but, in my judgment, betray a lack of seriousness about the Constitution, the separation of powers and the carefully balanced relationship of checks and balances between Congress and the President that was wisely crafted by the framers.

A resolution of censure, to mean anything, must punish if only to tarnish his reputation. But we have no authority under the Constitution to punish the President. It's called separation of powers.

As you know, we've been attacked for not producing fact witnesses. But this is the first impeachment inquiry in history with the Office of Independent Counsel in place, and their referral to us consisted of 60,000 pages of sworn testimony, grand jury transcripts, depositions, statements, affidavits, video and audio tapes.

We had the facts and we had them under oath.

We had Ms. Lewinsky's heavily corroborated testimony under a grant of immunity that would be revoked if she lied.

We accepted that and so did they. Else why didn't they call any others whose credibility they questioned as their own witnesses? Now there was so little dispute on the facts, they called no fact witnesses and have even based a resolution of censure on the same facts.

Let's be clear. The vote that all of us are asked to cast is, in the final analysis, a vote on the rule of law.

Now the rule of law is one of the great achievements of our civilization, for the alternative is the rule of raw power. We here today are the heirs of 3,000 years of history in which humanity slowly, painfully, at great cost evolved a form of politics in which law, not brute force, is the arbiter of our public destinies.

We are the heirs of the Ten Commandments and the Mosaic Law, a moral code for a free people, who, having been liberated from bondage, sought in law a means to avoid falling back into the habits of slaves.

We are the heirs of Roman Law, the first legal system by which peoples of different cultures, languages, races and religions came to live together in a form of political community.

We are the heirs of the Magna Carta, by which the free men of England began to break the arbitrary and unchecked power of royal absolutism.

We're the heirs of a long tradition of parliamentary development in which the rule of law gradually came to replace royal prerogative as a means for governing a society of free men and women.

We're the heirs of 1776 and of an epic moment in human affairs, when the founders of this Republic pledged their lives, their fortunes and their sacred honor. Think of that—sacred honor—to the defense of the rule of law.

We are the heirs of a hard-fought war between the states, which vindicated the rule of law over the appetites of some for owning others.

We are the heirs of the twentieth century's great struggles against totalitarianism, in which the rule of law was defended at immense cost against the worst tyrannies in human history.

The phrase "rule of law" is no pious aspiration from a civics text book. The rule of law is what stands between all of us and the arbitrary exercise of power by the state. The rule of law is the safeguard of our liberties. The rule of law is what allows us to live our freedom in ways that honor the freedom of others, while strengthening the common good.

The rule of law is like a three-legged stool. One leg is an honest judge, the second leg is an ethical bar, and the third is an enforceable oath. All three are indispensable to avoid political collapse.

In 1838, Abraham Lincoln celebrated the rule of law before the Young Men's Lyceum of Springfield, Illinois, and linked it to the perpetuation of American liberties and American political institutions. Listen to Lincoln, from 1838: "Let every American, every lover of liberty, every well-wisher to his posterity, swear by the blood of the revolution never to violate in the least particular the laws of the country; and never to tolerate their violation by others. As the patriots of '76 did to support the Declaration of Independence, so the support of the Constitution and laws, let every American pledge his life, his property and his sacred honor. Let every man remember that to violate the law is to trample on the blood of his father and to tear the character of his own and his children's liberty.

"Let reverence for the laws be breathed by every American mother to the lisping babe that prattles on her lap. Let it be taught in the schools, seminaries, colleges. Let it be written in primers, spelling books, almanacs. Let it be preached from the pulpit, proclaimed in legislative halls and enforced in the courts of justice."

So said Lincoln.

My colleagues, we have been sent here to strengthen and defend the rule of law—not to weaken it, not to attenuate it, not to disfigure it. This is not a question of perfection. It's a question of foundations. This isn't a matter of setting the bar too high. It's a matter of securing the basic structure of our freedom, which is the rule of law. No man or woman, no matter how highly placed, no matter how effective a communicator, no matter how gifted a manipulator of opinion or winner of votes, can be above the law in a democracy. That is not a counsel of perfection. That is a rock-bottom, irreducible principle of our public life.

There's no avoiding the issue before us—much as I wish we could. We are, in one way or another, establishing the parameters of permissible presidential conduct.

In creating a presidential system, the framers invested that office with extraordinary powers. If those powers are not exercised within the boundaries of the rule of law; if the President breaks the law by perjury and obstructs justice by willfully corrupting the legal system, that President must be removed from office.

We cannot have one law for the ruler and another law for the ruled. This was once broadly understood in our land. If that understanding is lost or if it becomes seriously eroded, the American democratic experiment and the freedom it guarantees is in jeopardy. That and not the fate of one man, or one political party, or one electoral cycle is what we're being asked to vote on today.

In casting our votes we should look not simply to ourselves, but to the past and to the future. Let's look back to Bunker Hill, Concord, Lexington. Let's look across the river to Arlington Cemetery where American heroes who gave their lives for the sake of the rule of law lie buried.

And let us not betray their memory.

Let's look to the future, to the children of today who are the presidents and members of Congress of the next century. And let's not crush their hope that they too will inherent a law-governed society.

Let's declare unmistakably that perjury and obstruction of justice disqualify a man from retaining the presidency of the United States.

There is a mountain of details which are assembled in a coherent mosaic in the committee report. It reads like a novel, only it's non-fiction. It really happened. And the corroboration is compelling. Read the report and be convinced.

What we're telling you today are not the ravings of some vindictive political crusade but a reaffirmation of a set of values that are tarnished and dim these days, but it is given to us to restore them so our Founding Fathers would be proud.

Listen, it's your country. The President is our flag bearer. He stands out in front of our people when the flag is falling. Catch the falling flag as we keep our appointment with history.

I yield back.

AL GORE

Concession Speech

While we yet hold and do not yield our opposing beliefs, there is a higher duty than the one we owe to political party.

Albert Gore, Jr., the son of a long-time Democratic congressman and senator from Tennessee, was born in Washington, D.C., in 1948. He graduated from Harvard University in 1969 and took courses at Vanderbilt University's divinity and law schools. Though opposed to the war in Vietnam, Gore accepted induction into the U.S. Army and served as a military reporter for *Stars and Stripes*. He later worked as an investigative reporter for the *Nashville Tennessean*. In 1976, he was elected to the first of four terms in the U.S. House of Representatives and, in 1984, to the U.S. Senate. Gore ran unsuccessfully for his party's presidential nomination in 1988 but, four years later, became the vice presidential running mate of Arkansas Governor Bill Clinton.

In 2000, campaigning on the strong economy and America's relatively peaceful standing in the world, Gore gained the Democratic presidential nomination. The result of the general election was a narrow victory for Gore in the popular vote, but a 271-267 electoral victory for his Republican opponent, George W. Bush. The election's outcome hinged on results from the state of Florida. On election night, the television networks prematurely declared Bush the winner, and Gore, as tradition dictates, called his opponent to concede. He retracted that concession soon thereafter when it was announced that the election was too close to call, thus sparking a five-week legal battle that would ultimately end in the Supreme Court.

On December 13, 2000, in a prime-time television address, Gore offered his concession. With grace, eloquence, humor, and patriotism, he joined President-elect Bush in calling upon the nation for unity.

Just moments ago, I spoke with George W. Bush and congratulated him on becoming the 43rd President of the United States. And I promised I wouldn't call him back this time.

I offered to meet with him as soon as possible, so that we can start to heal the divisions of the campaign, and the contest through which we have just passed.

Almost a century and a half ago, Senator Stephen

Douglas told Abraham Lincoln, who had just defeated him for the Presidency, "Partisan feeling must yield to patriotism. I am with you, Mr. President, and God bless you."

In that same spirit, I say to President-elect Bush that what remains of partisan rancor must now be put aside. And may God bless his stewardship of this country.

Neither he nor I anticipated this long and difficult road. Certainly, neither of us wanted it to happen. Yet it came. And now it has ended, resolved as it must be resolved—through the honored institutions of our democracy.

Over the library of one of our great law schools is inscribed the motto: "Not under man but under God and law." It is the ruling principle of American freedom, the source of our democratic liberties; I have tried to make it my guide throughout this contest, as it has guided America's deliberations of all the complex issues of the past five weeks.

Now the U.S. Supreme Court has spoken. Let there be no doubt: while I strongly disagree with the Court's decision, I accept it. I accept the finality of this outcome, which will be ratified next Monday in the Electoral College. And tonight, for the sake of our unity as a people and the strength of our democracy, I offer my concession.

I also accept my responsibility, which I will discharge unconditionally—to honor the new President-elect, and do everything possible to help him bring Americans together in fulfillment of the great vision that our Declaration of Independence defines, and that our Constitution affirms and defends.

Let me say how grateful I am to all those who supported me—and supported the cause for which we have fought.

Tipper and I feel a deep gratitude to Joe and Hadassah Lieberman, who brought passion and high purpose to our partnership—and opened new doors not just for our campaign, but for our country.

This has been an extraordinary election. But in one of God's unforeseen paths, this belatedly broken impasse can point us all to a new common ground. For its very closeness can serve to remind us that we are one people, with a shared history and a shared destiny.

Indeed, that history gives us many examples of contests as hotly debated, as fiercely fought, with their own challenges to the popular will. Other disputes have dragged on for weeks before reaching resolution. And each time, both the victor and the vanquished have accepted the result peacefully, and in a spirit of reconciliation.

So let it be with us.

I know that many of my supporters are disappointed. I am, too. But our disappointment must be overcome by our love of country.

And I say to our fellow members of the world community: let no one see this contest as a sign of American weakness. The strength of American democracy is shown most clearly through the difficulties it can overcome.

Some have expressed concern that the unusual nature of this election might hamper the next President in the conduct of his office. I do not believe it need be so.

President-elect Bush inherits a nation whose citizens will be ready to assist him in the conduct of his large responsibilities. I, personally, will be at his disposal.

And I call on all Americans—I particularly urge all who stood with us—to unite behind our next President.

This is America. Just as we fight hard when the stakes are high, we close ranks and come together when the contest is done.

And while there will be time enough to debate our continuing differences, now is the time to recognize that that which unites us is greater than that which divides us.

While we yet hold and do not yield our opposing beliefs, there is a higher duty than the one we owe to political party.

This is America—and we put country before party. We will stand together behind our new President.

As for what I'll do next, I don't know the answer to that one yet. Like many of you, I'm looking forward to spending the holidays with family and old friends.

I know I'll spend time in Tennessee and mend some fences—literally and figuratively.

Some have asked whether I have any regrets, and I do have one regret: that I didn't get the chance to stay and fight for the American people for the next four years. Especially for those who need burdens lifted and barriers removed. Especially for those who feel their voices have not been heard.

I heard you—and I will not forget.

I've seen America in this campaign. And I like what I see. It's worth fighting for. And that's a fight I'll never stop.

As for the battle that ends tonight, I do believe, as my father once said, that "No matter how hard the loss, defeat may serve as well as victory to shake the soul and let the glory out."

So for me, this campaign ends as it began—with the love of Tipper and our family; with faith in God and in the country I have been so proud to serve—from Vietnam to the vice presidency; and with gratitude to our truly tireless campaign staff and volunteers, including all those who worked so hard in Florida for the last 36 days.

Now the political struggle is over and we turn again to the unending struggle for the common good of all Americans, and for those multitudes around the world who look to us for leadership in the cause of freedom.

In the words of our great hymn, "America, America": "Let us crown thy good with brotherhood, from sea to shining sea."

And now, my friends, in a phrase I once addressed to others—it is time for me to go.

Thank you, and good night. And God bless America.

President George W. Bush sits at his desk in the Oval Office for the first time on Inaugural Day, January 20, 2001, as his father, former President George H.W. Bush, looks on.

My City of Ruins

"The Boss," as Bruce Springsteen is known to his fans, ranks as one on the most influential songwriters in American history. Born in 1949 in Freehold, New Jersey, near the beach town of Asbury Park, Springsteen released his first album in 1973 and quickly established himself as one on the world's premiere showmen, giving concert performances that were part rock revival and part music marathon.

Volumes have been written about the appeal of his music, but perhaps the best explanation comes from Stephen Holden of *The New York Times*, who wrote: "Forged from the simple vernaculars of blues, folk, country and gospel … hard Saturday night party music for the common people wasn't invented to help examine the hard realities of life but to find a release from those realities. [Springsteen] has transfused rock and roll and social realism into one another, and the compassion and the surging brawn of his music make his very despairing vision of American life into a kind of celebration."

"My City of Ruins" was originally written in 2000 for a benefit show to promote the revitalization of Asbury Park. The song took on an entirely new meaning soon after the terrorist attacks of September 11, 2001. On September 21, during the *America: A Tribute To Heroes* national telethon, Springsteen opened the program with a guitar and harmonica rendition of the song as "a prayer for our fallen brothers and sisters" while modifying a few verses. A studio recording of "My City of Ruins," with the lyrics printed here, was then incorporated as the concluding track of Springsteen's September 11-themed album, *The Rising* (2002).

There's a blood red circle
On the cold dark ground
And the rain is falling down
The church door's thrown open
I can hear the organ's song
But the congregation's gone
My city of ruins
My city of ruins

Now the sweet bells of mercy
Drift through the evening trees
Young men on the corner like scattered leaves,
The boarded up windows,
The empty streets
While my brother's down on his knees
My city of ruins
My city of ruins

Come on rise up!
Come on rise up!
Come on rise up!
Come on rise up!
Come on rise up!
Come on rise up!
Come on rise up!

Now there's tears on the pillow
Darlin' where we slept
And you took my heart when you left
Without your sweet kiss
My soul is lost, my friend
Tell me how do I begin again?
My city's in ruins
My city's in ruins

Now with these hands,
With these hands, With these hands
With these hands, I pray Lord
With these hands, With these hands,
I pray for the strength, Lord
With these hands, With these hands,
I pray for the faith Lord
With these hands, With these hands,
I pray for your love, Lord
With these hands, With these hands,
I pray for the strength, Lord
With these hands, With these hands,
I pray for your love, Lord
With these hands, With these hands,
I pray for your faith, Lord
With these hands, With these hands,
I pray for the strength, Lord
With these hands, With these hands

Come on, rise up!

Come on rise up!

Come on rise up!

Come on rise up!

Come on rise up!

Come on rise up!

Come on rise up!

GEORGE W. BUSH

War Message to Congress

We will direct every resource at our command—every means of diplomacy, every tool of intelligence, every instrument of law enforcement, every financial influence, and every necessary weapon of war—to the destruction and to the defeat of the global terror network.

George Walker Bush, the eldest son of the forty-first president of the United States, was born in 1946 in New Haven, Connecticut, and grew up in Midland, Texas, where his father worked in the oil business. He attended Philips Andover Academy in Massachusetts, graduated from Yale University, then returned to Texas and served as a fighter pilot with the Texas Air National Guard. In 1972, Bush entered Harvard Business School, earning his M.B.A. in 1975. He then ventured into the oil business and, in 1978, ran unsuccessfully for the U.S. Senate. In 1988, after working in his father's presidential campaign, Bush organized a group of investors and arranged the purchase of the Texas Rangers professional baseball team. In 1994, he shocked the political world and came to national prominence when he was elected governor of Texas, defeating the popular Democrat incumbent Anne Richards. In November 1998, he became the first Texas governor to be elected to consecutive four-year terms. That same year, his brother Jeb was elected governor of Florida. Billing himself as a "compassionate conservative," Bush announced in June 1999 his intention to run for president of the United States.

Bush's 2000 election victory was the fourth time the nation elected a president who did not win the popular vote. By a remarkable coincidence, the first president to hold this distinction was John Quincy Adams, also the son of a former president. In 1876, Rutherford B. Hayes lost the popular vote to Samuel Tilden by 247,000 votes, but won the electoral college by one vote, 185 to 184. In 1888, Benjamin Harrison lost the popular vote by 90,000 votes, but defeated the incumbent president, Grover Cleveland, 233-168 in the electoral college.

Initially, it seemed that the new president would focus on pursuing an ambitious domestic agenda and bridging the party divide after such a hotly contested election. Instead, his administration became immersed in unexpected cataclysmic events—the terrorist attacks of September 11; wars in Afghanistan and Iraq; devastation in New Orleans caused by Hurricane Katrina; and a widespread financial crisis resulting in part from the collapse in the housing market.

The following is Bush's address to a joint session of Congress following the attack of 9/11, delivered September 20, 2001.

... Tonight, we are a country awakened to danger and called to defend freedom. Our grief has turned to anger and anger to resolution. Whether we bring our enemies to justice or bring justice to our enemies, justice will be done. ...

On behalf of the American people, I thank the world for its outpouring of support. America will never forget the sounds of our national anthem playing at Buckingham Palace, on the streets of Paris, and at Berlin's Brandenburg Gate. We will not forget South Korean children gathering to pray outside our embassy in Seoul, or the prayers of sympathy offered at a mosque in Cairo. We will not forget moments of silence and days of mourning in Australia and Africa and Latin America. Nor will we forget the citizens of 80 other nations who died with our own: dozens of Pakistanis; more than 130 Israelis; more than 250 citizens of India; men and women from El Salvador, Iran, Mexico, and Japan; and hundreds of British citizens.

America has no truer friend than Great Britain. Once again, we are joined together in a great cause. I'm so honored the British Prime Minister has crossed an ocean to show his unity with America. Thank you for coming, friend.

On September the 11th, enemies of freedom committed an act of war against our country. Americans have known wars—but for the past 136 years they have been wars on foreign soil, except for one Sunday in 1941. Americans have known the casualties of war—but not at the center of a great city on a peaceful morning. Americans have known surprise attacks—but never before on thousands of civilians. All of this was brought upon us in a single day—and night fell on a different world, a world where freedom itself is under attack.

Americans have many questions tonight. Americans are asking, "Who attacked our country?"

The evidence we have gathered all points to a collection of loosely affiliated terrorist organizations known as al Qaeda. They are some of the murderers indicted for bombing American embassies in Tanzania and Kenya, and responsible for bombing the USS *Cole*.

Al Qaeda is to terror what the mafia is to crime. But its goal is not making money. Its goal is remaking the world and imposing its radical beliefs on people everywhere. The terrorists practice a fringe form of Islamic extremism that has been rejected by Muslim scholars and the vast majority of Muslim clerics; a fringe movement that perverts the peaceful teachings of Islam. The terrorists' directive commands them to kill Christians and Jews, to kill all Americans, and make no distinctions among military and civilians, including women and children.

This group and its leader—a person named Usama bin Laden—are linked to many other organizations in different countries, including the Egyptian Islamic Jihad and the Islamic Movement of Uzbekistan.

There are thousands of these terrorists in more than 60 countries. They are recruited from their own nations and neighborhoods and brought to camps in places like Afghanistan, where they are trained in the tactics of terror. They are sent back to their homes or sent to hide in countries around the world to plot evil and destruction.

The leadership of al Qaeda has great influence in Afghanistan and supports the Taliban regime in controlling most of that country. In Afghanistan, we see al Qaeda's vision for the world. Afghanistan's people have been brutalized; many are starving and many have fled. Women are not allowed to attend school. You can be jailed for owning a television. Religion can be practiced only as their leaders dictate. A man can be jailed in Afghanistan if his beard is not long enough.

The United States respects the people of Afghanistan. After all, we are currently its largest source of humanitarian aid—but we condemn the Taliban regime. It is not only repressing its own people, it is threatening people everywhere by sponsoring and sheltering and supplying terrorists. By aiding and abetting murder, the Taliban regime is committing murder. And tonight the United States of America makes the following demands on the Taliban:

Deliver to United States authorities all of the leaders of al Qaeda who hide in your land. Release all foreign nationals, including American citizens you have unjustly imprisoned. Protect foreign journalists, diplomats and aid workers in your country. Close immediately and permanently every terrorist training camp in Afghanistan, and hand over every terrorist, and every person in their support structure, to appropriate authorities. Give the United States full access to terrorist training camps, so we can make sure they are no longer operating.

These demands are not open to negotiation or discussion. The Taliban must act and act immediately. They will hand over the terrorists, or they will share in their fate.

I also want to speak tonight directly to Muslims throughout the world. We respect your faith. It's practiced freely by many millions of Americans and by millions more in countries that America counts as friends. Its teachings are good and peaceful, and those who commit evil in the name of Allah blaspheme the name of Allah.

The terrorists are traitors to their own faith, trying, in effect, to hijack Islam itself. The enemy of America is not our many Muslim friends; it is not our many Arab friends. Our enemy is a radical network of terrorists and every government that supports them.

Our war on terror begins with al Qaeda, but it does not end there. It will not end until every terrorist group of global reach has been found, stopped and defeated.

Americans are asking, "Why do they hate us?"

They hate what they see right here in this chamber: a democratically elected government. Their leaders are self-appointed. They hate our freedoms: our freedom of religion, our freedom of speech, our freedom to vote and assemble and disagree with each other.

They want to overthrow existing governments in many Muslim countries such as Egypt, Saudi Arabia, and Jordan. They want to drive Israel out of the Middle East. They want to drive Christians and Jews out of vast regions of Asia and Africa.

These terrorists kill not merely to end lives, but to disrupt and end a way of life. With every atrocity, they hope that America grows fearful, retreating from the world and forsaking our friends. They stand against us because we stand in their way.

We're not deceived by their pretenses to piety. We have seen their kind before. They're the heirs of all the murderous ideologies of the 20th century. By sacrificing human life to serve their radical visions—by abandoning every value except the will to power—they follow in the path of fascism, Nazism and totalitarianism. And they will follow that path all the way to where it ends: in history's unmarked grave of discarded lies.

Americans are asking, "How will we fight and win this war?"

We will direct every resource at our command—every means of diplomacy, every tool of intelligence, every instrument of law enforcement, every financial influence, and every necessary weapon of war—to the destruction and to the defeat of the global terror network.

Now this war will not be like the war against Iraq a decade ago, with a decisive liberation of territory and a swift conclusion. It will not look like the air war above Kosovo two years ago, where no ground troops were used and not a single American was lost in combat.

Our response involves far more than instant retaliation and isolated strikes. Americans should not expect one battle, but a lengthy campaign unlike any other we have ever seen. It may include dramatic strikes visible on TV and covert operations secret even in success.

We will starve terrorists of funding, turn them one against another, drive them from place to place until there is no refuge or no rest.

And we will pursue nations that provide aid or safe haven to terrorism. Every nation in every region now has a decision to make: Either you are with us, or you are with the terrorists.

From this day forward, any nation that continues to harbor or support terrorism will be regarded by the United States as a hostile regime. Our nation has been put on notice: we're not immune from attack. We will take defensive measures against terrorism to protect Americans.

Today, dozens of federal departments and agencies, as well as state and local governments, have responsibilities affecting homeland security.

These efforts must be coordinated at the highest level. So tonight, I announce the creation of a Cabinet-level position reporting directly to me—the Office of Homeland Security.

And tonight, I also announce a distinguished American to lead this effort, to strengthen American security: a military veteran, an effective governor, a true patriot, a trusted friend—Pennsylvania's Tom Ridge. He will lead, oversee, and coordinate a comprehensive national strategy to safeguard our country against terrorism and respond to any attacks that may come.

These measures are essential. The only way to defeat terrorism as a threat to our way of life is to stop it, eliminate it, and destroy it where it grows. Many will be involved in this effort, from FBI agents, to intelligence operatives, to the reservists we have called to active duty. All deserve our thanks, and all have our prayers.

And tonight, a few miles from the damaged Pentagon, I have a message for our military: Be ready. I have called the Armed Forces to alert, and there is a reason. The hour is coming when America will act, and you will make us proud. This is not, however, just America's fight. And what is at stake is not just America's freedom. This is the world's fight. This is civilization's fight. This is the fight of all who believe in progress and pluralism, tolerance and freedom. We ask every nation to join us.

We will ask, and we will need the help of police forces, intelligence services, and banking systems around the world. The United States is grateful that many nations and many international organizations have already responded with sympathy and with support—nations from Latin America, to Asia, to Africa, to Europe, to the Islamic world.

Perhaps the NATO charter reflects best the attitude of the world: An attack on one is an attack on all. The civilized world is rallying to America's side. They understand that if this terror goes unpunished, their own cities, their own citizens may be next. Terror unanswered cannot only bring down buildings, it can threaten the stability of legitimate governments. And you know what? We're not going to allow it.

Americans are asking, "What is expected of us?"

I ask you to live your lives and hug your children. I know many citizens have fears tonight, and I ask you to be calm and resolute, even in the face of a continuing threat. I ask you to uphold the values of America and remember why so many have come here. We're in a fight for our principles, and our first responsibility is to live by them. No one should be singled out for unfair treatment or unkind words because of their ethnic background or religious faith. I ask you to continue to support the victims of this tragedy with your contributions. …

The thousands of FBI agents who are now at work in this investigation may need your cooperation, and I ask you to give it. I ask for your patience with the delays and inconveniences that may accompany tighter security and for your patience in what will be a long struggle. I ask your continued participation and confidence in the American economy. Terrorists attacked a symbol of American prosperity; they did not touch its source.

America is successful because of the hard work, and creativity, and enterprise of our people. These were the true strengths of our economy before September 11th, and they are our strengths today.

And finally, please continue praying for the victims of terror and their families, for those in uniform, and for our great country. Prayer has comforted us in sorrow and will help strengthen us for the journey ahead.

Tonight, I thank my fellow Americans for what you have already done and for what you will do. And ladies and gentlemen of the Congress, I thank you, their representatives, for what you have already done and for what we will do together.

Tonight, we face new and sudden national challenges. We will come together to improve air safety, to dramatically expand the number of air marshals on domestic flights, and take new measures to prevent hijacking. We will come together to promote stability and keep our airlines flying, with direct assistance during this emergency. We will come together to give law enforcement the additional tools it needs to track down terror here at home. We will come together to strengthen our intelligence capabilities to know the plans of terrorists before they act, and to find them before they strike. We will come together to take active steps that strengthen America's economy and put our people back to work.

Tonight, we welcome two leaders who embody the extraordinary spirit of all New Yorkers: Governor George Pataki, and Mayor Rudolph Giuliani. As a symbol of America's resolve, my administration will work with Congress and these two leaders to show the world that we will rebuild New York City.

After all that has just passed—all the lives taken, and all the possibilities and hopes that died with them—it is natural to wonder if America's future is one of fear. Some speak of an age of terror. I know there are struggles ahead and dangers to face. But this country will define our times, not be defined by them. As long as the United States of America is determined and strong, this will not be an age of terror; this will be an age of liberty here and across the world.

Great harm has been done to us. We have suffered great loss. And in our grief and anger, we have found our mission and our moment. Freedom and fear are at war. The advance of human freedom—the great achievement of our time, and the great hope of every time—now depends on us.

Our nation, this generation, will lift a dark threat of violence from our people and our future. We will rally the world to this cause by our efforts, by our courage. We will not tire, we will not falter, and we will not fail.

It is my hope that in the months and years ahead, life will return almost to normal. We'll go back to our lives and routines, and that is good. Even grief recedes with time and grace. But our resolve must not pass. Each of us will remember what happened that day, and to whom it happened. We'll remember the moment the news came—where we were and what we were doing.

Some will remember an image of a fire, or a story of rescue. Some will carry memories of a face and a voice gone forever. And I will carry this: It is the police shield of a man named George Howard, who died at the World Trade Center trying to save others. It was given to me by his mom, Arlene, as a proud memorial to her son. This is my reminder of lives that ended, and a task that does not end.

I will not forget this wound to our country or those who inflicted it. I will not yield; I will not rest; I will not relent in waging this struggle for freedom and security for the American people.

The course of this conflict is not known, yet its outcome is certain. Freedom and fear, justice and cruelty, have always been at war, and we know that God is not neutral between them.

Fellow citizens, we'll meet violence with patient justice—assured of the rightness of our cause, and confident of the victories to come. In all that lies before us, may God grant us wisdom, and may He watch over the United States of America.

Barack Obama is sworn in as president by Chief Justice John Roberts. This was the first time the president was sworn into office by a chief justice he voted against confirming. As a senator in 2005, Obama joined twenty-one of his fellow Democrats in voting against Roberts's appointment. The inaugurations with the most potential for conflict included the 1801 swearing in of Thomas Jefferson by Chief Justice John Marshall, whom Jefferson despised. In 1861, Abraham Lincoln was sworn in by Chief Justice Roger Taney, who ruled in favor of slavery in the Dred Scott v. Sandford *decision and who continued to frustrate Lincoln for the three years he remained chief justice after the beginning of the Civil War. In 1937, Chief Justice Charles Hughes knew of the hostile plan to "pack the court" when he inaugurated Franklin D. Roosevelt.*

BARACK OBAMA

A More Perfect Union

I am the son of a black man from Kenya and a white woman from Kansas ... I will never forget that in no other country on Earth is my story even possible.

Barack Hussein Obama II, forty-fourth President of the United States, was born in Hawaii in 1961 to a Kenyan father and an American mother. Obama's parents met at the University of Hawaii at Mānoa, where his father was a foreign student on scholarship. His parents separated when he was two years old and they divorced in 1964. Obama Sr. remarried and returned to Kenya; he visited his son in Hawaii only once, in 1971, before dying in an automobile accident in 1982. From ages six to ten, Obama lived in Jakarta, Indonesia, with his mother and new stepfather, an Indonesian student who had also attended college in Hawaii. Obama returned to Honolulu in 1971 to live with his maternal grandparents. He went on to graduate from Columbia University and Harvard Law School, where he served as president of the *Harvard Law Review*. He worked as a community organizer, university lecturer, and civil rights lawyer before running for public office and serving three terms in the Illinois Senate. After an unsuccessful bid for a seat in the U.S. House of Representatives in 2000, he announced his campaign for U.S. Senate in 2003. The following year, while still an Illinois state legislator, Obama came to national prominence when he delivered the keynote address at the 2004 Democratic National Convention. He was elected to the U.S. Senate in November of that year with an impressive seventy percent of the vote.

Obama's presidential campaign began in February 2007. He secured the 2008 Democratic Party presidential nomination after a close campaign against the former First Lady, New York Senator Hillary Rodham Clinton. He defeated the Republican nominee, John McCain, in the general election and was inaugurated as president on January 20, 2009, becoming the first African American to hold the nation's highest office. He was re-elected in 2012, narrowly defeating Republican nominee Mitt Romney.

The following remarks were made by Obama while campaigning for the Democratic presidential nomination in Philadelphia on March 18, 2008. This speech was prompted by criticism of the Reverend Jeremiah Wright, an unpaid campaign adviser and pastor at Obama's Chicago church. Wright had made several highly publicized pronouncements that most Americans regarded as overtly racist. He made additional inflammatory remarks about the United States, accusing the country of bringing on the September 11, 2001, attacks by spreading terrorism. Here, Obama denounced those remarks while attempting to explain them in a historical and sociological context.

"We the people, in order to form a more perfect union." Two hundred and twenty one years ago, in a hall that still stands across the street, a group of men gathered and, with these simple words, launched America's improbable experiment in democracy. Farmers and scholars; statesmen and patriots who had traveled across an ocean to escape tyranny and persecution finally made real their declaration of independence at a Philadelphia convention that lasted through the spring of 1787.

The document they produced was eventually signed but ultimately unfinished. It was stained by this nation's original sin of slavery, a question that divided the colonies and brought the convention to a stalemate until the founders chose to allow the slave trade to continue for at least twenty more years, and to leave any final resolution to future generations.

Of course, the answer to the slavery question was already embedded within our Constitution—a Constitution that had at is very core the ideal of equal citizenship under the law; a Constitution that promised its people liberty, and justice, and a union that could be and should be perfected over time.

And yet words on a parchment would not be enough to deliver slaves from bondage, or provide men and women of every color and creed their full rights and obligations as citizens of the United States. What would be needed were Americans in successive generations who were willing to do their part—through protests and struggle, on the streets and in the courts, through a civil war and civil disobedience and always at great risk—to narrow that gap between the promise of our ideals and the reality of their time.

This was one of the tasks we set forth at the beginning of this campaign—to continue the long march of those who came before us, a march for a more just, more equal, more free, more caring and more prosperous America. I chose to run for the presidency at this moment in history because I believe deeply that we cannot solve the challenges of our time unless we solve them together—unless we perfect our union by understanding that we may have different stories, but we hold common hopes; that we may not look the same and we may not have come from the same place, but we all want to move in the same direction—towards a better future for our children and our grandchildren.

This belief comes from my unyielding faith in the decency and generosity of the American people. But it also comes from my own American story.

I am the son of a black man from Kenya and a white woman from Kansas. I was raised with the help of a white grandfather who survived a Depression to serve in Patton's Army during World War II and a white grandmother who worked on a bomber assembly line at Fort Leavenworth while he was overseas. I've gone to some of the best schools in America and lived in one of the world's poorest nations. I am married to a black American who carries within her the blood of slaves and slaveowners—an inheritance we pass on to our two precious daughters. I have brothers, sisters, nieces, nephews, uncles and cousins, of every race and every hue, scattered across three continents, and for as long as I live, I will never forget that in no other country on Earth is my story even possible.

It's a story that hasn't made me the most conventional candidate. But it is a story that has seared into my genetic makeup the idea that this nation is more than the sum of its parts—that out of many, we are truly one.

Throughout the first year of this campaign, against all predictions to the contrary, we saw how hungry the American people were for this message of unity. Despite the temptation to view my candidacy through a purely racial lens, we won commanding victories in states with some of the whitest populations in the country. In South Carolina, where the Confederate Flag still flies, we built a powerful coalition of African Americans and white Americans.

This is not to say that race has not been an issue in the campaign. At various stages in the campaign, some commentators have deemed me either "too black" or "not black enough." We saw racial tensions bubble to the surface during the week before the South Carolina primary. The press has scoured every exit poll for the latest evidence of racial polarization, not just in terms of white and black, but black and brown as well.

And yet, it has only been in the last couple of weeks that the discussion of race in this campaign has taken a particularly divisive turn.

On one end of the spectrum, we've heard the implication that my candidacy is somehow an exercise in affirmative action; that it's based solely on the desire of wide-eyed liberals to purchase racial reconciliation on the cheap. On the other end, we've heard my former pastor, Reverend Jeremiah Wright, use incendiary language to express views that have the potential not only to widen the racial divide, but views that denigrate both the greatness and the goodness of our nation; that rightly offend white and black alike.

I have already condemned, in unequivocal terms, the statements of Reverend Wright that have caused such controversy. For some, nagging questions remain. Did I know him to be an occasionally fierce critic of American domestic and foreign policy? Of course. Did I ever hear him make remarks that could be considered controversial while I sat in church? Yes. Did I strongly disagree with many of his political views? Absolutely—just as I'm sure many of you have heard remarks from your pastors, priests, or rabbis with which you strongly disagreed.

But the remarks that have caused this recent firestorm weren't simply controversial. They weren't simply a religious leader's effort to speak out against perceived injustice. Instead, they expressed a profoundly distorted view of this country—a view that sees white racism as endemic, and that elevates what is wrong with America above all that we know is right with America; a view that sees the conflicts in the Middle East as rooted primarily in the actions of stalwart allies like Israel, instead of emanating from the perverse and hateful ideologies of radical Islam.

As such, Reverend Wright's comments were not only wrong but divisive, divisive at a time when we need unity; racially charged at a time when we need to come together to solve a set of monumental problems—two wars, a terrorist threat, a falling economy, a chronic health care crisis and potentially devastating climate change; problems that are neither black or white or Latino or Asian, but rather problems that confront us all.

Given my background, my politics, and my professed values and ideals, there will no doubt be those for whom my statements of condemnation are not enough. Why associate myself with Reverend Wright in the first place, they may ask? Why not join another church? And I confess that if all that I knew of Reverend Wright were the snippets of those sermons that have run in an endless loop on the television and YouTube, or if Trinity United Church of Christ conformed to the caricatures being peddled by some commentators, there is no doubt that I would react in much the same way. …

Like other predominantly black churches across the country, Trinity embodies the black community in its entirety—the doctor and the welfare mom, the model student and the former gang-banger. Like other black churches, Trinity's services are full of raucous laughter and sometimes bawdy humor. They are full of dancing, clapping, screaming and shouting that may seem jarring to the untrained ear. The church contains in full the kindness and cruelty, the fierce intelligence and the shocking ignorance, the struggles and successes, the love and yes, the bitterness and bias that make up the black experience in America.

And this helps explain, perhaps, my relationship with Reverend Wright. As imperfect as he may be, he has been like family to me. He strengthened my faith, officiated my wedding, and baptized my children. Not once in my conversations with him have I heard him talk about any ethnic group in derogatory terms, or treat whites with whom he interacted with anything but courtesy and respect. He contains within him the contradictions—the good and the bad—of the community that he has served diligently for so many years.

I can no more disown him than I can disown the black community. I can no more disown him than I can my white grandmother—a woman who helped raise me, a woman who sacrificed again and again for me, a woman who loves me as much as she loves anything in this world, but a woman who once confessed her fear of black men who passed by her on the street, and who on more than one occasion has uttered racial or ethnic stereotypes that made me cringe.

These people are a part of me. And they are a part of America, this country that I love. …

Race is an issue that I believe this nation cannot afford to ignore right now. We would be making the same mistake that Reverend Wright made in his offending sermons about America—to simplify and stereotype and amplify the negative to the point that it distorts reality.

The fact is that the comments that have been made and the issues that have surfaced over the last few weeks reflect the complexities of race in this country that we've never really worked through—a part of our union that we have yet to perfect. And if we walk away now, if we simply retreat into our respective corners, we will never be able to come together and solve challenges like health care, or education, or the need to find good jobs for every American.

Understanding this reality requires a reminder of how we arrived at this point. As William Faulkner once wrote, "The past isn't dead and buried. In fact, it isn't even past." We do not need to recite here the history of racial injustice in this country. But we do need to remind ourselves that so many of the disparities that exist in the African-American community today can be directly traced to inequalities passed on from an earlier generation that suffered under the brutal legacy of slavery and Jim Crow.

Segregated schools were, and are, inferior schools; we still haven't fixed them, 50 years after *Brown v. Board of Education*. And the inferior education they provided, then and now, helps explain the pervasive achievement gap between today's black and white students.

Legalized discrimination—where blacks were prevented, often through violence, from owning property, or loans were not granted to African-American business owners, or black homeowners could not access FHA mortgages, or blacks were excluded from unions, or the police force, or fire departments—meant that black families could not amass any meaningful wealth to bequeath to future generations. That history helps explain the wealth and income gap between black and white, and the concentrated pockets of poverty that persists in so many of today's urban and rural communities.

A lack of economic opportunity among black men, and the shame and frustration that came from not being able to provide for one's family, contributed to the erosion of black families—a problem that welfare policies for many years may have worsened. And the lack of basic services in so many urban black neighborhoods—parks for kids to play in, police walking the beat, regular garbage pick-up and building code enforcement—all helped create a cycle of violence, blight and neglect that continue to haunt us.

This is the reality in which Reverend Wright and other African-Americans of his generation grew up. They came of age in the late fifties and early sixties, a time when segregation was still the law of the land and opportunity was systematically constricted. What's remarkable is not how many failed in the face of discrimination, but rather how many men and women overcame the odds; how many were able to make a way out of no way for those like me who would come after them.

But for all those who scratched and clawed their way to get a piece of the American Dream, there were many who didn't make it—those who were ultimately defeated, in one way or another, by discrimination. That legacy of defeat was passed on to future generations—those young men and increasingly young women who we see standing on street corners or languishing in our prisons, without hope or prospects for the future. Even for those blacks who did make it, questions of race, and racism, continue to define their worldview in fundamental ways. For the men and women of Reverend Wright's generation, the memories of humiliation and doubt and fear have not gone away; nor has the anger and the bitterness of those years. That anger may not get expressed in public, in front of white co-workers or white friends. But it does find voice in the barbershop or around the kitchen table. At times, that anger is exploited by politicians, to gin up votes along racial lines, or to make up for a politician's own failings.

And occasionally it finds voice in the church on Sunday morning, in the pulpit and in the pews. The fact that so many people are surprised to hear that anger in some of Reverend Wright's sermons simply reminds us of the old truism that the most segregated hour in American life occurs on Sunday morning. That anger is not always productive; indeed, all too often it distracts attention from solving real problems; it keeps us from squarely facing our own complicity in our condition, and prevents the African-American community from forging the alliances it needs to bring about real change. But the anger is real; it is powerful; and to simply wish it away, to condemn it without understanding its roots, only serves to widen the chasm of misunderstanding that exists between the races.

In fact, a similar anger exists within segments of the white community. Most working and middle-class white Americans don't feel that they have been particularly privileged by their race. Their experience is the immigrant experience—as far as they're concerned, no one handed them anything. They built it from scratch. They've worked hard all their lives, many times only to see their jobs shipped overseas

or their pension dumped after a lifetime of labor. They are anxious about their futures, and feel their dreams slipping away; in an era of stagnant wages and global competition, opportunity comes to be seen as a zero sum game, in which your dreams come at my expense. So when they are told to bus their children to a school across town; when they hear that an African American is getting an advantage in landing a good job or a spot in a good college because of an injustice that they themselves never committed; when they're told that their fears about crime in urban neighborhoods are somehow prejudiced, resentment builds over time.

Like the anger within the black community, these resentments aren't always expressed in polite company. But they have helped shape the political landscape for at least a generation. ...

Just as black anger often proved counterproductive, so have these white resentments distracted attention from the real culprits of the middle class squeeze—a corporate culture rife with inside dealing, questionable accounting practices, and short-term greed; a Washington dominated by lobbyists and special interests; economic policies that favor the few over the many. And yet, to wish away the resentments of white Americans, to label them as misguided or even racist, without recognizing they are grounded in legitimate concerns—this too widens the racial divide, and blocks the path to understanding.

This is where we are right now. It's a racial stalemate we've been stuck in for years. Contrary to the claims of some of my critics, black and white, I have never been so naïve as to believe that we can get beyond our racial divisions in a single election cycle, or with a single candidacy—particularly a candidacy as imperfect as my own.

But I have asserted a firm conviction—a conviction rooted in my faith in God and my faith in the American people—that, working together, we can move beyond some of our old racial wounds, and that in fact we have no choice if we are to continue on the path of a more perfect union.

For the African-American community, that path means embracing the burdens of our past without becoming victims of our past. It means continuing to insist on a full measure of justice in every aspect of American life. But it also means binding our particular grievances—for better health care, and better schools, and better jobs—to the larger aspirations of all Americans—the white woman struggling to break the glass ceiling, the white man who has been laid off, the immigrant trying to feed his family. And it means taking full responsibility for our own lives—by demanding more from our fathers, and spending more time with our children, and reading to them, and teaching them that while they may face challenges and discrimination in their own lives, they must never succumb to despair or cynicism; they must always believe that they can write their own destiny.

Ironically, this quintessentially American—and yes, conservative—notion of self-help found frequent expression in Reverend Wright's sermons. But what my former pastor too often failed to understand is that embarking on a program of self-help also requires a belief that society can change.

The profound mistake of Reverend Wright's sermons is not that he spoke about racism in our society. It's that he spoke as if our society was static; as if no progress has been made; as if this country—a country that has made it possible for one of his own members to run for the highest office in the land and build a coalition of white and black, Latino and Asian, rich and poor, young and old—is still irrevocably bound to a tragic past. But what we know—what we have seen—is that America can change. That is the true genius of this nation. What we have already achieved gives us hope—the audacity to hope—for what we can and must achieve tomorrow.

In the white community, the path to a more perfect union means acknowledging that what ails the African-American community does not just exist in the minds of black people; that the legacy of discrimination—and current incidents of discrimination, while less overt than in the past—are real and must be addressed. Not just with words, but with deeds—by investing in our schools and our communities; by enforcing our civil rights laws and ensuring fairness in our criminal justice system; by providing this generation with ladders of opportunity that were unavailable for previous generations. It requires all Americans to realize that your dreams do not have to come at the expense of my dreams; that investing in the health, welfare, and education of black and brown and white children will ultimately help all of America prosper.

In the end, then, what is called for is nothing more, and nothing less, than what all the world's great religions demand—that we do unto others as we would have them do unto us. Let us be our brother's keeper, Scripture tells us. Let us be our sister's keeper. Let us find that common stake we all have in one another, and let our politics reflect that spirit as well. …

The Taxpayer March on Washington was a Tea Party protest march from Freedom Plaza to the United States Capitol that was held on September 12, 2009, in Washington, D.C. The Tea Party Movement is a reference to the historic Boston Tea Party of 1773 and uses the acronym "TEA" for "Taxed Enough Already." This event coincided with other similar protests organized in cities and towns all across the nation. Millions rallied against a succession of big government spending projects beginning in the George W. Bush administration and greatly expanded under President Obama. Protestors were particularly concerned with the dismantling of free market capitalism due to government intervention in the banking industry, the automobile industry, healthcare, potential cap-and-trade legislation, and other Obama administration projects that projected a multi-trillion-dollar deficit in the coming decade and threatened the economic security of the United States.

DAVID MCCULLOUGH

The Course of Human Events

For a free, self-governing people, something more than a vague familiarity with history is essential, if we are to hold on to and sustain our freedom.

David Gaub McCullough, among the most noted of historians, was born in 1933 in Pittsburgh, Pennsylvania. He is a two-time winner of the Pulitzer Prize and is a recipient of the Presidential Medal of Freedom, the nation's highest civilian award. McCullough earned a degree in English literature from Yale University and released his first book, *The Johnstown Flood*, in 1968. He has since written on a variety of subjects, to include the Brooklyn Bridge, the Panama Canal, and U.S. Presidents Theodore Roosevelt, Harry Truman, and John Adams. His book *1776* chronicles the founding year of the United States, focusing on George Washington, the amateur army, and the military struggle for Independence. His more recent work, *The Greater Journey: Americans in Paris*, is an accounting of the "American artists, writers, doctors, politicians, architects, and others of high aspiration who set off for Paris" in the Victorian era, eager for adventure and ambitious to excel in their work.

On May 15, 2003, McCullough was selected for the thirty-second Jefferson Lecture in the Humanities at the Ronald Reagan Building and International Trade Center in Washington, D.C. Established in 1972, the Jefferson Lecture is the highest honor the federal government bestows for distinguished intellectual and public achievement in the humanities. McCullough's lecture was entitled "The Course of Human Events."

... Among the darkest times in living memory was the early part of 1942—when Hitler's armies were nearly to Moscow; when German submarines were sinking our oil tankers off the coasts of Florida and New Jersey, within sight of the beaches, and there was not a thing we could do about it; when half our navy had been destroyed at Pearl Harbor. We had scarcely any air force. Army recruits were drilling with wooden rifles. And there was no guarantee whatever that the Nazi war machine could be stopped.

It was then, in 1942, that the classical scholar Edith Hamilton issued an expanded edition of her book, *The Greek Way*, in which, in the preface, she wrote the following:

> I have felt while writing these new chapters a fresh realization of the refuge and strength the past can be to us in the troubled present. ... Religion is the great stronghold for the untroubled vision of the eternal, but there are others too. We have many silent sanctuaries in which we can find breathing space to free ourselves from the personal, to rise above our harassed and perplexed minds and catch sight of values that are stable, which no selfish and timorous preoccupations can make waver, because they are the hard-won permanent possessions of humanity. ...

> When the world is storm-driven and the bad that happens and the worse that threatens are so urgent as to shut out everything else from view, then we need to know all the strong fortresses of the spirit which men have built through the ages.

In the Rotunda of the Capitol hangs a large painting of forty-seven men in a room. The scene is as familiar, as hallowed a moment in our history as any we have.

John Trumbull's *Declaration of Independence* has been a main attraction on Capitol tours for a very long time, since 1826. It draws crowds continuously, as it should, every day—from three to five million people a year. It's probably been seen by more Americans than any painting ever—and the scene as portrayed never took place.

Trumbull said it was meant to represent July 4, 1776, and that's the popular understanding. But the Declaration of Independence was not signed on July 4. The signing began on August 2, and continued through the year as absent delegates returned to Philadelphia. No formal signing ceremony ever took place.

The scene comes closer to portraying June 28, when Thomas Jefferson submitted his first draft of the Declaration. But then, too, there was no such dramatic gathering.

The room is wrong, the doors are in the wrong place. The chairs are wrong. (They were Windsor chairs of the plainest kind.) There were no heavy draperies at the windows. The decorative display of military trophies and banners on the back wall is purely Trumbull's way of dressing the set.

Yet none of this really matters. What does matter greatly—particularly in our own dangerous, uncertain time—is the symbolic power of the painting, and where Trumbull put the emphasis.

The scene proclaims that in Philadelphia in the year 1776 a momentous, high-minded statement of far-reaching consequence was committed to paper. It was not the decree of a king or a sultan or emperor or czar, or something enacted by a far-distant parliament. It was a declaration of political faith and brave intent freely arrived at by an American congress. And that was something entirely new under the sun.

And there Trumbull has assembled them, men like other men, each, importantly, a specific, identifiable individual.

The accuracy is in the faces. John Adams, Thomas Jefferson, and Benjamin Franklin were painted from life. Before he was finished, Trumbull painted or sketched thirty-six of the faces from life. It took him years and he spared no expense, because he wanted it right. He wanted us to know who they were.

Adams, Jefferson, and Franklin stand front and center exactly as they did in the real drama of the Revolution.

A number who signed the Declaration are not shown. Several who did not sign are present.

Most conspicuous by his absence is George Washington who had departed Congress the year before to take command of the army.

Lord Bolingbroke, the eighteenth century political philosopher, said that "history is philosophy teaching by examples." Thucydides is reported to have said much the same thing two thousand years earlier.

Jefferson saw history as largely a chronicle of mistakes to be avoided.

Daniel Boorstin, the former Librarian of Congress, has wisely said that trying to plan for the future without a sense of the past is like trying to plant cut flowers.

One might also say that history is not about the past. If you think about it, no one ever lived in the past. Washington, Jefferson, John Adams, and their contemporaries didn't walk about saying, "Isn't this fascinating living in the past! Aren't we picturesque in our funny clothes!" They lived in the present. The difference is it was *their* present, not ours. They were caught up in the living moment exactly as we are, and with no more certainty of how things would turn out than we have.

Nor were they gods. Indeed, to see them as gods or god-like is to do disservice to their memories. Gods, after all, don't deserve a lot of credit because they can do whatever they wish.

Those we call the Founders were living men. None was perfect. Each had his human flaws and failings, his weaknesses. They made mistakes, let others down, let themselves down.

Washington could be foolhardy and ill-tempered. Adams could be vain, irritable; Jefferson evasive, at times duplicitous. And even in their day, many saw stunning hypocrisy in the cause of liberty being championed by slave masters.

They were imperfect mortals, human beings. Jefferson made the point in the very first line of the Declaration of Independence. "When in the course of human events … " The accent should be on the word *human*.

And of course their humanity is not evident only in their failings. It's there in Adams's heart-felt correspondence with his wife and children, in Jefferson's love of gardening, his fascination, as he said, in every blade of grass that grows.

Washington had a passionate love of architecture and interior design. Everything about his home at Mt. Vernon was done to his ideas and plans. Only a year before the war, he began an ambitious expansion of the house, doubling its size. How extremely important this was to him, the extent of his esthetic sense, few people ever realized. He cared about every detail—wallpaper, paint color, hardware, ceiling ornaments—and hated to be away from the project even for a day.

The patriotism and courage of these all-important protagonists stand as perhaps the most conspicuous and enduring testaments to their humanity. When those who signed the Declaration of Independence pledged their "lives, their fortunes, their sacred honor," that was no mere verbiage. They were putting their lives on the line. They were declaring themselves traitors to the King. If caught they would be hanged.

Stephen Hopkins of Rhode Island, who suffered from palsy, is said to have remarked as he signed his name, "My hand trembles, but my heart does not."

Hopkins was a grand old figure who had seen a lot of life. You can't miss him in the Trumbull painting. He's at the back with his broad-brimmed Quaker hat on. In after-hours he loved to drink rum and expound on his favorite writers. "He read Greek, Roman, and British history, and was familiar with English poetry," John Adams wrote. "And the flow of his soul made his reading our own, and seemed to bring recollection in all we had ever read."

We must never forget either how hard they worked. Nothing came easy. Nothing. Just getting through a day in the eighteenth century meant difficulties, discomforts, and effort of a kind we seldom even think about.

But it is in their ideas about happiness, I believe, that we come close to the heart of their being, and to their large view of the possibilities in their Glorious Cause.

In general, happiness was understood to mean being at peace with the world in the biblical sense, under one's own "vine and fig tree." But what did they, the Founders, mean by the expression "pursuit of happiness"?

It didn't mean long vacations or material possessions or ease. As much as anything it meant the life of the mind and spirit. It meant education and the love of learning, the freedom to think for oneself.

Jefferson defined happiness as "tranquility and occupation." For Jefferson, as we know, occupation meant mainly his intellectual pursuits.

Washington, though less inclined to speculate on such matters, considered education of surpassing value, in part because he had had so little. Once, when a friend came to say he hadn't money enough to send his son to college, Washington agreed to help—providing a hundred pounds in all, a sizable sum then—and with the hope, as he wrote, that the boy's education would "not only promote his own happiness, but the future welfare of others…" For Washington, happiness derived both from learning and employing the benefits of learning to further the welfare of others.

John Adams, in a letter to his son John Quincy when the boy was a student at the University of Leiden, stressed that he should carry a book with him wherever he went. And that while a knowledge of Greek and Latin were essential, he must never neglect the great works of literature in his own language, and particularly those of the English poets. It was his *happiness* that mattered, Adams told him. "You will never be alone with a poet in your pocket."

The Revolution was another of the darkest, most uncertain of times and the longest war in American history, until the Vietnam War. It lasted eight and a half years, and Adams, because of his unstinting service to his country, was separated from his family nearly all that time, much to his and their distress. In a letter from France he tried to explain to them the reason for such commitment.

> I must study politics and war [he wrote] that my sons may have liberty to study mathematics and philosophy. My sons ought to study mathematics and philosophy, geography, natural history, naval architecture, navigation, commerce, and agriculture in order to give their children a right to study paintings, poetry, music, architecture, statuary, tapestry, and porcelain.

That was the upward climb envisioned for the good society in the burgeoning new American republic. And Adams was himself vivid proof of the transforming miracle of education. His father was a farmer, his mother almost certainly illiterate. But with the help of a scholarship, he was able to attend Harvard, where, as he said, he discovered books and "read forever."

His Harvard studies over, Adams began teaching school at Worcester, then virtually the frontier. One crystal night, twenty years before the Declaration of Independence, he stood beneath a sky full of stars, "thrown into a kind of transport." He knew such wonders of the heavens to be the gifts of God, he wrote, but greatest of all was the gift of an inquiring mind.

> But all the provisions that He has [made] for the gratification of our senses … are much inferior to the provision, the wonderful provision, that He has made for the gratification of our nobler powers of intelligence and reason. He has given us reason to find out the truth, and the real design and true end of our existence.

He had decided to study law. "It will be hard work," he told a friend. "But the point is now determined, and I shall have the liberty to think for myself."

Of all the sustaining themes in our story as a nation, as clear as any has been the importance put on education, one generation after another, beginning with the first village academies in New England and the establishment of Harvard and the College of William and Mary. The place of education in the values of the first presidents is unmistakable.

Washington contributed generously, some $20,000 in stock to the founding of what would become Washington and Lee University in Virginia. His gift was the largest donation ever made to any educational institution in the nation until then, and has since grown to a substantial part of the endowment.

Jefferson founded the University of Virginia. But then it may be fairly said that Jefferson was a university unto himself.

The oldest written constitution still in use in the world today is the Constitution of the Commonwealth of Massachusetts, drafted by John Adams in 1778, just two years after the Declaration of Independence and fully a decade before our national Constitution. In many respects it is a rough draft of our national Constitution. But it also contains a paragraph on education that was without precedent. Though Adams worried that it would be rejected as too radical, it was passed unanimously. Listen, please, to what it says:

> Wisdom and knowledge, as well as virtue, diffused generally among the body of the people being necessary for the preservation of their rights and liberties. [Which is to say that there must be wisdom, knowledge, and virtue or all aspirations for the good society will come to nothing.] And as these depend on spreading the opportunities and advantages of education in various parts of the country, and among the different orders of the people [that is, *everyone*], it shall be the duty [not something they might consider, but the *duty*] of legislatures and magistrates in all future periods of this commonwealth to cherish the interests and literature and the sciences, and all seminaries of them … public schools, and grammar schools in the towns.

And he goes on to define what he means by education. It is literature and the sciences, yes, but much more: agriculture, the arts, commerce, trades, manufacturers, "and a natural history of the country." It shall be the duty, he continues,

> to countenance and inculcate the principles of humanity and general benevolence, public and private charity, industry and frugality, honesty [we *will* teach honesty] … sincerity, [and, please note] good humor, and all social affections, and generous sentiments among the people.

What a noble statement!

Years before, while still living under his father's roof, Adams had written in his diary, "I must judge for myself, but how can I judge, how can any man judge, unless his mind has been opened and enlarged by reading."

They were nearly all young men in 1776, it should be remembered, young men who believed, as Thomas Paine proclaimed, that the birth of a new world was at hand.

Jefferson was thirty-three, Adams, forty, Benjamin Rush, the Philadelphia physician, was all of thirty when he signed the Declaration of Independence. Rush, one of the most interesting of them all, was a leader in the anti-slavery movement, a leader in prescribing humane treatment for the insane, and the first to champion the elective system in higher education.

When George Washington took command of the army, he was forty-three. He had never led an army in battle before in his life, any more than the others had had prior experience as revolutionaries or nation builders.

And what of Franklin? Franklin, oldest and wisest, is for me a special case.

I met my first revisionist historian when I was six.

His name was Amos and he was a mouse, an eighteenth century church mouse to be exact, one of twenty-six children who with their mother and father lived in Old Christ Church in Philadelphia. I can never be in Old Christ Church without wondering if perhaps some of Amos's line are still there, back behind the paneling.

Amos, who took up lodging in Benjamin Franklin's fur hat, is the narrator of a little book called *Ben and Me* by Robert Lawson.

Most so-called historians have had Franklin all wrong, according to Amos. "Ben was undoubtedly a splendid fellow, a great man, a patriot and all that," he writes, "but he was undeniably stupid at times and had it not been for me—well, here's the true story … "

I was six, as I say, and I was hooked. I learned all about Philadelphia, printing presses, electricity, Franklin stoves, and the Palace of Versailles. I got to know Benjamin Franklin and, like Amos, relished his company.

And that was the start. I learned to love history by way of books. …

There should be no hesitation ever about giving anyone a book to enjoy, at any age. There should be no hesitation about teaching future teachers with books they will enjoy. No harm's done to history by making it something someone would want to read.

We are what we read more than we know. And it was true no less in that distant founding time. Working on the life of John Adams, I tried to read not only what he and others of his day wrote, but what they read. And to take up and read again works of literature of the kind we all remember from high school or college English classes was not only a different kind of research, but pure delight.

I read Swift, Pope, Defoe, Sterne, Fielding, and Samuel Johnson again after forty years, and Tobias Smollett and *Don Quixote* for the first time.

I then began to find lines from these writers turning up in the letters of my American subjects, turning up without attribution, because the lines were part of them, part of who they were and how they thought and expressed themselves.

But we do the same, more often than we realize. Every time we "refuse to budge an inch," or speak of "green-eyed jealousy," or claim to be "tongue-tied," we're quoting Shakespeare. When we say "a little learning is a dangerous thing," or "to err is human," or observe sagely that "fools rush in where angels fear to tread," we're borrowing from Alexander Pope, just as when you "slept not a wink," or "smell a rat," or "turn over a new leaf," or declare "mum's the word," you're quoting Cervantes.

When young Nathan Hale was hanged by the British as a spy in New York in 1776, he famously said as his last words, "My only regret is that I have but one life to lose for my country." That's a line from the popular play of the eighteenth century, *Cato*, by Joseph Addison, a play they all knew. Washington, who loved the theater, is believed to have seen it half a dozen times.

Imagine how it must have been for Nathan Hale, about to be hanged. Who, in such a moment, could possibly think of something eloquent to say. I think he was throwing that line right back at those British officers. After all, *Cato* was *their* play.

I imagine him delivering the line, "I only regret that I have but one life to lose for *my* country."

One needs to read the great political philosophers—Hume, Locke, Ferguson, Montesquieu—whose writings had such profound influence on the founders. Yet there is hardly a more appealing description of the Enlightenment outlook on life and learning than a single sentence in a popular novel of the day, *A Sentimental Journey*, by Laurence Sterne.

What a large volume of adventures may be grasped

within this little span of life by him who interests his heart in everything.

The stimulation, the motivation, the hard work and pleasures of writing history are mainly in the material. It's the finding and figuring out that keep you in pursuit. And you never know … you never know where you will find something, see something that's gone unnoticed, or make some unexpected connection that brings things into focus in a new or different way.

The truth of history is the objective always. But the truth isn't just the facts. You can have all the facts imaginable and miss the truth, just as you can have facts missing or some wrong, and reach the larger truth.

As the incomparable Francis Parkman wrote:

Faithfulness to the truth of history involves far more than a research, however patient and scrupulous, into special facts. Such facts may be detailed with the most minute exactness, and yet the narrative, taken as a whole, may be unmeaning or untrue. The narrator must seek to imbue himself with the life and spirit of the time. He must study events in their bearings near and remote; in the character, habits, and manners of those who took part in them. He must himself be, as it were, a sharer or spectator of the action he describes.

"I hear all the notes, but I hear no music," is the old piano teacher's complaint. There has to be music. History at best has to be literature or it will go to dust.

The work of history—writing history, teaching history—calls for mind and heart. Empathy is essential. The late J. H. Plumb, the eminent British historian, said that what is needed is more "heart-wise" historians.

What happened? And why? Who were those people? What was it like to have been alive then, in their shoes, in their skins? Of what were they afraid? What didn't they know?

Studying his face in the mirror, John Adams decided, "I am but an ordinary man. The times alone have destined me to fame." He was fishing. He was anything but ordinary and it is not possible to understand what happened in that tumultuous, protean time without knowing and understanding him and the others.

There are, of course, great sweeping tides in history—plague, famine, financial panic, the calamities of nature and war. Yet time and again, more often than not history turns on individual personality, or character.

I am presently at work on a book about the Revolution, with the focus on Washington and the army in the year 1776, which in the last months was the nadir of the fortunes of the United States of America, when the army was down to little more than three thousand men. By December, by all signs, the war was over and we had lost. Fortunately Washington did not see it that way. Had it not been for Washington and his little ragtag army, the Declaration of Independence and all it promised would have truly been "a skiff made of paper."

There are no paintings or sketches of the soldiers done at the time. Most that we have are by Trumbull, himself a veteran of the war, but his were all painted afterward.

It's in the surviving diaries, journals, letters, pension files, in descriptions posted for deserters that those in the ranks begin to emerge as flesh-and-blood individual men caught up in something far bigger than they knew.

There was Jabez Fitch, for example, a Connecticut farmer with eight children, who liked soldiering and kept a diary describing the war as he saw it day by day. There was young John Greenwood, a fifer boy, who at age sixteen walked all alone 150 miles from Maine to Boston to join up with Washington's army. And Mathias Smith, a deserter, who was described as: "a small smart fellow, a saddler by trade, grey headed, has a younger look in his face, is apt to say, 'I swear, I swear!' And between his words will spit smart; had on a green coat, and an old red greatcoat; he is a right gamester, although he wears something of a sober look."

"Greece," wrote Edith Hamilton, "never lost sight of the individual." And neither should we, ever.

They were hungry, starving some of them, and without warm clothes as winter set in. Not all were patriots. Not all were heroes. Not all came home. But they were once as alive as you and I.

"Posterity who are to reap the blessings," wrote Abigail Adams, "will scarcely be able to conceive the hardships and sufferings of their ancestors."

History is—or should be—a lesson in appreciation. History helps us keep a sense of proportion.

History teaches that there is no such thing as a self-made man or woman, that we are all shaped by the influences of others, including so many we've never seen because they are back there in history.

History teaches that nothing happens in isolation, or

without cause and effect, and that nothing ever had to happen as it did.

History teaches tolerance, and the value of common sense, and as Voltaire (and who knows how many others) observed, common sense is anything but common.

History is about high achievement, glorious works of art, music, architecture, literature, philosophy, science and medicine—not just politics and the military—as the best of politicians and generals have readily attested. History is about leadership, and the power of ideas. History is about change, because the world has never *not* been changing, indeed because life itself is change.

History is the course of human events. And it must therefore be, if truthful, about failure, injustice, struggle, suffering, disappointment, and the humdrum. History demonstrates often in brutal fashion the evils of enforced ignorance and demagoguery. History is a source of strength, a constant reminder of the courage of others in times more trying and painful than our own. As Churchill reminded us, "We have not journeyed all this way … because we are made of sugar candy."

History is filled with voices that reach out and lift the spirits, sometimes from the distance of centuries.

Is it possible to imagine *not* learning from the wisest, most thoughtful people who shaped the world, or to fail to take heart from manifest courage?

Is life not infinitely more interesting and enjoyable when one can stand in a great historic place or walk historic ground, and know something of what happened there and in whose footsteps you walk?

For a free, self-governing people, something more than a vague familiarity with history is essential, if we are to hold on to and sustain our freedom.

But I don't think history should ever be made to seem like some musty, unpleasant pill that has to be swallowed solely for our civic good. History, let us agree, can be an immense source of pleasure. For almost anyone with the normal human allotment of curiosity and an interest in people, it is a field day.

Why would anyone wish to be provincial in time, any more than being tied down to one place through life, when the whole reach of the human drama is there to experience in some of the greatest books ever written.

I guess if I had to boil it down to a few words, I would say history is a larger way of looking at life.

One of our innumerable advantages as a nation and a society is that we have such a specific moment of origin as the year 1776. And that we know who the Founders were—indeed we know an immense amount about an immense number of those at all levels who in that revolutionary time brought the United States of America and the reality of freedom into being.

But while it is essential to remember them as individual mortal beings no more perfect than are we, and that they themselves knew this better than anyone, it is also essential to understand that they knew their own great achievements to be imperfect and incomplete.

The American experiment was from its start an unfulfilled promise. There was much work to be done. There were glaring flaws to correct, unfinished business to attend to, improvements and necessary adjustments to devise in order to keep pace with the onrush of growth and change and expanding opportunities.

Those brave, high-minded people of earlier times gave us stars to steer by—a government of laws not of men, equal justice before the law, the importance of the individual, the ideal of equality, freedom of religion, freedom of thought and expression, and the love of learning.

From them, in our own dangerous and promising present, we can take heart. As Edith Hamilton said of the Greeks, we can "catch sight of values that are stable because they are the hard-won possessions of humanity."

Blessed we are. And duty bound, to continue the great cause of freedom, in their spirit and in their memory and for those who are to carry on next in their turn.

There is still much work to be done, still much to learn.

We hold these truths to be self-evident, that all men are created equal, that they are endowed by their Creator with certain unalienable Rights, that among these are Life, Liberty, and the pursuit of Happiness. …

On we go.

* * *

Author Index

A.

"A Nation at Risk," 448

Adams, John, "Letter to Abigail," 31

Ager, Milton, and Jack Yellen, "Happy Days Are Here Again," 330

Allen, Thomas B., "A Place for Memories," 431

"Amendments to the Constitution," 67

American Legion, "Preamble to the American Legion Constitution," 323

Anthony, Susan B., "Women's Right to Vote," 234

"Articles of Confederation," 38

B.

"Ballad of John Henry, The," 226

Ballou, Sullivan, "Letter to His Wife," 194

Baruch, Bernard, "The Baruch Plan for Control of Atomic Energy," 374

Bates, Katherine Lee, "America the Beautiful," 251

Benét, Rosemary and Stephen Vincent, "U.S.A.," 370

Bennett, Henry Holcomb, "The Flag Goes By," 275

Berlin, Irving: "Oh, How I Hate to Get Up in the Morning," 345; "God Bless America," 345

Black Hawk, "Speeches of Surrender and Reconciliation," 103

Brown, John, "Last Statement to the Court," 173

Brooks, Gwendolyn, "The Mother," 387

Bryan, Alfred, and Al Piantadosi, "I Didn't Raise My Boy to Be a Soldier," 292

Bryan, William Jennings, "The Cross of Gold," 254

Bryant, William Cullen: "Oh Mother of a Mighty Race," 192; "Our Country's Call," 192

Bush, George W., "War Message to Congress," 483

C.

Calhoun, John C., "Fort Hill Address," 154

Cash, Johnny, "Ragged Old Flag," 438

Chief Joseph, "Speech of Surrender," 238

Chief See-Yahtlh, "Address to the White Man," 139

"Clementine," 232

Cleveland, Grover, "Patriotism and Holidays," 276

Clinton, Hillary, "Women's Rights Are Human Rights," 468

Cohan, George M.: "Yankee Doodle Boy," 319; "Over There," 319

"Columbia, the Gem of the Ocean," 116

"Constitution of the United States, The," 51

Crawford, Robert, "The U.S. Air Force," 356

Crèvecoeur, Michel-Guillaume Jean de, *Letters from an American Farmer*, 45

D.

Darrow, Clarence, "Against Prohibition," 282

Daly, John Jay, "A Toast to the Flag," 306

Davis, Jefferson, "Farewell to the U.S. Senate," 184

Dickinson, John, "The Liberty Song," 16

Douglass, Frederick: "Fourth of July Address," 123; "Letter to His Former Master," 126; "Speech to the American Anti-Slavery Society," 215; "In Memory of Abraham Lincoln," 219; "Speech to the National Convention of Colored Men," 239; "I Have No Apology," 241

Drake, Joseph Rodman, "The American Flag," 92

Driftwood, Jimmy, "Battle of New Orleans," 89

Du Bois, W.E.B.: "The Talented Tenth," 272; "Advice to a Student," 274

Dylan, Bob, "Blowin' in the Wind," 418

E.

Edwards, Adrian, "Letter to His Mother," 307

Edwards, Jonathan, "Sinners in the Hands of an Angry God," 9

Eisenhower, Dwight D., "Farewell Address," 396

Emerson, Ralph Waldo: "Self-Reliance," 107; "Concord Hymn," 110

Emmett, Daniel Decatur, "Dixie," 197

Evans, Dale, and Roy Rogers, "Happy Trails," 389

F.

"Flag Day," 347

Franklin, Benjamin, *Poor Richard's Almanack*, 3

Finch, Francis Miles: "Nathan Hale," 35; "The Blue and the Gray," 223

Foster, Stephen: "Oh! Susanna," 141; "Old Folks at Home," 141; "Camptown Races," 141; "My Old Kentucky Home, Good Night," 141

Friedman, Milton and Rose, "Free to Choose," 445

Frost, Robert: "The Road Not Taken," 287; "Stopping by Woods on a Snowy Evening," 287; "The Gift Outright, 287"

G.

Garnet, Henry Highland, "An Address to the Slaves of the United States of America," 165

Garrison, William Lloyd, Prospectus for *The Liberator*, 160

Gehrig, Lou, "Farewell," 346

Gilmore, Patrick S., "When Johnny Comes Marching Home," 205

Glass, Carter, "The Court-Packing Plan," 338

"Go Down Moses," 180

Gompers, Samuel, "What Does the Working Man Want?," 245

Gore, Al, "Concession Speech," 479

Gorney, Jay, and E. Y. Harburg, "Brother, Can You Spare a Dime?," 331

Grant, Ulysses S., "Appomattox," 217

Gruber, Edmund L., "The Caisson Song," 321

Guiterman, Arthur, "Daniel Boone," 74

Guthrie, Woody, "This Land Is Your Land," 348

H.

Hamilton, Alexander, and James Madison, and John Jay, "The Federalist Papers," 58

Hamilton, Andrew, "Freedom of the Press," 7

Hand, Learned, "The Spirit of Liberty," 359

Harburg, E. Y., and Jay Gorney, "Brother, Can You Spare a Dime?," 331

Harlan, John Marshall, Dissent from *Plessy v. Ferguson*, 257

Harrison, Benjamin, "True Patriotism," 244

Hayne, Robert, "States' Rights," 149

Henry, Patrick: "An Appeal to Arms," 21; "Against Ratification," 64

Hewes, George R. T., "Recollections of the Boston Tea Party," 17

Holland, Josiah Gilbert, "God, Give Us Men!," 172

Holmes, Oliver Wendell: "The Flower of Liberty," 100; "Old Ironsides," 100

"Home on the Range," 231

Hopkinson, Joseph, "Hail, Columbia," 80

Howe, Julia Ward, "Battle Hymn of the Republic," 203

Hughes, Charles Evans, "National Symbol," 311

Hughes, Langston: "Dark Youth of the U.S.A.," 384; "Let America Be America Again," 384; "Refugee in America," 384

Hyde, Henry, "The Rule of Law," 476

I.

"I've Been Working on the Railroad," 231

J.

Jackson, Jesse, "Speech to the Democratic National Convention," 457

Janvier, Francis de Haes, "God Save Our President," 191

Jay, John, and Alexander Hamilton, and James Madison, "The Federalist Papers," 58

Jefferson, Thomas: "The Declaration of Independence," 28; "A Bill for Establishing Religious Freedom in Virginia," 43; "First Inaugural Address," 82

"John Brown's Body," 202

Johnson, Lyndon B., "The American Promise," 419

Jones, Stan, "Riders in the Sky," 388

K.

Key, Francis Scott, "The Star-Spangled Banner," 90

Kennedy, John F.: "Speech to the Greater Houston Ministerial Association," 402; "Inaugural Address," 405; "Speech at the Berlin Wall," 412

Kennedy, Robert F.: "Ending the War in Vietnam," 422; "On the Death of Martin Luther King, Jr.," 429

Kilmer, Joyce, "Trees," 304

King, Martin Luther, Jr.: "Letter from Birmingham City Jail," 408; "March on Washington Address," 414

Kittredge, Walter, "Tenting on the Old Camp Ground," 204

L.

La Follette, Robert M., Sr., "Free Speech in Wartime," 300

Lazarus, Emma, "The New Colossus," 241

Lee, Robert E., "Farewell to His Army," 218

"Letter from a Navy Pilot," 360

Lieberman, Elias, "I Am an American," 308; "Credo," 309

Lincoln, Abraham: "The House Divided Speech," 169; "The Cooper Union Speech," 174; "First Inaugural Address," 187; "Emancipation Proclamation," 206; "The Gettysburg Address," 212; "Second Inaugural Address," 214

Lindsay, Vachel, "Abraham Lincoln Walks at Midnight," 292

Lodge, Henry Cabot, "American Sovereignty," 325

Loesser, Frank, "Praise the Lord and Pass the Ammunition," 366

Longfellow, Henry Wadsworth: "Paul Revere's Ride," 112; "A Psalm of Life," 112; "The Village Blacksmith," 112; "The Ship of State," 112

Lowell, James Russell, "The Present Crisis," 161

M.

MacArthur, Douglas, "Farewell Address at West Point," 393

Madison, James, and Alexander Hamilton, and John Jay, "The Federalist Papers," 58

Mann, Horace, "The Case For Public Schools," 118

"Marines' Hymn, The," 322

Marshall, George C., "The Marshall Plan Speech," 375

Marshall, John, Marbury v. Madison, 85

"Mayflower Compact, The," 2

McCarthy, Eugene, "Kilroy," 426

McCarthy, Harry, "The Bonnie Blue Flag," 198

McCullough, David, "The Course of Human Events," 493

McKay, Claude: "America," 330; "If We Must Die," 330

Miles, Alfred H., and Charles A. Zimmerman, "Anchors Aweigh," 357

Miller, Alice Duer, "Evolution," 279

Minow, Newton, "Address to the Broadcasting Industry," 466

Mitchell, George J., "The Iran-Contra Hearings," 455

Monroe, James, "The Monroe Doctrine," 93

Moore, Robert L., and Barry Sadler, "Ballad of the Green Berets," 430

Morris, George Pope, "Woodman, Spare That Tree," 101

N.

Nixon, Richard, "Final Remarks at the White House," 436

Norris, George, "Against the War in Europe," 297

Norworth, Jack, and Albert Von Tilzer, "Take Me Out to the Ball Game," 278

O.

Obama, Barack, "A More Perfect Union," 488

O'Hara, Theodore, "The Bivouac of the Dead," 106

"On Top of Old Smoky," 116

Otis, James, "Against Writs of Assistance," 14

P.

Page, William Tyler, "The American's Creed," 310

Paine, Thomas: Common Sense, 23; "Liberty Tree," 27; The American Crisis, 32

Parker, Hubbard, "Old Flag," 305

Patton, George S., Jr.: "Speech to the Third Army," 361; "Through a Glass, Darkly," 364

Payne, John Howard, "Home, Sweet Home," 95

Piantadosi, Al, and Alfred Bryan, "I Didn't Raise My Boy to Be a Soldier," 292

R.

Randall, Dudley, "Ballad of Birmingham," 417

Randall, James Ryder, "Maryland, My Maryland," 201

Read, Thomas Buchanan, "The Flag of the Constellation," 196

Reagan, Ronald: "First Inaugural Address," 442; "Speech on the Challenger Disaster," 450; "Brandenburg Gate Speech," 452; "Speech at Moscow State University," 460

Revels, Hiram R., "On Readmission of Georgia to the Union," 228

Rogers, Roy, and Dale Evans, "Happy Trails," 389

Roosevelt, Franklin D.: "First Inaugural Address," 332; "Second Inaugural Address," 335; The Four Freedoms," 350; "War Message to Congress," 353

Roosevelt, Theodore: "The Duties of American Citizenship," 260; "True Americanism," 265; "The Strenuous Life," 268

Root, George F., "Battle Cry of Freedom," 199

Rose, Billy, "The Unknown Soldier," 327

S.

Sadler, Barry, and Robert L. Moore, "Ballad of the Green Berets," 430

Sandburg, Carl, "Grass," 322

Sanger, Margaret, *Woman and the New Race*, 280

Seeger, Pete, "Where Have All the Flowers Gone?," 407

"Seneca Falls Declaration of Sentiments and Resolutions," 120

Shapiro, Karl, "Elegy for a Dead Soldier," 367

Shepherd, Nathaniel Graham, "Roll-Call," 213

"Slaves' Appeal to the Royal Governor of Massachusetts," 20

Smith, Margaret Chase, "Declaration of Conscience," 381

Smith, Samuel F., "America," 102

Springsteen, Bruce, "My City of Ruins," 482

Stanton, Elizabeth Cady, "The Solitude of Self," 247

Stevenson, Adlai E., "The Nature of Patriotism," 390

Sunday, Billy, "Heaven," 314

"Swing Low, Sweet Chariot," 180

T.

Taft, Robert A., "Against the New Deal," 342

Thayer, Ernest Lawrence, "Casey at the Bat," 242

Thomas, Clarence, "Remarks to the National Bar Association," 471

Thoreau, Henry David: "Civil Disobedience," 130; *Walden*, 134

Travis, William Barret, "Dispatch from the Alamo," 105

Truman, Harry S., "Inaugural Address," 378

Truth, Sojourner, "Address to the Ohio Women's Rights Convention," 122

V.

"Valley Forge," 37

Van Dyke, Henry, "America For Me," 311

Von Tilzer, Albert, and Jack Norworth, "Take Me Out to the Ball Game," 278

W.

Walker, David, "Walker's Appeal," 146

Webster, Daniel: "Bunker Hill Oration," 96; "Against Nullification," 152

"We Shall Overcome," 416

Washington, Booker T., "The Atlanta Exposition Address," 251

Washington, George: "Answer to Congress on His Appointment as Commander-in-Chief," 23; "Rejecting a Crown," 50; "First Inaugural Address," 72; "Second Inaugural Address," 76; "Farewell Address," 77

Whittier, John Greenleaf, "Stanzas for the Times," 207; "Maud Muller," 207; "Barbara Frietchie," 207

Whitman, Walt: "I Hear America Singing," 221; "O Captain! My Captain!," 221

Wilson, Woodrow, "War Message to Congress," 293

Woodworth, Samuel, "The Old Oaken Bucket," 91

Y.

"Yankee Doodle," 34

Yellen, Jack, and Milton Ager, "Happy Days Are Here Again," 330

Z.

Zimmerman, Charles A., and Alfred H. Miles, "Anchors Aweigh," 357

Permissions and Credits

Reasonable care has been taken to trace ownership and, when necessary, obtain permission for each selection included. Grateful acknowledgment is made to the following:

The poem "Daniel Boone" by Arthur Guiterman. Reprinted with the permission of Richard E. Sclove.

The song "Battle of New Orleans" by Jimmy Driftwood. © Copyright 1959 Warden Music Company, Inc. Used by Permission of Don Warden Music Co., Inc.

The poems "The Road Not Taken," "Stopping by Woods on a Snowy Evening," and "The Gift Outright" from the book THE POETRY OF ROBERT FROST, edited by Edward Connery Lathem. Copyright © 1923, 1969 by Henry Holt and Company, copyright © 1942, 1951 by Robert Frost, copyright © 1970 by Lesley Frost Ballantine. Reprinted by permission of Henry Holt and Company, LLC.

The song "I Didn't Raise My Boy to Be a Soldier." Words by ALFRED BRYAN. Music by AL PIANTADOSI. Copyright © 1915 (Renewed) EMI FEIST CATALOG, INC. All Rights outside the U.S. controlled by EMI FEIST CATALOG, INC. (Publishing) and ALFRED PUBLISHING CO., INC. (Print). PD in U.S.

The poem "A Toast to the Flag" by John Jay Daly. Reprinted by Permission of National Sojourners, Inc.

The selection entitled "Heaven" by Billy Sunday from *The Best of Billy Sunday: 17 Burning Sermons from the Most Spectacular Evangelist the World Has Ever Known*, compiled and edited by John R. Rice. © Copyright 1965 Sword of the Lord Publishers, Murfreesboro, TN. All Rights Reserved. Used By Permission.

The song "Over There." Words and Music by GEORGE M. COHAN. © 1917 EMI FEIST CATALOG INC. for the World

Excluding the U.S. Exclusive Print Rights Administered by ALFRED MUSIC PUBLISHING CO., INC. PD in U.S.

The song "Yankee Doodle Boy" by GEORGE M. COHAN. With appreciation, the George M. Cohan Music Publishing Company.

The song "Happy Days Are Here Again." Words and Music by JACK YELLEN and MILTON AGER. Copyright © 1929 (Renewed) WB MUSIC CORP. All Rights Reserved. Used by Permission.

The song "Brother, Can You Spare a Dime?" Lyric by E.Y. "Yip" Harburg. Music by Jay Gorney. © 1932 (Renewed) Glocca Morra Music and Gorney Music. All Rights Administered by Next Decade Entertainment, Inc. All Rights Reserved. Used by Permission. *Reprinted by Permission of Hal Leonard Corporation.*

The song "God Bless America" by Irving Berlin. © Copyright 1938, 1939 by Irving Berlin. © Copyright Renewed 1965, 1966 by Irving Berlin. © Copyright Assigned the Trustees of the God Bless America Fund. International Copyright Secured. All Rights Reserved. Reprinted by Permission.

The song "Oh, How I Hate to Get Up in the Morning" by Irving Berlin. © Copyright 1918 by Irving Berlin. © Copyright Renewed. International Copyright Secured. All Rights Reserved. Reprinted by Permission.

The selection "Flag Day" reprinted from *The New York Times*. Copyright © 1940 by The New York Times Company. Reprinted by permission.

The song "This Land Is Your Land." Words and Music by Woody Guthrie. WGP/TRO-© Copyright 1956, 1958, 1970 and 1972 (copyrights renewed) Woody Guthrie Publications, Inc. & Ludlow Music, Inc., New York, NY. Administered by Ludlow Music, Inc. International Copyright Secured.

Illustrations

p. xiii ushistory.org

p. xxx Brooklyn Museum

p.3 Library of Congress

p.14 Library of Congress

p.19 Library of Congress

p.31 Architect of the Capitol

p.35 Library of Congress

p.38 National Archives and Records Administration

p.44 The Metropolitan Museum of Art

p.48 Architect of the Capitol

p.57 Architect of the Capitol

p.76 The Metropolitan Museum of Art

p.81 National Archives and Records Administration

p.88 National Archives and Records Administration

p.91 U.S. Senate Collection

p.98 Gilcrease Museum, Tulsa, OK , accession # 0226.1032

p.102 The Granger Collection, New York

p.104 Picture History

p.111 Library of Congress

p.117 Picture History

p.126 National Portrait Gallery, Smithsonian Institution; purchased with funds from an anonymous donor

p.138 Courtesy of The Bancroft Library, University of California, Berkeley

p.144 U.S. Senate Collection

p.159 Courtesy Encyclopedia Virginia, Virginia Foundation for the Humanities

p.164 St. Louis Art Museum, Gift of Bank of America, oil on canvas, accession # 43:2001

p.168 The Library Company of Philadelphia

p.180 Library of Congress

p.182 Library of Congress

p.191 Courtesy Union Pacific Railroad Museum

p.194 National Archives and Records Administration

p.200 National Archives and Records Administration

p.203 National Archives and Records Administration

p.212 Corbis

p.219 Library of Congress

p.224 Courtesy Union Pacific Railroad Museum

p.227 Collections of Seward House Museum, Auburn, NY

p.233 Library of Congress

p.238 White House Historical Association (White House Collection)

p.250 Thomas N. Athey Collection, Oklahoma Historical Society Research Division

p.264 Library of Congress

p.271 National Baseball Hall of Fame and Museum

p.275 National Archives and Records Administration

p.279 National Archives and Records Administration

p.286 Corbis

p.290 National Archives and Records Administration

p.304 Library of Congress

p.307 Library of Congress

p.310 National Archives and Records Administration

p.313 Library of Congress

p.324 Department of Defense

p.328 AP Photo—Joe Rosenthal

p.334 National Archives and Records Administration

p.337 Corbis

p.349 Printed by permission of the Norman Rockwell Family Agency. Book Rights Copyright © 1954 The Norman Rockwell Family Entities. Images provided by Curtis Publishing Company

p.353 Photograph by George Strock—Time & Life Pictures—Getty Images

p.355 Naval Historical Foundation

p.358 National Archives and Records Administration

p.360 National Archives and Records Administration

p.364 Franklin D. Roosevelt Library

p.367 National Archives and Records Administration

p.372 Photograph by J. R. Eyerman—Time & Life Pictures—Getty Images

p.377 Library of Congress

p.384 Library of Congress

p.389 National Archives and Records Administration; with thanks to Chuck Chriss of Olive-Drab.com and the U.S. Army Medical Department, Office of Medical History

p.392 Corbis

p.400 Photograph by Bernie Boston—RIT Archive Collections, Rochester Institute of Technology

p.404 Corbis

p.413 Corbis

p.419 LBJ Library, photograph by Cecil Stoughton

p.425 Photograph © 1970 John Paul Filo, courtesy of the photographer

p.428 National Archives and Records Administration

p.440 Courtesy Ronald Reagan Library

p.449 Courtesy National Atlas

p.451 NASA

p.452 NASA

p.464 Photograph by Thomas E. Franklin—The Record (Bergen County, NJ)—Getty Images

p.481 Photograph by Eric Draper, Courtesy of the George W. Bush Presidential Library

p.487 Department of Defense, photograph by MSgt Cecilio Ricardo

p.493 Wikipedia user "Freedom Fan"

p. 513 Corbis

In a November 5, 1994, letter to the nation, Ronald Reagan announced that he had been diagnosed with Alzheimer's disease. "Let me thank you, the American people, for giving me the great honor of allowing me to serve as your president," wrote Reagan. "When the Lord calls me home, whenever that day may be, I will leave with the greatest love for this country of ours and eternal optimism for its future. I now begin the journey that will lead me into the sunset of my life. I know that for America there will always be a bright dawn ahead."